HANDBOOK OF
Counseling Military Couples

The Family Therapy and Counseling Series
Series Editor
Jon Carlson, Psy.D., Ed.D.

Kit S. Ng
Global Perspectives in Family Therapy: Development, Practice, Trends

Phyllis Erdman and Tom Caffery
Attachment and Family Systems: Conceptual, Empirical, and Therapeutic Relatedness

Wes Crenshaw
Treating Families and Children in the Child Protective System

Len Sperry
Assessment of Couples and Families: Contemporary and Cutting-Edge Strategies

Robert L. Smith and R. Esteban Montilla
Counseling and Family Therapy With Latino Populations: Strategies That Work

Catherine Ford Sori
Engaging Children in Family Therapy: Creative Approaches to Integrating Theory and Research in Clinical Practice

Paul R. Peluso
Infidelity: A Practitioner's Guide to Working With Couples in Crisis

Jill D. Onedera
The Role of Religion in Marriage and Family Counseling

Christine Kerr, Janice Hoshino, Judith Sutherland, Sharyl Parashak, and Linda McCarley
Family Art Therapy

Debra D. Castaldo
Divorced Without Children: Solution Focused Therapy With Women at Midlife

Phyllis Erdman and Kok-Mun Ng
Attachment: Expanding the Cultural Connections

Jon Carlson and Len Sperry
Recovering Intimacy in Love Relationships: A Clinician's Guide

Adam Zagelbaum and Jon Carlson
Working With Immigrant Families: A Practical Guide for Counselors

David K. Carson and Montserrat Casado-Kehoe
Case Studies in Couples Therapy: Theory-Based Approaches

Shea M. Dunham, Shannon B. Dermer, and Jon Carlson
Poisonous Parenting: Toxic Relationships Between Parents and Their Adult Children

Bret A. Moore
Handbook of Counseling Military Couples

Len Sperry
Family Assessment: Contemporary and Cutting-Edge Strategies, 2nd ed.

HANDBOOK OF

Counseling Military Couples

Edited by Bret A. Moore

Routledge
Taylor & Francis Group
New York London

The views expressed in this book are those of the authors and do not reflect the official policy or position of the Department of the Army, Department of the Navy, Department of the Air Force, Department of Defense, or the U.S. Government.

This book is part of the Family Therapy and Counseling Series, edited by Jon Carlson.

Routledge
Taylor & Francis Group
711 Third Avenue
New York, NY 10017

Routledge
Taylor & Francis Group
27 Church Road
Hove, East Sussex BN3 2FA

Printed in the United States of America on acid-free paper
Version Date: 2011902

International Standard Book Number: 978-0-415-88730-4 (Hardback)

Library of Congress Cataloging-in-Publication Data

Moore, Bret A.
Handbook of counseling military couples / Bret A. Moore. -- 1st ed.
p. cm. -- (The family therapy and counseling series)
Includes bibliographical references and index.
ISBN 978-0-415-88730-4 (hbk. : alk. paper)
1. Families of military personnel--Services for--United States. 2. Couples--Counseling of--United States. 3. Marital psychotherapy--United States. 4. Military spouses--Services for--United States. 5. Soldiers--Family relationships--United States. 6. Soldiers--United States--Psychology. I. Title.

UB403.M67 2011
616.89'156208835500973--dc23 2011029452

Visit the Taylor & Francis Web site at
http://www.taylorandfrancis.com

and the Routledge Web site at
http://www.routledgementalhealth.com

To Katie Grace, Quincy, and Gracie

Contents

SECTION 3 SPECIFIC ISSUES IN MILITARY RELATIONSHIPS

SECTION 4 RESOURCES

Series Editor's Foreword

"Freedom is never free."

Anonymous

For several years I worked on military bases teaching graduate counseling and psychology classes to military men and women. Since I was known as someone who had written on couples and marriage, I was frequently cornered and asked to help with couples issues. I realized that the military couple has all of the stresses of regular couples plus frequent separation, stress of combat and job, and perhaps most important is that they are married to the military first. This loyalty causes challenges that are not easy to identify, let alone treat.

Bret Moore and the contributors to this volume present insight into the military culture and its impact on the military couple. They present the problems military families are dealing with as a result of the wars in Iraq and Afghanistan. These include issues of PTSD, depression, long deployments, frequent moves, chronic pain, substance abuse and dependence, and other psychiatric and physical problems. They highlight methods of treatment and provide resources for those who work with this population.

This book clearly shows the importance of mental health services for the military couple. I applaud Bret Moore and his contributors for creating the first book that deals exclusively with the challenges of being a military couple.

Jon Carlson, PsyD, EdD
Distinguished Professor
Governors State University

Contributors

Nathan D. Ainspan, PhD, is the Senior Personnel Psychologist with the Civilian Personnel Evaluation Agency. He has conducted research, written, and spoken about psychological issues impacting our wounded and transitioning warriors. He edited the book *Wars' Returning Wounded, Injured and Ill: A Handbook,* which was published last year, and wrote the chapter on how returning service members with physical and psychological disabilities can obtain employment in the civilian sector. He served as a facilitator for the "Beyond the Front" program as part of the Army's training on suicide prevention.

Christina Balderrama-Durbin, MA, is a doctoral candidate in clinical psychology at Texas A&M University. She has contributed to the Strong Bonds program for military couples with its founders at the University of Denver and to a longitudinal study of Air Force personnel deployed to Iraq. Her research interests include self-disclosure and infidelity in a military context.

James Kelly Barnett, PhD, is Assistant Professor of Psychology and Counseling and Director of Practicum and Internship Programs at Texas A&M University Central Texas in Killeen. A Licensed Marriage and Family Therapist and AAMFT Approved Supervisor, Dr. Barnett is also a U.S. Army Chaplain (Colonel), U.S. Army Reserve. He previously served on active duty in support of Operation Enduring Freedom in Afghanistan.

Paul Bliese, PhD, is the Director of the Center for Military Psychiatry and Neuroscience at the Walter Reed Army Institute of Research. COL Bliese has served as commander of the U.S. Army Medical Research Unit–Europe (Heidelberg, Germany) and the Chief of the Military Psychiatry Branch at the WRAIR. He deployed to Iraq in 2005, 2007, and 2009, and to Afghanistan in 2010 as part of the annual Mental Health Advisory Team. Dr. Bliese has published numerous scientific articles, and developed and maintains the multilevel library for the open-source statistical language *R*.

Patrick S. Calhoun, PhD, serves as an Associate Director of the VA Mid-Atlantic Mental Illness Research, Education, and Clinical Center, directs psychology fellowship training at the Durham VA Medical Center, and is an Assistant Professor of Psychiatry and Behavioral Sciences at Duke University Medical Center. In his role as a direct services provider, Dr. Calhoun specializes in the assessment and treatment of the posttraumatic stress disorder. He has co-authored over 70 articles and book chapters in his area of interest, which has focused primarily on the psychological, behavioral, and health consequences of traumatic stress including difficulties with violence and aggression.

Kevin M. Connolly, PhD, is a staff psychologist and operations manager of the Trauma Recovery Program at the G.V. (Sonny) Montgomery VAMC. He also holds an appointment as Assistant Professor in the Department of Psychiatry and Human Behavior, Division of Psychology, at the University of Mississippi Medical Center in Jackson. He currently serves as faculty for the University of Mississippi Medical Center/VA Medical Center internship training consortium.

Michael R. DeVries is a U.S. Army psychologist. He has served as the Regiment Psychologist for the 160th Special Operations Aviation Regiment (Airborne) as well as Brigade and Division Psychologist for the 82nd Airborne Division. He is a veteran of operations in both Iraq and Afghanistan.

Jacobus Donders, PhD, is the Chief Psychologist at Mary Free Bed Rehabilitation Hospital in Grand Rapids, Michigan. He is board-certified by the American Board of Professional Psychology in both clinical neuropsychology and rehabilitation psychology. He has served on multiple editorial and executive boards, has authored or co-authored more than 100 publications in peer-reviewed journals, and has co-edited three books. He is a Fellow of the National Academy of Neuropsychology and of Divisions 40 (Clinical Neuropsychology) and 22 (Rehabilitation Psychology) of the American Psychological Association.

Samuel Fiala, PhD, is Assistant Professor at Texas A&M University Central Texas in Killeen. He is a licensed psychologist and supervises therapists at Fort Hood involved in a clinical intervention trial targeting couples struggling with issues of infidelity.

Caitlin Fissette, BS, is a doctoral candidate in clinical psychology at Texas A&M University. She previously worked at Fort Hood for STRONG STAR, a research consortium developing interventions to detect, prevent, and treat combat-related posttraumatic stress disorder (PTSD) in active-duty military personnel and recently discharged veterans. Her research interests include PTSD assessment, military couple functioning, and couple-based interventions.

Sharon Morgillo Freeman, PhD, PMHCNS-BC, is the CEO of the Center for Brief Therapy, Secretary/Treasurer of the International Association for Cognitive Psychotherapy, and Associate Faculty, Indiana/Purdue University, Fort Wayne, Indiana. She is a Certified Member of the Academy of Cognitive Therapy and is certified as an Advanced Practice Psychiatric Clinical Nurse Specialist (PMHCNS-BC) with prescriptive authority. Dr. Freeman has a PhD in sociology, a Master of Arts in psychology, and a Master of Science in advanced practice psychiatric nursing.

Veronica Gutierrez, PhD, received her doctorate from the University of California, Santa Barbara in 2004. She is an Assistant Professor at Alliant International University in San Diego, California and a Fellow of the Rockway Institute. She is a member of the American Psychological Association. She teaches courses on issues involving diversity; human sexuality; and lesbian, gay, bisexual, and transgendered (LGBT) individuals. She also teaches students on how to conduct therapy in Spanish and how to develop competence in working with the LGBT community as straight therapists. She has conducted research in these areas and works as a psychologist in the community.

Kathryn S. Hahn, PhD, is an Assistant Professor at Millsaps College. Her clinical specialty and teaching focus on the cognitive, emotional, and behavioral intersect of psychopathology. She has authored several articles and professional presentations related to the role of information processing biases and emotion dysregulation in the development and maintenance of anxiety and depression. She enjoys inspiring student interest in the science and application of psychology.

Lynn Hall, EdD, is the Dean of the College of Social Sciences at the University of Phoenix. She spent seven years as a counselor educator at Western New Mexico University, leaving as a full Professor. Prior to that, she spent almost 10 years as a school counselor at both the middle and high school levels for the Department of Defense Schools in Germany. Lynn received both her Master's degree and Doctorate from the University of Arizona. Her experience as a school counselor working with military dependent children, as well as her work as a counselor educator, led to her interest in military families and to the 2008 publication of the book entitled *Counseling Military Families: What Mental Health Professionals Need to Know.*

H. Kent Hughes, PhD, earned his doctorate in 1993 from George Fox University. He is a civilian psychologist currently working for the Department of the Army attached to the 160th Special Operations Aviation Regiment (Airborne). Dr. Hughes has been in private practice for 17 years working with military families in the Fort Campbell, Kentucky area and has been working specifically for the Department of Defense since March 2009.

Desireé King, MA, earned a Master's degree in clinical psychology and is currently a doctoral candidate in clinical psychology at Argosy University-Schaumburg. She is presently developing a community-focused caregiver support resource group for partners of chronically injured veterans living with the long-term effects TBI/PTSD/Polytrauma. As the widow of a Marine with posttraumatic stress disorder, she has had the opportunity to experience deployment effects firsthand from the spousal perspective and is able to bring this wisdom and insight to her work with military and veteran families.

Jason M. Lavender, PhD, is a postdoctoral research fellow at the Neuropsychiatric Research Institute in Fargo, North Dakota. He completed his predoctoral internship at the University of Mississippi Medical Center/G.V. (Sonny) Montgomery

VAMC consortium in Jackson and received his PhD in clinical psychology from the University at Albany, State University of New York.

Dolores Little, PhD, is retired from the Department of Veterans Affairs. She held positions as Associate Hospital Director at VA medical centers in Big Spring, Texas; Bedford, Massachusetts; Providence, Rhode Island; and Loma Linda, California. Her topics of clinical interest have centered on patient health care, through training programs for interns and residents in medicine, nursing, psychology, and social work.

Judith A. Lyons, PhD, studied in Montreal (B.A., 1979, McGill University; M.A., 1982 and Ph.D., 1985, Concordia University) then completed her clinical internship in Jackson, Mississippi (1984-85). After serving as the founding Clinical Director of the Traumatic Stress Disorder Center at the Boston VA (1985-87), she returned to Jackson to establish the Trauma Recovery Program at the G. V. ("Sonny") Montgomery VA Medical Center. She assesses and treats traumatic stress through her work with the VA, consults on personal injury and criminal cases, and participates in disaster response work with the American Red Cross. She is an Associate Professor of psychiatry and human behavior at the University of Mississippi Medical Center and conducts research with the support of VA's South Central Mental Illness Research, Education and Clinical Center (MIRECC).

Nicole Pukay-Martin, PhD, is currently a postdoctoral fellow in the PTSD Clinic at the Durham VAMC. She received her doctoral degree at the University of North Carolina at Chapel Hill where she specialized in couple-based interventions for psychopathology and health problems. She assisted in the creation and implementation of a couple-based intervention for obsessive–compulsive disorder, and has co-authored several articles focused on a couple-based intervention for breast cancer. Dr. Pukay-Martin is currently concentrating on research and clinical work examining the interpersonal effects of PTSD, relational factors involved in the development and maintenance of PTSD, and couple-based treatments for PTSD.

Julie Merrill, MS, is a research psychologist in the Military Psychiatry Branch of the Center for Military Psychiatry & Neuroscience at the Walter Reed Army Institute of Research. She received her Master's from Portland State University in 2004.

R. Roudi Nazarinia Roy, PhD, is an Assistant Professor in the School of Family Studies and Human Services at Kansas State University. She teaches classes in the areas of family transitions, cultural and family diversity, couple relationships and parent–child interaction. Her research is in the areas of relationship satisfaction, family transitions and gender and cultural influences on family roles. She is also involved in multidisciplinary research involving money and relationships.

Robert P. O'Brien, PhD, is a clinical psychologist. He is a Supervisory Psychologist at the Central Texas Veterans Health Care System where he supervises the psychology staff in the Mental Health Clinic, the Family program, the PTSD program, the Substance Abuse program and the Primary Care Mental Health program. He is also the Evidence Based Psychotherapy Coordinator at Central Texas Veterans Health Care System. He holds appointments in the Clinical Psychology and Counseling Psychology departments of the University of Texas at Austin and in the Department of Psychiatry at Texas A&M University. He is a Gottman Certified Therapist, Workshop Leader, Trainer and Consultant. An ex-Army psychologist and a graduate of the U.S. Army Command and General Staff College, he lives with his wife in Austin, Texas.

Walter Penk, PhD, ABPP, is Professor in Psychiatry and Behavioral Sciences at Texas A&M College of Medicine and Consultant with VA Rehabilitation Research and Development. During his career, he served as a clinical and research psychologist in VA medical centers in Houston, Dallas, Boston, and Bedford, Massachusetts, with clinical appointments in Southwestern, Tufts, Boston University, University of Massachusetts, and Harvard medical schools. His health care research interests are in posttraumatic stress disorder.

Matthew C. Porter, PhD, is Assistant Professor of Clinical Psychology at Alliant International University, San Diego, California, and a Fellow of the Rockway Institute. He received his doctorate from the New School for Social Research, New York City, in 2005. His research focuses on social cognition in health psychology, cognitive-affective components of resilience and psychological development in the face of stressful life events (war trauma, cancer, HIV/AIDS), and the intersection of coping and lifespan development. His research has been featured in *JAMA*, and has been funded by the NIH and the Templeton Foundation. He was also a UN Peacekeeper, deployed to the former Yugoslavia in 1996-1997.

Kathryn Rheem, EdD, LCMFT, Director, Washington Baltimore Center for EFT, and founder and Director, along with Dr. Sue Johnson, of Strong Bonds, Strong Couples, a post-combat deployment retreat. She has trained U.S. Army Medical Command & Chaplains in EFT and worked with soldier couples at Forts Hood, Bragg, Leavenworth, Belvoir and in Germany; Marine couples at Camp Lejeune; and the Dutch Military. She has a private practice in Bethesda, Maryland, and Falls Church, Virginia.

Lyndon Riviere, PhD, is a research psychologist in the Military Psychiatry Branch of the Center for Military Psychiatry & Neuroscience at the Walter Reed Army Institute of Research (WRAIR). Dr. Riviere is the principal investigator of the Land Combat Study II protocol, "Impact of deployment and combat experiences on the mental health and well-being of military service members and their families," which will survey soldiers and spouses throughout the deployment cycle.

David Scheider, DMin, is Director of the Family Life Chaplain Training Center at Fort Hood in Killeen, Texas. He is a Licensed Marriage and Family Therapist and AAMFT Approved Supervisor. Dr. Scheider is a U.S. Army Chaplain (Lt. Colonel) and previously served as Deputy Garrison Chaplain in Grafenwoehr, Germany.

Walter R. Schumm, PhD, is Professor of Family Studies in the School of Family Studies and Human Services at Kansas State University in Manhattan, where he has taught since 1979. He is also a retired colonel, U.S. Army, having spent nearly 30 years on active duty and in the Reserve Components between 1972 and 2002, including a 12-month mobilization to Fifth Army Headquarters, San Antonio, Texas, for the first Persian Gulf War.

Douglas K. Snyder, PhD, is Professor of Psychology and Director of Clinical Training at Texas A&M University in College Station. He has written extensively on clinical assessment and treatment of couple distress. He has co-authored two books (*Getting Past the Affair* and *Helping Couples Get Past the Affair: A Clinician's Guide*) and has co-edited two others (*Treating Difficult Couples* and *Emotion Regulation in Couples and Families*). Dr. Snyder received the 2005 Award from the American Psychological Association for Distinguished Contributions to Family Psychology and serves on the editorial boards of numerous journals in clinical psychology and family therapy.

Carrie-Ann Strong, PsyD, is a psychologist at Mary Free Bed Rehabilitation Hospital in Grand Rapids, Michigan. She is board-certified by the American Board of Professional Psychology in Clinical Neuropsychology. Her clinical work involves both assessment and treatment of traumatic brain injury (TBI). She has also co-authored a number of publications in peer-reviewed journals, primarily in the area of neuropsychological test validation in TBI.

Rebecca Tews-Kozlowski, PhD, has been working with children and families since 1984, both as an educator and as a clinician. She has earned a PhD in counseling psychology from Marquette University and an MA in clinical psychology from Middle Tennessee State University. She is on the faculty of Argosy University-Schaumburg, Illinois where she has established a research program aimed at improving quality of life for veterans and their families through development and community integration of programming designed to support their unique needs.

Vance P. Theodore, PhD, recently retired as a Colonel from the military serving as a United States Army Chaplain. He currently is serving a post doctoral internship in the military relations division at the LDS Church Headquarters–Salt Lake City, Utah, working on issues of deployment.

Jeffrey L. Thomas, PhD, is the Branch Chief of Military Psychiatry at the Walter Reed Army Institute of Research (WRAIR). MAJ Thomas has been involved in deployment mental health research throughout his Army career from Bosnia and Kosovo to Iraq and Afghanistan. He has deployed on three U.S. Army Mental Health Advisory Teams, twice to Iraq and once to Afghanistan. Dr. Thomas has published over 40 peer-reviewed scientific papers and book chapters.

Matthew B. Tully is the founding partner of Tully Rinckey PLLC, a veteran-owned business that is one of the nation's largest federal employment law firms and a pioneer in the field of military law. He is an Iraq war veteran who serves as a lieutenant colonel with the New York Army National Guard. He is a nationally-syndicated columnist who writes "Ask the Lawyer" columns for the Army Times Publishing Company and the *Saratogian* in upstate New York. His essays have been featured in *The Streetwise Small Business Book of Lists, The American Veterans and Servicemembers Survival Guide,* and *Human Rights.*

Harvey D. Watson, PhD, is a former U.S. Army Infantry Officer, with combat unit command experience in the grades from Lieutenant through Colonel. His PhD from Auburn University is in experimental psychology with areas of expertise in human cognitive function, learning, sensation and perception, physiology and research methods and statistics.

Neil Weissman, PsyD, is a staff psychologist at the Baltimore VA Medical Center. He holds an appointment as Clinical Assistant Professor in the Department of Psychiatry, University of Maryland Medical School and University of Maryland School of Nursing. Dr. Weissman is also a certified EFT supervisor by the International Center of Excellence for Emotionally Focused Therapy.

Joshua Wilk, PhD, is the Deputy Branch Chief in the Military Psychiatry Branch of the Center for Military Psychiatry and Neuroscience at the Walter Reed Army Institute of Research. Dr. Wilk's current research includes work on the rates of mental health and functional problems, the effects of combat experience on alcohol misuse, the effects of blast-related mTBI, and on PTSD treatment in Active Component and National Guard soldiers. He is also a practicing clinician in private practice in Columbia, Maryland.

Scott Woolley, PhD, is a Professor and the Systemwide Director of the MFT Masters and Doctoral Programs in the California School of Professional Psychology at Alliant International University. He a founder and Director of the San Diego Center for EFT and a founder and the Executive Director of the Training and Research Institute for EFT at Alliant (TRI EFT Alliant).

Acknowledgments

Without the support of many people in my life, this book would have not been possible. First, I would like to thank my wife, Lori, for her continued patience and support. Second, I am extremely grateful that the series editor, Jon Carlson, and Anna Moore and the rest of the staff from Routledge had enough confidence in me to edit this volume. Last, I would like to thank my military mentors, COL Bruce Crow, Dr. Dennis Grill, LTC Jay Earles, LTC Stan Breuer, and LTC Ted Swanton for their guidance, patience, and friendship.

DISCLAIMERS

1

Introduction to Counseling Military Couples

BRET A. MOORE

A great deal of attention has been given to the psychological and social hardships the men and women of the Armed Forces have endured since 2001. Thankfully and rightfully so, countless biopsychosocial issues that affect the individual service member have been covered in premier scientific journals, comprehensive authored and edited books, and all forms of popular media. In addition to the individual service member, the military family unit has garnered considerable interest, particularly with regard to issues of resiliency, growth, and overall functioning.

One area of military mental health that has been less studied and written about is the impact the military lifestyle has on the military couple. Whether it is long and back-to-back combat deployments, uncertainty about career trajectory, frequent moves, or frequent school changes for the military child, the impact on the military couple can be tremendous. This is in addition to the same stressors all couples face, such as finances, incompatible personality characteristics, loss of intimacy, infidelity, and more.

Some may argue that as the current conflicts in Iraq and Afghanistan wind down and eventually come to a close, the strain on military couples will decrease. Although this is true to an extent, the residual effects of over a decade of fighting two wars will reverberate in military couples for many years. How could it not considering that tens of thousands, if not hundreds of thousands, of service members are suffering from posttraumatic stress disorder (PTSD), depression, substance abuse and dependence, chronic pain, traumatic brain injury, and other psychiatric and physical disorders?

The focus of this book is the myriad relationship issues that many military couples battle on a daily basis. As noted, in addition to dealing with the same problems all couples endure, military couples face unique challenges. Consequently, it is important for the clinician working with military couples to appreciate these differences and understand them within a military context. This volume addresses this need.

Chapter 2, by Michael R. DeVries, H. Kent Hughes, Harvey Watson, and Bret A. Moore, begins Section 1 on military culture. This chapter addresses the unique aspects of the military culture that are important for clinicians treating military couples to understand. The experience of this group of authors includes special operations work, multiple combat deployments, and direct line command of combat troops. Topics such as rank, military hierarchy, spirituality, personality characteristics, and the "mission first" mentality are covered in detail.

Chapter 3, by Lyndon A. Riviere, Julie C. Merrill, Jeffrey L. Thomas, Joshua E. Wilk, and Paul D. Bliese, presents a study that reports the latest findings on marital functioning in the military. First, it examines 2003–2009 trends in three self-reported marital functioning indicators to investigate whether the percentage of soldiers reporting high marital quality has declined over the course of simultaneous combat operations in Iraq and Afghanistan and whether reports of infidelity and separation/divorce intent have increased over time. Second, it examines whether these marital functioning trends are reflected in soldier marital dissolution rates between 2003 and 2009. Last, the authors interpret their findings with both the trauma and stress hypotheses.

Robert P. O'Brien's Chapter 4 on cognitive-behavioral therapy for couples begins Section 2 on treatment approaches. This chapter details the most commonly used treatment approach in working with couples. The most current research is covered as well as the strengths and limitations of using this approach with military couples.

In Chapter 5, Rebecca Tews-Kozlowski, outlines the solution-focused model for couples treatment. Arguably the most suited treatment for military couples due to its pragmatic approach to solving problems, this chapter presents a well-written account of how the model can be applied to military couples, particulary by staying in the present, focusing on assets and strengths, and working on attainable goals.

Kathryn D. Rheem, Scott R. Woolley, and Neil Weissman cover the utility of emotionally focused couples therapy with military couples in Chapter 6. Outlining the main goals of this approach, expanding and reorganizing key emotional responses, creating a shift in partners' interactional positions, and fostering the creation of a secure bond between partners, the authors present a nicely written case vignette, which highlights the ease of use of the approach.

No other treatment for couples has seen such a recent increase in interest and research as the one presented in Chapter 7. Robert P. O'Brien details the Gottman method couples therapy model of treatment and how it is already being used with military couples. With the primary goals of increasing respect, affection, and closeness, breaking through conflict when feeling stuck, developing a better understanding of each other, and keeping conflicts civil and calm, O'Brien discusses many of the benefits as well as the limitations of this approach with military couples.

Chapter 8 opens Section 3, which addresses the most common and unique challenges facing military couples. In this chapter, Lynn K. Hall provides a broad and comprehensive review of how the military culture has an impact on the relationship. Specifically, she discusses the challenges of role ambiguity, deployment, childhood attachment, and stigma. This chapter is an excellent complement to Chapter 2.

The remaining 9 chapters in Section 3 cover the following topics: separation and divorce (Chapter 9, Walter R. Schumm, R. Roudi Nazarinia Roy, and Vance Theodore); PTSD (Chapter 10, Jason M. Lavender and Judith A. Lyons); depression (Chapter 11, Kevin M. Connolly and Kathryn S. Hahn); infidelity (Chapter 12, Douglas K. Snyder, Christina Balderrama-Durbin, Caitlin Fissette, David M. Scheider, J. Kelly Barnett, and Samuel Fiala); intimate partner violence (Chapter 13, Nicole D. Pukay-Martin and Patrick S. Calhoun); substance misuse (Chapter 14, Sharon Morgillo Freeman); traumatic brain injury (Chapter 15, Carrie-Ann Strong and Jacobus Donders); enhancing resilience with culturally competent treatment of same-sex military couples (Chapter 16, Matthew Porter and Veronica Gutierrez); and cultural differences (Chapter 17, Rebecca Tews-Kozlowski and Desireé King).

In Chapter 18, Mathew B. Tully, a former military lawyer, provides invaluable information about divorce for those military couples who decide that this is the most appropriate solution to their situation. And finally, in Chapter 19, Walter Penk, a four-decade veteran clinician and researcher of the Veterans Administration, Dolores Little, and Nathan Ainspan outline the most useful and tested military and civilian psychosocial rehabilitation programs for couples dealing with PTSD.

Section 1

Military Culture

2

Understanding the Military Culture

MICHAEL R. DEVRIES, H. KENT HUGHES,
HARVEY WATSON, and BRET A. MOORE

INTRODUCTION

At an annual formal military ball, speaking to service members, their spouses, and significant others, Distinguished Service Cross recipient Chief Warrant Officer Dave Cooper made the point clear: "The Army recruits Soldiers, but it re-enlists families." In other words, service members serve only as long as their spouses allow them to serve. Service members enlist for a defined number of years. When it comes time to decide if a service member will reenlist, it is highly unlikely that he or she will do so if his or her spouse is unhappy with the military lifestyle.

It is a well-known truism when working with military families that the most significant threat to a service member's effectiveness is family problems. The moment a couple is divided or suffers significant marital discord, the service member's effectiveness is compromised. A troubling example is the increase of suicides in the military. It has been well covered in the media that the suicide rate in the military has risen significantly in the last few years. The investigations of recent suicide attempts and completed suicides show a common theme of marital/relationship distress. From 2005 to 2009, relationship problems were a factor in over 50% of the suicides in the Army (Analysis of Army Suicides, 2009). The health of our military fighting force is directly related to the health of our military marriages. What we see in the military is a common drama of relationship problems played out in an environment of uncommon stressors.

To begin the discussion of treatment approaches for working with military couples, it is important to discuss military culture and how military families may differ from their civilian counterparts. This chapter provides an overview of the unique characteristics of service members and their families as well as the overall military organization and how a clear understanding of the military culture is relevant to clinical practice.

MILITARY CULTURE

As we discuss the culture of the military and how clinicians can understand the unique pressures military service places on relationships, we must be cautious not to create a simplistic description of the military culture and therefore the military marriage. The military is not a collection of homogeneous individuals and couples. Consequently, individual couples vary in how much their marriage resembles the prototypical military marriage. This variation is due to many factors commonly discussed in marital counseling literature that would be true of any couple, civilian or military. In addition to these factors that all marriages have in common, there are characteristics specific to the military and the wide variety of subcultures within the military that may affect martial relationships. Despite the variation across the military, the unifying factor that makes a discussion of the military marriage worthwhile is the similarities that exist between the individual cultures of the Armed Forces that are collectively very different from civilian culture. Our primary experience has been with the Army, so our perspective will undoubtedly reflect this experience. We have tried to avoid making the discussion specific to the Army as much as possible (see Christian, Stivers, & Sammons, 2009; Matthews, 2009, for further discussion of military culture).

In considering the military couple who presents for counseling, like any initial counseling session, one must assess the effects of each individual's culture on the marriage. This requires an understanding of the cultures of both the individuals and their degree of acculturation. As with any culture, two individuals may be a part of the same military culture, but they may identify with the culture to differing degrees.

A common misconception is that all soldiers are the same. For example, while people who are not associated with the military may intellectually know there are many different jobs in the military, they often do not truly appreciate the various roles service members play and skills they possess. This misconception likely comes from the representations of military service in the media. Whether it be the news media or Hollywood, it is rare to hear about soldiers who are supply clerks, mechanics, dental assistants, water purification specialists, and sheet metal workers. The media either portray an infantry soldier, face to face with the enemy, locked in mortal combat, or show the pilot flying an aircraft in dramatic dogfights with the enemy air force. Combat units such as Special Operations, infantry, armor, and aviation are often called the "tip of the spear." While these individuals are the most lethal and well-known personnel of the military, they would not be much without the rest of the spear. The reality is that the vast majority of service members are support personnel. While there are commonalities among the different military occupational groups, there are also significant differences.

Even when we consider different combat arms roles, one can see significant differences in culture. The Special Operations, aviation, and infantry soldiers may have much in common with each other when compared to those in more supportive roles, but there are significant differences between these communities as well. In addition, many service members in supportive roles may be similar in personality style to their combat arms peers. By way of illustration of the variation in culture within the military, we use Army Special Operations as an example. Service members in Special Operations typically are volunteers from all other branches of the Army. It is likely then that some of their peers in these branches may have very similar personalities and cultural experiences; however, they did not volunteer. Special Operations service members are often called triple volunteers because they volunteer for the Army, volunteer again to jump from airplanes, and volunteer a third time to serve in a special unit. In addition to rigorous training, Special Operations organizations have strict and highly selective assessment programs. What characteristics may lead them to volunteer for and be able to complete this specialized training? Matthews (2009) discussed the differences in character traits between West Point cadets who complete their basic training and those who drop out. Special Operations assessment programs select for certain traits and therefore create new environments with certain characteristics based on their missions. By nature of being smaller and more specialized, these units develop their own cultural norms, not the least of which is pride in being willing to volunteer more times than the average service member.

Another good illustration of differences in cultures that may look superficially similar is that of aviators across all branches of the military. We often refer to the personality of the pilot because there seems to be commonalities between aviators; however, aviators in the Army may show significant cultural differences from their peers in the Air Force and Navy. For both the Air Force and Navy, pilots are officers who attended college before becoming pilots. In the Army, the majority of pilots are warrant officers. Warrant officers are technical experts who are often drawn from the enlisted ranks or come from direct accession programs (so-called high school to flight school). Many times, Army pilots may have served in the infantry or other branches and chosen to switch to aviation. They may not have attended college and may have chosen to switch for common reasons. It is often said in jest, likely with a good dose of truth, that those who switch to Army aviation are those who are tired of carrying a heavy rucksack and sleeping in the mud. These different paths to aviation and different experiential backgrounds are likely to lead to differences in the cultures of Army, Navy, and Air Force aviation personnel.

RANK

If the military culture is so diverse, what can we say about the commonalities of military subcultures? One of the main characteristics of military culture is the hierarchical system of rank. The military is made up of three classes of ranks: enlisted, warrant officer, and commissioned officer. The enlisted ranks, denoted by E-1 through E-9, can be thought of as the blue-collar workers of the military. They are commonly divided further into junior enlisted, E-1 through E-4, and noncommissioned officers (NCOs), E-5 through E-9. NCOs are enlisted service members who are expected to take on additional leadership roles. As mentioned, warrant officers are technical specialists. They differ from commissioned officers in that commissioned officers are expected to fill leadership and staff roles. Commissioned officers could be called the white-collar workers. While much could be written about the significance of each of these ranks and their individual nuances, we discuss some of the important cultural differences between these groups and how the culture of rank is important in understanding service members seeking marital counseling specifically.

Enlisted soldiers make up the majority of the military and are figuratively the body of the force. The officers are the managers and chief executive officers (CEOs). The warrant officers are the teachers and resident experts. The junior enlisted are the workers, and the senior enlisted are the floor supervisors. The NCO ranks are often referred to as the backbone of the Army. Senior enlisted service members are also considered technical experts, although like commissioned officers, they are often called to hold leadership positions in addition to maintaining proficiency in their jobs. At the higher ranks of E-8 and E-9, NCOs become senior advisors to the command. While not technically second in command (command is an officer role), they typically function as the right hand of the commander.

Hierarchy is important within the enlisted ranks. Depending on how formal the unit is, junior enlisted service members are required to stand at parade rest (i.e., with their hands in the small of their back) when addressing a senior-ranking enlisted person. Enlisted service members are required to stand and come to attention (feet together, back straight, hands at the side) when speaking with an officer. Enlisted service members take an oath and are sworn to obey the orders of officers appointed over them. The enlisted chain of command, in addition to supervising the work of the military, is tasked with ensuring that standards of dress and military rules and regulations are upheld within the force. They are literally the standard-bearers of the military. It is not hard to see how this role of the standard bearer could translate into a rule orientation even in a service member's family and social lives. Standards are important for all military members, and rule consciousness is common in all ranks but may be more prevalent in those with an NCO background.

The enlisted and officer ranks have traditionally been separate. The enlisted service member, no matter how senior, is required to salute even the most junior commissioned officer or warrant officer. Commissioned officers and warrant officers are addressed as sir or ma'am by all enlisted service members and by junior officers. There are rules against becoming too friendly or fraternizing with those of different ranks. This is intended to avoid officers showing or appearing to show favoritism toward soldiers to whom they have a friendly relationship. In the modern military, this separation is not intended to yield a class system but rather encourage discipline in and protect the integrity of a chain of command that must be followed to ensure that crucial decisions pertaining to life-and-death matters are made without hesitation and favoritism.

HIERARCHY

A strict hierarchy is necessary in an environment in which following orders is crucial. The midst of battle is no place to have an argument about what to do next.

Quick action can save lives and mean the difference between mission success and mission failure. As one earns higher rank, there is an increasing expectation that orders will be followed without question. In fact, at senior levels of rank, every comment or statement becomes an implied task for the staff. The chain of command is inviolate. While there are times when officers and enlisted members are expected to question orders (e.g., if they are illegal or immoral), in the case of routine orders, authority is not questioned; rather, they acknowledge the order and comply. The understanding that orders are meant to be followed often carries over into a service member's home life. Service members often experience a culture shock when they return home from deployment, especially after an extended absence, to a family that does not respond promptly and eagerly to their direction.

A close corollary to the importance of hierarchy in the military is the value placed on leadership. From very early on, new and inexperienced service members are expected to become leaders. In the hierarchy of the military, those at the top of the pyramid must excel at leadership. As service members advance, they are encouraged and rewarded for taking charge and being responsible for their squad, platoon, company, and so on. In every household, there is a hierarchy; whether it is patriarchal or matriarchal, it is rarely exactly egalitarian. The service member in the family is likely to feel a strong responsibility to be the leader in the home. This may or may not be received well by the family member. When the service member is absent from the home, often unpredictably, the civilian spouse is required to take on many of the leadership roles in the family. The service member, given the value placed on being a leader, may have a difficult time relinquishing this control. The clinician working with the military couple may find it valuable to take into consideration how this military hierarchy and chain of authority have influenced the dynamics of the marriage.

For people to effectively follow orders, the orders must be clear, concise, and to the point. In the military, clear and direct communication is valued. Service members may be more direct and blunt than the general population due to this style of communication. This direct communication style, with the expectation of compliance without question, can also present significant challenges in the military marriage.

THE "MISSION"

The concept of "mission first" is important in the military. While the military works hard to value the family lives of service members and their welfare, the nature of the job is that the mission trumps all other concerns. The ultimate display of mission first is when a service member puts the welfare of his family and self aside to enter harm's way. This dedication to mission accomplishment is applied to all missions, regardless of their importance. While practically some missions are deemed more or less important and prioritized on a daily basis, whenever faced with the direct question of what is more important, mission success or some other outcome, the service member will likely have a visceral response and carry out the mission. The focus on the mission often places the service member in conflict between dedication to the mission and dedication to relationships outside work. As will be mentioned, this devotion to the mission may be both culturally and personality based.

SPIRITUALITY

Based on the Office of Army Demographics, fiscal year [FY]05 (Maxfield, 2005), 72% of active duty service members claimed either a Protestant or Catholic affiliation. All of the services employ chaplains to look after the spiritual well-being of their service members, regardless of their faith, background, or religious preference. The military could be characterized as a religious culture, although the actual levels of spirituality vary greatly from individual to individual. Knowing the role of faith for military couples is vital as religious and spiritual issues may be important in their lives. Professionals will need to be sensitive to faith issues and how they influence marital decisions. For example, people of faith will often move toward forgiveness following a betrayal. This could be seen as maladaptive by some, but for a deeply spiritual person, this is the path toward healing. Sensitivity to issues of faith and the impact on one's motivation is important. We are not implying that all military couples are Christian or even religious. What is important for professionals to know is that religion and the military have a strong relationship and those beliefs will often permeate the counseling process.

COMBAT EXPERIENCE

An important aspect of military culture, which can affect both the marriage and the counseling relationship, is the effect of combat experience on the perspective of the service member. Chapter 10 of Kindsvatter's *American Soldier* (2003) is titled, "Dwellers Beyond the Environment of War." This chapter deals with the attitudes of the combat soldier toward those who have not experienced combat. Kindsvatter quotes a Private Eugene B. Sledge as saying "In our myopic view, we respected and admired only those who got shot at." Kindsvatter also said that combat soldiers, particularly those closest to the front doing most of the fighting, believed that the rest of the soldiers, and more so the civilians back home, did not have any idea what the combat soldier experienced. This can develop into a resentment of the difficulties the frontline troops have to bear, while those in the "rear" and back home have a seemingly carefree and comfortable existence. Kindsvatter points out that there is an ironic dichotomy here, as the combat veteran simultaneously wants the respect and admiration of those back home for his or her service and yet resents them for not having been in combat themselves.

This resentment toward those who have not served in direct combat can present a problem of credibility for the therapist who has no military or combat experience. There seems to be two ways for the therapist to reach service members who struggle with this issue. For counselors who serve in the military, there are often opportunities to earn credibility by experiencing as many of the difficult military experiences as they are allowed. Mental health providers in the military are often encouraged to attend challenging schools like the Army's Airborne or Ranger Schools. In addition, in a deployed environment, they can visit service members in remote and hostile areas and experience firsthand their difficulties. While mental health providers will never be combatants, they can earn respect by being willing to leave the safety of the rear to meet with those who see combat on a regular basis. For the provider who does not have the opportunity to gain these experiences, it is often important to assume a one-down perspective of someone who does not know what it is like and encourage the service member to tell his or her story. This taps into the service member's desire for respect from those who have not experienced combat. Allowing the service member to be the teacher early on can communicate respect for his or her difficult experience and make the service member more likely, in turn, to respect the education and experience of the counselor.

The effect of combat experience on the marital relationship can be broad and even positive in many cases; however, in the context of the resentment toward the home front, there are common challenges to relationships. In a relationship in which one person has recently returned from combat, there is often a mutual misunderstanding of the other's sacrifice during the separation. The belief of the combat veteran that those in the rear cannot understand because they have not been in combat can lead to a serious and progressive lack of communication. Lack of communication can drive a wedge between the couple that can quickly expand beyond discussions of combat experiences and into communication in general. This can lead to both parties feeling misunderstood.

Mutual experience of the hardship of military service and combat can have a strong bonding effect on those who serve together. The term *band of brothers* denotes the family-like bonds that are formed under intense stress. Return from combat, or even coming home each night, often requires the service member to say good-bye to friends and "brothers" and return to his or her spouse and family. While deployed overseas, a service member may spend 18 hours a day with his or her peers. Coming home and sharing free time with a significant other may feel like a loss of the relationships built while serving away from home. Due to their intensity, these work relationships can often compete with the service member's marital relationship with regard to attention and loyalty. It is not uncommon for the soldier experiencing marital problems to be encouraged to turn away from the spouse and toward their work family. The effects of work relationships on a marriage may not be unique to the military, but they may be made more intense by the level of stress and the duration of separations.

VALUES

Many of the important facets of military culture can be related to the values the military encourages. The Navy and Marines have the core values of honor, courage, and commitment. The Air Force has integrity, service before self, and excellence in all we do. The Coast Guard values include honor, respect, and devotion to duty. The Army encourages adherence to the seven Army values, represented (like everything else in the military) by an acronym. The complete definitions of these terms by all of the services cover most all of the same values. We can use the Army values as an example. LDRSHIP is the acronym for the Army values. It stands for loyalty, duty, respect, selfless service, honor, integrity, and personal courage. The Army values are defined as follows:

Loyalty: Bear true faith and allegiance to the U.S. Constitution, the Army, your unit, and other soldiers
Duty: Fulfill your obligations
Respect: Treat people as they should be treated
Selfless service: Put the welfare of the nation, the Army, and your subordinates before your own
Honor: Live up to the Army values
Integrity: Do what is right, legally and morally
Personal courage: Face fear, danger, or adversity

While all of these values are positive and an individual who lives up to them would most likely be a good spouse, as written, they emphasize responsibilities to the Army over those in the family.

PERSONALITY TYPES IN THE MILITARY

When assessing a new couple presenting for counseling, it may be hard to tell the cultural influence from the personality influence. Persons with common personality traits may be drawn to the military culture or certain personality traits may be reinforced by the culture of the military, resulting in the expression of certain personality traits. This may be an important distinction given that personalities tend to be stable over a lifetime, whereas the influence of one's environment at work may be more easily molded (Costa & McCrae, 1988). For a clinician working with a military couple with problems that seem to be related to the culture of the work environment, the individual may be more amenable to change.

As we consider personality as a factor in military marital counseling, it is important to remember, as with culture, the person in front of us may be very different from the prototype. The military attracts people with a wide variety of personalities and cultural backgrounds. In addition, as stated, the military is made up of a wide variety of job types. The personality drawn to spend months aboard a ship or submarine may vary significantly from the personality drawn to the infantry or aviation. People join the military for many different reasons: college money, escape from a dead-end lifestyle or job, service to their country, and so on. There may be some commonalities in personality, either innate or acquired, in some people who choose to join the military, but to say there is a personality style of military service members would be terribly simplistic. New service members who enlist for a defined period of time, typically 2–6 years, display a cross section of the general population in their personality styles. It is after this initial enlistment, when they truly know what they have signed up for, that a winnowing occurs. It is likely that those who choose to reenlist (with officers and warrant officers, this process is not technically reenlisting, but they similarly choose to stay or resign their commission or warrant) have more in common than those serving their initial term of service. In addition, any environmental effects the military may have on personality traits are likely to be more significant the longer the service member is exposed to the culture. Matthews (2009) noted, that over 47 months of training at West Point, character strengths are relatively stable, so any adaptation that takes place may take many years. So, what then can we say about personality traits of military service members?

In general, service members are more willing to leave behind the safety and security of home. The typical soldier seems to be willing to sacrifice all that is valuable to him or her for a greater cause. In his book on the American soldier, Peter Kindsvatter (2003) discusses the reasons soldiers "rally to the flag" and choose to serve. He notes that motivations range from "enthusiastic volunteer to resentful draftee." While we no longer have the draft, our current military is still characterized by the same "mix of enthusiasm, resignation, and resentment" described by Kindsvatter. So, while we cannot assume all military members have the same level of motivation and reasons for service, some generalities can be made. A desire to serve may be one commonality. Kindsvatter stated that World War I provided an opportunity for young men to prove their courage and manhood. The young soldier was "fascinated by the prospect of adventure and heroism." This call to serve can often seem stronger than the service member's devotion to a spouse. Rarely do service members want to be separated from their spouse and family. What they do desire is the opportunity to fulfill their training, and that generally requires separation. From the outside looking in, and often in the marital relationship itself, that desire can be misinterpreted as apathy toward the marriage. The clinician working with a military couple needs to understand that value placed on independence and fulfilling one's duties rather than judge this dedication to work as "antimarriage." As this concept was mentioned as part of the cultural influence as well, it can be hard to distinguish whether this is a cultural influence or a function of a career-oriented, adventure-seeking personality style.

The military also reinforces traits that look much like the symptoms of obsessive-compulsive personality disorder. Structure, order, and precision are values that permeate the military environment. Nearly everything in the military comes with a checklist. It is common for soldiers to be encouraged to check and recheck the gear they have packed for a training event or mission. When these checks are complete, a commander or supervisor may come and check the gear again. This behavior clearly makes sense when one considers that the safety of a soldier and his or her teammates may depend on the individual soldier having all his or her gear. Often, these traits can find their way into the home in unwelcome ways. In the military, everything is governed by regulation. There is a "right" way to do everything. At home, in the absence of regulations, a soldier may come to see the way he or she does things as the "right" way. Spouses are expected to know what right looks like and execute without a discussion. The nonmilitary spouse likely has a personal understanding of how things should be. Being a good spouse often requires a transition from the military way of doing things at work and the rules of the home while making the commute each evening.

COMMON THEMES IN MILITARY MARRIAGES

Whether it is the effects of culture, personality, or other circumstances, there are several factors about military life that make the military marriage unique when contrasted with civilian marriages. An Army chaplain was quoted as saying that, for the service member, the "Army is his wife, and the wife is his mistress." This is not implying that the spouse of a service member is less important. Rather, the spouse of a service member learns quickly when the military "calls," the service member must go, regardless of his or her life circumstances. This often can leave a spouse feeling abandoned and insignificant. In fact, the spouse may begin to feel as if the service member is choosing work over the relationship, when the reality is that the service member faces punishment, financial and otherwise, if duties are not fulfilled. Whatever branch of service, that branch has incredible power over the individual. The chain of command has ultimate authority and responsibility for the service member to the point fines, confinement, loss of privileges, loss of rank, and even removal from the military can be imposed. Complicating matters is the possibility that service members may love what they do and are torn between responsibilities at home and at work. Working with couples in this culture requires educating young couples in how to live in this reality without personalizing the choice of work over home life. A common phrase quoted in Army circles is, "If the Army wanted you to have a wife, they would have issued you one." This can be seen as humorous, but it can also come across as cruel. The Army is the third party in the marriage and the one with the most authority. Having this third party in the relationship has real consequences, and clinicians must be aware of this fact when working with military couples.

Another glaring factor that defines military marriage is that separation from each other is standard. Over the course of a marriage, the time apart can be years. The first author works with couples who have been married for less than 10 years and spent upward of 5 of those years separated by deployment. Some of the consequences from this lifestyle include a loss of emotional closeness, changed roles in the home, and issues of reunification. Assisting military couples to cope in healthy ways with these consequences is an essential component to marital therapy. Providers may not be able to utilize many of the marital tools found in civilian literature because the military couple may not be together to implement them. Consequently, various strategies will need adaptation to become useful in the military culture.

One specific consequence of this lifestyle is the growth of independence in the marriage. While separated, both spouses learn to take care of their lives individually. They cannot depend on each other as much for day-to-day living. The longer this goes on, the more and more independent they can become. Although necessary and useful, this independence can be disruptive for emotional closeness. Some couples who have served for many years will say that when they are together for a long period of time, they actually look forward to a separation. Most civilian couples do not have to deal with this phenomenon. Helping couples reconnect and maintain a healthy dependence on each other can prove challenging for the clinician.

Reunification following long separations is a normal occurrence for military marriages. Couples must develop specific skills to facilitate reunification. As previously stated, roles have often changed, and responsibilities were taken over by the spouse left behind. Returning to life the way it was before deployment is delicate. This is an experience that is unique to the military marriage and often triggers underlying emotional issues. Recognizing the unique effects of long-term deployments compared to multiple short-term rotations is critical in the timing and approach used with couples as they come back together physically and emotionally.

Military couples often live in locations far away from extended family and close friends. Frequent moves disrupt the continuity and support that extended family brings. This adds to the isolation effect that couples experience and either strengthens or erodes their self-confidence. Healthy marriages rely on the community surrounding the marriage. For the military couple, that community is always in flux and rarely includes family. The military has programs intentionally designed to create new communities for military families, but this requires couples to reach out each time they move and reconnect with strangers. Consequently, the military couple has to be more intentional to build support around them.

CONCLUSION

Military couples face multiple challenges that are unique to the military culture. The challenge for the counselor is to go beyond providing tertiary care to providing prevention and healthy adaptation. Adapting in healthy ways that promote emotional closeness for couples can actually strengthen the marriage. Providers need to learn the language of the military, understand the military culture, and recognize some of the common personality traits that may be present in our fighting force to become better equipped in working through the issues that often present in the military marriage. Although problems are often similar across various cultural divides, there are aspects of military life that demand special attention in order to be effective counselors. By becoming more effective, counselors can improve service member performance, strengthen the marriage, and truly contribute to the defense of our country and the freedom we so value.

REFERENCES

Analysis of Army suicides: 1 January 2003–31 October 2009 (Epidemiological Report No. 14-HK-OBW9-10a). (2009). U.S. Army Public Health Command, p. 13.

The Army values. (2011). Retrieved February 12, 2011, from http://www.army.mil/values/

Christian, J. R., Stivers, J. R., & Sammons, M. T. (2009). Training to the warrior ethos: Implications for clinicians treating military members and their families. In S. M. Freeman, B. A. Moore, & A. Freeman (Eds.), *Living and surviving in harm's way* (pp. 27–49). New York: Taylor & Francis Group.

Costa, P. T., & McCrae, R. R. (1988). Personality in adulthood: A six-year longitudinal study of self-reports and spouse ratings on the NEO Personality Inventory. *Journal of Personality and Social Psychology, 54*, 853–863.

Freeman, S. M., Moore, B. A., & Freeman, A. (2009). *Living and surviving in harm's way: A psychological treatment handbook for pre- and post-deployment of military personnel*. New York: Taylor & Francis Group.

Homeport: Coast Guard core values. (2005). Retrieved February 12, 2011, from http://homeport.uscg.mil/mycg/portal/ep/contentView.do? contentTypeId=2&contentId=17456&programId=12608&pageTypeId=16440

Kindsvatter, P. S. (2003). *American soldiers: Ground combat in the World Wars, Korea, and Vietnam*. Lawrence: University Press of Kansas.

Learn about the Air Force. (2009). Retrieved on February 12, 2011, from http://www.airforce.com/learn-about/our-values/

Matthews, M. D. (2009). The soldier's mind: Motivation, mindset, and attitude. In S. M. Freeman, B. A. Moore, & A. Freeman (Eds.), *Living and surviving in harm's way* (pp. 27–49). New York: Taylor & Francis Group.

Maxfield, B. D. (2005). *Army demographics FY05 Army profile*. Retrieved February 15, 2011, from http://www.armyg1.army.mil/HR/docs/demographics/FY05%20Army%20Profile.pdf

Maxfield, B. D. (2009). *Army demographics FY09 Army profile*. Retrieved February 14, 2011, from http://www.armyg1.army.mil/hr/docs/demographics/FY09%20Army%20Profile.pdf

United States Navy. (2009). Retrieved on February 12, 2011, from http://www.navy.mil/navydata/navy_legacy_hr.asp?id=193

The values that define a Marine. (2011). Retrieved February 12, 2011, from http://www.marines.com/main/index/making_marines/culture/traditions/core_values

3

Marital Functioning in the Army
Marital Dissolution Trends and Correlates of Marital Dissolution Intent among US Soldiers following Combat Deployments

LYNDON A. RIVIERE, JULIE C. MERRILL,
JEFFREY L. THOMAS, JOSHUA E. WILK,
and PAUL D. BLIESE

INTRODUCTION

Divorce or more broadly marital dissolution[*] in the general population has been of significant concern to researchers, clinicians, clergy and others. This concern was likely fueled by noticeable increases in divorce rates in the 1970s (rates have declined slightly since then but have remained fairly stable) (Coontz, 2007). Among military personnel, marital dissolution trends have been particularly scrutinized in the context of wars since wars are considered to have a major influence on several family related phenomenon such as marriage, childbirth, and divorce rates (Lester, 1993).

Research examining the relationship of war to dissolution rates among military personnel has produced mixed findings. Studies on World War II, Korean, and Vietnam War veterans' marriage outcomes have found increased risk of separation and divorce for combat veterans compared to marriages of non-deployed service members (Pavalko & Elder, 1990; Ruger, Wilson, & Waddoups, 2002). Similar

[*] The term marital dissolution encompasses divorce as well as separations.

results were found for Gulf War veterans, but only among female soldiers (Angrist & Johnson, 2000). However, one study that looked at divorce rates between 1933 and 1986, found no effect of either mobilization or demobilization on divorce rates (Lester, 1993).

Nonetheless, an increase in divorce rates among service members has been expected to be the most visible manifestation of the strain that 10 years of war in the current conflicts in Afghanistan and Iraq would exert on military marriages. Contrary to that expectation, the most recent data on service members' marital dissolution trends (Fiscal Year (FY)1996-FY2005) indicate that any elevation in these rates cannot be attributed to deployments to Iraq or Afghanistan (Karney & Crown, 2007). In that monograph, divorce rates from 1996 to 2000 were contrasted with those from 2001 to 2005, the latter time period reflecting a period of intense combat deployments to Afghanistan and then Iraq. There was a pattern of increasing divorce rates since 2001, but the rates in 2005 were identical to those of 1996, a year of relatively limited military engagements (Karney & Crown, 2007). Karney and Crown concluded there was little empirical evidence to support the expectation that the intense combat deployment cycle between 2001 and 2005 was associated with increased divorce rates.

However, it is not known whether marital dissolution trends illustrated by Karney and Crown (2007) have remained largely unchanged as the wars have continued beyond 2005. These results may be explained by the idea that marital dissolution is a distal indicator of marital problems (McLeland, Sutton, & Schumm, 2008; Riviere & Merrill, 2010), as it may take several years before chronic relationship strain results in marital dissolution, if at all. It is therefore informative to assess more proximal measures of relationship difficulties such as marital dissolution intent, infidelity, and marital quality.

Some researchers have examined trends in these proximal measures among enlisted male soldiers who had deployed to either Iraq or Afghanistan. Generally, their analyses show that the percentage of soldiers reporting high marital quality has declined from close to 80% in 2003 to around 65% in 2009 (Riviere, Merrill, Thomas, Wilk, & Bliese, under review). Mirroring this decline in marital quality, trend data for infidelity reports and for separation/divorce intent also increased during the same period (Riviere et al., under review). Together these findings suggest that while the data on marital dissolution trends up through FY 2005 were basically stable, Army marriages have been adversely affected by Afghanistan and Iraq combat deployments without an increase in marital dissolution rates. However, while Riviere and colleagues examined the influence of time and several other variables such as mental and physical health on marital dissolution intent, they did not assess whether marital quality and infidelity, which are known to be associated with divorce, were associated with marital dissolution intent.

Separation/Divorce Intent and Divorce

Couples who intend to separate or divorce do not always follow through with those plans. Even if separations occur they may be followed by reconciliation (Wineberg, 1994). Among women, one study showed that there were three types of separations:

temporary ones, those than ended in divorce, and those that were long-term (Morgan, 1988). However, it appears that around 85-90% of couples who separate go on to get divorces (Doherty, Willoughby, & Peterson, 2011). Although separation/divorce intent is not equivalent to actual separation, it seems likely that the majority of couples who indicate that they plan to get a divorce will go on to do so.

Divorce has received considerable research attention because it is considered a major life event stressor that has implications not only for the well-being of the couple, but for any children that they might have. However, studies have not settled whether the health disadvantage of separated and divorced people is temporary or long term (Booth & Amato, 1991; Johnson & Wu, 2002). Nevertheless, the evidence suggests that the transition from being married to being divorced worsens health (Williams & Umberson, 2004).

Research has also explored the risk factors for divorce. These include mental health problems such as depression and alcohol abuse (Breslau et al., 2011) and marital problems particularly infidelity and relationship quality (Amato & Previti, 2003; Amato & Rogers, 1997). Among service members, being older, having children, and, surprisingly, longer deployments among Army, Marine, and Navy enlisted service members are associated with lower divorce likelihood especially for males (Karney & Crown, 2007). Karney and Crown (2007) could not consider either marital quality or infidelity as contributing factors because the data set they used did not contain these measures.

Marital Quality & Infidelity

The term "marital quality" is generally used to describe how well a marriage functions and incorporates marital satisfaction and marital happiness (Spanier, 1979). Poor marital quality does not inevitably result in marital dissolution but it is a risk factor (Karney & Bradbury, 1997). Marital quality is also affected by some of the factors mentioned above that influence divorce. Mental health problems such as posttraumatic stress disorder (PTSD) have been found to be associated with relationship problems especially among military personnel (Taft, Watkins, Stafford, Street, & Monson, 2011). However, the relationship between PTSD and relationship problems may be reciprocal in nature (Monson, Taft, & Fredman, 2009).

Infidelity, identified as one of the most common causes of divorce across cultures (Betzig, 1989), is also linked with relationship dissatisfaction (Atkins, Baucom, & Jacobson, 2001; Blow & Hartnett, 2005; Whisman, Gordon, & Chatav, 2007). Further, infidelity is a predictor of mental health problems, at least among women (Cano & O'Leary, 2000). Given the interrelationship between marital quality and infidelity, it is important to examine whether they are independently related to dissolution intent.

Stress and Trauma Hypotheses

It can be expected that the correlates of divorce or dissolution intent are similar among both civilian and military couples. However, factors such as mental health problems that are the consequence of traumatic combat exposure and the demands of military life are factors that uniquely affect military couples. Few researchers have developed models on military marriage functioning (Karney & Crown, 2007), but two perspectives have emerged that may be useful in interpreting military marital functioning and dissolution. These perspectives are the stress hypothesis and the trauma hypothesis (Karney & Crown, 2007). The former posits that the stressors of military life such as separations and relocations are detrimental to marital functioning. The trauma hypothesis is related to the stress hypothesis because of the focus on the stressors of military life, but its focus is on how the sequelae of service members' combat exposure such as mental health problems, alcohol misuse, and anti-social behavior can impair their relationships (Gimbel & Booth, 1994). So, while the stress hypothesis can be applied to military marriages irrespective of the occurrence of wars, the trauma hypothesis appears to be more limited in scope. We will consider whether these perspectives provide insight about our findings.

AIMS

This chapter has two main aims. First, we present data that extends Karney and Crown's study (Karney & Crown, 2007) looking at marital dissolution trends beyond FY2005 (from 2003-2009) as previously reported (Riviere et al., under review). Secondly, because of the limited data on the correlates of marital dissolution in military populations who have experienced combat, we examine the association of two of the proximal indicators (marital quality and infidelity) with marital dissolution intent (separation/divorce intent) using both a large cross-sectional sample, and a longitudinal sample of enlisted soldiers assessed at 6 months and 12 months post Afghanistan and Iraq deployments. Further, the relationships between combat exposure, mental health problems, and somatic symptoms with marital dissolution intent are also explored in both these samples.

Few prior studies have examined divorce in the military, particularly as related to the current conflicts. We are unaware of any that examined dissolution intent. We contend that dissolution intent is closely related to actual dissolution and for that reason is important to assess what are its correlates.

METHODS

Participants and Procedures

As reported by Riviere and colleagues (Riviere et al., under review), data were obtained from the Defense Manpower Data Center (DMDC) in order to report Army marital dissolution rates stratified by rank for fiscal years 2003-2009 (n=1,895,571). Marital dissolution rates were calculated as any change in status from married to non-married out of the number of married soldiers in each year. While changes from married to any other status were part of this rate, the majority of the changes were from married to divorced.

We also report data from two samples of enlisted soldiers, which were obtained from a larger study on health and well-being among Active Component (AC) U.S.

soldiers between 2003 and 2009. The soldiers in the samples were drawn from brigade combat teams, which typically have lower percentages of female soldiers than other brigades.

The first sample, which is cross-sectional, comprised of 6,309 soldiers, was collected approximately 3 to 6 months after the soldiers returned from deployments to Iraq or Afghanistan. The second sample is longitudinal (n=313). A subset of the soldiers assessed in 2008 and 2009 in the cross-sectional sample was followed up at 12 months post deployment in 2009. Across both samples, we selected the married or separated male, enlisted soldiers who had deployed to Afghanistan and Iraq for our analyses. Other groups such as females and officers had too few soldiers for meaningful analyses.

Measures

Marital dissolution intent. One yes/no item measured intent to separate or divorce by the soldier or spouse. Specifically, soldiers were asked: "Are you or your spouse currently planning to get a divorce or separation?"

Infidelity. Soldiers were asked to respond to a single item question "In the last year, has infidelity been a problem in my marriage?" The response options were no, yes, and unsure. We combined the unsure and the yes into one category since it seemed logical that those unsure about infidelity are more similar to those who indicated yes.

Marital quality was assessed with three items from the 6-item scale Quality of Marriage Index (Norton, 1983); the individual items could be used as single-item predictors (Norton, 1983). The three items were: "I have a good marriage," "My relationship with my spouse is very stable," and "I really feel like part of a team with my spouse." The items' response options ranged from 1 (strongly disagree) to 5 (strongly agree). We used both the sum of this variable and a dichotomous variable, which was created from a median split of the sum. In the regression models, marital quality score was recoded so that higher values indicated poorer marital quality.

Combat exposure was measured using 20 items from the Combat Experiences Scale (CES) that has been used in similar samples (Hoge et al., 2004) resulting in a total number of combat experiences ranging from 0 to 20. Participants were asked whether or not they had the experience during their latest deployment.

Mental health problems. Major depression was measured with the 9-item Patient Health Questionnaire (PHQ-9), a well-validated clinical scale used in primary care (Spitzer, Kroenke, Williams, & and the Patient Health Questionnaire Primary Care Study Group, 1999) and military survey research (Hoge et al., 2004). To meet screening criteria for major depression, soldiers needed to report 5 or more symptoms and indicate little interest or pleasure in doing things as well as feeling down, depressed, or hopeless more than half the days of the past month. PTSD was measured using the 17-item Posttraumatic Stress Disorder Checklist (PCL) (Weathers, Litz, Herman, Huska, & Keane, 1993), a well-validated scale in civilian (Weathers et al., 1993) and military (Bliese et al., 2008; Terhakopian, Sinaii, Engel, Schnurr, & Hoge, 2008) settings. To meet screening criteria, soldiers needed a score of at least 50 (range 17-85) and endorsement of at least 1 re-experiencing symptom, 3 avoidance or numbing symptoms, and 2 hyperarousal symptoms at a moderate or higher level (Hoge et al., 2004).

Alcohol misuse. Soldiers were asked two questions about their alcohol use using a modified Two-Item Conjoint Screen for Alcohol (TICS) (Brown, Leonard, Saunders, & Papasouliotis, 2001). The modified TICS is a validated measure widely used in post-deployment screening (Bliese, Wright, Adler, Hoge, & Prayner, 2005; Milliken, Auchterionie, & Hoge, 2007). A "yes" endorsement for either item was considered a positive screen (Santiago et al., 2010; Wilk et al., 2010).

Somatic symptoms were assessed with 12 items from the Patient Health Questionnaire (PHQ-15), which asks how much the individual has been bothered by each symptom in the past 4 weeks using a 3-point scale (0 = "not bothered," 1 = "bothered a little," and 2 = "bothered a lot") (Kroenke, Spitzer, & Williams, 2002). The items were summed (range 0-36).

Demographic measures included age, rank, education, and years married.

Analyses

Descriptive statistics such as percentages and means were used to describe all the variables used in the cross-sectional and longitudinal data. The bivariate relationships between key predictors and the three indicators of marital functioning (dichotomous marital quality, infidelity, and marital dissolution intent) were analyzed with χ^2 tests of association. ANOVAs were used to assess differences in mean marital quality (continuous measure) across these key predictors. Multivariate logistic regression models were used to determine whether there were significant associations between marital dissolution intent, and infidelity and marital quality adjusting for combat exposure, mental health, alcohol misuse, physical health, and demographics (age, rank, years married, and number of children).

Given the relatively small longitudinal sample, the association of each covariate with dissolution intent was first assessed with unadjusted logistic regression analyses to reduce the number of variables that were entered into the final model. These analyses showed that rank was the only covariate that had a significant association with the outcome. Consequently, the final model had three predictors: rank, marital quality, and infidelity.

RESULTS

Marital Dissolution Trends

Karney and Crown's data showed that the FY1996-FY2005 marriage dissolution rates for all enlisted male soldiers hovered between 2 and 3% (Karney & Crown, 2007). As reported by Riviere and colleagues (under review), the population data on marital dissolution trends (Figure 3.1) showed that the rates for these soldiers also remained stable between FY2006 and FY2009. The rates for male junior enlisted soldiers and non-commissioned officers (NCOs; data not shown) were indistinguishable from the overall rates for all enlisted male soldiers. The rates for officer males also did not change substantially. Between FY2005 and FY2007, the rates for

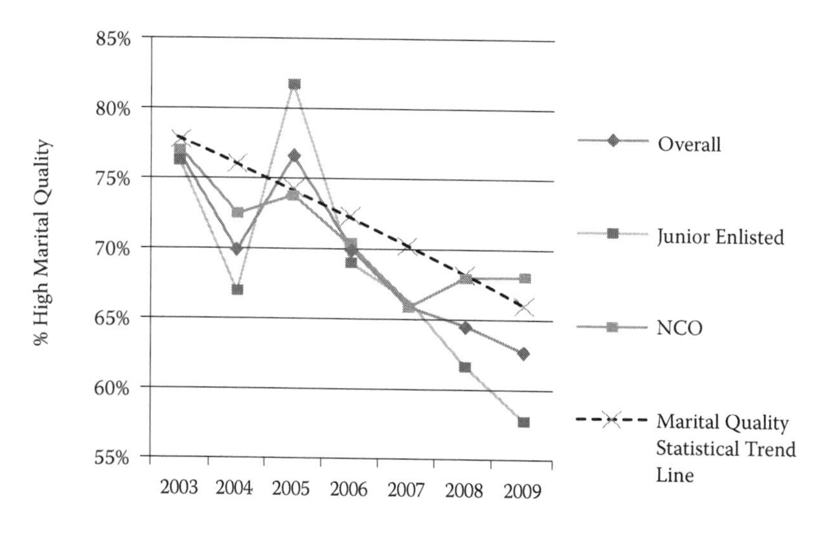

Figure 3.1 2003–2009 Marital dissolution rates among U.S. soldiers.

female officers remained under 5% but increased from about 5.5% in FY2008 to 8.7% in FY2009; the highest rate reported for that group since FY1996. The rates for enlisted females between FY2005 and FY2009 showed a slight increase from 8.2% to 9.7%; the highest rate reported since FY1996 (Riviere et al., under review).

Cross-sectional and Longitudinal Sample Descriptives

Table 3.1 displays the demographic characteristics of the samples. In both samples, around two-thirds of the sample was between 18-29 years old. NCOs (ranks E5-E9) comprised ~50% of the sample and the modal highest educational level reported across years was GED/high school diploma. The mean number of years married was under 5 years in both samples.

Also displayed in Table 3.1 are the number and percentage of soldiers who had low and high marital quality, reported past-year infidelity, dissolution intent, screened positive for depression, PTSD, alcohol misuse, and the means for combat exposure, somatic symptoms, and marital quality. Depression rates were slightly higher in the cross-sectional sample than in the longitudinal sample. PTSD was around 14% in both samples; but alcohol misuse was higher in the cross-sectional sample than in the longitudinal one. Close to two-thirds of the samples reported low marital quality (means were also similar). Percentages for both infidelity and dissolution intent were similar across samples as were the means for somatic symptoms. The mean level of combat exposure was higher in the cross-sectional than in the longitudinal sample.

Distribution of Marital Functioning Indicators by Select Covariates

Table 3.2 presents the distribution of the three marital functioning indicators by levels of combat, somatic symptoms, and marital quality. The bivariate relationship between these indicators and screening negative/positive for depression, PTSD,

TABLE 3.1 Demographic and Other Characteristics of the Samples

	Cross-sectional (N = 6309)		Longitudinal (N = 313)	
Variables	n	%	n	%
Age				
18–24	2,490	39.5	102	32.6
25–29	1,872	29.7	101	32.3
30–39	1,729	27.4	92	29.4
40+	217	3.4	18	5.8
Rank				
E1–E4	3,080	48.8	157	20.5
E5–E9	3,229	51.2	156	49.8
Education				
≤ GED/HS Diploma	3,525	56.5	169	54.5
Some college or other	2,370	38.0	134	43.2
≥ BA/BS degree	339	5.4	7	2.3
Depression (+)	513	8.1	20	6.5
PTSD (+)	874	13.9	45	14.4
Alcohol misuse (+)	1,362	21.9	52	16.8
Marital Quality	3,941	62.5	191	57.9
Low	3,795	60.3	190	61.3
High	2,499	39.7	120	38.7
Infidelity (Unsure/Yes)	1,344	21.4	63	20.3
Dissolution Intent (Yes)	850	13.5	45	14.6
	M	SD	M	SD
Years married	4.44	4.64	4.74	4.71
Combat exposure	9.00	5.54	7.79	4.72
Somatic symptoms	5.33	4.41	4.49	4.04
Marital Quality (sum)	11.40	3.62	11.23	3.77

and alcohol misuse are also displayed. Lastly we show the bivariate relationships among the three marital functioning indicators.

Of the soldiers who indicated that infidelity had been a problem in the past or who reported dissolution intent, higher percentages were in the high combat exposure group, in the groups that screened positive for depression, PTSD or alcohol misuse, and in the high somatic symptom group. Correspondingly, the marital quality means were statistically significantly lower in soldiers who had high combat exposure, who screened positive for the mental health problems or for somatic symptoms.

Lastly, as would be expected, mean marital quality was statistically lower in soldiers who reported infidelity was a problem, and for those who indicated dissolution intent. Similarly, among those who reported dissolution intent, two-thirds also reported infidelity had been a problem; while among those reporting infidelity, less than 50% also indicated that they or their spouse intended to dissolve their marriage.

TABLE 3.2 Distribution of Marital Functioning Indicators by Several Characteristics

Characteristics	Marital Functioning Indicators		
	Marital Quality (Mean)	Infidelity (% yes)	Dissolution Intent (% yes)
Combat Exposure			
Low	11.55	19.6	34.7
Medium	11.40	21.3	29.9
High	11.13*	23.9**	35.4*
Depression			
Screened –	11.56	19.7	12.5
Screened +	9.71***	40.3	24.8***
PTSD			
Screened –	11.60	19.3	12.2
Screened +	10.20	34.2***	21.6***
Alcohol misuse			
Screened –	11.77	17.7	10.5
Screened +	10.09***	34.3***	23.9***
Somatic Symptoms			
Low	11.6	19.4	12.4
Medium	10.63***	29.2	17.5
High	10.13***	35.8***	12.4***
Marital Quality			
Low	—	89.9	98.8
High	—	10.1***	1.2***
Infidelity			
No	12.34	—	31.6
Unsure/Yes	7.99***	—	68.4***
Dissolution Intent			
No	12.35	57.3	—
Yes	5.28***	42.7***	—

*$p < .05$; **$p < .01$; ***$p < .001$

Logistic Regression—Cross-Sectional Sample

Table 3.3 shows the results of the logistic regressions models with dissolution intent as the criterion variable. Of the demographic variables entered into the models, only rank remained a significant predictor in the final model; junior enlisted soldiers were more likely to report dissolution intent than NCOs. Since the sample had data from different years, we also included time as a covariate. In contrast to Model A, only soldiers in 2006 when compared to the soldiers in the reference year of 2003 were more likely to report dissolution intent. Neither combat exposure nor somatic symptoms were significantly associated with the outcome in any of the models. Surprisingly, while all the mental health indicators had significant associations with dissolution intent in Model A, only alcohol misuse remained a significant

TABLE 3.3 Logistic Regression Models Showing the Relationship Between the Key Predictors and Covariates With Dissolution Intent in the Cross-Sectional Sample

Variable	Model A OR (95% C. I.)	Model B OR (95% C. I.)	Model C OR (95% C. I.)
Age			
18–24	1.48 (0.84, 2.62)	1.05 (0.46, 2.37)	0.88 (0.38, 2.02)
25–29	1.69 (0.98, 2.93)	1.26 (0.58, 2.77)	1.08 (0.49, 2.40)
30–39	1.53 (0.91, 2.58)	1.30 (0.61, 2.74)	1.11 (0.52, 2.39)
40+ (Ref.)	1	1	1
Rank			
E1–E4	1.33 (1.11, 1.61)**	1.49 (1.13, 1.95)**	1.36 (1.02, 1.81)*
E5–E9 (Ref.)	1	1	
Education			
≤ GED/HS Diploma	1.65 (1.07, 2.59)*	1.10 (0.58, 2.06)	1.12 (0.59, 2.12)
Some college or other	1.75 (1.13, 2.72)*	1.32 (0.70, 2.48)	1.44 (0.75, 2.74)
≥ BA/BS degree (Ref.)	1	1	1
Years married	1.02 (1.00, 1.04)	0.68 (0.98, 1.04)	1.00 (0.97, 1.04)
Time			
2003 (Ref.)	1	1	1
2004	1.30 (0.98, 1.72)	1.37 (0.82, 2.30)	1.50 (0.99, 2.28)
2006	1.72 (1.21, 2.46)**	2.16 (1.40, 3.34)***	2.08 (1.21, 3.58)**
2007	1.70 (1.23, 2.37)**	3.21 (1.86, 5.54)***	0.96 (0.58, 1.60)
2008	1.69 (1.24, 2.31)**	1.36 (0.81, 2.27)	1.13 (0.70, 1.81)
2009	1.51 (1.06, 2.13)**	1.57 (0.97, 2.55)	0.67 (0.40, 1.13)
Combat Exposure	0.99 (0.98, 1.01)	1.00 (0.97, 1.02)	1.00 (0.98, 1.02)
Somatic symptoms	1.01 (0.99, 1.03)	0.98 (0.96, 1.01)	0.98 (0.95, 1.01)
Alcohol misuse	2.47 (2.09, 2.92)***	1.60 (1.24, 2.10)***	1.52 (1.17, 1.98)**
Depression	1.53 (1.17, 2.00)**	0.95 (0.65, 1.40)	0.91 (0.61, 1.35)
PTSD	1.31 (1.04, 1.66)*	0.98 (0.69, 1.38)	0.94 (0.66, 1.34)
Marital quality (sum)	—	1.97 (1.89, 2.06)***	1.89 (1.81, 1.98)***
Infidelity (no=ref.)	—	—	3.41 (2.69, 4.33)***

*$p < .05$; **$p < .01$; ***$p < .001$

predictor in the final model. Both marital quality and infidelity (added in the two subsequent models) increase the likelihood of dissolution intent.

Logistic Regression—Longitudinal Sample

Displayed in Table 3.4 is the longitudinal relationship between rank, marital quality, and infidelity (measured at 6 months post-deployment) and dissolution intent (at 12 months post-deployment). As previously noted, we included only the variables that were shown to have significant bivariate association with the outcome. Similar to the findings in the cross-sectional data, time 1 junior enlisted rank is significantly associated with time 2 dissolution intent (OR=2.73, CI=1.19, 6.31). Low

TABLE 3.4 Logistic Regression Models Showing the Relationship Between the Key Predictors and Covariates With Dissolution Intent in the Longitudinal Sample

Variable	Model A OR (95% C. I.)	Model B OR (95% C. I.)
Rank		
E1–E4	3.11 (1.37, 7.08)**	2.73 (1.19, 6.31)*
E5–E9 (Ref.)	1	1
Marital quality (sum)	1.37 (1.24, 1.52)***	1.32 (1.19, 1.47)***
Infidelity (ref. = no)	—	2.16 (0.92, 5.06)

marital quality also increased the odds of dissolution intent (OR=1.32, CI=1.19, 1.47 in the final model). Unlike the findings in the cross-sectional data, infidelity was not significantly associated with marital dissolution intent, which contrasts with findings (not shown), that soldiers who had low marital quality (dichotomous marital quality variable split at the median) was significantly associated with greater dissolution intent.

DISCUSSION

This chapter had two main aims: to examine whether Army population-wide marital dissolution trends had changed after FY2005, and to assess the association between marital quality and infidelity with marital dissolution intent within two samples of enlisted Army soldiers. The population trends demonstrate that marital dissolution rates have remained fairly stable after 2005 for male enlisted soldiers. That is, for males (enlisted and officers) such rates appear unaffected by the ongoing conflicts. However, rates for female enlisted and officers, while not showing dramatic changes, appear to be trending upwards.

Army FY10 demographic data shows that more AC male soldiers are married than are AC females soldiers (60% vs. 48%) (FY10 Army Profile, 2010) which could reflect female soldiers shorter marriage, higher divorce rates, or less potential to get married compared to male soldiers (perhaps it is a combination of all three). We do not have sufficient information to make definitive statements as to whether these gender-specific results reflect either the stress or trauma hypotheses. However, given that male and female soldiers have comparable post-deployment levels of mental health problems (Vogt et al., 2011), perhaps the stress hypothesis may be a better explanation; frequent deployment separations may have a more negative impact on the marriages of female AC soldiers.

One explanation for the relative stability of divorce rates may be the efforts that the Army had made to bolster marriages and prepare soldiers to adjust to their home lives when they return from deployments. Spouse Resilience Training (formerly Spouse Battlemind Training and Strong Bonds (Riviere & Merrill, 2010; Stanley, Allen, Markman, Rhoades, & Prentice, 2010) are examples of programs that have been implemented. A randomized controlled trial of one of the components of Strong Bonds–Prevention and Relationship Enhancement Program

(PREP) demonstrated that after one year couples in the program had one-third the marriage dissolution rate compared to the no-treatment control group (Stanley et al., 2010).

The DMDC marital dissolution population trend data do show that junior enlisted and NCO male soldiers have almost identical marital higher dissolution rates (data not shown). Our survey data findings are dissonant with that data as it shows that junior enlisted male soldiers are more likely than male NCOs to have dissolution plans even in the final logistic regression model that included marital quality and infidelity. The simplest explanation is the junior soldiers are younger and have been married a shorter periods; both of these are known risk factors of marital dissolution (Amato & Rogers, 1997). However, neither age nor years married were associated with dissolution intent in our findings, which may indicate that rank may be independently associated with the outcome.

Consistent with trauma hypothesis, our data showed that of the soldiers who indicated that infidelity had been a problem in the past year or that they intend to dissolve their marriages a greater proportion met criteria for depression, PTSD, or alcohol misuse. Further, marital quality was significantly lower among those who screened positive for either of the mental health problems. This is evidence that the wars have not only taken a toll on mental health, but also on marriages.

The association of the mental health problems with marital dissolution intent may not be a direct one, however, at least in the case of depression and PTSD. The results from the logistic regression analyses of the cross-sectional data showed that in the initial model, all three mental health problems were associated with dissolution intent. However, when marital quality was added to the model, depression and PTSD were no longer significantly associated with dissolution intent. This suggests that the relationship between depression and PTSD with dissolution intent could be mediated by marital quality. This, however, is not evidence to indicate that mental health problems such as PTSD *cause* low marital quality. Some researchers have posited the PTSD and relationship quality may have a reciprocal causal relationship: On the one hand, relationship problems can hamper recovery from PTSD, but on the other hand, PTSD symptoms such as avoidance likely have negative consequences on relationship dynamics (Monson et al., 2009).

The finding of a possible mediating function of marital quality in the relationship between depression and PSTD with marital dissolution intent was not found in the longitudinal data. Neither of the time 1 mental health problems was significantly associated with time 2 dissolution intent, which is at odds with previous research (Butterworth & Rodgers, 2008). We also assessed whether continuous measures of PTSD or depression (data not shown) would be significantly associated with dissolution intent, but the findings did not change. This suggests that findings from cross-sectional models that examine marital dissolution intent may not extend to longitudinal data, at least among soldiers where the time 2 follow-up comes 6 months after the initial assessment. However, given the relatively small number of soldiers who endorsed dissolution intent in the longitudinal sample (n=45), this is a tentative conclusion.

The finding that marital quality is associated with dissolution intent is consistent with previous studies, as was the significant association of infidelity in the cross-sectional sample. However, infidelity was not significantly associated with dissolution intent in the longitudinal data. This was an unexpected finding given the unadjusted significant relationship between infidelity and dissolution intent. Further, when a dimensional variable of marital quality was included in the model, infidelity had a significant adjusted association with the dissolution intent. This does not appear to be an issue of operationalization since the marital quality variable was similarly coded in the cross-sectional data. Clearly, it is too soon to conclude that infidelity, an often identified risk factor for divorce, is unrelated to dissolution intent over time.

The findings regarding alcohol misuse in the final model of the cross-sectional data indicate that alcohol misuse is independently associated with marital dissolution intent. This finding aligns with previous studies that have found such an association (Amato & Previti, 2003; Amato & Rogers, 1997). However, one study showed that it was discordant heavy alcohol use that affects marital dissolution (Ostermann, Sloan, & Taylor, 2005). That is, risk of divorce is lowest if both spouses are either heavy drinkers or teetotalers. We do not have the data to assess discordant drinking among couples, but it is known that alcohol misuse is elevated among soldiers who have deployed to Afghanistan or Iraq (Hoge et al., 2004), which may indicate that soldiers are drinking more alcohol than their spouses. However, as with depression and PTSD, time 1 alcohol misuse was unrelated to time 2 dissolution intent.

As is the case with most data, we would like to note a few limitations. The DMDC population trend data did not report separate rates for soldiers with deployment experience to Afghanistan or Iraq (with or without combat exposure) nor are rates reported for soldiers with marital quality differences or reports of infidelity. This limits the comparisons between the population and sample data. Likewise, the DMDC population data assessed dissolution behavior (including separations and divorces), while the survey sample data focused on dissolution plans. While we contend there is a link between the two (one has to first conclude that the marriage is no longer working and should be terminated before the actual dissolution is initiated) we do not have the necessary data to demonstrate such a link.

Both sets of data are limited because they could not follow soldiers once they had left the military. Some research suggests that military personnel have lower divorce rates while they are in the military, but higher rates once they have left the military (Pollard, Karney, & Loughran, 2008). The authors suggest that the higher divorce rates in veterans may reflect the loss of the incentives that the military provides to marriages, but it could also be posited that higher rates in veterans may reflect the eventual toll that relationship problems have on marriages.

Our measure of marital dissolution intent combined plans for separation and plans for divorce. Consequently we included in our cross-sectional and longitudinal samples both for soldiers who indicated that their current marital status was "married" and those who indicated that it was "separated". We expect that the soldiers who were married could be planning to either get separated or divorced, and that separated soldiers had plans to divorce. We do not expect that the relationships between the variables that we have shown would have been markedly different if separation intent and divorce intent were distinctly measured, but future studies should examine this.

Lastly, our survey sample data are generalizable to male enlisted soldiers from brigade combat teams. However, we did not have sufficient data to assess the correlates of dissolution intent among female soldiers. Given the DMDC population trend data showing higher dissolution rates among female soldiers, it is very important to identify what influences dissolution intent among this group of soldiers.

This chapter provided evidence that the wars in Afghanistan and Iraq have affected Army marriages. However, contrary to both the stress and trauma hypothesis, it appears relationship problems are the salient "predictors" of dissolution intent. Given that marital quality has been shown to have declined as the wars have progressed and that infidelity has increased (Riviere et al., under review), these results are concerning. It is plausible to expect that the dissolution rates may increase in the future, particularly among those who leave the military. We hope that marriage enrichment programs which have been demonstrated efficacious will be widely implemented and that they will successfully bolster the quality of these marriages, help couples cope with relationship problems, and reduce marital dissolution while they are still part of the military community.

REFERENCES

Amato, P. R., & Previti, D. (2003). People's reasons for divorcing: Gender, social class, the life course, and adjustment. *Journal of Family Issues, 24*(5), 602–626.

Amato, P. R., & Rogers, S. J. (1997). A longitudinal study of marital problems and subsequent divorce. *Journal of Marriage and the Family, 59*(3), 612–624.

Angrist, J. D., & Johnson, J. H. (2000). Effects of work-related absences on families: Evidence from the Gulf War. *Industrial and Labor Relations Review, 54*, 41–58.

Atkins, D. C., Baucom, D. H., & Jacobson, N. S. (2001). Understanding infidelity: Correlates in a national random sample. *Journal of Family Psychology : JFP : Journal of the Division of Family Psychology of the American Psychological Association, 15*(4), 735–749.

Betzig, L. (1989). Causes of conjugal dissolution: A cross-cultural study. *Current Anthropology, 30*(5), 654–676.

Bliese, P. D., Wright, K. M., Adler, A. B., Cabrera, O. A., Castro, C. A., & Hoge, C. W. (2008). Validating the primary care posttraumatic stress disorder screen and the posttraumatic stress disorder checklist with soldiers returning from combat. *Journal of Consulting and Clinical Psychology, 76*(2), 272–281.

Bliese, P. D., Wright, K. M., Adler, A. B., Hoge, C. W., & Prayner, R. (2005). Post-deployment psychological screening: Interpreting and scoring DD Form 2900. *U.S. Army Medical Research Unit-Europe Research Report 2005-003.*

Blow, A. J., & Hartnett, K. (2005). Infidelity in committed relationships II: A substantive review. *Journal of Marital and Family Therapy, 31*(2), 217–233.

Booth, A., & Amato, P. (1991). Divorce and psychological stress. *Journal of Health and Social Behavior, 32*, 396–407.

Breslau, J., Miller, E., Jin, R., Sampson, N. A., Alonso, J., Andrade, L. H., . . . Kessler, R. C. (2011). A multinational study of mental disorders, marriage, and divorce. *Acta psychiatrica Scandinavica*. doi: 10.1111/j.1600-0447.2011.01712.x

Brown, R. L., Leonard, T., Saunders, L. A., & Papasouliotis, O. (2001). A two-item conjoint screen for alcohol and other drug problems. *Journal of the American Board of Family Practice, 14*(2), 95–106.

Butterworth, P., & Rodgers, B. (2008). Mental health problems and marital disruption: Is it the combination of husbands and wives' mental health problems that predicts later divorce? [Research Support, Non-U.S. Gov't]. *Social psychiatry and psychiatric epidemiology, 43*(9), 758–763. doi: 10.1007/s00127-008-0366-5

Cano, A., & O'Leary, K. D. (2000). Infidelity and separations precipitate major depressive episodes and symptoms of nonspecific depression and anxiety. *Journal of Consulting and Clinical Psychology, 68*(5), 774–781.

Coontz, S. (2007). The origins of modern divorce. [Historical Article]. *Family process, 46*(1), 7–16.

Doherty, W., Willoughby, B., & Peterson, B. (2011). Interest in marital reconciliation among divorcing parents. *Family Court Review, 49* 313–321.

FY10 Army Profile. (2010) Retrieved 08/14/2011, from http://www.armyg1.army.mil/hr/docs/demographics/FY10_Army_Profile.pdf

Gimbel, C., & Booth, A. (1994). Why does military combat experience adversely affect marital relations? *Journal of Marriage and the Family, 56*(August), 691–703.

Hoge, C. W., Castro, C. A., Messer, S. C., McGurk, D., Cotting, D. I., & Koffman, R. L. (2004). Combat duty in Iraq and Afghanistan, mental health problems, and barriers to care. *New England Journal of Medicine, 351*(1), 13–22.

Johnson, D. R., & Wu, J. (2002). An empirical test of crisis, social selection, and role explanations of the relationship between marital disruption and psychological distress: A pooled time-series analysis of four-wave panel data. *Journal of Marriage and Family, 64*, 211–224.

Karney, B. R., & Bradbury, T. N. (1997). Neuroticism, marital interaction, and the trajectory of marital satisfaction. *Journal of Personality and Social Psychology, 72*(5), 1075–1092.

Karney, B. R., & Crown, J. S. (2007). *Families under stress*. Santa Monica, CA: RAND Corporation.

Kroenke, K., Spitzer, R. L., & Williams, J. B. W. (2002). The PHQ-15: Validity of a new measure for evaluating the severity of somatic symptoms. *Psychosomatic Medicine, 64*(2), 258–266.

Lester, D. (1993). The effect of war on marriage, divorce and birth rates. *Journal of Divorce & Remarriage, 19*(1–2), 229–231.

McLeland, K. C., Sutton, G. W., & Schumm, W. R. (2008). Marital satisfaction before and after deployments associated with the global war on terror. *Psychological Reports, 103*, 836–844.

Milliken, C. S., Auchterionie, J. L., & Hoge, C. W. (2007). Longitudinal assessment of mental health problems among active and reserve components soldiers returning from the Iraq War. *Journal of the American Medical Association, 298*(18), 2141–2148.

Monson, C. M., Taft, C. T., & Fredman, S. J. (2009). Military-related PTSD and intimate relationships: From description to theory-driven research and intervention development. [Review]. *Clinical Psychology Review, 29*(8), 707–714. doi: 10.1016/j.cpr.2009.09.002

Morgan, L. A. (1988). Outcomes of marital separations: A longitudinal test of predictors. *Journal of Marriage and the Family, 50*, 493–498.

Norton, R. (1983). Measuring marital quality: A critical look at the dependent variable. *Journal of Marriage and the Family, 45*(1), 141–151.

Ostermann, J., Sloan, F. A., & Taylor, D. H. (2005). Heavy alcohol use and marital dissolution in the USA. [Research Support, N.I.H., Extramural Research Support, U.S. Gov't, P.H.S.]. *Social Science & Medicine, 61*(11), 2304–2316. doi: 10.1016/j.socscimed.2005.07.021

Pavalko, E. K., & Elder, G. H. (1990). World War II and divorce: A life-course perspective. *American Journal of Sociology, 95*(5), 1212–1234.

Pollard, M., Karney, B. R., & Loughran, D. (2008). *Comparing rates of marriage and divorce in civilian, military, and veteran populations*. Paper presented at the Population Association of America, New Orleans. http://paa2008.princeton.edu/download.aspx?submissionId=81696

Riviere, L. A., & Merrill, J. C. (2010). The impact of combat deployment on military families. In A. B. Adler, P. D. Bliese & C. A. Castro (Eds.), *Deployment psychology: Evidence-based strategies to promote mental health in the military* (pp. 125–149). Washington, DC: American Psychological Association.

Riviere, L. A., Merrill, J. C., Thomas, J. L., Wilk, J. E., & Bliese, P. B. (under review). 2003–2009 Marital Functioning Trends among U.S. Enlisted Soldiers following Combat Deployments.

Ruger, W., Wilson, S. E., & Waddoups, S. L. (2002). Warfare and welfare: Military service, combat, and marital dissolution. *Armed Forces & Society, 29*(1), 85–107.

Santiago, P. N., Wilk, J. E., Milliken, C. S., Castro, C. A., Engel, C. C., & Hoge, C. W. (2010). Screening for alcohol misuse and alcohol-related behaviors among combat veterans. *Psychiatric Services, 61*(6), 575–581.

Spanier, G. B. (1979). The measurement of marital quality. *Journal of Sex and Marital Therapy, 5*(3), 288–300.

Spitzer, R. L., Kroenke, K., Williams, J. B. W., & and the Patient Health Questionnaire Primary Care Study Group. (1999). Validation and utility of a self-report version of PRIME-MD: the PHQ Primary Care Study. *Journal of the American Medical Association, 282*(18), 1737–1744. doi: 10.1001/jama.282.18.1737

Stanley, S. M., Allen, E. S., Markman, H. J., Rhoades, G. K., & Prentice, D. L. (2010). Decreasing divorce in army couples: Results from a randomized controlled trial using PREP for strong bonds. *Journal of Couple & Relationship Therapy, 9*(2), 149–160. doi: 10.1080/15332691003694901

Taft, C. T., Watkins, L. E., Stafford, J., Street, A. E., & Monson, C. M. (2011). Posttraumatic stress disorder and intimate relationship problems: A meta-analysis. *Journal of Consulting and Clinical Psychology, 79*(1), 22–33. doi: 10.1037/a0022196

Terhakopian, A., Sinaii, N., Engel, C. C., Schnurr, P. P., & Hoge, C. W. (2008). Estimating population prevalence of posttraumatic stress disorder: An example using the PTSD checklist. *Journal of Traumatic Stress, 21*(3), 290–300.

Vogt, D., Vaughn, R., Glickman, M. E., Schultz, M., Drainoni, M. L., Elwy, R., & Eisen, S. (2011). Gender differences in combat-related stressors and their association with postdeployment mental health in a nationally representative sample of U.S. OEF/OIF veterans. *Journal of Abnormal Psychology*. doi: 10.1037/a0023452

Weathers, F. W., Litz, B. T., Herman, D. S., Huska, J. A., & Keane, T. M. (1993). *The PTSD Checklist (PCL): Reliability, validity, and diagnostic utility*. Paper presented at the 9th annual conference of the ISTSS, San Antonio, TX.

Whisman, M. A., Gordon, K. C., & Chatav, Y. (2007). Predicting sexual infidelity in a population-based sample of married individuals. [Research Support, N.I.H., ExtramuralResearch Support, Non-U.S. Gov't]. *Journal of Family Psychology : JFP : Journal of the Division of Family Psychology of the American Psychological Association, 21*(2), 320–324. doi: 10.1037/0893-3200.21.2.320

Wilk, J. E., Bliese, P. D., Kim, P. Y., Thomas, J. L., McGurk, D., & Hoge, C. W. (2010). Relationship of combat experiences to alcohol misuse among U.S. soldiers returning from the Iraq War. *Drug and Alcohol Dependence, 108*, 115–121.

Williams, K., & Umberson, D. (2004). Marital status, marital transitions, and health: A gendered life course perspective. *Journal of Health and Social Behavior, 45*, 81–98.

Wineberg, H. (1994). Marital reconciliation in the United States—Which couples are successful. *Journal of Marriage and the Family, 56*(1), 80–88.

Section 2

Treatment Modalities

4

Cognitive-Behavioral Therapy With Military Couples

ROBERT P. O'BRIEN

INTRODUCTION

Cognitive-behavioral couples therapy (CBCT) has roots in (a) behavioral couples therapy, (b) cognitive therapy, and (c) the significant body of research associated with cognitive psychology. Behavioral couples therapy grew out of the application of standard behavioral interventions to couples, with the first application described by Stuart (1969). The key concept was that successful marriages were the result of a high frequency of positive acts exchanged reciprocally by the partners and was based on social exchange therapy (Thibaut & Kelly, 1959). Couples were happy if there was a balance in the number of positive reinforcers partners exchanged in their day-to-day life. Marriage was a social contract that provided positive reinforcers, and as long as each partner kept his or her part of the bargain, the marriage was satisfactory. Stuart's (1969) treatment involved obtaining a list of positive behaviors that each partner desired from the other and then establishing an agreement or contract between the partners to exchange tokens in response to these behaviors and to be able to redeem tokens for the desired behaviors. I was once advised by an early supervisor to determine which sexual behaviors the husband wanted (he made a detailed list) that were acceptable to the wife (she got to cross items she did not like off the list) and how many tokens each behavior was worth. The wife then listed the behaviors she was interested in (talking for at least 15 minutes, doing the dishes, washing the clothes, etc.), and the husband was able to cross off the items he did not agree with. The couple then discussed how many tokens could be earned by the husband for doing each of these tasks. With this in place, the couple went home, the husband earned his tokens, and the wife allowed him to redeem them for sex, all according to the agreed exchange plan.

While behavioral couples therapy has been shown to be effective (Baucom, Shoham, Mueser, Daiuto, & Stickle, 1998), several problems became apparent. First, outcome studies showed that improved behavioral exchange behaviors did not necessarily lead to improved marital satisfaction (Halford, Sanders, & Behrens, 1993). Second, studies that compared behavioral couples therapy with interventions that did not emphasize the modification of behavioral exchanges showed similar efficacy (Baucom, Epstein, & Gordon, 2000). Finally, studies showed marked discrepancies between partners' reports of positive and negative behaviors and between these self-reports and neutral observer reports (Fincham, Bradbury, & Scott, 1990). These and similar studies challenged the basic underpinnings of behavioral couples therapy and required an expansion of the model.

Behavioral couples therapy became more cognitive in its orientation with the growing cognitive therapy literature, which illustrated that an individual's emotional and behavioral reactions often depend on a rather unique and person-specific interpretation of events, and that these interpretations are subject to cognitive distortions. The integration of cognitive therapy principals into the treatment of couples emerged with Margolin and Weiss (1978) and Epstein (1982) and led to the expansion of the traditional behavioral model to include a focus on behavioral, cognitive, and emotional factors in both the development of couple distress and the treatment strategies employed to treat this distress. Cognitive-behavioral couple therapists believe that "partners' dysfunctional emotional and behavioral responses to relationship events are influenced by information processing errors, whereby cognitive appraisals of the events are either arbitrary or distorted" (Baucom, Epstein, Taillade, & Kirby, 2008, p. 33). CBCT has not abandoned its strictly behavioral roots and continues to hold that intervening to directly alter a partner's negative behaviors can result in behaviors that are more positive, cognitions, and emotions but has added cognitive interventions to its list of treatment strategies.

In sum, the original behavioral couples therapy has developed into CBCT. As with many models, there are different "versions" of CBCT, but two stand out from the rest; enhanced cognitive-behavioral couples therapy (from here on called ECBCT), reflected in the work of Baucom and colleagues, and integrative behavioral couples therapy (IBCT), which grew out of the work of Jacobson and Christensen (1996) and others (see, e.g., Dimidjian, Martell, & Christensen, 2008). To allow for a more detailed review, the rest of the chapter focuses on ECBCT. Given the space limitations for this chapter, refer to the work of Epstein and Baucom (2002) and Baucom, Epstein, Taillade, and Kirby (2008) for more detailed information on this model.

ENHANCED COGNITIVE-BEHAVIORAL COUPLES THERAPY

Epstein and Baucom (2002) and Baucom (2008) have called for enhancements (or expansions) in CBCT to better reflect the complex nature of couple interactions and the impact of other less-strictly behavioral (such as emotions) variables. One enhancement is the move from "microanalysis" of behavioral events to the inclusion of "macrolevel" patterns and core themes, such as differences between partners' desired levels of closeness and intimacy. A second enhancement has been the inclusion of what each partner brings to the relationship in terms of their personality, providing an explanation for why partners behave and interpret events in maladaptive ways. This reflects the research findings that suggest that individual differences among both psychologically healthy individuals and those manifesting psychopathology have an impact on the couple relationship. Third, stressors external to the couple and the presence of external support systems (or lack thereof) have a significant impact on couple interaction and couple distress. ECBCT now takes these directly into account in both understanding and intervening in couple distress. Fourth, emotion is held to be crucial to the couple relationship and has become the third major focus (the other two being behavior and cognition) of ECBCT. Finally, ECBCT has been expanded beyond the original goal of reducing negative interactions also to enhancing positive interactions. While the language is different, these enhancements demonstrate what might be considered a merging with emotionally focused couples therapy (stressing the primacy of emotion and the impact of early experiences with attachment styles) and Gottman's methodology (stressing, e.g., that attention must be given to meta-emotion mismatches as well as observing that removing distress must be augmented by increasing the positivity in the relationship).

Overview of Treatment Approach

Structure ECBCT is a brief therapy approach and typically takes from 5 to 20 sessions. Actual session length varies depending on the issues the couple brings to treatment. Sessions are generally held weekly (but this varies by case and situation), with the frequency of sessions decreased at the end of treatment. Booster sessions are often employed after termination. Some couple issues (intimate partner violence or infidelity being examples) or individual issues (such as the presence of a personality disorder in one or both partners) can be expected to lengthen the therapy process. Treatment is typically provided by a single therapist, although a cotherapist may be involved (particularly in training situations). Data do not suggest that cotherapy has better outcomes than working with a single therapist (Mehlman, Baucom, & Anderson, 1981). Sessions typically involve only the therapist and couple but may under unusual circumstances involve others important to the couple relationship (examples might include a mother who has come to live with the couple, adult children, etc.). This should always be discussed with the couple in advance. It is not unusual for one or both partners to be involved in individual psychotherapy or to be taking psychotropic medications. Neither of these is a contraindication for ECBCT but would require that the therapist take care not to foster the idea that the partner under treatment is "sick" or somehow more responsible for the couple distress than the other partner.

Role of Therapist The therapist plays multiple roles in ECBCT, including what Epstein and Baucom (2002) have called director, educator, facilitator, collaborator, and advocate. The therapist's ability to balance these roles while continuing to provide emotional support, guidance, and perspective is critical to the success of the treatment.

Assessment The assessment process includes both a joint couple interview as well as an individual interview with each partner. Unlike other models that use individual interviews with each partner (such as Gottman, 1999), ECBCT therapists inform each partner that what they tell the therapist during the individual session will be held confidential (although therapists will encourage the individual to bring up important information in the couple session). If a partner reveals an ongoing affair and refuses to divulge this information to the partner, the partner having the affair is asked to find a way to terminate couples therapy. The ECBCT therapist does not provide couples therapy under these circumstances. The formal clinical assessment for each couple takes two or three sessions (unless the couple enters treatment in acute distress). The major goals of the clinical assessment are (a) to identify the primary concerns and goals that the couple brings to the therapy; (b) to identify the cognitive, behavioral, and emotional factors with each individual, within the couple dyad, as well as within the couple's broader environment; and (c) to determine whether couples therapy is appropriate to address these concerns. The assessment process is multidimensional. It involves the use of an extensive battery of questionnaires, clinical interviews, and direct observation of the interaction of the couple. The therapist attempts to complete the assessment process within 1 or 2 weeks of the couple's initial presentation, using extended sessions that may last 2–3 hours. The assessment process, however, does not terminate with this initial evaluation, but continues throughout the course of treatment. While the therapist sees the assessment process as assessment, the couple often experiences the process as a therapeutic intervention.

Goal Setting After the initial assessment is completed, the therapist meets with the couple to provide treatment recommendations. The therapist presents the relevant couple, individual, and environmental factors that are having an impact on the couple relationship. The therapist then asks for feedback from the couple on this case conceptualization. The couple and therapist then work to translate negative complaints that are typical of couples seeking treatment (such as "He never talks to me") to descriptions of desired behaviors ("I would like him to spend some time every day talking about his day"). These goals include "microgoals" such as increasing the number of evenings the couple spends together and "macrogoals," such as increasing the couple's overall sense of togetherness.

Homework Treatment routinely involves the assignment of homework for the couple to complete between sessions. Homework is designed to take skills learned in the treatment session and to practice them in the expanded context of "the real world" of the couple.

Interventions ECBCT includes interventions that focus on behavior change (guided behavior change and skill-based interventions), interventions that focus on altering cognitions and interventions that focus on emotions. Each is briefly described in the following section; however, these interventions are quite detailed, and the reader is again referred to the work of Epstein and Baucom (2002).

INTERVENTIONS FOR BEHAVIOR CHANGE

Guided Behavior Change

Interventions for guided behavior change involve the therapist facilitating a conversation between the couple to help (a) each understand the kinds of behaviors or interactions that each partner would like and (b) work out a series of agreements between the couple aimed at increasing the desired interactions. These interventions focus on the needs of each partner and hope to produce general behavior change (as opposed to a more focused and specific behavior change, which would be the focus of the skill-based interventions). For this type of intervention, the therapist might say:

> I would like each of you to think about how you would behave if you were being the kind of partner you truly want to be. What does that mean you would do and not do? Behaving is this manner will likely have two very positive consequences. First, your partner is likely to be much happier. Second, you are likely to feel better about yourself. One thing that frequently happens when couples become distressed is that partners stray away the kinds of behaviors in which they themselves like to engage. So, I want you to get back to being the kind of person you enjoy being in the relationship and the best in you as an individual. (Baucom et al., 2008, p. 49)

The goal for this intervention is to help each partner identify what kinds of behaviors they might do more of and what kinds of behaviors their partner might do more of. In a sense, this process points the couple back to the behaviors that used to work well for them earlier in the relationship. It should be stressed that ECBCT does not see this process as a behavior exchange method. This form of intervention focuses on the general emotional tone of the relationship. It may also be used in a more focal manner and be directed toward a particular problem issue, such as giving the relationship a higher priority.

Skill-Based Interventions While the general emotional tone of the relationship may be altered by the guided behavior change intervention, this is usually insufficient to produce the full range of change that is needed to alter couple distress. In this case, it is important for the therapist to actively engage in helping the couple learn the specific behavioral skills involved in improving their interactions. Two types of skills are addressed in ECBCT: the couple's ability to have a conversation or discussion (in which partners share thoughts and feelings) or the more focused skill of having a decision-making or problem-solving conversation. Each type of intervention has a specific set of recommendations rather than rigid rules. Couples are provided a copy of these skills and given an opportunity to learn the skills in session and to practice the skills as homework. These are as follows:

Guidelines for Couple Discussion (General Discussion, *Not* Problem Solving)

- Skills for sharing thoughts and emotions:
  - State your views subjectively, from your perspective.
  - Express not only your thoughts but also your emotions and feelings.
  - State your feelings about your partner, not just the situation.
  - When expressing negative emotion, also include positive feelings.
  - Express one main idea and then stop to allow your partner to respond.
  - Express your thoughts and feelings with tact and timing.
- Skills for listening to your partner:
  - Show that you understand your partner's position.
  - Confirm the partner's right to these thoughts and feelings.
  - Demonstrate acceptance in your voice, body position, and expression.
  - Try to put yourself in your partner's place and see things from the partner's perspective.
- Ways to respond after your partner has finished speaking:
  - Summarize your partner's most important feelings and thoughts.
  - Do not:
    - Ask questions other than to request clarification.
    - Express your own viewpoint or position.
    - Interpret or change the meaning of what your partner says.
    - Try to solve the problem or offer solutions, just listen.
    - Make judgments or evaluations of what your partner has said.

Guidelines for Decision-Making Conversations (Problem Solving)

- Clearly and specifically state what the issue is.
  - Describe the issue with behaviors that are occurring or not occurring.
  - Break down big problems into smaller problems and deal with them separately.
  - Ensure both partners agree on the description of the problem *and* that they are willing to discuss it.
  - Clarify why the issue is important and what your needs are.
  - Clarify why the issue is important to you *and* how you understand the problem.
  - Explain or describe your needs; do not offer possible solutions yet.
  - Discuss possible solutions.
  - Suggest concrete and specific solutions that take your needs and your partner's needs into account.
  - Do not dwell on the past or try to blame each other; focus on right now and the future.
  - Consider brainstorming to increase the number of possible solutions.
  - Decide on a solution that is feasible and agreeable to both of you.

- If you cannot find a solution that satisfies both partners, see if there is a compromise solution.
- If a compromise cannot be developed, agree to follow one person's preferences.
- State the solution in clear behavioral terms.
- After reaching agreement, have one partner restate the solution.
- Do not accept a solution if you do not intend to follow through with it.
- Do not accept a solution that will make you angry or resentful.
- Decide on a trial period to implement the solution if it is a situation that will happen more than once.
- Allow for several attempts of the new solution.
- Review the workability of the solution at the end of the trial period.
- Revise the solution as needed based on what you have learned.

Interventions That Address Cognitions

Cognitive therapy has a rich tradition and empirical literature that describes interventions to change cognitions. ECBCT has identified a variety of cognitive variables that are critical in understanding couple interaction. These include selective attention, attributions, expectancies, assumptions, and standards (Baucom & Epstein, 1990; Epstein & Baucom, 2002). The standard interventions found in individually administered cognitive-behavioral therapy must be used with some caution in the couple context as the observing partner may understand such interventions as evidence that the partner being worked with is actually to blame for their problems (thinking that the partner's thinking is wrong and distorted, just like the therapist seems to be suggesting). With these cautions in mind, the following interventions are often used in ECBCT: Socratic questioning and guided discovery.

Socratic Questioning

- Evaluating experiences and the logic for supporting a cognition
- Weighing the advantages or disadvantages of a cognition
- Considering the best and worst possible outcomes
- Providing psychoeducation
- Using the more inductive "down-arrow" method
- Identifying macropatterns from cross-situational responses
- Identifying macrolevel patterns from past relationships
- Increasing schematic thinking by pointing out recurrent patterns in the couple's interaction

Guided Discovery The ECBCT therapist also uses guided discovery to create new experiences from which the couple may come to think differently or to question their thinking or perspective on an issue. As an example, a partner who has served in combat may return to the home at the end of the day and say nothing to the other partner, simply walking by the partner, going into their bedroom, and slamming the door. The observing partner might then become upset, feeling rejected and ignored. This situation might be addressed with Socratic questioning, or it could be addressed by facilitating a discussion between the couple about what each person was thinking and feeling in the moment. The goal here is for the couple to share each other's perspective on the event, a process that often leads to a change in cognition. After such an exchange, the observing partner might come to a different set of cognitions ("Oh, I guess he had a bad day, and it really looks like the PTSD [posttraumatic stress disorder] is kicking his butt tonight. I think I will be quiet to give him time to unwind").

Guided discovery might also involve a discussion of the inherent set of standards each partner holds for themselves and the relationship. Standards can rarely be altered via Socratic questioning because they are not based on logic. Issues involving standards are addressed primarily by asking the question how functional or helpful the standards for the relationship are. ECBCT addresses differences in standards in the following steps:

- Clarify each person's existing standard.
- Discuss the advantages and disadvantages of existing standards.
- If standards need to be changed, help revise them to form new more acceptable standards.
- Problem solve how these new standards will be taken into account behaviorally.
- If standards continue to differ, discuss how to accept differences.

Interventions That Focus on Emotions

One of the underlying assumptions of cognitive-behavioral therapy is that changing cognitions or behaviors changes emotions. While ECBCT continues to hold to this basic belief, ECBCT has developed interventions that pay more explicit attention to emotional factors. In some cases, the couple (or one partner) has difficulty understanding or even being aware of the emotions involved. At the other end of the spectrum, couples may be overwhelmed by intense and disruptive emotions. Some situations involve couples in which one or both partners (a) has difficulty with emotions in general or one emotion in particular, (b) has strong emotions but has difficulty differentiating these emotions, (c) has difficulty with the relationship between their emotions and their internal or external experience, or (d) tends to avoid primary emotions and focuses on secondary emotions. Specific interventions for developing greater awareness and connection to emotions include (a) normalizing both positive and negative emotional experiences; (b) clarifying thoughts about these emotions; (c) using questions, reflections, or interpretations to draw out primary emotion; (d) describing emotions with images, stories, and metaphors; (e) discouraging attempts to distract oneself from emotions; and (f) encouraging a partner's acceptance of the other partner's emotions.

Some couples have difficulty with emotional regulation or containing their emotions to allow for discussion or conversation. Interventions for this issue involve (a) scheduling times to discuss emotions and thoughts about emotions, (b) practicing "healthy compartmentalization," (c) seeking alternative means to communicate or share feelings and elicit support, and (d) developing skills to tolerate distressing emotions.

Research Base

Civilian Sector

ECBCT has an extensive research base in the civilian sector and is one of the most widely evaluated couple treatments, with about 24 well-controlled outcome studies already published and other studies under way. The findings suggest that between 30% and 66% of couples are in the nondistressed range after completing ECBCT. The data suggest that most couples maintain these gains over the short term, but long-term follow-up is not as encouraging. This general finding is true of virtually all couple interventions and is not unique to ECBCT.

Military Sector

A search of the PILOTS database, an extensive database that collects research related to exposure to military trauma, did not reveal any studies specific to ECBCT with PTSD or for the military population. The data do not suggest any contraindications for using this method with military or veteran couples.

Case Vignette – Hector and Samantha

INITIAL PRESENTATION

Hector (who is 27) and Samantha (who is 24 and known to all as Sam) have been married for 5 years and have a 3-year-old daughter, Laura. Hector was a career infantryman in the Army for 8 years until he was injured during his second deployment in an IED (improvised explosive device) explosion and lost his right arm at the elbow and his right leg at the knee. He is currently unemployed and receiving Veterans Affairs (VA) benefits. Sam was a medic in the Army for 6 years and deployed to Iraq twice. Sam elected to leave active duty so that she could care for Hector and their daughter. She is currently employed as an emergency medical technician (EMT) with the fire and ambulance service in her town. They sought couples therapy after an argument (over Hector's suspicion that Sam was having an affair) escalated to the point that Hector shoved Sam against a wall and sprained her shoulder. Sam called the police, and Hector spent a night in jail. The judge postponed any action pending the couple seeking couples therapy. Both Hector and Sam agreed that this had been the only episode of violence in their relationship. Both agreed that their relationship had been very good, and even did well through the first deployment, but had deteriorated since that time. Time spent together was minimal. Sexual encounters were rare and typically went badly. Hector was sullen, withdrawn, and angry.

The interaction that follows is from the couple's fifth session. It was thus early in the treatment phase of the process. It opens with Hector's ongoing complaint that Sam is not sexually receptive, and that she is turned off because he is a cripple and lost a leg. The general issue of Hector feeling rejected and unworthy after losing his leg had been a common theme for the couple, and the specific microdetails of their interactions involving initiating and accepting or refusing sex had been ongoing. The intervention involved some elements of guided discovery to help the couple capture and perhaps alter their cognitions around this event (particularly focused on Hector's cognitions), some guided behavior change in a rather focal manner around the specific issue of initiation and refusal of sex, as well as some emotional interventions (particularly to assist Hector in identifying more primary emotions [hurt] vs. the anger that was more overtly expressed).

The process of delivering ECBCT requires creativity on the part of the therapist, and each therapist does the work in a personal style. Other ECBCT therapists might have used Socratic questioning to help Hector deal with his cognitions or might have moved away from the specifics of the event to do a more skill-based intervention.

SESSION 5 DIALOGUE

Hector: She did it again *(looks sullen).*

Sam: *(Shrugs.)* Yeah right *(turns away and looks resigned).*

Therapist: What happened? *(asking for more behavioral specificity)*

Sam: He was drunk and wanted sex again. I just wasn't in the mood.

Hector: Yeah, you're never in the mood. But then, who would want to get it on with a one-legged crip.

Sam: You're not a crip; you keep bringing that up like it's a big deal.

Hector: Big deal? You're damn right is a big deal. I don't have a f*** leg any more *(pulls up his shorts and points to the stump).*

Therapist: This is one of those things that keeps coming up, right?

Sam: Yeah.

Hector: For sure.

Therapist: So, would you be up for some coaching about that?

Hector: Like that would do any good *(looking at the floor).*

Sam: OK *(hesitant).*

Therapist: So, if I get it, Hector you were feeling sexy and tried to start something with Sam?

Hector: But she wasn't interested and blew me off.

Therapist: Well, that's one way of thinking about it. Would you be willing to hear a bit more from Sam *(beginning a guided discovery process)*?

Hector: How else can I think about it? I come on to her, she takes one look at my stump, and we're done?

Therapist: I get it how much that hurt. Is it okay for us to check in with Sam?

Hector: *(Sighs.)* Okay.

Therapist: Sam … can you take us through what happened from your point of view?

Sam: Ah okay. So I was taking a shower, and I heard Hector kind of banging around in the bedroom and yelling.

Hector: I wasn't yelling. I …

Therapist: Hold on. Sam, what did you mean when you said yelling?
Sam: Oh, this is one of those times when you want me to be specific about his behavior, right? *(Sam has learned this is one thing the therapist works on with the couple.)*
Therapist: Right.
Sam: Yes, was talking in a loud voice.
Therapist: Great, you kept the judgment out of it. Could you hear what he said?
Hector: She heard all right. …
Therapist: Hold on. You don't know that yet. Let's check with her okay?
Hector: Okay.
Therapist: So, could you hear what he was saying?
Sam: He wanted sex.
Therapist: Is that what he actually said, or is that your interpretation?
Sam: Ah, okay it's my interpretation. But I know him pretty well.
Therapist: I get it, and maybe that is what he was interested in, but what did he actually say?
Sam: He said "Hey, you want some company in there?"
Hector: That's when she blew me off; she said some shit like she was almost finished so …
Therapist: Hector, I know this is really important to you and that you were pretty angry?
Hector: Hell yes.
Sam: He's always angry and pissed off.
Therapist: Hold on Sam; so Hector is angry. What other feelings were there? *(Deciding to work a bit on Hector's emotions, looking for primary and secondary emotions as this was preventing the guided discovery process.)*
Hector: I don't know *(looks down)*.
Therapist: Hurt? You really wanted to be close with Sam and felt pushed away?
Hector: Yeah, I guess.
Therapist: Can you tell Sam that?
Hector: I was hurt when you didn't ask me to get in the shower with you.
Therapist: Good job in describing what was behind the anger. Sam, did you know Hector was hurt?
Sam: I thought he was angry.
Therapist: Did you get the hurt that was underneath the anger?
Sam: No, I don't want to hurt him *(tear in her eye)*.
Therapist: So, you both got the angry part but kind of missed the hurt part? Hector, it sounds like you missed that feeling, too?
Sam: Yeah.
Hector: Yeah.
Therapist: So, Hector, can you talk more about what you were feeling when you went into the bathroom. Not the thinking part right now, but the feelings back in the bathroom?
Hector: I was feeling, ah well, you know about the angry part, and you're right, I was hurt.

Sam: *(Watching intently, noting later that Hector had never spoken about being hurt.)*
Therapist: Good job. How about before the hurt and anger showed up?
Hector: I had been thinking that I wanted some, you know …
Therapist: Yeah, you were missing that?
Hector: Right, and ah, I guess I was just missing all of it?
Therapist: All of it?
Hector: Well, the sex for sure but like just being with her, holding her, having her hold me *(looks up hesitantly toward Sam).*
Sam: You were missing me? I know about missing the sex, but missing me?
Hector: Yeah.
Sam: I didn't know; I thought that you just, well, wanted it.
Hector: To be honest, well I did want it, but ah, I wanted you, even if we didn't have sex right then.
Therapist: So, I think what I heard was that Hector, when you were heading into the bathroom, you were missing Sam and wanting some connection.
Hector: Yeah.
Therapist: Sam, what do you make of that? I take it that this is new information?
Sam: Yeah, I guess I was thinking about it wrong.
Therapist: Well, I don't like the word *wrong*, but it looks like you missed some stuff. Is there a different way to think about it?
Sam: I mean, we used to love sex and even more we used to love just being together. Showers would last until the hot water ran out and even then we didn't want to get out. I like the idea that he wants to be with me. It's been a long time since I thought that way.
Therapist: What's the feeling there?
Sam: It feels nice, ah, kind of warm, and well I like it a lot better. Next time, I won't be so ready to say no. I mean the water was still hot; it would have lasted for a while.
Hector: I like that idea.
Therapist: Let's go to back to the shower. Sam, you were in the shower, Hector asked to join you, did I remember that right?
Sam: Yeah.
Therapist: Do you remember what you thought when you heard that?
Sam: Ah, a bunch of thoughts.
Therapist: Like what?
Sam: Ah, well, I thought that we used to do that a lot, and I really enjoyed it. And I thought that he had been drinking, and I did not like that. And I thought that he was maybe drunk and could fall down 'cause it was like slippery and wet and you know.
Hector: Just say it; I got one leg, and that's a turnoff.
Sam: That's not it. Yeah, you got one leg, but if you're drunk and all, you might fall down and get hurt.
Therapist: So, Sam, you were worried he might get hurt?
Sam: Yeah.
Therapist: Hector, did you know that Sam worried about that?

Hector: No, I was a little drunk I guess.
Therapist: Is it reasonable to think you might have fallen in the shower?
Hector: Maybe *(looks a bit perplexed)*.
Therapist: Hector, you look you are thinking *(noting the perplexed feeling)*?
Hector: Yeah, I mean being worried about me is different than not wanting me.
Therapist: Yeah, it is.
Sam: I do worry, particularly when he drinks.
Therapist: Hector's drinking seems like a big part of what was in your head when you were in the shower.
Sam: Yeah, he has been drinking more.
Therapist: And that makes you worry more?
Sam: Yeah.
Therapist: So, let's go back and finish up reviewing the shower incident. You were worried Hector might fall? What else?
Sam: And I was upset because of the drinking.
Therapist: Anything else?
Sam: Well *(looking a bit hesitantly at Hector)*, we used to have some great times in the shower.
Hector: *(Looks a bit startled but says nothing.)*
Therapist: So, you were missing that? Is that what you were thinking?
Sam: Yeah, I was.
Therapist: Can you tell Hector that?
Sam: Ah *(looks away, then turns directly to Hector)*, I miss getting all soapy and all in the shower with you.
Hector: But you said there was no time?
Sam: Yeah, you were kind of drunk; I did not like that.
Hector: And my stump, you don't like that, that's a turnoff, right?
Sam: No, look I hate what the dam IED did, too. But, I did not even think about the leg then.
Hector: You didn't?
Sam: No.
Therapist: So, Sam, do I hear it right that you said no because you were worried Hector might fall, and you just were not well turned on by his being drunk? That this was what you were thinking about?
Sam: Yeah.
Therapist: And the stump. Hector worries a lot about what you think about that?
Sam: I mean like, I hate that it happened, and I guess in the beginning I was shocked to see it, but, well, its no big deal now.
Therapist: Hector, what do you think about this? Is this new?
Hector: Yeah. I thought she was thinking something else. I thought she just, well, could not stand the idea of me and my one leg in the shower with her.
Therapist: And now?
Hector: I guess she does worry about me, and well I have been drinking more lately.

Sam: Yeah.

Therapist: Sam, what do you make of Hector saying that he was hurt when you said no.

Sam: All I really saw or got was the angry part.

Therapist: Yeah, I get that, but now you know the hurt part also.

Sam: I don't want to hurt him. That is the last thing I want do do.

Therapist: Hector?

Hector: I guess I got all pissed off for no reason. *(Turning to Sam)* I am sorry.

Sam: Okay *(reaching out and touching his thigh).*

Therapist: Hector, let's not miss the hurt. It sounds like hurt came first; it's what we call a primary emotion, and the anger showed up, almost to cover up the hurt.

Hector: I do anger best.

Therapist: Yeah, I know. But Sam needs to know about the hurt, too. It helps her to think differently about the situation, too.

Sam: Yeah.

Therapist: So, Sam. Did I hear it right that if Hector had not been drinking and maybe not talking so angry, that you would have wanted him in the shower with you?

Sam: For sure! He does, ah, great soap downs.

Hector: *(With a smile.)* Yeah! And she, ah, she knows how to soap me up also.

Therapist: So, maybe you guys can make a shower appointment? *(Working on a more specific behavioral plan, but only when it was clear that both Sam and Hector found this workable.)*

Hector: Really?

Sam: How about tonight?

Hector: For real?

Sam: Yeah, but no drinking; can you ah do it that way?

Hector: For sure.

TREATMENT SUMMARY

The treatment process took 16 sessions. Both Hector and Sam became involved with individual and group treatment for PTSD (in a program specifically designed for veterans who saw combat in Iraq or Afghanistan). In addition, Hector completed an anger management group. All the components of ECBCT as described were employed, and considerable time was spent in skill-building exercises both during the session and as homework.

CONCLUSION

ECBCT reflects a natural extension of behavioral couples therapy. It has moved beyond the early behavioral exchange model to a more developed model, which includes traditional behavioral interventions (such as skill building and Socratic questioning) but also includes what might be understood as a more gentle way to address what each partner wants and needs from the relationship (guided behavior change) as well as helping couples become aware of the cognitions (guided discovery) and the underlying standards that might have an impact on the relationship. Unlike traditional behavioral couples therapy (and even some CBCTs), ECBCT directly addresses emotions and individual variables. The model allows for dealing with specific or microbehaviors or issues as well as more macrovariables. The model has consistently shown positive results (at least in the short term) in randomized clinical trials and has more published outcome studies than other couple treatment models.

REFERENCES

Baucom, D. H., & Epstein, N. B. (1990). *Cognitive behavioral marital therapy*. New York: Brunner/Mazel.

Baucom, D. H., Epstein, N. B., & Gordon, K. C. (2000). Martial therapy: Theory, practice and empirical status. In C. R. Synder & R. E. Ingram (Eds.), *Handbook of psychological change: Psychotherapy, processes and practices for the 21st century* (pp. 280–308). New York: Wiley.

Baucom, D. H., Epstein, N. B., Taillade, J. S., & Kirby, J. S. (2008). Cognitive-behavioral couple therapy. In A. S. Gurman (Ed.), *Clinical handbook of couple therapy* (4th ed., pp. 31–72). New York: Guilford Press.

Baucom, D. H., Shoham, V., Mueser, K. T., Daiuto, A. D., & Stickle, T. R. (1998). Empirically supported couples and family therapies for adult problems. *Journal of Consulting and Clinical Psychology, 66*, 53–88.

Dimidjian, S., Martell, C. R., & Christensen, A. (2008). Integrative behavioral couple therapy. In A. S. Gurman (Ed.). *Clinical handbook of couple therapy* (4th ed., pp. 73–103). New York: Guilford Press.

Epstein, N. (1982). Cognitive therapy with couples. *American Journal of Family Therapy, 10*(1), 5–16.

Epstein, N., & Baucom, D. H. (2002). *Enhanced cognitive-behavioral therapy for couples: A contextual approach*. Washington, DC: American Psychological Association.

Fincham, F. D., Bradbury, T. N., & Scott, C. K. (1990). Cognition in marriage. In F. D. Finsham & T. N. Bradbury (Eds.), *The psychology of marriage: Basic issues and applications* (pp. 118–149). New York: Guilford Press.

Gottman, J. M. (1999). *The marriage clinic*. New York: Norton.

Halford, W. K., Sanders, M. R., & Behrens, B. C. (1993). A comparison of the generalization of behavioral marital therapy and enhanced behavioral marital therapy. *Journal of Consulting and Clinical Psychology, 61*, 51–60.

Jacobson, N. S., & Christensen, A. (1996). Studying the effectiveness of psychotherapy: How well can clinical trials do the job? *American Psychologist, 51*, 1031–1039.

Margolin, G., & Weiss, R. L. (1978). Comparative evaluation of therapeutic components associated with behavioral marital treatments. *Journal of Consulting and Clinical Psychology, 46*, 1476–1486.

Melman, S. K., Baucom, D. H., & Anderson, D. (1981, November). *The relative effectiveness of co-therapists vs. single therapists and immediate vs. delayed treatment in a behavioral marital therapy outcome study.* Paper presented at the 15th annual meeting of the Association for the Advancement of Behavioral Therapy, Toronto, Canada.

Stuart, R. B. (1969). Operant marital treatment for marital discord. *Journal of Consulting and Clinical Psychology*, *33*, 675–682.

Thibaut, J. W., & Kelly, H. H. (1959). *The social psychology of groups.* New York; Wiley.

5

Solution-Focused Therapy With Military Couples

REBECCA TEWS-KOZLOWSKI

OVERVIEW OF THE TREATMENT APPROACH

Solution-focused therapies by their nature emphasize the resilience and strength of the couple as partners in a process of finding a path through the current difficulties. The emphasis of the approach combines an awareness of changing the way the couple defines their current difficulties and the way each individual can contribute to the overall movement through the problem or solution to the problem. It is important to note that the emphasis is on "solution" rather than on "problem," and the original proponents of this approach, including de Shazer and Berg (de Shazer et al., 1986), were quick to make this distinction. Problem-focused therapies often dwell more extensively on the "what" and "why" of the presenting situation rather than on the more active present and future emphasis on doing more of what works.

Of great importance in this model is the notion of collaborating with the couple to find strategies that they can then apply as a life skill to many other challenges they may face now or in the future. Because of this, the approach is seen as having great utility in complicated situations for which there are many competing stressors or ongoing challenges that may arise suddenly and often without warning given the environmental and lifestyle issues of the couple. This fosters a resiliency-based intervention that honors the strengths of the individuals and the process by which they combine those strengths as a couple. The shift in thinking moves from one of being victims of circumstance to a more empowered stance of belief in the strength of the couple to find an effective and sufficient resolution to the current challenges.

Notably, in reviewing training textbooks and materials on how to develop solution-focused clinical skills, two things are readily observed. First, most textbooks devote little time to this elegant and useful approach, often as few as one or two pages. Second, the methods through which these skills are transmitted are really through succinct writings with extensive vignettes and through intensive, immediate supervision during provision of therapy. For this reason, it is a real challenge to summarize a complex, dynamic approach that is essentially experientially taught by master practitioners into a basic rubric with which one might begin to work with the military population. Importantly, this therapeutic approach can be implemented at a basic level as part of other work, expanded as one has an opportunity to learn more, and ultimately developed into a more formalized personal and professional process (Pichot & Dolan, 2003, as cited in de Shazer et al., 2007, p. 160).

Drawing heavily on the writings of Berg, de Shazer, and the training team at Northwest Brief Therapy Training Center and material from the Solution-Focused Brief Therapy Association (SFBTA), this chapter overviews the basics of the approach and provides examples of what these strategies might accomplish with a military population. It is an approach that has not yet been presented in formally published research form for this population but offers so many advantages as part of a resiliency-based short-term model that it bears additional scrutiny and integration within the catalogue of military and Veterans Affairs (VA) therapy resources. It works across many levels of additional life change and challenge. Solution-focused brief therapy (SFBT) has a long history of producing positive change when therapies that are more traditional have failed.

THEORY

Solution-focused therapy (SFT), also known as SFBT, posits that clients inherently know what they need to do to fix their current problems and challenges. Suggesting that people are subject matter experts on themselves and their situation, the approach simply and elegantly establishes a platform in which the client can present the situation, explore his or her knowledge about how to solve the problem, and received collaborative support for moving toward more behavior and action that bring about sufficient solutions.

The approach emphasizes that one can only really work with the here-and-now situation, and however tempting it may be to reflect back on emotional experiences prior to this moment, effective progress with the current challenges is about examining which solutions are within the person's current grasp. Focusing the couples' attention on what they are doing right and helping them to continue to reflect on what they can do together to effectively solve the current challenges increases their sense of self-efficacy and empowers them to become the agents of their own progress. Langer (2010), of the Northwest Brief Therapy Training Center in Olympia, Washington, states that there are three basic rules in SFBT:

1. It it isn't broken, don't fix it;
2. If it works, do more of it;
3. If it's not working, do something different (from http://www.nwbttc.com, Berg & Dolan, 2001, p. 120).

In this approach, then, the therapist truly is a collaborator, *not* an expert, curative force, or director. The clinician's goal is to adopt an active listening position to attentively grasp the solution talk as it occurs and to occupy a positive, hopeful, and encouraging stance. Through the use of strategic questions and implementation of a series of proscribed strategies to facilitate the empowerment of the client or couple, the therapist generates a sense of hope and empowerment in the client or couple. Langer (2010) summarizes the approach in seven basic tenets:

1. Small steps can lead to big changes.
2. The future is both created and negotiable.
3. A solution is necessarily related to the problem.
4. Solution language is different from problem language.
5. Change is inevitable.
6. Problems do not happen all the time.
7. Find ways to cooperate with the client. (from http://www.nwbttc.com)

HOW THE BASIC TENETS WORK TOGETHER

Small steps in the right direction are observed by the therapist and acknowledged as progress. This attention to action in the right direction fosters the couple's sense of success and encourages more movement and autonomy. As people work together collaboratively, a concept of change as an inevitable part of life rather than a personalized negative experience begins to emerge. By focusing on solution language, the language of what works rather than what is wrong, it becomes clear that problems account for only a very small part of life. Although the problems may be large in magnitude, there is much ordinary successful daily living that occurs around the intrusions of the challenge at hand. Putting the spotlight on what works and discovering solutions in the here and now with the goal of improving the future keep the emphasis on doing more of what works. An outgrowth of this is that clients may realize that solutions do not always relate specifically to a problem. An observable truth is that sometimes presenting problems are just symptoms of other issues. These problems do not need to be "solved." Rather, when the couple begins to work on doing more of what works and concentrating on creating more time in which the problem does not occur, the solution actually evolves. This solution may not even correspond to the originally presented problem in the traditional cause/effect/solution models of therapy. It has, however, become a "good enough" alternative to the presenting problem because it reflects the reality of living life while moving toward the desired outcome (Berg, 1994; Berg & Dolan, 2001).

A couple may present with difficulty managing the marital strain of posttraumatic stress disorder (PTSD). They report that the husband's experience of nightly distress, daytime sleepiness, and general hypervigilance is creating extreme discord and isolation. Listening for strategies that the couple is effectively employing as coping mechanisms and observing their strength and resilience in being able to manage during the periods in which they are able to do so may mark those strategies as effective and encourage more frequent use. The couple may be seeking a solution to the underlying presenting problem. The problem itself may not have a clear solution, so they and their treating doctors may feel somewhat powerless to effect a change that restores life to the level of premorbid functioning. Utilizing the SFBT approach, the emphasis of therapy becomes evolving a solution of good enough coping by doing more of what works and avoiding what does not work. Eventually, successful coping crowds out the experience of being unable to cope, and although the problem-based solution may still be elusive, a daily living solution is now in place, and the future is secured.

IMPORTANT COMPONENTS

Early Sessions

Presession Change Questions The message that SFBT is different from other therapies begins with the intake or session-scheduling phone calls. "What has changed since you made the decision to call or begin therapy?" As an introductory question, this lets the client know that this interaction is going to be different. With couples, it is important to convey that not only the opinion of the person making the phone call is desired but also the partner's input is desired. This could take the form of asking the person on the phone what the person thinks his or her partner would say or in saying to the person calling that the partner's opinion on this will be solicited at the beginning of the first session. It creates a clear notion that the therapist is going to be interested in how things are changing and expects things will be changing. This establishes one of the basic tenets of SFBT: Change is part of life, and no problem remains static, but rather we are always evolving toward solutions, right from the start (Gordon, 2006; see the Appendix for intake forms).

Concrete Goals The hallmarks of concrete goals are that they are defined in measureable, observable terms and that the members of the couple and the therapist are able to accurately perceive whether the components of the goal are occurring and are independently able to agree on this. Many goals contain abstractions that are hard to measure and almost impossible to attain. Because of the abstract and ambiguous nature of such goals, one partner may think progress is happening, and the other may not. There is confusion in moving toward and accomplishing such goals. Often, there is a sense of hopelessness because the goals seem unattainable (de Shazer et al., 2007).

Concrete goals are derived through negotiation and must be relevant and meaningful to the couple and, by endorsement, to the therapist. Being doable, incremental, and realistic is essential. The goals must also be defined in small steps to ensure greater success and perception of accomplishment but should include the perception of involving effort on the part of the clients. This relates to a basic aspect of human perception that goals that require more work are more meaningful and more worth the effort. Finally, the goals should be stated in positive action terms rather than as what should "not" occur (e.g., "no shouting" becomes "speak calmly") (de Shazer et al., 2007).

For example, if the goal is a greater feeling of partnership and commitment between the partners, it may be easy to state this goal and hard to know if it is happening. Operationally defining the goal or placing it in behavioral action terms would include taking it from the abstract to the precise. It might now become (a) taking 10 minutes before work to go over a realistic to-do list for the day and deciding who will do what, (b) going over what was accomplished each day and giving positive feedback to the partner about what was accomplished, and (c) taking a half-hour media-free couple cuddle time each evening before bed to reward themselves for completing (a) and (b). This is more focused on achievable steps. This type of goal focuses on the process of completing the steps as the accomplishment rather than on the experience of an abstract feeling. It is empowering and lends itself to assessing progress through scaling (a way of demonstrably measuring progress). Over time, increased action on this type of concrete goal will create the experience of feeling connection and partnership. Gordon's (2006) client family scale and action plan are included in the Appendix as an example of how to track goals.

Miracle Question The miracle question is considered one of the unique hallmarks of SFT. It can be asked of individuals or of relationships. It is a simple but powerful tool. De Shazer (1988) related that in 1984 the Brief Family Therapy Center developed "the miracle question" as a framework for goal setting. It illustrates how the client already knows the solution and can often describe it in behavioral terms: "Suppose one night there is a miracle (or suppose a fairy godmother came with a magic wand) and while you are sleeping the problem is solved: What will you notice different the next morning that will tell you there has been a miracle" (http://www.nwbttc.com/sfmmirques.html)?

As practiced over the intervening 23 years, the way the question is presented has evolved somewhat. In the capstone book *More Than Miracles* (de Shazer et al., 2007), published after de Shazer's death, the treatment team at the Brief Family Therapy Center outlines a more structured manner of introducing the miracle question that they have found helpful for training beginning SFBT therapists. They note that the masters—de Shazer and Berg—pull this question off with such smoothness and intensive observation of the client that it looks deceptively simple. In practical training experience, though, having a bit more of a process to carry it off seems more effective.

De Shazer and Berg start by asking the client if it is okay to ask a question and strongly endorse waiting for the client's affirmative answer because it helps the client to recognize this as an important part of the process and prepares him to participate. This is followed by staging the question with a description of how the remainder of the day and evening might proceed for the client and how the client might go to bed and experience a restful evening in which this miracle occurs. This is then followed by the first line of the miracle question ("Suppose that during the night, while you are sleeping, a miracle happens"). This is followed by a pregnant pause of just the right length to look for the client's response. Then after a further description of the quality of the miracle as one that changes the problem that brought them to the office, further discussion takes place of the client being asleep and not knowing the miracle occurred. Finally, the morning reveal and follow-up questions are discussed (de Shazer et al., 2007, pp. 42–43).

The client's answer to the initial question is followed up by action-oriented questions about how often this experience occurs in real life, what the client would have to do to get more, how the client would act differently if the miracle occurred, and what the client would have to do to pretend that the miracle occurred. In exploring the impact on the relationship, the questions expand to include how the other person would know that the change had occurred and how the other person might act differently or might say the client were acting differently.

Scaling Scaling questions are designed to help draw out clients' subjective experience with regard to their problems and experience of distress and can be applied to both real situations and the discussion of idealized solutions. Within SFT, they are a means of information gathering for the therapist. Basically, clients are asked to explore their experience in the context of a subjective scale, such as 0–10, with 0 the lowest point (at which the client sought therapy) and ten the high postmiracle state.

The importance of scaling questions has been studied in greater detail by Strong, Pyle, and Sutherland (2009). They observed that the process of asking a client how the client will move from one point of progress to another on the scale creates a new conversation about what actions will be required to move from one point to another. In their research, they have begun a process of measuring how this dynamic works and what it needs to look like to facilitate the client's movement. Intentional and conscious dialogue on the part of the therapist is required to catch these opportunities (Gordon, 2006; Langer, 2004). Respect for the risk the client takes in emerging into this new paradigm and beginning to think in terms of moving from one point on the scale to another is also essential. Berg and de Shazer (Berg, 1994; de Shazer et al., 2007) often spoke of this as genuine curiosity and interest on the part of the therapist.

The scaling concept can be applied to the frequency of solution behavior as baseline. It can also be addressed to the client's level of hope, energy for change, or even other factors like trust, confidence, or motivation (Berg & Dolan, 2001, p. 70).

Every Session

Constructing and Paying Attention to Solutions and Their Exceptions Throughout each session, the therapist must pay rapt attention to the nuances of what the clients are saying. It is critically important that the therapist not miss the subtle shifts and changes in the way the couple discusses what is occurring and what they are observing. It is often through these shifts that it becomes clear that there are exceptions to the problems presented. For example, the couple may be describing the sleep difficulties experienced by the service member, and as they talk further, it becomes evident that this does not occur every day. The alert SFBT therapist will pick up on that subtlety and ask what makes the difference on those nights that sleep is better. By focusing on periods when there is an exception to the problem, it may be possible to identify solutions that are working at least part of the time and imagine forward how they might work more frequently. In this manner, solutions may be collaboratively constructed within the session (De Jong & Berg, 2002; Gordon, 2006).

Coping Questions Observing the strength of the individuals and the couple may be useful in engaging them in a conversation about what their secret is for managing so well under such difficult circumstances. This series of interactions can create a conversation that helps clients view themselves as more capable than they thought on entry to therapy and may also outline skills that they have already in place that do actually work for them. The coping questions may also remind them of skills they have utilized in past coping that perhaps they have forgotten to apply to the current problem. For example, a couple may present with intense marital distress around reintegrating a service member into the family after an extended absence. Their history together includes having coped with multiple deployments, seriously ill children, periods of separation due to injury, and the death of a child. The therapist might begin by observing that they are an amazing couple to have endured all of that. This may be followed by a genuine wondering out loud about how they have succeeded in preserving their marriage during such difficult times. As the couple creates an answer, they may revisit skills that they utilized previously in communicating, grieving together, seeking opportunities for renewal or togetherness, looking differently at their expectations, and so on. Through active and nonjudgmental listening and adroit questioning, the therapist can help them to clarify which of their previous coping strategies might be most useful to bring forward into this situation (Berg & Dolan, 2001; De Jong & Berg, 2002; Trepper et al., 2010).

Berg and Dolan (2001) suggested that formulating questions using "how" rather than "why" increases the positive action orientation and vote of confidence that the client is actually coping well amidst the stressors and crises that are occurring. An example might be asking the couple to tell how they managed to stay calm during a recent stressful experience rather than asking them why they do not manage better more often. Berg particularly has noted from her earliest writings that this gentle difference of celebrating success through positive questions that draw attention to what works brings about great change more quickly than any other approach (Berg, 1994).

COPING QUESTIONS

Solution-focused therapy builds on the strengths and resources clients have to help them develop solutions that uniquely fit them and their circumstances. This can be a particularly difficult challenge when dealing with the exceptional circumstance of clients who present as completely hopeless and helpless. They may see themselves as powerless over their situation and complain extensively about how impossible that situation is. Oftentimes these people have severe chronic medical problems and/or a personal history of severe abuse or mental illness. As a therapist it is easy to become discouraged and hopeless about this kind of client too.

Reassurance does not work with these clients. In fact, it is likely to have the opposite effect of the one intended. The client is not reassured but typically makes even more hopeless and desperate statements. She/he is picking up on the therapist's sense of helplessness and as a result may feel more out of control her/himself. All of a sudden it is the therapist's job to make the client feel better, not the client's job. In any case, a sense of empowerment and self confidence cannot be imposed from without, it must come from within.

Coping questions can solve this dilemma while cooperating with clients as well as accepting their view of the problem. The therapist can begin to help clients see their strengths and resources in trying circumstances and stay "behind" them rather than reassure them or take over and try to impose a solution (which is unlikely to fit well or be long-lasting).

Coping questions ask about how clients somehow manage to keep going in spite of the adversity they face. For example, someone who is suicidal obviously has not killed himself yet. Someone living with chronic pain is enduring it somehow. In spite of a terrible childhood, a client manages to get through the day and take care of her baby.

A solution-focused therapist is curious about this, and coping questions are designed to discover how clients manage to keep going in spite of all that is against them. Taking this approach helps clients discover resources and strengths they most likely did not know they had. When used properly and with persistence the result is empowering and uplifting. It helps shift their view of themselves in a positive, client-enhancing direction:

- "How did you manage to get up this morning (make it to this appointment, get through yesterday, etc.)?"
- "How do you keep going day after day when there seems to be no hope?"
- "How is it ("What do you do so) that things are not worse?"
- "How come you have not killed yourself yet? What has held you back?" (if thinking of suicide)
- "How did you learn to cope with such an awful situation, when you were still so young? Did you have to do it all by yourself?" (talking about childhood abuse/trauma)

This type of question helps the therapist let clients lead in telling what they are capable of, what is good about them and allows them to recognize strengths, resources, and abilities they oftentimes had not thought of themselves.

Once you get an answer to a coping question, the next task is to build on that answer, to expand it. So pursue their response and ask questions like:

- "What did you do to get up this morning (keep going yesterday, stay alive today, get through that period in your childhood, etc.)?"
- "What would it take for you to keep doing what you've been doing?"
- "Where did you learn to do that? Or did you figure it out by yourself?" (follow-up question: "How did you figure out this was a good way to do it?")

Caution: When working with clients who present as powerless and hopeless, make sure you're not "the customer" for your own services, that you're not the one who is most bothered by the problem or want a solution more than the client. Instead, stay with the **client's** identified problem/goal. You might ask how the concern you have relates to issue(s) the client has identified. Your work together has to be on the client's goal to succeed.

Langer (1995). ©1995 Northwest Brief Therapy Training Center, used with permission.

Is There Anything I Forgot to Ask? Taking the time to ask, "Is there anything I forgot to ask?" creates a space for the couple to reflect on what they are getting out of the session and whether they are feeling understood and have a sense of the direction of therapy. It is in any case a good customer service strategy. In SFBT, it is also a means of gauging what the clients are experiencing in the session and being certain that they feel seen, understood, and empowered.

Break Before the End of Session Another unique strategy of SFBT is the break before the end of the session. In the most traditional sense of the approach, this is a time to exit the therapy room to seek consult with the supervision team who participates in the therapy process. In some models of supervision, that team might even have been watching through a one-way mirror. For independently practicing therapists, it can be a few moments to reflect outside the dynamics of the session and to gather one's thoughts about the meaning of what has been covered or the progress that has been made. Inside the therapy room, the couple has the opportunity to reflect on what they have been doing and how they are feeling. Regardless of whether this has been a staffing opportunity or a moment for quiet reflection on the part of the therapist, on reentry the goal is to affirm the positive aspects of the work that has occurred. Second, the therapist asks the couple if they have changed in any way since the beginning of the session. Then, a conversation ensues about any additional insights that have been gleaned. Finally, this may be a segue into the session wrap-up and the assignment of homework or other experiments to further the therapeutic process during the space between sessions.

Within the SFBT model, compliments are often used to remark on or draw notice to the strengths and successes of the client. Most commonly, this occurs near the end of the session, perhaps following the break. De Jong and Berg (2002) also suggested that SFBT therapists find it useful to incorporate this strategy throughout the session if it feels natural and appropriate. As originally outlined by de Shazer and by Berg (Berg, 1994), the compliments were part of this final check in at the end of the session. The key is to remember that genuine compliments help to support the client's positive sense of self and self-efficacy. It is less important how a client reacts to the compliment and critical that the observation be made on those areas that relate to the client's own steps toward solution (De Jong & Berg, 2002).

Experiments and Homework Assignments The strategy of experiments and homework assignments is really more about giving empowering tasks that help the client look for what is changing, what is different, or what is working between sessions. The approach is about priming clients to pay attention to the salient information as it occurs and to look for information that supports the idea of themselves as agents of their own positive change. Human nature being what it is, there is a tendency only to see the information that fits with the current mental filter. So, if the client is preoccupied with the failings of a partner, the client will tend to notice the information that supports that view. Conversely if the task is changed to noticing the ways in which the partner actively shows love by doing what needs to be done or doing something nice, the client will be primed to look for those events rather than all the ways in which the partner falls short. Inevitably, in the next session the observation of even some of these positive points will come through in questions on progress scaling and what has changed. Ultimately, this should also lead to a sense of empowerment and an observation that the solution is on its way.

Strategies for the Second Session and Beyond

So, What Is Even a Little Better Since Last Time? Beginning subsequent sessions with the lead-in, "So, what is even a little better since last time?" orients the couple to be looking for the small steps of progress that again demonstrate the reality that change is constantly occurring and positively affirms their ability to be agents of that change. Master SFBT therapists note that the majority of clients are able to generate a positive statement of something that has improved in the intervening interval. These small progressions can be used to fine-tune movement toward the goal. They can also become a shared experience of changing the way the problem is viewed and moving from the all-negative or mostly negative thinking that accompanies the early entry into therapy.

This strategy extends the early notion of scaling into progress on those concrete goal steps. This can occur in each session as a measure of what is changing and can utilize the same or a similar scale of 0, the way things were when the client first decided to come to therapy, and 10, the way things would be right after the miracle occurred. Often, a couple will disagree on the progress they observe. This will create a fertile ground for discussion of how the goal needs fine-tuning or how their different views of progress are observations of different aspects of the situation. The person with the lower rating may be helped by being asked what it would take for them to be able to see increasing the scale score. This is a helpful action-oriented conversation that often moves the process forward significantly.

SECOND SESSION

Sometimes beginning solution-focused therapists have trouble maintaining a solution-focused approach after the first session. This handout is intended to help maintain that focus. Below are some suggestions for staying with it. Most likely you will come up with a number of your own ideas after some practice.

Probably the most important thing is to be **persistent** in asking solution-focused questions so that the clients notice what is good for them. Once they get started talking/thinking in this way, it is your job to follow along and help them stay solution-focused as they work toward their goal.

To start the second session, ask about **positive changes** that occurred between sessions. A good way to start out on the right foot is to ask one of the following questions:

- "What's better?"
- "What have you been doing that's good for you?"
- "On a ten point scale, where zero stands for how things were before our first session and 10 stands for the problems that brought you to therapy are completely solved, what number would you give it today?"

Often clients will not quite know what to do with such a question, since they still expect to talk about problems, difficulties etc. As a result they may answer with "Nothing's better." or something like it. It is useful to assume they did not hear the question properly, so **repeat** the question either directly or in some variation, such as:

- "What's happened to give you the idea there has been improvement?"
- "How far have you gotten in moving towards your goal since last time?"

If you still get a "Nothing." start asking about **differences**, such as:

- "So what's different?"
- "Tell me about what's happened since we met last time."
- "Were some times better than others since we met last time?"

If there has been a setback, you can ask questions around what has been **learned**:

- "What have you learned from this?"
- "What was different this time that you can use if this happens again?"
- "What kept you going through this?"
- "What would you do differently next time?"

Once you start getting positive changes, it is important to **expand and amplify** them for the clients. The clients may not have an answer to every one of your amplification questions, but that's O.K. You've got them thinking in the right direction:

- "How did you do that?" ("How did that happen?")
- "How did you know that was the right thing to do?"
- "What helped you to do this?"
- "What did your husband (wife, son, boss …) notice?"
- "Who else noticed?" (repeat as long as you get a new answer)
- "How did they react differently?"
- "Then what happened?"
- "How much difference did this make?"

Once you have gotten as much information as possible about a positive change, start over with the next one:

- "What else is better?"

After you have elicited changes/improvements, it is important to connect them with the **goal(s)** the client has for therapy, unless the client has done this already:

- "How is this related to what you came in here for?"
- "Supposing these changes continued, would you be satisfied you had achieved your goal for therapy?"
- "How far along are you now in achieving your therapy goal?" (use 10 point scale)
- "What else needs to happen?"

If there are no positive changes (which is unlikely), there may not be a goal you are working on together, in which case you may want to revisit the goal to make sure you're on track. If you find out there is no clear goal, you may want to renegotiate the goal (start over with first session questions, i.e., "So how can I help?"). In this instance it often turns out that after the first session the clients decided the goal discussed then actually isn't what they wanted to work on or they did not have a well-formed goal in the first place.

It is important to ask the questions above with **genuine curiosity** (and don't assume you know the answer beforehand—you'll often be surprised). The questions are intended to get clients started thinking in a solution-oriented way. Once they start, get out of the way and let them continue, asking questions only to keep them on task (solution-oriented and relevant to their goal). In other words, **follow rather than lead** as much as possible. After all, your goal is to get them to do this on their own and work yourself out of a job as soon as possible.

Progress Scaling

Gentle Homework Checks Checking on the outcome of homework or experiments is an essential next session follow-up item. In contrast perhaps to the more dogmatic homework follow-up of the cognitive-behavioral therapy (CBT) therapist, in SFBT great caution is taken to ask about this in a casual gentle manner. The conversation might include an aspect of respectful curiosity about what the couple learned or observed in completing their assignment. Great care is taken not to shift the power differential and activate a power dynamic in which the client now becomes the student. Remember the basic premise of this approach is that the therapist is the student. Therapists must be cautious and restrained if the homework has not been completed or if the client for some reason has shifted. A tentative observation that it would be interesting to know what might have happened if they had completed the homework should be the extent of any interaction around unfinished activity. The conversation could then be directed back to what is different since last session or to a progress scaling question.

Ask About Differences or Learning Since Last Time Asking about what is different or what has been learned since the last session keeps the flow and tone of the session squarely centered on the client's empowered process within a changing world. This affirms the client's role in the experience of life as it occurs both with and around the client. Returning to session to discuss what the client is learning and what is different from the previous session becomes a rhythm around which the continued work occurs. Clearly, this type of interaction supports the reality of SFBT as having a radically different cadence from other medical model approaches. The therapist genuinely looks forward to hearing from the client what has changed for and with the client and is there as a neutral, nonjudgmental platform for presenting what the experience has meant. Often in SFBT, the interval between sessions is a bit longer with no deleterious effects and is in fact an excellent outcome in terms of the clients' ability to observe the change process occurring within and around them.

What Makes It Effective?

Review of the Research in the Civilian Sector With the growing emphasis on evidenced-based therapies and intervention in clinical practice in general and within military and VA clinical services specifically, it is important to understand where SFT falls in terms of a measurable outcome. The original Milwaukee-based Brief Family Therapy Center conducted a number of small community-style studies looking at the outcome of their therapy model during the 1990s. Criticized as lacking in methodological rigor and containing more of an anecdotal quality (Fish, 1997; Kiser, 1996; Shoham et al., 1995, as cited in Lewis & Osborn, 2004), the broader community of mental health providers remained curious but unimpressed by the data. Current meta-analytic research is in press at this time according to the 2010 report of the Research Committee of the SFBTA (Trepper et al., 2010). The SFBTA does identify 18 outcome-based studies and notes that the Department of Juvenile Justice has endorsed SFBT as one of its approved evidenced-based practices.

One of the obvious challenges in the assessment of outcome is that the intervals for intervention vary widely by client; the model utilizes an approach that is radically different from most of the other therapeutic approaches currently in use, and therefore systematic program/intervention evaluation constructs may not fit a strictly SFT. To the traditionally, empirically trained practitioner then, the lack of empirical evidence may be somewhat distressing. The fact is that this therapeutic approach is quite comfortable as a stand-alone therapy or as an adjunctive therapeutic approach that makes its unique mark by flying in the face of the traditional Western medical model or problem-focused approach. The solution-focused therapeutic model emphasizes the role of the therapist as one who is learning about the client, a collaborator. The client is viewed as the subject matter expert on his or her life circumstances, problem, and reason for coming and ultimately as the one who already knows the solution.

So, rather than SFBT being a specific set of rigid techniques that accounts for change, it is a series of facilitated conversations, each as individually unique as the people who participate in them. This contributes to the idea that the approach be evaluated in a more anecdotal manner. However, from the earliest community data collected, it was apparent that 75% of clients reported having experienced a permanent change in the way they thought about their situation from even an initial session. Many reported specifically being impressed by the miracle question and finding themselves referring back to it over the years (De Jong & Berg, 2002).

The reason the approach has continued to gain in popularity over 30 years appears to be that it works so well with those who really may not be fully invested in the therapy process and for whom the concept of actively doing something to change their situation is much more preferable than having frequent protracted conversations about how they came to be at this point in their lives. Often, these clients feel that there is nothing "wrong" with them, and they are deeply resistant to being pathologized and made to feel as though there is something broken. Interviews with Insoo Berg (http://www.psychotherapy.net/interview/insoo-kim-berg) reveal how she came to find this as an approach that was satisfying for immigrant, working-class, and mandated individuals for whom the intellectual process of purely psychoanalytic approaches was worse than poison.

Berg and Dolan (2001) talked about the idea of "leading from behind." They stressed the importance of nonjudgmental demeanor and respect for the client as critical to the process of therapy. This approach is at once multicultural and ensures the stance of the therapist as the student in the interaction. This is a critical aspect of the approach because defense mechanisms are not triggered, and the work is not delayed and hampered by this dance of power and control. It is essential, however, for the therapist to suspend all judgment and to trust that as the clients explore their experience and find their voice within the therapy session they will arrive at the correct solution for them. In *Tales of Solutions,* Berg and Dolan (2001) explored the many different therapy stories that illustrate the application of this concept across culture, diagnosis, and severity of pathology. What is interesting in these stories is the patient, gentle acceptance, and freedom from expert advice giving in the voice of the therapists. Many of the stories addressed challenging issues like suicidal behavior, intensive PTSD, self-injury, substance abuse, domestic abuse, intense anger, and violence. Throughout the interactions described, and this volume alone contains many stories of how SFBT interactions that were seemingly simple generated significant changes in clients' lives, change occurred because a process of viewing life differently began in the conversation. The closest analogy is perhaps that of a small stone thrown into a pond with a small splash that generates ever-expanding ripples of impact.

If a criticism of the approach does exist, it is that the approach appears on the surface too anecdotal to be consistently applied. Once more research is done into the manner of how therapy is provided and how the therapist's skills are built up, this concern disappears. The SFBTA is making a concerted effort to create a uniform message, a consistent model of training, and to promulgate the wide range of research, including program outcome data, that supports the work of this unique approach (Trepper et al., 2010).

Review of the Research in the Military Population Currently, no published research exists looking at the model as strictly applied to military populations. The approach is being utilized within a number of strategies of time-limited prevention models and early intervention models for which data collection is occurring concurrently. The approach shows much promise within both active duty and veteran military populations because it is strength and resiliency focused, is time limited with opportunity to return as needed, and builds on existing skills. It is hoped that those who choose to use this model with military couples will join forces with the SFBTA in collecting data on the progress of their work with this growing population.

Strengths of Using This Approach With Military Personnel

What Sets It Apart From Others? This approach has unique benefits in the military community because it fosters a "can do" attitude that fits well with the other forms of training military personnel received. It establishes the couple as a functioning unit in which teamwork and solutions enhance the quality and satisfaction of the relationship. In a sense, this relationship building and the process of learning an active coping model that can be applied to many challenges unique to military families (e.g., sudden deployments, cross-country moves, sudden loss of income, anxiety regarding duty assignments, issues with children coping, etc.) becomes an additional reason for investing in the process.

The military culture observably tends to foster a sense of unity and cohesion in which repression or minimizing of individual needs or difficulties is rewarded by freedom from negative attention. Effectively, from basic training forward the tacit message is that you will be called out for weakness, personal problems, or neediness. While this may make sense on the battlefield, the reality of adopting this culture as a way of living over a lengthy period or even a lifetime can be problematic when the need for new coping and adaptation is required.

The solution-focused model disarms that sensitivity to being "called out" or having "weaknesses" noted by honoring the knowledge and skill that are present and reminding the client couple that they do actually know what to do and that they may just need to pay more attention to doing more of what works or using what they already know more efficiently. The respectful, supportive, and nondirective/non-judgmental tone of the therapy is also likely to be a welcome support to those with a military background. Often, the very fact that they are sitting in a therapy office is viewed internally by them as a statement of their incompetence. Finding instead a space of acceptance, respect, encouragement, and empowerment cannot help but be a welcome alternative to being pathologized, labeled, and deconstructed.

It is rewarding to see the tension and distress visibly lift from the shoulders of the service member when this approach is employed. The misconceptions about what the therapeutic process will be like and the perception of weakness and pathology and what that will mean for them often create incredible tension in the referral period. While a good therapist, regardless of orientation, can often help to alleviate this distress and normalize the therapeutic process, solution-focused therapists establish this positive orientation prior to the first session, and it is the persistent theme through every session from first to last. Anecdotal responses regarding the therapy suggest that this is often what clients value most in the solution-focused therapeutic process.

Why Might It Be Better Than Others? There are reasons this therapy might be better than the others. The solution-focused model is adaptable, and while advanced training is recommended for the most effective utilization of the approach, key concepts from the approach are easily integrated into other formats that may be utilized by chaplains, commanders, social workers, and even peer support programs.

As previously discussed, because this approach empowers and allows clients to discover coping strategies, it is time limited, emphasizes strength and capacity, and fits well within the military lifestyle. Since it does not foster dependence on the therapist, it creates a vision of the therapeutic process as collaborative, flexible, and responsive to current situations. Clients can expect a consistent approach from one solution-focused therapist to another and may find a real benefit from working with challenges from this perspective at whatever duty station they find themselves.

Stephen Langer (2004) of the Northwest Brief Therapy Training Center, experienced in working with military populations, offered some considerations for working with individuals with physical health concerns. These are summarized in the inset.

Limitations of This Approach With Military Couples

The approach tends to focus on here-and-now issues and to look at specific challenges and find sufficient resolution to the issues at hand. If there is a weakness in the approach, it is that the facilitator often holds the line on closing down discussions of underlying issues and intense emotionality that may represent underlying grief, trauma response, or anger. The strong emphasis on resolving challenges in the here and now and going forward can be viewed as a Band-Aid when intense

BRIEF SOLUTION-FOCUSED APPROACH WORKING WITH THE SOMATICALLY FOCUSED

Several Types of Somatically Focused Individuals

Clients with chronic illnesses/chronic pain, people who are exquisitely aware of body functions, individuals with fear of disease or disorder based on misinterpretation of bodily symptoms, others with multiple somatic complaints where no physical basis can be found.

Typical Issues Presented by Somatically Focused

Not feeling heard by medical system, negative self-definition, feeling overwhelmed by persistent symptoms, because of physical symptoms focus on body even more in problem-oriented ways, either-or thinking, drug and alcohol issues, unaware of personal resources.

Special Challenges for Solution-Focused Therapist

Being respectful and learning what to ignore and what to pay attention to with clients with lots of physical complaints: gripes vs. complaints, what client perceives he/she can change vs. what needs others' help for, when and how to get family involved, recognizing potential solutions already present, staying "behind the client."

Therapist Tasks With Somatically Focused Clients

Developing well-formed goals: reorienting patients to solutions rather than to problems, painting a realistic goal picture with a somatically preoccupied person, noticing what the therapist can use to compliment, deciding on an intervention, asking about connections between improvements/changes and somatic complaints/focus, using coping questions for setbacks or unchangeable physical problems and persistent complainant relationship about physical problems, projecting into the future and working back to the present.

Implications for the Practice of Solution-Focused Therapy

Emphasis on coping with what one cannot change in life, working towards clear and small goals, helping family/friends to be helpful and be resources for the client, persistence in staying with what client wants, creating web of connections between physical issues and what the client wants to solidify movement toward realistic goals, staying in a collaborative mode.

Langer (2004).

underlying issues of the couple may be part of what is creating the current distress. Even so, the model, when it is implemented by qualified professionals, can be used as a resource for breaking those issues down into a step-by-step format and working through the underlying concerns with a solution-oriented focus. For example, Jim and Jane may come to discuss their escalating fights over how to cope with an upcoming deployment. The underlying issues may include grief over the loss of Jim's presence during the early childhood of their son, fear that infidelity on Jane's part might overwhelm the marital commitment, and anger that a third yearlong deployment is being scheduled without regard to the human needs of this family. A solution-focused approach, as we have seen, will emphasize coping solutions in the here and now that address the presenting problem of how to cope more peaceably and productively with the reality of preparing for a third year of overseas duty. The tendency of the couple to emote and want to be heard regarding the emotional underpinnings will be a strong pressure to which a solution-focused facilitator would respond with strong emphasis on staying on the present situation by hearing the solutions the couple has used in the past to successfully deal with deployment. When supported, couples can see the utility of the approach and the point of postponing or potentially letting go of the journey through the history and emotions. Pragmatically, those underlying issues will need to be addressed at some point, whether in these sessions once the solution is in process for the current challenge or at some point down the road. The couple may however have learned through the use of SFT to focus on what they are doing right to address the needs and issues rather than to focus on the distress that less-functional strategies cause.

General Therapeutic Considerations

Training According the SFBTA (Trepper et al., 2010), the preferred training for solution-focused therapists is a solid underpinning in therapeutic skills such as one would find in a graduation program preparing one for work, certification, and licensure as a mental health practitioner. Minimum skills include a master's degree in a mental health field and formalized training and supervision in the provision of SFT. There are many paths to acquire this training and supervision, including taking a series of workshops or university classes and completing online training. Ideally, supervision is provided by a "master" practitioner of SFT. The formal course of training should include information on the history and philosophy of the approach, SFBT-specific session construction and format, video of masters doing their work with clients and video examples of specific strategies for doing SFBT, opportunities to play both the therapist and the patient in role play, and both practice and training with video feedback.

The SFBTA (2010) also recommends that the therapists

a. are warm and friendly;
b. are naturally positive and supportive (are often told that they see the good in people);
c. are open-minded and flexible to new ideas;

d. are excellent listeners, especially the ability to listen for clients' previous solutions embedded in "problem-talk";
e. are tenacious and patient. (p. 15)

Transference/Countertransference The unique position of the therapist in SFT is to assume the stance of student. In this nonjudgmental position, the therapist learns to utilize a listening approach that pays particular attention to "solution talk" being presented inside the clients' presentation of the problem. Inherent in this process, then, is the establishment of the clients as subject matter experts on themselves and their situation. Unlike nearly every other therapeutic approach, the strength of SFT comes from the building up of this teacher/student relationship with the therapist as student. Insoo Berg strongly argued that this approach reduces and perhaps even completely disarms the transference/countertransference process (Berg, 1994; Berg & Dolan, 2001) because there is no filter being applied by the therapist, and the client no longer needs to enroll in the typical dynamics of the therapeutic process by assuming the lower position. The collaborative nature of the model establishes the clients as the ultimate authority, and it is through the use of basic strategies of focusing on solutions and doing more of what the client already knows will work that the process moves along.

Resistance is another issue that often becomes a barrier to progress in most therapeutic models. Within the paradigm of the solution-focused model, resistance is addressed by adopting a stance that disarms resistant clients by allowing them to see that they are in fact in charge of their experience, making progress with steps in the right direction and not being evaluated, criticized, or instructed (Berg, 1994; Berg & Dolan, 2001). For this reason, this approach has been widely adopted with mandated clients and was actually fine-tuned in Berg's work with court-ordered single parents who were working on having their children removed by the Department of Child and Family Services returned to them (Berg, 1994). This challenging population, with its many issues related to chaotic lifestyle, lack of financial resources, unexpected single parenting, abusive relationships, and lack of personal control over lifestyle decisions, mirrors our military and veteran populations in surprising ways. Providing those who have come to view the "system" as intrusive and negative with a means of changing their focus to one of empowerment and ability to find solutions is one of the hallmarks of resistance reduction. From the premeeting stage of therapy through discharge, SFT integrates this approach at every level.

Therapy Fidelity The most effective utilization of the solution-focused model comes from therapists who are able to incorporate the primary tenet of treating the client as expert and allowing themselves to be in the nondirective "learner" position. Insoo Berg's training materials and those now being utilized by the SFBTA talk about the lifelong process of the therapist increasing the "listening ear" that focuses on what the clients are saying about the solutions they are using rather than applying their personal filter to what the clients are saying (Berg, 1994; De Jong & Berg, 2001). This is obviously an acquired skill that takes time and patience to develop. One of the reasons that the SFT model requires such intensive supervision during training is to ensure development of this skill. Berg developed a "phone-in" approach to supervision by which the therapist in training would pause for a break near the end of the session to receive feedback or, if during the session the therapist were to begin to stray back into a more traditional model of interaction, the phone would ring and the therapist in training would be advised regarding how to bring the session back on course in keeping with the tenets of SFT. Berg's stance was that the more immediate the supervision response the better, especially in the initial stages of training (De Jong & Berg, 2002).

Lehmann and Patton (2012) have been conducting research on a measure of solution-focused fidelity. They looked at how well 12 student therapists felt they were able to apply the SFT-consistent interventions of alliance building, solution talk, and provision of end-of-session feedback and a client outcome evaluation. They concluded that there is enough consistency in the model to allow for the creation of reliable fidelity instruments that can be combined in later research to look at therapy outcome analysis.

Supervision

To attain true proficiency with this approach and to reach the deepest level of skill that includes integrating it into both personal and professional use, a process of working with others who are master practitioners of the modality is truly required. Unlike many approaches, a few intensive seminars or trainings can get you started, but the skill set is very much viewed as a developmental process that requires ongoing training to reach the level of master practitioner.

The official position of the NWBTTC is that formal training and ongoing supervision are required to be able to practice at an advanced level of competency. The founders de Shazer and Berg also argued in favor of an intensive training process with a group of more advanced practitioners and students observing via one-way mirror and participating in the session through the phone-in technique and during the break at the end of the session.

At a minimum, it appears evident that it would be challenging for an individual therapist to begin to adopt this as a primary approach to therapy without having supervision support. The model is the antithesis of the traditional problem-focused or medical models, and particularly in top-down clinic settings where that focus is king, budding SFBT therapists could frequently find themselves at odds with and struggling for support from more traditionally trained mental health providers (Pichot & Dolan, 2003). It seems wise, then, that SFBT therapists seek the support of others in their modality and, both for the sake of ethical provision of care and for their own professional development, outline a course of training and supervision that allows them to develop and advance their skill set. Certainly, after reading a chapter like this, various strategies could be incorporated into a basic Stage 1 skill set that is open to learning more about this process and providing a more open solution-focused and encouraging therapeutic stance. Relatively quickly, the need for feedback and consultation becomes apparent, and it is here that membership in the SFBTA and further training will be most welcome. The SFBTA makes available a wealth of information in the form of downloads to assist in developing an SFBT practice. In addition, in-person training is available each year at their annual conference and through online interactive training programs that can be completed at the practitioners' own pace. The SFBTA also makes organizational training available for individual sites interested in creating a more formalized SFBT-oriented practice (http://www.sfbta.org).

Case Vignette – Ben and Julie

BACKGROUND

Ben and Julie had been referred for counseling because of marital distress. Several factors had contributed to this referral. Ben was at the time awaiting a medical discharge after two tours in Iraq. He had been diagnosed with mild brain injury, was experiencing some PTSD and fluctuating agitation, and was having a great deal of difficulty reintegrating into his family life with wife, Julie, and three young children ages 5, 3, and 13 months. The pressures were fairly intense as Julie, who was more independent now than she had been in the early years of the marriage, was unwilling to put up with the "temper tantrums" and daily restrictions that her husband was imposing. She reported that he was anxious about everything and was scaring the children because he did not want them to go outside as he was fearful that they would be harmed. He expressed concern about Julie's use of social media to keep in touch with family and friends, expressing fear that bad guys would know that they were a soldier's family and come after them. He seemed unwilling to do anything toward the household needs and refused to clean up after himself, engage in self-care, or help with errands. Increasingly, he was becoming forgetful, angry when reminded of what he needed to do, and often reported that Julie had not told him to do the things she said he was forgetting and was just setting him up. His medications had been changed frequently, but none of them seemed to be helping, and Julie was just fed up with trying to work, go to school, parent three little kids, and manage Ben's behavior. There had been involvement with the military police when neighbors had intervened during several loud verbal arguments, and the couple was about to split. Traditional psychotherapy had been tried, but Ben rejected it, stating that he did not want to discuss his childhood, and that he felt that everyone was blaming him and not seeing that Julie was the problem. He tended to come to session and say that everything was fine. After the fourth session, he no longer came. Social work had assigned a case manager, and it was through this route that the family was referred for couples counseling. Neither Julie nor Ben felt good about divorcing as the potential for losing contact with the children would be high for Ben, who had always been a loving father. Both of them could see this current situation as a problem related to wartime experience and wanted to address how they could move forward positively.

SOLUTION-FOCUSED BRIEF THERAPY

SESSION 1

Once given the referral, the SFBT therapist called the family to set up an appointment. She asked during this phone session about how things had improved since the referral was made. Julie had taken the call and informed her that since the referral they had been fighting less because they were both hoping to address their concerns in session instead of in their living room. The therapist complimented Julie on that progress and let her know that she would be looking forward to hearing Ben's thoughts on the change in the session. On entry to the session, the SBFT therapist welcomed the couple and complimented them on the fact that they had taken the first step in the right direction by coming to the session. She went on to ask them about how things had changed since they had made the initial phone call to set up the appointment. She patiently waited through the silence while Ben thoughtfully formulated his answer that he was trying to be more helpful by putting his things away and helping the kids to put their things away. Julie remarked that she had noticed this change and very much appreciated it. As the session proceeded, the therapist inquired about how the couple was managing through such very challenging circumstances and what actions they were finding most helpful to creating a calm day. At first, Julie had a tendency to resort back to her laundry list of what was not working and how upset she was. Notably, Ben would roll his eyes and seem to check out while she went on. With genuine curiosity and patience, the therapist noted the inconsistencies in Julie's statements, observing, "Julie, first you said that Ben had really been trying to do more and that you noticed and appreciated that. Then you said he never picks up or helps out no matter what you say or do. I am not sure I understand how those two points go together." Julie stopped for a moment and went on to say that it was true there had been a change lately, and that maybe things were already improving. Ben added that he thought they were getting through these difficulties because at the end of the day they were able to hug each other and agree to start fresh each morning.

Ben seemed more engaged at this point, so the therapist asked the couple if she might ask them a question. They replied affirmatively. Following the general script for asking the miracle question, the therapist introduced it by recalling the aspects of a good night's sleep, followed by the intervention of a fairy godmother, and then a morning reveal. She then asked them each to tell her what they would first notice that would indicate something was different. Ben shared that Julie would be cuddling him and that their little ones would be playing quietly in their rooms. Julie observed that she would be surprised that she had gotten a whole night's sleep, and that Ben had not had any night terrors and was sleeping next to her peacefully like in the old days. Next, their children would notice that they were not crabby and arguing, but that they were peaceful, working together to make breakfast and get them ready for their day. Next, Julie observed that on her drive to work she would not be feeling like the whole day was ruined, and instead of feeling guilty about the impact of fighting on her children, she would have a sense of well-being that they had a happy start to the day. Ben reported that he would be feeling like he had done a good thing in helping his kids and wife get out of the house happy, and that he might feel good enough to go work out and maybe start cleaning up the downstairs for a surprise for his wife. In short, their observations related to a positive contagion of good feelings and how that would motivate additional positive actions and behaviors.

The therapist followed this up with another question about how often they got a few hours or a day like this. Ben said he could remember 1 day last week. Julie thought that there might have been 2 or 3 days in the last 2 weeks. The therapist remarked on how wonderful it was to hear that there were good days even as they were under such stress. Applying the scaling principle she then asked the couple to rate their current level from 0 (the level you were at on the day of your referral for therapy) to 10 (the day of the miracle). Ben put it at a 4, and Julie put it at a 3. The therapist asked Julie what it would take to make it a 4, and Julie thoughtfully replied that being able to see it happen from here forward would make it a 4.

Out of this miracle question then came a small goal of seeing if there were any additional hours or days that were more like this and observing what it was they were doing differently on those days. The therapist then asked the couple if there was anything that she missed or that she should have asked about and did not. Ben said that he was sad that his homecoming had been so hard. Julie expressed feeling that she had a lot of hope that they could move past this. The therapist then explained about taking a break before ending and encouraged them to talk about the session while she excused herself. During the break, Ben and Julie observed that there were positive things happening, and Julie affirmed how much she appreciated Ben's presence in their home and the fact that they did have some good days. Ben, for his part, expressed that he had not understood how guilty Julie was feeling about the kids starting each day so roughly. Julie was able to share that it was that feeling that made her think of leaving—for the kids' sake. Ben was able to say that he also was struggling with guilt over his behavior. When the therapist returned, she shared her observation that they were a very strong couple. She remarked on their strength in being able to find several good days even when things were so hard. She also asked if they had learned anything new during the session, and they summarized the observations about appreciation and guilt. The task was reaffirmed, and the couple left the session.

Session 2

Session 2 began with the SFBT therapist inquiring about what had changed even a little bit since last time. Ben reported that he had been feeling like his medication was helping his anxiety better, and that he was not feeling so scared to go out of the house. Julie reported that she had been able to see 3 days this week when things were calm and they did not fight. The therapist responded with compliments regarding the positive progress and wondered about how they would scale their progress from 0 to 10. Ben reported being at 5, and Julie reported being at 6. Exploring the discrepancy allowed room for discussion of the homework task and what specifically they had observed occurring. Out of this conversation, it was learned that Julie was now interpreting Ben's PTSD behaviors more accurately and either walking away to give him space or encouraging him to take a break until they passed. The bottom line was that she was no longer thinking that he was doing it on purpose. She felt that this awareness had come to her in the last session when she realized how much guilt he was carrying about how this was happening. Ben felt less judged by Julie and that in turn helped him to be less anxious about losing her and his family. The reduction in anxiety helped him to think more clearly about how to solve problems in a way that would not scare his kids. The therapist was able to gather information from this conversation about strategies that were working for this couple. Summarizing the progress, they were able to create a short list of ideas that were effective in creating a solution. From here, additional goals and tasks about increasing the use of these strategies could be addressed. Julie felt she could continue to use understanding and backing off to support Ben. Ben felt he could continue to work on letting go of the anxiety. Together, they developed a plan for Ben to be clearer with Julie when he was feeling an increase in anxiety. Julie agreed to help Ben develop a plan for what to do when the anxiety seemed not to respond (e.g., calling the help line, going to a prearranged safe place, using the meditation he had previously learned). The therapist was able to compliment the couple on their teamwork and creative use of strategies they already had on board.

During the end-of-session break, the therapist also realized that the couple was conveying support to each other nonverbally by increased closeness and touching. On returning to the session, she remarked on her observation and noted that human contact has often been associated with reduced stress ratings and wondered aloud if it might be helping in this particular situation. This allowed a clarifying conversation in which Ben was able to say that most of the time it was reassuring to have the contact, but that when he was having a flashback he did not feel safe being touched because he was afraid he would hurt Julie without meaning to do so. This led to a discussion about exploring the potential of getting a service dog.

Third Session and Beyond

By the third session, the couple was reporting progress scaling at 8, and they were in agreement. The solution in their mind had been to create a plan for managing the distress of the PTSD and to be able to find ways of creating a new approach to work together in which they were not trying to get back to the way it was before but rather to manage the way it was now. They both felt that this shift in their thinking had created enough behavior change for them to stop fighting and using their approach of "each day is a fresh start," to let each day really be a fresh start. Julie was reporting feeling that she was managing better, and that the kids were more relaxed and seemed to be behaving more calmly. Ben had been enjoying playing in the yard with them and was now working out each day. He was making progress with a transition plan and beginning to think about his postmilitary future in concrete goals. At this point, the couple agreed to take a 2-month break from therapy to see how things developed. They understood that they were welcome to return at any time if things began to slip back but were also observed as a couple for whom this would be unlikely because they had so many positive strategies for managing in place already.

At the 2-month check, the progress was maintained. New stressors were beginning to appear around the impending discharge from the service and the move into civilian life. The couple was able to go through the miracle question with regard to this new transition and to identify what they could do more of to improve their progress. They did attend two more sessions around transition planning and left with a referral to an SFBT therapist at the VA nearest the town where they planned to live.

REFERENCES

Berg, I. K. (1994). *Family-based services: A solution-focused approach*. New York: Norton.

Berg, I. K., & Dolan, Y. (2001). *Tales of solutions: A collection of hope-inspiring stories*. New York: Norton.

De Jong, P., & Berg, I. K. (2001). *Interviewing for solutions* (2nd ed.). Pacific Grove, CA: Brooks/Cole.

De Jong, P., & Berg, I. K. (2008). *Interviewing for solutions* (3rd ed.). Belmont, CA: Thomson Brooks/Cole.

De Shazer, S. (1988). *Clues: Investigating solutions in brief therapy*. New York: W.W. Norton and Company.

De Shazer, S., Berg, I. K., Lipchik, E., Nunnally, E., Molnar, A., Gingerich, W., & Weiner-Davis, M. (1986). Brief therapy: Focused solution development. *Family Process, 25*, 207–221.

De Shazer, S., Dolan, Y., Korman, H., Trepper, T., McCollum, E., & Berg, I. K. (2007). *More than miracles: The state of the art of solution-focused brief therapy*. New York: Haworth Press.

Gordon, A. B. (2006). *Solution-focused forms for work with children and families*. Families Facing Solutions. Retrieved from http://www.sfbta.org/traininglinks.html

Langer, S. (1994). *Second session*. Retrieved from http://www.nwbttc.com/

Langer, S. (1995). *Coping questions*. Retrieved from http://www.nwbttc.com/

Langer, S. (2004). *Brief solution-focused approach: Working with the somatically focused*. Retrieved from http://www.nwbttc.com/

Langer, S. (2010). *Northwest Brief Therapy Training Center*. Retrieved from http://www.nwbttc.com

Lehmann, P., & Patton, J. A. (2010). The development of a solution-focused fidelity instrument: A pilot study. In C. Franklin, T. Trepper, & E. McCollum (Eds.), *Solution-focused brief therapy*. New York: Oxford University Press.

Lewis, T., & Osborn, C. (2004). Solution-focused counseling and interviewing: A consideration of confluence. *Journal of Counseling and Development, 82*, 38–48.

Northwest Brief Therapy Training Center (NWBTTC) (2007) Solution focused management: Miracle questions. http://www.nwbttc.com/sfmmirques.html

Pichot, T., & Dolan, Y. (2003). *Solution-focused brief therapy: Its effective use in agency settings*. New York: Haworth.

Strong, T., Pyle, N., & Sutherland, A. (2009). Scaling clients' problems and solutions via questions and answers in counseling.

Trepper, T. S., McCollum, E. E., De Jong, P., Korman, H., Gingerich, W., & Franklin, C. (2010). *Solution focused therapy treatment manual for working with individuals: Research Committee of the Solution-Focused Brief Therapy Association*. http://www.sfbta.org/researchDownloads.html

APPENDIX
Family Assessment*

Family Name: ____________________ Date: __________________________

I. Family's understanding of the reason for the referral:
(What has happened to bring me here to meet with you?)

____

____

____

II. Family Genogram (refer to Figure 5.1). (*I am going to ask you about your family and draw a family map. This will help me to learn more about your family and how I might be helpful to you.*)

III. Family's Past Successes (Listen to your client's story. What are some things that tell you something positive about your client/family and the good choices family members made … their successes). *(What are some of the good things that people notice about you and your family?)*

1. ____
2. ____
3. ____

IV. Family's Resources (Family Members and Community Support): (*Who are the family members and/or friends that are helpful to you? … in what ways? Are you a member of a faith-based or social group? What other community programs are helpful to you?*) Together develop an ecogram on Figure 5.2 to include other folks/services in the family's lives.

1. ____
2. ____
3. ____

V. In what ways has the family tried to solve their concerns in the past? (*When the family has had problems before, how were you able to solve them?*)

____

____

____

* From Families Facing Solutions (2006), copyright Arlene Brett Gordon. Reproduced by permission.

VI. Family's Goal/Miracle: (Tell the family that you are going to ask them a very unusual question. ... *Suppose when you go to sleep tonight, a miracle occurs and the problems that brought us together today are solved. Since you are sleeping, you don't know that a miracle has happened and that your problem is solved. What do you suppose you will notice different the next morning that will tell you there has been a miracle?*)

____

____

____

VII. Scaling

____

1 2 3 4 5 6 7 8 9 10

On a scale from one to ten, ten meaning the most hopeful you can be that you will reach your goal and one meaning having no hope at all ... how hopeful are you that you will reach your goal? ______________. *What needs to happen for you to feel one point closer to your goal?*

____

____

____

Notes:

Family Name: ____________ Worker: ____________ Date: ____________

Family Genogram: Family Map

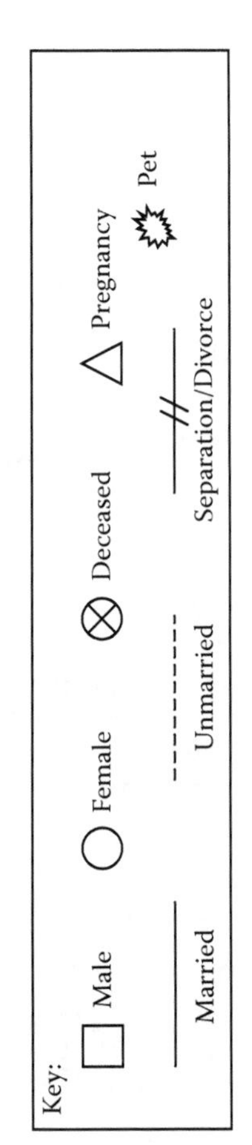

Figure 5.1 Family genogram: family map.

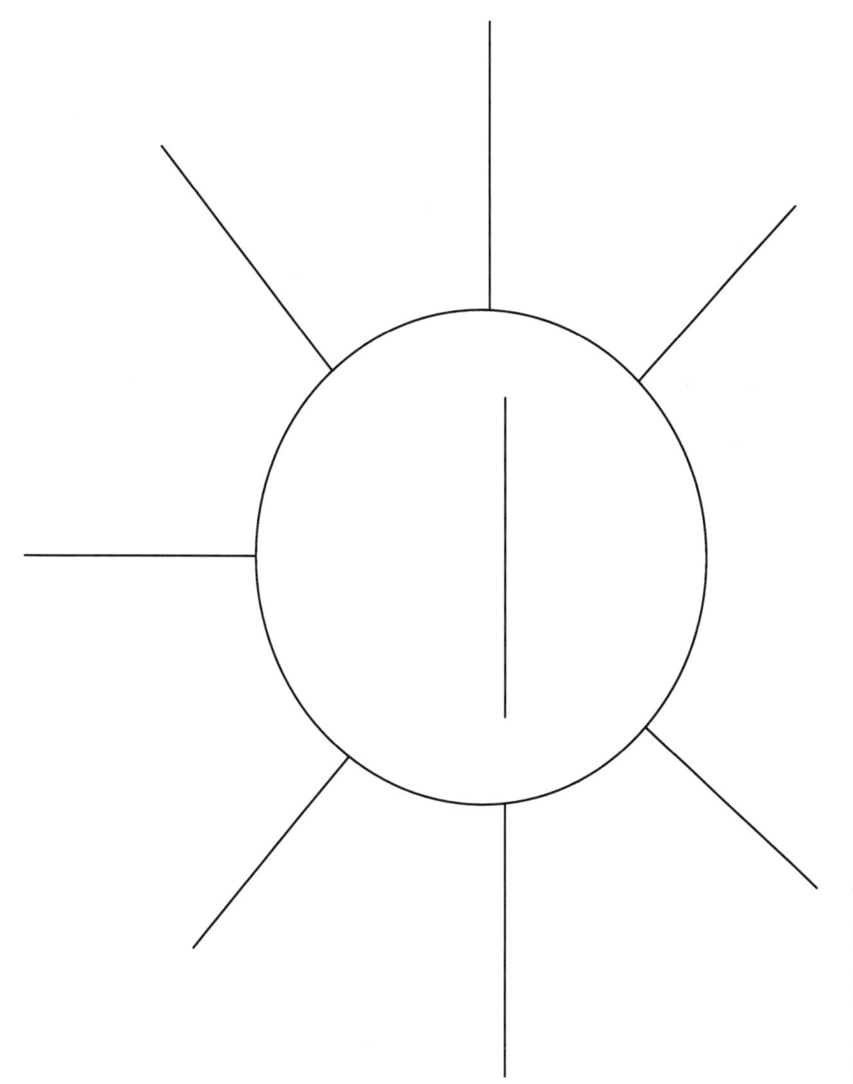

Figure 5.2 Family ecogram: resource map.

Family Assessment Update*

Family Name: ____________________ Date: ____________________________
Worker's Name: ____________________

I. Positive Change: *"What's better?"* (*"What are some of the positive changes that you have noticed over the past three to six months?"*)

____

____

____

II. Miracle: Discover if the miracle needs to be updated. (*"Since last our meeting, has your miracle stayed the same? If so, how have you been able to get closer to your miracle? If not, how is the miracle changed?"*)

____

____

____

III. Scaling

____

1 2 3 4 5 6 7 8 9 10

"On a scale from one to ten, ten meaning the most hopeful you can be that you will reach your goal and one meaning having no hope at all … how hopeful are you that you will reach your goal?" ______________.
"What needs to happen for you to feel one point closer to your goal?"

____

____

____

IV. Tasks:

1. Worker: (*"Let us discuss the things I am going to do from now until our next meeting."*)

2. Client: (*"From now until our next meeting, what are some of the things you and your family will need to do?"*)

Family Name: __________ Worker: _____________ Date: _______________
Supervisor: _____________ Date: _______________

* From Families Facing Solutions (2006), copyright Arlene Brett Gordon. Reproduced by permission.

Family Action Plan*

Family Name: ____________________ Date: ____________________
Worker's Name: ____________________ Agency: ____________________

Family Members Present:

____

Successes: *What is better since our last meeting?*

1. ____
2. ____

Goal/Miracle: (Ask the family to recall their miracle as stated on the Family Assessment. Check to make sure that the miracle is the same. If not, repeat the Miracle Question:

Suppose when you go to sleep tonight, a miracle occurs and the problems that brought us together today are solved. Since you are sleeping, you don't know that a miracle has happened and that your problem is solved. What do you suppose you will notice different the next morning that will tell you there has been a miracle?)

____

____

Steps: What steps will you have taken to reach this goal? (*What was the first thing done to reach your miracle/goal? What was the next step? ... the next step?*)

5. ____
4. ____
3. ____
2. ____
1. ____

Tasks:

I. Worker: (*What will I have done to help get closer to the miracle from now until our next meeting?*)

1. ____
2. ____
3. ____

* From Families Facing Solutions (2006), copyright Arlene Brett Gordon. Reproduced by permission.

II. Family: (*From now until our next meeting, what are some of the things you and your family will have done to get closer to the miracle?*)

1. ______________________________
2. ______________________________
3. ______________________________

Scaling Question and Number: *On a scale from one to ten, ten meaning the most hopeful you can be that you will reach your miracle/goal, and one having no hope at all. How hopeful are you that you will reach your miracle/goal?* ____________.

What needs to happen for you to feel one point closer to your miracle/goal?

____

____

Notes:

Family Member(s): ____________ Therapist: __________ Date: __________

Family Name: ____________________ Date: __________________________
Worker: __________________________

Family Goal: ____

____

Work together to assign a number during each session. *How close are you to your goal?*

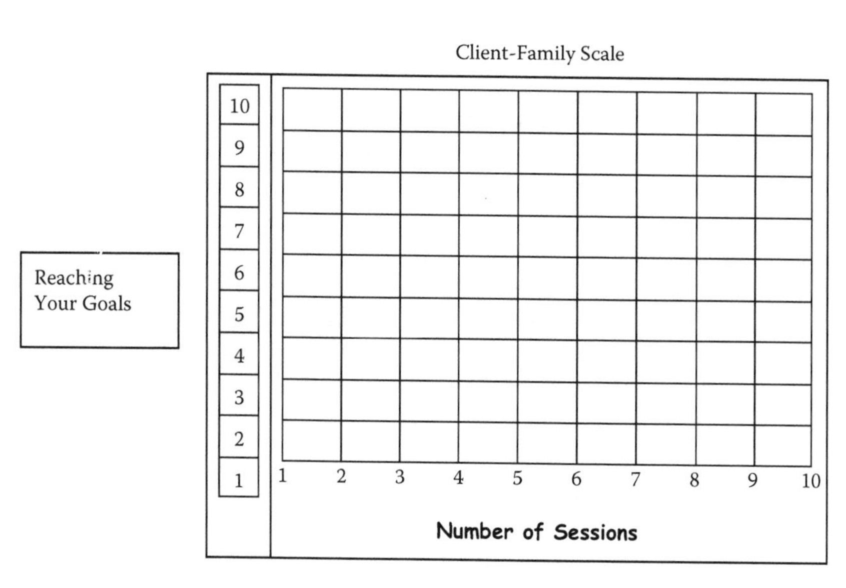

Figure 5.3 Client-family scale.

What's Better?

Transition Summary*

Family Name: ________________ Agency/Program: ________________

Intake Date: ________ Goal Date for Service Completion: ____________

I. If it is the family's understanding that services were completed successfully, what would they say is different? ("*Envision the time in the future when you know that our work together is done—what would be different?*")

____

____

____

II. List some of the positive changes the family has made. ("*Your family has changed the way they work together. Let's list the positive changes you have made.*")

____

____

____

III. Review the family's past successes. ("*This family has shown so many successes during our work together. Which may be helpful in the future?*")

____

____

____

IV. Suppose you kept up with the progress you have made. What will you continue to do? ("*You and your family have worked so hard. What are some of the things that you will continue to do?*")

____

____

____

V. Family's Ongoing Miracle: ("*Envision your family six months from now and all your hard work has paid off. What will you be doing? Your husband? Your children?*")

____

____

____

* From Families Facing Solutions (2006), copyright Arlene Brett Gordon. Reproduced by permission.

VI. Scaling:

____

1 2 3 4 5 6 7 8 9 10

a. Hopefulness:

"On a scale from one to ten, ten meaning the most hopeful you can be that you will continue to meet your goals and one meaning having no hope at all … how hopeful are you? ____________ *. What can you do to stay hopeful?"*

____

____

____

b. Change:

"On a scale from one to ten, ten meaning the best family you could ever imagine to be, and one stands for your family the first time we met, where are you today? ______________ *. Suppose your family was one point closer to your goal. How did you do it?"*

____

____

____

Family Member: __________ Worker: ____________ Date: ____________

Supervisor: ____________ Date: ____________

Program Information

Total of sessions: __________________

Reason for closing: ____

____

Referrals made (include date): ______________________________

____

6

Using Emotionally Focused Couples Therapy With Military Couples

KATHRYN D. RHEEM, SCOTT R. WOOLLEY, and NEIL WEISSMAN

INTRODUCTION

The impacts of deployment and combat-related trauma have once again been pushed to the fore due to the current conflicts in Iraq and Afghanistan. Similar to shell shock from the World Wars and combat fatigue from the Vietnam War, combat-related psychological symptoms have now impacted 31–38% of our postcombat deployed military service members (Munsey, 2007). Of those with psychological symptoms, 17% are diagnosed with posttraumatic stress disorder (PTSD), major depression, or generalized anxiety (Hoge et al., 2004). Typically, the military service member with PTSD or combat stress has been treated individually (APA Military Deployment Services Task Force Report, 2007), despite the known negative relational impacts of deployment and combat stress on the service member and the individual's spouse and children (Sherman, Zanotti, & Jones, 2005). Just as deployment and combat stress are associated with mental health disorders such as PTSD, depression, anxiety, suicidality, and substance abuse (Hoge, Terhakopian, Castro, Messer, & Engel, 2007), marital distress often increases (Basham, 2008). Emotionally focused therapy (EFT; Johnson, 2004) for couples, with its focus on emotions as the leading elements in couple dynamics and with its ability to treat individual symptomology within a relational context, is particularly well suited for military couples facing the echoes of battle and the distress resulting from deployment and combat stress (Johnson, 2002; Johnson & Rheem, 2006).

THE ROLE OF EMOTIONS

From a systemic perspective, "emotions link self and system" (Johnson, 2004, p. 15). PTSD symptoms generally involve intense emotional deregulation. PTSD sufferers typically alternate between numbness, anxiety, depression, anger, and hypervigilance, which have an impact on and are impacted by couple relationships (Johnson, 2002). In EFT, the therapist helps structure and organize each partner's emotional experience, which creates new emotional states and helps prompt new interactional cues and responses. "Emotion guides and gives meaning to perception; motivates and cues attachment responses; and, when expressed, communicates to others and organizes their responses" (Johnson & Denton, 2002, p. 229). Facilitating the expression of organized, expanded, and better-regulated emotional states loosens the grip of constricted, dysregulated emotional patterns and shifts the couple's interaction patterns to create safe, healing connections (Johnson, 2004).

Attachment Theory

Attachment theory (Bowlby, 1969) holds the built-in answers to human vulnerability with its primary goals of protection and security. Seeking and maintaining contact with a significant other, as Bowlby (1988) postulated, "is viewed as the primary motivating principle in human beings and an innate survival mechanism" (Johnson, 1999). Threats (real or perceived) activate the attachment system, which compels proximity-seeking behaviors toward a protective figure. Proximity seeking and connection with a protective attachment figure help individuals cope with threats and regulate emotionally. The need to seek comfort and protection from attachment figures is a biologically hard-wired response that is integral to survival and emotional balance. It helps us understand the intense bonding that often happens among troops in combat, as well as the bonding and healing power that can happen in committed, romantic couple relationships.

When an attachment figure is responsive and attentive, the sense of threat and resultant unwanted emotional state is mitigated. The protection and comfort provided by the attachment figure provides the security that alters "undesirable emotional states" (Mikulincer & Shaver, 2007, p. 190) and facilitates changes in the emotional states that help individuals feel protected, secure, and nonthreatened.

Predictably, when an attachment figure is nonresponsive, "undesirable emotional states" (Mikulincer & Shaver, 2007, p. 190) persist, and emotional balance is not attained. The lack of emotional regulation can lead to intense affect, such as anger, sadness, and fear, which floods the nervous system. This intense affect can have control precedence (Tronick, 1989), which overrides other cues, even positive ones, and inhibits positive coping strategies while intensifying distress. This intense affect creates rigid, negative, interactional patterns between partners.

In short, attachment theory "addresses how relational partners deal with their emotions, process and organize information about the self and others, and communicate with loved ones" (Johnson, 2004, p. 36). Proximity to and connection with an attachment figure creates a safe haven and secure base (Bowlby, 1988), which allows for the processing of threats in an emotionally balanced, nondefensive manner.

EMOTIONALLY FOCUSED THERAPY

Emotionally focused therapy views the relationship between partners as an emotional bond, not a bargain to be negotiated (Johnson, 2004, p. 7). Since affect dysregulation is a primary experience of those coping with the echoes of battle, providing treatment that can address the emotional climate within and between a service member and his or her partner makes sense. EFT, based on attachment theory (Bowlby, 1969), prioritizes "the crucial significance of emotion and emotional communication in the organization of patterns of interaction and key defining experiences in close relationships" (Johnson, 2004, p. 4).

The process of change in EFT has been delineated in nine steps within three stages. The first four steps involve assessment and the deescalation of problematic interactional cycles. In Stage 2, Steps 5 to 7 emphasize the creation of specific change events in which new bonding experiences occur and basic interactional positions shift. Stage 3, the last two steps of therapy (Steps 8 and 9), addresses the consolidation of change and the integration of these changes into the everyday life of the couple. These steps are described in linear form. In fact, the therapist circles through them in an interactive, spiral fashion.

The nine steps and three stages of EFT are as follows:

Stage 1: Cycle deescalation

Step 1: Assessment and creating an alliance and explicating the core issues in the marital conflict using an attachment perspective.

Step 2: Identifying the negative interactional cycle that maintains attachment insecurity and marital distress.

Step 3: Accessing the unacknowledged primary, attachment-related, vulnerable emotions that underlie interactional positions.

Step 4: Reframing the problem in terms of the cycle, the underlying emotions, and attachment needs.

Stage 2: Changing interactional positions

Step 5: Promoting identification with disowned needs and aspects of self and integrating these into relationship interactions.

Step 6: Promoting acceptance of the partner's new construction of experience in the relationship and new interactional behavior.

Step 7: Facilitating the expression of specific needs and wants and creating emotional engagement.

Stage 3: Consolidation/integration

Step 8: Facilitating the emergence of new solutions to old problematic relationship issues.

Step 9: Consolidating new positions and new cycles of attachment behavior.

The goal of the first stage of EFT is deescalation. After assessing if the couple is appropriate for couples therapy, treatment is started by building an alliance with the couple (Step 1). Step 2 is to formulate the couple's negative pattern of interaction, such as demand-withdraw, in which one partner is the critical demander and the other placates and withdraws. That is, when distress reaches a certain level, absorbing negative affect creates rigid patterns of response from each partner. As partners interact with each other, these rigid patterns tend to keep each partner stuck and disconnected from the other. Unexpressed underlying emotions, often driven by unmet attachment needs, keep the rigid response pattern intact. Accessing these underlying emotions and connecting how they fuel the interactions with their partner are the foci of Step 3 of EFT. The final step of Stage 1, Step 4, reframes the couple's distress in terms of their attachment significance and helps them see that their relationship has been caught in a vicious cycle. The cycle is framed as the enemy, rather than each other.

After achieving deescalation, the goal of Stage 2 is to restructure the couple's interactional pattern. The focus of Stage 2 of EFT is creating experiences of bonding, sharing, and responsiveness that redefine the couple's experiences of each other and changes the negative cycle to a pattern that involves the healing of accessibility, responsiveness, and safety.

To create a new interactional pattern, two main change events are necessary: withdrawer reengagement and pursuer/blamer softening. These two change events are the focus of Steps 5–7, which typically are done twice, the first time with the focus on the withdrawer and then with the focus on the pursuer. In Step 5, the most intrapsychic of EFT, the EFT therapist works with the withdrawer's disowned attachment needs, fears, and longings, helping deepen, distill, and disclose underlying experiences and integrating these into the interactions of the relationship. Withdrawn partners needs to access primary, vulnerable emotions, feel entitled to their experience, and assert themselves emotionally. Step 6 involves helping the pursuing partner accept the withdrawer's assertions and emotional experiences. In Step 7, the new experience of the withdrawer crystallizes in the sharing of the withdrawer's needs from a position of vulnerability and asserting him- or herself emotionally to the listening, more accepting partner. In Step 7, these moments of mutual accessibility and responsiveness soothe the past pain and become the building blocks of the couple's new pattern of interaction. The EFT therapist then goes back to do Step 5 with the pursuing partner to deepen, distill, and disclose attachment vulnerabilities, needs, and fears. As pursuers access their softer, more primary emotions, the therapist promotes acceptance from the withdrawer (Step 6). As the withdrawer remains emotionally engaged with the pursuing partner, the pursuer shares deep fears, needs, and vulnerabilities and asks for basic attachment needs to be met (Step 7).

The final stage of EFT is Stage 3, consolidation (Steps 8 and 9). In Step 8, the partners are able to emotionally connect and start solving old relationship issues from this new place of connection and togetherness. Previous differences—differences that used to threaten the couple's connection and block problem solving—are now resolved with openness, compassion, and tenderness. In the final step (Step 9), the therapist helps the couple identify the changes that have occurred and integrate them into all aspects of their lives. At times, the therapist will help the couple develop attachment rituals that help the couple continue to connect and find safety and healing in their relationship. Each partner has a new position in the cycle of the relationship in which there is clear expression of and response to attachment needs and signals.

THE STANCE OF THE EFT THERAPIST

Since EFT is systemic (Bertalanffy, 1968), Rogerian (Rogers, 1951) and experiential in nature, the EFT therapist identifies and tracks the couple's pattern of interaction and the underlying emotion that fuels their interactions from a position of collaboration. With empathetic attunement and unconditional positive regard, the therapist helps each partner access and organize his or her underlying emotion and share these emotions from a place of vulnerability, rather than in a critical or a distant manner. "The EFT therapist is a process consultant who supports partners in restructuring and expanding their emotional responses to each other" (Johnson & Denton, 2002, p. 221).

LITERATURE ON EMOTIONALLY FOCUSED THERAPY

The literature on EFT (Johnson, 2004) is robust. EFT is empirically validated; there are a growing number of published outcome studies (Cloutier, Manion, Gordon-Walker, & Johnson, 2002; Denton, Burleson, Clark, Rodriguez, & Hobbs, 2000; Johnson, Hunsley, Greenberg, & Schindler, 1999), and others in are progress. In a meta-analysis of the four most rigorous studies, Johnson and colleagues (1999) found a 70–73% rate of recovery for distressed relationships, and 86% showed significant improvement.

Many studies explored the application of EFT with specific populations. Four studies with couples impacted by trauma have been completed. Naaman, Radwan, and Johnson (2009) studied the use of EFT with breast cancer survivors in distressed relationships, Dalton, Johnson, Classen, and Greenman (in press) examined the effectiveness of EFT with female survivors of childhood sexual abuse, MacIntosh and Johnson (2008) studied couples in which one or both partners had a history of childhood sexual abuse, and combat veterans with PTSD and their partners in distressed marriages have been studied (Weissman, Batten, Dixon, Pasillas, Potts, Decker, & Brown, 2011) and are reviewed next.

An outcome study on the use of EFT in couples struggling with major depression has also been completed (Denton, Nakonezny, & Jarrett, 2009) that followed an earlier pilot study on EFT with depression (Dessaulles, Johnson, & Denton, 2003). A study of using EFT with chronic illness has been completed (Stiell, Naaman, & Lee, 2007), and a study of couples with chronically ill children with a 2-year longitudinal follow-up has been completed (Cloutier et al., 2002; Walker, Johnson, Manion, & Cloutier, 1996). EFT studies have begun to address areas of sexuality (Honarparvaran, Tabrizy, & Navabinejad, 2010; Johnson & Zuccarini, 2010), cultural diversity (Greenman, Young, & Johnson, 2009), and relationship enhancement and education (Johnson, 2008).

Along with outcome studies and studies with specific populations, the process research on EFT is extensive. After Johnson and Greenberg's (1988) initial process study, two main process study threads have emerged in the EFT literature: the process of pursuer/blamer softening, one of the main change events in EFT (Bradley & Furrow, 2004, 2007; Bradley & Johnson, 2005), and the process of naming and repairing attachment injuries between partners (Halchuk, Makinen, & Johnson, 2010; Johnson, Makinen, & Millikin, 2001; Makinen & Johnson, 2006).

Review of EFT Literature With Military Populations

The Mental Illness Research and Clinical Center of the Veterans Affairs (VA) Maryland Healthcare System supported a pilot study examining the feasibility and effectiveness of providing EFT for couples to veterans with PTSD and their partners (Batten et al., 2011). The study explored whether participating in EFT can assist in reducing psychiatric symptoms and distress and increase marital satisfaction. Seven couples completed the protocol. Veterans were assessed pre- and posttreatment on measures of PTSD, depression, psychiatric distress, quality of life, and marital satisfaction. Partners completed pre- and posttreatment measures of psychiatric distress, quality of life, and marital satisfaction.

The couples presented with complex and complicated histories. The veterans had all experienced combat trauma, and one veteran also experienced military sexual trauma. In four of the seven couples, the partner, in the course of therapy, also reported having experienced severe interpersonal stresses prior to marriage, such as childhood abuse or neglect, domestic violence, or abandonment in previous marriages.

The couples attended an average of 30 sessions (range 19–34). The findings demonstrated statistically significant improvement in marital satisfaction and reduction in psychological distress. A decrease in severity of PTSD symptoms as measured by the PCL (PTSD Checklist) was also statistically significant. On the Clinician-Administered PTSD Scale (CAPS), a second measure of PTSD, total scores did not improve. Posttreatment interviews of the veterans and partners revealed comments such as the following: "I feel more trust in my spouse"; "Our communications are more open and effective"; "Conflict has decreased"; "I have greater appreciation of my spouse and the trauma and its impact on him"; "I don't have to put up the wall"; "It brought us closer together."

While the results are promising, further research such as a randomized controlled study would provide greater clarity regarding the impact of EFT on couples and veterans' improvements.

Importance of Treating the Service Member and Partner Sherman et al. (2005) highlighted the need to involve the partner in the treatment of combat stress for a military service member and the multiple benefits for both the soldiers and their partners. These authors also found that partners and caregivers of service members with PTSD experience higher relationship distress and less ability to cope with adjustments when war comes home. Providing effective interventions that help the service members and their partners as well as improving relationship dynamics is imperative. Increased relationship tension and stress can exacerbate PTSD symptomology, and those who are hurt by PTSD symptomology are less likely to continue providing care (Sherman et al., 2005).

In her study on traumatized military couples and the application of attachment theory, Basham's (2008) study highlighted the need for social support provided for the returning service member. She named two problems for the military marriage postdeployment: Deployment disrupts the attachment bond between spouses and family members. Second, the relational impacts of affect dysregulation, commonly characterized by emotional numbing and avoidance, are pervasive. Since the predictable expression of affect between spouses and family members helps build a secure bond between them, when relationships become characterized by poor affect regulation, the couple's bond is threatened. When redeployed military couples can be treated with attachment-based couples therapy such as EFT, both partners receive the benefits of learning to regulate their affect and learning how to "be there" for their loved ones. These couples have a chance to work together and help each other cope with life after returning from war. In this time of war, multiple deployments are common, and "with each separation and reunion, the attachment systems of the partners are activated as they must face saying good-bye along with the whole range of feelings that accompany the farewell" (Basham, p. 90).

Treatment of Posttraumatic Stress Disorder The research includes many studies on the impacts of and treatment options for deployment and combat stress as well as for combat-related PTSD. The treatment of PTSD has typically been an individualized treatment focusing on changing behaviors by containing symptoms and setting and reaching goals (Monson & Friedman, 2006). The success of these treatments depends on many factors. In the context of the military, resources to treat PTSD have been scarce, yet the rates of military service members with PTSD continue to increase (APA Military Deployment Services Task Force Report, 2007; Hoge et al., 2004). The individual military service member with PTSD faces many challenges in receiving adequate treatment, which has an impact on the service member and his or her partner and family. When the impacts on partners and family members are not addressed or contained, the success of the treatment is diminished, and the service member could experience an increase in PTSD symptoms. EFT does the double duty of addressing the PTSD symptoms within the context of strengthening the couple's and family's cohesiveness and supportiveness (Johnson, 2002) as well as dealing with relationship issues and problematic interactions that arise as a result of PTSD (Sherman et al., 2005).

STRENGTHS OF USING EFT WITH MILITARY COUPLES

To date, focus on the impacts of deployment and combat trauma on the soldier's marital relationship and family has been sparse (Basham, 2008). If the echoes of battle are not contained, the result for military service members and their partners is increased impacts of trauma resulting from deployment and combat. In a securely attached relationship, partners become a protective factor against the echoes of battle and help the soldier contain, heal, and ameliorate the effects of deployment and combat. In an insecurely attached marriage, deployment and combat exacerbate the lack of relationship safety and connection and typically increase distrust, vigilance, and fear (Basham, 2008), leading to greater stresses for both spouses. Most mental health services provided for soldiers and their families are based on cognitive-behavioral interventions (Armstrong, Best, & Domenici, 2006; Riggs, 2000), which fail to address the soldier's marital and familial attachment bonds. Not only does a soldier bring the battle home, but also the battle lives on within the couple's relationship, threatens their bond, and can add additional traumas to both members of the couple.

EFT, with its focus on attachment and affect, can be a good fit with military couples coping with the echoes of battle (Johnson & Rheem, 2006). Both partners are framed as warriors: one with a mission overseas and the other with the mission of protecting the home front. As both partners come together after deployments, the EFT therapist frames the new mission as one of fighting this new enemy of emotional disconnect and isolation and the negative cycle. This new mission supports the couple in working together just as each did with other comrades and battle buddies while deployed. We encourage each to think of his or her partner as their newest battle buddy, a concept that all military service members and their partners know and respect.

Another strength of EFT with military couples is the ability of EFT to work with each partner's defenses. The Battlemind™ training that each soldier receives before deploying to a combat zone helps the soldier develop mental toughness and build defenses necessary to fight. These defenses are the best survival strategy for each military service member and are imperative to survive combat and stressors of life while deployed and endure multiple and back-to-back deployments. On homecoming, these defenses do not naturally go away. For many service members, living with these defenses feels more natural and provides more safety even after redeploying home. In couple therapy, the EFT therapist makes no attempt to "get rid of defenses" (Johnson, 2009, p. 275) but normalizes the need for strong defenses and helps the service member and partner make sense of their defensive stances. When these defenses come between partners, the EFT therapist helps each partner talk about his or her defenses, the event or emotion that fueled the need for the defenses, and the vulnerabilities behind the defensive walls. In this way, each partner can let the other in—let the other behind—the defenses to create connection between them. As fears and defenses are validated and developed, the meaning and context for each is explored. As this process unfolds, fears are better tolerated, and impermeable defenses become more porous and situation appropriate. These explorations and discoveries are integrated into the couple's interactional pattern.

Particularly for military culture, emotional constriction has many advantages. Emotional avoidance has evolutionary benefits to protect society. Highly regulated emotional responses are adaptive for dangerous environments that demand a cognitive focus on tasks to accomplish the mission, which allows a service member to stay calm under duress. Values such as toughness, assertiveness, fearlessness, a focus on tasks and logistics, confidence, and perseverance become the measure for success. Anger feels empowering and mobilizes one out of fearful paralysis and helplessness. Other emotions, particularly the softer emotions, feel threatening.

Particularly at home, emotional constriction also has disadvantages. Success in combat can come with a price to pay at home. The emotional constriction needed from combat becomes a habit that is automatically applied at home or in other settings, which limits connection with a loved one and intimacy. In a secure, loving relationship, healthy and effective dependency is important. In my moments of need, for example, can I reach for you? Can I let you know that I am struggling so that you can be more patient and supportive? Being self-reliant leaves little room for healthy and effective dependency. The armor used to carry out the mission makes it difficult to connect and feel alive when not in combat. Other impacts of emotional constriction are increased risk for depression, anxiety, PTSD, substance abuse, domestic violence, divorce, and suicide (Johnson, 2002).

In EFT, the therapist normalizes the need to shut down to complete the mission as well as the need for flexibility to adapt to being home again. Shutting down emotionally is adaptive and makes perfect sense for combat, deployment stress, and the military culture. But, as all good leaders learn, the need for flexibility is paramount. Military couples in EFT learn to slow their interaction pattern to consider the context before responding to each other, much like a unit leader slows enough to choose a strategy for the firefight, placement of the troops to protect them, or the type of weapon needed to be successful. While we normalize and value the need to shut down emotionally, we also support and value the need for flexibility to increase success regardless of the type of mission.

Because the ability to shut down emotionally is not foolproof, often rapid shifts in emotions occur, such as moving from anger to numbing and back to anger. Knowing how to work with these shifts in extreme emotional states and understanding the context for these emotions can be very normalizing and helpful for the military couple. Within military culture, emotions are pathologized and misunderstood. Many couples present for therapy with one partner complaining of or misunderstanding the strength of the other's emotions.

The role of adrenaline in these rapid shifts also needs to be understood. During deployment, the service member never lets his or her guard down. Doing so could be deadly in these ongoing conflicts in Iraq and Afghanistan, where there is no back line. Adrenaline helps solders keep their guard up and be ready to fight at any moment. After months of relying on adrenaline to feel safe, coming home and not feeling this intensity can be unsettling. Often, service members will find methods of feeling their adrenaline kick in, even when it makes their partner feel unsafe.

When deployed to a combat zone, the basic goal of the mission is to survive. This goal, among others, provides a sense of purpose and focus that is unparalleled in the nondeployment world. On redeployment, the military couple often needs to help each other find new purpose and meaning. When service members struggle to find purpose and focus after combat, this can lead to more distress for the couple.

Due to military culture and Battlemind training, showing fear can be particularly difficult. For a service member, admitting fear can be stigmatizing, can evoke shame, or can convey a sense of weakness or poor leadership. For the partner protecting the home front, showing fear can also be seen as a weakness or heard as a complaint about the mission that is frowned on. In the context of couple relationships, sharing fears and asking for comfort is necessary and part of building a secure connection. For the military couple, however, sharing fears and asking for comfort can feel particularly risky and unfamiliar.

The EFT therapist normalizes how difficult and foreign it feels to touch our basic human fears and then to consider asking for comfort from a loved one. In session, the EFT therapist helps each partner tolerate personal fears and hear his or her partner's fears and helps each ask for comfort from the other. In combat, battle buddies do a version of this with each other when they talk about the highlights of a firefight, share the intensity of battle over a cigarette, or clean their weapons and restock their vehicle together after a mission. These shared rituals provide a sense of connection and camaraderie necessary for cohesion and morale. At home, a felt sense of connection with a partner is one of the fundamental strategies of protecting against the common feelings of helplessness and meaninglessness when adjusting to being home again.

The attachment frame of adult love helps the EFT therapist make sense of a common point of distress for military couples: competing attachments between military command, obligations, and battle buddies and partner and family needs. These two main priorities for a service member often conflict, which can lead to misunderstandings and increased distress for each partner and the relationship. When a couple is caught in distress, these competing attachments can add fuel to the fire or pull loved ones away just when they are needed most by their partner or family members. Understanding military culture and framing these competing attachments as a bind the couple must work together on can be helpful in decreasing the stress and tension that result.

In our EFT-based postdeployment retreats (Johnson & Rheem, 2006), we discuss how the echoes of battle scramble the signals of the relationship. Signals sent between partners are not clear, needs are not expressed, it is hard to turn to a partner and seek comfort, and the silence, distance, and tension take up more space in the house. As a result, distress and escalation intensify and leave each partner emotionally isolated. Fear is reduced by a cohesive unit (Johnson, 2002). In theater, the cohesive unit is the battle buddy. At home, the cohesive unit is the partner or family member. Connection with a loved one—creating a cohesive unit—helps us cope and deal with our fears and the echoes of battle. It is easier to find courage when we are not alone. Deriving comfort from another is a sign of strength as it increases each partner's personal strength and resilience as it strengthens the couple's relationship.

Strengths of EFT With Military Couples Struggling With Trauma

EFT has a strong empirical base and has been proven successful for distressed couples. As Johnson and Williams-Keeler (1998) stated, "The marital relationship can be considered one of the most important elements of the recovery environment" (p. 27). In a secure marriage, the proximity of a soothing, loving partner (Schore, 1994), the immediacy of the partner during symptomatic times, and the longevity of the partner's presence may all be important factors in a service member's recovery (Rheem, 2008). An emotionally accessible and responsive partner can help service members regulate their affect, one of the main symptoms of PTSD (Johnson & Williams-Keeler, 1998). When partners can be responsive to one another, especially during times of distress and vulnerability, bonding occurs, and the relationship can be strengthened. For this reason, among other reasons, treating the military service member suffering from PTSD and his or her spouse together can be an effective treatment for combat-related trauma (Johnson, 2002).

Previously, our field has lacked a theoretical framework for treating an individual's PTSD in the context of couples therapy. EFT fills this lack as its "application is now used to address more and more 'individual' symptomatology, such as depression, anxiety disorders, and chronic illness" (Johnson, 2004, p. 3). The individual symptomology of PTSD as an anxiety disorder with elements of depression fits this newer application of treating an individual's symptoms within the context of couple treatment.

Typically, the partner knows the soldier he or she sent off to war is not the same one coming home. The partner sees and feels the impacts of combat trauma on their loved one as well as experiences the impacts directly. Often, the partners of military service members report being alienated, misunderstood, and targeted by their soldier's unpredictable outbursts. The soldiers often do not understand their outbursts or their mood changes. They also report knowing and feeling they are different now but are as confused as their loved one about these differences. Including the partner in the treatment of PTSD allows the partner to become part of the healing environment necessary for the military service member's recovery. By addressing the impacts of trauma on the couple's dynamics and helping the partners become soothing forces in each other's lives again, the soldier's trauma symptoms may be better contained and eventually ameliorated.

LIMITATIONS OF USING EFT WITH MILITARY COUPLES

The military mind-set of not experiencing, revealing, or disclosing vulnerabilities can make doing experiential therapies difficult. The approach of not experiencing or revealing vulnerabilities served them well as combatants and to some degree helped them cope in some situations, albeit not effectively, with their PTSD symptoms. In the combat theater, not feeling or giving in to fear may have helped keep them alive but, as mentioned, once home it can become debilitating, particularly for intimate relationships. Revealing traumatic events or associated feelings (which can involve fear, sadness, and other vulnerable feelings) with others who "have not been there" can be difficult and can emphasize that the partner is an outsider. Service members at times find validation and safety with their peers. Often due to feeling shame and not being understood or accepted, talking with civilians, including partners, can be very difficult.

With this population, there is often an array of comorbidities, such as severe mood disorders, addictions, traumatic brain injury (TBI), and other medical problems, that need to be addressed. The couples therapy can be overloaded by these issues if they are not attended to in other venues. Often, the PTSD symptoms are so intense they prevent people from being present with emotional content. Ideally, the service member with PTSD would benefit by being in another primary treatment specifically for PTSD. For troops and veterans with PTSD, avoidance is both a defining symptom and perceived (erroneously) as a good coping strategy. If I feel, a soldier may think, I may get angry, and that would be bad for everyone.

The military, Department of Defense, and Department of Veterans Affairs have cultures of focusing on the veteran, while partners and family members remain an afterthought. Sometimes, partners or family members were considered an interference to care. Gratefully, this culture is changing. However, the frontline clinicians are not used to considering the need to involve family members and typically do not get the specific training (or make appropriate referrals) to effectively treat the service member and family members together.

In military or veteran settings accustomed to only seeing a client for four or six sessions, it can be an uphill effort to engage service member couples and clinicians in longer-term, experiential treatments, even though it can be effective and cost effective (Caldwell, Woolley, & Caldwell, 2007).

THERAPEUTIC CONSIDERATIONS

When working with military couples, the EFT therapist needs to carefully build and monitor the alliance. Transparency and collaborativeness are vital to convey respect for the service member and the relationship. Providing rationale frequently in the early stages of therapy is important and helps increase safety, predictability, and comfort. It is important not to make assumptions about military or combat experiences and to ask for more details when you are not sure. Each service member and military couple experience many unique experiences during their deployments. These uniquenesses are often misunderstood, not respected, and need to be explored for personal and relationship meaning and significance.

When working with military couples, the EFT therapist also needs to move slowly when helping each partner encounter his or her emotional experiences. Based on their military culture and mission, as previously stated, the need to shut down emotionally is a survival adaption. "Because attachment needs are higher and at the same time emotional engagement is experienced as more dangerous, the steps toward more emotional engagement are smaller with more frequent blocks and impasses" (Johnson, 2002, p. 60).

Obtaining training in EFT is paramount when using EFT in the treatment of military couples. The governing body for EFT, the International Center for Excellence in EFT (ICEEFT; http://www.iceeft.com), sanctions many training opportunities in North America and around the world. Individual and group supervision is available in person in many locations and around the world through distance supervision. Supervision provides helpful case-specific consultation to support the EFT therapist. Specialized advanced training in using EFT with trauma would also be useful since the therapist needs to be familiar with and prepared to work with the echoes of battle, combat stress, and PTSD.

Case Vignette – Jackie and Mike

Jackie and Mike, both in their mid-20s, were among the few couples in the family day program at the VA hospital to respond to an invitation to participate in a new couples therapy program. They knew their marriage of 8 years was in serious jeopardy. Mike, an army veteran, had returned 13 months earlier from his second deployment to Iraq. On his return home, there was the initial excitement of this family of five, two parents and three young children, being finally reunited. However, the joy and togetherness dissipated almost immediately. Mike began to drink heavily and was spending more time alone with his liquor bottle than alone with his wife. With the encouragement of family, the guidance and intervention of the VA, as well as Mike's own resolute determination, he was able to stop drinking. During the recovery, Mike was diagnosed with PTSD. He joined a trauma treatment program and had been progressing, albeit slowly. Mike found steady employment, and it appeared that the family was regaining its balance. However, this was not the case for the marital relationship. Jackie and Mike remained distressed; their relationship was punctuated by arguments and periods of avoidance and isolation. Jackie told her husband, "I had to learn to depend on myself because you were not here. Now you are back but still aren't here. If I need to I can and will manage on my own."

Prior to the treatment, each partner completed the Dyadic Adjustment Scale (Spanier, 1976). Both partners revealed a high level of dissatisfaction in the marriage, but both also indicated a commitment to making it right. They were in emotional pain but were motivated to work on their relationship.

THE FIRST SESSION

Mike and Jackie arrived on time for their first session. They entered the office with evident trepidation mixed with an eagerness to begin their work. The therapist set up the chairs such that they were gently angled toward one another and at the same time facing the therapist. The therapist provided an overview of the treatment process as well as a brief discussion of the potential risks and benefits. Confidentiality and its limits were explained. The EFT therapist made sure to articulate that he respected and valued the experience of both partners and recognized that they were the experts on their own experience. The therapist framed his role as a consultant to *their* process. In this light, the therapist explained that he would consistently check with them to make sure his comments and observations accurately reflected their experience. He made it clear that the process was a collaborative joint partnership between him and them.

The therapist also assured the couple of transparency: He had no hidden agendas—all questions were welcome. When working with survivors of trauma, highlighting the collaboration and transparency of the process can help to allay the inherent anxiety and distrust a trauma survivor brings to new experiences, or any experience, that may feel out of his or her control. In the overview, the therapist explained the importance of an early task in treatment, that of discovering how and why the couple were stuck that led them to feeling unhappy and frustrated. He explained that it was critical they learn how trauma has an impact on each of them and their relationship. Indeed, this awareness would assist them in standing together against the negative interactions and the symptoms of trauma. The therapist then inquired about whether the couple had questions or concerns. Jackie and Mike thanked the therapist for the explanation and stated they were ready to begin the session.

Jackie was eager to share her dismay and frustration. She openly and emphatically described her own history of abandonment by her biological father and stepfather. She also described the emotional unavailability alternating with contention and disapproval that characterized her relationship with her mother. Mike was more reticent and described his family of origin as cold, distant, and devoid of closeness and affection. Jackie summarized, "We were both raised with no affection. He [Mike] is like his parents and shows no feelings, while I … I need more attention and love."

The therapist asked about the history of their relationship. He inquired regarding their perception of the strengths of their relationship and asked for a description of what they were like as a couple when they get along and when they feel or have felt close and happy. The therapist was careful to attend to each partner, to join with each, and to convey in action and in words that they each would be respected and would have the opportunity to share personal views, feelings, and perspectives. The therapist then asked the couple to describe what happened when they disagreed, what they disagreed about, and how they disagreed. It was with this inquiry that the negative interactions that formed their negative cycle began to emerge.

Wife (W): I always feel so alone with the burden of fixing problems in the family. I just want to be able to ask him for help. I know it sounds like I am nagging or complaining. But, Mike is just not there. Ever since he came back from Iraq, he is so distant, and he gets so easily frustrated and even mean. It's not fair. I walk on eggshells.

Therapist (TH): It's so hard for you to continue to feel alone. You want to turn to Mike for support and for help at home … but he often seems upset with you or unavailable. … Is that right?

W: *(Nods; tears start forming in her eyes.)*

TH: what happens for you when you feel that loneliness?

W: I get angry. … I complain more. … I guess … get critical … loud. … I am so frustrated. … I just don't know how to reach him. I say the wrong thing, and he is gone. Sometimes, I chase after him, really, room to room.

TH: You try to get his attention—when you can't, you feel anger and frustration. Sure, it is frustrating for you. So, you keep on trying to get his attention, even room to room. What happens then?

W: Mike either shuts the door, turns on a videogame or something. Thank God he no longer drinks. Sometimes, he gets really mad, we argue, we fight … then we go our separate ways.

The therapist reflects and summarizes Jackie's experiences, validating her feelings. He then turns to Mike.

TH: How would you describe the typical arguments at home?

Husband (H): Jackie is right. I have, like, no patience anymore. I have a really short fuse. When she starts complaining, I get all mixed up inside … so I try to stay away so I don't do anything wrong. She complains, gets loud so often—I know I can be mean … *(looks down and away).*

TH: When Jackie gets upset with you, you get all confused inside … sounds like you also quickly feel angry, but you pull away so you don't get into a fight. Is that what happens? *(Husband nods, continues to look down.)*

TH: Mike, what is it like for you now as you describe these events?

H: I don't want to hurt Jackie. Sometimes I don't even hear what she is saying. I get mad so fast; I just got to get away.

TH: You really care about your wife. It sounds like getting angry is hard for you, too. So you pull away, go into another room, to prevent a fight, yes?

TH: Jackie, when your husband pulls away, what happens for you?

W: I get more angry. … I'm like, where are you going? Why are you leaving me? I guess I get more down on him. It doesn't help; he shuts me out more.

The therapist begins to see the problematic dance of disconnection fueled by anger, a stand-in for their hurt and fear. The therapist "explicates the cycle," providing the couple with a new frame. This expanded understanding of their experience preempts blame and helps reduce defensiveness.

TH: You have both described well what you get caught up in, the interaction that keeps on reoccurring which causes such unhappiness. May I share my observations?

(They both nod and appear curious regarding what will follow. The therapist continues.)

Partners in a couple want to feel emotionally connected and valued by their spouse. When that feeling is threatened, each partner responds in a way, copes in a way, that makes sense for them. However, those reactions create more insecurity and reactivity in their partner. It is a cycle that both of you get caught in, almost automatically. Because it is a circle, there is no real beginning. For example, Jackie when you need Mike, reach for him and feel he is not there for you, you get angry. Actually, you described the deeper experience of feeling alone and then you get angry. You sort of protest, to get his attention, perhaps to pull him back. Mike, when you see Jackie get upset with you, anxiety begins to churn inside, you get that uneasy feeling, and to prevent your anger to erupt, you pull away. When you pull away, Jackie you feel the hurt and anger and protest. This leads Mike to withdraw more ... and now you are stuck in a cycle. Does that sound right to you? Is that what happens?

(The couple nods, and the therapist continues.)

There is an added dimension which fuels this stuck pattern even after. When a person has experienced trauma, their bodies and minds become more sensitive—more reactive. So, he or she is prone to more reactivity, such as anxiety or anger. They are also more prone to responding to that feeling with avoidance, emotional numbing, or withdrawal. Mike, when you feel that tension, which you did not seem to feel with Jackie earlier in your relationship, before your deployment, you do feel more confused ... and you want to withdraw more. Mike and Jackie, the goal of this therapy is for you to learn to stand together against the cycle and against the symptoms of trauma—which as you can see—accelerates and deepens the cycle.

Jackie and Mike listened to this new frame. The therapist explored their reactions and inquired about their questions. At the close of the session, they were given a handout on the impact of trauma on a couple's relationship and were asked to review it at home and to highlight for the next session the information relevant to their lives. The session closed on a hopeful note as the therapist explicitly honored their courage in being open and in listening to each other. The couple left with a new, expanded view of their own experience and of their relationship.

STAGE I: DEESCALATION OF THE CYCLE

The first stage of EFT focuses on identifying the cycle and the underlying attachment-related hurts and fears. Many times over the next several sessions, as the couple described arguments over different issues, the therapist slowed the process such that each could appreciate the emotions triggered, the ensuing behaviors, and the resulting cycle of negative interactions.

In one typical sequence, Jackie explained her unrequited needs and the resulting pain.

W: When I feel anxious, I look to hold onto someone ... so I reach for my husband.
TH: You turn to your husband for comfort, for reassurance.
H: She gets so clingy. ... It's too much.
TH: What happens for you when she turns to you ... when you feel she is too clingy?
H: I get this tight, pressured, tight feeling ... so I try to get away or push her away.
TH: A tight feeling ... where do you feel that?

H: Right in my chest, like a knot of pressure, also in my throat.
TH: Tight feeling … sounds like tension, anxiety. … When else have you felt that … ?

Mike spontaneously described an experience in Iraq when he went out on patrol. He described how he felt trapped, and while protected in his vehicle—he also felt fearful—vigilant of attacks. He never shared these fears with his peers or with his wife until that moment.

TH: You had the tight, pressing feeling when you were in real danger. Now safe at home, your body triggers the same reaction when you sense tension or conflict. Yes?
W: *(Tearful.)* But why am I a source of anxiety for him, not comfort? When will I ever be able to turn to him? You know I rode 50 miles here with Mike on the back of his motorcycle. I trust him with my life. … When will I be able to trust him with my feelings. When will he trust me with his?
TH: You so much want to be there for Mike and need him there for you. It hurts, truly hurts and confuses you when he feels pressured—threatened by you, your needs.
H: Jackie does not understand that I also want to be a good husband, a good father. I don't want to feel that tense and clinched-up feeling. … I don't want to numb out.
TH: Mike, you are explaining all this to let her in—so she can see that this is hard for you and not what you want. Can you tell her that? Can you tell Jackie directly that this is a struggle for you, but that you want to be there for her? Can you turn to Jackie; explain that to your wife?
H: She heard me tell you.
TH: I know she did, but the message is so much more important and real when you tell her directly.
H: *(Awkwardly at first)* Jackie, I don't like feeling tight. But it is not your fault … and it does not mean that I don't want to be with you. I just get that feeling when I feel stuck. … I am trying. … I do want to be there for you.

The therapist asked the husband to directly convey his heartfelt struggle to his wife. This exchange, called an *enactment*, can be difficult for some couples as it entails greater emotional contact and risk. This dialogue was enabled by the slowing of the cycle at home and in the session. Jackie was able to hear and to be momentarily soothed by Mike's opening up to her about his inner experience as he did so directly and empathically. Small, more contained enactments are encouraged in the first stage of EFT, while deeper and more emotionally vulnerable enactments are facilitated in Stage 2 of the process. In each enactment, the therapist attempts to sufficiently "slice thin" the emotional content so as not to overwhelm either partner.

The couple discussed several topics over the following sessions. Two topics in particular generated a great deal of emotional intensity. Jackie had been carrying an emotional injury for several months but had never discussed it with

Mike. In session, Jackie reported that there was a several-week period while Mike was in Iraq that she had not heard from him. He had later explained in a letter that he did not call her because he did not want to wait in the lengthy line for the phone. Jackie was deeply wounded by his insensitivity toward her, the nervous and lonely wife back home. The couple never discussed the matter after his return until this session. Jackie revealed her feelings and her hurt. Rather than become defensive, Mike explained that actually he had been on several dangerous patrols during that period, and he felt he would not be able to talk with her without revealing his fears. This would worry her more. Mike explained he had never opted to explain this to her because he was fearful of her anger. As an indication of the progress made by this couple, they did not revert to their negative cycle, but instead shared their various experiences and feelings. Each was able to provide understanding and compassion to the partner.

The second issue did not go as well. Indeed, the issue and the way they each handled it at home resulted in a relapse, an exacerbation of their cycle. Jackie wanted another child; Mike did not. Jackie felt he was not responding to her, and he was not. Mike avoided her, closing himself in "his room"—playing video games and music.

W: I am so sick of not getting what I want. He just won't deal with me *(tearful)*.

TH: It really hurts, makes you feel so sad when you feel that Mike does not care about what you want.

W: He doesn't … he shuts the door on me.

H: I am tired of talking about it *(annoyed)*.

TH: Mike, what happened for you just now? The moment before you said you wanted to end this conversation. What was going on for you?

H: I can't stand to see her upset … so I try to end the conversation … fast.

TH: You care so much about her—you don't want to see her upset. It's hard for you, not sure what to do, so you try and end the conversation.

H: Right, but she doesn't believe me … that I care about her. I really don't know what to do.

TH: You do care about her feelings. Her pain is hard for you. But ending the conversation seems to make her more upset. I wonder if you can tell Jackie about what happens for you. Can you tell her about not knowing what to do but not wanting to see her in pain? Can you tell her directly what you struggle with?

H: *(Hesitation.)* … I don't stop talking to you because I don't care. … I don't want to see you hurt … so I guess I do my old thing and shut down. Now you are still hurt, aren't you?

TH: Right, right *(turning to Jackie)*. What is it like for you to hear that actually Mike shuts down not because he doesn't care—but because he cares so much, but doesn't know what to do?

W: I know he doesn't want me to be upset. I can see now that it breaks his heart to see me sad. That is so important for me to hear.

STAGE II: RESTRUCTURING THE BOND

In the second stage of EFT, once the cycle has deescalated, each partner is asked to reach deep within. They reflect on, discover, reveal, and share their fears, needs, and even longings for the other's love and presence. This exchange of emotion and its mutual acceptance restructures the bonds between the couple. The withdrawer is more fully present, and the pursuer can reach in a softer, more empathy-inducing manner. In the process, a partner's very sense of self is often strengthened and healed.

The following discussion occurred in the 18th session. Again, the veteran had distanced himself from his wife as he felt the "tightness" of pressure and anxiety. Jackie, in turn, felt rejected and reported feeling "guilty" that she is so shamefully needy that she pushes her husband away.

W: When Mike pulls away or pushes me back, I feel I am just too needy.

TH: Jackie, you describe the inner conflict of wanting to reach for him—but fearing that you will overwhelm him, and he will disappear. There are tears in your eyes, a sadness … what is happening for you now?

W: One time, I just wanted to tell my mom about my day. So, I guess I kept on trying to get her attention. Finally, she said to me, "Go to your room; you just talk too damn much."

TH: Such a hurtful memory, hurtful message.

W: I could never approach my mom; I was always afraid of being pushed away. I was always walking on eggshells—I didn't want to ask for too much. She was always angry, always in a bad mood.

TH: So painful. … Jackie, are you saying you sometimes feel the same way with Mike?

W: I do feel rejected—like there is something just wrong with me.

TH: You need so much to feel accepted. Whatever your needs may be. You long for acceptance and caring. It hurts you when you feel your husband is not available to you. You wonder is it me, am I worth it, am I too much? Too needy?

The pain is right there, in your heart right now. Can you please tell Mike what that feeling is like, the rejection from Mom and sometimes with Mike? Can you tell what it feels like when you need his attention—but fear his rejection?

W: *(Turns to husband.)* Mostly I feel rejected like I am not worthy of your attention, your love. I think your needs to not be pressured or whatever are more important than me.

TH: Sometimes you feel not worthy of Mike's attention and love.

W: Especially when I am not feeling good. I do need more comfort and … *(Silence, tears rolling down her cheeks. She looks down at the floor.)*

TH: I know it hurts; I see that. Mike is here, and he is listening to you. Can you tell him what you really need from him?

W: I need your attention. I want to feel important to you. I need you to care about me … to take care of me!

TH: You deeply long to feel that you are worth his attention, his care, his love. This something that you did not feel with your mom. There is so much pain from the past … you take the risk to tell your husband of your pain and how he can comfort you.

W: Uh huh *(gentle tears)*.

TH: You need to know you are not a burden and that Mike can and does care about you. Can you tell him that?

W: I do, I feel like a burden. I want to know how important I am to you—that you appreciate me. …

(Long silence; husband looks at wife, then at the therapist, then back to his wife.)

TH: Jackie, you have taken a real risk by telling Mike what you need, sharing a hurt—being vulnerable. … Mike, has been so attentive. … I want to check with him. … *(Turns to Mike.)* I can see how you are looking at your wife with deep attention; what is going on for you now? What are you feeling inside as you listen to her tell you of her fears and needs?

H: Jackie, I do value … love … appreciate you. Sometimes it just slips away from me, and then I consider my own feelings, that tight feeling—and I don't consider what you are feeling. I hear you, I understand you more. *(Turns to therapist.)* I just feel pressured, wound tight, even now, when I can't give her what she wants. …

TH: You feel that tightness even now … and when you feel not capable, not sure what Jackie wants and how to help her.

H: My chest feels so tight, my palms get sweaty, and I don't think straight.

TH: That is anxiety, which you explained before occurs when you feel you can't control the situation or when you feel you won't measure up, or that something bad is going to happen and you don't know what to do. … That's when you feel anxious, tight.

Mike, your body remains sensitized by the trauma, by the fears you experienced in Iraq. The flood of anxiety is triggered when you feel I can't do this, and I have nowhere to escape.

H: I don't want to feel this. Jackie, I don't want to hurt you. It is not that I don't want to be with you, or that you are too needy. I just need some time to calm my body down.

TH: You are telling your wife, the tight feeling does not mean you don't want to be with her—the opposite is true, but the tension does take over. Can you tell her that—so she knows what you struggle with inside.

H: I want the pressured feeling to go away so I can be with you. *(He looks at his wife, waiting for a response.)*

TH: It's so important to you that Jackie understands that you do love her, value her, want to be with her.

H: I do understand you. I would also feel rejected. Deep down it is not what I feel at all. I also need you, and I don't want to be away from you.

TH: *(Turning to Jackie.)* Can you hear that? Can you hear your husband's deeper wish to be with you? What is that like for you, now?

W: I think … I know he means it, and that is truly comforting, so good.

TH: This is a different message than what you felt growing up. *(Jackie tears.)* What do the tears mean?

W: He has told me before that he loves me, but I never really knew if he meant it. I am not used to believing that. … It is hard for me to believe.

TH: Tears of sadness and of joy. You do feel and believe his love today; you hear him differently. Mike explains he can feel tense inside and still love you. You hear your husband explain that you are not too needy. It is so important for you to feel his love like you do now. Can you tell Mike what you are feeling?

W: I feel more safe. You put me first in your heart even as you struggle with your anxieties.

TH: You have both taken such remarkable risks today. You shared with each other, reached for each other, extending trust that your partner will be there for you. Mike, what is it you heard from Jackie just now?

H: I hear her sadness, not feeling worthy. It's me; I don't feel capable. Jackie, I never want you to feel rejected by me. I want you to feel safe.

TH: So much caring. When you talk from your hearts, reveal softer feelings, you both respond with love and care.

STAGE III: CONSOLIDATION

Jackie and Mike continued in therapy for a few more sessions over the following month. They reported an occasional tendency to enter the cycle but were able to avoid it and instead talk with one another heart to heart. Mike stated that he had asked for a "time-out" when he felt pressured and was able to reassure Jackie that they would talk at a later time, and they did. The couple jointly stated they felt ready to conclude the therapy. They each felt confident in each other's presence and love. They stated they were ready and able to contend with their inevitable life challenges as life partners.

CONCLUSION

The individual military service member with PTSD faces many challenges in receiving adequate treatment that has an impact on the service member and his or her spouse and family. When the impacts on spouse and family members are not addressed or contained, the success of the treatment is diminished, and the service member could experience an increase in PTSD symptoms. "Treatment aimed at the interpersonal context does the double duty of addressing the PTSD symptoms within the context of strengthening the family's cohesiveness and supportiveness (Johnson, 2002) as well as dealing with family problems that arise as a result of PTSD" (Sherman et al., 2005, p. 627).

REFERENCES

APA Military Deployment Services Task Force Report. (2007). *The psychological needs of U.S. military service members and their families: A preliminary report.* Washington, DC: American Psychological Association.

Armstrong, K., Best, S., & Domenici, P. (2006). *Courage after fire: Coping strategies for troops returning from Iraq and Afghanistan and their families*. Berkeley: Ulysses Press.

Basham, K. (2008). Homecoming as safe haven or the new front: Attachment and detachment in military couples. *Clinical Social Work Journal, 36*, 83–96.

Batten, S., Dixon, L., Weissman, N., Pasillas, W., Potts, W., & Decker, M. (2011). *The effectiveness of emotionally focused couple therapy (EFT) with veterans with PTSD.* Unpublished data.

Bertalanffy, L. (1968). *General system theory*. New York: George Braziller.

Bowlby, J. (1969). *Attachment and loss* (Vol. 1). New York: Basic Books.

Bowlby, J. (1988). *A secure base.* New York: Basic Books.

Bradley, B., & Furrow, J. L. (2007). Inside blamer softening: Maps and missteps. *Journal of Systemic Therapies, 26*(4), 25–43.

Bradley, B., & Furrow, J. L. (2004). Toward a mini-theory of the blamer softening event: Tracking the moment-by-moment process. *Journal of Marital and Family Therapy, 30*, 233–246.

Bradley, B., & Johnson, S. M. (2005). Task analysis of couple and family change events. In D. H. Sprenkle & F. P. Piercy (Eds.), *Research methods in family therapy* (pp. 254–271). New York: Guilford Press.

Caldwell, B. E., Woolley, S. R., & Caldwell, C. J. (2007). Preliminary estimates of cost-effectiveness for marital therapy. *Journal of Marital and Family Therapy, 33*, 392–405.

Cloutier, P., Manion, I., Gordon-Walker, J., & Johnson, S. M. (2002). Emotionally focused interventions for couples with chronically ill children: A two year follow-up. *Journal of Marital and Family Therapy, 28*, 391–399.

Dalton, J., Johnson, S. M., Classen, C., & Greenman, P. (In press). Treating relationship distress and the effects of childhood abuse with emotionally focused couple therapy: A randomized controlled trial. *Journal of Marital and Family Therapy.*

Dessaulles, A., Johnson, S. M., & Denton, W. H. (2003). Emotion focused therapy for couples in treatment for depression: A pilot study. *American Journal of Family Therapy, 31*, 345–353.

Denton, W. H., Burleson, B. R., Clark, T. E., Rodriguez, C. P., & Hobbs, B. V. (2000, September). A randomized trial of emotion focused theory for couples in a training clinic. *Journal of Marital and Family Therapy, 26*, 65–78.

Denton, W. H., Nakonezny, P. A., & Jarrett, R. B. (2009). *Augmenting antidepressant medication treatment of women with EFT*. Paper presented at the annual conference of the American Association for Marriage and Family Therapy, Sacramento, CA.

Greenberg, L. S., & Johnson, S. M. (1985). Emotionally focused therapy: An affective systemic approach. In N. S. Jacobson & A. S. Gurman (Eds.), *Handbook of clinical and marital therapy*. New York: Guilford Press.

Greenman, P., Young, M., & Johnson, S. M. (2009). Emotionally focused therapy with intercultural couples. In M. Rastogi & V. Thomas (Eds.), *Multicultural couple therapy* (pp. 143–166). Los Angeles: Sage Publications.

Halchuk, R. E., Makinen, J. A., & Johnson, S. M. (2010). Resolving attachment injuries in couples using emotionally focused therapy: A three-year follow-up. *Journal of Couple and Relationship Therapy, 9(1)*, 31–47.

Hoge, C. W., Castro, C. A., Messner, S. C., McGurk, D., Cotting, D. I., & Koffman, R. L. (2004). Combat duty in Iraq and Afghanistan, mental health problems, and barriers to care. *New England Journal of Medicine, 351*, 13–22.

Hoge, C. W., Terhakopian, A., Castro, C. A., Messer, S. C., & Engel, C. C. (2007). Association with posttraumatic stress disorder with somatic symptoms, health care visits, and absenteeism among Iraq War veterans. *American Journal of Psychiatry, 164*, 150–153.

Honarparvaran, N., Tabrizy, M., & Navabinejad, Sh. (2010). The efficacy of emotionally focused couple therapy (EFT-C) training with regard to reducing sexual dissatisfaction among couples. *European Journal of Scientific Research, 43*, 538–545.

Johnson, S. M. (1999). Emotionally focused therapy: Straight to the heart. In J. Donovan (Ed.), *Short term couple therapy* (pp. 11–42). New York: Guilford Press.

Johnson, S. M. (2002). *Emotionally focused couple therapy with trauma survivors: Strengthening attachment bonds*. New York: Guilford.

Johnson, S. M. (2004). *The practice of emotionally focused couple therapy: Creating connection* (2nd ed.). New York: Brunner-Routledge.

Johnson, S. M. (2008). *Hold me tight: Seven conversations for a lifetime of love*. New York: Little, Brown.

Johnson, S. M. (2009). Extravagant emotion: Understanding and transforming love relationships in emotionally focused therapy. In D. Fosha, D. J. Siegel, & M. F. Solomon (Eds.), *The healing power of emotion: Affective neuroscience, development and clinical practice* (pp. 257–279) New York: Norton.

Johnson, S. M., & Denton, W. (2002). Emotionally focused couple therapy: Creating secure connections. In A. S. Gurman & N. S. Jacobson (Eds.), *Clinical handbook of couple therapy* (3rd ed., pp. 221–250). New York: Guilford Press.

Johnson, S. M., & Greenberg, L. S. (1988). Relating process to outcome in marital therapy. *Journal of Marital and Family Therapy, 14*, 175–183.

Johnson, S. M., Hunsley, J., Greenberg, L. S., & Schindler, D. (1999). Emotionally focused couples therapy: Status and challenges. *Journal of Clinical Psychology: Science and Practice, 6*, 67–79.

Johnson, S. M., Makinen, J. A., & Millikin, J. (2001). Attachment injuries in couple relationships: A new perspective on impasses in couples therapy. *Journal of Marital and Family Therapy, 27*, 145–155.

Johnson, S. M., & Rheem, K. D. (2006). *Becoming a couple again: A post-deployment retreat for military couples*. Washington, DC: Strong Bonds, Strong Couples.

Johnson, S. M., & Williams-Keeler, L. (1998). Creating healing relationships for couples dealing with trauma. *Journal of Marital and Family Therapy, 24*, 25–40.

Johnson, S. M., & Zuccarini, D. (2010). Integrating sex and attachment in emotionally focused couple therapy. *Journal of Marital and Family Therapy, 36* 431–445.

MacIntosh, H. B., & Johnson, S. M. (2008). Emotionally focused therapy for couples and childhood sexual abuse survivors. *Journal of Marital and Family Therapy, 34*, 298–315.

Makinen, J. A., & Johnson, S. M. (2006). Resolving attachment injuries in couples using emotionally focused therapy: Steps toward forgiveness and reconciliation. *Journal of Consulting and Clinical Psychology, 74*, 1055–1064.

Mikulincer, M., & Shaver, P. R. (2007). *Attachment in adulthood: Structure, dynamics, and change.* New York: Guilford Press.

Monson, C. M., & Friedman, M. J. (2006). Back to the future of understanding trauma: Implications for cognitive-behavioral therapies for trauma. In V. M. Follette & J. I. Ruzek (Eds.), *Cognitive-behavioral therapies for trauma* (2nd ed.), New York: Guilford Press.

Munsey, C. (2007). Serving those who serve: Transforming military mental health. *APA Monitor on Psychology, 38*(8), 38–41.

Naaman, S., Radwan, K., & Johnson, S. M. (2009). Coping with early breast cancer: Couple adjustment processes and couple-based intervention. *Psychiatry: Biological and Interpersonal Processes, 72*, 321–345.

Rheem, K. D. (2008, June). *Emotionally focused therapy with military veterans*. Presentation to Canadian Veterans Administration, Montreal, Quebec.

Riggs, D. (2000). Marital and family therapy. In E. B. Foa, T. M. Keane, & M. J. Friedman (Eds.), *Effective treatments for PTSD* (pp. 280–301). New York: Guilford Press.

Rogers, C. (1951). *Client-centered therapy*. Boston: Houghton-Mifflin.

Schore, A. (1994). *Affect regulation and the organization of self.* Hillsdale, NJ: Erlbaum.

Sherman, M. D., Zanotti, D. K., & Jones, D. E. (2005). Key elements in couples therapy with veterans with combat-related posttraumatic stress disorder. *Professional Psychology: Research and Practice, 36*, 626–633.

Spanier, (1976). Measuring dyadic adjustment. *Journal of Marriage and the Family, 38*, 15–28.

Stiell, K., Naaman, S., & Lee, A. (2007). Couples and chronic illness: An attachment perspective and emotionally focused therapy interventions. *Journal of Systemic Therapies, 26*(4), 59–74.

Tronick, E. Z. (1989). Emotions and emotional communication in infants. *American Psychologist, 44*, 112–119.

Walker, M. S., Johnson, S. M., Manion, I., & Cloutier, P. (1996). An emotionally focused marital intervention for couples with chronically ill children. *Journal of Consulting and Clinical Psychology, 64,* 1029–1036.

Weissman, N., Batten, S. V., Dixon, L. B., Pasillas, R. M., Potts, W., Decker, M., & Brown, C. H. (2011, August). *The Effectiveness of Emotionally Focused Couples Therapy (EFT) with Veterans with PTSD.* Presented at the Veterans Affairs National Annual Conference: Improving Veterans Mental Health Care for the 21st Century, Baltimore, MD.

7

Gottman Method Couples Therapy With Military Couples

ROBERT P. O'BRIEN

INTRODUCTION

Distressed couples present immense clinical challenges. A quick walk through the self-help area of any large bookstore reveals hundreds of books that attempt to answer two basic questions: Why and how do some relationships deteriorate, while some relationships flourish? What makes relationships better? Almost everyone has an opinion on this topic. What is generally missing, however, is observational research on how real couples actually interact across time. The answers to these questions can only be known by observing couples over time and actually seeing what works and what does not work. Gottman (along with his colleague Bob Levenson) came to couples work first as researchers and only later to the challenging task of therapy. His groundbreaking research focused on following nonclinical samples (over 700 couples to date) for up to 20 years. The research was directly observational and multidimensional. It was only after the majority of this research had been done that we had an answer to the questions. Gottman method couples therapy (GMCT) is the outgrowth of these studies and is described in detail in this chapter. Further details of this research base can be found in the work of Driver and Gottman (2004); Gottman, Coan, Carrere, and Swanson (1998); Gottman, Driver, Yoshimoto, and Rushe (2002); Gottman and Levenson (1984, 1985, 1988, 1992, 2002); Katz and Gottman (1993); Levenson, Carstensen, and Gottman (1993); Shapiro, Gottman and Carrere (2000); Shapiro and Gottman (2005); and Tabares, Driver, and Gottman (2004), as well as the hundreds of other papers written by Gottman and his colleagues.

OVERVIEW OF TREATMENT APPROACH

GMCT is emotion focused, experiential, and centered in the here and now. It is grounded in several decades of research involving actual observations of couples across time. This research has allowed, for example, the accurate prediction of which couples will divorce and which will not with approximately 87% accuracy (a finding that has been replicated in four longitudinal studies) as well as the ability to predict eventual marital satisfaction among newlyweds. It has allowed the development of an assessment methodology and a series of clinical interventions designed to interrupt the processes associated with divorce or marital distress and teach the skills that increase relationship satisfaction. Thus, both the assessment methodology and the clinical interventions are research derived. The entire model is explained in more detail in the work of Gottman (1999) and more recently in that of Gottman and Gottman (2008).

KEY RESEARCH FINDINGS

Gottman has conducted seven long-term, longitudinal studies, following over 700 couples, some for as long as 20 years. These studies have included couples from a variety of cultural, ethnic, and socioeconomic backgrounds. Studies have also been done with same-sex couples. The studies allowed for the following conclusions (Gottman & Gottman, 2008):

1. In most relationships, conflict is not solvable but rather perpetual and is based on lasting personality differences between partners. Some perpetual problems become gridlocked and highly destructive. Developing the ability to have a dialogue about the problem breaks the gridlock but does not remove the issue.
2. Gridlocked conflict is not about negative affect reciprocity (returning negativity in response to negativity) but rather about escalating reciprocity (in which the interaction becomes increasingly negative and destructive and may lead to the highly destructive "Four Horseman of the Apocalypse" (criticism, defensiveness, contempt, and stonewalling).
3. Escalating negativity is characteristic of couples who divorce early in their relationship. A second pattern was found, one that features emotional disengagement in which both negative and positive affect are lacking. The finding leads to the clinical conclusion that reducing negativity is not sufficient, but that positivity must be increased, particularly during conflict situations.
4. Masters of marriage exhibit a gentle approach (characterized by a softened startup, accepting influence, compromise, humor, affection, and low levels of physiologic arousal) to conflict. The disasters of marriage do not exhibit these behaviors.

   Diffusing physiologic arousal (measured by elevated heart rate) is critically important. Couples who can soothe (reduce) their physiologic arousal have improved marital satisfaction over time.

5. Dialogue and conversation about perpetual problems do not solve the problem but keep the problem from becoming gridlocked. This dialogue must be about the core meaning of the issue. Trying to develop a budget in the face of a gridlocked money problem will not eliminate gridlock. The conversation must be about the meaning of money, the hopes and dreams associated with money, and each partner's experiences with money in their family of origin.
6. Building general positivity in the relationship during both conflict and nonconflict interactions is essential for long-term marital satisfaction.

   Friendship processes (which show up via sentiment overrides) control both the effectiveness and thresholds of the repair of both conflict and regrettable incidents.

   Developing shared meaning facilitates stability and happiness.
7. These three systems (conflict, friendship/intimacy/positive affect, and shared meaning) interact bidirectionally, and all are important to maintain stability and relationship satisfaction and success.

THE SOUND RELATIONSHIP HOUSE

The sound relationship house model is the culmination and integration of 30 years of longitudinal research with couples. The model captures the key findings of this research and allows for both a clear description of what problems might exist and a road map for treatment. Each level captures the key tasks that must be accomplished and maintained for a relationship to last.

1. Build love maps: Be interested in, have room for, and attend to your partner's inner world.
2. Build fondness and admiration: Express both admiration and fondness and affection for your partner in small, everyday moments.
3. Turn toward: Respond to your partner's bids for connection rather than turning away or against these bids.
4. Allow positive sentiment override: The natural consequence of success in the first three levels is to be contrasted with negative sentiment override, which is the consequence of failure in the first three levels.
5. Manage conflict: Take a gentle approach to solvable problems and developing a dialogue about perpetual problems that attends to the existential meaning of the problem rather than the details of the conflict.
6. Honor each other's life dreams: Build the shared meaning system by establishing both formal and informal rituals of connection, creating shared goals, and values and supporting each other in life roles.

TREATMENT GOALS

The key research conclusions described and the sound relationship house yield the following five treatment goals:

1. Downregulate negative affect during conflict.
2. Upregulate positive affect during conflict.
3. Build positive affect during nonconflict.
4. Bridge meta-emotion mismatches.
5. Create and nurture a shared meaning system.

The importance of each goal for a particular couple depends on their relationships. The assessment procedure will help the therapist determine which goals are important and assist in prioritizing the goals. As a general rule, virtually all couples entering couples therapy will need to work on downregulating negative affect during conflict before they can make much progress on the other goals.

ROLE OF ASSESSMENT

GMCT begins with a standardized assessment process that typically takes three sessions. The first session is used to establish rapport, obtain informed consent, hear the couple's narrative of why and how they chose to come to therapy, and to observe a 10-minute sample (uninterrupted by the therapist) of the couple having a conflict discussion (that is, talking directly to each other about a problem that they have not been able to solve). The couple also completes a standard set of assessment instruments that measure the dimensions of the sound relationship house, along with scales to measure general mental health, suicide risk, and the presence of domestic violence, affairs, or substance abuse. The second session is spent individually with each partner. The couple is informed ahead of time that this is not an individual therapy session, and that the information discussed with the therapist should not be considered confidential. This session is used to learn more about each partner's history as well as to ask questions about domestic violence, abuse, substance use, and affairs outside the hearing of the other partner. The final session is spent providing feedback to the couple on their areas of strength and challenges using the sound relationship house as the model for the discussion. Feedback from the couple is invited. The general format of therapy is then described, and the couple is invited to enter into a treatment contract.

TREATMENT FORMAT

The nature of the interaction between therapist and couple shifts as the process shifts from assessment to treatment. Treatment sessions become mostly dyadic in nature (that is, the couple talks directly to each other rather than through the therapist), with the therapist acting as guide or coach. Sessions are not manualized and typically begin with the question, "So, how was your week?" and go from there.

INTERVENTIONS

GMCT has an inventory of over 50 interventions. In general practice, however, most Gottman therapists use a core group of interventions for 90% of their work. The sound relationship house model allows for most therapeutic work to be implemented with three intervention blueprints. These include a friendship and intimacy blueprint, a meanings blueprint, and a conflict blueprint. The friendship and intimacy blueprint and the meanings blueprint can be duplicated on one page, and the conflict blueprint can be duplicated on another page. When these blueprints are presented to the couple, they typically look at the pages and turn them over to make sure there is no additional material on the reverse side. Then, they look up with a smile and say, "That's it? All we have to learn is two pages? We can do that, right?"

The content of each blueprint is discussed next.

Friendship and Intimacy Blueprint

Step 1: Build emotional connection during everyday moments.
- a. Build love maps via open-ended questions.
- b. Build a culture of appreciation and respect, catch the partner doing something right.
- c. Turn toward bids. Increase awareness and understanding of the partner's bids for connection and the partner's needs.
- d. Emotion coaching.
- e. Build positive affect.

Step 2: Daily stress-reducing conversation: Each partner gets 10 minutes to whine and complain about his or her day; the partner listens and validates.

Step 3: Build affection, sex, romance, and passion.

Meanings Blueprint

Step 1: Create shared meaning through making rituals intentional.
- Nurture the shared feeling of developing something valuable.
- Create formal and informal rituals of connection.
- Define yearly holiday and special-day cycles and their meaning.

Step 2: Create shared meaning through making goals and values intentional.
- Talk about shared goals, missions, and legacy.
- Support central roles (mother, father, friend, sister, etc.).
- Support central values and symbols.

Conflict Blueprint

Step 1: Listening and validation (dual perspectives).
Step 2: Compromise and problem solving (solvable problems).
Step 3: Dreams within conflict (existential meaning).
Step 4: The aftermath of regrettable incidents (repair).

Each step has a specific intervention that can be clearly described, illustrated, and learned in therapy. Couples typically find the interventions to be a positive affective experience and can begin to see changes in their relationship with the first session or two.

Treatment Length

Gottman method couples therapy is not a time-limited treatment or a manualized treatment process. Low-distress couples typically require 5–10 sessions, high-distress couples 15–20 sessions, and couples with significant comorbidities or struggling with the aftermath of an affair 25–50 sessions.

USE OF APPROACH WITH GROUPS (WORKSHOPS)

There is emerging data to suggest that couples who attend a 2-day, highly structured, workshop for couples report a significantly positive result. This is even more significant given the data that suggest that couples who attend such workshops arrive at the workshop with a higher level of marital distress than is typical for couples when they arrive in the couple's therapist's office. The success of these workshops, given that they are structured and manualized, suggests that a manualized approach to working with a couple by themselves might also be successful.

RESEARCH BASE

Civilian Sector

All of the research currently available in the literature has been conducted with couples drawn from community samples. The initial screening and the demographic database for these couples does not include information on whether they had ever served in the military. There is minimal outcome research on treatment effects to date, and all involves nonmilitary couples.

Military Sector

There is no outcome research on the use of GMCT with military couples. Use of the Gottman method after combat trauma has been described by O'Brien (2007, 2008a, 2008b, 2010) in a variety of workshops.

STRENGTHS OF APPROACH WITH MILITARY POPULATION

There are a number of reasons that GMCT is well suited for military couples.

1. The samples involved in the initial research were large (involved over 700 couples) and involved couples with a variety of cultural, ethnic, and economic backgrounds as well as a variety of sexual orientations. The samples are representative of our current military population in a way that is not typically true of other models of couples therapy.
2. These research samples were collected among nonclinical samples and are likely to better represent the wide variability found in the military.
3. The inclusion of psychophysiologic measures in the research and the development of specific couple interventions that target diffuse physiologic arousal make the approach uniquely suited to the hyperarousal symptom cluster of posttraumatic stress disorder (PTSD).

4. The interventions are easy to describe and easy for most couples to learn. This is well suited to the action orientation of military personnel and illustrated by an active duty spouse telling me that "I don't need to know all the research or the rationale behind all of this; just tell me what I need to do to make it better."
5. The material can be presented in a variety of clinical and nonclinical contexts, including bibliotherapy and couples workshops. Outcome research from the couples workshops has demonstrated that attending a 2-day workshop has a significant impact on marital satisfaction, this despite the fact that the initial distress level of couples attending the workshop is actually higher than the typical distress level of couples entering couples therapy (Gottman & Gottman, 2008). Of particular interest is a project involving a military social worker who held an ongoing group for the deployed spouses (working from Gottman's "Seven Principles That Make Marriage Work"; Gottman & Silver, 1999), while another social worker held another ongoing group for the nondeployed spouses back in the United States, with exercises done via phone link (Gottman, Gottman, & Atkins, 2011).
6. Gottman has written a variety of books specifically for couples that are typically well received by military couples and allow the couple to take the material home (in my clinic, our couples are routinely given a copy of *The Seven Principals That Make Marriage Work*; Gottman & Silver, 1999). For many couples, this is sufficient intervention to make a significant difference.
7. The Army has developed both a soldier resiliency program and a couple/family resiliency program. The couple/family resiliency program is being written by Gottman and is based on the research described. This allows for significant continuity between the couple/family resiliency program, the books that can be given to couples (or used with a cohort of deployed soldiers and nondeployed partners located thousands of miles away), the couples workshops, and the more focused couples therapy.

GENERAL THERAPEUTIC CONSIDERATIONS, INCLUDING RECOMMENDED TRAINING OF THE THERAPIST, TRANSFERENCE/COUNTERTRANSFERENCE, AND MORE

There is a formal training process developed by Gottman that includes what is called Level 1, Level 2, and Level 3 training. Formal certification requires a consultation process that involves having an approved Gottman consultant review video of work of the therapist in training. On completion, the student is allowed to call him- or herself a Gottman-certified therapist. Additional training is needed to be certified as a Gottman workshop leader, Gottman trainer, or Gottman consultant. While the training process to become a Gottman certified therapist is recommended, clinical proficiency can be reached by attending other training events. Formal case supervision by a fully certified Gottman therapist or trainer is recommended.

The description of GMCT and the underlying research base presented is necessarily brief. Additional information about the model can be found in the references at the end of the chapter, particularly Gottman (1999) and Gottman and Gottman (2008).

Case Vignette With Sam and Hector

INITIAL PRESENTATION

Hector (who is 27) and Samantha (who is 24 and known to all as Sam) have been married for 5 years and have a 3-year-old daughter, Laura. Hector was a career infantryman in the Army for 8 years until he was injured during his second deployment in an improvised explosive device (IED) explosion and lost his right arm at the elbow and his right leg at the knee. He is currently unemployed and receiving Veterans Affairs (VA) benefits. Sam was a medic in the Army for 6 years and deployed to Iraq twice. Sam elected to leave active duty so that she could care for Hector and their daughter. She is now employed as an emergency medical technician (EMT) with the fire and ambulance service in her town. They sought couples therapy after an argument (over Hector's suspicion that Sam was having an affair) escalated to the point that Hector shoved Sam against a wall and sprained her shoulder. Sam called the police, and Hector spent a night in jail. The judge has postponed any action pending the couple seeking couples therapy. Both Hector and Sam agreed that this had been the only episode of violence in their relationship.

ASSESSMENT DATA

The assessment interviews suggested that the sound relationship house had been fractured from top to bottom. Both Sam and Hector agreed that the other person was "not the person I married," but Hector disagreed with the idea that he had changed and was angered when Sam or his family told him that he had changed. He insisted that Sam was no longer the warm and caring women he married. Sam, unlike Hector, agreed that she was much different after two deployments and getting "stuck" with Hector's limitations and injuries. Both were sullen and withdrawn, although Hector more so than Sam. While Sam reported great admiration for Hector and all he has had to endure, Hector discounted these statements as "something she says to make me feel better, but she doesn't really mean it." Sam was angry with Hector's drinking and at times compared him to his alcoholic father, which infuriated him. There was little affection, and sex was infrequent. Sam "gave in under pressure," and Hector was convinced that she was put off by his injuries and had been seeing someone else who was "a complete man." Sam denied being involved in an affair but said with resignation that it "might come to that." Hector spent most of his time alone in his room, and Sam was either working or taking care of their daughter. They spent little time together, and Hector said he was content with this, while Sam felt ignored and angry. The four horsemen were present much of the time. Sam was critical and biting in her attempts to manage conflict, and Hector was defensive, increasingly contemptuous, and stonewalled.

Individual sessions revealed that both Hector and Sam met criteria for PTSD, and that Sam also met criteria for major depressive disorder. Neither had been involved with mental health professionals prior to their current episode of care. Both denied any trauma exposure prior to the military. Sam did not drink alcohol at all, and Hector downplayed his drinking (but did admit to some drinking "to help me sleep and deal with stuff"). Sam reported that Hector drank almost every day and got drunk multiple times a month. There was no evidence of any illicit drug use. Sam insisted that she was not having an affair, and Hector tended to believe her unless he had been drinking. He worried that his injuries "make me less than a man" and, with some hesitation, noted difficulty with sexual performance. Both Sam and Hector were raised in intact families, although Hector noted that his father sometimes drank too much and was sometimes violent toward both his mother and himself.

ORAL HISTORY DATA

Both Sam and Hector exhibited considerable positive affect in discussing how they met and dated. They were physically affectionate (touching each other) and smiled frequently while relating the story of how they met and courted. This surprised them, and when Sam suggested "We still have some good stuff here," Hector agreed. Sam noted some changes in Hector after his first deployment, with even bigger changes after his second deployment (and the loss of his arm and leg). Hector had difficulty acknowledging any changes other than "what would be natural if you lost an arm and a leg." He saw Sam as "not as soft" as she had been when they met, "more independent," and "I think she needs me less than she did." While Sam and Hector had shared many hopes and dreams for themselves and their family (Laura was planned, and "we had hoped to have more children, but well, we don't know now"). Now, they "focus on just getting by." Hector and Sam were looking forward to a career in the Army. They were excited about their daughter, and Hector got tears in his eyes when he talked about her birth. He immediately lapsed into sadness and even despair at "what the future holds for her; the world sucks; we shouldn't have brought her into such a mess."

CONFLICT DISCUSSION

When asked to find a problem to discuss, they were silent; finally, Sam noted, "There are too many to pick just one." The major issues that came up at this point were Hector's fear that Sam was having an affair, sex (minimal since Hector was released from the hospital), and Hector's drinking. They finally settled on Hector's fear that Sam was having an affair. Hector started the conversation with a string of criticisms, Sam became defensive, and Hector muttered several contemptuous comments and stonewalled. Since I use a pulse oximeter on each partner, I knew that Hector had become flooded during the initial burst of criticism, and his pulse hit 135 by the time he stonewalled. Sam's pulse rose to about 95 until Hector stonewalled, at which point she also flooded. They sat in silence for a few moments and then slowly made eye contact. Sam made a repair attempt, to which Hector did not respond, but about a minute later he made his own repair attempt, which Sam accepted. Sam's pulse went under 90, then under 80, and Hector's pulse ended at 91.

SAM AND HECTOR'S SOUND RELATIONSHIP HOUSE

Love Maps

Hector and Sam did not feel that they knew each other very well anymore, and neither felt known by the other. Both said that the other person "had changed, were not the same person I married." Both kept the most important aspects of his or her experiences at war away from the partner, stating with a shrug that they did not want "to burden them with my shit; they have enough of their own to deal with." Sam captured the feeling best when she noted "getting into bed with Hector is like sleeping with a stranger."

Fondness and Admiration

Neither Sam nor Hector treated each other with much respect (Hector less so than Sam). Both had withdrawn, leaving little opportunity for small expressions of fondness or admiration. Hector "knew" that Sam was no longer attracted to his "half a man's body," although Sam insisted that this was not true.

Turning Toward

Both Sam and Hector were preoccupied with their own issues, and neither seemed to take time or even have interest in spending time with the other. Both Hector and Sam had stopped making bids for connection, and both had stopped responding to bids.

Sentiment Override

The sentiment override was strongly negative.

Conflict Management

Conflict management skills were poor for solvable problems and perpetual problems. Escalating negativity during the conflict discussion was high, and the four horsemen dominated their interaction. Sam was critical and used a harsh startup most of the time ("How else can I get him to listen to me? If I say it nice, he doesn't even hear me, at least this way he hears me … maybe."). Diffuse physiological arousal (DPA) was common and Hector became flooded much of the time. Multiple problem areas were gridlocked.

Honoring Life Dreams

Both Sam and Hector had "lost" their life dream of a career in the military. Many of their earlier dreams no longer seemed possible or even relevant. Both doubted their capacity to be good parents, with both being haunted by images of injured, dying, or dead children, none of which they had yet discussed. They were resigned to having their parents (although they argued which parents) raise Laura.

Shared Meaning

Both Sam and Hector agreed that they were "just plodding through life; nothing really means much anymore." They had stopped attending church and no longer shared prayer time or Bible study as they had done before. Hector had not "seen any reason to get all excited or worked up about the holidays; it's all commercial crap anyway." They had done nothing special for Thanksgiving and had not put up a tree for Christmas.

CASE CONCEPTUALIZATION

The oral history data suggest that the couple had been doing well leading up to Hector's first deployment, and that they had managed the first deployment with minimal damage to the sound relationship house. They had not managed their second deployments well. Hector's injuries, their loss of careers, and the growing impact of PTSD had shaken the relationship to its foundation. Verbal fights were commonplace; withdrawal and stonewalling were the norm (particularly on Hector's part, but also not uncommon for Sam). Sex was infrequent and only occurred when Hector was drunk and Sam complied to avoid a fight. Laura was spending more and more time with either Sam or Hector's families, and there was little awareness or interest in the future. The four horsemen were present most of the time, and both partners had withdrawn into an angry, often sullen, isolation. Key issues to focus on were negativity during conflict (the four horsemen), improving positive affect during nonconflict (improving the "marital friendship"), and creating and nurturing a meaning system. All three blueprints would be needed.

FEEDBACK TO THE COUPLE

The first part of the feedback session consisted of a review of the sound relationship house and the status of each level for Sam and Hector. Feedback focused on a key strength (their strength and resiliency in the face of terrible traumas and their apparent dedication to each other, as illustrated by Hector's comment that he would rather not live if he lost Sam and Laura). The therapist highlighted the positive affect that emerged during the initial sections of the oral history interview and noted that this had apparently surprised both of them and was a good sign for the future of their relationship. Their key challenges were the virtual destruction of their love maps, the ever-present negativity when dealing with conflict, and their shattered dreams.

The following conversation ended the feedback session:

Therapist: Do either of you have any questions or reactions to our work so far or the issues we talked about?

Hector: *(Looking at the floor, silent.)* [Possible flooding, but therapist did not see it as flooding.]

Sam: *(Glancing at therapist and then at Hector.)*

Hector: I guess you don't think there is much hope? [Negative sentiment override at work.]

Therapist: No, actually, I think there is. There are skills and ways of talking that I think can help a lot.

Hector: *(Continues to look at the ground, but some reduction in foot tapping.)*

Sam: What would we do in therapy?

Therapist: Well it's basically about learning new ways to talk, to learn new ways to deal with things like when each of you gets flooded [this concept had already been described in the feedback portion and thus was familiar and did not need to be described in more detail at this point], to get to know each other all over again. Basically about getting back on track with each other.

Hector: You mean like communication training; we did that once, and it didn't help.

Therapist: It's not so much like communication training; more like learning to talk about the right stuff.

Hector: What do you mean? [Hector's interest has been captured.]

Therapist: Well, we would need to work on that in sessions, but as an example, I think it is clear that you really really love Sam, and that you go off by yourself or shut her out not because you don't love her anymore, but because you love her so much that you can't stand the idea that maybe you hurt her. [This is an abbreviated form of an intervention that Gottman has called "doing a Dan Wile."]

Hector: *(Looking intently at therapist, then glancing almost shyly at Sam.)* Yeah, I do, I really do. *(Then to therapist.)* How did you figure that out?

Sam: Really? I mean for real?

Hector: Yeah.

Sam: *(Silent but with a tear running down her cheek.)*

Therapist: Knowing that underneath all of this that Hector really really loves you brings tears to your eyes?

Sam: Yeah; I thought he didn't love me anymore.

Hector: Yeah, I do *(looking at Sam directly).*

Sam: *(Leans over and puts her hand on Hector's thigh and squeezes.)* Me, too.

Hector: *(Looking at the hand, which is resting just above the amputation point.)*

Sam: I hate the damn IED, too.

Hector: Hard to get turned on by a gimp with no arm and no leg *(looks down again).*

Sam: No, it's not hard.

Therapist: *(Allows both to sit in silence for a few moments.)* [Note that this conversation is dyadic; the couple is talking to each other not the therapist. The therapist lets it go as long as the four horsemen do not show up.]

Therapist: How does this feel? Different than at home?

Sam: For sure.

Hector: Yeah.
Therapist: That's what I mean by learning to talk about the right stuff.
Hector: We don't talk much any more, and when we do it gets pretty bad.
Therapist: That's where I come in. So, what do you want to do *(referring to their pending decision on beginning therapy and knowing that their time in session is almost up)*?
Hector: You *really* want to know?
Therapist: Yeah.
Hector: Go home and get it on with her *(looking at Sam)*, and I promise, no drinking this time. Just us.
Sam: Really? *(A big smile.)*
Hector: Really!
Sam: *(Both Sam and Hector are smiling, and Sam is laughing a bit.)* Doc, this stuff really works!

Note the return of positive affect. Also, had Sam's reaction to the suggestion of sex been hesitant or uncomfortable, the therapist would have intervened to try to slow things down.

Although the therapist sees the assessment process and the feedback session preliminary to treatment, the couple often experiences both as treatment. In the brief excerpt presented, there is a significant increase in positivity, a bit of movement on enhancing love maps, as well as a change in the fondness and admiration system. Formal treatment would begin in the next session, but the change process is under way. This illustrates one of the underlying expectations of GMCT: The experience should be a positive affective experience for the couple.

TREATMENT

COMORBIDITIES

Significant comorbidities existed for both Hector and Sam, and both were referred to our PTSD program for their own issues; Hector was seen by one of the PTSD/SUD (substance use disorder) specialists to assist with his drinking. Both also saw a PTSD psychiatrist and were started on SSRI (selective serotonin reuptake) medications. The most noticeable impact of the medication was on reducing Hector's irritability a bit. Both Sam and Hector were slightly less depressed (as measured by the Beck Depression Inventory II), but their scores continued in the severely depressed range. These individual interventions were not sufficient to have an impact the couple's relationship, and ongoing relationship issues led to difficulties in treatment compliance in the PTSD and SUD programs. This was most poignantly illustrated by Hector's statement shortly after he began PTSD and substance abuse treatment that "If I am going to lose Sam and Laura, then f*** it; I'll just blow my brains out and be done with all this s***." Appropriate safety plans were developed, and there was routine monitoring of Hector's suicide risk throughout treatment. But, there was little change until relationship issues were dealt with.

Couples Therapy

GMCT is not a manualized treatment process. When Sam and Hector returned the following week, the session began as follows:

Therapist: Hi guys. How was the week? [This is the standard opening for GMCT sessions.]

Hector: *(Looking at the floor, saying nothing.)*

Sam: *(Looking angry and hurt.)* It was a typical crappy week. I mean it started good, really good. We went home and had the best sex we've had in maybe a year. But then, hell, once I let him f**k me, he was back to being his asshole self. [The four horsemen emerge almost immediately.]

Hector: Yeah, well, you didn't even wait for the sex to be over before you were back to being a bitch. [Four horsemen continue.]

Therapist: Whoa. Talking like this is really hurtful and doesn't work at all.

[Therapist has observed several of the four horsemen, one of the targets for therapy. When the four horsemen appear, they almost always become the immediate focus of an intervention as the four horsemen derail almost every intervention if not dealt with. This often involves rather direct and firm interruption of the couple.]

Sam: Yeah, but he …

Therapist: Hold on. We have to find a better way to talk.

Hector: But, it's true she is …

Therapist: Hold on. I get it that both of you are angry and hurt. Do I get that right? Sam, you are feeling hurt and angry?

Sam: Yes, but …

Therapist: Hold on. Let's just stick with that, angry and hurt. Hector? Are you are angry and hurt?

Hector: Sure, wouldn't …

Therapist: Time out *(puts hands up in time-out signal)*. I think that both of you have some very important things to say. But when you start out by calling each other names or making fun of each other, that really doesn't work very well. We call that criticism and contempt.

Sam: But …

Therapist: *(Gives time-out signal.)* When you jump in to defend yourself, without hearing the other person, that's defensiveness; it only makes things worse.

Sam: *(Sits back on couch, sighs.)* Okay, I get it, that only makes it worse.

Therapist: Right.

Hector: *(Sullen, arms across chest, looking away from Sam.)*

Therapist: Before we talk about that some more, I want to check in with Hector. Hector, how are you doing?

Hector: *(Does not respond.)*

Therapist: Remember when we learned how to take your pulse? Can each of you do that? Hector? Could you take your pulse? *(Both Sam and Hector find their pulse and nod.)* Okay, when I say go count: Go. *(15 seconds pass.)* What did you get, Hector?

Hector: 34 [flooded].

Sam: 21 [not flooded].

Therapist: Hector, so if you got 34, your pulse is 136. You're really flooded. What does it feel like?

Hector: I can feel my heart pounding; it's like I can't breathe, like I have to get out of here. It's crazy; I can't even think straight. I hate it.

Therapist: Right. That's the flooding we were talking about. We need to fix that before we do anything else. Can you do something with me to help fix that?

Hector: Okay.

Therapist: Can you do it along with us, Sam? [Although Sam was not flooded, it will likely benefit her and the couple if she does the exercise also, but this is not mandatory.]

Sam: Sure, okay.

Therapist: *(Leads couple in 10- to 15-minute sitting muscle relaxation exercise with both Sam and Hector participating and the therapist illustrating the activities.)*

Therapist: Ok, so let's take your pulses again. Do you have the pulse?

Hector: Yes.

Sam: Yes.

Therapist: Go *(pauses for 15 seconds)*. Hector, what was your count?

Hector: 19.

Sam: 17.

Therapist: Great. Hector, how does it feel now?

Hector: Better.

Sam: Better.

Therapist: Okay, so that's a very important skill. Research tells us that when people get flooded, it is almost impossible to have a good conversation with your partner.

Sam: You got that right.

Hector: Right.

Therapist: This business of flooding is really important. It's even more important when, in your guys' case, both of you have PTSD. PTSD makes it easier to get flooded, and you get flooded faster than a lot of people who don't have PTSD. Can you remember back to before you went to Iraq? Did you get flooded then?

Sam: I don't think so. Maybe once in a while, but not like now.

Hector: Sam's right on that.

Therapist: Okay, so it's really important to be able to recognize when you are flooded.

Sam: How, I mean when I get flooded I'm not sure I know my own name!

Hector: Me either.

(Couple then has a 5-minute discussion about flooding and how they experience flooding and how they might identify flooding in themselves and each other.)

Therapist: Do you think you can agree on a way to let each other know when you are flooded?
Hector: Like using the time-out signal like you did?
Therapist: That would work. You can use any signal you want, but a signal is a great idea.

(A longer conversation then occurred in which Sam and Hector negotiated a specific signal to identify flooding [or suspected flooding], agreed on their willingness to take their pulses at this point, and agreed either to engage in the relaxation exercise learned in session or to take a 20- to 30-minute break and to return to continue the conversation after the break. They did two brief practice sessions in which one would request a break with the signal and the other would accept influence and agree.)

Therapist: I'd like to end with another exercise, one that I call "the PTSD monster." Can I tell you about it? *(There would be more education about PTSD and trauma in many cases. This was not done at this point as both Sam and Hector were in a PTSD treatment program, had accepted the diagnosis as accurate for them, and had been in psychoeducational groups on the signs and symptoms of PTSD, but never in the same group and never with a focus of discussion on the impact on their relationship.)*
Hector: Monster sounds about right.
Sam: For sure.
Therapist: Okay, you up to giving it a try?
Sam: Sure, I guess.
Hector: *(Nods.)*
Therapist: Okay, this is a cheat sheet to take us through the exercise *(hands a laminated exercise guide to each partner)*. Here is how this works: Each of you will take a turn talking as we work through each section of the exercise. When you are talking, the task is to answer the question as it applies to you to the best of your ability. Remember, you are talking about yourself, and not the other person. You are only trying to describe your perspective or thoughts. Don't drift into trying to persuade your partner to agree with you. Okay? Who wants to start?
Hector: It doesn't matter to me.
Sam: Me, either *(looks at Hector)*. Do you want to start?
Hector: Okay. *(Looks at the exercise card and reads the question.)* "How have I changed since deployment?" Okay, I get angry a lot.

Sam: That's for sure. You just ....
Therapist: Hold on Sam. Just listen. I know it's hard. But just listen to Hector.
Sam: That's hard, but okay.
Hector: Okay, so like I said, I get angry a lot. There are a lot of jerks out there. I don't want to be around people, and like I hate Wal-Mart, it is so crowded. I don't sleep very well. I have a lot of pain from, you know, my wounds. I hate that dam IED.
Therapist: Sam, can you ask a question? Remember, you just want to understand Hector's point of view. [Goal is to keep a dyadic conversation going.]
Sam: But, you get angry with me, and it's not my fault ...
Hector: *(Sits back in his chair.)* Did I say it was? God, I don't ...
Therapist: Hold on guys. Sam, this is about Hector telling you his point of view. You are going to get a chance to tell Hector your point of view. You don't have to agree, just listen. I know it's hard. Ask him, "What about the wounds gets you so angry?" [Therapist suggests a question since Sam does not seem able to find one on her own.]
Sam: *(Almost like reciting badly learned lines in a play.)* Okay, what about the wounds gets you angry? [Note that the therapist did not ask the question but suggested that Sam ask the question, keeping the conversation dyadic.]
Hector: What gets me angry? I got no f***ing leg or arm, I lost my f***ing job, and it hurts like hell. That good enough?
Sam: *(Backing away at the anger, but then leaning forward.)* I get it.
Therapist: Good job, you stayed with him. [Reinforcing Sam for not getting defensive.]
Hector: You do? How the hell do you get it?
Sam: *(Looks at the floor and says nothing.)*
Therapist: Sam, can you tell Hector what you get? [This is asking Sam to validate Hector's experience and is perhaps a bit risky, but the therapist thought that Sam did actually get it.]
Sam: Okay *(wipes a tear from her eye)*. I get it that you loved the Army and lost your career, and your dreams, and I get it that the phantom pain the docs talked about hurts like hell. I get it that you can hardly stand to see yourself in the mirror, and that you think that I can't stand seeing you either, and that maybe I won't want to be with you anymore.
Hector: *(Looking at the floor.)*
Therapist: Does that come close to Sam getting it?
Hector: Yeah, I guess so.
Therapist: Can you tell her that? [Returning to the dyadic conversation.]
Hector: *(Turning and looking hesitantly at Sam.)* I think that you got it pretty good.
Sam: I want to get it, I do.
Therapist: Is there a part that she could get better?
Hector: Maybe.

Therapist: Can you try to tell Sam that part again, the part that you want her to get better?

Hector: *(This time looking directly at Sam.)* When I see myself in the mirror, I just hate what I see, and I think you won't be able to stand it either.

Sam: Is that why you won't let me take a shower with you anymore? Why you won't let me see you naked anymore? You think that I'll be turned off or something?

Hector: Yeah, I figure you'll be disgusted like I am.

Sam: And, ah God, ah, maybe that's why you have to get drunk to want sex? Cause then I'm going to see?

Hector: Yeah, no one wants to get it on with a freak.

Sam: Hey, you're not a freak. That's one of those contempt things right, Doc, but he's saying it about himself?

Therapist: Right. Hector, can you ask Sam if she sees you as a freak?

Hector: Maybe I don't want to know.

Therapist: I get it, but, can you look at her? I mean really look at her?

Hector: *(Looking at Sam.)* She's crying.

Therapist: Right, does she look disgusted?

Hector: No.

Therapist: Ask her, see if you can ask even though it's scary.

Hector: *(Looking at Sam.)* Do you think I am a freak?

Sam: No, I never had that thought.

Hector: But, look at me? I mean …

Sam: I hate the damn IED, too, and I hate what it did to you. But you are not a freak. I don't like to see the wounds and all that, but I love seeing you. Remember when I was preggo with Laura, and I thought I was ugly and that you weren't turned on by me anymore? I used to use that stupid cream to fix the stretch marks. God, I think I hated all of that.

Hector: Yeah, I remember. But you were sexy as hell.

Sam: I was fat, and could hardly walk, and we had a hard time finding a position we could use that would work around my fat old belly. *(Both laugh.)*

Hector: But … *(suddenly smiles)*. You mean that this is like that? That I worry about it but you don't?

Sam: Yeah. *(She leans over and puts her hand on his thigh above the amputation.)* It sucks that you lost your leg, I get it.

Hector: But you say no all the time. [A complaint, not a criticism, so acceptable.]

Sam: I say no when you are drunk and just want to nail me and be done with it.

Hector: I do that, don't I?

Sam: Yeah, that's what I get disgusted about. Invite me to take a shower when you are sober and see what happens; you just might be surprised!

Therapist: Do you get what Sam is saying?
Hector: Yeah, I think so.
Therapist: Tell her what you get.

The conversation continues in this way for the rest of the session. Note that the therapist is at times very active and even directive, but that when the conversation is going well, the therapist stays out of the way. The couple is encouraged to talk directly to each other as much as possible. The therapist intervenes to keep the conversation going and to deal with the four horsemen. The goal of the intervention was twofold: to help the couple understand each other's perspective (thus providing a way out of gridlock) and to expand each partner's understanding of the other (thus expanding love maps).

KEY LEARNING POINTS

1. There is a high probability of comorbidities when one or both partners have been exposed to war. These must be dealt with directly by providers skilled in these areas.
2. Comorbidities should not be used to rule out couples therapy and couples therapy should not be delayed pending treatment of the comorbidities. Clearly, there can be a point at which the severity of the symptoms may require a delay in couples therapy, but this should be avoided unless there is serious immediate risk to either partner.
3. Effective couples therapy enhances compliance and improves the outcome of the individual treatments (in this case for PTSD and substance abuse).

While couples therapy is not considered a first-line treatment for PTSD, it is clear that many of the tasks involved in Gottman method therapy (examples include improving love maps by sharing some of the trauma material [a version of exposure and a counter to experiential avoidance], reducing the four horsemen, and teaching self-soothing [a way to help with irritability, anger, and withdrawal], building fondness and admiration [expanding emotionality and reducing interpersonal avoidance]) allow for interventions in areas that are key PTSD symptoms.

GMCT has face validity to the couple, can be delivered in a way that makes it a positive affective experience, and teaches skills that can make an immediate difference in the relationship and easily generalize to other relationships. In Hector and Sam's case, the early work with the four horsemen and dealing with flooding not only had an immediate impact on their relationship, but also improved their interactions with Laura, with Sam's parents, and with Sam's supervisor. Hector's group therapist spontaneously asked what had happened with Hector as he was better able to navigate the challenges of both the PTSD program and the substance abuse program.

CONCLUSION

The key points in the chapter are:

- The research base for GMCT is extensive and includes multidimensional and longitudinal observation of couples across up to 20 years. The couples represent a variety of cultural, economic, ethnic, and sexual orientations and are representative of the couples serving in the military.
- This research allows for an empirically derived model (the sound relationship house) and does not rely on either experience with small clinical samples or hunches about what might go wrong with a relationship.
- The sound relationship house model allowed for the development of assessment instruments, which were then validated against actual observation and coding of couple interactions. The assessment tools are tied directly to observations of couples.
- The research base allowed for the creation of specific interventions that target what is going wrong in a relationship and for teaching what needs to go right for the relationship to succeed.
- The therapist's role is often quite active and involves direct coaching of the skills involved.
- GMCT is highly dyadic, with the therapist working to get the couple talking directly to each other rather than talking through the therapist.
- While initial work may focus on conflict management, this is not sufficient. The therapist must also target the marital friendship, positive affect systems, as well as the meanings system.
- GMCT is immediately experiential and affective in focus. The therapist stays in the moment with the couple. There is no recipe or predetermined sequencing of session content or focus.

REFERENCES

Driver, J. L., & Gottman, J. M. (2004). Daily marital interactions and positive affect during marital conflict among newlywed couples. *Family Process*, *43*, 301–314.

Gottman, J. M. (1999). *The marriage clinic.* New York: Norton.

Gottman, J. M., Coan, J., Carrere, S., & Swanson, C., (1998). Predicting marital happiness and stability from newlywed interactions. *Journal of Marriage and the Family*, *60*, 5–22.

Gottman, J. M., Driver, J., Yoshimoto, D., & Rushe, R. (2002). Approaches to the study of power in violent and nonviolent marriages, and in gay male and lesbian cohabiting relationships. In P. Noller & J. A. Feeney (Eds.), *Understanding marriage: Developments in the study of couple interaction* (pp. 323–347). Cambridge: Cambridge University Press.

Gottman, J. M. & Gottman, J. S. (2008). Gottman Method Couple Therapy. In A. S. Gurman (Ed.). *Clinical handbook of couple therapy* (pp. 138–164). New York: Guilford Press.

Gottman, J. M., Gottman, J. S., & Atkins, C. L. (2011). The Comprehensive Soldier Fitness Program: Family skills component. *American Psychologist*, *66*(1), 52–57.

Gottman, J. M., & Levenson, R. W. (1984). Why marriages fail: Affective and physiological patterns in marital interactions. In J. Masters (Ed.), *Boundary areas in social and developmental psychology* (pp. 110–136). New York: Academic Press.

Gottman, J. M., & Levenson, R. W. (1985). A valid procedure for obtaining self-report of affect in marital interactions. *Journal of Consulting and Clinical Psychology, 53*, 151–160.

Gottman, J. M., & Levenson, R. W. (1988). The social psychophysiology of marriage. In P. Noller & M. A. Fitzpatrick (Eds.), *Perspectives on marital interaction* (pp. 182–200). Clevedon, UK: Multilingual Matters.

Gottman, J. M., & Levenson, R. W. (1992). Marital processes predictive of later dissolution: Behavior, physiology and health. *Journal of Personality and Social Psychology, 63*, 221–233.

Gottman, J. M., & Levenson, R. W. (2002). A two-factor model for predicting when a couple will divorce: Exploratory analyses using 14 year longitudinal data. *Family Process, 41*, 83–96.

Gottman, J. M., & Silver, N. (1999). *The seven principles for making marriage work.* New York: Crown Publishing.

Katz, L. F., & Gottman, J. M. (1993). Patterns of marital conflict predict children's internalizing and externalizing behaviors. *Developmental Psychology, 29*, 940–950.

Levenson, R. W., Carstensen, L. L., & Gottman, J. M. (1993). Long term marriage: Age, gender and satisfaction, *Psychology and Aging, 8*, 301–313.

O'Brien, R. P. (2007, September 28). *The effect of combat related exposure on marital therapy and the sound relationship house*. Paper presented at the fourth annual Gottman Institute Conference, Seattle, WA.

O'Brien, R. P. (2008a, October 30). *Couples work after combat trauma: A Gottman perspective*. Paper presented at Pre-conference Institute, AAMFT annual meeting, Nashville, TN.

O'Brien, R. P. (2008b, November 20). *Couples work and combat trauma.* Paper presented at Texas Psychological Association annual meeting, Austin.

O'Brien, R. P. (2010). *Research based conflict management after combat trauma.* Presented at the American Association of Marriage and Family Therapy Annual Meeting, Atlanta, GA.

Shapiro, A. F., & Gottman, J. M. (2005). Effects on marriage of a psycho-communicative-educational intervention with couples undergoing transition to parenthood, evaluation at 1 year post intervention. *Journal of Family Communication, 5*, 1–24.

Shapiro, A. F., Gottman, J. M., & Carrere, S. (2000). The baby and the marriage: Identifying factors that buffer against decline in marital satisfaction after first baby arrives. *Journal of Family Psychology, 14*, 59–70.

Tabares, A. A., Driver, J. L., & Gottman, J. M. (2004). Repair attempts observational coding system: Measuring de-escalation of negative affect during marital conflict. In P. K. Kerig & D. H. Baucom (Eds.), *Couple observational coding systems* (pp. 227–241). Hillsdale, NJ: Erlbaum.

Section 3

Specific Issues in Military Relationships

8

The Military Lifestyle and the Relationship

LYNN K. HALL

INTRODUCTION

Readers were introduced in Chapter 1 of this volume to significant aspects of the unique culture of the military. In this chapter, I define how that military culture has an impact on the couples who serve and what challenges military couples regularly face because of that culture. I first look at a short overview of the basic elements of military culture, then consider four dynamics that are created specifically because these couples are in the military and address some of the common challenges faced within each of these dynamics.

ELEMENTS OF MILITARY CULTURE

As outlined in Chapter 1, there are numerous unique characteristics of military culture that often are foreign to civilian mental health professionals working with military couples. It is important to remember that the study of military culture is "limited … to the study of those particular beliefs, values, rituals, and other symbolic productions that organize and sustain military organization [which] includes the reception of these by the larger society to which the military belongs" ("Military Culture," 2008, p. 1). However, while these beliefs and values may be accepted by the society at large, that does not necessarily mean that the society at large actually understands the impact of this culture on the functioning of service members and their families.

Authors of the article in the *Encyclopedia of Violence, Peace and Conflict* ("Military Culture," 2008) define *military culture* as a "symbolic 'toolkit' of rituals, ceremonies, assumptions and beliefs that grow out of and guide a military force"

(p. 1). The authors of this article help us understand military culture by identifying "at least four distinct and commonly used tools, or elements" (p. 2) in the culture that not only define the culture but also give us insight into how the culture is used by the military to reach its ultimate goal, which is "to deal with (and, if possible, to overcome) the uncertainty of war, impose some pattern on war, control war's outcome, and invest it with meaning or significance" (p. 2). This reflects one of the major tenets from Adlerian psychology, that is, the psychology of use versus possession. Just knowing the characteristics or elements is not as valuable as knowing how these are used to maintain the culture. These tools or elements include discipline, professional ethos, ceremonies and etiquette, and esprit de corps and cohesion.

Discipline was defined as the "the orderly conduct of military personnel [which is] perfected through repetitive drill that makes the desired action a matter of habit" ("Military Culture," 2008, p. 5). The obvious goal of this kind of ritualistic discipline is to "minimize the confusion and disintegrative consequences of battle by imposing order" (p. 5), but a more subtle or perhaps psychological goal is to "ritualize the violence of war, to set it apart from ordinary life" (p. 5). It is important, however, to understand that the manner of discipline within the military still has to be sanctioned by the larger society ("Military Culture," 2008), thereby creating a style of discipline that is honored and sometimes even emulated by other parts of society. If the form and substance of our U.S. military discipline resembled other more violent or militant systems, it would not be tolerated by U.S. society.

Professional ethos can be defined as "a corporate identity based on expert knowledge of and control over the means of violence" ("Military Culture," 2008, p. 5) with a commitment that "presumes personal willingness to kill and accepts the risk of being killed, for oneself and for those one commands" (p. 5). Again, this identity must not only be sanctioned but also be in the service of the state, as well as maintain a relatively "explicit normative code of conduct" (p. 5), as society in general would not tolerate a professional ethos that is outside a reasonable norm of the majority culture. A further explanation is possible through a comparison of the military with the U.S. civilian society, in which the "military expresses a collectivistic vs. individualistic ethos, has clearly defined and codified social hierarchies, explicitly regulates the expression of emotion … , does not use material wealth as an index of social standing … , and promotes a self-concept rooted in history" (Christian, Stivers, & Sammons, 2009, p. 31).

Military ceremonies and etiquette are often the "most readily observable elements of modern military culture … [with] bright colored uniforms and unfurled flags … , drum rolls and bugle calls … , foot parades and the more contemporary air shows" ("Military Culture," 2008, p. 6). Military ritual plays the same role in society as other rituals do, which is often "to control or mask our anxieties and ignorance; to affirm our solidarity with one another; and to celebrate our being, usually in connection with some larger universe" (p. 6). However, perhaps an even more important purpose of military ceremonies is to "connect the burdens of military service with the larger society … [and] to convey the full meaning of military service, to show how central military service is to the life and well-being of the country" (p. 7).

Esprit de corps and cohesion basically address and also create the issue of morale. "Military cohesion refers to the feelings of identity and comradeship that soldiers hold for those in their immediate military unit ... [while] esprit de corps ... refers to the commitment and pride soldiers take in the larger military establishment to which their immediate unit belongs" ("Military Culture," 2008, p. 8). The long-held belief that cohesion and esprit de corps are the results of "love of country and attachment to ideological commitments of the state" (p. 8) actually may not adequately explain how these important elements develop. Social science research has shown instead that "cohesion among soldiers ... rests on concrete and primary experiences ... [suggesting] that cohesion results from military drill ... not very different from the bonding that occurs among those engaged in a collective dance or enacting a common religious ritual" (p. 8).

While knowledge of these basic elements of military culture are essential in working with and understanding military couples, it is also important to realize that, to a great degree, some of these "traditional" elements of the military have been greatly impacted by the move from a conscripted military to voluntary service in the 1970s. This move has, in fact, created a number of value conflicts within the military, one of which is the priority of military over family life. During the days of the draft, a much lower percentage of enlisted military were married, while since the inception of the volunteer military, the number of service members who are married, and often married with children, has drastically increased. "The bonds of loyalty on which esprit de corps and cohesion exist depend on bonds among a community of warriors. They entail a commitment to self-sacrifice that places the well-being of the outfit above all else, including the responsibilities of family life" ("Military Culture," 2008, p. 14). With the introduction of spouses and children into the military system, the military must find the balance between providing families with enough support to limit the service members' worries about their families' well-being, while maintaining the required morale and necessary cohesion between the warriors.

DYNAMICS FACED BY MILITARY COUPLES

With that in mind, it is important to understand the dynamics and challenges for military couples. For this chapter, the four dynamics to be discussed are boundary ambiguity, attachment issues, children and spouse concerns, and family readiness.

In the discussion about boundary ambiguity, the issues faced by the couple during deployment and other absences of the service member from the family, and the authoritarian nature of the military, which often is reflected in the family structure as well as in the military communities, are covered. While addressing the dynamic of attachment, this chapter focuses on the mobility of the military families, including the frequent moves and the isolation felt by being far from extended family and community support, often during the early adult years, when major developmental adult transitions normally occur, such as marriage and parenting.

While discussing the third dynamic, this chapter looks at the specific concerns of the military spouse, who must also make the commitment to the military, usually at a young age and without having developed sufficient career or educational goals to find personal fulfillment. In addition, the issues faced by children as they are raised as "military brats" in a culture far different from most other American children are discussed. How military couples address the concerns faced by spouses and children, including their role as parents, is often key to the success of the couple relationship. Last, the dynamic of family readiness, often described as the "third leg" (Henderson, 2006) of military readiness, and how issues around the importance of the mission and the constant preparation for disaster have an impact on the couple are explored.

Boundary Ambiguity

Boundary ambiguity is defined as "a state in which family members are uncertain in their perception about who is in or out of the family and who is performing which roles and tasks within the family" (Faber, Willerton, Clymer, MacDermid, & Weiss, 2008, p. 222). While boundary ambiguity is not exclusive to the military, it is often one of the consequences of the elements of esprit de corps and cohesion. The inherent authoritarian structure of the military based on hierarchy is practiced continually through discipline and rituals. The practices of deployment, as well as numerous training opportunities and frequent TDYs (temporary duties), have an impact on the couple's relationship boundaries. For instance, Faber et al. (2008) state that "during deployment, all family members experienced boundary ambiguity" (p. 222), but it is obvious that the issue of boundary ambiguity is experienced not only during deployment, but also as a regular experience by most military couples throughout their career.

Authoritarian Structure As suggested, the tools of the military are used to produce a service in which order is maintained, confusion is minimized, necessary action is a matter of habit, and violence is ritualized. This cannot happen without the requisite authoritarian structure. "Rank plays a fundamental role … [where] enlisted soldiers, noncommissioned officers, warrant officers, and commissioned officers represent discrete groups with unique roles and corresponding power. … Rank represents important implications for power in relationships" (Reger, Etherage, Reger, & Gahm, 2008, p. 25). Because of the external locus of control of military service, this authoritarian structure often contributes to the manner in which couples and family relationships are developed and maintained. While extreme, an interesting example is in the movie *The Great Santini*, from the book of the same title by Pat Conroy, based on his life as the son of a military officer. As Reger et al. (2008) suggest, service members "live with the expectation of deployment, the inability to quit their job, a loss of control over significant life decisions … and the requirement to respond to others" (p. 29).

In 1984, Keith and Whitaker suggested that military tradition expects that the service member must "run a tight ship at home," which would be advantageous to the career of the service member, and advised that "the military family lives in a community in which no one dies from old age, only violently … lead[ing] to an illusion of eternal youth and vigor" (p. 156), and that the father (who is military) outranks his wife because he has a closer affiliation with the base commander. This imbalance between the couple can cause problems within the family (Hall, 2008) and certainly within partner relationships. For instance, when service members set themselves up as the authoritarian head of the household while they are at home, the boundaries can become ambiguous for both members of the couple when the service members are deployed and again on returning home. "The great paradox of the military is that its members, the self-appointed front-line guardians of our cherished American democratic values, do not live in a democracy themselves" (Wertsch, 1991, p. 15).

McKay and Maybell (2004) suggested that the "upheaval in all of our social institutions: government, education, the workplace, race relationships, gender relationships and families" (p. 64) have resulted in these institutions operating from an equality identity that includes attitudes of equal values and respect. These societal changes have been accepted by most of society so that when one joins the military and accepts the inherent authoritarian structure at work, it is not necessarily guaranteed that the person he or she marries will also accept the authoritarian structure within their relationship. "The military family still lives, at least to some degree, in a democratic society and often struggles in their movement back and forth from the authoritarian world of the military to the democratic world in which they both come from and continually have to step back into" (Hall, 2011, p. 48).

American society has made great strides to affirm and equalize the differences in society, but all military systems function in a rigid hierarchical system based on dominance and subordination. Housing on military installations is separated, with single military in one area, enlisted family housing in another and officers' quarters in another, with clear distinctions in appearance, quality, and size. "In speaking with numerous adult military brats, when the subject of rank comes up, virtually all will share that, as kids, they could, almost instantaneously, recognize an officer's kid or an enlisted kid. It is not a distinction to be taken lightly by civilian mental health professionals" (Hall, 2011, p. 38).

There are many ways in which the authoritarian rank system affects spouses and families. In the past, most installations included separate officers' and enlisted clubs; those no longer exist and have been replaced with the more generic "food court"-type facilities used by all members of the military and their families. In the past, spouses (usually wives) had clearly defined roles based on whether the military spouse was enlisted or an officer; again, this has been modified somewhat, with spouses working together on volunteer projects or in jobs on military installations. School officials, while cognizant of rank/grade of the service member, clearly attempt to be inclusive so that there is no differentiation between officer and enlisted kids in supporting them academically or in extracurricular activities. While it is still true that spouses and children can almost immediately recognize members of an officer or enlisted family, the boundaries have become quite permeable in terms of the rules that guide the behavior of the two groups, sometimes causing conflict within the family if the service member does not approve of the action of the spouse or children.

Deployment "Spouses of military members have reported that deployments result in loss of emotional support, loneliness, role overload, role shifts and concerns about the safety and well-being of the deployed military members" (Faber et al., 2008, p. 223). Findings suggest that family members are constantly faced with the need to "stretch the family boundary enough both to psychologically retain the service member as a viable family member and to temporarily reassign his or her responsibilities" (Faber et al, 2008, p. 223). In reporting the results of their study of reservists and their families, these authors wrote that during the deployment phase, boundary ambiguity issues center around "safety, redistribution of roles and responsibilities and rejoining the family … [and that] boundary ambiguity was elevated when the family members heard of bombings or attacks" (p. 223). Spouses especially experienced high levels of boundary ambiguity around family roles and household decisions, having to make all of the household and family decisions done previously either by or at least in partnership with the service member.

Bowling and Sherman (2008) summarized the "four of the major tasks of deployment, which are redefining of roles, expectations and division of household responsibilities; managing strong emotions; abandoning emotional construction and creating intimacy in relationships; and creating a sense of shared meaning surrounding the deployment experience" (p. 451), all of which demand a certain level of boundary ambiguity and permeability in the work of completing these tasks.

By the end of deployment, boundary ambiguity often changes from concerns about the safety of the deployed service member and household decisions, to concern about the upcoming reunion. "The transition from physical absence to physical presence was characterized by concerns about how the reservist would rejoin the family system, as well as about the reservist's personality and behavior upon return" (Faber et al., 2008, p. 225). Once home, the couple often feels that they have to start over, reconstructing their relationship based on often-substantial personal changes they have made during the service member's absence. "Some partners will feel that they were tested and strengthened by their experiences; others may feel overwhelmed and isolated. As partners get to know one another again, they must renegotiate how to communicate with one another, make decisions together, divide up tasks and assign roles within the family, deal with finances, raise children, and once again rely upon one another" (Erbes, Polusny, MacDermid, & Compton, 2008, p. 974).

Reunion boundary ambiguity is centered on how to resume the roles and responsibilities for both the spouse and the service member.

> Family members felt hesitant about asking their reservist to resume certain roles, as they felt unsure of whether the reservist was ready to take back some of his or her roles or exactly how much more time the reservist needed. Reservists also wondered about how to take up roles without interfering with the family members' new routine and how exactly to fit back into the family. (Faber et al., 2008, p. 226)

Couples expressed concerns about the transition from a closed-communication to an open-communication system, with the at-home spouse sharing that while the reservist was gone, there was no need to share daily activities or coordinate schedules with anyone. In addition, family members found it difficult to understand the service member who has returned home physically but did not seem the same psychologically, with the majority of the reservists in the study sharing that they were having a hard time letting their guard down on returning home (Faber et al., 2008).

Reservists also expressed concerns about their "soldier-to-civilian" transition, compounding the issue of boundary ambiguity as they struggled to make the switch back from soldier to civilian. "Boundary ambiguity surrounding work was often related to financial stressors, which created relationship stress and, in turn, struggles with sharing roles" (Faber et al., 2008, p. 227). While reservists often return to the same or similar employment, active duty service members usually do not. The soldier-to-civilian concern is therefore also expressed by active duty service members who return to the civilian world after one or more tours of duty; their world has changed, their perspective on life has changed, and their relationships will have to adjust to that change. After living even for a short time in a world of discipline, rituals, and warrior cohesion, many service members experience the civilian world as a "messy" place, with no order and little external direction (Hall, 2008).

Attachment Issues

One of the most well-known characteristics of military culture is the high level of mobility of military families, often resulting in issues associated with isolation and alienation from extended family and commitment to communities of support. "On average, active duty military families move every two to three years within the United States or overseas. … Secondary school-age students move three times more often than their civilian counterparts do" (Park, 2011, p. 66).

Children feel rootless and often have difficulties building relationships or maintaining commitments, especially during adolescence. Separation from a parent because of military assignments often has a negative impact on a child's school performance and mental health. Frequent moves pose additional challenges for academic achievement due to differing state graduation requirements (Hall, 2008; Park, 2011). This kind of mobility serves the military well and is the result of the professional ethos that the military comes first; the work and mission of the military must not be outweighed by the needs of the family. In addition, even the experience of moving (or PCSing, ironically called permanent change of station) comes with rituals, taking up to 2 or 3 weeks to get all the permissions, requisite signatures, school records, household goods packed and shipped, and so on, which reinforce the needs of the military over the family.

"Attachment theory has provided the core foundation for several contemporary theorists who write about and practice couple therapy … [and who] talk about 'attachment injuries' where one partner experiences a sense of violation and betrayal, while the other partner fails to offer comfort and caring in the face of distress" (Basham, 2008, p. 84,). If the military service member or the spouse is "poorly differentiated from their families of origin, or originate from failed (or abusive) family backgrounds" (Everson & Camp, 2011, p. 21), these premilitary service issues would certainly place them at a higher risk of later developing problems in the face of the stressful military lifestyles. Sherwood (2009) reminded us that "attachment styles that are insecure pose a challenge to relationships as partners can eventually become incapable of the responsiveness needed for secure bonding to take place" (p. 337). Rigid attachment styles in general might pose difficulties in military couples, and separation may be more difficult for those couples "who struggle with trust and have deep-seated fears of rejection wherein such fears are not easily alleviated" (Sherwood, 2009, p. 337). In addition,

> insecure-avoidant or dismissive partners may be nonresponsive to keeping closeness alive while away, and may also have a difficult time re-engaging upon return. How such couples maintain their needs for intimate closeness, and how one's sense of security remains unaffected by multiple absences would be of particular interest to attachment-focused clinicians. (p. 337)

Traumatic experiences, such as those often experienced by the service member, point to a "state of discomfort, extreme stress, and memories of a catastrophic event. … [Not] unlike the impact of a car accident or a natural disaster, combat trauma comes closer to Type II trauma, which involves chronic and repetitive life threatening events that render a victim powerless" (Basham, 2008, p. 84). Warriors return home changed, perhaps having "suffered profound disillusionment with the senselessness and immorality of some combat-related actions and the political decisions affecting the war" (p. 84). A newly gained set of skills and strengths, on the other hand, helped them survive in a combat zone but may not be useful with the stressors they face on returning home.

> Soldiers learn to control fears and suppress emotions, to master the art of deception while cunningly devising ways to survive, and to parse information while restricting communication. As they gain physical strength, endurance, and quickness to respond to dangerous situations, they also develop the capacity to respond immediately and instantly with violent lethal force. They maintain a vigilant watchful stance at all times, preparing to respond to danger and recognize that the fixed rules of hierarchy can be broken when they pose threat to safety. (Basham, 2008, p. 84)

When faced with traumatic events and sometimes ethical dilemmas about some of their wartime actions, one's sense of self and trust in others is often shattered, thereby disrupting attachments with others. "Attachments transform from secure connections into tenuous insecure connections managed through ambivalence or avoidance. … Relationships can become very chaotic and disorganized in response to the assault upon the basic relationship patterns" (Basham, 2008, p. 84). Often, an additional response to these injuries is "irritability and grandiose entitlement [in which] small slights may be experienced as major offenses resulting in rage responses" (Basham, 2008, p. 84). These responses on returning home lead to difficulties for couples to reattach or find new meaning in their changed relationship.

Traumatized couples often have difficulties with adjusting to the many shifts in family roles and the balancing of power in decision making as the stay-at-home partner has had to assume responsibility for virtually all parenting and household management. "In these families, we see the insidious effects of affect dysregulation on the parents and children, disrupted attachments, and erratic parenting, which fuel disorganized attachments and increased behavioral problems in children" (Basham, 2008, p. 90). As the military service member experiences a series of separations and reunions, the attachment systems of each of the partners is activated. The partner who remains behind may actually begin to develop a sense of accomplishment and pride, even while being overwhelmed with financial, household, and parenting hardships.

> If we think of attachment theory constructs applied to the warfighter's homecoming process, we can say that, during active deployment, many of these men and women experience something like a "preoccupied" attachment bond with their superiors. In these situations, the soldier's day-to-day life is governed by the directives issued by the commanding officer. … Consequently these warriors often worry about returning home to their partners and families with potentially de-stabilized and insecure attachments. (Basham, 2008, p. 90)

A therapist using "the lens of attachment relationship to understand the emotional cycle of deployment, can be a real lifeline to hurting and confused military couples" (Sneath & Rheem, 2011, p. 131).

Attachment issues are also a part of military dependents' experience as they almost always have a sense of being different from the nonmilitary students while attending schools and living in communities in the continental United States. Wertsch (1991) stated that it is "next to impossible to grow up in the warrior society without absorbing the notion that civilians are very different and sometimes incomprehensible" (p. 315), leaving military dependent kids unattached to the larger civilian childhood population. This isolation and unattachment is often manifested with a focus turned inward to the military world, rather than outward to the local community or even the world in general (Hall, 2011). "Due to frequent moves, many military children experience disrupted relationships with friends, and must repeatedly adapt to new schools and cultivate new community supports" (National Child Traumatic Stress Network, 2009, p. 1).

In addition to experiencing a sense of isolation from their civilian counterparts, the authoritarian rank and grade structure of the military creates a certain amount of isolation within the military itself. While, as mentioned, there has been significant movement toward parity for families of enlisted and officers, there is always a subtle difference as spouses and children learn to understand that they are not, in fact, equal. Wertsch (1991) pointed out that the military has its reasons to make these distinctions and more than likely could not exist without them, but it seems that "the only equality among officers and enlisted is in dying on the battlefield" (p. 288).

During the times that families live abroad, the isolation can seem overwhelming as U.S. military housing areas are secluded from the outside culture, so the world of military families becomes "an oddly isolated life, one in which it is possible to delude oneself that one is still on American soil" (Wertsch, 1991, p. 330). Instead of making this experience one that could positively last a lifetime, often families are anxious about the experience and may spend the majority of the duty tour within the fences of the military installation (Hall, 2008).

An additional result of the mobility of military families is the constant giving up of attachments and having to forge new ones. Even if the family does not experience a death or injury of the service member, the family is constantly in the midst of transitions and change, therefore experiencing ongoing and unfinished grief and loss. These issues are rarely dealt with and can eventually lead to symptoms or behavior problems that resemble Type II trauma. Basham (2008) noted previously that combat trauma resembled Type II trauma or the "chronic and repetitive life threatening events that render a victim powerless" (p. 84), but it was the author's experience that many of the children of military service members also began to show many similar behavioral issues, often the result of feeling that sense of powerlessness over their own lives (Hall, 2008). By working with the children and the parents to help them uncover some of their earlier fears and anxieties, as well as giving them permission to express their long-denied grief over the many transitions they had lived, young people can begin to value their unique experiences and build on the strengths that living in the military can provide.

Smith (2011) believes that professionals who combine techniques from the two fields of family play therapy and attachment theory can make a major impact on the healing of relationships within military families "in such a way as to restore family roles and reconstruct levels of intimacy after multiple short-term separations or even extended deployments" (p. 153), as well as other interruptions in the lives of the family that have long been denied.

CHILDREN AND SPOUSE CONCERNS

The Children

Pat Conroy (1991) wrote, in the introduction of Mary Wertsch's (1991) book about military brats, that

> The gathering of military men should be thanking their children, their fine and resourceful children, who were strangers in every school they entered, thanking them for their extraordinary service to their country, for the sacrifices they made over and over again to the United States of America, to its ideals of freedom, to its preservation, and to its everlasting honor. … Military brats, my lost tribe, spent their entire youth in service to this country and no one even knew we were there. (Conroy, 1991, p. xxv)

Most military families will have to contend with numerous stressors related to deployment, including separation, reunification, and reintegration. Many children, of course, will also have to face the loss of a parent, or having a parent return home with combat-related mental health problems or physical injuries, along with the stress resulting from multiple deployments. The children who are most at risk for experiencing trauma are those who are young; have preexisting problems; have parents in the Guard or Reserves; experience multiple deployments; live far from military installations; are in isolated communities with limited mental health resources; come from single-parent families with the parent deployed; or come from dual-military families and both parents are deployed (National Child

Traumatic Stress Network, 2009). Although military children and families, for the most part do well, "these challenges can take a toll on their health and well-being" (Park, 2011, p. 65).

Deployment has been shown to affect physical health, academic performance, behavior problems, depression, and anxiety. Adolescent children of deployed parents show higher levels of stress, systolic blood pressure, and heart rate. "More than one third of school-age children showed high risk for psychosocial difficulties during parental deployment, 2.5 times the national norm … [and] the longer the parental deployment is, the greater these problems are, during and after deployment" (Park, 2011, p. 65).

Deployment issues, however, are not the only concerns of the typical military child. As Wertsch (1991) pointed out in her study of military brats, children of the military face unique challenges, including having a sense of homelessness, a need to become very adaptable to numerous and often new situations, living their entire childhood (at least for career military families) under an external locus of control, and living in what Wertsch describes as the Fortress, which refers "to the physical communities in which military service members live, as well as to the psychological world that is created for the children as they grow up" (Hall, 2008, p. 106). These challenges of military living, as well as the many other characteristics described throughout this book, have enormous impact on the lives of children, which often are considered negative but can also become strengths.

Some of the potential strengths that military life creates for children are the ability to get along with everyone; being resilient and flexible; being loyal and self-sacrificing; having the ability to face risks and challenges; being productive, accepting, and living with diversity; and having a need to continue to serve or take care of the world (Hall, 2008; Wertsch, 1991). While the majority of children develop at least some degree of each of these strengths during their life in the military, those children who are more fragile or do not have the necessary personality traits or family support to cope with this unique culture, can have significant problems. In addition, these strengths, taken to the extreme as sometimes happens, can also lead to behavioral problems in adolescents and even difficulties in adulthood for these children.

Adult military children often describe themselves as rootless and often do not have the ability to maintain long-term relationships or set down roots for long periods of time. As Wertsch (1991) said, they are often "leaving one foot in the realm of the temporary, and one foot in the realm of potential" (p. 354). Military children might also grow up believing in a sense of powerlessness as they have lived under this external locus of control most of their lives and may not have developed the belief that they can take control over their lives. In addition, "military children often have difficulty reconciling the paradoxical contradictions of their life, particularly the need for autonomy versus the need for structure … as the need for structure and order is built into the family, the environment, the community, and often the individual" (Hall, 2008, p. 108). The consequences of these contradictions sometimes lead these adults to pushing limits, having problems with authority, and finding it difficult to function in more stable communities (Hall, 2008).

The Spouses

Park (2011) points out that members of the military tend to marry earlier than their civilian counterparts, which is an important consideration in comparing military and civilian families because research has clearly documented that marriage at a younger age often results in more problems than marriage at an older age. Park quotes the 2009 U.S. Department of Defense Manpower Data Center, saying that "seventy-four percent of the spouses of service members report personal growth, despite also reporting increased loneliness, stress and anxiety" (Park, 2011, p. 68).

As noted in this chapter, changes have been made in the military because of the transition to a volunteer force; these changes have been required because of the introduction of spouses (and families) into the military and the need for the military to meet the support needs of the family. For example, in 1989 when I first became a school counselor in the Department of Defense school system in Germany, there were over 7,000 civilian teachers in Germany alone, there solely to meet the educational needs of military dependent children. While that has decreased over the years because of the drawdown required at the end of the "cold war," there remain today well over 3,000 Department of Defense teachers in Germany. The entire Department of Defense school system throughout the world was developed, and in the 1970s greatly expanded after the change to a volunteer service, simply to accommodate the families of service members.

This support of the family is very different from what in the past defined military life when couples were seen as part of a two-person career (Durand, 2000), which meant that the military spouse's job was to create the right family setting so that her husband's work reflected his life at home, by staying positive, being interested in his duty, and being flexible and adaptable (Hall, 2008). Durand's study (2000) found that a key difference in the beliefs of military spouses from the military of the past and today's military is that today's military is viewed as the service member's career, not the spouse's. "While women's sacrifices on behalf of their husband's career continue to be glorified in the Army, many wives today believe they have an equal right to an income and job of their own" (Houppert, 2005, p. 226).

A study of over 1,000 participants in the late 1990s (Bourg & Segal, 1999) showed that "recruitment, retention, morale, and commitment of married military members have all been shown to be related to their spouse's attitudes towards military service" (p. 637). The results of the study point out that the degree of military support for families clearly has an impact on the adaptation to and satisfaction with military life. In addition, the satisfaction of the spouse is also impacted by the amount the military interferes in the life of the family, suggesting that the service members' attitudes toward the military are influenced by their spouses' satisfaction and commitment. Bourg and Segal (1999) summarized the findings by sharing that the spouses' satisfaction and commitment are determined by the level of the military's support for families and the amount of interference with family needs and demands.

The study supports the assertion that military responsiveness to families will indeed lessen the degree of conflict "between the two greedy institutions of the military and the family" (Bourg & Segal, 1999, p. 647). Another important aspect of this responsiveness to families, from the military perspective, is that "Army–family conflict affects the organizational commitment of soldiers ... through the wife's commitment" (p. 647). One might argue, as Houppert (2005) did, that this is the reason why the military has put the resources into supporting the family. She suggested that the support programs are not really to support the spouses or families but to "teach them to be self reliant" (p. 86) so that when something happens to the service member, the families are not so dependent on the military.

So, what are the needs of the spouse who will then contribute to the steadiness and commitment of the service member to the military mission? As indicated, the support services necessary to carry out the responsibilities as a parent are obvious, but in addition, spouses (the majority of whom are still women) want the opportunity to continue their education or support the financial needs of the family through employment. What is often not understood is that the young, particularly newly enlisted families, live on meager incomes, despite having their housing and other necessities provided. In most cases, in the early years of service, many families actually qualify for food stamps and other government assistance, such as free and reduced meals in schools. Therefore, the need for the spouse to earn additional income is significant.

Bourg and Segal's (1999) study also indicates that "rank, age, and presence of a child all positively affect the organizational commitment of the soldier ... [and the] presence of a child also positively influences the commitment of the wife to the organization" (p. 643). While in this study the wife's employment had no significant effect on Army–family conflict or the commitment of the service member or the spouse (Bourg & Segal, 1999), other authors have defined some of the challenges of employment for the military spouse. Russo, Dougherty, and Martin (2000) suggested that as female spouses of the military are now more and more being joined by civilian male spouses of female service members, the issue of spouse employment is being recognized by the Department of Defense as an important quality-of-life issue.

Being employed as a military spouse includes the unique aspects of (a) the additional commitment to military service; (b) little control over when the military spouse spends time away from home; (c) the necessary secondary nature of the civilian spouses' work; (d) the fact that military spouses often function in their careers as if they were single; (e) the determination by the military member's rank of the control he or she has over aspects of the military career that have an impact on the spouse; and (f) family responsibilities, which usually fall on the nonmilitary partner (Hall, 2008; Russo et al, 2000). With these constraints, employment and further education for the military spouse become a difficult issue for the spouse, and therefore the couple and the family, eventually having an impact on their satisfaction with the military. Again, we see that the focus on military cohesion, esprit de corps, and ethos demands that the family, particularly the spouse, comes second to the military commitment. Even the discipline and rituals required by the military often mean the service member is not available for family functions or support of the spouse. Ceremonies and rituals also often demand attendance and protocol that can impinge on the spouses' time.

FAMILY READINESS

"A common saying in the military is that when one person joins, the whole family serves" (Park, 2011, p. 65). The 2009 Mental Health Advisory Team reported that positive family relationships are a source of resilience to service members, and relationship problems are a source of stress (Park, 2011). "Any efforts to build a strong, effective, and sustainable military force must also consider military families, improving the relationships of the soldier with his or her family members and strengthening the family itself" (p. 65). Henderson (2006) told us that deployed warriors believe that those who are left behind have a profound impact on their ability to hold up under fire, and she suggested that "military readiness is like a three-legged stool. The first leg is training, the second equipment. The third leg is the family. If any of these three legs snaps, the stool tips over and America is unprepared to defend herself" (p. 5). The norms, values, and beliefs that form the basis for acculturation and standards for conduct must be adhered to by military dependents since "disruptions in family life can negatively impact the service member in terms of potential assignments that enhance opportunities for promotion or the family being asked to leave the installation because of misdeeds by family members" (Everson & Camp, 2011, p. 26). It was not unusual in the Department of Defense schools in Europe for a child with significant behavior problems to be sent back to the United States to live with an aunt, an uncle, or a grandparent if there were inadequate services to meet the child's needs and the service member was too valuable to be reassigned.

Mental health professionals who work with the military must understand why people join the military and why they serve. While there are numerous references to this (Hall, 2008; Wertsch, 1991), the bottom line is that both the service member and the spouse are in service to this country. While there are definite benefits to this service, these young men and women have shared beliefs that the military mission is to provide national defense, which requires personal sacrifices. "Anyone who joins … should be ready to fight; personality characteristics that are adaptive for fighting are valued; characteristics that could put other team members at risk are devalued" (Reger et al., 2008, p. 27).

The conditions and demands of a total commitment to the military are the very essence of military unit cohesion (Martin & McClure, 2000) and esprit de corps. "This felt sense of mission is, after all, the purpose of the military; for each service member, the commitment is not just about having a better education or training for a job but is, in fact, a felt sense of mission to make the world a better and safer place" (Hall, 2011, p. 40). Houppert (2005) suggested that the purpose of basic training is to shift the dependence of the young civilian from the family to the military team: "The soldier must learn that he can trust no one but his buddies" (p. 84). As "incongruous as it may seem … [service members] on the front line are proud to be there and willing to serve again. The overall effect is to heighten the sense that the military is becoming a proud cult that fewer and fewer outsiders want to join" (Gegax & Thomas, 2005, p. 26).

Fenell (2008) notes a number of common values shared by military personnel that related closely to the elements or tools of the military addressed in this chapter. These include maintaining physical fitness, training hard prior to deployment to reduce casualties, never abandoning fellow soldiers in combat, always placing the mission and the unit before the individual, and never showing weakness to fellow soldiers or the enemy. These values clearly reflect the elements of discipline, professional ethos, and esprit de corps and cohesion, but they also relate to the imperative of readiness preparation.

While changes in the policies of the military noted previously have been to provide services for the families of service members, spouses and children see themselves as part of two families. Conflict often emerges when this second "military family" is perceived to be more important than the family left at home. It is a difficult balance to be part of two families who are so integral to the success of the mission (Fenell & Weinhold, 2003). The military mission is to constantly prepare and be ready for disaster, which means the family also lives under the constant potential for death or injury of the military service member (Hall, 2011). Mary Wertsch (1991), in describing her life as a military brat, called the military mission that "all powerful presence that went with them everywhere and without which their lives would have no meaning" (Hall, 2008, p. 54). In the end, "families that function most effectively are active, optimistic, self-reliant, and flexible. [They] find meaning in military life and identify with the work of their uniformed family member. Family preparedness for deployment as well as community and social support lead to better adjustment" (Park, 2011, p. 68).

IMPLICATIONS FOR WORKING WITH COUPLES

Risk and Protective Factors

To work effectively with military couples, we might also consider how the elements and dynamics of the military create risk factors, as well as what protective factors are available to couples. Faber et al. (2008) reported that "military families' adaptation to stressful events depends upon family resources and strengths, the 'pileup' of demands on the family system, and the family perceptions of the situation" (p. 223). Deployments and reunions affect families differently, depending on personal characteristics and availability of social support, which can buffer the effects of deployment. Families who have the most trouble adapting are usually those "whose members are young, newly married, financially unstable, and experiencing their first deployment" (p. 223). Factors that seem to buffer the negative effects include positive attitudes toward relocation, social support, previous relocation experience, and active coping styles (Park, 2011).

It also has been shown that children respond more positively if they are given the chance to take on responsibilities and to be more independent and mature during parental separation. As Park (2011) points out, the hierarchical structure of the military often produces resentment in military children and has the possibility of decreasing their independent thinking, but as noted, it can also foster many of the military values: "Service, sacrifice, honor, teamwork, loyalty, sense of purpose, sense of community, and pride can work as resilience factors to overcome difficulties of military life" (p. 67).

Risk factors that can increase the negative effects of deployment on families include a

> history of family problems, younger families, less educated families, foreign-born spouses, families with young children, those with lower pay grades or reduced income, those without a unit affiliation such as National Guard and Reserve families, families with children who have disabilities, families with pregnancies, single-parent families and families with mothers in the military. (Park, 2011, p. 68)

Bowling and Sherman (2008) added to our understanding of the risk and protective factors associated with military service when they reported that "flexible gender roles, the use of active coping strategies, and the use of community and social supports all serve as protective factors. On the other hand, families without support, young or new families, and families with other stressors are all at increased risk for mental health issues and relationship distress" (p. 452). These are important factors to look for in the initial assessment of couples as therapy with military families is often transitory and short term. Finding protective factors in their personal experience or communities that can add to the support during therapy is essential. Often, families, particularly new to the military, are not aware of what is available through the military or in the community, so it is imperative that therapists use all available support to assist in working with the couple. These support services will more than likely be available at the next duty station, while the therapist will not.

Stigma One of the risk factors for the military has been, and continues to be, the stigma against seeking mental health services. Often, it is the actual commitment, as well as the overarching mission of the military, that leads to this stigma, and it frequently encompasses issues faced by the couple or the family when they find themselves in need of help. One young Air Force noncommissioned officer (NCO) decided to go to a civilian counselor when he and his wife were having difficulties, but not until after a lot of concern and deliberation about how this might be viewed by his chain of command. At their first appointment, he made it clear that the client records must show that it was his civilian wife who was the "identified client," even though this civilian therapist had no responsibility to report their relationship issues to the military.

Dahn (2008) described the double bind in which military personnel often find themselves, with a restriction from seeking counseling but then being "admonished by their chain of command for any domestic matter in which the police are called" (p. 56), often leading to frustration and sometimes domestic violence, which has to stay hidden and therefore is allowed to continue. Sometimes, the concept of honor and sacrifice, so essential to military service and part of the professional ethos, presents difficulty in therapy because the service member may believe that he or she should be "given a pass when it comes to relationship issues with family and children" (Hall, 2008, p. 63). The service members often believe that their military commitment comes first, regardless of what happens at home, and they have been warned that "seeking professional counseling could be detrimental to career advancement or seen as a sign of weakness by their chain of command" (Dahn, 2008, p. 56).

Nash (2007) compared the genius of great athletes that "lies in the ability to perform as if there is no distance or weight or danger" to overcome with the genius of the warrior to "fight as if there is no terror, horror, or hardship" (p. 14). He warned helping professionals that "they may do more harm than good by asking warriors in an operational theater to become more aware of their own stressors and stress reaction" (p. 15). In fact, "searching for ways to become more comfortable or safe in war can be not only a distraction from the real business at hand, but also a serious hazard to success and even survival" (p. 15).

Despite improved outreach to all members of the military, rank is an important issue during treatment as higher-ranking individuals often struggle more with the belief that seeking mental health service may put their career in jeopardy. "To the extent that seeking psychological treatment is defined as weakness soldiers may be slow to pursue services. 'Weakness' is not adaptive for combat, and some may view it as dangerous to have individuals who require psychological support on a combat team" (Reger et al., 2008, p. 27), particularly in a leadership position.

Research has shown that it is not just the military who suffer from this stigma against seeking mental health services but "that people with concealable stigmas (people who are gay, of minority faith-based communities, or with mental illness) decide to avoid this harm by hiding their stigma and staying in the closet" (Corrigan, 2004, p. 616). In addition to the possibility of having potential negative effects on a service member's career, research has shown that people avoid the stigma of mental illness because of its potential effects on one's sense of self, which is "typically operationalized as diminished views about personal worth and is often experienced as shame … [which has been shown to have] a significant relationship … with avoiding treatment" (Corrigan, 2004, p. 618).

Corrigan's (2004) reflections are valuable to those considering working with military service couples, as shame is a significant issue, particularly in working with men in general and military men specifically. Mejia (2005) suggested that, in the traditional socialization process of boys, strategies for dealing with shame are suppressed, and boys who are socialized from a shame-based perspective often find themselves a good fit with the military culture. Joining the military is a natural extension to the socialization that "taught them to avoid shame at all costs, to wear a mask of coolness, to act as though everything is going all right, as though everything is under control" (p. 33). Gilligan (1996) wrote that the "most dangerous men on earth are those who are afraid that they are wimps. Wars have been started for less" (p. 6). While this does not apply to all, or perhaps even the majority, of male service members, it is to some extent an essential part of military culture and often has a significant impact on whether service members seek mental health care.

Another way of understanding the source of this stigma is to understand three dynamics that are the result of living in the "fortress" of the military. After her research with military children, Mary Wertsch (1991) identified three overarching themes that define how military families function. These include secrecy, stoicism, and denial, all of which contribute to the stigma against seeking mental health services.

1. Secrecy is the dictate that work is kept separate from home as well as the opposite, that what goes on at home stays at home, such as an incident of domestic violence or child abuse. Not talking about what goes on at work is often demanded of many military job categories, so there can be a shutting down of dialogue related to important job-related stressors that the service member cannot share with the spouse.
2. Stoicism is the need to have a public face of stability as well as the appearance of having the ability to handle any stress the family experiences so that stress does not have an impact on the work of the service member. This constant "putting on a good face" means that the anxiety, fears, and other uncomfortable feelings often go unexpressed; family concerns may be pushed aside instead of dealt with openly, for example, sending a child to a relative instead of reassigning the service member so the child can obtain needed services.
3. Denial is the need, then, to keep all the feelings, fears, and even normal developmental stressors of the family under wraps. While this denial may not reach the troubling levels of domestic violence, child abuse, or other offenses, it does mean that feelings are not expressed, fears are not shared, and the need to request assistance goes unnoticed. This can lead to behavioral and interpersonal issues noted previously with children who exhibit Type II unfinished grief symptoms.

"Secrecy, stoicism and denial are, in fact, crucial for success of the warrior, success of the mission and ultimately success of the military" (Hall, 2011). However, these restrictions often do not allow military families the chance to work with professionals, whether it is in schools or through mental health services, to experience the growth that can come from the "work" done when assistance is sought. To the extent that the culture encourages secrecy, stoicism, and denial, it also encourages the continuation of the stigma against seeking assistance for many of the stressors service members and their spouses face during their military service.

CONCLUSION

The purpose of this chapter was to understand how the characteristics of the military culture have an impact on the lifestyle of military couples. It is valuable to understand how certain elements of the military are used to actually create the necessary characteristics of the culture, and why these characteristics are important to the functioning of the military. In addition, the chapter showed how these elements have an impact on the dynamics of the couple, which then creates the challenges that military couples must face to be successful military couples. These dynamics of boundary ambiguity, attachment issues, spouse and children concerns, and family readiness will invariably be raised regardless of the issues couples bring to therapy. This chapter has also looked at some of the implications for mental health interventions by considering a few of the risk and protective factors faced by military couples, particularly the risk factor of the stigma against seeking mental health services.

In an early work about counseling military families, Keith and Whitaker (1984) reminded mental health professionals that "the military family does not come to the clinic to learn how to become a civilian family, but rather it needs help to live inside the military system" (p. 150). That holds true today. Our goal in working with military couples is not to move them toward being well-functioning civilian couples, but to find ways to help them make the necessary personal and relationship adjustments to become successful couples and parents during that period of time when they are in service to our country and, when necessary, to make the transition back to the civilian world.

REFERENCES

Basham, K. (2008). Homecoming as a safe haven or the new front: Attachment and detachment in military couples. *Clinical Social Work Journal, 36*, 83–96.

Bourg, C., & Segal, M. W. (1999, Summer). The impact of family supportive policies and practices on organizational commitment to the Army. *Armed Forces and Society, 25*, 633–652.

Bowling, U. B., & Sherman, M. D. (2008). Welcoming them home: Supporting service members and their families in navigating the tasks of reintegration. *Professional Psychology: Research and Practice, 39*, 451–458.

Christian, J. R., Stivers, J. R., & Sammons, M. T. (2009). Training to the warrior ethos: Implications for clinicians treating military members and their families. In S. M. Freeman, B. A. Moore, & A. Freeman (Eds.), *Living and surviving in harm's way: A psychological treatment handbook for pre-and post-deployment of military personnel* (pp. 27–49). New York: Routledge, Taylor and Francis Group.

Conroy, P. (1991). Introduction. In M. E. Wertsch, *Military brats: Legacies of childhood inside the fortress* (pp. xvii-xxv). St. Louis, MO: Brightwell. (Original work published by Harmony Books)

Corrigan, P. (2004, October). How stigma interferes with mental health care. *American Psychologist, 59*, 614–625.

Dahn, V. L. (2008, October). Silent service in the soldier's shadow. *Counseling Today, 51*(4), 55–57.

Durand, D. (2000). The role of the senior military wife—then and now. In J. S. Martin, L. N. Rosen, & L. R. Sparcino (Eds.), *The military family: A practice guide for human service providers* (pp. 73–86). Westport, CT: Praeger.

Erbes, C. R., Polusny, M. A., MacDermid, S., & Compton, J. S. (2008). Couple therapy with combat veterans and their partners. *Journal of Clinical Psychology: In Session, 64*, 972–983.

Everson, R. B., & Camp, T. G. (2011). An introduction to systemic approaches with military families. In R. B. Everson & C. R. Figley (Eds.), *Families under fire: Systemic therapy with military families* (pp. 3–29). New York: Routledge, Taylor and Francis Group.

Faber, A. J., Willerton, E., Clymer, S. R., MacDermid, S. M., & Weiss, H. M. (2008). Ambiguous absence, ambiguous presence: A qualitative study of military reserve families in wartime. *Journal of Family Psychology, 2*, 222–230.

Fenell, D. (2008, June). A distinct culture: Applying multicultural counseling competencies to work with military personnel. *Counseling Today, 50*(12), 8–9, 35.

Fenell, D. L., & Weinhold, B. K. (2003). *Counseling families: An introduction to marriage and family therapy* (3rd ed.). Denver, CO: Love.

Gegax, T. T., & Thomas, E. (2005, June 20). The family business. *Newsweek, 145*(25), 24–31.

Gilligan, J. (1996). *Violence: Reflections on a national epidemic.* New York: Random House.

Hall, L. K. (2008). *Counseling military families: What mental health professionals need to know.* New York: Routledge, Taylor and Francis Group.

Hall, L. K. (2011). The military culture, language, and lifestyle. In R. B. Everson & C. R. Figley (Eds.), *Families under fire: Systemic therapy with military families* (pp. 31–52). New York: Routledge, Taylor and Francis Group.

Henderson, K. (2006). *While they're at war: The true story of American families on the homefront.* New York: Houghton-Mifflin.

Houppert, K. (2005). *Home fires burning: Married to the military—for better or worse.* New York: Ballantine Books.

Keith, D. V., & Whitaker, C. A. (1984). C'est la Guerre: Military families and family therapy. In F. W. Kaslow & R. I. Ridenour (Eds.), *The military family: Dynamics and treatment* (pp. 147–166). New York: Guilford Press.

Martin, J. A., & McClure, P. (2000). Today's active duty military family: The evolving challenges of military family life. In J. A. Martin, L. N. Rosen, & L. R. Sparacino (Eds.), *The military family: A practice guide for human service providers* (pp. 3–24). Westport, CT: Praeger.

McKay, G. D., & Maybell, S. A. (2004). *Calming the family story: Anger management for moms, dads, and all the kids.* Atascadero, CA: Impact.

Mejia, Z. E. (2005). Gender matters: Working with adult male survivors of trauma. *Journal of Counseling and Development*, 83(2), 29–40.

Military culture. (2008). In *Encyclopedia of Violence, Peace and Conflict.* Retrieved January 18, 2011, from http://www.credoreference.com/entry/estpeace/military_culture

Nash, W. P. (2007). The stressors of war. In C. R. Figley & W. P. Nash (Eds.), *Combat stress injury: Theory, research and management* (pp. 11–32). New York: Routledge, Taylor and Francis Group.

National Child Traumatic Stress Network. (2009, November). *NCCTS leadership: Military children and families.* (2009, November). Retrieved January 18, 2011, from http://www.NCTSN.org/sites/default/files/assets/pdfs/MilitaryFamilies_Info-Brief_FINAL.pdf

Park, N. (2011, January). Military children and families: Strengths and challenges during peace and war. *American Psychologist, 66*(1), 65–72.

Reger, M. A., Etherage, J. R., Reger, G. M., & Gahm, G. A. (2008). Civilian psychologists in an Army culture: The ethical challenge of cultural competence. *Military Psychology, 20*, 21–35.

Russo, T. M., Dougherty, L. M., & Martin, J. A. (2000). Military spouse employment: Challenges and opportunities. In J. S. Martin, L. N. Rosen, & L. R. Sparcino (Eds.), *The military family: A practice guide for human service providers* (pp. 87–102). Westport, CT: Praeger.

Sherwood, E. (2009). Clinical assessment of Canadian military marriages. *Clinical Social Work Journal, 37*, 332–339.

Smith, G. W., (2011). Attachment as a consideration in family play therapy with military families. In R. B. Everson & C. R. Figley (Eds.), *Families under fire: Systemic therapy with military families* (pp. 153–165). New York: Routledge.

Sneath, L., & Rheem, K. D. (2011). The use of emotionally focused couples therapy with military couples and families. In R. B. Everson & C. R. Figley (Eds.), *Families under fire: Systemic therapy with military families* (pp. 127–151). New York: Routledge.

Wertsch, M. E. (1991). *Military brats: Legacies of childhood inside the fortress.* St. Louis, MO: Brightwell. (Originally published by Harmony Books)

9

Separation and Divorce

WALTER R. SCHUMM, R. ROUDI NAZARINIA ROY,
and VANCE THEODORE

INTRODUCTION

The military is a unique system that is very demanding of its members and their families; in return, it can give them a sense of community, social support structures, and economic stability. Only a few decades ago, the U.S. military included mostly single young men; today, most members are part of families (Booth et al., 2007, p. 12). Therefore, counseling with military members will often involve partners, spouses, or children as significant others. The numerous pressures of military life, in an era of persistent conflict (Casey, 2011) can lead to serious conflicts among significant others, possibly leading to formal separations or divorce. Laser and Stephens (2011) have indicated that "there is a growing need for mental health providers in and outside the military" (p. 29), citing estimates of more than 300,000 service members suffering from posttraumatic stress disorder (PTSD) and/or traumatic brain injury (TBI) (p. 33). However, referring to the multiple problems often faced by military families (including financial problems, role conflicts, children's reactions, PTSD, depression, multiple injuries, relocations, deployments, etc.), Sayers (2011) stated, "Existing treatments do not fully address how to help service members and their families with this level of complexity" (p. 108). Perhaps, as a consequence, at least some interventions have apparently proved ineffective. For example, in a study of 133 active-duty Army personnel stationed in Korea who had deployed to combat zones, Kotlowski (2010) found that military programs designed to help soldiers manage deployment stress did not appear to reduce divorce rates.

What should a counselor know about separation and divorce with respect to military clients? First, we discuss the state of knowledge about divorce in the military, highlighting some of the current controversies. Second, we discuss some implications for counselors, along with suggestions for deeper study. Accordingly, we begin by addressing some of the empirical realities of separation and divorce in the military, as well as some of the underlying causes, especially as they relate to overseas deployments and family separations. When evaluating reported divorce rates, it may be helpful to keep in mind that national U.S. data indicate a divorce rate of 2–4% per year for young couples (Raley & Bumpass, 2003), that is, about a 30% divorce rate at the first 10-year mark of heterosexual unions. Although some research on combat stress and family life has been reported for veterans of Vietnam and previous wars (Call & Teachman, 1991, 1996; Card, 1983; Frey-Wouters & Laufer, 1986; Kulka, Schlenger, Fairbank, Hough, Jordan, Marmar.... Grady, 1990; Laufer & Gallop, 1985; Ruger, Wilson, & Waddoups, 2002), our focus in this chapter will be on the aftermath of wars after 1990.

RESEARCH: SEPARATION AND DIVORCE IN THE MILITARY

More Deployments/More Family Separation

Military families are having to deal with family separation issues more than ever. Most scholars recognize that military families have been exposed to tremendous stress since 2001, with more and longer deployments (Booth et al., 2007; Karney & Crown, 2011). Booth et al. (2007) noted, "Army family life today is characterized by more frequent and less predictable separation than it used to be" (p. 29), a quotation reiterated by Spera (2009, p. 288). Many U.S. service members have been spending more time deployed away from home than at home (Huebner, Mancini, Bowen, & Orthner, 2009). Park (2011) described lengthy deployments of service members to combat zones as the "major challenge for military children and families during war" (p. 67). Reviews of the literature generally conclude that families perceive deployment-related separation as one of their greatest emotional challenges (Padden, Connors, & Agazio, 2011). Gottman, Gottman, and Atkins (2011) have detailed many of the specific relationship challenges faced today by families of deployed military members. Of course, not all families have the social resources needed to manage deployment separation effectively (Orthner & Rose, 2003). When families find deployments unmanageable, such family concerns can have an adverse impact on the morale or combat effectiveness of the deployed service members (Warner, Appenzeller, Warner, & Grieger, 2009). Accordingly, it would be natural to wonder what the consequences have been as a result of these changes. Some consequences are clear; others are less so.

Marriage and Divorce in the Military

Numerous research studies have reported higher separation and divorce rates in the military as compared to the civilian population (Adler-Baeder, Pittman, & Taylor, 2005; Gimbel & Booth, 1994; Hogan & Seifert, 2010; Lundquist, 2007; Stellman, Stellman, & Sommer, 1988). Females in the military have been reported to have higher divorce rates than their male counterparts (Adler-Baeder et al., 2005; Karney & Crown, 2007). Lundquist (2007), in an analysis of longitudinal data for enlisted military personnel compared to civilians, found that veterans were more likely to divorce, with women more likely to divorce than men (for both civilians and veterans). Pollard, Karney, and Loughran (2008) found that military service was associated with higher rates of marriage and lower rates of divorce for men, but higher rates of divorce for women; after leaving the military, both male and female veterans had higher rates of divorce than civilian counterparts. Hogan and Seifert (2010) found that military service was associated with both higher rates of marriage and higher rates of divorce, using data from the 2005 American Community Survey. However, rates of divorce might be associated with military service but not with deployment experience.

Deployments and Divorce: The Controversy

Combat exposure and longer or multiple military deployments have been strongly linked to psychological outcomes (Booth et al., 2007, p. 38; McFarlane, 2009; Reger, Gahm, Swanson, & Duma, 2009; Rona et al., 2007), especially for Reserve Component soldiers (Laser & Stephens, 2011; Milliken, Auchterlonie, & Hoge, 2007; Renshaw, Rodrigues, & Jones, 2009; Tollefson, 2008). In particular, deployments of more than a year (Booth et al., 2007; McFarlane, 2009) or of unknown length (Spera, 2009) seem to be especially challenging for families. The fact that deployments are stressful on families is undisputed (Karney & Crown, 2011, p. 26). However difficult deployments might be for military members or their family members as *individuals*, it might not necessarily be true that deployments would be associated with increased divorce rates for military *couples*. For example, Karney and Crown (2011) have cited Bell and Schumm (2000) for lack of evidence linking deployments to higher divorce rates and have cited Schumm, Hemesath, Bell, Palmer-Johnson, and Elig (1996) for lack of evidence linking deployment to declines in marital satisfaction.

The RAND Report

Evidence along those lines appeared in a report (Karney & Crown, 2007) released from the RAND National Defense Research Institute (NDRI). Results from the RAND report indicated that the longer service members were deployed for the wars in Iraq and Afghanistan, the *lower* their chances of divorce. That result was interpreted as a rejection of the so-called stress hypothesis, which would predict that stressful deployments would lead to higher divorce rates. In contrast, the results were taken as support for the selection hypothesis, in which individuals at higher risk for divorce were more likely to join the military or to marry veterans. For example, demographic factors such as earlier age at marriage, minority race/ethnicity, and lower education levels have been consistent predictors of divorce across multiple studies (Sweeney & Phillips, 2004), and military members would appear to often have similar risk factors. The tremendous impact of the Karney and Crown (2007) RAND report is clear, as it has been cited favorably numerous times (Behnke, MacDermid, Anderson, & Weiss, 2010; Hogan & Seifert, 2010; Huebner et al., 2009; Monson, Fredman, & Taft, 2011; Orthner & Rose, 2009; Sayers, 2011;

Sayers, Farrow, Ross, & Oslin, 2009), as well as being summarized in a book chapter (Karney & Crown, 2011).

DEPLOYMENTS AND DIVORCE: ALTERNATIVE RESEARCH

Given the scholarly acceptance granted the RAND report, some might suppose that the relationship between military deployments and marital outcomes, despite media interest or lay acceptance, was now a dead issue. However, there have been a number of research projects that have detected an association between deployments and declines in either marital stability or marital satisfaction or related outcomes; some of these studies have not previously been published.

Published Studies

Rosen and Durand (2000b) surveyed 776 soldiers of 1,274 who had participated in a predeployment survey before Operations Desert Shield/Storm (ODS/S); they found that 7% had divorced by the spring of 1992, while another 14% were considering divorce (5% said they had been considering divorce before the war). Using data from a 1992 survey of 1,064 civilian wives of soldiers who had been deployed for ODS/S, Pittman, Kerpelman, and McFadyen (2004) found that perceived coping with deployments during ODS/S predicted both internal family adaptation (including measures of marital quality) and external family adaptation (including satisfaction or family fit with Army life). Adler-Baeder et al. (2005) used census data and several military surveys to conclude that military personnel were more likely to marry and to divorce than comparable civilians, with female service members more likely to avoid marriage and to divorce than male service members; enlisted personnel were more likely to divorce than officers.

Burrell, Adams, Durand, and Castro (2006) analyzed data from 346 military spouses stationed in Europe in 2002 (13% response rate). They used four items to measure the perceived impact of deployments: "The separations from my spouse are stressful," "The number of deployments has put a strain on our family," "The number of deployments has hurt the stability of our marriage," and "I worry about the effects of my spouse's deploying on our children" (p. 47). Norton's (1983) Quality of Marriage Index was used to measure marital satisfaction. They found that perceived deployment impact significantly and negatively predicted psychological well-being, physical well-being, satisfaction with Army life, and marital satisfaction.

McLeland and Sutton (2005) and McLeland, Sutton, and Schumm (2008) found limited evidence of lower marital satisfaction among military personnel preparing for or having returned from a deployment, compared to civilian counterparts. Orthner and Rose (2009), using data from 8,056 female spouses of soldiers (43% response rate), found that number of months separated in the past 3 years significantly predicted lower psychological well-being, while age, informal social support, and comfort working with formal support systems predicted better well-being. They noticed some nonlinear patterns (a significant quadratic effect) between deployment and adjustment.

The Survey of Total Army Military Personnel Study of the ODS/S Deployment

Previous research reports have had numerous limitations, including low response rates, a cross-sectional rather than a longitudinal design, and unclear links between some of their key variables. Fortunately, some longitudinal data were available to the authors that have not been widely available elsewhere. To investigate the effects of ODS/S deployments, in late 1991 through early 1992, the U.S. Army Research Institute implemented a Survey of Total Army Military Personnel (STAMP), mailed to a stratified random sample of 22,264 veterans, of whom 6,516 officers and 4,741 enlisted personnel responded, an overall response rate of 50.7% (Schumm, Tiggle, Bright, Bell, & Gade, 1996). Nonrespondents were mailed follow-up surveys in April and May 1992; data collection was completed by the end of July 1992. Our analyses here were restricted to personnel who retrospectively reported having been married as of August 1, 1990, 68.8% of the officers and 60.0% of the enlisted personnel (the sample also included those who were dating, engaged, or not involved romantically).

Independent variables included gender, race (white/minority), ethnicity (Hispanic/non-Hispanic), rank (officer/enlisted), deployment status (deployed overseas/did not deploy during ODS/S), marital status (remarried/first marriage), and marital instability as of August 1, 1990 (unstable meant the veteran indicated that his or her marriage was in trouble or that they had been thinking about or discussing getting a divorce). Single-item measures (with seven response categories) of current marital satisfaction as well as retrospective marital satisfaction as of August 1, 1990, were also available. One advantage of the data was that it included a substantial number of female veterans, a group that needs much further research (Cohen & Segal, 2009, p. 35).

Predicting Marital Instability The first research question involved predicting marital instability (separation, legal separation, or divorce, paralleling the inclusive approach used by Karney and Crown, 2007, 2011) from prior instability, ethnicity, race, gender, rank, marital status, and deployment status, using binary logistic regression ($N = 6{,}743$, Nagelkerke $R^2 = 0.242$). Race and ethnicity were not significant. Instability was predicted from being in a remarriage (odds ratio [OR] = 1.35, 95% confidence interval [CI] 1.04–1.74, $p < .05$); enlisted rank (OR = 2.08, 95% CI 1.63–2.66, $p < .001$); female gender (OR = 1.98, 95% CI 1.54–2.55, $p < .001$); predeployment instability (OR = 12.73, 95% CI 10.1–16.1, $p < .001$); and having been deployed (OR = 1.77, 95% CI 1.40–2.25, $p < .001$). Deployment did significantly predict marital instability, controlling for the other predictors, but prior instability was the strongest predictor.

For example, female veterans who deployed had a 14.1% marital instability rate, compared to 6.7% for those who did not deploy (one-sided Fisher exact test, $p < .001$), compared to 5.4% and 3.5%, respectively, for male veterans (one-sided Fisher exact test, $p < .002$). Those with unstable marriages who deployed had a 28.8% instability rate, compared to 25.0% for those who did not deploy (n.s.), while those with stable marriages who deployed had a 3.7% instability rate, compared to 1.9% for those who did not deploy (one-sided Fisher exact test, $p < .001$). If we combine the best of all combinations (male officers in first and stable marriages), deployment made a difference of 1.9% versus 0.7% instability (one-sided Fisher exact test, $p < .02$); if we combine the worst of all combinations (female enlisted in unstable remarriages), deployment made a difference of 61.5% versus 34.4% (one-sided Fisher exact test, $p < .10$).

Causes for Marital Instability Another research question was whether the veterans themselves viewed increases in instability as caused by ODS/S. Veterans were asked if each type of instability had been caused by ODS/S. Of the 2,308 veterans who had deployed, 158 (6.8%) reported marital instability. Of those reporting instability, 109 (69%) blamed ODS/S. Of the 4,697 veterans who had not deployed, 207 (4.4%) reported marital instability. Discounting the 109 deployed veterans who blamed ODS/S for their marital instability, the instability rate would have been 2.2% (49/2,199). In other words, the higher instability rates among veterans did not just occur without explanation; the veterans themselves attributed much of that instability to their deployment for ODS/S.

Changes in Marital Satisfaction The next research question was whether deployment status would predict a perceived change in marital satisfaction, that is, predict current marital satisfaction, controlling for marital satisfaction as of August 1, 1990, among those whose marriages had been stable. Using linear multiple regression, for only those veterans whose marriages were stable ($N = 6,129$), the only significant predictors were prior marital satisfaction ($b = .69$, $p < .001$) and prior instability ($b = -.04$, $p < .001$), with adjusted $R^2 = 0.500$. Neither deployment status nor marital status, rank, race, ethnicity, or gender significantly predicted current marital satisfaction. Thus, while deployment predicted significantly greater risks of marital instability, it did not appear to predict declines in marital satisfaction among those veterans whose marriages were stable. Paradoxically, deployment effects were more often significant among veterans with more favorable relationship characteristics, while absolute rates of instability (regardless of deployment status) were much higher for veterans with less-favorable relationship characteristics.

Other Army Research Institute Deployment Studies

In a study of a deployment to Bosnia from U.S. Army units in Italy, it was observed that about 5–10% of the spouses reported improved mental health while their soldiers were deployed, apparently because they received less emotional or physical abuse while their soldiers were absent (Bell et al., 1997), a finding that further indicated the complexities of assessing the impact of deployments. In other words, adverse effects of deployments for well-adjusted families could be partly masked by the welcome effects of deployments for dysfunctional families.

In a true longitudinal study (August/October 1995 to January 1997) of soldiers deployed to the Sinai desert for a peacekeeping operation, we found that 21% of the marriages ended between the start of the deployment and a telephone survey nearly 2 years later (Schumm, Bell, & Gade, 2000). Subsequent conversations with unit members of that deployment suggested that low morale associated with poor unit leadership may have enhanced the risks to marriages for that particular mission. However, similar to what we found with the STAMP data, marital satisfaction after the Sinai deployment appeared to recover from any declines during deployment, after discounting marriages that ended.

Fort Riley and Fort Leavenworth Deployment Studies

In unpublished quasi-longitudinal studies of veterans from Fort Riley (Schumm, Crock, Likcani, Akagi, & Bosch, 2008) and Fort Leavenworth, Kansas, we have found that divorce rates were significantly higher among those soldiers who had been deployed than among those who had not, and that deployment experience featured a curvilinear relationship with marital instability, which peaked at about two or three deployments, lower for both fewer and for more deployments. We also observed that the perceived risk of divorce was most strongly correlated with recency of reunion, that those who had just returned from their deployments were most likely to expect their marriage to end in divorce than were those who had been back for longer periods of time.

Deployments and Marital Outcomes: Conclusions

We conclude that deployments do, on average, have an adverse impact on marital stability but that those effects occur within a matrix of other, often more important, factors, including no doubt many positive factors (increased pay, tax incentives, greater sense of purpose, helping local citizens, etc.) (Sayers, 2011; Sundin et al., 2010). Even so, if there are positive factors, their presence may statistically suppress evidence for underlying negative factors, which may account for the mixed results seen in the literature. If marriages survive reunion, their quality usually returns to predeployment levels or better. While weaker marriages are much more likely to dissolve after a deployment, even strong marriages entail significantly greater divorce risks after a deployment, although absolute levels of risk are much lower. Because military service remains voluntary in the U.S. military, those couples who find they cannot cope well with frequent deployments are probably "voting with their feet" and leaving the military, which may account for the curvilinear patterns that we and others (Orthner & Rose, 2009) have observed. One way to reconcile Karney and Crown's (2011) predominantly null findings with their sense that the media and many laypersons believe that deployments do increase divorce may lie in our finding of "pockets" of high divorce for either selected units that had low morale (Schumm et al., 2000) or more vulnerable subgroups within the overall military population, as discussed. However, Karney and Crown's (2007, 2011) results may be an artifact of legal restrictions regarding divorce while military members are deployed; those who are not deployed can arrange divorce at their convenience, but those who are deployed must wait until they return.

Implications of Separation/Divorce Research for Counselors

Our results led to implications for counselors working with military couples considering divorce. First, couples who feel that military stress has complicated their family relationships are not imagining the stress or are uninformed about the consequences of stress. Despite some evidence for the selection hypothesis, we believe there are also data that support the stress hypothesis. Second, some couples may prefer to give priority to their family life and change from military to civilian careers; they should not be shamed for making such decisions. Some families may simply find adaptation to military demands too difficult to manage effectively. That does not mark them as "bad" couples; in fact, some relationships of lower apparent quality may seem to achieve a better "fit" with military life than other relationships. In other words, not "fitting in" might be a sign of strength rather than of weakness. Third, there is much hope that if marriages can survive the difficult moments after reunion and avoid divorce, predeployment levels of quality or satisfaction are likely to be regained, which may be a "vote" against hasty decisions in favor of divorce. However, even if marriages were viewed as "in trouble" or unstable before a deployment, their chances of breaking up were still less than 30%; at the same time, even among marriages not seen as "in trouble" or unstable, nearly 4% broke up, despite the much more favorable circumstances. Thus, apparent trouble does not guarantee divorce; an apparent lack of problems also does not guarantee that divorce will be avoided. Consequently, stereotypes should be taken less than seriously.

We think the best evidence indicates that family separation and deployments are associated with higher levels of divorce, albeit through intervening factors such as combat stress and subsequent mental health developments. So, why are individuals who have served in the military divorcing at a higher rate than their civilian counterparts? What is it about military life that can lead to higher rates of divorce? It is important to emphasize that divorce is not a singular event but rather a process. As such, it is important to remember that there is no one absolute reason for any military member to divorce, but rather there can be multiple reasons or cumulative effects. For that reason, we want to explore some of the underlying causes of separation and divorce that are unique to military service members and their families.

UNDERLYING CAUSES OF SEPARATION AND DIVORCE

Age at Marriage

In general, young age at marriage is one of the strongest demographic predictors of divorce (Karney & Crown, 2011; Sweeney & Phillips, 2004). In research comparing military personnel ages 23 to 25 to their civilian counterparts and controlling for sex, age, race, and education levels, Hogan and Seifert (2010) found that military personal were three times more likely to be married. Karney and Crown (2011) found that older age at marriage predicted a lower divorce rate across most branches of service of the U.S. military. However, Karney and Crown (2011, p. 37) found that "younger" (based on age at marriage, not duration of marriage) marriages were less likely to divorce after deployments than were "older" marriages.

Because the military allows even 17-year-olds to enlist, with parental permission, it creates a condition in which someone with only a secondary education can immediately accept employment with a moderate salary and unmatched health and vacation benefits. If a service member marries, the individual is often entitled to an additional tax-free housing allowance or to free housing with utilities at a very low cost. Pregnancy and newborn care are covered as well.

Findings suggest that men are more likely to get married when they earn more and have greater economic stability (Loyd & South, 1996; Oppenheimer, 2003; Sweeney, 2002; Teachman, Polonko, & Leigh, 1987). Phillips and colleagues (1992) reported that the income available to recruits, for example, is higher than they could earn in the civilian world, and perhaps this is what makes military service more appealing to new recruits. Hogan and Seifert (2010) have suggested that the compensation that married military personal receive in both monetary resources and in-kind resources may promote earlier entry into marriage. Financial barriers that might intimidate nonmilitary youth from marrying or having children are much weaker for military members. The risk, of course, is that they will enter into marriage or parenthood prematurely for their level of emotional maturity. Some may marry before a deployment as part of an extended "friends-with-benefits" arrangement, in which the benefits might include free rent, medical care, and insurance benefits (if the service member is killed on duty) for the time the service member is deployed. Some may marry in haste to provide more of a reason to come back alive or to enjoy married life at least briefly in case they do not come back from combat alive. The implication is that counselors may wish to ask about the reasons for the marriage, which may be other than for "love."

Emotional/Sexual Infidelity

Sayers (2011) reports, "Infidelity is a common concern among military service members and their spouses in wartime deployments" (p. 112). An Army brigade commander deployed to Afghanistan made the news after being relieved of command in the aftermath of a lurid affair and divorce (Gould, 2011). Less has been researched on this topic in the military because of its sensitivity. However, some commanders, and even chaplains, may condone sexual activities overseas that would not be accepted within the United States (what happens in Iraq stays in Iraq). Aside from the availability of some local nationals or fellow comrades for sexual interaction, Internet access to pornography can create issues of emotional fidelity. Even when nothing has occurred, unit rumors can create such appearances. Service members will probably be exposed overseas to unfamiliar cultural norms and practices regarding sexuality, challenging their traditional assumptions. Just knowing that one's husband lives on a military base overseas complete with, for example, a swimming pool and bikini-clad female service members might create anxiety in the most trusting of wives. Some local nationals may view enticement of an American as their ticket to political freedom and a remarkably improved socioeconomic status. Even though we know less about these issues from a research perspective, there are plenty of complications for family conflicts and counselor concern.

Traumatic Brain Injury

Marital adjustment after TBI has become a concern (Blais & Boisvert, 2005, 2007; Hammond, Davis, Whiteside, Philbrick, & Hirsch, 2011). Arango-Lasprilla et al. (2008) have reported that "TBI often causes high levels of stress and strain on family relationships" (p. 566). In a research study conducted by Kreutzer, Marwitz, Hsu, Williams, and Riddick (2007), it was claimed that brain injury did not predict a higher risk of separation or divorce. With a sample of 120 individuals who had sustained mild, moderate, or severe brain injury, Kreutzer et al. (2007) found that 17% divorced and 8% separated over a period of 30 to 96 months. Arango-Lasprilla et al. (2008) followed 976 individuals with moderate-to-severe TBI and found that, over 2 years, 15% had divorced or separated (nearly 13% of Caucasians, over 20% of minorities). However, one study of 626 veterans with mild brain injuries found that after an average of 8 years, marriage rates were much lower—rather than in a range of 63–74% for veterans without head injuries or any motor vehicle accidents, they ranged as low as 29% (Vanderploeg, Curtiss, Duchnick, & Luis, 2003, p. 158). Another study found a 49% marriage failure rate, with marriages most likely to end approximately 5–6 years after the TBI incident (Wood & Yurdakul, 1997). The most recent review of TBI treatment (Godwin, Kreutzer, Arango-Lasprilla, & Lehan, 2011) recommends the use of marriage and family relational models along with standard medical and rehabilitation interventions.

Combat Exposure and PTSD

It appears to be well established that combat is associated with subsequent risk of mental health concerns (Walker, 2010; Wells et al., 2010). Combat-related PTSD has been linked to family adjustment problems (Galovski & Lyons, 2004; Laufer & Gallops, 1985; Monson, Taft, & Fredman, 2009). Monson et al. (2011) have argued that combat exposure rather than deployment may better explain divorce among military veterans. Research has highlighted some specifics about current family problems being experienced by recent war veterans. For example, of 754 veterans receiving Veterans Affairs (VA) medical care, Sayer, Noorbaloochi, Frazier, Carlson, Gravely, and Murdoch (2010) found that 35% had experienced divorce or separation problems since returning from combat in Iraq or Afghanistan. More specifically, Sayers, Farrow, Ross, and Oslin (2009) found that, among 199 combat veterans who had been referred for VA care, 36% had been divorced, while among those still married, 56% reported a troubled relationship—only 22% reported no family issues. Jordan et al. (1992) found that, within a sample of 967 male Vietnam veterans, of whom 231 (24%) had PTSD, those with PTSD were six times more likely to report a high level of marital problems (49% vs. 9%, $p < .001$).

In a small sample of 47 Vietnam veterans, Hendrix, Jurich, and Schumm (1995) found some significant relationships between combat exposure, especially the witnessing of atrocities (Sareen et al., 2007), and family environment as many as 15 years after Vietnam. Riggs, Byrne, Weathers, and Litz (1998) found that among a sample of 50 couples in which the man was a Vietnam veteran, 72% of those veterans with a PTSD diagnosis were distressed on the Dyadic Adjustment Scale

(Spanier, 1976) compared to 24% of those veterans without that diagnosis ($p < .005$); scores on a measure of marital stability were similar between the two groups ($p < .05$). Dekel, Goldblatt, Keidar, Solomon, and Polliack (2005) found that civilian wives of military personnel suffering from PTSD often thought about divorce, but fear of how their husbands would react deterred them from filing. Cohan, Cole, and Davila (2005) studied matched groups of Navy aviators who had been or not been prisoners of war, finding that the former prisoners of war (POWs) had higher rates of divorce, especially within the first 2 years after their repatriation. Sayer et al. (2010) found that Iraq/Afghanistan veterans diagnosed with PTSD were significantly ($OR = 2.21$, 95% CI 1.37–3.56, $p < .05$) more likely to report divorce or separation since homecoming (46% vs. 27%) than similar veterans without PTSD. In a study of 473 Israeli veterans, Solomon, Debby-Aharon, Zerach, and Horesh (2011) found that PTSD predicted lower marital adjustment among war veterans as many as 20 years after their combat experiences.

DEPLOYMENT ISSUES AND INTERVENTIONS

Phases of Deployments

Many mental health specialists have come to define deployment in terms of at least three phases (Kalamdien, 2008; Kalamdien & Van Dyk, 2009; Laser & Stephens, 2011). Each phase of deployment—before, during, and after—presents its own challenges. Booth et al. (2007) have summarized much of what we know from research about the issues associated with each phase. Sometimes before a deployment, couples will fight, as part of the emotional separation process, without understanding what is happening and with anger masking underlying anxiety and pain (Laser & Stephens, 2011). There is often an inherent conflict as the spouse wants to hold on while the service member is reorienting toward the mission as part of increasing chances of survival. Furthermore, most service members enjoy their jobs and look forward to doing them under challenging conditions (game day). Spouses will be split between appreciating their service member's enthusiasm for going and their own emotional loss at their absence. There may be impulsive actions, to live life fully before the service member departs (Laser & Stephens, 2011). As much as possible, families should write down key information on questions or problems that may arise during the deployment (emergency phone numbers, where to get things repaired, where key documents are located, etc.). As always, unit leadership plays a critical role at this time, keeping families informed of deployment dates (and changes), affirming their commitment to family support, and encouraging public support for the mission (Bell & Schumm, 2000). Cacioppo, Reis, and Zautra (2011) recommend that soldiers and families develop social resilience, which includes a capacity and motivation to perceive others accurately and empathically, to feel connected with others, to communicate respect and caring, to recognize others' regard for yourself, to value the welfare of both yourself and others, to respond appropriately in a timely way to social problems, to express social emotions effectively, to trust others, and to be tolerant and open to others.

During deployment, new routines will have to be established at home. Depending on the level of communications available in the war zone, it may be sooner or later before the service member can make contact with home by e-mail, telephone, or other means (Bell, Schumm, Knott, & Ender, 1999; Schumm, Bell, Ender, & Rice, 2004). Spouses may resent having to play the single-parent role ("I did not get married so I could be a single parent!"). Easy access to news about casualties in the combat zone can keep spouses on edge continually, worrying if their service member is safe. Anxiety attends not only their possible death but also, perhaps worse, severe brain injuries or loss of limbs, so that the service member who returns is far from the same person who left, aside from any psychological injuries or changes associated with combat exposure or cultural encounters. Research suggests that maintaining a positive attitude, focusing on what you can control, developing individual and family goals, maintaining family routines, remaining active, seeking social support from constructive sources, keeping communication open with the deployed service member, and evaluating rumors carefully are helpful behaviors (Bell & Schumm, 2000). Unit family readiness or support groups are often helpful, but some are dysfunctional or ineffective (Booth et al., 2007, p. 41; Laser & Stephens, 2011, p. 32) and may be best avoided. Unit leaders should do their best to limit damaging rumors, provide communication access to and from families, and provide accurate and timely information on the deployment, including return dates and procedures (Bell & Schumm, 2000). It appears best if deployments are kept to under a year (Booth et al., 2007, p. 46), but, of course, that is beyond the control of families or counselors.

After deployment, it is likely that both partners will want a "vacation" at the same time, even though there may be much household work to be caught up. Even under the best of circumstances, the service member may finally have a chance to admit to their exhaustion and want to spend much time catching up on sleep—at the same time that his or her spouse and family want them to catch up on just about everything else. If a child was born just before the deployment or just after, the child may resent the return of the other parent (Who is this?), giving a lukewarm reception (Sayers, 2011, p. 109), which may greatly disappoint the service member and lead to years of misunderstanding, especially if other children are more delighted to have their other parent back home. It may take several months, even years, for children to reestablish emotional bonds with the service member (Laser & Stephens, 2011, p. 33). The horrors of war may be something the service member feels uncomfortable sharing with the family, but at the same time, this makes him or her seem distant and uncommunicative. Even so, the service member has most likely lived for months in crisis mode, in which even simple mistakes can lead to serious injury or death. The service member can "blow up" at what may seem like small matters to the family. Accustomed to instant obedience from subordinates during crises, the service member may be astonished and feel threatened when family members are not so responsive. Intermediate military leaders often carry a great deal of guilt if they have lost unit members who were under their care and protection. Survivor guilt is another possibility (Laser & Stephens, 2011, p. 34).

One example of postwar adjustment involves driving habits. To survive IED (improvised explosive device) and sniper attacks in Iraq, soldiers had to drive unpredictably and aggressively, habits that are less-functional back home (Sayers, 2011, p. 110). Sayer et al. (2010) found that 35% of the veterans surveyed in their study reported dangerous driving noticed by others.

If the service member is affected by PTSD, he or she may show detachment, emotional unavailability, a lack of impulse control, overactive startle reflex, emotional numbing, and lack of interest, which will complicate reintegration with their family (Laser & Stephens, 2011, p. 34; McFarlane, 2009; Solomon et al., 2011). Divorce rates are likely much higher for couples in which the service member returns with PTSD or brain injuries (Laser & Stephens, 2011, p. 36).

Sayers (2011) has explained that "the lowest point of marital satisfaction likely occurs from the 4th to the 9th month into the reintegration period" (p. 109). Unit leaders should help service members have realistic expectations about their return and provide time off as promised and as needed (Bell & Schumm, 2000). Doyle and Peterson (2005) have provided more information on postdeployment military programs.

SPECIAL COUNSELING ISSUES

Weak Use of Theory

Rosen, Teitelbaum, and Westhuis (1993) developed a theoretical model in which deployment factors, moderated by social support (including family support groups, rear detachments, unit leadership climate), influence perceived family stress, which influences psychological outcomes. In their survey of 1,274 military spouses (37% to 65% response rates by mail), they found empirical support for their model and that most of their model's variables were also predicted significantly by spouse's age (older doing better), soldier's rank (higher ranks doing better), and soldiers' training (better training doing better). Prior military experience, greater comfort dealing with Army agencies, better extended family support, and lower prior life stress also made positive contributions to the model. Padden et al. (2011) surveyed 105 female spouses of deployed Army soldiers and found that perceived stress was the strongest predictor of psychological well-being; they also found that younger wives whose husbands had fewer years of active duty experience reported more stress, and that optimistic coping was associated with lower stress levels. Deployment characteristics by themselves did not predict either stress or well-being.

Overall, research seems to suggest a theory in which duration of deployment is a relatively weak and distal factor compared to deployment experiences (combat, brain injury, emotional trauma), which predict deployment stress, which predicts a variety of psychological outcomes, which then influence postdeployment adjustment, which then may lead to separation or divorce. Attempting to model a direct path from duration of deployment to marital instability is a great leap over numerous intervening (and some moderating) variables. Counselors must avoid oversimplification of the processes involved before, during, and after deployments and recognize that almost none of the current research has attempted to evaluate even the modest theoretical model presented here.

Priorities: Family versus Military

Studies assessing family members' satisfaction with military life have consistently found that service members whose families are happy with military life are significantly more likely to reenlist compared with members whose families are less satisfied with military life (e.g., Bourg & Segal, 1999; Rosen & Durand, 2000a). However, for some couples, reunion issues may seem to boil down to a choice between the military as a career and the survival of the marriage or partnership. Either way, a couple may feel like they failed, being unable somehow to manage both simultaneously. However, shame is unwarranted. Some couples may have wonderful relationships that simply cannot be sustained at high-quality levels under a military environment. For other couples, the secret to military success may be *not* having the closest emotional relationship, which may provide better military-family "fit" even if it does not appear to promote the highest levels of relationship quality. Our research suggests that some couples do vote with their feet and leave the military after one or two deployments, while others figure out how to survive, even thrive, in spite of multiple, long separations. The counselor must be willing to work with each family to help them decide their own best courses of action.

Counselor Conflicts of Interest

Most counselors focus on the needs and goals of their clients. Some counselors may work with military families when being hired or paid by the military itself. Warner, Appenzeller, Grieger, Benedek, and Roberts (2009) have discussed some of the issues involved in cases of dual responsibility. Is the counselor working for the client or for the military? What if an outcome of treatment is that the family decides to leave the military—is that a betrayal of the military? Under what conditions will the counselor release private information to the military? What disclosures should the counselor make to the clients about the counselor's obligations to the military? Many service members and their families feel that receiving mental health support formally will stigmatize them and will jeopardize their military careers (Gould et al., 2010; Green-Shortridge, Britt, & Castro, 2007; Iversen et al., 2011; Laser & Stephens, 2011; Pietrzak, Johnson, Goldstein, Malley, & Southwick, 2009). Because of such stigma, many military clients bring their mental health concerns to primary care physicians (Eaton et al., 2008), possibly bypassing the specialists who could help them the most. Other couples, to minimize stigma, may use counselors who are not formally connected with the military. Counselors need to consider what to do to reduce such perceptions and to safeguard their clients' privacy interests.

Do Not Generalize

There is no single counseling approach that is appropriate for all clientele (Hall, 2008), and we believe there is no one family issue that brings all military families to seek professional support. Although military life can have an impact on the lives of military service members and their families in similar ways, it is important that we emphasize the existence of great diversity within military families. Since 1970, the military has become more diverse in terms of gender, race, and ethnicity (Martin & McClure, 2000), but it has also become more diverse in terms of other family issues. Not only do we see a higher portion of military service members with spouses and dependent children, but also there has been an increase in military wives working outside the home and dual-career military families (Rotter & Boveja, 1999). In the civilian population, issues of work and family can be taxing on a marriage, and it is important that the professional working with military families focus on the unique issues that each family brings to counseling rather than generalizing all families as simply having similar military issues.

Professional Resources

It would be presumptuous of us to pretend that everything a counselor might need to know about dealing with military clients could be presented in one chapter. First, there are numerous resources available for military members, usually at low or no cost. Moore, a clinical psychologist with two tours in Iraq (2011), listed some of them, including the following:

Military OneSource (http://www.militaryonesource.com; 800-342-9647), providing mental health and other referrals
Coming Home Project (http://www.cominghomeproject.net; 415-353-5363), providing support for combat veterans and their families before, during, and after deployments
Employer Support of the Guard and Reserve (http://www.esgr.org; 800-336-4590), helping to resolve employer-veteran conflicts
Disabled American Veterans (http://www.dav.org; 859-441-7300), for help for disabled veterans
Operation: Military Kids (http://www.operationmilitarykids.org), with information on resources for military children
National Veterans Foundation (http://www.nvf.org; 310-642-0255), with crisis management and referral services
Fallen Patriot Fund (http://www.fallenpatriotfund.org; 214-658-7125), for families of veterans killed or seriously wounded
Center for Women Veterans (http://www.va.gov/womenvet), with information for female veterans
National Suicide Prevention Lifeline (800-273-8255), with a toll-free 24-hour suicide crisis line with special help for veterans

Other Web sites of interest include Military Homefront (http://www.militaryhomefront.dod.mil), CareerOneStop resources for military spouses (http://www.careeronestop.org/militaryspouse), National Guard Family Program (http://www.jointservicessupport.org/FP), National Military Family Association (http://www.militaryfamily.org), and Patriot Outreach (http://www.PatriotOutreach.org).

ADVANCED THERAPIES

As mentioned, Sayers (2011) noted that current treatments do not fully take into account the entire complexity of challenges, problems, or stressors being faced by military families in the middle of persistent conflict (Casey, 2011). In fact, Sayers (2011) argued, "There is no existing research providing significant support for the use of any therapy for military couples with multiple comorbidities and problems" (p. 117). Most of the approaches for counseling military families appear now to be based on cognitive-behavioral models (Basham, 2008; Laser & Stephens, 2011), with some focused on PTSD (Fredman, Monson, & Adair, 2011). As recognized by Sayers (2011), Nelson-Goff and Smith (2005) have developed a model specifically focused on helping couples deal with wartime traumatic stress.

Sayers (2011, p. 115) recommended the use of behavioral couples therapy combined with psychoeducational approaches, including the Battlemind™ program (Laser & Stephens, 2011) developed by the U.S. Army, which was designed to help soldiers modify wartime responses to better reflect civilian conditions back home. The Complicated Family Reintegration Scale is also available as part of assessment of military families (Sayers, 2011). Laser and Stephens (2011) also cited the use of family-focused treatment (Miklowitz, 2008) with returning service members.

Monson et al. (2009) have developed a cognitive-behavioral conjoint therapy for PTSD designed to ameliorate the symptoms of PTSD and enhance relationships at the same time. Monson et al. (2009) also reported the use of Johnson's (2002) emotionally focused couples therapy (EFT) and the Army's Strong Bonds program for families (http://www.strongbonds.org), among others, as alternative approaches for working with veterans.

Stanley et al. (2005) have adapted the Prevention and Relationship Enhancement Program (PREP) for interventions with military families. Basham (2008) has followed up on an idea from Vormbrock (1993), to use attachment theory as a basis for interventions with military families.

The military has developed master resilience training in an attempt to prepare all soldiers for deployment stress (Reivich, Seligman, & McBride, 2011), although Basham (2008) viewed negative mental health outcomes as a risk after deployments, regardless of predeployment resilience. Sherman, Zanotti, and Jones (2005) have recommended combining Gottman's ideas (Gottman et al., 2011) with Johnson's (2002), as well as couple communication skills training and assessment for domestic violence, as part of a comprehensive treatment program. Pargament and Sweeney (2011) have recently discussed the role of spiritual factors in soldier resiliency.

CONCLUSIONS

Whether military deployments are associated with marital instability will remain controversial. However, it is clear that deployments involve higher risk of combat exposure, PTSD, and TBI, all of which have been linked at least in some research to higher rates of separation or divorce. Without doubt, the military environment is ripe with difficulties, challenges, and the complex issues that accompany separation, deployments, and the constant give and take of reintegration and the cyclical nature of training, and combat tours. Also, common in this environment is the collateral damage to soldiers and families caused by such events as PTSD, mild TBIs, and the secondary affects that families, spouses, and children experience from primary exposure (military personnel) to traumatic material. This traumatic material can affect marital relationships, job security, parent-child communication, and reintegration of soldiers, airmen and -women, sailors, and marines who have been engaged in and involved with hazardous environments for the last 10 years.

In this milieu of events to include issues of separation and divorce, the counselors with their training and their theories that help to guide individuals and families in a healing process are confronted with this complexity of effect. Complexity of effect for this chapter is defined for the counselor as the fabric of the military, which includes the stressful events and outcomes of these hazardous environments that influence the lives of the men and women who serve in the military. This fabric is complex in nature and requires an understanding of the military culture for the counselor to be effective in providing care that is appropriate and time sensitive.

This chapter primarily has focused on research, theories, and reports that have explained and detailed the effects of these events in the lives of military personnel. More specifically, it has focused on separation and divorce. However, counselors should take into consideration the following when working with a military population: culture, carryover effects, finding time for counseling, stigma, and complexity of effect.

Culture

What cultural issues (military) are presented by the clients? How am I taking into effect the context of the service member's experiences? What exposure to traumatic material has the client witnessed? What specific issues are particular to the client's military branch? For example, a soldier who has gone on 200 combat patrols will have different issues compared to an airman who is stationed in an airbase and provides support for air combat missions. Both individuals may have experienced traumatic material; however, exposure to traumatic events may be of a different degree. This in no way negates the experience of each individual but puts into context the environments in which military personnel provide support and in which they conduct combat missions.

Carryover Effects

Assessment tools and clarifying questions will help the counselor understand the complex environments from which military personnel operate and from which individuals can suffer from the effects of that environment. Of particular interest to the counselor should be the rank of the individual. Military personnel work in a hierarchical system. The duties and responsibilities of each system provide its own set of hazardous conditions. In today's military, there are no delineated lines of combat. This means that men and women can be affected by the trauma of hazardous duty. For example, many of the battlefield injuries come from IEDs. Most, if not all, of our military personnel in Afghanistan and Iraq experience the effects of mortar and shelling of their compounds. The constant need of hypervigilance and awareness of the situation can provide a steady source of stress that may not even be conscious, but on return may provide events that need to be dealt with (e.g., an individual who has a weapon constantly nearby for safety). This type of behavior is no longer needed but has become a conditioned response of the individual's daily activities. Most, if not all, of these instances can be normalized in the weekly process of counseling. However, the counselor needs to be aware of the environments that produce these effects and are normal for combat situations.

Finding Time for Counseling

Counseling military personnel comes with its own set of difficulties. Many military families and individuals are in a constant flux of change. This includes training, promotions, and schools that military personnel have to attend to progress (i.e., retention) and to make rank. Many times, after complex deployments, enlisted, noncommissioned officers, and officers have to fit this (schooling) into their schedules, which increases the amount of time spent away from home. This means that military personnel not only are separated from families and friends due to combat environments but also are separated from families due to training and schools to maintain their military status. This provides the counselor with another set of parameters to understand in helping individuals and families with their concerns. It is not that many do not want help; it is *when* they can get the help that is needed. Counselors can become frustrated with this cycle of career maintenance if they are not aware of the culture in which these men and women serve. This also has consequences for the type of interventions that are used by counselors who provide therapy for military personnel. Are these therapies time sensitive, that is, do they have a beginning and an end? What type of interventions or counseling techniques are being used for military personnel? Do they require several sessions? Will the counselors have time to develop trust and a client counselor relationship in which complex issues can be discussed and comprehended? These and other questions like them are important to consider when working with a military population.

Stigma

As mentioned, counselors need to be aware that many military personnel perceive counseling services as counterproductive (i.e., it will hamper their career). Some senior military personnel feel that they do not need it (i.e., counseling or interventions to solve personal concerns). Although they may publically endorse mental health initiatives and military-wide policies, privately, they may not see the need for help. Many times, only after heartbreaking circumstances do people get help. This is specific not only to the military, but also to the general population. Consequently, counselors need to be sensitive to this issue. Because of this, resources like Military OneSource were created so military personnel could receive off-base mental health services in a timely manner where confidentiality was paramount. Nonetheless, the military provides a myriad of mental health services and resources to help with issues caused by frequent separations and the effects of hazardous duty assignments as discussed in this chapter.

Complexity of Effect

For counselors, *complexity of effect* is a term that needs further research. It is best understood as the complex nature of working with military personnel and families. It can be challenging when counseling with those who suffer from concerns like PTSD, mild traumatic brain injury (MTBI), marital issues, death, separation, divorce, abuse, etc. Nevertheless, like an intricate maze, the counselor needs to negotiate complexity of effect with care. Counselors who work with military environments should be aware of the concept, although there is a paucity of research concerning this factor. Nonetheless, studies by Drummet, Coleman, and Cable (2003), Figley (1995), and Karney and Crown (2007) allude to this construct implicitly but not explicitly.

As a final thought, counselors should understand that the military is like an intricately woven tapestry. The threads that make up its fabric can be ordinary, yet complex; simple, yet elaborate; and easily understood, yet difficult to comprehend. The fabric comes in all colors, shapes, and sizes. It is woven with its own history and complexity of effect. Born in the historical context of strife, and pictured as a blend of what has happened in the past, it is full of honor, service, and duty. Nevertheless, within its fabric there is also much pain and years of sacrifice that many have rendered often with their lives in service to their country. It is a tapestry that is constantly being worked on and grows with each succeeding generation of those who enter and provide service in the military. Counselors should strive to understand it. It should be respected and when worked with understood within the context of the individual and military structure as a whole.

AUTHORS' NOTE

The views expressed in this manuscript are those of the authors and do not reflect the views or official policy or position of Kansas State University, the U.S. Army Research Institute for the Behavioral and Social Sciences, the U.S. Department of Defense, or the U.S. government.

REFERENCES

Adler-Baeder, F., Pittman, J. F., & Taylor, L. (2005). The prevalence of marital transitions in military families. *Journal of Divorce and Remarriage*, *44*, 91–106.

Arango-Lasprilla, J. C., Ketchum, J. M., Dezfulian, T., Kreutzer, J. S., O'Neil-Pirozzi, T. M., Hammond, F., & Jha, A. (2008). Predictors of marital stability 2 years following traumatic brain injury. *Brain Injury*, *22*, 565–574.

Basham, K. (2008). Homecoming as safe haven or the new front: Attachment and detachment in military couples. *Clinical Social Work Journal*, *36*, 83–96.

Behnke, A. O., MacDermid, S. M., Anderson, J. C., & Weiss, H. M. (2010). Ethnic variations in the connection between work-induced family separation and turnover intent. *Journal of Family Issues, 31*, 626–655.

Bell, D. B., Bartone, J., Bartone, P. T., Schumm, W. R., Rice, R. E., & Hinson, C. (1997, October 24–26). *Helping U.S. Army families cope with the stresses of troop deployment in Bosnia-Herzegovina.* Paper presented at the Inter-University Seminar on Armed Forces and Society Biennial International Conference, Baltimore.

Bell, D. B., & Schumm, W. R. (2000). Providing family support during military deployments. In J. A. Martin, L. N. Rosen, & L. R. Sparacino (Eds.), *The military family: A practice guide for human service providers* (pp. 153–165). Westport, CT: Praeger.

Bell, D. B., Schumm, W. R., Knott, B., & Ender, M. G. (1999). The Desert Fax: A research note on calling home from Somalia. *Armed Forces & Society, 25*, 509–521.

Blais, M. C., & Boisvert, J. M. (2005). Psychological and marital adjustment in couples following a traumatic brain injury (TBI): A critical review. *Brain Injury, 19*, 1223–1235.

Blais, M. C., & Boisvert, J. M. (2007). Psychological adjustment and marital satisfaction following head injury. Which critical personal characteristics should both partners develop? *Brain Injury, 21*, 357–372.

Booth, B., Segal, M. W., Bell, D. B., Martin, J. A., Ender, M. G., Rohall, D. E., & Nelson, J. (2007). *What we know about Army families: 2007 update*. Fairfax, VA: ICF International.

Bourg, C., & Segal, M. W. (1999). The impact of family supportive policies and practices on organizational commitment to the army. *Armed Forces and Society, 25*, 633–652.

Burrell, L. M., Adams, G. A., Durand, D. B., & Castro, C. A. (2006). The impact of military lifestyle demands on well-being, Army, and family outcomes. *Armed Forces & Society, 33*, 43–58.

Cacioppo, J. T., Reis, H. T., & Zautra, A. J. (2011). Social resilience: The value of social fitness with an application to the military. *American Psychologist, 66*, 43–51.

Call, V., & Teachman, J. (1991). Military service and stability in the family life course. *Military Psychology, 3*, 233–250.

Call, V., & Teachman, J. (1996). Life-course timing and sequencing of marriage and military service and their effects on marital stability. *Journal of Marriage and the Family, 58*, 219–226.

Card, J. (1983). *Lives after Vietnam: The personal impact of military service*. Lexington, MA: Lexington Books.

Casey, G. W., Jr. (2011). Comprehensive soldier fitness: A vision for psychological resilience in the U.S. Army. *American Psychologist, 66*, 1–3.

Cohan, C. L., Cole, S., & Davila, J. (2005). Marital transitions among Vietnam-era repatriated prisoners of war. *Journal of Social and Personal Relationships, 22*, 777–795.

Cohen, J., & Segal, M. W. (2009). Veterans, the Vietnam Era, and marital dissolution. *Armed Forces & Society*, 36, 19–37.

Dekel, R., Goldblatt, H., Keidar, M., Solomon, Z., & Polliack, M. (2005). Being a wife of a veterans with posttraumatic stress disorder. *Family Relations, 54*, 24–36.

Doyle, M. E., & Peterson, K. A. (2005). Re-entry and reintegration: returning home after combat. *Psychiatric Quarterly, 76*, 361–370.

Drummet, A. R., Coleman, M., & Cable, S. (2003). Military families under stress: Implications for family life education. *Family Relations, 52*(3), 279–287.

Eaton, K. M., Hoge, C. W., Messer, S. C., Whitt, A. A., Cabrera, O. A., McGurk, D., … Castro, C. A. (2008). Prevalence of mental health problems, treatment need, and barriers to care among primacy care-seeking spouses of military service members involved in Iraq and Afghanistan deployments. *Military Medicine, 173*, 1051–1056.

Figley, C. R. (1995). Compassion fatigue as secondary traumatic stress disorder: An overview. In C. R. Figley (Ed.), *Compassion fatigue: Coping with secondary traumatic stress disorder in those who treated the traumatized* (pp. 1–20). New York: Brunner-Routledge.

Fredman, S. J., Monson, C. M., & Adair, K. C. (2011). Implementing cognitive-behavioral conjoint therapy for PTSD with the newest generation of veterans and their partners. *Cognitive and Behavioral Practice*, *18*, 120–130.

Frey-Wouters, E., & Laufer, R. (1986). *Legacy of a war: The American soldier in Vietnam*. Armonk, NY: Sharpe.

Galovski, T., & Lyons, J. A. (2004). Psychological sequelae of combat violence: A review of the impact of PTSD on the veteran's family and possible interventions. *Aggression and Violent Behavior*, *9*, 477–501.

Gimbel, C., & Booth, A. (1994). Why does military combat experience adversely affect marital relations? *Journal of Marriage and the Family*, *56*, 691–703.

Godwin, E. E., Kreutzer, J. S., Arango-Lasprilla, J. C., & Lehan, T. J. (2011). Marriage after brain injury: Review, analysis, and research recommendations. *Journal of Head Trauma Rehabilitation*, *26*, 43–55.

Gottman, J. M., Gottman, J. S., & Atkins, C. L. (2011). The comprehensive soldier fitness program: Family skills component. *American Psychologist*, *66*, 52–57.

Gould, J. (2011, April 11). The fall of an airborne commander: Fired 173rd leader faces possible court-martial—and a lurid divorce. *Army Times*, *71*(39), 16–17.

Gould, M., Adler, A., Zamorski, M., Castro, C., Hanily, N., Steele, N., … Greenberg, N. (2010). Do stigma and other perceived barriers to mental health care differ across Armed Forces? *Journal of the Royal Society of Medicine*, *103*, 148–156.

Greene-Shortridge, T. M., Britt, T. W., & Castro, C. A. (2007). The stigma of mental health problems in the military. *Military Medicine*, *172*, 157–161.

Hall, L. K. (2008). *Counseling military families: What mental health professionals need to know*. New York: Routledge.

Hammond, F. M., Davis, C. S., Whiteside, O. Y., Philbrick, P., & Hirsch, M. A. (2011). Marital adjustment and stability following traumatic brain injury: A pilot qualitative analysis of spouse perspectives. *Journal of Head Trauma Rehabilitation*, *26*, 69–78.

Hendrix, C. C., Jurich, A. P., & Schumm, W. R. (1995). Long-term impact of Vietnam war service on family environment and satisfaction. *Families in Society*, *76*, 498–506.

Hogan, P. F., & Seifert, R. F. (2010). Marriage and the military: Evidence that those who serve marry earlier and divorce earlier. *Armed Forces & Society*, *36*, 420–438.

Huebner, A. J., Mancini, J. A., Bowen, G. L., & Orthner, D. K. (2009). Shadowed by war: Building community capacity to support military families. *Family Relations*, *58*, 216–228.

Iversen, A. C., van Staden, L., Hughes, J. H., Greenberg, N., Hotopf, M., Rona, R. J., … Fear, N. T. (2011). The stigma of mental health problems and other barriers to care in the U.K. Armed Forces. *BMC Health Services Research*, *11*, 31.

Johnson, S. M. (2002). *Emotionally focused couple therapy with trauma survivors: Strengthening attachment bonds*. New York: Guilford Press.

Jordan, B. K., Marmar, C. R., Fairbank, J. A., Schlenger, W. E., Kulka, R. A., Hough, R. L., & Weiss, D. S. (1992). Problems in families of male Vietnam veterans with posttraumatic stress disorder. *Journal of Consulting and Clinical Psychology*, *60*, 916–926.

Kalamdien, D. J. (2008). A psychological support programme for peacekeeping soldiers and their families: a model for discussion. In G. A. J. Van Dyk (Ed.), *Strategic challenges for African Armed Forces for the next decade* (pp. 83–101). Stellenbosch, South Africa: Sun Press.

Kalamdien, D. J., & Van Dyk, G. A. J. (2009). A psychological support for peacekeeping soldiers and their families: A preliminary model. *Journal of Psychology in Africa*, *19*, 281–288.

Karney, B. R., & Crown, J. S. (2007). *Families under stress: An assessment of data, theory, and research on marriage and divorce in the military* (MG-599-OSD). Santa Monica, CA: RAND.

Karney, B. R., & Crown, J. S. (2011). Does deployment keep military marriages together or break them apart? Evidence from Afghanistan and Iraq. In S. M. Wadsworth & D. Riggs (Eds.), *Risk and resilience in U.S. military families* (pp. 23–45). New York: Springer Science + Business Media.

Kotlowski, C. A. (2010). An exploratory study of military deployment and its impact on marriage and family of soldiers. *Dissertation Abstracts International*, *70*(09), 3614A.

Kreutzer, J., Marwitz, J., Hsu, N., Williams, J., & Riddick, A. (2007). Marital stability after brain injury: An investigation and analysis. *NeuroRehabilitation, 22*, 53–59.

Kulka, R. A., Schlenger, W. E., Fairbank, J. A., Hough, R. L., Jordan, K. B., Marmar, C. R., ... Grady, D. A. (1990). *Trauma and the Vietnam War generation*. New York: Brunner/Mazel.

Laser, J. A., & Stephens, P. M. (2011). Working with military families through deployment and beyond. *Clinical Social Work Journal*, *39*, 28–38.

Laufer, R., & Gallops, M. S. (1985). Life-course effects of Vietnam combat and abusive violence: marital patterns. *Journal of Marriage and the Family*, *47*, 839–853.

Lloyd, K. M., & South, S. J. (1996). Contextual influences on young men's transition to first marriage. *Social Forces, 74,* 1097–1119.

Lundquist, J. H. (2007). A comparison of civilian and enlisted divorce rates during the early All Volunteer Force era. *Journal of Political and Military Sociology, 35,* 199–217.

Martin, J. A., & McClure, P. (2000). Today's active duty military family: The evolving challenge of military family life. In J. A. Martin, L. N. Rosen, & L. R. Sparacino (Eds.), *The military family: A practice guide for human service providers* (pp. 3–23). Westport, CT: Praeger.

McFarlane, A. C. (2009). The duration of deployment and sensitization to stress. *Psychiatric Annals*, *39*(2), 81–88.

McLeland, K. C., & Sutton, G. W. (2005). Military service, marital status, and men's relationship satisfaction. *Individual Differences Research*, *3*, 177–182.

McLeland, K. C., Sutton, G. W., & Schumm, W. R. (2008). Marital satisfaction before and after deployments associated with the Global War on Terror. *Psychological Reports*, *103*, 836–844.

Miklowitz, D. (2008). *Bipolar disorder: A family focused treatment approach*. New York: Guilford.

Milliken, C. S., Auchterlonie, J. L., & Hoge, C. W. (2007). Longitudinal assessment of mental health problems among Active and Reserve Component soldiers returning from the Iraq War. *Journal of the American Medical Association*, *298*, 2141–2148.

Monson, C. M., Fredman, S. J., & Taft, C. T. (2011). Couple and family issues and interventions for veterans of the Iraq and Afghanistan wars. In J. I. Ruzek, P. P. Schurr, J. J. Vasterling, & M. J. Friedman (Eds.), *Caring for veterans with deployment-related stress disorders* (pp. 151–169). Washington, DC: American Psychological Association.

Monson, C. M., Taft, C. T., & Fredman, S. J. (2009). Military-related PTSD and intimate relationships: From description to theory-driven research and intervention development. *Clinical Psychology Review*, *29*, 707–714.

Moore, B. A. (2011, April 11). Useful community resources available for service members. *Army Times*, *71*(39), OFFduty insert, p. 13.

Nelson-Goff, B. S., & Smith, D. B. (2005). Systemic traumatic stress: The couple adaptation to traumatic stress model. *Journal of Marital and Family Therapy*, *31*, 145–157.

Norton, R. (1983). Measuring marital quality: a critical look at the dependent variable. *Journal of Marriage and the Family*, *45*, 141–151.

Oppenheimer, V. K. (2003). Cohabiting and marriage during young men's career-developing process. *Demography, 40,* 127–149.

Orthner, D. K., & Rose, R. (2003). Dealing with the effects of absence: Deployment and adjustment to separation among military families. *Journal of Family Consumer Sciences*, *95*, 33–37.

Orthner, D. K., & Rose, R. (2009). Work separation demands and spouse psychological well-being. *Family Relations, 58*, 392–403.

Padden, D. L., Connors, R. A., & Agazio, J. G. (2011). Stress, coping, and well-being in military spouses during deployment separation. *Western Journal of Nursing Research, 33*, 247–267.

Pargament, K. I., & Sweeney, P. J. (2011). Building spiritual fitness in the Army: An innovative approach to a vital aspect of human development. *American Psychologist, 66*, 58–64.

Park, N. (2011). Military children and families: Strengths and challenges during peace and war. *American Psychologist, 66*, 65–72.

Phillips, R. L., Andrisani, P. J., Daymont, T. N., & Gilroy, C. L. (1992). The economic returns to military service: Race-ethnic differences. *Social Science Quarterly, 73*, 340–359.

Pietrzak, R. H., Johnson, D. C., Goldstein, M. B., Malley, J. C., & Southwick, S. M. (2009). Perceived stigma and barriers to mental health care utilization among OEF-OIF veterans. *Psychiatric Services, 60*, 1118–1122.

Pittman, J. F., Kerpelman, J. L., & McFadyen, J. M. (2004). Internal and external adaptation in Army families: Lessons from Operations Desert Shield and Desert Storm. *Family Relations, 53*, 249–260.

Pollard, M., Karney, B., & Loughran, D. (2008, April 17). *Comparing rates of marriage and divorce in civilian, military, and veteran populations.* Poster session, P2–48, Population Association of America, New Orleans.

Raley, R. K., & Bumpass, L. (2003). The topography of the divorce plateau: Levels and trends in union stability in the United States after 1980. *Demographic Research, 8*, 245–260.

Reger, M. A., Gahm, G. A., Swanson, R. D., & Duma, S. J. (2009). Association between number of deployments to Iraq and mental health screening outcomes in U.S. Army soldiers. *Journal of Clinical Psychiatry, 70*, 1266–1272.

Reivich, K. J., Seligman, M. E. P., & McBride, S. (2011). Master resilience training in the U.S. Army. *American Psychologist, 66*, 25–34.

Renshaw, K. D., Rodrigues, C. S., & Jones, D. H. (2009). Combat exposure, psychological symptoms, and marital satisfaction in National Guard soldiers who served in Operation Iraqi Freedom from 2005 to 2006. *Anxiety, Stress, & Coping, 22*, 101–115.

Riggs, D. S., Byrne, C. A., Weathers, F. W., & Litz, B. T. (1998). The quality of the intimate relationships of male Vietnam veterans: problems associated with posttraumatic stress disorder. *Journal of Traumatic Stress, 11*, 87–101.

Rona, R. J., Fear, N. T., Hull, L., Greenberg, N., Earnshaw, M., Hotopf, M., & Wessely, S. (2007). Mental health consequences of overstretch in the U.K. armed forces: First phase of a cohort study. *British Medical Journal, 335*, 603.

Rosen, L. N., & Durand, D. B. (2000a). Coping with the unique demands of military family life. In J. A. Martin, L. N. Rosen, & L. R. Sparacino (Eds.), *The military family: A practice guide for human service providers* (pp. 55–72). Westport, CT: Praeger.

Rosen, L. N., & Durand, D. B. (2000b). Marital adjustment following deployment. In J. A. Martin, L. N. Rosen, & L. R. Sparacino (Eds.), *The military family: A practice guide for human service providers*. (pp. 153–165). Westport, CT: Praeger.

Rosen, L. N., Teitelbaum, J. M., & Westhuis, D. J. (1993). Stressors, stress mediators, and emotional well-being among spouses of soldiers deployed to the Persian Gulf during Operation Desert Shield/Storm. *Journal of Applied Social Psychology, 23*, 1587–1593.

Rotter, J. C., & Boveja, M. E. (1999). Counseling military families. *Family Journal: Counseling and Therapy for Couples and Families, 7*, 379–382.

Ruger, W., Wilson, S. E., & Waddoups, S. L. (2002). Warfare and welfare: Military service, combat, and marital dissolution. *Armed Forces & Society, 29*, 85–107.

Sareen, J., Cox, B. J., Afifi, T. O., Stein, M. B., Belik, S. L., Meadows, G., & Asmundson, G. J. (2007). Combat and peacekeeping operations in relation to prevalence of mental disorders and perceived need for mental health care: Findings from a large representative sample of military personnel. *Archives of General Psychiatry, 64*, 843–852.

Sayer, N. A., Noorbaloochi, S., Frazier, P., Carlson, K., Gravely, A., & Murdoch, M. (2010). Reintegration problems and treatment interests among Iraq and Afghanistan combat veterans receiving VA medical care. *Psychiatric Services, 61*, 589–597.

Sayers, S. L. (2011). Family reintegration difficulties and couples therapy for military veterans and their spouses. *Cognitive and Behavioral Practice, 18*, 108–119.

Sayers, S. L., Farrow, V. A., Ross, J., & Oslin, D. W. (2009). Family problems among recently returned military veterans referred for a mental health evaluation. *Journal of Clinical Psychiatry, 70*, 163–170.

Schumm, W. R., Bell, D. B., Ender, M. G., & Rice, R. E. (2004). Expectations, use, and evaluation of communication media among deployed peacekeepers. *Armed Forces & Society, 30*, 649–662.

Schumm, W. R., Bell, D. B., & Gade, P. A. (2000). Effects of a military overseas peacekeeping deployment on marital quality, satisfaction, and stability. *Psychological Reports, 87*, 815–821.

Schumm, W. R., Crock, R. J., Likcani, A., Akagi, C. G., & Bosch, K. R. (2008). Reliability and validity of the Kansas Marital Satisfaction Scale with different response formats in a recent sample of U.S. Army personnel. *Individual Differences Research, 6*, 26–37.

Schumm, W. R., Hemesath, K., Bell, D. B., Palmer-Johnson, C. E., & Elig, T. W. (1996). Did Desert Storm reduce marital satisfaction among Army enlisted personnel? *Psychological Reports, 78*, 1241–1242.

Schumm, W. R., Tiggle, R., Bright, A., Bell, D. B., & Gade, P. A. (1996). *Did Desert Storm increase marital instability among Active and Reserve Component Army personnel?* Unpublished working paper. Alexandria, VA: U.S. Army Research Institute for the Behavioral and Social Sciences.

Sherman, M. D., Zanotti, D. K., & Jones, D. E. (2005). Key elements in couples therapy with veterans with combat-related posttraumatic stress disorder. *Professional Psychology: Research and Practice, 36*, 626–633.

Solomon, Z., Debby-Aharon, S., Zerach, G., & Horesh, D. (2011). Marital adjustment, parental functioning, and emotional sharing in war veterans. *Journal of Family Issues, 32*, 127–147.

Spanier, G. B. (1976). Measuring dyadic adjustment: New scales for assessing the quality of marriage and similar dyads. *Journal of Marriage and the Family, 38*, 15–28.

Spera, C. (2009). Spouses' ability to cope with deployment and adjust to Air Force family demands. *Armed Forces & Society, 35*, 286–306.

Stanley, S. M., Allen, E. S., Markman, H. J., Saiz, C. C., Bloomstrom, G., Thomas, R., … Bailey, A. E. (2005). Dissemination and evaluation of marriage education in the Army. *Family Process, 44*, 187–201.

Stellman, J. M., Stellman, J. M., & Sommer, J. F. (1988). Social and behavioral consequences of the Vietnam experiences among American Legionnaires. *Environmental Research, 47*, 129–149.

Sundin, J., Fear, N. T., Hull, L., Jones, N., Dandeker, C., Hotopf, M., … Rona, R. J. (2010). Rewarding and unrewarding aspects of deployment to Iraq and its association with psychological health in U.K. military personnel. *International Archives of Occupational and Environmental Health, 83*, 653–663.

Sweeney, M. M. (2002). Remarriage and the nature of divorce: Does it matter which spouse chose to leave? *Journal of Family Issues, 23*, 410–440.

Sweeney, M. M., & Phillips J. A. (2004). Understanding racial differences in marital disruption: Recent trends and explanations. *Journal of Marriage and Family, 66*, 639–650.

Teachman, J. D., Polonko, K. A., & Leigh, G. K. (1987). Marital timing: Race and sex comparisons. *Social Forces, 66,* 239–268.

Tollefson, T. T. (2008). Supporting spouses during a military deployment. *Family and Community Health, 31,* 281–286.

Vanderploeg, R. D., Curtiss, G., Duchnick, J. J., & Luis, C. A. (2003). Demographic, medical, and psychiatric factors in work and marital status after mild head injury. *Journal of Head Trauma Rehabilitation, 18,* 148–163.

Vormbrock, J. K. (1993). Attachment theory as applied to wartime and job-related marital separation. *Psychological Bulletin, 114,* 122–144.

Walker, S. (2010). Assessing the mental health consequences of military combat in Iraq and Afghanistan: A literature review. *Journal of Psychiatric and Mental Health Nursing, 17,* 790–796.

Warner, C. H., Appenzeller, G. N., Grieger, T. A., Benedek, D. M., & Roberts, L. W. (2009). Ethical considerations in military psychiatry. *Psychiatric Clinics of North America, 32,* 271–281.

Warner, C. H., Appenzeller, G. N., Warner, C. M., & Grieger, T. (2009). Psychological effects of deployments on military families. *Psychiatric Annals, 39,* 56–63.

Wells, T. S., LeardMann, C. A., Fortuna, S. O., Smith, B., Smith, T. C., Ryan, M. A., … Millennium Cohort Study Team. (2010). A prospective study of depression following combat deployment in support of the wars in Iraq and Afghanistan. *American Journal of Public Health, 100,* 90–99.

Wood, R. L., & Yurdakul, L. K. (1997). Change in relationship status following traumatic brain injury. *Brain Injury, 7,* 491–502.

10

Posttraumatic Stress Disorder

JASON M. LAVENDER and JUDITH A. LYONS

INTRODUCTION

Posttraumatic stress disorder (PTSD) as defined by the fourth edition of the *Diagnostic and Statistical Manual of Mental Disorders* (*DSM-IV*; American Psychiatric Association [APA], 2000) requires that an individual experience a traumatic stressor. This requirement for the PTSD diagnosis (referred to as a Criterion A event) specifies both the nature of the trauma, "the person experienced, witnessed, or was confronted with an event or events that involved actual or threatened death or serious injury, or a threat to the physical integrity of self or others" (APA, 2000, p. 467), and the individual's reaction to the trauma, "the person's response involved intense fear, helplessness, or horror" (APA, 2000, p. 467). The symptoms of PTSD fall under three categories: reexperiencing the traumatic event, avoidance/numbing, and hyperarousal. Within the reexperiencing category, the individual must meet at least one of five possible criteria, examples of which include distressing dreams (i.e., nightmares) of the event, feeling as if the trauma were recurring (e.g., flashbacks), and intrusive trauma-related memories, images, or thoughts. In the avoidance/numbing category, the individual must meet at least three of seven criteria, examples of which include feeling detached from others, experiencing substantially decreased interest in significant activities, and efforts to avoid thoughts, places, or people that remind the individual of the trauma. In the third symptom category, the individual must meet at least two of five possible hyperarousal criteria, examples of which include sleep disturbance, exaggerated startle response, and irritability or angry outbursts.

PREVALENCE IN THE GENERAL POPULATION

Large, population-based epidemiological studies indicate that approximately 80% of individuals in the United States will experience at least one traumatic event within their lifetime, and the majority of individuals reporting trauma exposure endorse having experienced more than one traumatic event (Kessler et al., 2005; Sledjeski, Speisman, & Dierker, 2008). However, the lifetime prevalence of PTSD within the general U.S. population has recently been estimated at only 6.8% (Kessler et al., 2005). Further, studies reported consistent gender differences in the prevalence of PTSD. Although research suggests that men are more likely to experience a traumatic event, the lifetime prevalence of PTSD is higher among women than among men (Kessler et al., 2005; Sledjeski et al., 2008).

PREVALENCE IN VETERANS

Since the diagnosis of PTSD was first introduced, there has been substantial controversy about the prevalence of PTSD among veterans who served in combat zones. For instance, the prevalence of PTSD among veterans of the Vietnam War continues to be debated, with estimates ranging between approximately 15% and 31%, with a recent estimate suggesting a lifetime prevalence of approximately 19% and a 9.1% point prevalence 10 to 12 years after the war (Dohrenwend et al., 2006, 2007; Kulka, 1990). A similar controversy exists regarding the prevalence of PTSD among Operation Iraqi Freedom (OIF) and Operation Enduring Freedom (OEF) veterans (Ramchand et al., 2010; Sundin, Fear, Iversen, Rona, & Wessely, 2010). In a review of studies reporting on PTSD among personnel deployed to Iraq, Sundin and colleagues found that the prevalence rates ranged between 1.4% and 31%, with rates between 10% and 17% for combat-deployed troops and lower rates of 2.1–11.6% for representative samples of all deployed forces. In a review of PTSD prevalence among OIF and OEF service members, Ramchand and colleagues reported similar prevalence estimates of approximately 5% to 20% among non-treatment-seeking samples.

RISK AND PROTECTIVE FACTORS

Given strong evidence that the majority of individuals (both civilians and military personnel deployed to combat zones) who are exposed to traumatic events do not go on to develop PTSD, studies have sought to determine what variables function as either risk or protective factors in the etiology of PTSD. Overall, research suggests that proximal risk factors, including those that occur around the time of the trauma exposure or during the period after the trauma (e.g., perceived life threat and perceived support), are more strongly predictive of PTSD onset than distal, pretrauma factors such as a history of psychological difficulties and prior exposure to traumatic events (Brewin, Andrews, & Valentine, 2000; Ozer, Best, Lipsey, & Weiss, 2003).

Among the most salient predictors of PTSD that have been identified in recent reviews are peri- or posttraumatic factors, including severity of the trauma, lack of social support, and additional life stress during the period after the trauma (Brewin et al., 2000; Ozer et al., 2003). The impact of trauma severity has been reported as one of the strongest predictors of PTSD, particularly among combat Veterans (Brewin et al., 2000). For example, Rona and colleagues (2009) found that combat exposure was significantly associated with PTSD and that specific forms of combat exposure, including witnessing comrades being wounded or killed, being subjected to small arms fire, and being in close contact with enemy soldiers, were particularly strong predictors of the development of PTSD. Similarly, a review by Ozer and colleagues (2003) reported that the perceived life threat of a traumatic event, a factor that is associated with the severity of the trauma, was one of the strongest predictors of PTSD.

Numerous empirical studies and meta-analytic reviews strongly suggest that a lack of social support following the experience of a traumatic event is an important variable related to the development of PTSD. In reviews by both Brewin and colleagues (2000) and Ozer and colleagues (2003), the level of perceived support following a trauma was found to be one of the two strongest predictors of PTSD onset. However, the majority of the research has focused on the role of emotional support; therefore, the impact of other forms of support, such as tangible support (e.g., financial assistance), remains unclear.

A related variable that has also been shown to serve as a predictor of PTSD onset is the degree of life stress following exposure to the traumatic event (Brewin et al., 2000). It may be that increased life stress subsequent to the traumatic exposure interferes with the natural recovery processes that occur after exposure to a trauma. This may be of particular relevance in combat Veteran populations, given the inherent stresses associated with postdeployment reintegration in civilian and family life. Although research studies commonly focus on combat exposure as the primary stressor among military personnel, researchers have also examined the role of noncombat deployment-related stressors (Booth-Kewley, Larson, Highfill-McRoy, Garland, & Gaskin, 2010). These factors include tangible stressors such as excessive heat or cold and lack of adequate supplies, as well as issues back home. For example, in a study of U.S. Marines who had completed at least one war-zone deployment, Booth-Kewley and colleagues found that deployment-related stressors were more strongly associated with PTSD symptoms than combat exposure. Specifically, Marines who expressed high concerns about issues at home and problems communicating with home were much more likely to report symptoms consistent with a diagnosis of PTSD than Marines who did not express such concerns.

Although research suggests that variables that play a role around the time of the trauma or after the traumatic exposure tend to be stronger predictors than those that are established prior to the trauma, studies have also examined the predictive power of pretrauma variables. The most widely studied pretrauma predictors of the development of PTSD include variables such as past traumatic exposures and history of psychological difficulties, as well as family history of psychopathology. With regard to the impact of prior trauma exposure, two reviews of PTSD predictors both found previous exposure to a traumatic event to be only weakly associated with the development of PTSD (Brewin et al., 2000; Ozer et al., 2003). Similarly, these reviews and more recent studies among military personnel reported that a history of psychological difficulties prior to the trauma exposure, as well as a family history of psychopathology, were only weakly predictive of PTSD onset (Brewin et al., 2000; Ozer et al., 2003; Rona et al., 2009).

Although studies have historically focused on identifying variables that are associated with an increased risk of psychopathology, more recently researchers have begun to conduct studies investigating constructs that may function as protective factors that reduce the likelihood of an individual developing PTSD after exposure to a traumatic event. Given research suggesting that posttrauma lack of social support may function as a risk factor for the development of PTSD, researchers have also examined social support as a potential protective factor. For example, in a study of OIF/OEF veterans, higher levels of postdeployment social support were associated with lower PTSD and depression symptoms (Pietrzak, Johnson, et al. 2010). Similarly, postdeployment social support has been found to function as a protective factor for suicidal ideation among combat veterans (Pietrzak, Goldstein, et al., 2010). Research also suggests that the availability of early postdeployment social support may reduce the incidence of PTSD symptoms and co-occurring psychological difficulties among veterans following war-zone deployment (Milliken, Auchterlonie, & Hoge, 2007). Another factor that has recently received attention in the literature is military unit support and the associated variable of group cohesion. Studies suggest that unit support may function as a protective factor, with higher levels of unit support associated with fewer PTSD symptoms (Pietrzak, Johnson, et al., 2010; Rona et al., 2009). Specifically, one study (Pietrzak, Johnson, et al., 2010) showed that greater unit support was associated with higher levels of psychological resilience, which in turn was associated with fewer symptoms of PTSD.

CHALLENGES

One of the major challenges in researching, identifying, and treating PTSD among military personnel is the stigma associated with psychological difficulties and being labeled with a psychological diagnosis. Concerns related to this stigma are particularly relevant among military personnel who may be anxious about how a mental health diagnosis could affect their job status or opportunities for promotion. Concerns about mental health stigma have been documented as a barrier for veterans receiving appropriate mental health care, and veterans who screen positive for a psychiatric disorder are more likely to report greater stigma concerns (Hoge et al., 2004). Studies also suggested that certain factors, including lower unit support and negative beliefs about mental health care in general, are associated with greater stigma and a reduced likelihood of seeking mental health counseling (Pietrzak, Johnson, Goldstein, Malley, & Southwick, 2009). In contrast, protective factors such as marriage and social support are associated with reduced stigma and may promote the utilization of mental health care services (Pietrzak et al., 2009).

HOW PTSD HAS AN IMPACT ON RELATIONSHIPS

Evidence from a large body of research suggests that PTSD symptoms affect functioning in a variety of domains, including in the context of intimate relationships and more broadly in the area of overall family functioning (Galovski & Lyons, 2004). Although much of the research has focused on the impact of PTSD on military couples, the negative effects of PTSD often extend beyond the intimate relationship to the broader family unit, with effects on parenting and overall family functioning (Cloutier, Manion, & Walker, 2002). Compared to those who have been exposed to a trauma without developing PTSD, veterans suffering from PTSD exhibit more impairments in emotional expression, greater variety and severity of relationship difficulties, higher rates of physical and verbal aggression against their partners and children, and higher rates of divorce (Monson, Fredman, & Adair, 2008). Further, patients with PTSD have a substantially greater chance of experiencing impairments in occupational functioning (e.g., unemployment) and marital instability, and evidence suggests that OIF/OEF veterans diagnosed with a psychiatric disorder such as PTSD commit suicide at a higher rate than the general population (Kang & Bullman, 2008; Kessler, 2000).

Of the three primary clusters of PTSD symptoms, studies suggest that the avoidance/numbing symptoms are perhaps the most strongly associated with problems in family and intimate relationship functioning (Monson, Taft, & Fredman, 2009). Studies have shown that the avoidance/numbing symptom cluster (e.g., emotional numbing, feelings of detachment) is associated with intimate relationship difficulties and reduced parenting satisfaction, likely due in part to the negative impact these symptoms have on interpersonal communication (Berz, Taft, Watkins, & Monson, 2008; Samper, Taft, King, & King, 2004). In contrast, the hyperarousal cluster of symptoms has been more strongly implicated in the perpetration of aggression against an intimate partner, and evidence suggests that veterans who also exhibit difficulties in regulating negative emotions such as anger are at greater risk of engaging in intimate partner aggression (Monson et al., 2009; Savarese, Suvak, King, & King, 2001). Co-occurring substance use disorders may serve as an additional risk factor for the perpetration of intimate partner aggression among veterans with PTSD (Taft et al., 2005).

In their review of the association between military-related PTSD and intimate relationships, Monson and colleagues (2009) addressed the potential effects of caregiver burden in the role of PTSD as a causal factor for relationship difficulties. Caregiver burden, defined as a caregivers' perception that caring for an impaired relative affects their social life, health, or financial status (Zarit, Todd, & Zarit, 1986), has been the focus of several studies of family functioning among patients with PTSD. The results of these studies suggest a positive association between severity of veterans' PTSD symptoms and degree of caregiver burden among intimate partners (Calhoun, Beckham, & Bosworth, 2002; Manguno-Mire et al., 2007). Research also suggests that caregiver burden is associated with the degree of PTSD-related impairments in the partner's occupational functioning (Dekel, Solomon, & Bleich, 2005).

In an effort to better clarify the effects of PTSD on intimate relationships, Nelson Goff and Smith (2005) developed the couple adaptation to traumatic stress (CATS) model, which proposes that a couple's adaptation to traumatic stress is based on the interactions among three factors: the level of individual functioning of each partner, predisposing factors and resources, and the functioning of the couple. Unlike other theories that have focused on unidirectional relationships (e.g., PTSD causing relationship difficulties or relationship difficulties contributing to the onset or maintenance of PTSD), the CATS model incorporates the notion of a bidirectional transmission of stress, as well as accounting for predisposing factors among both partners (Dekel & Monson, 2010).

Given that the symptoms of psychological disorders are often ambiguous and difficult to discern, relatives who observe behavior changes in a family member with PTSD may interpret the changes in a negative way due to limited understanding of how such behaviors function as symptoms of PTSD (Barrowclough, Gregg, & Tarrier, 2008). Such interpretations may result in criticism or hostility from family members (Tarrier, 1996). In studies that have examined expressed emotion (EE) among family members of patients with PTSD, patients living with a high-EE relative (i.e., those who are more critical and hostile toward the patient) exhibited smaller improvements following cognitive-behavioral treatment. Hostility and criticism from family members have also been found to be significant predictors of later PTSD symptoms (Tarrier, Sommerfield, & Pilgrim, 1999). Research suggests that high-EE relatives make more attributions that the patient with PTSD patient is responsible for bad outcomes, including psychological difficulties (Barrowclough et al., 2008). Taken together, these findings emphasize the need to consider and assist the family, particularly intimate partners, when developing a treatment plan for a veteran with PTSD.

TREATMENT STRATEGIES

Assessment and Monitoring of Symptoms

Numerous structured and semistructured interviews are available for clinicians to assess for the presence of PTSD. Examples of diagnostic interviews that can be used to assess for a variety of Axis I disorders include the Structured Clinical Interview for *DSM-IV* Disorders (SCID-IV; First, Spitzer, Gibbon, & Williams, 1997) and the Anxiety Disorders Interview Schedule (ADIS-IV; Brown, DiNardo, & Barlow, 2004), which focuses on anxiety disorders and commonly co-occurring conditions, including mood, somatoform, and substance use disorders. To assess PTSD specifically, the Clinician-Administered PTSD Scale (CAPS; Blake et al., 1995) is considered to be the gold standard structured interview for determining PTSD diagnostic status and symptom severity. This structured interview was initially validated with combat veterans and has been used with a wide variety of trauma-exposed populations (Weathers, Keane, & Davidson, 2001). The CAPS contains 30-items that correspond to the 17 *DSM-IV* criteria for PTSD. It also addresses overall PTSD severity, the impact of symptoms on social and occupational functioning, and frequency and intensity of five associated symptoms (depersonalization, derealization, survivor guilt, guilt about actions, and gaps in awareness). The full CAPS interview takes approximately 45–60 minutes to administer.

In addition to interviews, several self-report measures of PTSD symptoms are available. Such measures are particularly useful for repeated administration during therapy sessions to track progress in PTSD treatment.

Perhaps the most widely used self-report measure of PTSD symptoms, particularly among military populations, is the PTSD Checklist (PCL; Weathers, Litz, Herman, Huska, & Keane, 1993). The 17 items of the PCL correspond to the *DSM-IV* diagnostic criteria of PTSD. Several versions of the PCL are available depending on the purpose of the assessment and the particular patient. The PCL-M (military), which asks about symptoms in response to "stressful military experiences," is recommended for use with veterans and service members. Clinicians who wish to determine the extent to which PTSD symptoms are directly associated with a particular trauma may also choose to administer the PCL-S (specific), which asks about symptoms in relation to a specific "stressful experience" identified by the patient. The PCL is freely available for use in research and clinical contexts (http://www.pdhealth.mil/clinicians/assessment_tools.asp#ptsdc).

Veterans Health Administration Evidence-Based Psychotherapy Initiative

The Veterans Health Administration (VHA) has recently placed an emphasis on the dissemination of therapies with strong empirical support, with the goal of training clinicians in evidence-based psychotherapies for a variety of disorders commonly encountered among veterans (McHugh & Barlow, 2010). For example, the VHA has begun offering trainings in cognitive-behavioral therapy (CBT) and acceptance and commitment therapy (ACT) for depression and anxiety. Within the context of PTSD treatment, the VHA has focused their dissemination efforts on two evidence-based treatments that have been widely researched in civilian and veteran populations: prolonged exposure (PE) therapy (Foa, Hembree, & Rothbaum, 2007) and cognitive processing therapy (CPT; Resick, Monson, & Chard, 2008). According to the Department of Veterans Affairs, VHA *Uniform Mental Health Services Handbook* (Kussman, 2008), all veterans with PTSD must be provided access to PE or CPT for PTSD treatment. Given the strong empirical support for these two interventions, as well as the emphasis of the VHA on dissemination of these psychotherapies, this section focuses specifically on reviewing PE and CPT for the treatment of PTSD.

Prolonged Exposure

PE therapy is a cognitive-behavioral treatment and perhaps the most widely studied psychological intervention for PTSD. Exposure therapy is the treatment of choice for anxiety disorders, and within the context of PTSD treatment, a substantial research literature strongly supports the efficacy of PE for PTSD (Powers, Halpern, Ferenschak, Gillihan, & Foa, 2010). PE consists of four primary components: psychoeducation, breathing retraining, in vivo exposure, and imaginal exposure. The therapy is delivered in 10–15 weekly or twice-weekly sessions that are recommended to be approximately 90 minutes each to accommodate the various goals that are outlined for each session.

In the psychoeducation component of the PE protocol, patients are provided with an overview of the treatment protocol, and common reactions to trauma are discussed. A general rationale for PE is provided, focusing on the role of avoidance. Specifically, cognitive avoidance (i.e., avoiding or suppressing memories, thoughts, or emotions related to the trauma) and behavioral avoidance (i.e., avoiding situations, people, or places that serve as reminders of the trauma) are highlighted, and the patient is asked to indicate how these forms of avoidance have applied in their own experience. This discussion of avoidance leads to the introduction of imaginal and in vivo exposure, and a brief description and rationale for each form of exposure is provided. Finally, the role of irrational cognitions and beliefs in the maintenance of PTSD (e.g., guilt, hindsight bias, belief that no place is safe) are reviewed.

The second primary component of PE is breathing retraining, which is introduced by explaining the negative physiological and emotional effects of hyperventilation and shallow breathing (i.e., increased anxiety and associated physical symptoms such as muscle tension). As taught in PE, breathing retraining focuses on teaching slow breathing rather than deep breathing. Given that the body is physiologically more relaxed during the process of exhalation, the goal of breathing retraining is to help the patient learn to take normal breaths, but to extend the process of exhaling to enhance relaxation.

The third major component of PE is in vivo, or real-life, exposure. When first introduced, the patient is presented with a rationale for this form of exposure, with a focus on the goal of fear reduction by reducing avoidance and confronting previously avoided and feared situations. The Subjective Units of Discomfort Scale, a 0 (no discomfort at all) to 100 (the most upset the individual has ever been) scale, is used to assess the subjective experience of anxiety during exposure exercises. The therapist and patient work together to develop an in vivo exposure hierarchy that is composed of previously avoided situations that the patient will confront during in vivo exposure exercises. The patient then engages in these in vivo exposure exercises as homework between sessions for the remainder of the treatment, working up the hierarchy from the more easily confronted situations to the most difficult.

Finally, the fourth major component of PE, which is the focus of the majority of the sessions, is imaginal exposure. A detailed rationale for imaginal exposure is presented to the patient, with a focus on explaining how the exposure will allow the individual to organize the memory of the trauma, develop a stronger sense of self-control, and ultimately experience less distress in response to internal and external reminders of the trauma. Although the majority of individuals exposed to a trauma report more than one traumatic experience, this portion of PE requires the therapist and patient to select one trauma to be the focus of the imaginal exposure exercises. During the imaginal exposure sessions, patients are asked to repeatedly describe their trauma aloud in detail and in the present tense. A recording is made for the patient to listen to as daily homework. The therapist and patient then discuss the exposure exercise, and the patient is encouraged to speak about his or her reactions to revisiting the trauma. Given the inherently distressing nature of these exposure sessions, it is also important to explain that patients may temporarily experience a slight worsening of symptoms when first starting imaginal exposure, and that such experiences are normal and are not related to the ultimate success of the treatment.

Cognitive Processing Therapy

Another form of CBT, CPT, has also received substantial empirical support in the treatment of trauma-related psychopathology, including symptoms of PTSD and depression. Originally developed as a treatment for PTSD among victims of sexual assault, the CPT protocol has since been adapted for use specifically with veteran/military populations (Resick, Monson, & Chard, 2008). Numerous studies have supported the effectiveness of CPT in treating PTSD among veterans, and findings suggest that PE and CPT tend to be associated with equivalent outcomes (Powers et al., 2010). The therapy is delivered either in an individual format consisting of 12 weekly 60-minute sessions or in a group format consisting of 12 sessions 90 minutes long. In both formats, each session is structured such that the general format consists of practice assignment review, education and discussion about the primary target for that session, cognitive restructuring, and a review of the session, followed by assigning the practice exercise for the following week. The 12 sessions of CPT can be categorized broadly into four primary components: psychoeducation, trauma processing, cognitive interventions, and closure. Further, there is an alternate and equally effective form of CPT, termed CPT-C (cognitive only), which includes all elements of the full CPT protocol described, with the exception of the trauma-processing component. This form of the treatment may be particularly useful for patients with poor memories of the traumatic event, such as individuals with memory difficulties resulting from a traumatic brain injury.

Similar to PE, the CPT protocol begins with psychoeducation, particularly focused on explaining the symptoms of PTSD, the rationale for therapy, and the basic foundations of cognitive theory. An overview of the treatment protocol is also provided, and the therapist and patient work together to identify the worst traumatic experience, which will be the focus of the trauma-processing portion of the therapy. The other initial sessions focus on helping the patient to understand the meaning of the traumatic event, with an emphasis on identifying how the event changed the patient's beliefs about self, the world, or other people. Patients are also provided with information regarding the link between events, thoughts, and emotions, and patients then monitor their thoughts and feelings throughout the course of the treatment. Beginning in the early sessions, the therapist and patient work to identify stuck points, which are the patient's problematic beliefs and conclusions regarding the nature and meaning of the traumatic experience. Identifying and challenging these stuck points remains a primary treatment goal during the remaining course of the protocol.

The second primary component of the CPT protocol is trauma processing. Specifically, patients are asked to write down a detailed account of their worst trauma, and they are then asked to read this account aloud to the therapist in session. Patients are also asked to read this account daily between sessions. In contrast to the full CPT protocol, the CPT-C protocol does not include the trauma-processing component described, with this alternate form focusing entirely on cognitions about the trauma rather than details of the actual event.

During the middle phase of the protocol, the focus of sessions turns primarily to cognitive interventions, including identifying stuck points and problematic patterns of thinking, as well as challenging automatic and irrational interpretations and beliefs. The final sessions of the protocol focus on various difficulties that individuals who have been exposed to a trauma commonly report, including issues with safety, trust, control, self-esteem, and intimacy. CPT is concluded by having the patient review his or her progress during the treatment, with a specific focus on identifying how their trauma-related thoughts, beliefs, and interpretations have changed since the beginning of therapy.

Family Involvement in PTSD Treatment

Studies have shown that the inclusion of family members in treatment may improve outcomes for a variety of psychiatric disorders, including schizophrenia and bipolar disorder, and evidence also suggests that family members can play a major role in the etiology and course of PTSD (Brewin et al., 2000). In a study of partner engagement in PTSD treatment among a sample of Vietnam War veterans, Sautter and colleagues (2006) found that both partner/caregiver burden and patient-partner involvement were significantly associated with how engaged the female partner was in the veteran's PTSD treatment. In another study, Tarrier and colleagues (1999) found that greater EE from important relatives was predictive of PTSD symptoms, with negative family relationships accounting for nearly 20% of the variance in the outcomes of PTSD treatment.

Batten and colleagues (2009) conducted a studying to examine veteran interest in the involvement of family members in PTSD treatment. Approximately three quarters of veterans in the sample expressed interest in greater family involvement in their treatment, and nearly the same percentage expressed the belief that a family member would be interested in attending a couples or family support group. Given these results, as well as other research findings that intimate partners can serve as sources of both interpersonal support and interpersonal stress (Laffaye, Cavella, Drescher, & Rosen 2008), it is important to assess couples and family functioning and to consider addressing these areas when improvements could enhance PTSD or other mental health treatment outcomes.

Sherman, Blevins, Kirchner, Ridener, and Jackson (2008) examined factors associated with engaging significant others in the treatment of veterans with PTSD. The authors proposed seven recommendations to reduce barriers to family treatment involvement:

1. In multidisciplinary settings, promote family involvement to all mental health staff because direct case managers may be the most persuasive referral sources.
2. Emphasize the benefits of family involvement to both the veteran and the partner.
3. Be flexible and accommodating of the partner's availability for treatment sessions.
4. Be aware of and address possible interfering beliefs (e.g., wanting to keep family issues private).

5. Address and normalize fears (e.g., concerns about confidentiality or about revealing disturbing material to the partner).
6. Overtly assess and address possible behavioral dysregulation (e.g., intimate partner violence, child abuse, or suicidal tendencies).
7. Be aware that family involvement is not indicated for all patients.

LIMITATIONS OF TREATMENT STRATEGIES

Comorbidity

Individuals diagnosed with PTSD frequently exhibit either lifetime or current co-occurring psychological disorders, including major depressive disorder, substance use disorders, and other anxiety disorders. For example, among adults with chronic PTSD, approximately one half experience co-occurring depression (Kessler, Sonnega, Bromet, Hughes, & Nelson, 1995; Orsillo et al., 1996). Co-occurring anxiety disorders are also common among adults with PTSD, and a substantial percentage of individuals experience co-occurrence of multiple disorders, including anxiety, depression, and PTSD (Ginzburg, Ein-Dor, & Solomon, 2010). Similarly, a substantial research literature suggests a high rate of co-occurrence between PTSD and substance use disorders, and veterans with PTSD tend to exhibit more severe substance use disorder problems than veterans without PTSD (Jacobsen, Southwick, & Kosten, 2001; Rotunda, O'Farrell, Murphy, & Babey, 2008). Given that the co-occurrence of other psychological disorders among patients with PTSD is common, understanding the clinical and treatment implications of disorders that frequently co-occur with PTSD is of particular importance.

Individuals with depression may experience low energy, a lack of motivation, and various symptoms of avoidance; therefore, it may be important to assess for co-occurring depression to be aware of symptoms that negatively affect engagement in treatment. Both CPT and PE require active involvement on the part of the PTSD patient, including regular attendance to therapy sessions and engagement in practice exercises between sessions. When depression is present, it should be carefully monitored to determine whether mood symptoms may interfere with the patient's involvement in the PTSD treatment. Fortunately, studies examining the efficacy of PE for PTSD have found that depression symptoms tend to decrease following treatment, suggesting that for some patients, the depression symptoms may be primarily PTSD related. Although some studies suggested that the presence of co-occurring depression may require an increase in the duration of cognitive-behavioral treatment (i.e., a great number of sessions), overall evidence suggests that both PE and CPT are associated with improvements in both the primary PTSD symptom outcomes and secondary outcomes such as broader anxiety and depression (Foa et al., 2005; Resick et al., 2008; Resick, Nishith, Weaver, Astin, & Feuer, 2002).

In considering the ability for a patient to successfully engage in psychotherapy for PTSD, the co-occurrence of substance use disorders is of particular concern.

Similar to symptoms of depression, substance use can potentially interfere with the ability for a patient to adequately engage in PE or CPT, particularly with regard to completing the necessary and important practice exercises between sessions. Further, given that PE requires actively confronting previously avoided thoughts, feelings, and situations, the use of substances as a way of avoiding unpleasant cognitive or emotional experiences would hinder the effectiveness of the intervention. Similarly, within CPT, the exposure-based component, the monitoring of beliefs and feelings, and the challenging of automatic thoughts and interpretations would be negatively impacted by the current presence of a substance use disorder. Foa and colleagues (2007) indicated that individuals with current substance abuse or dependence can participate in PE treatment for PTSD, but concurrent substance use disorder treatment is highly recommended, and substance use must be carefully monitored. Resick and colleagues (2008) recommended that substance dependence be treated before addressing PTSD, but patients with substance abuse can engage in CPT if substance use is directly addressed as a possible avoidance behavior and the patient agrees not to abuse the substance during the course of the therapy.

Treatment Engagement

Although cognitive-behavioral treatments of PTSD, including PE and CPT, have received support in the literature, a substantial percentage of patients who receive these treatments continue to experience clinically significant PTSD symptoms. Researchers have suggested that one factor contributing to this reduced treatment response may be poor treatment engagement due to ambivalence or a lack of awareness regarding the need to address trauma-related symptoms (Murphy, Rosen, Thompson, Murray, & Rainey, 2004). In particular, combat veterans may not believe that the avoidance behaviors associated with PTSD (e.g., emotional detachment) require treatment because such behaviors are viewed as adaptive responses to what the veterans may perceive as a potentially dangerous world (Murphy, Thompson, Murray, Rainey, & Uddo, 2009). Other patient populations, such as individuals with substance use disorders, are also known to exhibit high levels of ambivalence that can interfere with treatment engagement and successful treatment completion. Research has shown motivational interviewing (Miller & Rollnick, 2002), a therapy designed to reduce ambivalence and increase motivation for positive behavior change, is an effective brief intervention for substance users, although more research on the underlying mechanisms of the intervention is needed (Apodaca & Longabaugh, 2009). Other studies have sought to determine whether motivational enhancement therapy can produce improvements in PTSD treatment engagement among veterans (Murphy, Rosen, Cameron, & Thompson, 2002). Evidence from these studies suggests that addressing readiness to change and ambivalence prior to beginning psychological treatment for PTSD may have a positive impact on veterans' engagement in cognitive-behavioral PTSD treatment, including improvements in treatment attendance and retention (Murphy et al., 2009).

SPECIFIC POPULATIONS

Female Veterans

Research suggests that PTSD may be underdiagnosed among female veterans compared to their male counterparts (Grossman et al., 1997). Given a gender discrepancy within the general population that suggests that women are more likely than men to develop PTSD following exposure to a trauma, it is especially important to assess for and provide appropriate treatment for PTSD among female veterans. Compared to their male counterparts, female OIF/OEF veterans have fewer social supports and are more economically disadvantaged, both of which function as risk factors for postdeployment onset of PTSD (Fontana, Rosenheck, & Desai, 2010). Women currently make up approximately a seventh of the U.S. military force, and as a result of the recent OIF/OEF conflicts, the number of female veterans seeking mental health treatment is higher than ever (Nunnink et al., 2010). Combat veterans have historically been the focus of research due to their greater likelihood of exposure to traumatic events; the increasing number of women serving in combat roles has been associated with an increased focus in the literature on the mental health and access to treatment services among female veterans. Furthermore, women may also be at an elevated risk for developing PTSD in response to noncombat trauma exposures. This notion is supported by studies that suggest that women are at greater risk of exposure to certain traumatic events, such as military sexual trauma (Fontana et al., 2010).

National Guard and Reserve Troops

National Guard and Reserve members have comprised approximately 40% of the OIF/OEF combat forces, and studies suggest that Guard and Reserve troops are at a higher risk for mental and general physical health problems, including PTSD, than active duty personnel following deployment (Milliken et al., 2007; Shea, Vujanovic, Mansfield, Sevin, & Liu, 2010). Several explanations for these higher rates of mental and physical health problems have been proposed. Schnurr, Lunney, Bovin, and Marx (2009) note that Guard and Reserve soldiers are on average older than their active duty counterparts, and the additional stressors of reintegrating into established civilian careers and families may function as a risk factor. Further, Milliken and colleagues (2007) suggest that Guard and Reserve veterans may be at greater risk for mental health problems due to the lack of ongoing support from fellow combat veterans, as well as experiencing greater concerns about maintaining postdeployment health care than their active duty counterparts.

DIRECTIONS FOR FUTURE RESEARCH AND PROGRAM DEVELOPMENT

Telehealth/Internet Delivery

One issue that remains a barrier for veterans seeking psychological treatments for PTSD is the availability of mental health providers who have received specialized training to deliver a treatment protocol such as PE and CPT. This is particularly a challenge for veterans who live in rural areas and seek care at their local Veterans Affairs (VA) community-based outpatient clinic (Tuerk, Yoder, Ruggiero, Gros, & Acierno, 2010). The VHA has focused on developing a telemedicine infrastructure to increase the availability of treatment services to veterans living in rural areas, and research studies have examined the utility of PTSD treatments delivered in a telemedicine format. For instance, in a pilot study, Tuerk and colleagues (2010) found that PE delivered in a telemedicine format appeared to be feasible, acceptable, safe, and effective in reducing PTSD symptoms among a small sample of OIF/OEF veterans.

Given the treatment barriers, including limited availability of specially trained PTSD treatment providers, as well as the patient time and resources required to successfully complete cognitive-behavioral PTSD treatments, researchers have also proposed the need to examine the utility of self-management and Internet-based treatments (Taylor & Luce, 2003). For example, Litz, Engel, Bryant, and Papa (2007) conducted a study examining the efficacy of an 8-week therapist-assisted, self-management CBT for PTSD among service members with PTSD. The authors found a dropout rate similar to what is normally seen in cognitive-behavioral PTSD treatment, and both depression and PTSD symptoms were significantly lower among after treatment and at a 6-month follow-up among treatment completers. In sum, although these preliminary studies provided support for the utility of PTSD treatments delivered in a telemedicine or Internet-based format, further research is necessary to determine how effective treatments delivered in these alternative formats will be compared to delivery in a standard in-person format.

Specific Populations

To date, most research on military PTSD has focused on male veterans from past war eras, during which Guard and Reserve units played a much more limited role than is currently the case. Recent studies have begun to explore unique needs associated with gender, Guard/Reserve status, and multiple deployments, but these areas remain fertile ground for additional study. Particularly lacking is research on the impact of PTSD on the relationships of female veterans with their partners and children. As the number of female veterans expands, such research is sorely needed.

CONCLUSION

As veterans and service members continue to present with new or decades-old PTSD, the need for mental health services is essential. Compared to earlier war eras, many more assessment tools and manualized treatments are available. Promoting engagement and ensuring universal access to the highest-quality care in the context of constrained budgets will continue to present challenges and require ongoing innovation.

REFERENCES

American Psychiatric Association. (2000). *Diagnostic and Statistical Manual of Mental Disorders* (4th ed., text revision). Washington, DC: Author.

Apodaca, T. R., & Longabaugh, R. (2009). Mechanisms of change in motivational interviewing: A review and preliminary evaluation of the evidence. *Addiction, 104*, 705–715.

Barrowclough, C., Gregg, L., & Tarrier, N. (2008). Expressed emotion and causal attributions in relatives of post-traumatic stress disorder patients. *Behaviour Research and Therapy, 46*, 207–218.

Batten, S. V., Drapalski, A. L., Decker, M. L., DeViva, J. C., Morris, L. J., Mann, M. A., & Dixon, L. B. (2009). Veteran interest in family involvement in PTSD treatment. *Psychological Services, 6*, 184–189.

Berz, J. B., Taft, C. T., Watkins, L. E., & Monson, C. M. (2008). Associations between PTSD symptoms and parenting satisfaction in a female sample. *Journal of Psychological Trauma, 7*, 37–45.

Blake, D. D., Weathers, F. W., Nagy, L. M., Kaloupek, D. G., Gusman, F. D., Charney, D. S., & Keane, T. M. (1995). The development of a clinician-administered PTSD scale. *Journal of Traumatic Stress, 8*, 75–90.

Booth-Kewley, S., Larson, G. E., Highfill-McRoy, R. M., Garland, C. F., & Gaskin, T. A. (2010). Correlates of posttraumatic stress disorder symptoms in Marines back from war. *Journal of Traumatic Stress, 23*, 69–77.

Brewin, C. R., Andrews, B., & Valentine, J. D. (2000). Meta-analysis of risk factors for posttraumatic stress disorder in trauma exposed adults. *Journal of Consulting and Clinical Psychology, 68*, 748–766.

Brown, T. A., DiNardo, P., & Barlow, D. H. (2004). *Anxiety Disorders Interview Schedule Adult Version (ADIS-IV): Client Interview Schedule*. Albany, NY: Graywind.

Calhoun, P. S., Beckham, J. C., & Bosworth, H. B. (2002). Caregiver burden and psychological distress in partners of veterans with chronic posttraumatic stress disorder. *Journal of Traumatic Stress, 15*, 205–212.

Cloutier, P. F., Manion, I. G., & Walker, J. G. (2002). Emotionally focused interventions for couples with chronically ill children: A 2-year follow up. *Journal of Marital and Family Therapy, 28*, 391–398.

Dekel, R., & Monson, C. M. (2010). Military-related post-traumatic stress disorder and family relations: Current knowledge and future directions. *Aggression and Violent Behavior, 15*, 303–309.

Dekel, R., Solomon, Z., & Bleich, A. (2005). Emotional distress and marital adjustment of caregivers: Contribution of level of impairment and appraised burden. *Anxiety, Stress, and Coping, 18*, 71–82.

Dohrenwend, B. P., Turner, J. B., Turse, N. A., Adams, B. G., Koenen, K. C., & Marshall, R. (2006). The psychological risks of Vietnam for U.S. veterans: A revisit with new data and methods. *Science, 313*, 979–982.

Dohrenwend, B. P., Turner, J. B., Turse, N. A., Adams, B. G., Koenen, K. C., & Marshall, R. (2007). Continuing controversy over the psychological risks of Vietnam for U.S. veterans. *Journal of Traumatic Stress, 20*, 449–465.

First, M. B., Spitzer, R. L., Gibbon, M., & Williams, J. B. W. (1997). *Structured Clinical Interview for* DSM-IV *Axis-I Disorders (SCID-I)*. Washington, DC: APA.

Foa, E. B., Hembree, E. A., Cahill, S. P., Rauch, S. A. M., Riggs, D. S., Feeny, N. C., & Yadin, E. (2005). Randomized trial of prolonged exposure for posttraumatic stress disorder with and without cognitive restructuring: Outcome at academic and community clinics. *Journal of Consulting and Clinical Psychology, 73*, 953–964.

Foa, E. B., Hembree, E. A., & Rothbaum, B. O. (2007). *Prolonged exposure therapy for PTSD: Emotional processing of traumatic experiences, therapist guide*. New York: Oxford University Press.

Fontana, A., Rosenheck, R., & Desai, R. (2010). Female veterans of Iraq and Afghanistan seeking care from VA specialized PTSD programs: Comparison with male veterans and female war zone veterans of previous eras. *Journal of Women's Health, 19*, 751–757.

Galovski, T., & Lyons, J.A. (2004). Psychological sequelae of combat violence: A review of the impact of PTSD on the veteran's family and possible interventions. *Aggression and Violent Behavior, 9*, 477–501.

Ginzburg, K., Ein-Dor, T., & Solomon, Z. (2010). Comorbidity of posttraumatic stress disorder, anxiety and depression: A 20-year longitudinal study of war veterans. *Journal of Affective Disorders, 123*, 249–257.

Grossman, L. S., Willer, J. K., Stovall, J. G., McRae, S. G., Maxwell, S., & Nelson, R. (1997). Underdiagnosis of PTSD and substance use disorders in hospitalized female veterans. *Psychiatric Services, 48*, 393–395.

Hoge, C. W., Castro, C. A., Messer, S. M., McGurk, D., Cotting, D. I., & Koffman, R. L. (2004). Combat duty in Iraq and Afghanistan, mental health problems, and barriers to care. *The New England Journal of Medicine, 351*, 13–22.

Jacobsen, L. K., Southwick, S. M., & Kosten, T. R. (2001). Substance use disorders in patients with posttraumatic stress disorder: A review of the literature. *American Journal of Psychiatry, 158*, 1184–1190.

Kang, H. K., & Bullman, T. A. (2008). Risk of suicide among U.S. veterans after returning from the Iraq or Afghanistan war zones. *Journal of the American Medical Association, 300*, 652–653.

Kessler, R. C. (2000). Posttraumatic stress disorder: The burden to the individual and to society. *Journal of Clinical Psychiatry, 61*, 4–12.

Kessler, R. C., Berglund, P., Demler, O., Jin, R., Merikangas, K. R., & Walters, E. E. (2005). Lifetime prevalence and age-of-onset distributions of *DSM-IV* disorders in the National Comorbidity Survey Replication. *Archives of General Psychiatry, 62*, 593–602.

Kessler, R., Sonnega, A., Bromet, E., Hughes, M., & Nelson, C. (1995). Posttraumatic stress disorder in the National Comorbidity Survey. *Archives of General Psychiatry, 52*, 1048–1060.

Kulka, R. A. (1990). *Trauma and the Vietnam War generation: Report of findings from the National Vietnam Veterans Readjustment Study*. New York: Brunner/Mazel.

Kussman, M. J. (2008). *Uniform mental health services in VA medical centers and clinics*. Retrieved December 3, 2010, from http://www1.va.gov/vhapublications/ViewPublication.asp?pub_ID=1762

Laffaye, C., Cavella, S., Drescher, K., & Rosen, C. (2008). Relationships among PTSD symptoms, social support, and support source in veterans with chronic PTSD. *Journal of Traumatic Stress, 21*, 394–401.

Litz, B. T., Engel, C. C., Bryant, R. A., & Papa, A. (2007). A randomized, controlled proof-of-concept trial of an Internet-based, therapist-assisted self-management treatment for posttraumatic stress disorder. *Journal of American Psychiatry, 164*, 1676–1683.

Manguno-Mire, G., Sautter, F., Lyons, J. A., Myers, L., Perry, D., Sherman, M., … Sullivan, G. (2007). Psychological distress and burden among female partners of combat veterans with PTSD. *Journal of Nervous and Mental Disease, 195*, 144–151.

McHugh, R. K., & Barlow, D. H. (2010). The dissemination and implementation of evidence-based psychological treatments: A review of current efforts. *American Psychologist, 65*, 73–84.

Miller, W. R., & Rollnick, S. (2002). *Motivational interviewing* (2nd ed.). New York: Guilford.

Milliken, C. S., Auchterlonie, J. L., & Hoge, C. W. (2007). Longitudinal assessment of mental health problems among active and reserve component soldiers returning from the Iraq war. *Journal of the American Medical Association, 298*, 2141–2148.

Monson, C. M., Fredman, S. J., & Adair, K. C. (2008). Cognitive-behavioral conjoint therapy for posttraumatic stress disorder: Application to Operation Enduring and Iraqi Freedom veterans. *Journal of Clinical Psychology, 64*, 958–971.

Monson, C. M., Taft, C. T., & Fredman, S. J. (2009). Military-related PTSD and intimate relationships: From description to theory-driven research and intervention development. *Clinical Psychology Review, 29*, 707–714.

Murphy, R. T., Rosen, C. S., Cameron, R. P., & Thompson, K. E. (2002). Development of a group treatment for enhancing motivation to change PTSD symptoms. *Cognitive and Behavioral Practice, 9*, 308–316.

Murphy, R. T., Rosen, C. S., Thompson, K. E., Murray, M., & Rainey, Q. (2004). A readiness to change approach to preventing PTSD treatment failure. In S. Taylor (Ed.), *Advances in the treatment of posttraumatic stress disorder: Cognitive-behavioral perspectives* (pp. 67–92). New York: Springer.

Murphy, R. T., Thompson, K. E., Murray, M., Rainey, Q., & Uddo, M. M. (2009). Effect of a motivation enhancement intervention on veterans' engagement in PTSD treatment *Psychological Services, 6*, 264–278.

Nelson Goff, B. S., & Smith, D. B. (2005). Systemic traumatic stress: The couple adaptation to traumatic stress model. *Journal of Marital and Family Therapy, 31*, 145–157.

Nunnink, S. E., Goldwaser, G., Heppner, P. S., Pittman, J. O. E., Nievergelt, C. M., & Baker, D. G. (2010). Female veterans of the OEF/OIF conflict: Concordance of PTSD symptoms and substance misuse. *Addictive Behaviors, 35*, 655–659.

Orsillo, S. M., Weathers, F. W., Litz, B. T., Steinberg, H. R., Huska, J. A., & Keane, T. M. (1996). Current and lifetime psychiatric disorders among veterans with warzone-related posttraumatic stress disorder. *Journal of Nervous & Mental Disease, 184*, 307–313.

Ozer, E. J., Best, S. R., Lipsey, T. L., & Weiss, D. S. (2003). Predictors of posttraumatic stress disorder and symptoms in adults: A meta-analysis. *Psychological Bulletin, 129*, 52–73.

Pietrzak, R. H., Goldstein, M. B., Malley, J. C., Rivers, A. J., Johnson, D. C., & Southwick, S. M. (2010). Risk and protective factors associated with suicidal ideation in veterans of Operations Enduring Freedom and Iraqi Freedom. *Journal of Affective Disorders, 123*, 102–107.

Pietrzak, R. H., Johnson, D. C., Goldstein, M. B., Malley, J. C., Rivers, A. J., Morgan, C. A., & Southwick, S. M. (2010). Psychosocial buffers of traumatic stress, depressive symptoms, and psychosocial difficulties in veterans of Operations Enduring Freedom and Iraqi Freedom: The role of resilience, unit support, and postdeployment social support. *Journal of Affective Disorders, 120*, 188–192.

Pietrzak, R. H., Johnson, D. C., Goldstein, M. B., Malley, J. C., & Southwick, S. M. (2009). Perceived stigma and barriers to mental health care utilization among OEF-OIF veterans. *Psychiatric Services, 60*, 1118–1122.

Powers, M. B., Halpern, J. M., Ferenschak, M. P., Gillihan, S. J., & Foa, E. B. (2010). A meta-analytic review of prolonged exposure for posttraumatic stress disorder. *Clinical Psychology Review, 30*, 635–641.

Ramchand, R., Schell, T. L., Karney, B. R., Osilla, K. C., Burns, R. M., & Caldarone, L. (2010). Disparate prevalence estimates of PTSD among service members who served in Iraq and Afghanistan: Possible explanations. *Journal of Traumatic Stress, 23*, 59–68.

Resick, P. A., Monson, C. M., & Chard, K. M. (2008). *Cognitive processing therapy treatment manual: Veteran/military version*. Boston: Veterans Administration.

Resick, P. A., Nishith, P., Weaver, T. L., Astin, M. C., & Feuer, C. A. (2002). A comparison of cognitive-processing therapy with prolonged exposure and a waiting condition for the treatment of chronic posttraumatic stress disorder in female rape victims. *Journal of Consulting and Clinical Psychology, 70,* 867–879.

Rona, R. J., Hooper, R., Jones, M., Iverson, A. C., Hull, L., Murphy, D., & Wessely, S. (2009). The contribution of prior psychological symptoms and combat exposure to post Iraq deployment mental health in the UK military. *Journal of Traumatic Stress, 22,* 11–19.

Rotunda, R. J., O'Farrell, T. J., Murphy, M., & Babey, S. H. (2008). Behavioral couples therapy for comorbid substance use disorders and combat-related posttraumatic stress disorder among male veterans: An initial evaluation. *Addictive Behaviors, 33,* 180–187.

Samper, R., Taft, C. T., King, D. W., & King, L. A. (2004). Posttraumatic stress disorder and parenting satisfaction among a national sample of male Vietnam veterans. *Journal of Traumatic Stress, 17,* 311–315.

Sautter, F., Lyons, J., Manguno-Mire, G., Perry, D., Han, X., Sherman, M., … Sullivan, G. (2006). Predictors of partner engagement in PTSD treatment. *Journal of Psychopathology and Behavioral Assessment, 28,* 123–130.

Savarese, V. W., Suvak, M. K., King, L. A., & King, D. W. (2001). Relationships among alcohol use, hyperarousal, and marital abuse and violence in Vietnam veterans. *Journal of Traumatic Stress, 14,* 717–732.

Schnurr, P. P., Lunney, C. A., Bovin, M. J., & Marx, B. P. (2009). Posttraumatic stress disorder and quality of life: Extension of findings to veterans of the wars in Iraq and Afghanistan. *Clinical Psychology Review, 29,* 727–735.

Shea, M. T., Vujanovic, A. A., Mansfield, A. K., Sevin, E., & Liu, F. (2010). Posttraumatic stress disorder symptoms and functional impairment among OEF and OIF National Guard and Reserve veterans. *Journal of Traumatic Stress, 23,* 100–107.

Sherman, M.D., Blevins, D., Kirchner, J., Ridener, L., & Jackson, T. (2008). Key factors involved in engaging significant others in the treatment of Vietnam veterans with PTSD. *Professional Psychology: Research and Practice, 39,* 443–450.

Sledjeski, E. M., Speisman, B., & Dierker, L. C. (2008). Does number of lifetime traumas explain the relationship between PTSD and chronic medical conditions? Answers from the National Comorbidity Survey-Replication (NCS-R). *Journal of Behavioral Medicine, 31,* 341–349.

Sundin, J., Fear, N. T., Iversen, A., Rona, R. J., & Wessely, S. (2010). PTSD after deployment to Iraq: Conflicting rates, conflicting claims. *Psychological Medicine, 40,* 367–382.

Taft, C. T., Pless, A. P., Stalans, L. J., Koenen, K. C., King, L. A., & King, D. W. (2005). Risk factors for partner violence among a national sample of combat veterans. *Journal of Consulting and Clinical Psychology, 73,* 151–159.

Tarrier, N. (1996). An application of expressed emotion to the study of PTSD: Preliminary findings. *Clinical Psychology and Psychotherapy, 3,* 220–229.

Tarrier, N., Sommerfield, C., & Pilgrim, H. (1999). Relatives' expressed emotion (EE) and PTSD treatment outcome. *Psychological Medicine, 29,* 801–811.

Taylor, C. B., & Luce, K. H. (2003). Computer- and Internet-based psychotherapy interventions. *Current Directions in Psychological Science, 12,* 18–22.

Tuerk, P. W., Yoder, M., Ruggiero, K. J., Gros, D. F., & Acierno, R. (2010). A pilot study of prolonged exposure therapy for posttraumatic stress disorder delivered via telehealth technology. *Journal of Traumatic Stress, 23,* 116–123.

Weathers, F. W., Keane, T. M., & Davidson, J. R. (2001). Clinician-Administered PTSD Scale: A review of the first 10 years of research. *Depression and Anxiety, 13,* 132–156.

Weathers, F. W., Litz, B. T., Herman, D. S., Huska, J. A., & Keane, T. M. (1993). *The PTSD Checklist: Reliability, validity, and diagnostic utility.* Paper presented at the annual meeting of the International Society for Traumatic Stress Studies, San Antonio, TX.

Zarit, S. H., Todd, P. A., & Zarit, J. M. (1986). Subjective burden of husbands and wives as caregivers: A longitudinal study. *The Gerontologist, 26,* 260–266.

11

Depression

KEVIN M. CONNOLLY and KATHRYN S. HAHN

INTRODUCTION

The consideration of depression difficulties within the context of interpersonal relations is not a new development to the field of psychology (Whisman, 2001). For many, successful navigation of the challenging arena of intimate partnerships is a primary goal that people often spend a lifetime pursuing (Roberts & Robins, 2000). Consideration of the reciprocal impact of interpersonal relations and emotional stability is incorporated in several prominent theories of depression, including attachment theory (Bowlby, 1973); interpersonal theory (Weissman, Markowitz, & Klerman, 2000); cognitive theory (Beck, Rush, Shaw, & Emery, 1979); and behavioral theory (Lewinsohn & Gotlib, 1995). Many have found that marital distress and depression are related (Cano & O'Leary, 2000; Davila, Bradbury, Cohan, & Tochluk, 1997; Whisman & Bruce, 1999); however, some have found evidence to the contrary (Riggs, Hiss, & Foa, 1992). Thus, the consideration of couples therapy for depression may be specific to unique circumstances contributing to their depressive symptoms. As such, determining when couples therapy for the treatment of depression is clinically indicated, in addition to the exact procedures to be applied, are key considerations within the literature at large.

In the current chapter, we begin by discussing depressive disorders and how they have an impact on military personnel. Then, we provide a discussion of conceptual models of depression within an interpersonal context. A review of couples therapy activities, including assessment and active treatment protocols that have been examined in the literature, is provided, followed by a review of the treatment efficacy of such activities. We conclude the chapter with a discussion of limitations within the literature and additional considerations applicable to providing couples therapy for depression.

DESCRIPTION OF DEPRESSIVE DISORDERS

Major depressive disorder and dysthymic disorder are the two primary depressive disorders listed in the text revision of the fourth edition of the *Diagnostic and Statistical Manual of Mental Disorders* (*DSM-IV-TR*; American Psychiatric Association [APA], 2000). Although these two disorders are distinct, they share overlapping elements. Major depressive disorder is diagnosed by documenting the presence of one or more major depressive episodes. Diagnosis of a major depressive episode requires the presence of five or more of a collection of nine symptoms across a 2-week period. At least one of the symptoms must be depressed mood or anhedonia. The remaining symptoms include significant weight loss/gain, insomnia/hypersomnia, psychomotor agitation/retardation, fatigue/loss of energy, worthlessness/guilt, cognitive difficulties such as poor concentration, and recurrent thoughts of death such as suicidal ideation (APA, 2000). Dysthymic disorder is diagnosed by documented presence of depressed mood in conjunction with two (or more) additional symptoms for the majority of days across a 2-year period (APA, 2000). Additional symptoms include poor appetite/overeating, insomnia/hypersomnia, low energy/fatigue, low self-esteem, cognitive difficulties, and feelings of hopelessness. The last three symptoms are distinct from major depressive disorder diagnostic criteria. Functional impairment in the activities of daily life must be present to receive such diagnoses. It is necessary to define depression in terms of the research reviewed herein. Research examining both major depressive disorder and dysthymic disorder is included in this review. However, for the sake of brevity, we refer to these disorders as *depression* throughout the text.

Increasing evidence asserts that depressive disorders are commonly chronic, and depressive episodes tend to recur across time. Estimates suggest that approximately 80% of individuals who experience one major depressive episode will go on to experience a second (Judd, 1997). Clinical presentation, risk factors, and predictors of initial episodes may be distinct from recurring episodes (Daley, Hammen, & Rao, 2000). In support, research has found that past depressive episodes are the most prominent predictor of future episodes, suggesting unique predictor sets for initial episodes (Daley et al., 2000). In addition, witnessing violence and both chronic and episodic periods of stress are predictive of subsequent depressive episodes. Although these findings are based on a civilian population, the processes are highly relatable to combat veterans, who commonly witness violence and are exposed to chronic and episodic periods of intense stress. Overall, depressive disorders tend to present as chronic difficulty with numerous aspects influencing clinical presentation.

When considering the difficulties associated with depression, feelings of hopelessness commonly enter into the discussion. Such experiences have been strongly connected with suicide. In a review of the literature, Kleespies et al. (1999) summarized findings from community samples suggesting that depression was present in approximately 50% of individuals who completed suicides. Desai, Rosenheck, and Desai (2008) estimated that approximately 35–38% of suicides occur among veterans with depression. Further, among military samples, estimates suggested that individuals with mood disorders have an estimated three times greater risk of suicide compared to those without mood disorders (Ilgen et al., 2010). Such findings highlight the potential impact and clinical severity of depression.

It is apparent from the diagnostic criteria that clinical presentations of depression can vary widely among individuals (Kendler, Gardner, & Prescott, 1999). Numerous complex inter- and intrapersonal issues interact to result in how a person functions in daily life. For example, deployment to a combat zone can complicate family relations, resulting in a more complex clinical case conceptualization (Sayers, 2011). The varied combinations of symptom presentations all resulting in the same diagnosis can make research and applied endeavors complicated. Adding another person's history, interpersonal style, emotional tendencies, and life experiences can result in an extremely challenging situation from a clinical standpoint, not to mention a difficult life for each party involved.

PREVALENCE IN THE MILITARY

Prevalence estimates of depression vary depending on the sample studied. Estimates for veterans of the Korean War fluctuate around 15% (Ikin, Creamer, Sim, & McKenzie, 2010). Following recent deployments to Iraq, depression estimates ranged from 9% to 31% (Thomas et al., 2010). Ginzburg, Ein-Dor, and Solomon (2010) reported prevalence estimates of depression among Israeli veterans across the past 20 years. They found prevalence rates escalating to approximately 30%. These estimates for men are considerably elevated compared to national lifetime prevalence estimates ranging from 5% to 12% (APA, 2000). Such elevations are not surprising when considering how stressful life events can serve as precipitating and maintaining factors in the development of psychological disorders. This consideration functions at the core of our model of depression.

CONCEPTUAL MODEL OF DEPRESSION

Stress has been conceptualized as a life event that disrupts an individual's ability to maintain stability of their physiology, emotion, cognition, and behavior (Ingram & Price, 2001). A large body of literature demonstrates the role of stressful life events as a precipitant in the development, exacerbation, and maintenance of depressive symptoms (e.g., Kendler, Karkowski, & Prescott, 1999; Lewinsohn, Hoberman, & Rosenbaum, 1988; Stroud, Davila, & Moyer, 2008). Stressful events are intimately tied to the lives of deployed military personnel. Such stressors may include combat and separation from loved ones (Erbes, Polusny, MacDermid, & Compton, 2008). Stress plays a central role in two developmental models of depression: the diathesis-stress model and the stress generation model.

The development and maintenance of depressive symptomatology can be conceptualized from a diathesis-stress model. This model posits that an interaction of stress with vulnerability factors increases the likelihood of developing psychopathology (Zuckerman, 1999). This model allows for a framework to better understand causal factors in symptom development (Ingram & Price, 2001). For example, soldiers who have a genetic predisposition for depression (diathesis) and are deployed to a war zone (stressor) will be at increased risk for the development of depression than if the diathesis or stressor occurred alone.

Diathesis refers to an underlying mechanism that sets the stage for the development of a specific disorder. Psychological diatheses are conceptualized as relatively stable individual differences that increase one's vulnerability to stress and to the development of psychological disorders. These psychological vulnerabilities are defined as stable, endogenous, and not easily observable until interacting with a life stressor (Ingram & Price, 2001). Common psychological diatheses associated with depression include negative cognitive styles (e.g., Safford, Alloy, Abramson, & Crossfield, 2007), hopelessness (e.g., Joiner, Wingate, & Otamendi, 2005), and avoidance coping (e.g., Holahan, Moos, Holahan, Brennan, & Schutte, 2005).

Research has suggested that deployment to a war zone likely serves as a stressor increasing the risk for the development of depression. In support, postdeployment depression rates have been found to be significantly elevated compared to predeployment rates (Hoge et al., 2004). Differential rates of psychological difficulties have been found to be dependent on whether one serves in a combat zone. Hoge, Auchterlonie, and Milliken (2006) found that soldiers endorsed a 19% rate of mental health problems 2 weeks after returning from deployment in war zones. However, only 9% of their noncombat military counterparts returning from deployment endorsed clinically significant mental health problems. Deployment serves as a military-specific stressor that may play a causal role in the development of depression.

The stress generation model is another model of depression development with particular relevance to the military population. This model suggests that individuals who possess a vulnerability to depression are more likely to influence and create life stressors such as loss of social support, increased illness due to poor health behaviors, or financial problems (Hammen, 1991b; Kendler, Karkowski, et al., 1998; see Liu & Alloy, 2010, for a full review). The stress generation model differs from the diathesis-stress model in that depression-prone people will create stress related to their own behavior. This model does not focus on major life stressors that are independent from an individual's behavior (e.g., deployment, natural disasters, death of relatives) and may better explain the maintenance of depressive symptoms or relapse.

Based on the stress generation model, marital discord could be a stressor that is created or exacerbated by the individual who is suffering from depressive symptoms. Milliken, Auchterlonie, and Hoge (2007) measured depression rates in soldiers returning from deployment at 2 weeks and then again at 6 months. Rates of depression doubled from 5% to 10% in this time frame, suggesting additional influential mechanisms beyond the initial stressor of deployment. According to this theory, the soldiers may have been engaging in behavior that caused additional stressors and exacerbated their symptoms. One common stressor related to depression is a loss of social support. Pietrzak et al. (2010) found that decreases in social support (including marital problems) are associated with an increase in depressive symptoms.

Both the diathesis-stress model and the stress generation model take into consideration the influence of life stressors. The diathesis-stress model emphasizes major life events, such as military deployment, that suggest an etiology to depressive disorders. On the other hand, the stress generation model implicates the behavior of the individual in producing additional life stressors that may maintain or exacerbate depressive symptoms. Taken together, these models paint a picture of development and maintenance of depression particularly relevant in military samples.

DEPRESSION IN THE INTERPERSONAL CONTEXT

It has been well established that psychological disorders and marital discord are related (e.g., Jacobson, Holtzworth-Munroe, & Schmaling, 1989). Lewinsohn and Shaffer (1971) drew our attention to the importance of interpersonal issues in depression and marital concerns. Specifically, they highlighted that the examination of interpersonal reinforcement is a topic to be considered in the evaluation and treatment of depression. Hammen (1991a) proposed a specific theory to explain the relation between depression and relationships. This theory asserts that the stress generated by a depressed individual has an impact on family relations. In turn, family stress reactions inform the depressed individual's reaction, exacerbating the condition. In support of this theory, several studies have found that depression predicts marital difficulties (e.g., Cano & O'Leary, 2000; Denton, Golden, & Walsh, 2003). Studies have also found that stressful marital events can result in two to six times increased risk for depression (e.g., Cano & O'Leary, 2000; Whisman & Bruce, 1999), and that marital distress predicts subsequent depression (Davila et al., 1997), supporting the notion that marital distress may serve as a precipitating factor in depressive disorders. Regardless of etiology, it is likely that once depression and co-occurring marital discord are established, their relationship is likely maintained within a reciprocal causation model. Following this line, theoretical speculation has suggested that depression may benefit from therapy aimed at improving dysfunctional interpersonal relations.

Increased focus on the challenges associated with combat deployment is becoming more necessary as we understand more about not only the impact combat has on the individual, but also the individual's family system (Gimbel & Booth, 1994). Erbes et al. (2008) discussed various aspects of how the military experience can have an impact on couples. They highlighted a variety of concerns with an impact on the veteran and his or her family. It was noted that the burden of deployment can last much longer than the duration of deployment due to preparation efforts prior to deployment and recovery efforts after deployment. In addition, persistent worry about the potential for injury or death during deployment takes a toll on emotional resources. Concerns for family strength during deployment in addition to the potential to learn of negative life events during deployment also contribute to chronic stress. Plus, couples can experience difficulties in relearning how to communicate and function as a cohesive family unit following the soldier's return home. Overall, there are numerous stressors before, during, and postdeployment. The impact on couples can be immense, setting the stage for the development of a variety of psychological difficulties, including depression (Hoge et al., 2004). In considering such stressors, it is not surprising that the prevalence of depression in military samples is elevated compared to national estimates.

REVIEW OF COUPLES TREATMENT STRATEGIES FOR DEPRESSION

Although several empirically supported therapies exist for depressive disorders (e.g., behavioral activation, cognitive therapy [CT]) and several empirically supported therapies exist for marital/couple discord (e.g., integrative behavioral couples therapy), there have been few examinations of therapies specifically designed for this relatively common overlap. However, given the reciprocal relationship between depression and intimate relationships, it is possible that providing individual therapy specifically for depression or marital therapy (MT) aimed specifically at correcting interpersonal difficulties could effectively treat the presenting problem. Veterans Affairs (VA) has made great strides in training clinicians and providing evidence-based treatments to veterans. Included in these treatments are cognitive-behavioral therapy (CBT) for depression and integrated behavioral couples therapy for marital discord. Although CBT for depression and couples therapy to improve marital relations may result in reduced depression and increased interpersonal functioning, neither treatment is specifically designed as couples treatment for depression.

Couples Therapy for Depression

Beach, Sandeen, and O'Leary (1990) developed an initial couples treatment for depression based on earlier versions of behavioral marital therapy (BMT). Previously, it had been shown that depressive couples exposed to BMT had significant treatment gains (e.g., Jacobson, Follette, & Pagel, 1986). In the following years, our conceptualization of depressive disorders and their link to interpersonal relations has broadened (e.g., Hammen, 2005). However, prior to initiating couples therapy for the treatment of depression, it is important to complete a thorough assessment of relevant factors to develop a clear and concise case conceptualization that will guide treatment activities.

Assessment Considerations

It becomes apparent in examining the processes and relations among interpersonal relations and depression that it is necessary to complete a comprehensive evaluation prior to referring for couples therapy for depression. Initially, evaluation of mental status is necessary to rule out more severe psychopathology that may interfere with couples therapy (Beach, Dreifuss, Franklin, Kamen, & Gabriel, 2008). Such illnesses may include but are not limited to psychotic disorders, certain personality disorders, substance-related disorders, or bipolar disorders. Further, extreme reactions such as suicidal or homicidal risk must be assessed throughout therapy. If safety becomes a concern, a shift from couples therapy to individual therapy may be indicated. Once it has been established that more severe pathology is not present, further evaluation of couple functioning and depression can ensue. Several relevant factors must be assessed prior to initiating couples therapy for depression. We provide a brief review of relevant topics.

Providing a treatment that exhibits a clear conceptual connection with their perception of the cause of their depression may be influential in treatment success (O'Leary, Riso, & Beach, 1990). Beach and O'Leary (1992) highlighted the necessity to assess the level of marital discord and maladaptive cognitive reactions. Specifically, they found evidence to suggest that participants are more likely to benefit from couples therapy for depression compared to CT when there is a high level of couple distress and low level of cognitive distortion. Further, previous work has suggested that the sex of the depressed person may influence treatment outcome. Isakson et al. (2006) found that couples with similar levels of distress benefited from couples therapy. However, female participants with greater levels of initial distress compared to their spouse experienced significantly fewer treatment gains with couples therapy compared to individual therapy. Males experienced treatment gains regardless of modality. However, their gains appeared in fewer couples therapy sessions compared to individual sessions. These findings suggest that specific patient characteristics may be important when considering couples therapy compared to individual therapy.

Expanding on assessment of current functioning, Proulx, Buehler, and Helms (2009) found evidence suggesting that interpersonal hostility and warmth predict variation in depression. Such considerations will inform clinical case conceptualization and subsequent treatment activities. Further, the concept of perceived relationship instability has been found to prospectively predict subsequent depression (Whitton & Whisman, 2010).

Finally, Beach and colleagues (2008) noted that it is important to meet with each person individually to assess for individual situations that may hinder treatment. Such occurrences may include domestic violence, personal perceptions of the relationship, whether or not divorce/separation is pending, infidelity, and personal commitment to therapy. These findings highlight the importance of assessing a variety of interpersonal factors longitudinally, which may help determine clinical status and if interpersonally focused interventions are clinically indicated. Accordingly, areas to assess for the purpose of case conceptualization and treatment recommendations include current and historic marital discord, current and historic stability of perceived relationship satisfaction, maladaptive cognitive patterns, personal concerns/reactions, and the sex of the person experiencing depression. Each of these domains has been linked to clinical status and intervention success and warrant clinical attention prior to treatment.

Goals of Couples Therapy for Depression

Beach et al. (2008) detailed two overarching goals for MT for depression: (a) enhance marital quality and (b) reduce the symptom severity of depression. Inherent within these two goals are several additional, more specific goals designed to target the constructs likely to maintain depression and marital discord. They noted three primary targets for couples therapy for depression. The first target focuses on interpersonal behavior modification for the purpose of increasing shared social engagement and enhancing stress management. The second target focuses on problem solving and addressing concerns unique to the couple and their history. The final target focuses on relapse prevention. The extant literature has identified a number of therapeutic activities designed to target these goals. The following sections discuss these therapies and review their empirical status.

Couples Therapy for Depression Treatment Programs

The literature has empirically examined several variations of couples therapy in terms of its effect on depression. Much of the literature has focused on interpersonal behavioral modification, although some have targeted cognition as well as medication. Here, we briefly describe the components of the interventions that have been previously examined for their impact on depression. Then, we provide an empirical review of treatment outcome literature examining the effectiveness of the reviewed interventions.

Behavioral marital therapy (Jacobson, Dobson, Fruzzetti, Schmaling, & Salusky, 1991) incorporates elements of both behavior therapy and CT, with emphasis on building communication skills, problem-solving skills and conflict resolution. Treatment activities include contingency management, behavioral rehearsal, and cognitive restructuring. BMT is typically complete after 15–20 sessions.

Marital therapy (Beach et al., 1990; Emanuels-Zuurveen & Emmelkamp, 1996) was specifically designed for the treatment of depression within a couples format. Similar to BMT, MT incorporates skill-building exercises focused on communication and problem solving, in addition to assertiveness training and behavioral rehearsal and modeling within the dyad. However, MT initially targets aspects of depression (e.g., isolation) that may interfere with MT. Then, more interpersonal activities are incorporated with both members of the couple participating. Unlike BMT, MT is designed as a 10-session intervention.

Cognitive marital therapy (CMT; Teichman, Bar-El, Shor, Sirota, & Elizur, 1995; Teichman & Teichman, 1990) is a modified version of individual CT. This treatment specifically focuses on cognitive functioning within the interpersonal realm. This therapy provides education concerning the relation among cognition, emotion, and behaviors and aims to identify the cognitive components maintaining depressive symptoms. Treatment is designed to last approximately 15 sessions.

Systemic couples therapy (SCT; Jones & Asen, 1999) for depression attempts to place depressive reactions within an interpersonal context and then to disrupt such relations through modification of attributes and behaviors. Thus, the targets appear to be cognitive and behavioral as they relate to interpersonal context. SCT is designed to be complete in approximately 12–20 sessions.

Coping-oriented couples therapy (COCT; Bodenmann et al., 2008) is based on cognitive and behavioral treatments aimed at reducing stress and enhancing coping skills within the dyad. This treatment incorporates many similar activities as other cognitive and behavioral interventions, including behavioral rehearsal, communication skills training, and problem-solving skills training. However, this treatment specifically aims to strengthen "dyadic coping" by enhancing each individual's ability to communicate stress, react to the partner's stress, and modify reactions based on the partner's reactions. Contingency management techniques are incorporated into this therapy. COCT was designed to be complete in ten 2-hour sessions occurring every other week.

Brief couples therapy (BCT; Cohen, O'Leary, & Foran, 2010) for depression occurs across five 2-hour sessions. The focus of this therapy is to provide education about depression and to enhance cognitive and behavioral coping skills as they relate to depression. Elements of contingency management, communication skill training, cognitive modification, and interpersonal behavioral interactions are included in this intervention.

It is clear that current couples treatments aimed at ameliorating depressive symptoms incorporate a variety of therapeutic procedures in a number of ways. Many of these treatment protocols overlap in terms of procedural components; however they are commonly packaged in differing formats, making direct comparisons from one study to another difficult. The following section details the treatment outcome findings of the interventions previously discussed.

Couples Therapy for Depression Treatment Outcome Research

Outcome research has begun to pave the way for our current understanding of the impact of MT on depressive symptoms. Historically, couples therapy was considered one component in the treatment of depression. Early findings suggested that the inclusion of MT along with medication can have a positive effect on depression (e.g., Friedman, 1975). This treatment avenue has gained empirical attention in recent years. Researchers have synthesized the literature examining the role of couples therapy for depression in relation to more typical forms of individual therapy for depression (Gilliam & Cottone, 2005). A review of the literature has revealed relatively few treatment studies examining couples therapy specifically designed for the treatment of depression. We were unable to find any studies within the extant literature examining couples therapy for depression with military samples. Further, the studies that are present have been noted to have methodological limitations, making firm statements regarding the impact of the intervention difficult (e.g., Barbato & D'Avanzo, 2008; Gupta, Coyne, & Beach, 2003).

Several studies have examined the impact of BMT compared to individual therapy on depressive symptoms (Beach & O'Leary, 1992; Emanuels-Zuurveen & Emmelkamp, 1996; Jacobson et al., 1991). Accordingly, BMT is the most tested couples therapy for depression to date. Jacobson and colleagues (1991) examined the impact of BMT compared to individual CT and a combination condition incorporating both treatments on depressive symptoms in females. Participants were randomly assigned to one of the three groups. No wait-list (WL) control condition was included. All treatments resulted in reduced depressive symptoms. Results varied depending on whether the couple was experiencing distress at the outset of the study. Individuals reporting low levels of marital distress benefited more from CBT compared to BMT or the combined treatment condition. Couples high in marital distress benefited equally from BMT and CBT in reduction of depressive symptoms. BMT resulted in greater benefit on relationship satisfaction compared to competing conditions. These preliminary findings suggest that BMT may be clinically indicated when the wife is clinically depressed and the dyad is reporting marital distress. However, BMT may be clinically contraindicated when no marital distress is present.

Beach and O'Leary (1992) compared the impact of BMT to individual CT and a WL control group on depressive symptoms of randomly assigned female participants. All three conditions resulted in improved depression symptoms from pre- to posttreatment, with the two active conditions resulting in equivalent improvement and greater improvement compared to WL. BMT resulted in significantly improved marital adjustment compared to the alternative conditions. Further, analyses revealed that depression improvements were mediated by improvements in marital functioning among the BMT condition. The authors went on to suggest that secondary analyses of their data indicated that women with greater marital distress with limited maladaptive cognitive distortions may benefit more from BMT compared to CT. Such findings suggest the use of BMT with individuals who are depressed and in a distressing relationship. These findings will need to be replicated due to small sample size (n = 15).

In 1996, Emanuels-Zuurveen and Emmelkamp reported on findings comparing individual CBT and MT on depressive symptoms such as mood, behavioral activity, and depressive cognition. Participants were randomly assigned to one of the two conditions. No WL condition was included. Both treatments evidenced benefits across depressive symptoms; however, the authors reported that the MT condition had a greater impact on interpersonal variables compared to the CBT condition. Again, these findings suggest that couples therapy for depression is clinically indicated when the couple is experiencing marital distress in conjunction with individual depression.

Results comparing behavioral couples therapy to individual therapies appeared equivocal across studies when examining depression. However, as one might expect, marital discord improved to a greater extent with couples therapy compared to individual therapy. This supports previous reports suggesting that assessment of the presence of marital discord prior to initiating treatment is indicated.

Moving beyond behavioral couples therapy, one study examined a modified version of interpersonal psychotherapy (IPT; Klerman, Weissman, Rounsaville, & Chevron, 1984) for couples (Foley, Roundsaville, Weissman, Sholomaskas, & Chevron, 1989). Compared to individual IPT, couples IPT produced equivalent results, with both conditions reducing depression symptoms. However, similar to treatment outcome research examining behavioral couples therapy, IPT couples therapy resulted in an advantageous gain in marital satisfaction compared to individual therapy.

Another examination looked at individual CT compared to CMT (Teichman et al., 1995). This study included both male and female depressed participants and a WL condition. Participants were not randomly assigned to all conditions. In addition, some participants were provided antidepressant medication. Across all measurements, CMT benefited depressive symptoms. Results for the CT group at postassessment approached significance, and the WL group did not evidence statistical benefit. At follow-up, both CT and CMT conditions did not differ in their improvement of depressive symptoms. The authors concluded that CMT appeared to have a more immediate effect on depression compared to CT. It was suggested that this may be due to increased support from the spouse and coverage of a broader spectrum of relevant interpersonal constructs. However, concerns of random assignment and inclusion of medication therapy make firm conclusions about specific mechanisms of change difficult.

Leff et al. (2000) reported findings supporting the use of SCT for depression compared to antidepressant medication. Participants were randomly assigned to either SCT or medication treatment. A WL condition was not included. Both treatments resulted in significant postintervention change; however, SCT achieved significantly greater reductions in depression compared to antidepressant medication at posttreatment and 2-year follow-up. These findings support the long-term effects of couples treatment for depression compared to medication.

Further expanding our comparisons between treatment modalities for depression, COCT was compared to both CT and IPT in terms of impact on depression and interpersonal constructs (Bodenmann et al., 2008). CT and IPT were delivered individually, although at times the spouse was incorporated into several IPT sessions, primarily for educational purposes. Sixty male and female participants were randomly assigned to one of the three treatment conditions. The authors found that COCT was as effective in reducing depressive symptoms as the other two treatments. However, COCT did not evidence statistical improvement in couple satisfaction or interpersonal coping. Contrary to previous research, these findings suggest that COCT does not have an interpersonal advantage over individual therapy for depression. This study suggested equivalent findings among established treatments for depression compared to couples-oriented treatment for depression without additional interpersonal benefits. However, similar to other studies, the current study may have had insufficient power to detect true differences.

Finally, a randomized study examined the impact of BCT on depression (Cohen et al., 2010). Participants were depressed women who were randomly assigned to either a BCT (n = 18) or a WL group (n = 17). Findings suggest that brief couples interventions may benefit depressive symptoms more than WL will. Significant findings occurred at postassessment and follow-up assessments. Further, the authors reported that couple satisfaction, understanding, and acceptance of depression improved, as did general psychological distress. Again, these findings support what several previous studies found in that cognitive-behavioral couples treatments appeared beneficial in terms of ameliorating depressive symptoms and interpersonal difficulties.

Currently, the literature conceptualizes the function of MT for depression as an avenue to interrupt the self-perpetuating cycle between marital discord and depression. There is much room to grow in this literature. We are unaware of any published studies examining the impact of couples therapy for depression in military veterans. Thus, our current considerations for use of this therapy are based on civilian samples. The extant literature is limited, and we are unable to draw firm conclusions about the efficacy of couples therapy for depression at this time due to several notable limitations, discussed next. It appears at present that couples therapy for depression may be as effective as individual therapy for depression, with the possibility of additional benefits for the dyad relationship. More rigorous randomized controlled trials are necessary to make more conclusive statements.

LIMITATIONS OF THE EXTANT LITERATURE

A number of methodological and conceptual concerns have led several researchers to further question the empirical status of couples therapy for the treatment of depression (Barbato & D'Avanzo, 2008; Gilliam & Cottone, 2005; Gupta et al., 2003). Some limitations we have noted in our discussion of the treatment outcome literature. However, there are additional limitations to be considered when evaluating the extant literature. For example, several studies have found that participants questioned the rationale for MT for depression and specifically stated that they did not believe it directly addressed depression and focused more on the relationship (see Gilliam & Cottone, 2005, for a review). In fact, several authors have noted that couples therapy is not typically modified to more directly address difficulties related to depression (Denton et al., 2003). It appears as though interpersonal treatments focused on treating depression would benefit from increasing the salience of specific treatment components to address difficulties clearly related to depression (Gilliam & Cottone, 2005).

Examining the state of the literature, Barbato and D'Avanzo (2008) conducted a meta-analysis reviewing the efficacy of couples therapy as a treatment for depression. Their analyses supported the previous findings noted here in that couples therapy for depression did not result in greater benefit for depression symptoms compared to individual therapy for depression. However, generally issues pertaining to relationship discord did improve to a greater degree for those receiving couples therapy compared to individual therapy recipients. The authors reported a number of notable limitations in the literature. Namely, there are few studies utilizing no treatment control groups or studies comparing couples therapy for depression to pharmacological interventions. Further, they noted that the findings are plagued by small sample sizes, unclear randomization procedures, lack of randomization, lack of blind evaluative conditions, and reports of treatment completers only. Disparate attrition rates also make interpretation difficult (Gupta et al., 2003). In addition, most studies are confined to middle-age samples and samples who fall within the mild-to-moderate levels of depression. Thus, older and younger individuals and individuals with major depression are quite underrepresented in the treatment outcome literature. Further, among the few studies existing, it is difficult to compare the findings of one study to another due to great variability in terms of methods, treatment interventions, and sample characteristics.

At this time, it is unclear when and under what circumstances such a treatment would be indicated above empirically established individual psychotherapy for depression. Currently, MT for depression might best be limited to veterans with depressive disorders who also have clinically significant marital difficulties and are contraindicated with veterans who do not have marital difficulties. Further studies are necessary to determine if additional benefit would result from supplemental treatments such as medication management or individual therapy.

ADDITIONAL ISSUES TO CONSIDER

Ethical considerations are of paramount importance when considering couples therapy in military populations. The unique elements involved in couples therapy in a VA setting provides for some novel ethics-relevant situations that may have an impact on therapeutic activities and outcomes. It is important to enter into such a therapeutic situation with a level of familiarity with potential ethical considerations and to address such concepts early in the therapy process. We provide a brief review of ethical issues to consider when conducting couples therapy for depression.

Gottlieb, Lasser, and Simpson (2008) detailed a number of ethical issues to be considered in couples therapy. In accordance with the American Psychological Association ethics code (American Psychological Association, 2002), at the outset of therapy the psychologist is to make clear the relationship he or she has with each family member, including who is the client and potentially how this agreed-on course of action may have an impact on therapy (informed consent). We are taught to ask ourselves, "Who is our client?" The answer to this question is, in most cases, rather clear when conducting individual therapy. However, in couples therapy there are typically at least three individuals involved: the therapist and both individuals in the couple. Couples therapy commonly operates under the premise that the therapist is a neutral party focused on the overall benefit of both parties involved. However, within a VA setting, the clinician's official client is the veteran. If only one person in the couple is a veteran, then on initiation of therapy, the therapist's allegiance is to the veteran. As a result, the concept of therapeutic neutrality is weakened. This scenario immediately puts the couple on slightly uneven ground in terms of their relationship to the therapist and could have an impact on treatment activities.

The American Psychological Association ethics code is explicit about the terms of when confidentiality does and does not apply. However, each state exhibits some variability in terms of how this ethics code is enforced. Given that the client is the veteran, confidentiality is applied to the veteran's treatment. However, where does that leave the nonveteran spouse? Again, such a dynamic can create concerns about what the couple does and does not share in session. Such a concern could potentially have an impact on the effectiveness of therapy if the couple or even one individual is concerned about sharing private information with confidentiality concerns. This mimics most situations when a family member provides collateral information in the context of individual treatment sessions. Perhaps it would be best to treat this scenario the same way. Regardless, it is imperative that all individuals understand their relationship with the therapist and the limitations of confidentiality.

Also, issues of record keeping come into play. Only the veteran has access to chart documentation (unless the veteran consents for his or her spouse to have chart access). This should be discussed prior to initiation of therapy. However, a collateral chart can be opened for the nonveteran to document clinically relevant information. If both individuals are veterans, then the clinician can document in both charts. We recommend caution in the content of documentation in such cases. A number of ethical dilemmas could surface if the couple were to legally divorce and request records. Overall, during couples therapy numerous ethical concerns could arise. Each situation deserves to be examined on a case-by-case basis with consideration of the ethics code and all potential courses of action and the associated outcomes. In addition, when necessary consult with other professionals to help determine the most ethical course of action.

FUTURE DIRECTIONS

Theoretical speculation and empirical findings have yielded tentative support for the use of couples therapy for depressive disorders. However, as noted, the literature has a number of notable limitations. Our understanding and successful application of couples therapy for depression would benefit from future studies examining a number of conceptual issues. First, to our knowledge, there has not been a treatment outcome study examining couples therapy for depression using a military sample. Currently, we must draw from the civilian literature; however, it will be necessary to extend such studies to veterans. Also, the literature would benefit from additional description of the specific procedures used and how such procedures relate in a systematic way to previous studies. This will make comparing study methods and, as a result, their findings more meaningful. Variability in the presentation of depressive disorders and marital discord can result in numerous case conceptualizations. Varied case conceptualization may lead to differential treatment efficacy. Additional research is necessary to determine what specific intervention works best for whom and under what circumstances.

In terms of methodology, future research will benefit from adequately powered studies that compare a variety of empirically established treatments to uncover when specific interventions may be of greater benefit than others. In other words, where does the benefit of a specific treatment lie, and how do we accurately assess the necessary constructs on the front end? Much work needs to be done to more fully understand exactly where couple therapy fits in among our currently empirically supported depression treatments.

REFERENCES

American Psychiatric Association. (2000). *Diagnostic and statistical manual of mental disorders* (4th ed., text revision). Washington, DC: Author.

American Psychological Association. (2002). Ethical principles and code of conduct. *American Psychologist, 57,* 1060–1073.

Barbato, A., & D'Avanzo, B. (2008). Efficacy of couple therapy as a treatment for depression: A meta-analysis. *Psychiatry Quarterly, 79,* 121–132.

Beach, S. R. H., Dreifuss, J. A., Franklin, K. J., Kamen, C., & Gabriel, B. (2008). Couple therapy and the treatment of depression. In A. S. Gurman (Ed.), *Clinical handbook of couple therapy* (4th ed., pp. 545–566). New York: Guilford Press.

Beach, S. R. H., & O'Leary, K. D. (1992). Treating depression in the context of marital discord: Outcome and predictors of response for marital therapy versus cognitive therapy. *Behavior Therapy, 17,* 43–49.

Beach, S. R. H., Sandeen, E. E., & O'Leary, K. D. (1990). *Depression in marriage: A model for etiology and treatment.* New York: Guilford Press.

Beck, A. T., Rush, A. J., Shaw, B. F., & Emery, G. (1979). *Cognitive therapy of depression.* New York: Guilford Press.

Bodenmann, G., Plancherel, B., Beach, S. R. H., Widmer, K., Gabriel, B., Meuwly, N., ... Schramm, E. (2008). Effects of coping-oriented couples therapy on depression: A randomized clinical trial. *Journal of Consulting and Clinical Psychology, 76,* 944–954.

Bowlby, J. (1973). *Attachment and loss.* New York: Basic Books.

Cano, A., & O'Leary, K. D. (2000). Infidelity and separations precipitate major depressive episodes and symptoms of non-specific depression and anxiety. *Journal of Consulting and Clinical Psychology, 68,* 774–781.

Cohen, S., O'Leary, K. D., & Foran, H. (2010). A randomized clinical trial of a brief, problem-focused couple therapy for depression. *Behavior Therapy, 41,* 433–446.

Daley, S. E., Hammen, C., & Rao, U. (2000). Predictors of first onset and recurrence of major depression in young women during the 5 years following high school graduation. *Journal of Abnormal Psychology, 109,* 525–533.

Davila, J., Bradbury, T. N., Cohan, C. L., & Tochluk, S. (1997). Marital functioning and depressive symptoms: Evidence for a stress generation model. *Journal of Personality and Social Psychology, 73,* 849–861.

Denton, W. H., Golden, R. N., & Walsh, S. R. (2003). Depression, marital discord and couple therapy. *Current Opinion in Psychiatry, 16,* 29–34.

Desai, M. M., Rosenheck, R. A., & Desai, R. A. (2008). Time trends and predictors of suicide among mental health outpatients in the department of Veterans Affairs. *The Journal of Behavioral Health Sciences and Research, 35,* 115–124.

Emanuels-Zuurveen, L., & Emmelkamp, P. M. (1996). Individual behavioral-cognitive therapy versus marital therapy for depression in martially distressed couples. *British Journal of Psychiatry, 169,* 181–188.

Erbes, C. R., Polusny, M. A., MacDermid, S., & Compton, J. S. (2008). Couple therapy with combat veterans and their partners. *Journal of Clinical Psychology: In Session, 64,* 972–983.

Foley, S. H., Roundsaville, B. J., Weissman, M. M., Sholomaskas, D., & Chevron, E. (1989). Individual versus conjoint interpersonal therapy for depressed patients with marital disputes. *International Journal of Family Psychiatry, 10,* 29–42.

Friedman, A. (1975). Interaction of drug therapy with marital therapy in depressive patients. *Archives of General Psychiatry, 32,* 619–637.

Gilliam, C. M., & Cottone, R. R. (2005). Couple or individual therapy for the treatment of depression?: An update of the empirical literature. *The American Journal of Family Therapy, 33,* 265–272.

Gimbel, C., & Booth, A. (1994). Why does the military combat experience adversely affect marital relations? *Journal of Marriage and Family, 56,* 1150–1152.

Ginzburg, K., Ein-Dor, T., & Solomon, Z. (2010). Comorbidity of posttraumatic stress disorder, anxiety and depression: A 20-year longitudinal study of war veterans. *Journal of Affective Disorders, 123,* 249–257.

Gottlieb, M. C., Lasser, J., & Simpson, G. L. (2008). Legal and ethical issues in couple therapy. In A. S. Gurman (Ed.), *Clinical handbook of couple therapy* (4th ed., pp. 698–717). New York: Guilford Press.

Gupta, M., Coyne, J. C., & Beach, S. R. H. (2003). Couples treatment for major depression: critique of the literature and suggestions for some different directions. *Journal of Family Therapy, 25,* 317–346.

Hammen, C. (1991a). *Depression runs in families: The social context of risk and resilience in children of depressed mothers.* New York: Springer-Verlag.

Hammen, C. (1991b). Generation of stress in the course of unipolar depression. *Journal of Abnormal Psychology, 100,* 555–561.

Hammen, C. (2005). Stress and depression. *Annual Review of Clinical Psychology, 1,* 293–319.

Hoge, C. W., Auchterlonie, J. L., & Milliken, C. S. (2006). Mental health problems, use of mental health services, and attrition from military service after returning from deployment to Iraq or Afghanistan. *Journal of the American Medical Association, 295*, 1023–1032.

Hoge, C. W., Castro, C. A., Messer, S. C., McGurk, D., Cotting, D. I., & Koffman, R. L. (2004). Combat duty in Iraq and Afghanistan, mental health problems, and barriers to care. *New England Journal of Medicine, 351*, 13–22.

Holahan, C. J., Moos, R. H., Holahan, C. K., Brennan, P. L., & Schutte, K. K. (2005). Stress generation, avoidance coping, and depressive symptoms: A 10-year model. *Journal of Consulting and Clinical Psychology, 73*, 685–666.

Ikin, J. F., Creamer, M. C., Sim, M. R., & McKenzie, D. P. (2010). Comorbidity of PTSD and depression in Korean War veterans: Prevalence, predictors and impairment. *Journal of Affective Disorder, 125*, 279–286.

Ilgen, M. A., Bohnert, A. S. B., Ignacio, R. V., McCarthy, J. F., Valenstein, M. M., Kim, M., & Blow, F. C. (2010). Psychiatric diagnoses and risk of suicide in veterans. *Archives of General Psychiatry, 67*, 1152–1158.

Ingram, R. E. & Price, J. M. (2001). *Vulnerability to psychopathology: Risk across the lifespan.* New York: Guilford Press.

Isakson, R. L. Hawkins, E. J., Harmon, S. C., Slade, K., Martinez, J. S., & Lambert, M. J. (2006). Assessing couple therapy as a treatment for individual distress: When is referral to couple therapy contraindicated? *Contemporary Family Therapy, 28*, 313–322.

Jacobson, N. S., Dobson, K., Fruzzeti, A. E., Schmaling, D. B., & Salusky, S. (1991). Marital therapy as a treatment for depression. *Journal of Consulting and Clinical Psychology, 59*, 547–557.

Jacobson, N. S., Follette, W. C., & Pagel, M. (1986). Predicting who will benefit from behavioral marital therapy. *Journal of Consulting and Clinical Psychology, 54*, 518–522.

Jacobson, N. S., Holtzworth-Munroe, A., & Schmaling, K. B. (1989). Marital therapy and spouse involvement in the treatment of depression, agoraphobia, and alcoholism. *Journal of Consulting and Clinical Psychology, 57*, 5–10.

Joiner, T. E., Wingate, L. R., & Otamendi, A. (2005). An interpersonal addendum to the hopelessness theory of depression: Hopelessness as a stress and depression generator. *Journal of Social and Clinical Psychology, 24*, 649–664.

Jones, E., & Asen, E. (1999). *Systemic couple therapy and depression.* London: Karnac.

Judd, L. L. (1997). The clinical course of unipolar major depressive disorders. *Archives of General Psychiatry, 54*, 989–991.

Kendler, K. S., Gardner, C. O., & Prescott, C. A. (1999). Clinical characteristics of major depression that predict risk of depression in relatives. *Archives of General Psychiatry, 56*, 322–327.

Kendler, K. S., Karkowski, L. M., & Prescott, C. A. (1999). Causal relationship between stressful life events and the onset of major depression. *American Journal of Psychiatry, 156*, 837–841.

Kleespies, P. M., Deleppo, J. D., Gallagher, P. L., & Niles, B. L. (1999). Managing suicidal emergencies: Recommendations for the practitioner. *Professional Psychology: Research and Practice, 30*, 454–463.

Klerman, G. L., Weissman, M. M., Rounsaville, B. J., & Chevron, E. (1984). *Interpersonal psychotherapy of depression.* New York: Basic Books.

Leff, J., Vearnals, S., Wolff, G., Alexander, B., Chisholm, D., Everitt, B., … Dayson, D. (2000). The London Depression Intervention Trial: Randomised controlled trial of antidepressants versus couple therapy in the treatment and maintenance of people with depression living with a partner: clinical outcome and costs. *The British Journal of Psychiatry, 177*, 95–100.

Lewinsohn, P. M., & Gotlib, I. H. (1995). Behavioral theory and treatment of depression. In E. E. Becker & W. R. Leber (Eds.), *Handbook of depression* (pp. 352–375). New York: Guilford Press.

Lewinsohn, P. M., Hoberman, H. M., & Rosenbaum, M. (1988). A prospective study of risk factors for unipolar depression. *Journal of Abnormal Psychology, 97,* 251–264.

Lewinsohn, P. M., & Shaffer, M. (1971). Use of home observations as an integral part of the treatment of depression: Preliminary report and case studies. *Journal of Consulting and Clinical Psychology, 37,* 87–94.

Liu, R. T., & Alloy, L. B. (2010). Stress generation in depression: A systematic review of the empirical literature and recommendations for future study. *Clinical Psychology Review, 30,* 582–593.

Milliken, C. S., Auchterlonie, J. L., & Hoge, C. W. (2007). Longitudinal assessment of mental health problems among active and reserve component soldiers returning from the Iraq war. *Journal of the American Medical Association, 298,* 2141–2148.

O'Leary, K. D., Riso, L. P., & Beach, S. R. H. (1990). Attributions about the marital discord/depression link and therapy outcome. *Behavior Therapy, 21,* 413–422.

Pietrzak, R. H., Johnson, D. C., Goldstein, M. B., Malley, J. C., Rivers, A. J., Morgan, C. A., & Southwick, S. M. (2010). Psychosocial buffers of traumatic stress, depressive symptoms, and psychosocial difficulties in veterans of operations enduring freedom and Iraqi freedom: The role of resilience, unit support, and postdeployment social support. *Journal of Affective Disorders, 120,* 188–192.

Proulx, C. M., Buehler, C., & Helms, H. (2009). Moderators of the link between marital hostility and change in spouses' depressive symptoms. *Journal of Family Psychology, 23,* 540–550.

Riggs, D. S., Hiss, H., & Foa, E. B. (1992). Marital distress and the treatment of obsessive compulsive disorder. *Behavior Therapy, 23,* 585–597.

Roberts, B. W., & Robins, R. W. (2000). Broad dispositions, broad aspirations: The intersection of personality traits and major life goals. *Personality and Social Psychology Bulletin, 26,* 1284–1296.

Safford, S. M., Alloy, L. B., Abramson, L. Y., & Crossfield, A. G. (2007). Negative cognitive style as a predictor of negative life events in depression-prone individuals: A test of the stress generation hypothesis. *Journal of Affective Disorders, 99,* 147–154.

Sayers, S. L. (2011). Family reintegration difficulties and couples therapy for military veterans and their spouses. *Cognitive and Behavioral Practice, 18,* 108–119.

Stroud, C. B., Davila, J., & Moyer, A. (2008). The relationship between stress and depression in first onsets versus recurrences: A meta-analytic review. *Journal of Abnormal Psychology, 117,* 206–213.

Teichman, Y., Bar-El, Z., Shor, H., Sirota, P., & Elizur, A. (1995). A comparison of two modalities of cognitive therapy (individual and marital) in treating depression. *Psychiatry, 58,* 136–148.

Teichman, Y., & Teichman, M. (1990). Interpersonal view of depression: Review and integration. *Journal of Family Psychology, 3,* 349–367.

Thomas, J. L., Wilk, J. E., Riviere, L. A., McGurk, D., Castro, C. A., & Hoge, C. W. (2010). Prevalence of mental health problems and functional impairment among Active Component and National Guard soldiers 3 and 12 months following combat in Iraq. *Archives of General Psychiatry, 67,* 614–623.

Weissman, M. M., Markowitz, J. C., & Klerman, G. L. (2000). *Comprehensive guide to interpersonal psychotherapy.* New York: Basic Books.

Whisman, M. A. (2001). The association between depression and marital dissatisfaction. In S. R. H. Beach (Ed.), *Marital and family processes in depression: A scientific foundation for clinical practice* (pp. 3–24). Washington, DC: American Psychological Association.

Whisman, M. A., & Bruce, M. L. (1999). Marital distress and incidence of major depressive episode in a community sample. *Journal of Abnormal Psychology, 108,* 674–678.
Whitton, S. W., & Whisman, M. A. (2010). Relationship satisfaction instability and depression. *Journal of Family Psychology, 24,* 791–794.
Zuckerman, M. (1999). Mood disorders. In M. Zuckerman (Ed.), *Vulnerability to psychopathology: A biosocial model* (pp. 151–208). Washington, DC. American Psychological Association.

12

Infidelity

DOUGLAS K. SNYDER, CHRISTINA BALDERRAMA-DURBIN,
CAITLIN FISSETTE, DAVID M. SCHEIDER,
J. KELLY BARNETT, and SAMUEL FIALA

INTRODUCTION

The disclosure or discovery of an extramarital affair by one's partner reliably results in significant emotional and behavioral disruption in both the individual partners and their relationship. Couples report infidelity as a leading cause of divorce, and couple therapists describe infidelity as among the most difficult problems to treat. The recent upsurge in both the frequency and duration of deployments related to the Operation Iraqi Freedom/Operation Enduring Freedom (OIF/OEF) conflicts, as well as changing demographics in the all-volunteer U.S. armed forces, have contributed to increased vulnerability of military marriages to sexual infidelity. In this chapter, we first summarize research findings regarding the prevalence of infidelity in civilian and military populations, as well as its impact on both individual and relationship functioning. We describe a structured, three-stage integrative treatment tailored specifically to couples struggling with infidelity, and report initial evidence regarding the effectiveness of this intervention. We present evidence indicating that military counselors receiving training in this structured protocol not only can learn information regarding the conceptual underpinnings and specific interventions comprising this treatment but also can apply it appropriately in analog clinical situations. We then conclude with suggestions for future research and for extending dissemination efforts to reduce acute adverse consequences experienced by service members and their partners experiencing infidelity.

PREVALENCE OF INFIDELITY IN CIVILIAN AND MILITARY POPULATIONS

Extramarital affairs occur with high frequency both within the general U.S. population and among treatment-seeking samples. Representative community surveys indicate a lifetime prevalence of sexual infidelity of approximately 21% among men and 11% among women (Laumann, Gagnon, Michael, & Michaels, 1994); broadening infidelity to encompass emotional as well as sexual affairs increases these rates among men and women to 44% and 25%, respectively (Glass & Wright, 1992). Recent evidence indicates that the rates for both physical and emotional infidelity among women are approaching those for men. Studies examining the annual incidence of extramarital sex suggest that approximately 2–4% of all married men and women are likely to have engaged in extramarital sex in the past year (Treas & Giesen, 2000; Wiederman, 1997). Infidelity is the most frequently cited cause of divorce (Amato & Rogers, 1997), with approximately 40% of divorced individuals reporting at least one extramarital sexual contact during their marriage (Janus & Janus, 1993). These prevalence rates of infidelity stand in bold contrast to studies indicating that most individuals (70–85%) report that extramarital affairs violate their expectations for acceptable behavior in committed relationships (Laumann et al., 1994; Smith, 1994).

Although the incidence of infidelity among couples in which one or both partners serve in the U.S. Armed Forces is unknown, anecdotal evidence suggests comparable or higher rates compared to civilian samples. Soldiers tend to enlist young and marry young; just 1% of the civilian population under 20 is married, compared with nearly 14% of military members in the same age group—and marriage at a young age is a strong predictor of subsequent infidelity (Atkins, Baucom, & Jacobson, 2001). Moreover, in the past decade, these marriages have been tested by the longest and most recurrent deployments in the history of the volunteer military. Among combat-exposed troops, the high incidence of stress-related mental health problems evidenced 3–4 months after returning from deployment (estimated by the Army's surgeon general at 30%) further strains couples' relationships and renders them more vulnerable to infidelity (Monson, Fredman, & Adair, 2008; Sayers, Farrow, Ross, & Oslin, 2009; Tichenor, Armstrong, Vann, & Green, 2002). Indeed, among military couples seeking marital therapy from U.S. Army family life chaplains, roughly 50–60% seek assistance with issues of infidelity—a rate strikingly higher than for the percentage of civilian couples in marital therapy (approximately 15%) (Atkins, Eldridge, Baucom, & Christensen, 2005).

Thus, whether working predominantly within a civilian or military setting, clinicians are frequently likely to encounter individuals coping with infidelity, whether in the context of couples therapy aimed at recovery from an extramarital affair, individual therapy with someone struggling with his or her own affair or responding to a partner's affair, or interventions with children contending with consequences of a parent's infidelity. Surveys of couple therapists indicate that they regard extramarital affairs as among the most difficult conflicts to treat, and that they often feel inadequately trained to conduct effective interventions targeting them (Whisman, Dixon, & Johnson, 1997).

Several factors render working with military and veteran couples struggling with issues of infidelity potentially even more challenging. Because of the deployment cycle, interventions may be difficult to implement when an affair is first disclosed or discovered; organizing interventions with partners separated geographically requires coordinating professional as well as technological resources. Second, issues of confidentiality assume special importance for some individuals because infidelity remains a punishable offense under Article 134 of the Uniform Code of Military Justice (UCMJ). Finally, comorbid emotional and behavioral difficulties having increased prevalence among personnel exposed to combat—particularly emotional expressiveness and regulation deficits accompanying posttraumatic stress disorder (PTSD) and other stress-related disorders—may both contribute to relationship vulnerability to infidelity or complicate the recovery process.

IMPACT OF INFIDELITY ON INDIVIDUAL AND RELATIONSHIP FUNCTIONING

Adverse individual and relationship consequences of infidelity are well documented (Allen et al., 2005). For persons recently learning of their partner's affair, research documents a broad range of negative emotional and behavioral effects, including partner violence, depression, suicidal ideation, acute anxiety, and symptoms similar to PTSD (Beach, Jouriles, & O'Leary, 1985; Cano & O'Leary, 2000; Charny & Parnass, 1995; Glass & Wright, 1997). Among persons having participated in an affair, similar reactions of depression, suicidality, and acute anxiety are also common effects—particularly when disclosure or discovery of infidelity results in marital separation or threats of divorce (Beach et al, 1985; Spanier & Margolis, 1983; Wiggins & Lederer, 1984).

Consequences of infidelity for a couple's relationship are equally well documented. Infidelity is the most frequently cited cause of divorce (Amato & Rogers, 1997). An unpublished reanalysis of the 1991–2002 General Social Surveys based on 8,637 community respondents found that having an affair nearly doubled the likelihood of divorce (from 21% to 40%) in that sample (D. Atkins, personal communication, 2006). Anecdotal evidence suggests that, regardless of culmination in separation or divorce, couples responding to infidelity exhibit disproportionately high rates of severe conflict and verbal or physical aggression, compared to maritally distressed couples not reporting an affair.

Infidelity has an adverse impact on not only the adult partners, but also the children affected by parental conflict or divorce. In the United States, approximately 17% of children experience their parents' divorce each year. Considerable evidence confirms that marital distress, conflict, and disruption are associated with a wide range of deleterious effects on children, including depression, withdrawal, poor social competence, health problems, poor academic performance, a variety of conduct-related difficulties, and markedly decreased longevity (Gottman, 1999).

In sum, sexual and emotional infidelity has a high prevalence in both civilian and military populations, has significant adverse impact on individual partners and their relationship, and can be particularly difficult to treat.

A THREE-STAGE INTEGRATIVE TREATMENT PROMOTING RECOVERY FROM INFIDELITY

Until recently, there has been almost no empirical study of interventions for couples dealing with affairs. To date, the *only* intervention designed specifically for couples struggling with issues of infidelity to be empirically evaluated and supported as efficacious is an integrative approach designed by Snyder, Baucom, and Gordon (Baucom, Snyder, & Gordon, 2009; Gordon, Baucom, & Snyder, 2004; Snyder, Baucom, & Gordon, 2007).

This intervention for couples struggling with issues of infidelity builds on strengths of two empirically supported treatments for couple distress, specifically cognitive-behavioral couples therapy (CBCT) and insight-oriented couples therapy (IOCT). CBCT is a skills-based approach emphasizing communication skills (e.g., emotional expressiveness and problem solving) as well as behavior change skills (e.g., constructing independent or shared behavior change agreements), with additional emphasis on cognitive processes (e.g., relationship beliefs and standards, expectancies, and interpersonal attributions) that moderate the initiation, maintenance, or impact of these relationship skills (Epstein & Baucom, 2002). IOCT is a developmental approach emphasizing the identification, interpretation, and resolution of conflictual emotional processes in the couple's relationship related to enduring maladaptive interpersonal patterns established in previous relationships (Snyder & Mitchell, 2008). Although theoretically grounded primarily in these two approaches to couples therapy, the specific interventions comprising our treatment are fully congruent with a broad range of alternative theoretical approaches fostering change in couples' problem-solving interactions (e.g., solution-focused therapy) and emotional responsiveness (e.g., emotion-focused therapy).

In addition to integrating empirically supported components from CBCT and IOCT, the affair-specific intervention outlined here builds on the empirical literature regarding recovery from interpersonal trauma and recovery from relationship injuries. Specifically, infidelity is viewed as a traumatic event to the relationship that dramatically disrupts partners' assumptions about themselves and their relationship, causing both emotional and behavioral upheaval related to perceived loss of control and unpredictability of their future. Among other individual symptoms, reactions to infidelity frequently include intrusive and persistent rumination about the affair, hypervigilance to relationship threats and the partner's interactions with others, vacillation of emotional numbing with affect dysregulation, physiological hyperarousal accompanied by disrupted sleep or appetite, difficulties in concentration, and a broad spectrum of symptoms similar to those exhibited in PTSD.

Consistent with conceptualization of infidelity as an interpersonal trauma, this affair-specific intervention for couples also draws on literature regarding recovery from interpersonal injury, including an emerging empirical literature on stages and processes of forgiveness. Similar to trauma-based approaches, across diverse conceptualizations of recovery from interpersonal injury a crucial component involves developing a changed understanding of why the injury or betrayal occurred and reconstructing a new meaning for the event. Preliminary evidence concerning interventions aimed at promoting recovery from interpersonal injury—heretofore developed almost exclusively from an individual- rather than couple-based perspective—indicates that such interventions can facilitate a more balanced appraisal of the injuring person and event, decreased negative affect and behaviors toward the offender, and increased psychological and physical health (Gordon, Baucom, & Snyder, 2005).

Detailed guidelines for clinical assessment and intervention—along with extended case examples and representative dialogues between therapist and partners—have been provided in a published clinician's guide (Baucom et al., 2009). This clinician's guide also describes how to integrate a self-help book designed for affair couples (Snyder et al., 2007) into treatment as a supplemental resource. We organize our treatment for affair couples into three stages: (a) dealing with the initial impact; (b) exploring context and finding meaning; and (c) moving on. Descriptions of each of these three stages follow.

Stage 1: Dealing With the Initial Impact

The first stage of this intervention addresses the impact of the affair. The first goal involves assessment of individual and relationship functioning to identify immediate crises requiring intervention (e.g., suicidality or physical aggression) and develop a shared intervention plan outlining each participant's responsibilities. Following this assessment and formulation, initial interventions assist partners in articulating desired boundaries or guidelines for interaction between themselves and with others. For example, partners often need to negotiate how much time to spend together or apart; whether to sleep together or to maintain sexual relations; what further contact, if any, the participating partner will have with the outside affair person; and what information to share with potential interested parties (e.g., children, in-laws, or friends). Even couples with a previous history of effective problem-solving skills often find it difficult without assistance to resolve basic boundary issues due to the emotional turmoil following an affair.

Because of frequent negative interactions between partners during this initial stage of recovery, most couples need a strategy that allows them to disengage when their level of emotion becomes too high. Consequently, both "time-out" and appropriate "venting" strategies are presented, with partners instructed on when and how to implement these strategies effectively.

After some degree of stabilization has been achieved, the couple can begin to examine the impact of the affair on themselves and their relationship. Couples are taught to use appropriate emotional expressiveness skills for both speaker and listener to promote more effective communication regarding the impact of the affair. In addition to facilitating discussion of this impact within sessions, supervised letter writing is used as a means for helping partners to explore and exchange their feelings in a more reflective manner.

Despite initial stabilization and emotional containment, many couples recovering from an affair continue to wrestle with episodic "flashbacks" involving the injured partner's reexperiencing of intense emotional reactions to the affair. These are particularly frequent during the initial stage of recovery but may persist at a reduced intensity and frequency for months or even years following the initial discovery or disclosure. Thus, couples are helped to achieve a greater understanding of what flashbacks are and why they occur, and partners are advised in specific steps they can take both individually and as a couple to cope with these more effectively.

Finally, because common reactions to affairs include acute anxiety, depression, and shame, partners are provided with specific strategies to facilitate physical self-care (e.g., sleep, diet, exercise), engaging social support while maintaining appropriate boundaries, and spiritual support if consistent with the partner's belief system. The supportive nature of these sessions also aids in strengthening rapport with each partner.

Stage 2: Exploring Context and Finding Meaning

The second stage of this intervention involves exploring factors that contributed to the occurrence of the affair and evaluating both their ongoing effects and potential response to intervention. Toward this end, a comprehensive conceptual model is proposed to the couple that integrates both recent (proximal) and early developmental (distal) factors across multiple domains influencing vulnerability to, engagement in, and recovery from an affair. Domains of potential contributing factors include (a) aspects of the couple's own relationship (e.g., high conflict, low emotional warmth); (b) situational factors outside their relationship (e.g., work-related stressors, pursuit by a potential partner outside their relationship); (c) characteristics of the participating partner (e.g., anger at the injured partner, insecurities about self, unrealistic relationship expectations, developmental history, or enduring personality disorders); and (d) characteristics of the injured partner (e.g., discomfort with emotional closeness, avoidance of conflict, developmental history, and long-standing emotional or behavioral difficulties).

Factors from each of these domains are explored as potential contributors to the course of an extramarital affair, including (a) preexisting and enduring vulnerabilities; (b) initial approach behaviors (e.g., flirtatious behavior outside the couple's own standards); (c) implicit or explicit decisions to engage in or maintain the affair; (d) disclosure or discovery of the affair (e.g., participating partner's feelings of guilt, injured partner's increased vigilance); and (e) the couple's immediate and potential long-term response (e.g., capacity for emotional self-regulation and containment of intense couple conflict). In discussing these various factors, individual responsibility is placed on the partner involved in the affair, but a careful assessment of the context within which the individual decided to have an affair is important. It is essential to differentiate between understanding the context for the affair versus "blaming the victim" for the affair.

An overriding objective during Stage 2 of this intervention involves deriving a comprehensive explanatory formulation of the affair that facilitates a realistic appraisal regarding potential reoccurrence of this traumatic experience and aids in creating a new understanding of the couple's relationship—both as it functioned prior to the affair and its current dynamics. The injured partner's recovery of perceived relational security is critical to his or her ability to move beyond the hurt, anger, and anxiety that typify their initial response to an affair. A second goal is to promote the participating partner's tolerance for the injured partner's continued emotional reactivity and persistent "need to know" why the affair occurred. Partners often have conflicting timelines for recovery, with participating partners preferring to "move on" and put the affair behind them well before their injured partners feel emotionally prepared to do so. Unless this difference is understood and normalized, and the participating partner's engagement in exploring the context is facilitated, a couple's long-term recovery following some initial stabilization of affect is frequently compromised. Third, examination of contributing factors promotes initial problem-solving processes and provides the couple with an opportunity to evaluate their ability to initiate changes critical to the long-term viability of their relationship.

Finally, through the process of examining enduring developmental processes potentially contributing to vulnerability and response to the affair, both partners have an opportunity to understand their own and each other's emotions and behaviors in a more comprehensive manner. This new understanding often reduces the intensity of negative emotions surrounding the affair, diminishes confusion and anxiety about partners' own reactivity, and often facilitates an optimism regarding potential for change and greater emotional fulfillment in their relationship. That is, understanding persistent dysfunctional relationship patterns from a developmental perspective often promotes more effective modification of these patterns using cognitive and behavioral strategies.

Stage 3: Moving On

The final stage of this intervention begins by integrating information obtained in previous sessions in preparing to reach an informed decision about how to move on. An integrative summary provided to the couple, along with letters written by each partner to the other, are used to converge on a shared formulation regarding factors contributing to the occurrence of the affair. Similar to the cognitive processing therapy for PTSD, any remaining questions or fears about their relationship are addressed, and reconstructed beliefs about the relationship are evaluated. Once this goal is achieved, handouts and written exercises are used to promote partners' evaluation and discussion of the viability of their relationship, its potential for change, and partners' commitment to work toward change based on what they have learned about themselves and each other. Partners explore the process of moving on by examining the meaning of this construct as it relates to both their personal and relationship values and belief systems.

For many couples, this process involves examining personal beliefs about forgiveness. We advocate a view of forgiveness as a process by which partners pursue increased understanding of themselves, each other, and their relationship to free themselves from being dominated by negative thoughts, feelings, and behaviors. This process is distinguished from a view of forgiveness as excusing or forgetting that the affair occurred or requiring a decision to reconcile and remain in the couple's relationship. An important aspect of this conceptualization of forgiveness is that it does not stipulate that partners must reconcile for forgiveness to occur.

Rather, forgiveness is conceptualized as meaning that negative feelings no longer dominate their lives or control their actions toward their partner, and that the affair event has been resolved to such an extent that the injured partner no longer carries its negative effects into other relationships. The forgiveness process also allows for the possible development of warmer and more positive feelings toward the participating partner.

Thus, partners' beliefs about forgiveness are explored, along with their apprehensions or fears regarding moving on. Potential risks and benefits of moving on emotionally are examined, including research on adverse consequences of sustained anger on individuals' physical and emotional health as well as relationships with others. If the couple decides during this stage to continue their relationship, interventions aid the couple in identifying areas of their relationship that require additional assistance and provide them with strategies to address these difficulties. Alternatively, if the couple decides to separate or pursue divorce, additional sessions help partners plan how to pursue this goal in a manner that is least hurtful to them and others they care about (e.g., children and extended family) and that promotes a process of moving on emotionally and rebuilding healthy, but separate, lives.

TAILORING TREATMENT TO ACTIVE DUTY OR VETERAN COUPLES

There may be circumstances that require adapting the general treatment strategies and specific components described to a highly structured, abbreviated protocol. Especially for military couples for whom consideration of the deployment cycle precludes treatment lasting several months or longer, an abbreviated intervention protocol may be essential. For military couples recovering from infidelity, Snyder and colleagues articulated an eight-session intervention protocol based on the full-length treatment previously demonstrated to be efficacious. This abbreviated protocol is outlined in Table 12.1 and is designed to be administered in 12 hours, with sessions 1–3 and 7 lasting 2 hours each. An intervention procedures manual (Snyder, 2008) outlines the basic tasks of each session, along with handouts and reference to the self-help resource guide developed for affair couples.

Sometimes, deployment or other factors initially preclude conjoint sessions. However, both technological advances (e.g., videoconferencing) and coordination of interventions (e.g., by two separate counselors adopting the same basic protocol) can facilitate couple-based interventions enhancing recovery. For example, the self-help resource book for affair couples (Snyder et al., 2007) guides partners through specific exercises aimed at promoting understanding of individual and relationship processes impacted by an affair and specific steps essential to restoring a healthy relationship. Partners separated geographically can be provided with readings targeting a given stage of recovery, handouts summarizing key points, and exercises for partners to complete separately or to share and work through together. Both partners and therapists separated geographically can more readily coordinate interventions and recovery efforts by drawing on these common resources.

TABLE 12.1 Structure of an Eight-Session Abbreviated Affair-Specific Intervention

Stage 1: Dealing with the initial impact
Session 1: Understanding what has happened and preventing further damage
Session 2: Reaching good decisions to manage the crisis and contain its impact
Session 3: Dealing with painful feelings and engaging in self-care
Stage 2: Exploring context and finding meaning
Session 4: Factors in and around your relationship that contributed to the affair
Session 5: Characteristics of partners that contributed to vulnerability
Session 6: Putting the pieces together—Developing a shared formulation
Stage 3: Moving on
Session 7: Understanding forgiveness—Exploring personal perspectives
Session 8: Reaching and implementing an informed decision about how to move on

Note: Listed "sessions" may be conceptualized as therapeutic tasks to be accomplished in one or more actual sessions or in extended sessions lasting 90–120 minutes.

EVIDENCE OF TREATMENT EFFICACY

Using a replicated case-study design, Gordon et al. (2004) demonstrated that, following this three-stage integrative treatment, injured spouses whose partner had participated in an extramarital relationship showed significant decreases in depression and PTSD-related symptomatology, reductions in state anger and global marital distress, and decreases in negative assumptions and increases in forgiveness toward their partner (see Figure 12. 1). Similarly, participating partners showed significant decreases in PTSD-related symptoms, depression, and initial anger toward their spouse. Effect sizes reflecting reductions in marital distress for injured spouses were moderate to large and generally exceeded average effect sizes for efficacious marital therapies not targeting affair couples.

DISSEMINATION OF THE INTERVENTION PROTOCOL WITHIN THE MILITARY SETTING

Since 2006, we have provided training in this intervention protocol to a broad spectrum of providers, including chaplains, social workers, marriage and family therapists, and psychologists employed by the military to provide counseling and related services. The training formats have varied in length (1 versus 2 days), structure (primarily didactic versus engagement in role plays), and composition (professional backgrounds and numbers of participants). Given that couples more often seek the assistance of clergy than mental health professionals when pursuing relationship preparation or counseling (Doss, Rhoades, Stanley, Markman, & Johnson, 2009), and that chaplains are the first-ranked counseling resource sought by soldiers (Shinseki, 2003), we have been particularly interested in the impact of structured training in this affair-specific intervention protocol with military chaplains. Specifically, we have examined whether a brief training protocol could have

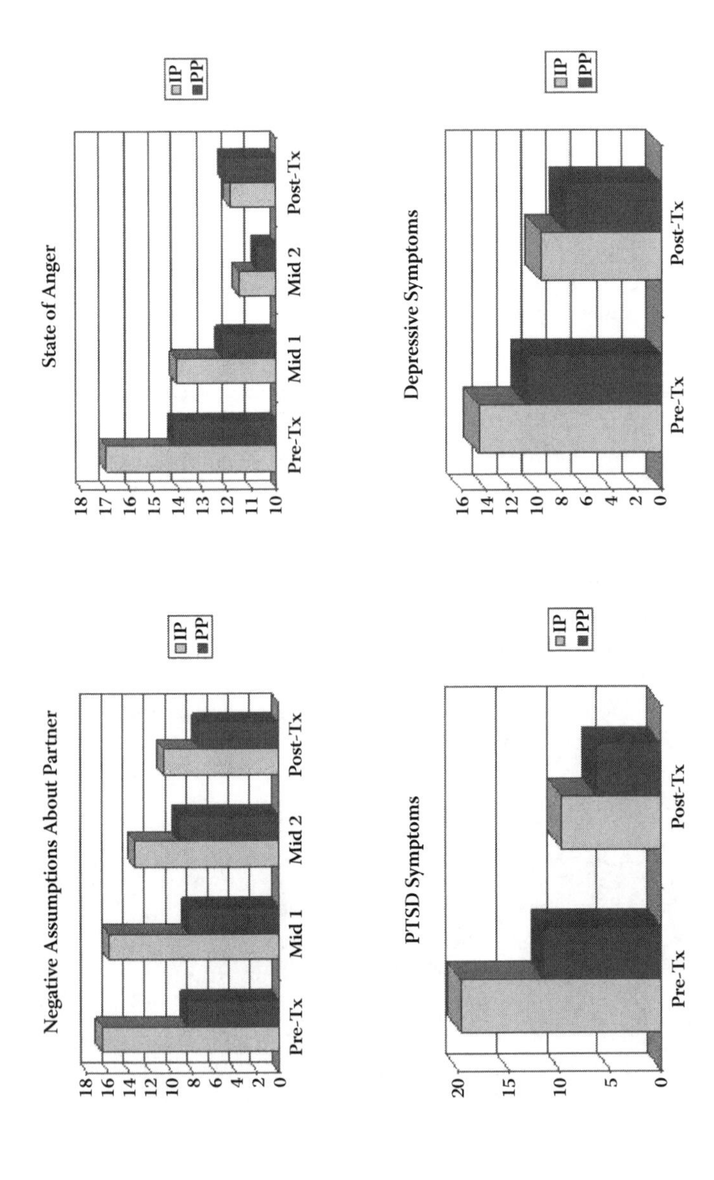

Figure 12.1 Changes in negative assumptions about partner, state anger, PTSD symptoms, and depressive symptoms for injured partners (IP) and participating partners (PP) during an integrative treatment (Tx) for marital infidelity. Mid-1 and Mid-2 assessments were conducted following Stage 1 and Stage 2 interventions, respectively.

a significant impact on chaplains' (a) knowledge about marital infidelity and the impact of infidelity, (b) basic understanding of the composition and content of the brief structured intervention for affair couples, and (c) ability to use that training to make preliminary decisions about how to intervene with couples presenting with particular issues at various stages of treatment (Snyder, Gasbarrini, Doss, & Scheider, in press).

U.S. Army chaplains were sampled in two separate trainings in the affair-specific intervention. The first training included 57 family life chaplains from the U.S. Army stationed in the continental United States; the second training was provided to 17 U.S. Army family life chaplains stationed in Europe. Each of the two training workshops provided information in each of the following domains: (a) the prevalence and impact of infidelity; (b) an overall conceptual model and rationale for this intervention protocol integrating diverse theoretical approaches to couples therapy, as well as literature regarding interpersonal trauma and forgiveness; and (c) detailed descriptions of interventions comprising each of the eight sessions in the structured three-stage intervention protocol as well as videotaped examples of clinical implementation of those interventions. The first group of chaplains received 1 day of training, whereas the second group of chaplains received 2 days.

Findings affirmed that chaplains receiving either a 1- or 2-day training gained significantly in overall knowledge and skills relevant to treating couples recovering from an affair. The format of the training (1 versus 2 days) did not have a significant overall effect on knowledge acquired; however, when given the opportunity for a 2-day training, chaplains not only learned about affair-specific interventions but also acquired increased knowledge of general couple therapy interventions as well. Moreover, chaplains in both groups reported a high likelihood of integrating the affair-specific protocol into their own counseling practices.

ETHICAL ISSUES SPECIFIC TO INTERVENING WITH AFFAIR COUPLES

Snyder and Doss (2005) have discussed a broad range of ethical issues that become particularly salient when working with clients struggling with issues of infidelity—including issues of professional competence specific to working with this unique population, managing potential conflicts of interest, addressing undisclosed infidelity in situations involving HIV or other sexually transmitted diseases, and handling more general issues of confidentiality. Managing issues of confidentiality in couples therapy can be difficult under any circumstances but it becomes increasingly complex when the issues relate to infidelity. Ongoing infidelities known by the therapist but not disclosed to the nonparticipating partner undermine a clinician's ability to conduct couples therapy. A common stance is to inform participants in the initial session that anything revealed outside conjoint sessions becomes a part of the couples therapy and, *at the discretion of the therapist*, may be disclosed in subsequent sessions involving both partners. The qualifier regarding the therapist's discretion permits clinical judgments concerning the potential consequences for all participants of sharing or withholding specific information on either an interim or permanent basis.

Issues of confidentiality are further complicated for military couples because infidelity remains a punishable offense under Article 134 of the UCMJ. This general article of the UCMJ permits nonspecified "conduct of a nature to bring discredit upon the armed forces" to be subject to court-martial and "punished at the discretion of that court." Although not routinely pursued, military participants may still be at risk if their participation in an affair is deemed prejudicial to good order or discipline or is "service discrediting"—with consideration given to marital status and military rank of the participating or injured partner as well as the outside person, in addition to the impact of the affair on the respective parties' ability to perform any relevant military responsibilities. Some providers within the military may *not* have the option of keeping the nature or basis of couple counseling separate from medical records available to command personnel, and any such limits to confidentiality should be clearly explained to partners at the outset of any individual or conjoint sessions.

Case Vignette – Sherry and Mike

Toward the end of her husband's most recent cruise, Sherry could sense that something was wrong. Mike, a naval lieutenant assigned to a carrier force supporting OEF operations, had largely stopped communicating with her. His e-mails were sporadic, brief, and lacked the warmth or reassurances that he typically had included in the past. After his return, his distance continued and seemed greater than during the reintegration periods they had weathered in the past. Sherry repeatedly asked him what was wrong, but Mike generally responded with silence. At times, she saw his eyes tear up before turning away.

A month following his return, Mike informed Sherry that he did not think he loved her anymore. Panicked and demanding explanation, Sherry eventually elicited his disclosure that he had become sexually involved with someone on ship. The sexual aspects of the relationship had lasted only a week, and Mike had been consumed with guilt, but the emotional aspects had lingered for several months. He was no longer in contact with the other woman—she had been reassigned to another task group for reasons unrelated to their affair—but he continued to think of her and miss that relationship.

Mike agreed to accompany Sherry to a counselor off base for one session. During that session, Sherry declared that she not only wanted to save her marriage but also acknowledged numerous challenges the couple had faced prior to Mike's most recent deployment. Their two daughters, ages 6 and 8, had struggled with Mike's recurring absences, and the older one had become rebellious and difficult to manage. Mike had struggled with extended family stressors involving a terminally ill father, whom he had barely seen since his parents' divorce when he was 11. Sherry reported family stressors of her own, including a psychiatrically disordered sister who had tried on several occasions to commit suicide. Sherry struggled with chronic sinus infections of her own that were resistant to antibiotics, and her recurring health issues had taken a toll on her and Mike's physical intimacy.

Mike did not want his marriage to end but described overwhelming guilt that made it difficult for him to interact with Sherry or tolerate her distress. Their counselor described some simple guidelines for disrupting negative escalations and using time-outs, as well as basic self-care strategies each could use independently of the other to promote better emotional regulation on their own. Mike agreed to return for three or four more sessions but could offer no commitment beyond that.

When they returned for their second session, the counselor described a three-stage model of recovery and then focused on immediate decisions facing the couple. Mike and Sherry agreed that they could sleep together but, at Mike's request, would not have sex until they decided what to do about their marriage in the long run. The counselor helped them to construct shared plans for how to deal with their daughters and how to let each other know when they felt overwhelmed without anger or blame. When they reported some increased stability in their marriage at the beginning of the third session, their counselor began to help them each describe how this crisis had an impact on their thoughts and feelings about themselves and each other—and encouraged Sherry to write a letter to Mike that conveyed not only her pain and fears but also her continuing hopes for their marriage.

Following exchange and discussion of Sherry's letter, Mike's attitudes toward the counseling shifted. He was better able to tolerate Sherry's distress and his own guilt as inevitable consequences of the affair, but to view them as indicators of the importance of their marriage to each of them and reasons to continue working at recovery—rather than as evidence of the demise of the marriage and reasons to divorce. In addition to examining numerous stressors, including recurring deployments, challenges of parenting and dealing with extended family, and physical health problems, Sherry and Mike were each willing to reflect on their own emotional styles that had made communicating about these challenges difficult.

Mike acknowledged that, by nature, he was avoidant of conflict. He preferred not to confront issues in their marriage so he did not "expose himself to aversive stimuli" any more than necessary. By contrast, the absence of discussions felt progressively anxiety arousing for Sherry; she sought comfort in talking about their relationship struggles and felt reassured when they did so. But, she acknowledged that in the past she had escalated or "cranked up the volume" to provoke Mike's engagement, even recognizing that this made it more difficult for him to engage in discussions productively. Their counselor framed this cycle as common among distressed couples and offered specific strategies for how to work against it.

A major struggle for Mike was confronting his discomfort with conflict. When he described how easy it had been to be with the other woman on ship, the counselor challenged him about the inherent differences between an affair relationship and a marriage—with the latter not having the luxury of being devoted exclusively to positive experiences. Mike acknowledged that Sherry had also been "easy to be with" during their courtship before the challenges of marriage beset them. Sherry learned to lower the intensity of her approaches to Mike, give him advance notice of her wish to have a relationship talk so he would not feel "blindsided," and provide him more time to formulate his responses during their discussions. Their ability to talk about relationship issues improved but remained a challenge.

The couple's fifth session was devoted exclusively to discussing their sexual relationship. Sherry acknowledged that her recurring sinus infections had made it difficult for her to enjoy intercourse, during which she sometimes felt as though she was suffocating. But, she had been reluctant to disappoint Mike and typically had agreed to sex when he initiated it, but without conveying her own experience. Mike had sensed her reluctance but attributed it to Sherry's no longer being attracted to him, and gradually he approached her less frequently to avoid his own feelings of inadequacy and rejection. In turn, Sherry interpreted his withdrawal as his displeasure with her, and the couple gradually lapsed into progressive avoidance of sexual intimacy. Their counselor encouraged them to "lower the stakes" of both initiating and declining sexual overtures and to communicate more openly their respective desires and discomforts. She also facilitated more candid discussion of alternative sexual exchanges they could offer one another when Sherry's health condition rendered a particular activity less comfortable than another. The couple's response to greater transparency and permission to suggest sexual encounters, decline, or suggest alternatives was immediate and dramatic—and their physical intimacy improved significantly, with both partners taking turns in initiating sexual intimacy.

Within 6 weeks after their initial presentation, Sherry and Mike had recommitted to their marriage and had a better understanding of the factors that had placed them at risk. At their counselor's suggestion, Mike wrote a letter to Sherry expressing his understanding of how the affair had come about, the traumatic impact it had on Sherry, his appreciation for her willingness to work with him toward recovery, and his request for her forgiveness. Sherry had never experienced such emotional depth from Mike in the past and extended to him a letter in exchange that reaffirmed her commitment to Mike and their marriage, offered her forgiveness, and pledged to "move on"—learning from the affair but no longer allowing its aftermath to dominate their lives together.

The couple suspended their counseling but returned a few months later when Mike received temporary orders to a joint forces training offshore for 3 weeks. Although the other woman with whom Mike had his affair would not be involved in the training, the anticipated separation elicited strong flashback responses from Sherry, which Mike found distressing. Their counselor reframed Sherry's responses as part of the "normal" recovery cycle rather than as a "setback." She helped the couple develop more constructive strategies for discussing these experiences, for Mike to extend understanding and support to Sherry, and for Sherry also to find independent ways of regulating her own fears during these times. The couple also discussed specific ways for staying connected during Mike's training exercises and for Sherry to elicit both emotional and strategic support on the home front from close friends. A follow-up session after Mike's return affirmed that they had been able to implement these strategies successfully, and no further sessions were scheduled.

DIRECTIONS FOR FUTURE RESEARCH

Although preliminary quantitative findings from a replicated case study as well as qualitative findings from diverse clinical settings affirm significant positive effects of this three-stage intervention protocol for couples struggling to recover from infidelity, further clinical trials are warranted to affirm the generalizability of these findings across diverse clinical samples and providers. In addition to studies of overall effectiveness, it will be important to identify both moderators and mediators of treatment outcome. For example, preliminary evidence suggests that, similar to emerging data from trials of treatments for general couple distress, affair couples in which one or both partners suffer from comorbid Axis II disorders (particularly antisocial or borderline personality disorder) struggle more and derive less benefit from couple-based treatments. Each of the three stages of treatment likely has its own mediating mechanisms of therapeutic impact; for example, the (a) ability to self-regulate and develop conflict management skills to disrupt negative escalations in Stage 1, (b) capacity for introspection and empathic responding in Stage 2, and (c) modifiability of attitudes toward forgiveness and restoration of secure attachment in Stage 3 may all comprise essential paths toward recovery. The specific benefits of supervised letter writing interwoven throughout treatment also warrant further study regarding their role in discovery, cathartic expression, and empathic response facilitating partners' recovery of trust and intimacy.

Surveys of soldiers returning from tours abroad confirm the adverse impact of extended deployments on military marriages. For example, between 2001 and 2007, the divorce rate in the Army more than doubled (Defense Manpower Data Center, 2009). In a survey of more than 2,200 OEF soldiers, the percentages of noncommissioned officers and enlisted ranks planning separation or divorce tripled over a 15-month deployment. Moreover, the U.S. Army estimates that approximately 50–65% of suicides among active-duty soldiers in recent years were precipitated by the breakup of an intimate relationship (Suicide Risk Management and Surveillance Office, 2008). Universal prevention programs promoting basic communication skills may have limited effectiveness for couples having elevated risk for infidelity because their generality precludes individualizing components targeting specific mechanisms underlying vulnerability factors and promoting resilience. Hence, it will be critical to develop empirically informed predeployment assessment of both relationship and individual functioning to identify those couples having moderate or higher distress for whom more intensive support could mitigate adverse impacts of deployment. Such support might include structuring specific methods for communicating during deployment, developing plans for addressing crises or dealing with feelings of loneliness, cultivating support networks that value fidelity, and promoting a sense of shared commitment to the military lifestyle.

CONCLUSION

Evidence abounds that stresses of the deployment cycle place military couples at increased risk for a broad range of relationship difficulties, including an affair by either the service member or civilian partner. Effective treatment requires an integrative approach that (a) builds relationship skills essential to initial containment of trauma and effective decision making, (b) promotes partners' greater understanding of factors within and outside themselves that increased their vulnerability to an affair and influence their recovery, and (c) addresses emotional, cognitive, and behavioral processes essential to forgiveness and moving on—either together or separately. The integrative treatment approach described here is the first treatment designed specifically to assist couples' recovery from an affair to garner empirical evidence of its efficacy. Additional evidence is emerging in support of abbreviated adaptations of the intervention tailored to contextual constraints of the military environment and implementation by a broad range of service providers.

REFERENCES

Allen, E. S., Atkins, D. C., Baucom, D. H., Snyder, D. K., Gordon, K. C., & Glass, S. P. (2005). Intrapersonal, interpersonal, and contextual factors in engaging in and responding to extramarital involvement. *Clinical Psychology: Science and Practice, 12,* 101–130.

Amato, P. R., & Rogers, S. J. (1997). A longitudinal study of marital problems and subsequent divorce. *Journal of Marriage and the Family, 59,* 612–624.

Atkins, D. C., Baucom, D. H., & Jacobson, N. S. (2001). Understanding infidelity: Correlates in a national random sample. *Journal of Family Psychology, 15,* 735–749.

Atkins, D. C., Eldridge, K. A., Baucom, D. H., & Christensen, A. (2005). Infidelity and behavioral couple therapy: Optimism in the face of betrayal. *Journal of Consulting and Clinical Psychology, 73,* 144–150.

Baucom, D. H., Snyder, D. K., & Gordon, K. C. (2009). *Helping couples get past the affair: A clinician's guide.* New York: Guilford Press.

Beach, S. R. H., Jouriles, E. N., & O'Leary, D. K. (1985). Extramarital sex: Impact on depression and commitment in couples seeking marital therapy. *Journal of Sex and Marital Therapy, 11,* 99–108.

Cano, A., & O'Leary, K. D. (2000). Infidelity and separations precipitate major depressive episodes and symptoms of nonspecific depression and anxiety. *Journal of Consulting and Clinical Psychology, 68,* 774–781.

Charny, I. W., & Parnass, S. (1995). The impact of extramarital relationships on the continuation of marriages. *Journal of Sex and Marital Therapy, 21,* 100–115.

Defense Manpower Data Center. (2009). *Selected manpower statistics.* Arlington, VA: Department of Defense.

Doss, B. D., Rhoades, G. K., Stanley, S. M., Markman, H. J., & Johnson, C. A. (2009). Differential use of premarital education in first and second marriages. *Journal of Family Psychology, 23,* 268–273.

Epstein, N. B., & Baucom, D. H. (2002). *Enhanced cognitive-behavioral therapy for couples: A contextual approach.* Washington, DC: American Psychological Association.

Glass, S. P., & Wright, T. L. (1992). Justifications for extramarital relationships: The association between attitudes, behaviors, and gender. *Journal of Sex Research, 29,* 361–387.

Glass, S. P., & Wright, T. L. (1997). Reconstructing marriages after the trauma of infidelity. In W. K. Halford & H. J. Markman (Eds.), *Clinical handbook of marriage and couples intervention* (pp. 471–507). New York: Wiley.

Gordon, K. C., Baucom, D. H., & Snyder, D. K. (2004). An integrative intervention for promoting recovery from extramarital affairs. *Journal of Marital and Family Therapy, 30,* 1–12.

Gordon, K. C., Baucom, D. H., & Snyder, D. K. (2005). Forgiveness in couples: Divorce, affairs, and couples therapy. In E. Worthington (Ed.), *Handbook of forgiveness* (pp. 407–421). New York: Routledge.
Gottman, J. M. (1999). *The marriage clinic: A scientifically based marital therapy*. New York: Norton.
Janus, S. S., & Janus, C. L. (1993). *The Janus report on sexual behavior*. New York: Wiley.
Laumann, E. O., Gagnon, J. H., Michael, R. T., & Michaels, S. (1994). *The social organization of sexuality: Sexual practices in the United States.* Chicago: University of Chicago Press.
Monson, C. M., Fredman, S. J., & Adair, K. C. (2008). Cognitive-behavioral conjoint therapy for posttraumatic stress disorder: Application to Operation Enduring and Iraqi Freedom veterans. *Journal of Clinical Psychology, 64*, 958–971.
Sayers, S. L., Farrow, V. A., Ross, J., & Oslin, D. W. (2009). Family problems among recently returned military veterans referred for a mental health evaluation. *Journal of Clinical Psychiatry, 70*, 163–170.
Shinseki, E. K. (2003). *The Army family: A white paper*. Washington, DC: U.S. Army Publishing Directorate.
Smith, T. W. (1994). Attitudes toward sexual permissiveness: Trends, correlates, and behavioral connections. In A. S. Rossi (Ed.), *Sexuality across the life course* (pp. 63–97). Chicago: University of Chicago Press.
Snyder, D. K. (2008). *Treatment procedures manual: Intervening with military couples at acute risk from marital infidelity*. Unpublished manuscript, Texas A&M University, College Station, TX.
Snyder, D. K., Baucom, D. H., & Gordon, K. C. (2007). *Getting past the affair: A program to help you cope, heal, and move on—together or apart*. New York: Guilford Press.
Snyder, D. K., & Doss, B. D. (2005). Treating infidelity: Clinical and ethical directions. *Journal of Clinical Psychology: In-Session, 61*, 1453–1465.
Snyder, D. K., Gasbarrini, M. F., Doss, B. D., & Scheider, D. M. (in press). Intervening with military couples struggling with issues of sexual infidelity. *Journal of Contemporary Psychotherapy*.
Snyder, D. K., & Mitchell, A. E. (2008). Affective reconstructive couple therapy: A pluralistic, developmental approach. In A. S. Gurman (Ed.), *Clinical handbook of couple therapy* (4th ed., pp. 353–382). New York: Guilford Press.
Spanier, G. B., & Margolis, R. L. (1983). Marital separation and extramarital sexual behavior. *The Journal of Sex Research, 19*, 23–48.
Suicide Risk Management and Surveillance Office. (2008). *Army suicide event report*. Tacoma, WA: Madigan Army Medical Center.
Tichenor, V., Armstrong, K., Vann, V., & Green, R. J. (2002). Interventions for couples with post-traumatic stress disorder. In C. R. Figley (Ed.), *Brief treatments for the traumatized: A project of the Green Cross Foundation* (pp. 266–291). Westport, CT: Greenwood Press.
Treas, J., & Giesen, D. (2000). Sexual infidelity among married and cohabitating Americans. *Journal of Marriage and the Family, 62*, 48–60.
Whisman, M. A., Dixon, A. E., & Johnson, B. (1997). Therapists' perspectives of couple problems and treatment issues in couple therapy. *Journal of Family Psychology, 11*, 361–366.
Wiederman, M. W. (1997). Extramarital sex: Prevalence and correlates in a national survey. *Journal of Sex Research, 34*, 167–174.
Wiggins, J. D., & Lederer, D. A. (1984). Differential antecedents of infidelity in marriage. *American Mental Health Counselors Association Journal, 6*, 152–161.

13

Intimate Partner Violence

NICOLE D. PUKAY-MARTIN and PATRICK S. CALHOUN

INTRODUCTION

Once viewed as a "private" problem, intimate partner violence (IPV) among military couples has recently received increased public attention. In 2002 at Fort Bragg, North Carolina, four Army wives were killed by their husbands during a 6-week period, with two of the husbands then committing suicide. Following this tragedy, wives' requests for support and treatment of relationship problems increased dramatically. In 2000, the Department of Defense (DOD) began reviewing policies surrounding the identification and treatment of domestic violence and issued a new directive regarding these policies in 2004. Demonstrating the military's recognition of IPV as a significant issue, this directive enhanced programming to aid in prevention, identification, treatment, and follow-up for victims and families experiencing domestic violence.

IPV has been increasingly recognized as a prevalent problem within the couples therapy literature. Many researchers have called for systematic screening for IPV in all couples therapy clients who present for treatment (e.g., Holtzworth-Munroe, Clements, & Farris, 2005). Recent studies suggested, however, that the majority of clinicians do not regularly screen for or recognize IPV in couple clients (Hansen, Harway, & Cervantes, 1991; Schacht, Dimidjian, George, & Berns, 2009). Clinicians treating military couples must be even more vigilant about IPV, as both military service members and couples seeking treatment have been shown to be at increased risk for IPV compared to the general population (Cascardi, Langhinrichsen, & Vivian, 1992; Heyman & Neidig, 1999). Because domestic violence has many negative consequences, including physical injury, psychological distress, and even death (Centers for Disease Control and Prevention, 2003), it is extremely important for clinicians to recognize IPV and provide appropriate and effective treatment.

In an effort to increase awareness surrounding this important issue in military couples, we first present an overview of literature investigating prevalence rates, risk factors for violence perpetration, and effects of IPV in military and civilian populations. Next, we discuss recommendations for screening and assessment of IPV, give an overview of the available literature focused on treatment for IPV within a couple context, and describe the limitations associated with this literature. Finally, we outline relevant information specific to clinicians working with this population and identify areas for future research. As the majority of research is focused on male-to-female violence, this chapter mainly focuses on male-perpetrated violence.

DEFINITIONS OF VIOLENCE

Throughout the chapter, we use the term *intimate partner violence* or *aggression* to denote any type of violence perpetrated by a spouse, ex-spouse, boyfriend, girlfriend, or former boyfriend or girlfriend. This term is thought to be more inclusive than marital violence because it encompasses partners who are not married, partners who are no longer in a romantic relationship, and partners of the same sex. Physical violence is the most frequently researched type of violence; however, studies are increasingly differentiating between physical, psychological, and sexual violence. Physical violence ranges from mild (e.g., slapping, pushing, and grabbing) to severe (e.g., kicking, hitting with a closed fist, and attacking with a weapon). Psychological violence can be defined as "non-physical behaviors that represent an attempt to control, dominate, or gain power over one's partner" (Holtzworth-Munroe, Smutzler, Bates, & Sandin, 1997). Psychological aggression includes hostile withdrawal, disparaging the partner, threats of violence, and restriction of the partner in terms of freedom, access to financial resources, and social support. Sexual violence consists of attempting to force a partner to perform a sexual act when (s)he is unwilling or cannot consent. Efforts may include coercion, threats, and physical force (Monson, Langhinrichsen-Rohling, & Taft, 2009).

In addition to distinguishing between these types of violence, researchers are increasingly recognizing that aggression is a heterogeneous construct. Johnson (2006) identified four types of violence seen in couples: intimate terrorism (originally called patriarchal terrorism; Johnson, 1995); violent resistance; situational couple violence (originally called common couple violence, Johnson, 1995); and mutual violent control. In intimate terrorism, the individual is violent and controlling and uses violence in an effort to dominate and control the partner. This type of violence is consistent with the common view of battering, is perpetrated almost solely by men (97%), and is likely to escalate (e.g., 76% of men characterized as perpetrating intimate terrorism in Johnson [2006] were reported to become more violent over time as reported by wives). In violent resistance, the individual is violent but not controlling and acts in response to a violent and controlling partner. This type of violence is consistent with self-defense and is committed mostly by women (96%). In situational couple violence, one or both individuals are violent, but neither is seen as controlling. This is the most common type of violence measured in survey approaches and seen in couple therapy clinics. In situational couple violence, violent acts are typically not as severe or frequent as those in intimate terrorism, are less likely to cause injury or fear in the partner, and are unlikely to escalate (e.g., 28% of these men characterized as perpetrating situational couple violence by Johnson [2006] were reported to become more violent over time as reported by wives). Situational couple violence usually occurs as a result of an escalation of conflict and poor anger management skills and is often bidirectional. In mutual violent control, both the individual and partner are violent and controlling. This type of violence is uncommon and not much is known about its frequency or associated features (Kelly & Johnson, 2008).

Johnson (1995, 2006) originally partitioned violence into separate categories due to the disparities in findings between feminist and family researchers. He argued that feminist researchers typically investigate IPV within agency settings, such as battered women's shelters. These agencies oversample for intimate terrorism and violent resistance due to the population utilizing agency assistance. Therefore, in these samples, violence has been found to be more severe and unilateral. In contrast, family researchers have typically used a survey approach, by which situational couple violence that is less severe and more often bidirectional in nature is more common. To the degree that severe batterers and victims refuse to participate in survey research, surveys may underestimate the rates of severe violence among couples (Johnson 1995). Both Johnson (2006) and Kelly and Johnson (2008) asserted the importance of distinguishing between these types of violence when conducting research involving IPV, as each type of violence is likely to have different correlates, risk factors, and effects, and each may respond differently to varied treatment approaches.

PREVALENCE

Prevalence studies indicated that 12% of couples experience male-to-female violence annually (Straus & Gelles, 1990). In addition, 1.3 million women are physically assaulted by a male partner each year, and nearly half of these women sustain injury (Centers for Disease Control and Prevention, 2003; Straus & Gelles, 1990; Tjaden & Thoennes, 2000). In a national survey, 22.1% of women and 7.4% of men reported experiencing IPV during their lifetime (Tjaden & Thoennes, 2000). Contrary to popular beliefs that aggression develops later in the marriage, studies demonstrated that half of newlywed couples (Lawrence & Bradbury, 2001) and almost half of community couples between the ages of 20 and 35 (Slep & O'Leary, 2005) experienced physical aggression. Estimates of prevalence in treatment-seeking populations are even higher. Studies suggested that between 50% and 70% of couples seeking couples therapy have experienced aggression (e.g., Cascardi et al., 1992; O'Leary, Vivian, & Malone, 1992). Among the majority of these couples, both partners are aggressive (85% in Cascardi et al., 1992).

Although psychological aggression is somewhat difficult to quantify because there is no standardized measure of psychological aggression, and a number of different measures were utilized in various studies (Holtzworth-Munroe et al., 1997), current evidence suggests that it is highly prevalent among couples. As compared to physical aggression, psychological aggression is even more common. In one survey, 74% of men and 75% of women reported using psychological aggression against their partner in the past year (Straus & Sweet, 1992). In clinical samples, the rate of psychological aggression is around 95% (Simpson & Christensen, 2005). Psychological aggression has similar or even more deleterious effects on victims' physical and psychological outcomes (O'Leary, 2001) and is a stronger predictor of marital dissolution than physical aggression (Jacobson, Gottman, Gortner, Berns, & Shortt, 1996). In terms of sexual aggression, 7.7% of women in a national survey reported being raped by an intimate partner during their lifetime, with an estimated 322,230 intimate partner rapes each year (Center for Disease Control and Prevention, 2003). Thirty-six percent of those who were raped sustained an injury (other than the rape), and about a third of these injured women sought medical care related to the rape. Based on the estimates of physical, psychological, and sexual aggression perpetrated by partners, it is clear that IPV occurs frequently and carries with it a high risk of injury.

Compared to civilian samples, military couples have been found to experience greater rates of IPV (Heyman & Neidig, 1999; McCarroll et al., 2000). Although rates of IPV in the military vary greatly due to sampling differences, studies that have obtained representative samples generally found one to three times the rate of intimate violence in the military compared to civilian populations (Straus & Gelles, 1990). In nonstandardized, smaller samples of military servicemen, rates of physical aggression have ranged from 30% to 47% (e.g., Pan, Neidig, & O'Leary, 1994). Thirty percent of active duty women reported adult lifetime physical IPV; 21.6% reported physical IPV during military service, and 44.3% reported lifetime emotional abuse or stalking (Campbell et al., 2003). Twenty-one percent of Navy personnel reported being victims of IPV, and 10.6% reported severe violence (Crouch, Thomsen, Milner, Stander, & Merrill, 2009). The Army has the highest rates of IPV, followed by the Marines, Navy, and finally Air Force (Stamm, 2009). Rates of IPV incidents that are reported, investigated, and substantiated by military police are around 1%, much lower than rates of IPV reported in surveys (McCarroll et al., 1999).

Why rates of violence are higher among military couples compared to civilian couples is unknown. There is some evidence that suggests higher rates may be due in part to demographic differences between civilian and military samples. In an investigation that compared a representative sample of Army servicemen to a demographically matched civilian sample based on age and race (Heyman & Neidig, 1999), Army servicemen reported similar rates of moderate aggression compared to civilian rates (10.8% vs. 9.9%) but higher rates of severe aggression (2.5% vs. 0.7%). When reported by the wives, however, rates of both moderate and severe physical aggression were higher in the military sample (13.1% vs. 10% for moderate and 4.4% vs. 2% for severe). The authors concluded that the higher rates of IPV in military samples were mostly due to differences in age and race rather than propensity for abuse. In addition, some have argued that couples in the military have higher rates of IPV due to increased rates of risk factors for violence among military service members, suggesting that those who choose to enlist in the military are already at higher risk for IPV (Merrill, Crouch, Thomsen, Guimond, & Milner, 2005). Therefore, it is important to understand the various risk factors for violence when interpreting the rates of IPV.

RISK FACTORS

Multiple characteristics have been identified as risk factors for IPV. These risk factors can be organized into three categories: individual, dyadic, and environmental/societal (e.g., Holtzworth-Munroe, Marshall, Meehan, & Rehman, 2003).

Individual Factors

Several demographic factors have been associated with increased risk of IPV perpetration. Younger age, lower socioeconomic status, less education, less income, unemployment, minority status, cohabiting status (as compared to married couples), and having children in the home confer greater risk of IPV (Campbell et al., 2003; McCarroll et al., 2003; Pan et al., 1994). In addition, IPV is more frequent among enlisted, low-ranking service members than among officers (Rosen, Kaminski, Parmley, Knudson, & Fancher, 2003). Researchers suggested that these variables reflect greater economic and life stressors combined with a general lack of resources to cope with these stressors.

Men who commit IPV are more likely to have psychological difficulties, including depression, posttraumatic stress disorder (PTSD), alcohol and drug use, low self-esteem, high levels of anger and hostility, increased jealousy, anxious attachment, and personality disorders, especially antisocial and borderline personality traits (Beckham, Moore, & Reynolds, 2000; Gerlock, 2004; Pan et al., 1994; Rosen, Kaminski, et al., 2003; Rosen, Parmley, Knudson, & Fancher, 2002). In a sample of veterans seeking couples therapy, 81% of those with depression and 81% of those with PTSD engaged in at least one act of IPV in the past year, while 42% of those with depression and 45% of those with PTSD engaged in at least one act of severe IPV (Sherman, Sautter, Jackson, Lyons, & Han, 2006). About one third of veterans with PTSD reported perpetrating physical violence, and 91% reported using psychological aggression against their partners in a year-long period (Taft et al., 2009). In addition to increased prevalence in psychiatric populations, severity of psychiatric problems is associated with IPV. For example, depression severity is correlated with frequency of IPV (Rosen, Kaminski, et al., 2003), and when depression is accompanied by trait hostility, the risk of violence increases. Similarly, PTSD severity is correlated with the frequency and severity of IPV (Gerlock, 2004). Specifically, the hyperarousal symptom cluster of PTSD is directly linked to IPV perpetration (King & King, 2000). Interestingly, the relationship between hyperarousal and violence varies as a function of alcohol use (Saverese, Suvak, King, & King, 2001). Hyperarousal has its strongest effect on IPV when drinking is low in frequency and quantity; however, when alcohol is frequently consumed at low quantities, the relationship between hyperarousal and IPV diminishes. Typically, alcohol and drug use is linked to more severe and frequent IPV (e.g., Pan et al., 1994). For example, in a sample of men entering substance abuse or IPV treatment, the likelihood of male-to-female physical aggression was 5 to 11 times higher on days of drinking or drug use compared with abstinent days (e.g., Fals-Stewart, Golden, & Schumacher, 2003).

In addition to psychopathology, past violence is a strong predictor of future violence (O'Leary et al., 1989). Physical aggression is relatively stable over time (O'Leary et al., 1989), and frequency and severity of IPV are correlated, such that those who report more severe violence also report more frequent violence (Ehrensaft & Vivian, 1996). However, men with lower levels of aggression are less likely to escalate in frequency and severity and are more likely to stop using violence. In fact, in a 2- to 3-year follow-up period, about one quarter to one half of less-violent men discontinued use of violence (Holtzworth-Munroe, Meehan, Herron, Rehman, & Stuart, 2000). Beyond violent behavior, violent thoughts, violent attitudes, threats of violence, criminality, and violation of court orders are all risks for future violence (see Kropp, 2008, for a review).

Many men who perpetrate IPV report violence in their family of origin. In military samples of partner-violent men, 39% reported witnessing interparental violence as children (Wasileski, Callaghan-Chaffee, & Chaffee, 1982), and between 11% and 49% reported being physically or emotionally abused by a parent (e.g., Wasileski et al., 1982). In fact, the frequency of childhood abuse is correlated with IPV perpetration (Rosen et al., 2002). In addition, studies among civilians suggested that there is a stronger relationship between family-of-origin violence and severe (as compared to moderate) IPV (e.g., Sugarman & Hotaling, 1989).

In terms of risk factors specific to military populations, several factors have been investigated. As several researchers have argued that those who enlist in the military have more risk factors for IPV, Merrill et al. (2005) examined the rates of IPV in Navy service members before enlistment and during the second year of service. Preenlistment rates were higher for women (20%) than for men (4%). In addition, the rates of IPV for men increased over time (4% preenlistment to 16% during the second year), while the rates for women decreased over time (20% preenlistment to 12% during the second year). By comparing these rates of IPV to those in a national survey, the authors concluded that the data did not support the theory that Navy recruits enlist with higher levels of IPV than civilians. Furthermore, they suggested that the changes in rates of IPV over time may be due to maturational factors; however, because the study did not include a civilian comparison group, no strong conclusions can be made.

In contrast to the theory that individuals who enlist in the military have higher risk factors for violence, others have hypothesized that the military experience confers a certain degree of risk for violence. Stressors that are unique to the military, such as frequent moves (leading to less social support), frequent deployments with lengthy separations from family, combat training, and exposure to violence, have been associated with increased IPV (e.g., McCarroll et al., 2000). In an Army-wide survey, severity of self-reported IPV perpetration was associated with length of deployment (McCarroll et al., 2000); as length of deployment increased, the percentage of servicemen perpetrating IPV also increased. However, in a sample of Army servicemen deployed to Bosnia, there was no difference in rates of IPV between those deployed to Bosnia and those who were not deployed (McCarroll et al., 2003). Combat exposure has been linked to IPV perpetration; however, this relationship appears to be mediated by PTSD symptoms (Beckham et al., 2000). The perception of threat in a war zone is also associated with IPV (Orcutt, King,

& King, 2003). These factors suggest that the experiences associated with military life may be associated with an increased risk of IPV.

In addition to these general demographic, psychological, and military-related factors, research has demonstrated that deficits in social skills are related to IPV perpetration (Holtzworth-Munroe, 1992). For example, men who engage in IPV are less assertive with their spouse (e.g., Rosenbaum & O'Leary, 1981) and demonstrate more frequent negative behaviors when interacting with their spouse (e.g., Margolin, John, & Gleberman, 1988) than nonviolent men. Violent men are also more likely to attribute hostile intent to their partner's actions than nonviolent men (e.g., Holtzworth-Munroe & Hutchinson, 1993). In addition, when provided with vignettes of marital conflict situations, violent men are less able to generate competent responses than nonviolent men (e.g., Holtzworth-Munroe & Anglin, 1991). Thus, violent men may choose violence in attempts to solve problems because they lack necessary skills to be effective in intimate relationships.

In sum, research suggests that a number of individual factors, including demographics, psychopathology, family-of-origin violence, military-related variables, and social skills deficits, distinguish violent from nonviolent men.

Dyadic Factors

In addition to individual characteristics, several dyadic factors have been found to relate to IPV. Lower marital satisfaction and adjustment have frequently been associated with more frequent and severe IPV (Pan et al., 1994; Rosen, Kaminski, et al., 2003; Simpson, Doss, Wheeler, & Christensen, 2007). More specifically, relationship discord and conflict are predictors of abuse (Rosenbaum & O'Leary, 1981). Communication patterns have also been associated with IPV. For example, couples who engage in IPV demonstrate more negative reciprocity, verbal attacks, anger, contempt, belligerence, and withdrawal, and this pattern of increased negativity is demonstrated through self-report and videotaped interactions (Margolin et al., 1988). More severely violent couples demonstrate difficulties in problem solving (Simpson et al., 2007). In addition, psychological aggression predicts the onset of later physical aggression and often precedes and co-occurs with physical aggression during conflict (O'Leary, Malone, & Tyree, 1994). Further, more severe IPV may be related to couple dynamics in which the male partner uses various methods to exert power and control over his female partner (Johnson, 2006). These dynamics tend to vary by perpetrator. For example, male violence tends to escalate in response to a number of female behaviors, and once this violence begins, nothing the female does has the effect of stopping the violence; however, this pattern is not true for female violence (Jacobson et al., 1994). Despite these findings, not a great deal is known about dyadic factors related to IPV, as many researchers are concerned that investigation into these factors may constitute victim blaming.

Environmental/Societal Factors

Focusing on societal rather than individual factors, feminist approaches to IPV theorize that violence is a method of controlling and dominating women in patriarchal society. Thus, violence is thought to be the result of a society in which men have greater privilege, power, and control (Holtzworth-Munroe et al., 2003). Despite the frequent use of this theory to understand IPV, relatively little empirical research has investigated societal or environmental factors related to IPV. One study conducted with Army servicemen investigated the relationship between IPV and various group-level factors, measuring group factors at the company level. The authors found that less leadership support, a hypermasculine culture, and lower support for spouses at the company level were related to increased IPV (Rosen, Kaminski, et al., 2003). This study lends some support to the idea that group culture may influence risk for IPV.

This overview suggests that a wide variety of individual, dyadic, and environmental factors are associated with IPV perpetration. (For a good review of literature addressing IPV in military and veteran populations, see the work of Marshall, Panuzio, & Taft, 2005). Because of the many various risk factors and different types of violence that exist, researchers have attempted to classify these risk factors and types of violence into categories to better understand perpetrators of violence in the hope that this information will inform conceptualization and treatment of IPV.

Researchers have increasingly recognized that violent men are a heterogeneous group. Multiple studies have used theoretical or empirical approaches to categorize violent men into separate subgroups based on personality inventories, character traits, and measures of violence. In their review of the literature, Holtzworth-Munroe and Stewart (1994) concluded that previous research classified violent men along three dimensions: (a) frequency and severity of violence, (b) generality of violence (e.g., restricted to family or not) and factors related to the extent of violence (e.g., criminal prosecution), and (c) the individual's psychopathology and personality disorder. See the work of Holtzworth-Munroe and Stewart (1994) for a review of the literature and suggested subtypes.

Although subtypes appear theoretically valid, research has demonstrated partial to no support for suggested typologies (Babcock, Green, Webb, & Graham, 2004; Holtzworth-Munroe et al., 2000). Therefore, it may be more helpful to conceptualize violent men from a continuous or dimensional approach rather than a categorical one (Langhinrichsen-Rohling, Huss, & Rohling, 2006). Regardless of method of classification, the heterogeneity within violent men suggests that certain treatment approaches may be more appropriate or effective for violent men as they vary along these dimensions (Edleson & Tolman, 1992).

EFFECTS OF IPV ON VICTIMS

IPV has deleterious effects on the victim, relationship, and family. Women who experience violence are at high risk for physical injury. In fact, IPV causes more injuries than road accidents, muggings, and rapes combined (D'Ardenne & Balakrishna, 2001). Women who experience violence also are at risk for a number of negative psychological effects, including emotional stress, PTSD, depression, anxiety, fear, alcohol and drug use, and low self-esteem (Cascardi et al., 1992). In addition, many abused women lack problem-solving and coping skills (Launius & Lindquist, 1988). Although both men and women perpetrate mild-to-moderate aggression at similar rates (Archer, 2000), women are more likely to be severely victimized, and the physical and psychological consequences of male violence are more frequent and severe (Cascardi et al., 1992). Women who are the target of IPV experience greater fear of their partner and more physical injury than men receiving IPV, likely due to the difference in size and strength of men and women (Browne, 1993).

Besides the effects on the individual, IPV has negative effects on the intimate relationship. Aggression is associated with lower relationship satisfaction and more frequent relationship dissolution (Lawrence & Bradbury, 2001; Pan et al., 1994), with psychological aggression acting as a stronger predictor of relationship dissolution than physical aggression (Jacobson et al., 1996). However, it is unclear whether IPV is the result or cause of relationship unhappiness as most studies were cross sectional rather than longitudinal in design.

IPV also has effects on others in the home besides the partner. Children are present during 80% of wife assaults (Jaffe, Wolfe, & Wilson, 1990), and children of parents who perpetrate IPV are more likely to experience physical, emotional, and sexual abuse than children of nonviolent parents. Of children exposed to IPV, 40% to 75% are victims of physical abuse (Emery & Laumann-Billings, 1998). In addition, children from maritally violent homes experience externalizing and internalizing behavior problems and impaired functioning in social competence and social problem solving (see Margolin, 1998, for a review). Children who witness IPV demonstrate more aggressive and violent behavior (Bailey, 1996), and they are more likely to assault siblings and parents, commit violent crimes, and perpetrate IPV in the future (Straus & Gelles, 1990). In sum, IPV has many negative effects on both direct and indirect victims.

TREATMENT APPROACHES

Given these negative consequences, many have attempted to create programs to reduce and eliminate IPV. Currently, there are generally two treatment approaches to IPV, gender-specific treatment, which is much more widespread, and conjoint treatment, which remains controversial. Gender-specific treatment involves men's (or batterers') groups that attempt to change attitudes toward women and violence by increasing awareness or attempt to change aggressive behavior through anger management strategies. The groups range from feminist to cognitive-behavioral in nature, but only treat the batterer. Gender-specific treatment has been shown to have only limited efficacy, and it has not conclusively been proven to be more effective than simply identifying or arresting violent men (Babcock, Green, & Robie, 2004). Women's (victims') support groups also exist to assist in providing women with support to manage the consequences of IPV.

Alternatively, conjoint treatment involves treating couples together in either individual or group formats. These treatments are often cognitive-behavioral in nature and often also draw from feminist principles. However, a great deal of controversy surrounds treating aggression in a conjoint format. Writers have suggested three main objections to treating IPV with both members of the couple present (McCollum & Stith, 2007; O'Leary, Heyman, & Neidig, 1999). First, many believe that treating the batterer and victim in a conjoint format is equivalent to blaming the victim, and these critics are concerned that this type of treatment will send the message that women are to blame for the violence. Second, some are concerned that having the violent partner present will cause women to be unable to be open and honest in treatment due to fears of retaliation by the violent partner. Third, many believe that treating the IPV and raising relevant relationship issues will increase conflict and violence between partners, increasing women's risk for injury.

Although these concerns seem valid, research has not supported these arguments against treating IPV in a conjoint format. In contrast to the fear of victim blaming, O'Leary et al. (1999) found that, through treatment, husbands reported less blame of wives for aggression, and wives accepted less responsibility for their husbands' aggression. In addition, despite the concern that conjoint therapy would result in increased violence outside therapy, O'Leary and colleagues found that couples therapy did not place women at higher risk for aggression. There were no differences between conjoint and gender-specific treatments in terms of violence between sessions. Furthermore, the majority of women did not fear participating in conjoint therapy, and through clinical observation, the authors suggested that women were very involved in treatment and did not appear to be hindered by their partners' presence. Given the results of this study, it appears that conducting conjoint therapy for IPV may be appropriate with lower levels of violence and is not likely to create higher-risk situations for women.

In support of conducting conjoint therapy with some types of IPV, proponents have suggested several strong arguments in favor of the approach (Bograd & Mederos, 1999; Holtzworth-Munroe et al., 2003, 2005). First, by including both partners, clinicians have the opportunity to gather more accurate and complete information regarding the violence. Because disagreement between partners regarding frequency and severity of violent acts is common, research recommends obtaining reports from both partners to gain a more complete understanding of the IPV. The clinician may also be able to gain more complete information regarding the interactional patterns that occur with IPV and may glean more insight into patterns of control within the couple when both partners are present. Second, some argue that gender-specific treatment may have negative effects on women (Dutton, 1986; Edleson & Tolman, 1992; Gondolf, 2002; Holtzworth-Munroe et al., 2003; Stith, McCollum, Rosen, Locke, & Goldberg, 2005). Of female partners, 10–15% reported that their lives worsened after their partner began attending a batterer program (Gondolf, 2002). Wives also reported increased verbal abuse following gender-specific treatment (Dutton, 1986). In fact, some critics contended that gender-specific treatment may support men's positive views of violence and negative attitudes toward women (Edleson & Tolman, 1992). For example, after hearing other men's reports of violence, some male partners believe their wives should not object to their behavior because their level of violence is less than the other group members' violence (Tolman, 1990, as cited in Stith, Rosen, & McCollum, 2003). In addition, some men misuse strategies taught in gender-specific treatment, such as time-outs, as a way to continue controlling their wives (Gondolf & Russell, 1986). If both partners are included in therapy, both will have the opportunity to understand the clinician's conceptualization of violence in the relationship, both will be taught the same skills, and both will gain the same understanding of the use and misuse of those skills. In addition, the partners will be guided in a collaborative approach to skill learning (as in the negotiated time-out; Rosen, Matheson, Stith, McCollum, & Locke, 2003), directed to plan for how and when they will use the skills, and coached to role-play the new skills in session. Through this collaborative approach, couples will be more likely to use skills such as time-out at home. In contrast to men who use violence to dominate, less-violent men may be insulted by programs that assume they wish to control their wives (Raab, 2000, as cited in Kelly & Johnson, 2008). Conjoint approaches offer an alternative for men who do not use violence as a means of dominating their partners. Third, a conjoint format provides couples with a controlled environment in which to raise difficult topics. In conjoint treatment, couples are taught communication skills to assist with discussion of conflictual topics. If partners are unable to discuss these topics alone, they are instructed to postpone discussion until therapy sessions (Holtzworth-Munroe et al., 2003). Allowing the couples a safe arena to discuss such topics may actually decrease violence outside of sessions, rather than increase it. Fourth, men's groups do not address underlying couple dynamics that may be contributing to incidents of domestic violence (Holtzworth-Munroe, Beatty, & Anglin, 1995; McCollum & Stith, 2007). Since discord leads to violence, many believe that relationship discord must be alleviated to decrease IPV (Pan et al., 1994); however, gender-specific treatment does not treat relationship discord. Conjoint therapy can address problematic interaction patterns through communication and problem-solving skills. Clinicians can aid the couples in changing their negative dynamics by interrupting them and asking couples to practice new skills with coaching during session. Fifth, some research suggested that women use violence as often as men (Archer, 2000) and are at greater risk for assault when they use violence (Gondolf, 2000). Therefore, including women in treatment may help decrease their risk for IPV victimization. Teaching anger management skills to both partners may be necessary to stop the IPV, as it is highly unlikely for one partner to stop being violent if the other continues to use violent tactics (Feld & Straus, 1989). Sixth, gender-specific treatment has not conclusively been proven to be more effective than simply identifying or arresting violent men (Babcock, Green, & Robie, 2004). Given this limited response to treatment, alternative approaches to treatment should be investigated. In addition, because violent men are heterogeneous, a "one-size-fits-all" approach to treatment is unlikely to be successful for all violent men (McCollum & Stith, 2007). Various treatment approaches may work more effectively for certain violent men. Conjoint treatment may be especially effective for certain couples experiencing mild-to-moderate levels of violence. Finally, many violent couples decide to remain in the relationship, and conjoint therapy can help improve the relationship (McCollum & Stith, 2007). In fact, by refusing to treat violent couples in conjoint therapy, clinicians may be disadvantaging the women who decide to stay in violent relationships (Heyman & Neidig, 1999; Stith et al., 2005). Conjoint therapy can assist couples in determining whether they can have a relationship free of violence, and if not, can help them decide whether to separate and how to do so in a nonviolent manner.

GUIDELINES FOR DETERMINING THE APPROPRIATENESS OF CONJOINT TREATMENT

Given the previous arguments, it is clear that conjoint therapy for IPV may be extremely helpful with some couples; however, even strong supporters of the approach agree that couples therapy is not appropriate for all types of violence (Holtzworth-Munroe et al., 1995, 2005; O'Leary, 1996). Most writers suggest that conjoint therapy is only appropriate for cases involving mild-to-moderate IPV (i.e., situational couple violence). Unfortunately, due to the strong stance against conjoint treatment, little research has been done to explore which couples may benefit most from conjoint therapy for IPV. Therefore, most studies investigating conjoint therapies utilize rationally derived, rather than empirically derived, criteria for establishing which couples should be included in the studies. Most studies exclude couples experiencing severe violence and battering in which there is a clear pattern of control and intimidation of the partner; however, researchers have used slightly different ways to identify which couples are appropriate for conjoint therapy. For example, Harris, Savage, Jones, and Brooke (1988) only included couples in which (a) the wife indicated she intended to continue the relationship and (b) the wife did not feel endangered by her partner's knowledge that she discussed violence. By contrast, O'Leary et al. (1999) only included couples in which (a) the wife had not sustained injuries requiring medical attention, (b) the wife reported feeling comfortable with the prospect of participating in couple therapy, (c) the wife did not feel unsafe and was not afraid of living with husband, (d) there was no alcohol abuse present, (e) no severe psychopathology existed in either partner, and (f) the man admitted perpetration of violent acts.

Several authors have published suggested guidelines for determining whether to provide conjoint therapy (Holtzworth-Munroe et al., 1995; O'Leary, 1996; Stith et al., 2005). Stith et al. (2005) suggested that both partners must wish to participate in couples therapy, and both must want to end violence and improve their relationship. The partners must both be willing to sign a nonviolence contract and remove weapons from the home. No severe violence can be present, including violence involving weapons, violence resulting in injuries requiring hospitalization, and violence outside the home. Others recommended conjoint therapy only in the context of low-to-moderate aggression, with the wife not in imminent physical harm and not fearing her husband. In addition, the wife must feel comfortable participating in conjoint therapy with her husband and must not report difficulties being honest due to intimidation (Holtzworth-Munroe et al., 1995; O'Leary, 1996). Both partners must be interested in staying in the relationship, and partners must acknowledge the existence and the problematic nature of violence and be willing to take steps to end violence. Clearly, the aim of these guidelines is to ensure the safety of the victim and make certain that therapy can be effective.

ASSESSMENT OF IPV

To determine whether couples therapy is appropriate, a thorough assessment of violence must be conducted with couples who present to therapy. The majority of couples who experience IPV do not identify violence as a presenting problem and do not spontaneously report violence. O'Leary et al. (1992) found that, although only 6% of wives described physical violence as a marital problem on a general intake form, 44% of them indicated that physical aggression was a problem in their marriage when interviewed, and 53% revealed the problem with the use of a self-report measure with specific questions about aggression. Similarly, Ehrensaft and Vivian (1996) found that fewer than 10% of couples reported violence as a presenting problem or spontaneously reported violence. However, when asked directly in a structured interview, 40% of wives and 34% of husbands reported engaging in IPV. Further, 53% of wives and 57% of husbands reported engaging in IPV on self-report measures. Couples who later reported violence were asked to rate reasons they did not originally report violence, and couples most frequently responded that (a) they did not believe aggression was a problem in their relationship, (b) the aggression was unstable or infrequent, and (c) the aggression was secondary to other marital problems. These results suggest the importance of multimodal assessment when determining the frequency and severity of violence.

Various self-report measures are available to use in violence assessment. The most widely used measure of aggression is the Conflict Tactics Scales (CTS1; Straus, 1979) and revised Conflict Tactics Scale (CTS2; Straus, Hamby, Boney-McCoy, & Sugarman, 1996), which lists numerous acts of varying severity and asks partners to rate frequency of each act in the past year by either partner. The CTS2 contains subscales of physical assault, psychological aggression, sexual coercion, injury, and negotiation. The CTS2 is helpful in terms of quantifying frequency and severity of aggression; however, it does not assist in determining precipitating events, intent of perpetrator, interpersonal patterns involved in aggression, or consequences of violence (Jacobson, 1994). For example, a partner hitting during an argument out of frustration versus a partner hitting in self-defense would both be tallied in the same way on the CTS2. Therefore, individual interviews with each partner are recommended to gather more information about aggression in the relationship. Besides the CTS1 and CTS2, there are a number of other self-report measures that may be used in the assessment of aggression (see Aldarondo & Straus, 1994; Kropp, 2008; Rathus & Feindler, 2004, for a detailed description of a number of written instruments). Regardless of the self-report measures chosen, partners should complete these measures separately to ensure that individuals are able to honestly complete the measures without fear of retaliation.

For this same reason, it is recommended that separate interviews be conducted with each partner so that the victim(s) is given the best chance to honestly report any violence occurring in the relationship. Interview questions should cover psychological aggression, physical aggression, and sexual aggression. Suggested assessment questions for these areas can be found in the work of Bograd and Mederos (1999). Detailed information about patterns of aggression, precipitating events, intent of aggressor, response of victim, consequences of aggression, and aftereffects should be gathered. In addition, interviews should include an assessment of risk factors associated with violence, including psychopathology (depression, PTSD); alcohol and drug use; personality traits (borderline, antisocial); anger and hostility; and social skills deficits. Child abuse or risk to children should also be assessed, as 40% to 70% of children of parents who commit IPV are victims of child abuse (Emery & Laumann-Billings, 1998).

Clinicians should attempt to distinguish between aggression with control and intimidation versus aggression that may be the result of frustration or an attempt to fight back (Jacobson & Christensen, 1996). Degree of intimidation and control over the victim should be established, as well as lethality and degree of danger, which includes asking about use of weapons, previous injuries, threats of lethality, fear of victim, steps the victim has taken toward separation, and involvement of alcohol or drug use (Aldarondo & Straus, 1994). If safety is at risk, safety planning should be completed with both the victim and the perpetrator to ensure victim safety. Victims should be provided with contact information for local agencies (e.g., battered women's shelters, support groups, police department) and should be informed of potential legal actions available to them.

CONJOINT TREATMENT

Because of the controversy surrounding treating violence and aggression in a conjoint format, there is limited research available on the efficacy of conjoint therapy for IPV and even fewer rigorous investigations on this topic. There are four main programs of research investigating conjoint therapy for IPV: (a) the domestic conflict containment program (DCCP; Neidig, 1986), which was modified to become physical aggression couples treatment (PACT); (b) the domestic violence focused couples treatment (DVFCT; Stith et al., 2005); (c) the couples abuse prevention program (CAPP; LaTaillade, Epstein, & Werlinich, 2006); and (d) the San Diego Navy Experiment (Dunford, 2000). In addition to these four programs, two other groups have shown success in decreasing IPV with treatment focused on other aspects of individual or relational functioning: (a) behavioral couples therapy (BCT) for addictions (O'Farrell & Fals-Stewart, 2000) and (b) BCT (Simpson, Atkins, Gattis, & Christensen, 2008). These various programs are described in more detail below.

As PACT is a conjoint therapy focused on IPV, the purpose of PACT is to eliminate violence in the relationship (Heyman & Neidig, 1997). PACT, originally DCCP, was created by Neidig (1986) in response to a request from the U.S. Marine Corps. DCCP utilized a skill-building approach based on social learning and cognitive restructuring principles. Methods of intervention included instruction, behavioral rehearsal, and feedback from group leaders. In the original trial of DCCP in a group of partner-violent Marines (Neidig, 1986), service members were ordered to participate, and the spouses were strongly encouraged to attend the program. Couples attended weekly 2-hour sessions for 10 weeks in multicouple groups consisting of 6 to 8 couples. Results from the trial indicated that 8 of 10 couples were violence free at 4-month follow-up. In addition, both husbands' and wives' relationship adjustment increased, and locus of control became more internal following the intervention (Neidig, 1986). Given the close monitoring and strict consequences for missing sessions that occurred in this military setting, it was uncertain whether the program would translate to civilian settings.

In several attempts to revise the treatment program, DCCP was modified to create PACT. PACT is based in feminist principles and uses cognitive-behavioral strategies to create behavior and attitude change. During the first half of PACT, aggressors are taught to take responsibility for their violence and are introduced to anger management skills. In the second half of PACT, couples discuss various relationship dynamics and are taught communication skills in an effort to increase alternatives to violence and decrease conflict that might lead to violence. Studies investigating the efficacy of DCCP and PACT in civilian samples found that the conjoint therapy resulted in the same or greater decreases in violent behavior compared to gender-specific treatment (e.g., O'Leary et al., 1999). In addition, husbands participating in the conjoint treatment had higher levels of marital satisfaction at posttest than husbands in the gender-specific treatment (O'Leary et al., 1999). Interestingly, participants in the gender-specific treatment requested additional therapy to focus on couples issues following the end of the gender-specific treatment. These results suggest that conjoint therapy for aggressive couples may decrease violence comparable to gender-specific treatments, as well as increase marital satisfaction by including the partner. However, there were large dropout rates in these studies (e.g., 44% in O'Leary et al., 1999), making it difficult to draw conclusions about the general effectiveness for all aggressors.

Similar to PACT, the DVFCT has as its goal the cessation of violence in the relationship. DVFCT is based on a solution-focused approach to treatment (Stith et al., 2005) and also integrates techniques from several family systems models. Couples are asked to develop a vision of a healthy relationship free of violence and are assisted in creating safety plans, awareness of anger signals, and negotiated time-out plans (Rosen, Matheson, et al., 2003). DVFCT can be conducted with an individual couple or in a multicouple group format and is co-led by two clinicians. Prior to the 12-week conjoint treatment, participants are required to attend a 6-week gender-specific group treatment focused on anger management skills to prepare for conjoint treatment. To ensure safety during the conjoint phase of treatment, therapists meet with gender-specific groups at the beginning of each conjoint session to assess for violent episodes during the week and at the end of each session to allow any irritations that were raised in the session to subside before returning home and to ensure all participants feel safe and calm. If partners are distressed, they are encouraged to use safety plans, meditation, or other skills learned in the group.

Research investigating the effectiveness of DVFCT compared outcomes for couples completing either a multicouple group format or an individual couple format with a wait-list control group (Stith, Rosen, McCollum, & Thomsen, 2004). Couples in the multicouple group format improved on the three measured outcome variables (i.e., level of aggression, marital satisfaction, attitudes about wife beating); however, neither the couples in the individual couple group nor those in the wait-list control couples improved on these measures. However, based on wife reports, husbands in either of the couple groups were less likely to relapse than husbands in the wait-list control group 6 months and 2 years following treatment. At 2-year follow-up, the relapse rate was 5.4%; only 1 of 19 women reported that her husband had been violent since the 6-month follow-up period. The authors suggested that the multicouple group format may have been more conducive to positive changes due to various factors occurring within the group process (e.g., the opportunity to learn and receive support from others, normalization of difficulties with violence, facilitation of discussion of difficult topics).

Similar to both PACT and DVFCT, CAPP is a project investigating the efficacy of a cognitive-behavioral couples treatment that was designed to increase marital functioning and decrease IPV and its risk factors through the use of psychoeducation about IPV, anger management, communication and problem-solving skills, and positive activities and mutual support (LaTaillade et al., 2006). The structured treatment consists of 10 weekly 90-minute sessions. A small pilot study comparing the structured cognitive-behavioral couples treatment with treatment as usual (i.e., couples therapy based on various systems theories) found that both treatments resulted in significantly lower rates of psychological aggression. Physical aggression did not change as a result of treatment; however, the authors speculated that this lack of change was due to low levels of physical aggression in the study. These results suggest that both couple therapies focused on IPV, and those that are more general in nature are effective in reducing aggression; however, because no control group was included, it is unclear whether psychological aggression would decrease over time without intervention.

The San Diego Navy Experiment was created to test the effectiveness of a cognitive-behavioral approach in decreasing IPV (Dunford, 2000). Two treatment "formats" were included: a men's group and a conjoint group. These treatments were compared to a group that was rigorously monitored and a control group that received minimal intervention. Both the men's group and the conjoint group met weekly for 6 months and then met monthly for another 6 months. Attitudes about women and violence toward women were addressed, and men were taught skills (e.g., time-out) to decrease violence. The last six monthly sessions were used to review material. At the end of treatment and at follow-ups, there were no differences between the four groups on measures of frequency and prevalence of violence. The author concluded that cognitive-behavioral treatment did not decrease aggression above and beyond simply being identified by the Navy as having a problem with violence. However, this study may not have provided a true test of a conjoint treatment (Stith et al., 2003). The curriculum in the conjoint group was similar to the men's group; however, the presence of the wives was hypothesized to change the dynamic present in the conjoint group as compared to the men's group. It was suggested that simply providing the women with the opportunity to see authority figures challenging male violence and teaching skills to manage conflict would be a source of empowerment to the women. Therefore, it does not appear that the conjoint treatment was created using known couple or family therapy approaches that focus on improving interpersonal dynamics. In addition, the wives were not required to attend the group; therefore, their attendance in the conjoint group was inconsistent. On average, there was a ratio of 2 women to 5 men in the conjoint group, with the ratio ranging from 1:10 to 7:10. Given these problems with the conjoint group, it may be premature to conclude that the conjoint therapy for IPV in Navy couples was no more successful than simply identifying violent men.

In contrast to these three approaches, BCT for addictions does not directly focus on decreasing IPV (e.g., Fals-Stewart & Clinton-Sherrod, 2009; O'Farrell &

Fals-Stewart, 2000). The goal of BCT is to reduce or eliminate drug and alcohol use and increase relationship functioning. BCT is based on behavioral principles and involves assisting a couple to create a sobriety contract, helping the partner support the individual in positive efforts, and encouraging the couple to save discussions of past substance use or fears of future use until sessions. In addition, couples are coached to focus on positive partner behaviors, shown how to increase positive shared activities, and taught communication skills. BCT also teaches partners of substance users specific actions to decrease the chance of violence on days of substance use. Therefore, BCT does not rely on abstinence as the only method of eliminating violence as individual treatment for substance use does (Fals-Stewart & Clinton-Sherrod, 2009). Couples typically attend 15 to 20 treatment sessions over the course of 5 to 6 months (O'Farrell & Fals-Stewart, 2000).

A program of research has demonstrated the effectiveness of BCT in reducing substance use and improving relationship functioning (see O'Farrell & Fals-Stewart, 2000, for a brief review). In fact, individuals who participate in BCT exhibit more abstinence, fewer substance-related problems, greater relationship satisfaction, and less risk of relationship dissolution than individuals participating in individual treatments. BCT for substance use has been shown to reduce overall IPV compared to both individual treatment and a control conjoint treatment. In addition, IPV decreases after BCT treatment as a function of substance use status (Fals-Stewart & Clinton-Sherrod, 2009). Individuals who continued to use substances following treatment had a reduced, although higher, rate of IPV perpetration compared to matched controls at 1- and 2-year follow-up. However, individuals who remained abstinent following treatment demonstrated rates of IPV that were similar to matched controls. These results have been shown for alcohol abuse and drug abuse, as well as both men and women abusers. The authors concluded that teaching the couple how to manage violence together may result in decreased violence due to preventive measures the partner takes on substance use days. Furthermore, a study investigating the use of BCT with individuals with comorbid substance use and PTSD found comparable reductions in substance use and IPV as well as similar increases in relationship satisfaction for individuals with both PTSD and substance use disorder (SUD) compared to individuals with SUD alone (Rotunda, O'Farrell, Murphy, & Babey, 2008). That is, the intervention was effective regardless of PTSD status. This intervention using behavioral principles in a conjoint format demonstrated the effectiveness of treatment targeting a major risk factor for IPV to reduce IPV, even when comorbidities are present.

In addition to BCT for substance use, several writers have argued that couples therapy may be effective despite the presence of IPV (Simpson et al., 2008). Due to the high rate of IPV in couples seeking conjoint therapy and the lack of IPV assessment in couples therapy trials, it logically follows that aggression must have been present during previous trials (O'Leary, 2008). These trials were successful in increasing marital satisfaction despite the unidentified IPV; therefore, couples therapy may be successful with couples experiencing IPV. In fact, the frequency of violent acts in couples seeking couples therapy is relatively low (O'Leary et al., 1999). Many of these couples do not believe the aggression is a problem in their relationship (Ehrensaft & Vivian, 1996), leading some couples to feel that couples therapy focused on IPV is irrelevant and does not meet their needs (O'Leary et al., 1999). To investigate the possibility of conducting couples therapy in the presence of IPV, one recent trial of couples therapy investigated whether IPV would affect treatment outcomes (Simpson et al., 2008). Couples with mild IPV and couples without mild IPV attended 26 sessions of treatment derived from BCT. Relationship and individual outcomes following therapy did not differ due to IPV; therapy was successful regardless of IPV status. Couples maintained such low levels of physical aggression during and after treatment that analyses could not be conducted to investigate changes in physical aggression over time. Psychological aggression decreased over the course of the study, and reductions in psychological aggression were related to increases in marital satisfaction and individual functioning. These two courses of research demonstrated that conjoint therapy focused on improving risk factors for IPV (e.g., substance use, marital dissatisfaction) actually reduces or eliminates IPV, and that these gains were maintained over long follow-up periods (i.e., 2 years).

LIMITATIONS

Taken together, these studies suggested that conjoint therapy for IPV or risk factors associated with IPV may be effective in decreasing IPV. However, these studies have many limitations. First, attrition rates in the studies investigating conjoint therapy for IPV were high (Holtzworth-Munroe et al., 2003; O'Leary, 2008). Stith et al. (2004) reported a 70% completion rate in individual couple format and 73% completion in the multicouple group format. However, they also reported that 32% of male partners were noncompliant with a required pretreatment men's group and therefore were not eligible for the conjoint therapy. An additional 49% were unable or unwilling to attend conjoint sessions. If men who were noncompliant and couples who were unwilling to attend were included in attrition, the dropout rate would be much higher than the 30% reported. These dropout rates make it difficult to determine whether the therapy was actually effective. In addition, in military samples, it is difficult to secure the participation of the nonmilitary partner in intervention and assessment (Dunford, 2000; Neidig, 1986). Therefore, it is difficult to assess how well received and effective conjoint therapy would be in a military setting. Second, investigators rarely compared conjoint therapy to a wait-list group, choosing instead to compare to gender-specific group treatment (O'Leary, 2008). However, research on gender-specific treatment has demonstrated very small, if any, decreases in IPV compared to simply being identified by the legal system as an offender and being arrested (Babcock, Green, & Robie, 2004). For example, 40% of men in gender-specific treatment achieved nonviolence, while 35% were nonviolent without treatment (Babcock, Green, Webb, et al., 2004). Therefore, it is imperative that conjoint treatments be compared not only to gender-specific treatment, but also to a wait-list control to evaluate the true effectiveness of the program above and beyond identification as violent.

The research on conjoint therapy for IPV is still in its infancy, and larger, more rigorously controlled studies should be conducted in this area to determine if conjoint treatment approaches are effective in the treatment of IPV. Most studies do not distinguish between types of violence or subtypes of offenders, factors that may distinguish between those who complete the program and achieve successful outcomes and those who drop out or relapse (Kelly & Johnson, 2008). Much more work needs to be done before the effectiveness of treatments for specific offenders can be determined.

ISSUES FOR THE CLINICIAN

As stated, comprehensive and systematic assessment of IPV in all clients presenting for couples therapy is extremely important. Without thorough assessment, clinicians often do not recognize IPV when it is present. For example, when clinicians were presented with vignettes describing couples therapy cases involving severe domestic violence (Hansen et al., 1991), less than half of clinicians listed violence as a clinical problem, and few identified the risk of lethality, even in the case that actually resulted in the death of the female partner. In addition to failure to identify IPV, research demonstrated that few clinicians follow recommended screening procedures for IPV, which includes screening all couples for IPV using behaviorally specific self-report measures (e.g., CTS2) and separate individual interviews.

In one survey, about half of clinicians who responded indicated that they screen all couples for IPV (Schacht et al., 2009). About 37% interviewed all couples separately when screening, but almost 8% interviewed couples conjointly, asking the victim about abuse in front of the perpetrator, which may place the victim at risk. Only 12% used questionnaires in their assessment of IPV, and of these, only 7.5% used behaviorally specific, standardized measures. Therefore, less than 4% of clinicians in this sample used all the recommended guidelines for screening for IPV. In considering whether couples therapy was appropriate, only 42% considered fear and safety of the victim, less than 20% considered whether the abuse was currently occurring, and less than 5% considered injury or lethality of past violence. Thus, the majority of clinicians did not consider major risk factors when considering the appropriateness of conjoint therapy.

In addition to the importance of increasing identification of IPV, routinely screening couples for IPV as part of a standardized battery may reduce stigma associated with violence (Punukollo, 2003). Women reported that being asked about IPV as part of a standard battery does, in fact, reduce their perception of stigma (Chang et al., 2005), which facilitates successful identification and treatment of violence by allowing women to speak more openly about their experiences with IPV.

In addition to initial assessments, ongoing assessment throughout the therapy should be routine. In this way, clinicians will be more likely to identify additional acts of violence and will have the opportunity to renew no-violence contracts or refer the couple elsewhere if the violence has become too severe.

Besides thorough assessment procedures, clinicians should be aware of community resources for violent couples. Due to the high levels of aggression in clinic samples, it is likely that some couples will be identified as experiencing severe violence and therefore be inappropriate for conjoint therapy. In these cases, clinicians should have relevant referrals on hand to facilitate the acquisition of appropriate treatment for these couples. Appropriate contacts include local battered women's shelters, victim support groups, gender-specific treatment groups, and local law enforcement. Women should be informed of their legal rights, including restraining orders or orders for protection (Goodwin, 1993). In addition, clinicians should be aware when violence is too severe to be appropriate for conjoint therapy or will challenge their level of expertise in this area. In these cases, clinicians should refer couples to more appropriate treatment sources.

However, if violent couples appear appropriate for conjoint treatment following thorough assessment, clinicians should be prepared to provide treatment for IPV in a couples format. Conjoint treatment for IPV should include several elements (Holtzworth-Munroe et al., 2005). First, the couple and clinician should collaboratively set goals for treatment, with the cessation of violence being one of the primary goals. The clinician should provide psychoeducation around IPV, including prevalence, risk factors, negative consequences, and potential to escalate to serious injury. The couple should be informed that each partner must take responsibility for their own aggressive behavior. In addition, the couple must sign a no-violence contract, agree to report any future violent episodes, and remove weapons from the home. The couple should be informed that the clinician will regularly inquire about violence, and if any incidents are reported, the treatment plan will be reevaluated. If the violence becomes severe, conjoint treatment should be terminated, and the couple should be referred to alternative treatment. Safety plans and plans to avoid violence should be created in individual sessions and agreed to in the conjoint session. Once all this groundwork has been laid, treatment should first focus on anger management, including increasing awareness of anger cues and utilizing use of negotiated time-outs to decrease violence. Following anger management, therapy should focus on teaching couples emotional expressiveness and problem-solving skills. Once these skills are learned, couples can begin to communicate around relevant relationship issues to address presenting complaints.

As clinicians work to identify and treat IPV in their couple clients, they must be aware of their level of professional experience with treating violence and their own attitudes toward IPV (Gauthier & Levendosky, 1996). Specialized, in-depth training is recommended before engaging in the treatment of IPV due to the potential safety issues involved (Kaufman, 1992). In addition, IPV is a phenomenon that is associated with strong feelings and opinions. Clinicians should be aware of their own biases in this area and ensure they approach assessment and treatment in the most therapeutically appropriate manner. Some have suggested that this involves taking a strong stance against domestic violence (Bograd & Mederos, 1999); however, clinicians may also have their own opinions about whether violent relationships should continue, and they should be careful to balance the clients' desire to continue the relationship with safety before making recommendations.

ISSUES SPECIFIC TO MILITARY COUPLES

Clinicians treating military couples for IPV not only must be alert to general issues surrounding conjoint therapy for IPV, but also must be aware of issues specific to military populations, including DOD directives and regulations targeting domestic violence and barriers to reporting IPV. To improve policies and programs for IPV, DOD created the Defense Task Force on Domestic Violence (DTFDV). From 2000 to 2003, the DTFDV reviewed the policies of the DOD surrounding domestic violence, releasing three reports containing almost 200 recommendations (DOD, n.d.). In 2004, the DOD issued a directive updating the Military Family Advocacy Program (FAP), an organization that was originally expanded from its focus on child abuse to include domestic violence programming in 1981 (Neidig, 1986). The new directive assigned FAP responsibility for addressing IPV through prevention, identification, treatment, and follow-up services for victims and families.

FAP has a four-phase response to domestic violence (Brannen & Hamlin, 2000). First, all suspected incidents of domestic violence occurring within the military must be reported to the FAP. Law enforcement, medical, and dental facilities are the most common sources of referral for domestic violence. Second, the FAP must establish the safety of the victim, creating a safety plan and notifying authorities. Third, the domestic violence must be substantiated. A case manager opens an investigation and prepares recommendations to present to a case review committee (CRC) within 30 days. The CRC, which consists of a variety of military and civilian professionals, then determines whether the violence is substantiated. To be substantiated, there must be a great deal of evidence that indicated abuse occurred. If the CRC believes the incident occurred but there is not enough evidence, the CRC can confer suspected status to the case. If it is unclear whether the incident occurred, the CRC determines the case to be unsubstantiated.

Once CRC establishes substantiation, the committee delivers treatment recommendations, and the command staff can determine appropriate disciplinary action. Command has four options: (a) no action; (b) administrative action, including counseling or administrative separation; (c) nonjudicial punishment, including reprimand or reduction in pay or grade; or (d) court-martial (Clark & Messer, 2006). In terms of treatment, FAP typically recommends gender-specific individual or group treatment, anger management, domestic conflict containment programs, or couple treatment after the offender completes individual or group treatment (Clark & Messer, 2006). Treatment is carefully monitored by assessing behavioral changes in the offender, and the victim's safety is safeguarded through efforts of the FAP, victim advocate, and command. If treatment is completed successfully, command can decide to suspend punishment. Through these efforts, the goal of the DOD is to achieve decreases in violent behavior in 50% of offenders.

With the efforts of FAP to address IPV in the military, requirements to report domestic violence and the associated consequences may lead to underreporting of IPV. In military settings, couples are not guaranteed confidentiality around IPV identification or treatment, and previously there was a mandatory reporting law in effect. However, a new policy allows victims to make restricted reports to health care providers or victim advocates (Stamm, 2009). As this is a relatively new policy, it is difficult to determine its impact on reporting of IPV. The identification of IPV may have negative consequences for the service member and the family. As discussed, possible disciplinary measures include reduction in pay or grade, arrest in quarters, and even court-martial (Clark & Messer, 2006). These negative consequences may lead to underreporting of frequency and severity of violent incidents. Therefore, clinicians must be alert to these influences when assessing for IPV.

When conducting IPV assessments with military couples, clinicians must consider risk factors specific to the military. Clinicians should assess pay, rank, education, financial stress, recent moves, and perceptions of group-level attitudes about domestic violence. In addition, length of recent deployments and adjustment issues when returning from deployment, including relationship difficulties, should be discussed. Finally, combat experience, perceived threat in the combat zone, and symptoms of PTSD, depression, and alcohol or drug use should be queried. If these factors are considered, clinicians will be able to conduct comprehensive assessments of IPV that are sensitive to the particular risk factors present in the military population.

FUTURE RESEARCH DIRECTIONS

Due to the controversial nature of conjoint therapy for IPV, few rigorous studies have been conducted to develop and test the efficacy for conjoint interventions for IPV. Therefore, there is a great deal of room for growth in this area. A number of writers argued that, because aggressors are a heterogeneous group, treatment should not take a "one-size-fits-all" approach (e.g., McCollum & Stith, 2007). Many believe that mild-to-moderate violence or situational couple violence should be the primary targets of conjoint approaches (Holtzworth-Munroe & Stewart, 1994). However, besides theorizing, no treatment studies have empirically investigated the characteristics of clients for whom conjoint treatments work. Little research has been conducted to determine the frequency and severity of violence that can be safely and effectively treated in conjoint therapy (Simpson et al., 2008). Due to large dropout rates, it is unclear whether a conjoint approach is effective for all situational couple violence. Therefore, studies distinguishing between treatment dropouts and completers and between those who remain nonviolent versus relapse should be conducted. Matching studies, which assign participants to treatments based on specific participant characteristics thought to be associated with each treatment's effectiveness, would be helpful in determining for whom the conjoint therapy is most useful and the effectiveness of conjoint therapy when applied to the optimal population. In addition, these studies would help to establish empirically supported guidelines for inclusion of couples in conjoint treatment.

As some research suggested that intervening on risk factors for IPV results in decreases in IPV (e.g., O'Farrell & Fals-Stewart, 2000), risk factors should be identified from the literature that could serve as potential treatment targets in conjoint treatment. For example, due to the high rate of IPV among veterans with PTSD, conjoint treatment for PTSD (Monson, Fredman, & Adair, 2008) may be helpful in reducing IPV, although the treatment focuses on trauma rather than IPV directly. Researchers should be creative in developing and implementing novel treatment approaches for IPV, as many of the current approaches are similar and may not be extremely effective.

In addition to treatment programs for IPV, research should continue to focus on development and implementation of prevention and early detection programs for IPV, especially within military populations (Marshall et al., 2005). Few programs have been implemented in an active duty population, and those that have been conducted provided contradictory results regarding the effectiveness of conjoint intervention (Dunford, 2000; Neidig, 1986). Further, identifying potential group factors in the military that lead to increased or decreased rates of IPV, such as hypermasculinity, may prove to be especially fruitful. Once these group factors are identified, prevention programs can be created to modify these characteristics. In addition, screening programs should be implemented in which service members are routinely screened for IPV and associated risk factors to aid in early identification of individuals at risk or of problematic interaction patterns. In this way, the negative effects of IPV may be minimized.

CONCLUSION

Despite the controversy surrounding conjoint therapy for IPV, a growing body of literature suggests that conjoint treatments may be safe and effective for the treatment of aggression. The research demonstrating the effectiveness of BCT for substance abuse provides a strong argument in favor of a conjoint approach for some violent couples. Even though couple researchers are becoming increasingly aware of the high prevalence of IPV in clinic samples, clinicians do not always assess for IPV and rarely conform to published guidelines for assessment. In addition, couples do not typically report IPV as a presenting problem, and specialized self-report measures and clinical interviews are necessary to increase detection. Therefore, IPV is likely underidentified in military couples seeking therapy, and treating these couples in a conjoint format without assessment of IPV may place the victims at increased risk for injury. Future research to identify specific individuals for whom conjoint treatment works and to develop new conjoint treatments to target risk factors for IPV will aid in increasing the effectiveness and reach of these conjoint interventions. These efforts will help more military couples receive the most efficacious treatments available, thereby reducing the deleterious impact of IPV on these individuals, families, the military, and society at large.

REFERENCES

Aldarondo, E., & Straus, M. (1994). Screening for physical violence in couple therapy: Methodological, practical, and ethical considerations. *Family Process, 33,* 425–439.

Archer, J. (2000). Sex differences in aggression between heterosexual partners: A meta-analytic review. *Psychological Bulletin, 126,* 651–680.

Babcock, J. C., Green, C. E., & Robie, C. (2004). Does batterers' treatment work? A meta-analytic review of domestic violence treatment. *Clinical Psychology Review, 23,* 1023–1053.

Babcock, J. C., Green, C. E., Webb, S. A., & Graham, K. H. (2004). A second failure to replicate the Gottman et al. (1995) typology of men who abuse intimate partners and possible reasons why. *Journal of Family Psychology, 18,* 396–400.

Bailey, S. (1996). Adolescents who murder. *Journal of Adolescence, 19,* 19–39.

Beckham, J. C., Moore, S. D., & Reynolds, V. (2000). Interpersonal hostility and violence in Vietnam combat veterans with chronic posttraumatic stress disorder: A review of theoretical models and empirical evidence. *Aggression and Violent Behavior, 5,* 451–466.

Bograd, M., & Mederos, F. (1999). Battering and couples therapy: Universal screening and selection of treatment modality. *Journal of Marital and Family Therapy, 25,* 291–312.

Brannen, S. J., & Hamlin, E. R. (2000). Understanding spouse abuse in military families. In J. A. Martin, L. N. Rosen, & L. R. Sparacino (Eds.), *The military family: A practice guide for human service providers* (pp. 169–183). Westport, CT: Praeger.

Browne, A. (1993). Violence against women by male partners: Prevalence, outcomes, and policy implications. *American Psychologist, 48,* 1077–1087.

Campbell, J. C., Garza, M. A., Gielen, A. C., O'Campo, P., Kub, J., Dienemann, J., … Jafar, E. (2003). Intimate partner violence and abuse among active duty military women. *Violence Against Women, 9,* 1072–1092.

Cascardi, M., Langhinrichsen, J., & Vivian, D. (1992). Marital aggression: Impact, injury, and health correlates for husbands and wives. *Archives of Internal Medicine, 152,* 1178–1184.

Center for Disease Control and Prevention. (2003). *Costs of intimate partner violence against women in the United States.* Retrieved January 5, 2011, from http://www.cdc.gov/violenceprevention/pdf/IPVBook-a.pdf

Chang, J. C., Decker, M. R., Moracco, K. E., Martin, S. L., Petersen, R., & Frasier, P. Y. (2005). Asking about intimate partner violence: Advice from female survivors to health care practitioners. *Patient Education and Counseling, 59,* 141–147.

Clark, J. C., & Messer, S. C. (2006). Intimate partner violence in the U.S. military: Rates, risks, and responses. In C. A. Castro, A. B. Adler, & T. W. Britt (Eds.), *Military life: The psychology of serving in peace and combat. Volume 3: The military family* (pp. 193–219). Westport, CT: Praeger Security International.

Crouch, J. L., Thomsen, C. J., Milner, J. S., Stander, V. A., & Merrill, L. L. (2009). Heterosexual intimate partner violence among navy personnel: Gender differences in incidence and consequences. *Military Psychology, 21,* S1–S15.

D'Ardenne, P., & Balakrishna, J. (2001). Domestic violence and intimacy: What the relationship therapist needs to know. *Sexual and Relationship Therapy, 16,* 229–246.

Department of Defense. (n.d.). *Military homefront: Supporting our troops and their families.* Retrieved January 5, 2011, http://www.militaryhomefront.dod.mil/

Dunford, F. W. (2000). The San Diego Navy Experiment: An assessment of interventions for men who assault their wives. *Journal of Consulting and Clinical Psychology, 68,* 468–476.

Dutton, D. G. (1986). The outcome of court-mandated treatment of wife assault: A quasi-experimental evaluation. *Violence & Victims, 1,* 163–175.

Edleson, J. L., & Tolman, R. M. (1992). *Intervention for men who batter: An ecological approach.* Thousand Oaks, CA: Sage.

Ehrensaft, M. K., & Vivian, D. (1996). Spouses' reasons for not reporting existing physical aggression as a marital problem. *Journal of Family Psychology, 10,* 443–453.

Emery, R. E., & Laumann-Billings, L. (1998). An overview of the nature, causes, and consequences of abusive family relationships: Toward differentiating maltreatment and violence. *American Psychologist, 53,* 121–135.

Fals-Stewart, W., & Clinton-Sherrod, M. (2009). Treating intimate partner violence among substance-abusing dyads: The effect of couples therapy. *Professional Psychology: Research and Practice, 40,* 257–263.

Fals-Stewart, W., Golden, J., & Schumacher, J. (2003). Intimate partner violence. *Journal of Substance Abuse Treatment, 22,* 87–96.

Feld, S. L., & Straus, M. A. (1989). Escalation and desistance of wife assault in marriage. *Criminology, 27,* 141–161.
Gauthier, L. M., & Levendosky, A. A. (1996). Assessment and treatment of couples with abusive male partners: Guidelines for therapists. *Psychotherapy, 33,* 403–417.
Gerlock, A. A. (2004). Domestic violence and post-traumatic stress disorder severity for participants of a domestic violence rehabilitation program. *Military Medicine, 169,* 470–474.
Gondolf, E. W. (2000). A 30-month follow-up of court-referred batterers in four cities. *International Journal of Offender Therapy and Comparative Criminology, 44,* 111–128.
Gondolf, E. W. (2002) *Batterer intervention systems: Issues, outcomes, and recommendations.* Thousand Oaks, CA: Sage.
Gondolf, E. W., & Russell, D. (1986). The case against anger control treatment programs for batterers. *Response, 9,* 2–5.
Goodwin, B. J. (1993). Psychotherapy supervision: Training therapists to recognize family violence. In M. Hansen and M. Harway (Eds.), *Battering and family therapy: A feminist perspective* (pp. 119–133). Newbury Park, CA: Sage.
Hansen, M., Harway, M., & Cervantes, N. (1991). Therapists' perceptions of severity in cases of family violence. *Violence and Victims, 6,* 225–235.
Harris, R., Savage, S., Jones, T., & Brooke, W. (1988). A comparison of treatments for abusive men and their partners within a family-service agency. *Canadian Journal of Community Mental Health, 7,* 147–155.
Heyman, R. E., & Neidig, P. H. (1997). Physical aggression couples treatment. In W. K. Halford & H. J. Markman (Eds.), *Clinical handbook of marriage and couples interventions* (pp. 589–617). Chichester, UK: Wiley.
Heyman, R. E., & Neidig, P. H. (1999). A comparison of spousal aggression prevalence rates in U.S. Army and civilian representative samples. *Journal of Consulting and Clinical Psychology, 67,* 239–242.
Holtzworth-Munroe, A. (1992). Social skills deficits in maritally violent men: Interpreting the data using a social information processing model. *Clinical Psychology Review, 12,* 605–617.
Holtzworth-Munroe, A., & Anglin, K. (1991). The competency of responses given by martially violent versus nonviolent men to problematic marital situations. *Clinical Psychology Review, 12,* 605–617.
Holtzworth-Munroe, A., Beatty, S. B., & Anglin, K. (1995). The assessment and treatment of marital violence: An introduction for the marital therapist. In N. S. Jacobson & A. S. Gurman (Eds.), *Clinical handbook of marital therapy* (2nd ed., pp. 317–339). New York: Guilford Press.
Holtzworth-Munroe, A., Clements, K., & Farris, C. (2005). Working with couples who have experienced physical aggression. In M. Harway (Ed.), *Handbook of couples therapy* (pp. 289–312). Hoboken, NJ: Wiley.
Holtzworth-Munroe, A., & Hutchinson, G. (1993). Attributing negative intent to wife behavior: The attributions of martially violent versus nonviolent men. *Journal of Abnormal Psychology, 102,* 206–211.
Holtzworth-Munroe, A., Marshall, A. D., Meehan, J. C., & Rehman, U. (2003). Physical aggression. In D. K. Snyder & M. A. Whisman (Eds.), *Treating difficult couples: Helping clients with coexisting mental and relationship disorders* (pp. 201–231). New York: Guilford Press.
Holtzworth-Munroe, A., Meehan, J. C., Herron, K., Rehman, U., & Stuart, G. L. (2000). Testing the Holtzworth-Munroe and Stuart (1994) batterer typology. *Journal of Consulting and Clinical Psychology, 68,* 1000–1019.
Holtzworth-Munroe, A, Smutzler, N., Bates, L., & Sandin, E. (1997). Husband violence: Basic facts and clinic implications. In W. K. Halford & H. J. Markman (Eds.), *Clinical handbook of marriage and couples interventions* (pp. 129–156). Chichester, UK: Wiley.

Holtzworth-Munroe, A., & Stewart, G. L. (1994). Typologies of male batterers: Three subtypes and the differences among them. *Psychological Bulletin, 116,* 476–497.

Jacobson, N. S. (1994). Rewards and dangers in researching domestic violence. *Family Process, 33,* 81–85.

Jacobson, N. S., & Christensen, A. (1996). *Integrative couple therapy: Promoting acceptance and change.* New York: Norton.

Jacobson, N. S., Gottman, J. M., Gortner, E., Berns, S., & Shortt, J. W. (1996). Psychological factors in the longitudinal course of battering: When do the couples split up? When does the abuse decrease? *Violence and Victims, 11,* 371–392.

Jacobson, N. S., Gottman, J. M., Waltz, J., Rushe, R., Babcock, J., & Holtzworth-Munroe, A. M. (1994). Affect, verbal content, and psychophysiology and the argument of couples with a violent husband. *Journal of Counseling and Clinical Psychology, 62,* 982–988.

Jaffe, P. G., Wolfe, D. A., & Wilson, S. K. (1990). *Children of battered women.* Newbury Park, CA: Sage.

Johnson, M. P. (1995). Patriarchal terrorism and common couple violence: Two forms of violence against women in U.S. families. *Journal of Marriage and the Family, 57,* 283–294.

Johnson, M. P. (2006). Conflict and control: Gender symmetry and asymmetry in domestic violence. *Violence Against Women, 12,* 1003–1018.

Kaufman, G. (1992). The mysterious disappearance of battered women in family therapists' offices: Male privilege colluding with male violence. *Journal of Marital and Family Therapy, 18,* 233–243.

Kelly, J. B., & Johnson, M. P. (2008). Differentiation among types of intimate partner violence: Research update and implications for interventions. *Family Court Review, 46,* 476–499.

King, L. A., & King, D. W. (2000). Male-perpetrated domestic violence: Testing a series of multifactorial family models. Summary (NCJRS Document No. 185695). Rockville, MD: National Institute of Justice/NCJRS.

Kropp, P. R. (2008). Intimate partner violence risk assessment and management. *Violence and Victims, 23,* 202–220.

Langhinrichsen-Rohling, J., Huss, M. T., & Rohling, M. L. (2006). Aggressive behavior. In M. Hersen (Ed.), *Clinician's handbook of adult behavioral* assessment (pp. 371–395). San Diego, CA: Elsevier.

LaTaillade, J. J., Epstein, N. B., & Werlinich, C. A. (2006). Conjoint treatment of intimate partner violence: A cognitive behavioral approach. *Journal of Cognitive Psychotherapy: An International Quarterly, 20,* 393–410.

Launius, M. H., & Lindquist, C. U. (1988). Learned helplessness, external locus of control, and passivity in battered women. *Journal of Interpersonal Violence, 3,* 307–318.

Lawrence, E., & Bradbury, T. N. (2001). Physical aggression and marital dysfunction: A longitudinal analysis. *Journal of Family Psychology, 15,* 135–154.

Margolin, G. (1998). Effects of domestic violence on children. In P. K. Trickett & C. J. Schellenback (Eds.), *Violence against children in the family and the community* (pp. 57–101). Washington, DC: American Psychological Association.

Margolin, G., John, R. S., & Gleberman, L. (1988). Affective responses to conflictual discussions in violent and nonviolent couples. *Journal of Consulting and Clinical Psychology, 56,* 24–33.

Marshall, A. D., Panuzio, J., & Taft, C. T. (2005). Intimate partner violence among military veterans and active duty servicemen. *Clinical Psychology Review, 25,* 862–876.

McCarroll, J. E., Newby, J. H., Thayer, L. E., Norwood, A. E., Fullerton, C. S., & Ursano, R.J. (1999). Reports of spouse abuse in the U.S. Army central registry (1989–1997). *Military Medicine, 164,* 77–84.

McCarroll, J. E., Ursano, R. J., Liu, X., Thayer, L. E., Newby, J. H., Norwood, A. E., Fullerton, C. S. (2000). Deployment and the probability of spousal aggression by U.S. Army soldiers. *Military Medicine, 165,* 41–44.

McCarroll, J. E., Ursano, R. J., Newby, J. H., Liu, X., Fullerton, C. S., Norwood, A. E., & Osuch, E. A. (2003). Domestic violence and deployment in U.S. Army soldiers. *Journal of Nervous and Mental Disease, 191,* 3–9.

McCollum, E. E., & Stith, S. M. (2007). Conjoint couple's treatment for intimate partner violence: Controversy and promise. In J. L. Wetchler (Ed.), *Handbook of clinical issues in couple therapy* (pp. 71–82). Binghamton, NY: Haworth Press.

Merrill, L. L., Crouch, J. L., Thomsen, C. J., Guimond, J., & Milner, J. S. (2005). Perpetration of severe intimate partner violence: Premilitary and second year service rates. *Military Medicine, 170,* 705–709.

Monson, C. M., Fredman, S. J., & Adair, K. C. (2008). Cognitive-behavioral conjoint therapy for posttraumatic stress disorder: Application to Operation Enduring and Iraqi Freedom veterans. *Journal of Clinical Psychology: In Session, 64,* 958–971.

Monson, C. M., Langhinrichsen-Rohling, J., & Taft, C. T. (2009). Sexual aggression in intimate relationships. In K. D. O'Leary & E. M. Woodin (Eds.), *Psychological and physical aggression in couples: Causes and interventions* (pp. 37–58). Washington, DC: American Psychological Association.

Neidig, P. H. (1986). The development and evaluation of a spouse abuse treatment program in a military setting. *Evaluation and Program Planning, 9,* 275–280.

O'Farrell, T. J., & Fals-Stewart, W. (2000). Behavioral couples therapy for alcoholism and drug abuse. *Journal of Substance Abuse Treatment, 2000,* 51–54.

O'Leary, K. D. (1996). Physical aggression in intimate relationships can be treated within a marital context under certain circumstances. *Journal of Interpersonal Violence, 11,* 450–452.

O'Leary, K. D. (2001). Psychological abuse: A variable deserving critical attention in domestic violence. In K. D. O'Leary & R. D. Maiuro (Eds.), *Psychological abuse in violent domestic relations* (pp. 3–28). New York: Springer.

O'Leary, K. D. (2008). Couple therapy and physical aggression. In A. S. Gurman (Ed.), *Clinical handbook of couple therapy* (4th ed., pp. 478–498). New York: Guilford Press.

O'Leary, K. D., Barling, J., Arias, I., Rosenbaum, A., Malone, J., & Tyree, A. (1989). Prevalence and stability of marital aggression between spouses: A longitudinal analysis. *Journal of Consulting and Clinical Psychology, 57,* 263–268.

O'Leary, K. D., Heyman, R. E., & Neidig, P. H. (1999). Treatment of wife abuse: A comparison of gender specific and conjoint approaches. *Behavior Therapy, 30,* 475–505.

O'Leary, K. D., Malone, J., & Tyree, A. (1994). Physical aggression in early marriage: Prerelationship and relationship effects. *Journal of Consulting and Clinical Psychology, 62,* 594–602.

O'Leary, K. D., Vivian, D., & Malone, J. (1992). Assessment of physical aggression against women in marriage: The need for multimodal assessment. *Behavioral Assessment, 14,* 5–14.

Orcutt, H. K., King, L. A., & King, D. W. (2003). Male-perpetrated violence among Vietnam veteran couples: Relationships with veteran's early life characteristics, trauma history, and PTSD symptomatology. *Journal of Traumatic Stress, 16,* 381–390.

Pan, H. D., Neidig, P. H., & O'Leary, K. D. (1994). Predicting mild and severe husband-to-wife physical aggression. *Journal of Consulting and Clinical Psychology, 62,* 975–981.

Punukollo, M. (2003). Domestic violence: Screening made practical. *The Journal of Family Practice, 52,* 537–543.

Rathus, J. H., & Feindler, E. L. (2004). *Assessment of partner violence: A handbook for researchers and practitioners.* Washington, DC: American Psychological Association.

Rosen, K. H., Matheson, J. L., Stith, S. M., McCollum, E. E., & Locke, L. D. (2003). Negotiated time-out: A de-escalation tool for couples. *Journal of Marital and Family Therapy, 29,* 291–298.

Rosen, L. N., Kaminski, R. J., Parmley, A. M., Knudson, K. H., & Fancher, P. (2003). The effects of peer group climate on intimate partner violence among married U.S. Army soldiers. *Violence Against Women, 9,* 1045–1071.

Rosen, L. N., Parmley, A. M., Knudson, K. H., & Fancher, P. (2002). Intimate partner violence among married male U.S. Army soldiers: Ethnicity as a factor in self-reported perpetration and victimization. *Violence and Victims, 17,* 607–622.

Rosenbaum, A., & O'Leary, D. (1981). The treatment of marital violence. In N. S. Jacobsen and A. S. Gurman (Eds.), *Clinical handbook of marital therapy.* New York: Guilford.

Rotunda, R. J., O'Farrell, T. J., Murphy, M., & Babey, S. H. (2008). Behavioral couples therapy for comorbid substance use disorders and combat-related posttraumatic stress disorder among male veterans: An initial evaluation. *Addictive Behaviors, 33,* 180–187.

Saverese, V. W., Suvak, M. K., King, L. A., & King, D. W. (2001). Relationships among alcohol use, hyperarousal and marital abuse and violence in Vietnam veterans. *Journal of Traumatic Stress, 14,* 717–732.

Schacht, R. L., Dimidjian, S., George, W. H., & Berns, S. B. (2009). Domestic violence assessment procedures among couple therapists. *Journal of Marital and Family Therapy, 35,* 47–59.

Sherman, M. D., Sautter, F., Jackson, M. H., Lyons, J. A., & Han, X. (2006). Domestic violence in veterans with posttraumatic stress disorder who seek couples therapy. *Journal of Marital and Family Therapy, 32,* 479–490.

Simpson, L. E., Atkins, D. C., Gattis, K. S., & Christensen, A. (2008). Low-level relationship aggression and couple therapy outcomes. *Journal of Family Psychology, 22,* 102–111.

Simpson, L. E., & Christensen, A. (2005). Spousal agreement regarding relationship aggression on the Conflict Tactics Scale-2. *Psychological Assessment, 17,* 423–432.

Simpson, L. E., Doss, B. D., Wheeler, J., & Christensen, A. (2007). Relationship violence among couples seeking therapy: Common couple violence or battering? *Journal of Marital and Family Therapy, 33,* 270–283.

Slep, A. M. S., & O'Leary, S. G. (2005). Parent and partner violence in families with young children: Rates, patterns, and connections. *Journal of Consulting and Clinical Psychology, 73,* 435–444.

Stamm, S. (2009). Intimate partner violence in the military: Securing our country, starting with the home. *Family Court Review, 47,* 321–339.

Stith, S. M., McCollum, E. E., Rosen, K. H., Locke, L. D., & Goldberg, P. D. (2005). Domestic violence-focused couples treatment. In J. L. Lebow (Ed.), *Handbook of clinical family therapy* (pp. 406–430). Hoboken, NJ: Wiley.

Stith, S. M., Rosen, K. H., & McCollum, E. E. (2003). Effectiveness of couples treatment for spouse abuse. *Journal of Marital and Family Therapy, 29,* 407–426.

Stith, S. M., Rosen, K. H., McCollum, E. E., & Thomsen, C. J. (2004). Treating intimate partner violence within intact couple relationships: Outcomes of multi-couple versus individual couple therapy. *Journal of Marital and Family Therapy, 30,* 305–318.

Straus, M. A. (1979). Measuring intrafamily conflict and violence: The Conflict Tactics Scale. *Journal of Marriage and the Family, 41,* 75–88.

Straus, M. A., & Gelles, R. J. (1990). *Physical violence in American families.* New Brunswick, NJ: Transaction.

Straus, M. A., Hamby, S. L., Boney-McCoy, S., & Sugarman, D. (1996). The revised Conflict Tactics Scales (CTS-2): Development and preliminary psychometric data. *Journal of Family Issues, 17,* 283–316.

Straus, M. A., & Sweet, S. (1992). Verbal aggression in couples: Incidence rates and relationships to personal characteristics. *Journal of Marriage and the Family, 54,* 346–357.

Sugarman, D. B., & Hotaling, G. T. (1989). Violent men in intimate relationships: An analysis of risk markers. *Journal of Applied Social Psychology, 19,* 1034–1048.

Taft, C. T., Weatherill, R. P., Woodward, H. E., Pinto, L. A., Watkins, L. E., Miller, M. W., & Dekel, R. (2009). Intimate partner and general aggression perpetration among combat veterans presenting to a posttraumatic stress disorder clinic. *American Journal of Orthopsychiatry, 79,* 461–468.

Tjaden, P., & Thoennes, N. (2000). *Extent, nature, and consequences of intimate partner violence: Findings from the National Violence Against Women Survey* (Report No. NCJ 181867). Washington, DC: U.S. Department of Justice.

Wasileski, M., Callaghan-Chaffee, M. E., & Chaffee, R. B. (1982). Spousal violence in military homes: An initial survey. *Military Medicine, 147,* 761–765.

14

Substance Misuse

SHARON MORGILLO FREEMAN

INTRODUCTION

Substance use disorders (SUDs) account for 8.9% of the total burden of diseases, including 4.1% for tobacco-related problems and 4% for alcohol-related problems according to the World Health Organization (Campanini, 2002). Illegal substances added an additional 0.8% in 2000 to the overall burden placed on health care systems worldwide. The total burden is due to a variety of health and social problems, including serious infectious diseases, crime, and secondary health problems such as chronic obstructive pulmonary disease (COPD), emphysema, and liver failure. Substance misuse problems cross all socioeconomic, occupational, and international boundaries. Therefore, it should not come as a surprise that individuals in military occupations would also be at risk for this particular human behavioral health problem. For example, an estimated 7.1% of individuals in military settings age 18 or older have met the criteria for a past-year SUD. This rate of SUDs translates into approximately 1.8 million veterans affected (Substance Abuse and Mental Health Services Administration [SAMHSA], 2008).

The most common substances of abuse among veterans are alcohol and nicotine, with binge-drinking patterns being most problematic, especially in deployed personnel with combat exposure. The Office of Applied Studies reported that within this group, National Guard and Reserve troops in younger age brackets are at the highest risk for problematic alcohol use disorders (SAMHSA, 2008).

The military is reinforcing the need for service members to seek marriage counseling as a sign of strength, especially postdeployment, if there are problems in the marriage. It has become apparent that service members who have problems at home are less effective in the workplace, which can have severe consequences in a warrior society.

This chapter addresses problems of alcohol and drug misuse in the military, specifically in intimate relationships. The majority of military members are either married or in a significant relationship; therefore, it would stand to reason that substance misuse would negatively affect military relationships similar to the way substance misuse disorders affect civilian relationships. Negative consequences related to SUDs eventually filter into the service member's personal relationships, work performance, and financial situation. The impact of SUDs on relationships in the civilian sector is well known; however, these problems become more complicated in the military as well as chosen methods of intervention.

BACKGROUND

The choice of mood-altering substance is generally based on three specific criteria: ease of access, rapidity of onset of action, and activation of the reward system of the brain (Dackis & O'Brien, 2001). The reward system of the brain is fairly complex, with a series of actions required in various structures before the individual experiences a reward response described as "euphoria." Substances and behaviors that result in the feeling of euphoria trigger increases in cell firing in a portion of the brain called the ventral tegmentum (VT). Stimulation of the VT increases the release of dopamine (DA) in another structure called the nucleus accumbens (NA). The release of DA alters the presence of another neurochemical, gamma-amino-butyric acid (GABA) at presynaptic sites (Portenoy & Payne, 1992). The resulting release of DA in the NA is experienced as a "rush" or "euphoria," which is highly rewarding and reinforcing. Given that humans tend to repeat experiences that are highly rewarding, the individual is likely to repeat the pleasurable experience again and again (Portenoy & Payne, 1992). In most societies, the use of a chemical to produce a rush is considered inappropriate (as in illicit drug use, illicit sexual experiences, etc.) and therefore described as "abuse."

The use of the substance alone is not in and of itself criteria for problematic substance-related disorders. There is much more that must occur for the criteria to be met. If an individual uses a substance for its pleasurable effect and continues to abuse the substance, experiencing negative consequences that are significant, the individual is at risk for the development of substance dependence. If the same individual experiences negative mood or physical changes due to their use and spends a great deal of time or effort to obtain that substance, then this person likely meets the criteria for substance dependence. The *International Classification of Disease Diagnostic Criteria for Substance Dependence* as published by the WHO (2010) is outlined in Table 14.1.

SUBSTANCE MISUSE IN THE MILITARY

Despite a popular misconception about substance use prevalence in military settings, statistics comparing military and civilian use do not demonstrate a significant difference in these populations. A review of substance abuse during the Vietnam era showed that only 5% of these veterans were found to be dependent on heroin

TABLE 14.1 Criteria for Substance Dependence in *ICD-10*

Three or more of the following must have been experienced or exhibited together at some time during the previous year:

(a) a strong desire or sense of compulsion to take the substance;
(b) difficulties in controlling substance-taking behaviour in terms of its onset, termination, or levels of use;
(c) physiological withdrawal state when substance use has ceased or been reduced, as evidenced by: the characteristic withdrawal syndrome for the substance; or use of the same (or a closely related) substance with the intention of relieving or avoiding withdrawal symptoms;
(d) evidence of tolerance, such that increased doses of the psychoactive substance are required in order to achieve effects originally produced by lower doses;
(e) progressive neglect of alternative pleasures or interests because of psychoactive substance use, increased amount of time necessary to obtain or take the substance or to recover from its effects;
(f) persisting with substance use despite clear evidence of overtly harmful consequences, such as harm to the liver through excessive drinking, depressive mood states consequent to heavy substance use, or drug-related impairment of cognitive functioning. Efforts should be made to determine that the user was actually, or could be expected to be, aware of the nature and extent of the harm.

Source: From World Health Organization. *ICD-10 Classification of Mental and Behavioural Disorders: Clinical descriptions and diagnostic guidelines.* Retrieved January 1, 2011, from http://www.who.int/substance_abuse/terminology/ICD10ClinicalDiagnosis.pdf.

after returning to the United States. Of those who were dependent on heroin, 12% relapsed within their first 3 years after returning. During the 1970s, heroin was inexpensive, easily accessible, and tolerated socially in many settings, which may account for the relapse rate on this substance (Rittenhouse, 1977). Health care providers often fail to remember that the years surrounding the Vietnam conflict coincided with a significant increase in the consumption of substances of abuse all over the world. Therefore, it would only be logical that there would be an overlap between the civilian and military sectors.

According to the Department of Defense, the 2008 rate for illicit drug use in the past month, including prescription drugs, was 12%, with a 2005 rate of 5%. The rate for illicit drug use, excluding prescription drugs, has been unchanged at 2% from 2002 to 2008. The difference in the rates for illicit drug use was explained as changed due to the addition of several questions regarding narcotic pain medications that had not been contained in the questions prior to 2008 (Military Health Services, 2009). SAMHSA examined the prevalence of illegal drug use in military and civilian populations. Tables 14.2 to 14.4 outline the results of one of these surveys.

MILITARY CODE OF CONDUCT

Military codes of conduct exist to address the behaviors of service members who demonstrate an inability to control behaviors that may discredit the uniform of the United States or whatever country that individual is serving. The majority of codes of conduct include multiple breaches before serious consequences occur for

TABLE 14.2 Illegal Drug Use

	2005	2006
Civilians		
Ages 18–20		
Past 30 days	22.3%	22.2%
Past 12 months	37.9%	37.6%
Ages 21–25		
Past 30 days	18.7%	18.3%
Past 12 months	31.8%	32.3%
Military		
Past 30 days	5%	Data not available
Past 12 months	10.9%	Data not available

Source: Data courtesy of the Substance Abuse and Mental Health Services Administration, Office of Applied Studies, *National survey on drug use and health*, 2008. Retrieved January 10, 2011, from http://oas.samhsa.gov/nhsda.htm.

TABLE 14.3 Sociodemographic Correlates of Illicit Drug Use, Past 30 Days, Active Duty Military

Marital Status	Prevalence (%)
Not married	6.6
Married, spouse not present	6.3
Married, spouse present	3.4

Source: Bray et al. (2006).Department of Defense Health Related Behaviors Among Active Duty Military Personnel.

TABLE 14.4 Stress in Family, Past 12 Months, by Drinking Levels (%)

Drinking Level	Nondrinker	Infrequent/Light	Moderate	Moderate/Heavy	Heavy
A lot	15.3	18.3	18.1	18.3	24.7
Some or a little	57.3	59.7	61.9	62.5	51.6
None at all	27.4	22	20	19.2	23.7

Source: Bray et al. (2006). Department of Defense Health Related Behaviors Among Active Duty Military Personnel.

the service member. Codes of conduct exist for service members who may exhibit behavioral problems related to substance abuse or use. Civilian practitioners who interact with military members should have cursory knowledge about military codes of conduct that may affect treatment planning, disciplinary action, and communication structures regarding confidential information related to substance use problems. A portion of the Army's Substance Abuse Program (ASAP) guide of the Uniform Code of Military Justice includes the following information regarding substances of abuse:

Section **8–13**: "If the unit commander determines that conduct, duty performance, and progress are unsatisfactory, and that further rehabilitation efforts cannot be justified, they will initiate a discharge from military Service. ASAP counseling services will be provided until the Soldier is separated. Referral to VA [Veterans Affairs] services will be offered."

Section **8–20. Unacceptable rehabilitation modalities**

a. Methadone maintenance will not be used.
b. Use of Disulfiram (Antabuse) will not be mandatory.

Section **8–21. Counseling staff standards/competency**

a. The ASAP clinical providers will have a master's degree in social work or psychology.

Section **10–4. Administrative and Uniform Code of Military Justice options**

a. Commanders may take the following actions against Soldiers who test positive for illegal drugs or for illicit use of legal drugs when a MRO determines the Soldier has no legitimate medical purpose for taking the drug:
(1) Administrative actions—
    (*a*) Oral or written counseling/reprimand.
    (*b*) Suspension of access to classified information.
    (*c*) Suspension of favorable personnel actions.
    (*d*) The commander must initiate administrative separation in accordance with paragraph 1–7*c*(7) the retention/separation authority will decide if the Soldier is retained or separated.

(Department of the Army, 2009.)

IMPACT OF SUBSTANCE ABUSE ON RELATIONSHIPS

Substance abuse affects not only the person using the substance but also the significant other or partner, albeit in different ways. The person using the substance is often convincing him- or herself that he or she has not changed, is still competent in his or her role, and entitled to do whatever he or she chooses to do because he or she can "handle it." The partner, however, is slowly losing his or her connection, helpmate, and friend to this "other" entity who is becoming more and more important in the loved one's life. At first, the changes may be subtle, such as oversleeping due to being hung over and acting "silly" or embarrassing in social settings. Gradually, the partner becomes disgusted, angry, and resentful that their loved one is "blind" to the negative changes occurring with continued use of the substance.

Some individuals who have developed problematic SUDs may be causing distress by spending monies meant for living expenses or failing to participate in shared household/child-rearing responsibilities. Eventually, the nonabusing partner begins to take over the lion's share of responsibilities, making excuses for the loved one, and engaging in shouting matches over alcohol or drug use. Anxiety increases as the nonabusing partner grows concerned over potential legal problems (arrest for driving under the influence), potential injury to the loved one or the loved one injuring someone else while driving, or losing control while angry, as well as concerns about the direct physical damage of the drug itself (Epstein & McCrady, 2002; O'Farrell & Birchler, 1987).

Couples therapists must also be aware of the potential for overreaction to a loved one's drinking based on personal past experience (e.g., being raised in an alcoholic home) that may mimic true addiction problems. In the example of the couple at the end of the chapter, Kathy and Bob, Bob feels Kathy is overreacting to "normal" drinking behaviors. To assess whether Bob has problematic drinking, certain empirically based screening instruments can be used directly in the session. For example, the therapist might stop and conduct a brief screening evaluation such as the CAGE questionnaire or the Alcohol Use Disorder Inventory Test (AUDIT) to help evaluate potential problems. The CAGE stands for the questions asked in the inventory: (a) Has anyone asked you to *C*ut down on your drinking? (b) Has anyone *A*nnoyed you by complaining about your drinking? (c) Have you ever felt *G*uilty about your drinking? And, (d) have you ever had a drink to avoid withdrawal symptoms like a hangover (*E*ye-opener)?

The AUDIT is used to identify persons with hazardous and harmful patterns of alcohol consumption. The AUDIT was developed by WHO as a simple method of screening for excessive drinking and to assist in brief assessment. The AUDIT is available along with the accompanying manual from the World Health Organization Web site (http://whqlibdoc.who.int/hq/2001/who_msd_msb_01.6a.pdf). Another screening test is the Michigan Alcohol Screening Test (MAST), which is a 22-question screening instrument for alcohol use disorders (Selzer, 1971). These screening tests are available free online from various sources (e.g., http://counsellingresource.com/quizzes/alcohol-mast/index.html).

The National Institute on Alcohol Abuse and Alcoholism (NIAAA) has published a downloadable user friendly guide for marriage and family therapists that includes a number of screening tools as well as decision trees for assessment of both the drinker and the family member. The guide is "Alcohol Problems in Intimate Relationships: Identification and Intervention: A Guide for Marriage and Family Therapists" (Roberts & McCrady, 2003). The Guide is in the public domain and may be copied or reproduced without further permission from NIAAA (http://www.niaaa.nih.gov/Publications/EducationTrainingMaterials/Documents/NIAAA_AAMF_%20Final.pdf). The NIAAA recommends using brief intervention guidelines as described next when treating an active substance-abusing client. Major elements of the brief intervention include (a) areful assessment of the drinking and its consequences, (b) feedback, (c) drinker choices, (d) emphasis on personal responsibility, (e) involvement of the family, and (f) follow-up. The screening instrument decision tree as published by NIAAA is reproduced as Figure 14.1.

Overview of Recommended Tools		
	Interview	Self-Administered
Screen	Q-F and CAGE	AUDIT
Problem Assessment		
Consumption	BDP	Q-F
Dependence	SCID	ADS
Consequences	SCID	DrInC

Acronym	Full Name	Source/Availability	Administration Time (minutes)
CAGE	Stands for main word in each of four questions	Mayfield, McLeod and Hall, 1974: Ewing, 1984. Available on pages A-2 and A-4.	1
Q-F	Basic Quantity-Frequency Items	NIAAA, 1995. Available on pages A-2 and A-4.	1
AUDIT	Alcohol Use Disorders Identification Test	Babor, et al., 1992 www.niaaa.nih.gov/publications/insaudit.htm	2
BDP	Brief Drinker Profile	Miller and Marlatt, 1984. Available on pages A-6 through A-10.	3-10*
SCID	Structural Clinical Interview for DSM IV-TR	First, et al., 2001. Dependence questions available on pages A-11 and A-12. Alcohol Abuse questions available through www.scid4.org	2-5*
ADS	Alcohol Dependence Scale	Skinner and Horn, 1984. www.niaaa.nih.gov/publications/ads.pdf	5
DrInC	Drinker Inventory of Consequences	Miller, Tonigan and Longabaugh, 1995. Available on pages A-13 through A-18.	10

*Times are estimates for the adapted versions presented in this Guide.

Figure 14.1 Recommended assessment tools. (From Roberts and McCrady, 2003.)

Screening is of course only the first step in treatment. Once a problem has been identified, it is important to choose the appropriate treatment option. If the therapist is competent in treating substance abuse problems, the therapist should begin one of the empirically supported treatment modalities. If the therapist is not trained specifically in the treatment of SUDs, then a referral to a competent therapist or treatment program based on empirically supported treatment is the next step. Some of the empirically validated treatment options include

- Cognitive-behavioral therapy (CBT).
- Motivational enhancement therapy (MET), which is a brief, two- to four-session treatment that combines assessment, feedback, and principles of motivational interviewing. MET is particularly effective for those clients who are angry and resistant at the onset of treatment (Miller & Rollnick, 2002).
- Behavioral couples therapy (BCT) (O'Farrell & Fals-Stewart, 2006).

BCT is the most widely utilized and most effective treatment for couples experiencing substance use problems (Epstein & McCrady, 2002; O'Farrell & Birchler, 1987). According to O'Farrell and Fals-Stewart (2006) the purposes of BCT are (a) to increase relationship factors conducive to abstinence; (b) to use of a daily sobriety contract to support abstinence; (c) to use behavioral therapy to increase positive feelings, shared activities, and constructive communication; and (d) to fits well with self-help groups, recovery medications, and other counseling. An overview of the BCT clinical guideline may be found at http://www.bhrm.org/guidelines/couples%20therapy.pdf. (Due to the large magnitude of materials available for purposes of screening, evaluation, and treatment of SUDs, refer to the cited primary resources for further information on the use of these various modalities).

According to O'Farrell and Fals-Stewart (2006):

> Family members often experience resentment about past substance abuse and fear and distrust about the possible return of substance abuse in the future. The substance abuser often experiences guilt and a desire for recognition of current improved behavior. These feelings experienced by the substance abuser and the family often lead to an atmosphere of tension and unhappiness in couple and family relationships. There are problems caused by substance use (e.g., bills, legal charges, and embarrassing incidents) that still need to be resolved. There is often a backlog of other unresolved couple and family problems that the substance use obscured. The couple frequently lacks the mutual positive feelings and communication skills needed to resolve these problems. As a result, many marriages and families are dissolved during the first 1 or 2 years of the substance abusers recovery. In other cases, couple and family conflicts trigger relapse and a return to substance abuse. Even in cases where the substance abuser has a basically sound marriage and family life when he or she is not abusing substances, the initiation of abstinence can produce temporary tension and role readjustment and provide the opportunity for stabilizing and enriching couple and family relationships. For these reasons, many alcohol abusers can benefit from assistance to improve their couple and family relationships. (p. 15)

REVIEW OF VARIOUS TREATMENT/REHABILITATION STRATEGIES

Treatment, and therefore rehabilitation, from problematic SUDs is contingent on the individual's motivation for change, support structures, and ability to change. For example, an individual who has high motivation to discontinue the use of cigarettes has the ability to use the treatment chosen (such as nicotine replacement gum) and has a good support system (a supportive spouse, for example) has a fairly high potential for success. The same individual, however, who resides with an active smoker would have a significantly lower chance of successfully quitting cigarettes due to the proximity of the drug and frequent triggers (e.g., sight and smell of smoke). These factors must be taken into consideration when evaluating potential for change. The Stages of Change Readiness and Treatment Eagerness Scale (SOCRATES) is an instrument designed to assess readiness for change in individuals with alcohol misuse disorders. The SOCRATES instrument was used before and after treatment completion in a pre-post test sample of substance-dependent military service members who completed an intensive SUD treatment program (Miller & Tonigan, 1996). The instrument yields three factorially derived scale scores: Recognition (Re), Ambivalence (Am), and Taking Steps (Ts). It is a public domain instrument and may be used without special permission (http://casaa.unm.edu/inst/SOCRATESv8.pdf).

Scores on two of the three SOCRATES subscales were significantly improved after treatment completion, suggesting that readiness to change (RTC) processes measurably change during treatment and further suggest that SOCRATES is an appropriate tool for assessing short-term changes in RTC (Mitchell, Angelone, & Cox, 2007).

In military settings, motivation to change is often tied to disciplinary action or termination from the military if the individual is not compliant and successful with a treatment program. Some military spouses have used threats of reporting their partner to their chain of command as a way to improve motivation for treatment, although the success of this technique is questionable regarding its efficacy. An individual is much more likely to remain in a "positive change mind-set" if he or she perceives support and experience success.

LIMITATIONS AND GAPS IN RESEARCH

Although there is a great deal known about assessment, intervention, and treatment for substance abuse problems in civilian populations, there is much to be learned about SUDs in military populations. The military culture is one that contains richer structure regarding behavioral boundaries, yet at the same time maintains a closed structure in keeping problems private within the family, the unit/organization, and the military itself. Access to service members may be restricted due to reporting structures and guidelines for disciplinary action. In some cases, there are clear-cut procedural mandates, and in other cases, there may be decision trees implemented for intervention purposes. As a result, access to information becomes more problematic as additional communication boundaries are crossed. Data regarding substance-using behaviors may not be available, may be only partly available or not available for years, may be compromised due to collection procedures (anonymous self-report, for example) and a desire by the service members themselves to protect their job by underreporting problems. More research is needed on the use of measures, interventions, and treatments that are commonplace in civilian populations that may not have the same utility in military populations, such as BCT.

Case Vignette – Kathy and Bob

Kathy and Bob were an Army National Guard couple residing in Northwest Indiana. Kathy was a stay-at-home mother, and Bob was a staff sergeant in an infantry combat unit. Bob has deployed twice to the Middle East. His unit redeployed back to Indiana approximately 6 months prior to their first appointment for couples counseling. They were referred by Bob's commander after observing a significant change in Bob's attitude and work performance since returning to the United States. Bob explained this change as difficulties in his marriage that had been progressively getting worse following this deployment. In the initial session, Bob was extremely polite, dressed in an Army-issue ACU (Army combat uniform). His wife was dressed casually in jeans and a long-sleeved T-shirt. Kathy arranged for the appointment and was the first to talk.

K: He is just unbearable on weekends when he is home. We used to enjoy watching football or working around the yard, and now he just sits by himself all weekend barely talking. It's like walking on eggshells any time we are in the same room together!

B: She exaggerates! I've been quieter sure, but she doesn't understand what I've been through over there! If she would just give me some space I would be fine. But no! She is always trying to get me to do something and is never happy even if I try to help her out. There's no winning!

Therapist: When did the two of you notice a change in your relationship?

K: Pretty much as soon as he came home this time. He started drinking at night, and then almost all weekend, and now it seems he always has a beer in his hands.

B: That's not true! I told you she exaggerates! What's wrong with having a beer once in a while? I'm not 16 anymore, but she treats me like she's my mother!

K: I don't treat you like you are 16. I treat you like a man that ignores me, is always sullen and rarely interacts with anyone except the other guys you deployed with! It's like they became your family, and we are just … I don't know, we're just not important anymore.

This situation is unfortunately not uncommon with redeployed military families trying to adjust to the experience of reintegrating into civilian life after a deployment. What is unusual, however, is the description of the use of alcohol in this soldier's daily life. The therapist will conduct a SUD assessment, evaluate the extent of the problem, and then decide on a plan for intervention and possibly treatment.

REFERENCES

Bray, R. (2009) *Department of Defense survey of health related behaviors among active duty military personnel*. Dane Publishing.

Bray, R. M., Hourani, L. L., Olmsted, K. L., Witt, M., Brown, J. M., Pemberton, M. R. … Hayden. (2006) Department of Defense Health Related Behaviors Among Active Duty Military Personnel, 2005. Research Triangle Institute (RTI). Department of Defense publication.

Bray, R. M., Spira, J. L., Olmsted, K., & Hout, J. J. (2010). Behavioral and occupational fitness. *Military Medicine*, 39–56.

Campanini, B. (Ed). 2002. World Health Report 2002: Reducing Risks, Promoting Healthy Life (pp. 9–10). World Health Organization. Geneva, Switzerland.

Dackis, C. A., & O'Brien, C. P. (2001). Cocaine dependence: A disease of the brain's reward centers. *Journal of Substance Abuse Treatment, 21,* 111–117.
Department of the Army. (2009). *U.S. Department of Defense's survey of health-related behavior among military personnel. The Army Substance Abuse Program, regulation 600–85; personnel—general.* Washington, DC. Retrieved March 1, 2011, from http://www.apd.army.mil/pdffiles/r600_85
Epstein, E. E., & McCrady, B. S. (2002). Couple therapy in the treatment of alcohol problems. In A. Gurman & N. Jacobson (Eds.), *Clinical handbook of marital therapy* (3rd ed.). New York: Guilford.
Federman, E., Bray, R. M., & Kroutil, L. A. (2000). Relationships between substance use and recent deployments among women and men in the military. *Military Psychology, 12,* 205–220.
Miller, W. R., & Rollnick, S. (2002). *Motivational interviewing: Preparing people for change* (2nd ed., pp. 217–250). New York: Guilford Press.
Miller, W. R., & Tonigan, J. S. (1996). Assessing drinkers' motivation for change: The Stages of Change Readiness and Treatment Eagerness Scale (SOCRATES). *Psychology of Addictive Behaviors, 10,* 81–89.
Mitchell, D., Angelone, D. J., & Cox, S. M. (2007). An exploration of readiness to change processes in a clinical sample of military service members. *Journal of Addictive Diseases, 26*(3), 53–60. doi:10.1300/J069v26n03_06
Military Health Services. (2009). *Department of Defense survey of health related behaviors among active duty military personnel: 2008 survey summary.* Washington, DC. Retrieved March 1, 2011, from http://www.health.mil/Content/docs/Health%20 Behaviors%20Survey%20QAs.pdf
O'Farrell, T. J., & Birchler, G. R. (1987). Marital relationships of alcoholic, conflicted, and nonconflicted couples. *Journal of Marital and Family Therapy, 13,* 259–274.
O'Farrell, T. J., & Fals-Stewart, W. (2006). *Behavioral couples therapy for alcoholism and drug abuse.* New York: Guilford Press.
Portenoy, R. K., & Payne, R. (1992). Acute and chronic pain. In J.H. Lowinson, P. Ruiz, R.B. Millman & J.G. Langrod (Eds.), Substance abuse: A comprehensive textbook (Second Edition). Baltimore: Williams & Wilkins.
Roberts, L., & McCrady, B. (2003). Alcohol problems in intimate relationships: Identification and intervention: A guide for marriage and family therapists. National Institute on Alcohol Abuse and Alcoholism, The Department of Health and Human Services.
Rittenhouse, J. D. (1977). The epidemiology of heroin and other narcotics: National Institute of Drug Abuse Research Monograph 16. Washington, DC: Alcohol Drug Abuse and Mental Health Administration, Department of Health, Education and Welfare.
Selzer, M. L. (1971). The Michigan Alcoholism Screening Test (MAST): The quest for a new diagnostic instrument. *American Journal of Psychiatry, 127,* 1653–1658.
Substance Abuse and Mental Health Services Administration. (2007). *Results from the 2006 National Survey on Drug Use and Health: National Findings* (Office of Applied Studies, NSDUH Series H-32, DHHS Publication No. SMA 07–4293). Rockville, MD.
Substance Abuse and Mental Health Services Administration, Office of Applied Studies. (2008) *National survey on drug use and health.* Retrieved January 10, 2011, from http://oas.samhsa.gov/nhsda.htm
World Health Organization. (2010) *The ICD-10 Classification of Mental and Behavioural Disorders: Clinical descriptions and diagnostic guidelines.* Retrieved January 1, 2011, from http://www.who.int/substance_abuse/terminology/ICD10ClinicalDiagnosis.pdf
World Health Organization. (2010). *Atlas on substance use: resources for the prevention and treatment of substance use disorders.* Geneva, Switzerland: Author.

15

Traumatic Brain Injury

CARRIE-ANN H. STRONG and JACOBUS DONDERS

INTRODUCTION

Traumatic brain injury (TBI) is a common neurological condition in which there is an external blunt or penetrating force to the skull, with at least temporary disruption of cerebral functioning. Particularly with more severe injuries, such as those associated with prolonged coma or diffuse intracranial lesions, there can be significant and lasting cognitive and behavioral sequelae that may affect participation in various psychosocial domains, including family, school, work, and broader community integration (Kothari, 2007; Selassie et al., 2008). The goal of this chapter is to provide a broad overview of TBI, followed by issues specific to injuries that were sustained in the context of recent military conflicts, Operation Enduring Freedom (OEF) and Operation Iraqi Freedom (OIF). Subjects surrounding these injuries that are salient to the treatment of couples are then described.

It is important to note that the vast majority of TBIs incurred in both civilian and military populations are mild in nature (McCrea et al., 2009). Furthermore, treatment approaches in mild TBI and moderate-severe TBI are very distinct. Patients with mild TBI should not be treated as "less-severe" counterparts to those with severe TBI (McCrea, 2008; Mittenberg, Canyock, Condit, & Patton, 2001). There is evidence that such an approach may be ineffective and potentially harmful (Hoge, Goldberg, & Castro, 2009). For this reason, treatment approaches for, respectively, mild and moderate-severe TBI are described separately in this chapter.

EPIDEMIOLOGY, PATHOPHYSIOLOGY, AND OUTCOME IN CIVILIANS WITH TBI

Each year in the United States, 1.7 million civilian people sustain a TBI. Of those people, 235,000 require hospitalization, and 50,000 are fatally injured (Faul,

Xu, Wald, & Coronado, 2010). Major risk factors for TBI in the civilian population include very young and old age, male gender, and low socioeconomic status (Corrigan, Selassie, & Orman, 2010). Civilians who sustain TBI frequently have preinjury comorbidities, which may range from learning disabilities in children, to substance abuse in young adults, to hypertension and diabetes mellitus in the elderly. Injuries resulting from motor vehicle accidents are the most common cause of TBI from adolescence through young adulthood; in this age range most cases of fatal TBI are firearm related, especially in African American males (Corrigan et al., 2010). In contrast, child abuse is the leading cause of severe TBI in infants and toddlers (Carty & Pierce, 2002), whereas older adults are at increased risk for TBI due to falls and associated subdural hematomas (Flanagan, Hibbard, Riordan, & Gordon, 2006; Langlois, Rutland-Brown, & Thomas, 2004).

The majority of TBIs (>80%) are classified as "uncomplicated mild" (also referred to as "concussion"). In contrast to the more severe injuries, mild TBI is defined as a brief alteration in mental status. In mild TBI, loss of consciousness and posttraumatic amnesia must not exceed 30 minutes or 24 hours, respectively. In uncomplicated mild TBI, one does not see any visible damage to intracranial structures, whereas in complicated mild TBI there are positive neuroimaging findings (Ruff et al., 2009).

Cognitive and other symptoms, such as headaches, dizziness, blurred vision, and fatigue, are commonly experienced by adults in the early acute stages of recovery from mild TBI. Nevertheless, a best-evidence synthesis of the literature suggests that the vast majority of patients (>90%) who sustain uncomplicated mild TBI show complete recovery within 3 months, with effects rarely persisting beyond 1 year in the absence of complicating premorbid or comorbid factors, such as prior psychiatric history or financial compensation seeking (Carroll et al., 2004; Iverson, 2005). Persons with otherwise mild injuries who do have intracranial lesions on neuroimaging typically have less-favorable outcomes (Rao et al., 2010; Smits et al., 2008). There are also a small minority (less than 5%) of civilians with uncomplicated mild TBI who show a less-complete recovery. Those people who do not recover quickly are at risk for developing a persistent postconcussive disorder (Iverson, Zasler, & Lange, 2007).

The postconcussive disorder is a highly controversial diagnosis and presents complex challenges for those involved in its research and treatment. This is due to its basis in self-reported complaints, as well as the nonspecificity of postconcussive symptoms (i.e., the symptoms are seen in numerous other medical and psychiatric disorders, as well as the normal population). This lack of specificity has also been demonstrated specifically in postdeployment military personnel (Fear et al., 2009). Moreover, while acute symptoms are known sequelae of organic disruption, persistent concussive symptoms are strongly influenced by nonneurological factors, including perception of and reaction to symptoms, psychological history, psychosocial environment, and personality variables (Boone, 2009; Iverson, Lange, Brooks, & Rennison, 2010; Whittaker, Kemp, & House, 2007). Factors such as litigation and iatrogenesis also play a role (Iverson, Zasler et al., 2007; Tsanadis et al., 2008).

Moderate-severe TBI is defined by the combination of any of the following: duration of loss of consciousness longer than 30 minutes, Glasgow Coma Scale

(GCS; Teasdale & Jennett, 1974) score less than 12, duration of posttraumatic amnesia more than 24 hours, or intracranial lesions on acute neuroimaging. In contrast to mild TBI, the cerebral compromise in moderate-severe TBI can be permanent and is the result of both primary and secondary factors (Fritz & Bauer, 2004). Primary forces include linear displacement due to acceleration or deceleration that causes focal lesions such as cortical contusions and intracranial rotation, which may result in diffuse lesions, such as axonal injury. Secondary injuries arise indirectly, may continue to develop over the course of several days, and are the result of disrupted cerebral circulation and an associated cascade of neurochemical events, leading to hypoxic-ischemic injury, diffuse edema, and neuronal excitotoxicity.

Computed tomographic (CT) scan is the most appropriate neuroimaging method on the day of injury because it can be done fairly quickly in medically unstable patients while still visualizing sequelae of TBI that require immediate intervention (e.g., epidural hematoma). However, follow-up magnetic resonance imaging (MRI) over more extended periods of time is necessary for a more accurate description of the degenerative changes after TBI (for a more detailed review of neuroimaging methods as applied to TBI, see Kurth & Bigler, 2008).

As patients with moderate-severe TBI emerge from coma, acute problem behaviors such as confusion, agitation, emotional lability, and diminished responsiveness to environmental cues are prominent. After acute recovery, there are a range of deficits that can persist. Although full recovery is possible, many people with this level of injury endure chronic problems in one or more areas of cognitive, emotional, or behavioral functioning. There is no invariant "signature" cognitive profile after moderate-to-severe TBI. However, in general terms, impairments in the areas of attention, executive functioning, memory, and processing speed are common during the first year of recovery (for review, see: Goldstein & Levin, 2010; Roebuck-Spencer, Baños, Sherer, & Novack, 2010). Insufficient self-awareness of cognitive deficits is another commonplace problem after this level of injury, even in those with acute sensitivity to physical losses, and shows only partial improvement over the first year postinjury (Hart, Seignourel, & Sherer, 2009). This can lead to poor compliance with treatment recommendations, longer lengths of stay in postacute rehabilitation, heightened caregiver distress, and worse educational and vocational outcomes (Flashman & MacAllister, 2002).

Moderate-severe TBI is also associated with a strong risk for developing new adjustment and mood disorders, as well as personality changes in the postacute phase, with affective lability, depression, and insufficient interpersonal pragmatics relatively most common (Nicholl & LaFrance, 2009; Silver, Kramer, Greenwald, & Weissman, 2001). These various problems stem from a combination of direct organic (especially prefrontal) effects of TBI, adjustment reactions related to grief and loss issues, and moderating preinjury personality variables and coping style (Patterson & Staton, 2009). Finally, substance abuse is a common problem after TBI. Premorbid alcohol abuse tends to be associated with worse outcomes after TBI in the areas of employment, independent living, neurobehavioral functioning, and satisfaction with life (Corrigan, 2005).

EPIDEMIOLOGY, PATHOPHYSIOLOGY, AND OUTCOME IN MILITARY TBI

TBI is often referred to as the "signature injury" of the wars in Iraq and Afghanistan. Between 2003 and 2009, it is estimated that more than 9,000 service members were wounded due to TBI in the OIF and OEF conflicts; the vast majority of these injuries would be classified as mild (French, Spector, Stiers, & Kane, 2010; McCrea et al., 2009). Since the adoption by the Department of Defense of screening post-deployment in 2006 (for a description, see Meyer, Marion, Coronel, & Jaffee, 2010), as many as 10–20% of soldiers screen positive for mild TBI, although most of those diagnoses are not confirmed after more thorough evaluation (Corby-Edwards, 2009; Hoge et al., 2009; Polusny et al., 2011). Similar to civilian patients sustaining mild TBI, most warriors report a complete recovery from concussive symptoms within 3 months of their injuries. However, there is a small percentage of warriors (about 8%) who experience persistent postconcussive symptoms, most commonly, headaches and dizziness (Terrio et al., 2009; Walker, Clark, & Sanders, 2010).

There continue to be questions regarding the true epidemiology of TBI in the OIF and OEF conflicts. There is concern that the rates of TBI (particularly mild TBI) being reported may be substantially inflated (Hoge et al., 2009). There are a number of reasons for this, beginning with the heightened appreciation of the issue of TBI, given a concerted focus to increase awareness by both the military and the news media. While TBI awareness is, at a surface level, a noble cause, the nuances and intricacies associated with mild TBI diagnosis are often not fully appreciated by media outlets. While moderate-severe TBI is quite easy to identify, even in theater of war due to acute neurological signs and subsequent neuroimaging, it is much more challenging to diagnose mild TBI, which is typically associated with very subtle injury characteristics, invisibility on neuroimaging, and symptoms that are highly nonspecific (Iverson, Langlois, McCrea, & Kelly, 2009). Furthermore, post-deployment screens for mild TBI are often conducted many months after initial injury, reliant on self-reports, which are inherently biased. Warriors are asked to recall whether they ever felt "dazed" or "confused" at the time of injury; so many months later, this recollection is prone to recall bias and can easily be faulty or suggestible. In a longitudinal study of mild TBI reporting rates in a large sample of National Guard soldiers (Polusny et al., 2011), the rate of mild TBI reported in theater, involving a zone of high combat exposure, was about 9%. A year later, this rate of mild TBI reporting increased to about 22%. It is also possible that the dazed and confused symptoms reported were caused by something other than TBI. Common alternative explanations in the theater of war may include acute stress, dissociation, syncope, sleep deprivation, or "confusion of war" (Hoge et al., 2009).

It is known, based on more thorough follow-up assessments, that the postdeployment TBI screening is sensitive, but produces a high number of false-positive rates of mild TBI (Belanger, Uomoto, & Vanderploeg, 2009). There are some potential benefits of this inflation, including insurance that no service member "falls through the cracks," and that warriors are treated for their injuries. Problems with this overidentification also exist. High numbers of soldiers need follow-up evaluation, which may be difficult and costly to obtain (Iverson et al., 2009). In the meantime, harmful effects can take root, including false attribution of symptoms as being the result of presumably permanent brain damage, diagnosis threat (i.e., the belief that one has a "brain injury" results in worsened cognitive performance during neuropsychological evaluation), and the "good old days bias" (i.e., having an overly idealistic view of life preinjury and falsely blaming *all* current problems postinjury on the mild TBI).

The mechanism of injury typified by the OEF and OIF conflicts is another issue being studied in military TBI. The enemy's choice of weapon in these conflicts is explosive devices; thus, injuries originating from a blast or explosion make up the vast majority. Of the TBIs associated with loss of consciousness sustained in the OEF and OIF conflicts, 79% were incurred as a result of a blast (Walker, Clark, & Sanders, 2010). It has been estimated that over 60% of blast injuries involve TBI (Pickett, Bender, & Gourley, 2010), although the vast majority of those injuries are still classified as mild (McCrea et al., 2009). Soldiers wounded as a result of blasts typically sustain one or more of the following four types of injuries: primary injury (the overpressurized blast wave leading to displacement of bodily tissue and organs), secondary injury (the displacement of the soldier when thrown through the air and then hitting a stationary object), tertiary injury (shrapnel and other objects being propelled through the air and striking the soldier), and quaternary injury (including blood loss from traumatic amputation or internal injuries, as well as effects from toxic gases and burns; Bochicchio et al., 2008; French et al., 2010). Direct neurological damage resulting from blasts may arise from various sources, including acceleration-deceleration forces, possible transference of kinetic energy through large blood vessels, and secondary effects of polytrauma (French et al., 2010). Indirect effects are often related to lung injury (which is the second most commonly affected organ by blast), which in severe cases can lead to cerebral hypoxia or pulmonary emboli, causing cerebral infarcts (Howe, 2009). Those sustaining significant moderate-severe TBI as the result of a blast are also vulnerable to developing sudden brain edema and vasospasms, as well as changes in blood chemistry and electrolyte imbalances (French et al., 2010).

While there may well be pathophysiological differences between blast and nonblast moderate-severe TBI, there is, so far, no evidence that the macroscopic damage resulting from blast mild TBI is at all divergent from similarly mild TBI sustained as a result of other etiologies. Furthermore, neuropsychological and functional outcomes of blast and nonblast mild TBI have been found to be commensurate (French et al, 2010; Jaffee & Meyer, 2009; Lippa, Pastorek, Benge, & Thornton, 2010). Studies have confirmed that the cognitive sequelae of TBI are more closely related to injury severity and not mechanism of injury (i.e., blast vs. nonblast; Belanger, Kretzmer, Yoash-Gantz, Pickett, & Tupler, 2009). In self-reported mild TBI after deployment, there is no evidence that one will typically have permanent cognitive impairment (Ivins, Kane, & Schwab, 2009). In addition, no difference has been found in the severity of reported postconcussive symptoms when looking at blast versus nonblast injury, even when considering the number of exposures to a blast and proximity to a blast (Lippa et al., 2010).

While cognitive and functional outcomes are ultimately similar when comparing military to civilian TBI, there are some challenges in the assessment and treatment of military TBI, given the presence of some unique premorbid and comorbid factors. The highly stressful environment in which combat-related TBI occurs, as well as the considerable risk for repetitive injuries without full recovery in between injuries, may place warriors at increased risk for complicated outcome (French & Parkinson, 2008). Furthermore, military culture fosters a code of conduct that emphasizes preparedness for, and acceptance of, adverse events. Consequently, many warriors may be reluctant to admit to problems, let alone seek help (Hall, 2011).

For military personnel, secondary gain by reporting embellished, persistent postconcussive symptoms may be more complex than its common correlate during financial compensation seeking in a civilian context. The avoidance of future conflicts may be a large motivation for some warriors (Nelson et al., 2010). Nevertheless, the compensation and pension system does play a role. Federal regulation passed in 2008 assigned a 40% disability rating to warriors with mild cognitive impairment, or those reporting three or more moderately disabling postconcussive symptoms (Hoge et al., 2009). As also seen in civilian medicolegal contexts, there appears to be a strong association between financial compensation seeking and the reporting of persistent concussive symptoms after mild TBI (Howe, 2009).

Warriors who are seen in forensic compensation-seeking contexts show much higher rates of poor effort performance on symptom validity tests used in neuropsychological evaluations to assess for response bias and exaggeration, in comparison to those evaluated in nonforensic contexts. In one study of forensic military evaluations (Nelson et al., 2010), insufficient effort accounted for a significant (20–33%) proportion of the variance of cognitive test performance, with 22% of the sample providing suboptimal effort on neuropsychological tests. After controlling for the effects of effort, there was no difference in the cognitive performance between warriors who had sustained a mild TBI during deployment and those who had not.

Secondary gain is only one of the many issues contributing to persistent subjective symptoms in warriors sustaining mild TBI. More salient issues for service members may be the presence of comorbid conditions. Physical injuries and symptoms can be associated with concussive-type symptoms. These may include sensory impairments, which are common after blast injury. The tympanic membrane is the most susceptible organ to blast injury; thus, sensorineural conditions, including hearing loss, tinnitus, and vertigo, can be evident and mistaken as sequelae of concussion (Bochicchio et al., 2008; Howe, 2009). Sleep disturbance, pain, and headache are also common physical conditions associated with blast injury, with associated symptoms that can mimic concussion (Walker, Clark, Nampiaparampil, et al., 2010). Ruff, Ruff, and Wang (2008) reported that warriors with neuropsychological deficits after mild TBI were more likely to have headaches, with more intense pain, more frequent episodes, and more migraine-like features. They also found that warriors with residual cognitive deficits were more likely to have sleep disturbance. Chronic pain (in regions of the body other than the head) is another frequent complaint, with and without TBI, of warriors wounded in OEF and OIF. Polytrauma sustained as a result of blast injury does not appear to be associated with greater severity of brain injury but is associated with more extensive physical injuries, greater pain levels, higher rates of opioid use, and more frequent emotional problems (Clark, Walker, Gironda, & Scholten, 2009). All of those problems can lead to what may be labeled or perceived as postconcussive symptoms, including cognitive problems and mood changes.

The most prominent comorbidities seen in the military mild TBI population, though, are psychological conditions, most commonly depression and post-traumatic stress disorder (PTSD). Depression rates in OEF and OIF warriors are estimated at about 8%, while PTSD rates range from approximately 12% to 20% (Polusny et al., 2011; Tuerk, Grubaugh, Hammer, & Foa, 2009). Those involved with killing during deployment are at especially high risk for development of PTSD (Maguen et al., 2010). Higher levels of PTSD are associated with higher levels of exposure to combat and physical injury, although no difference in stress symptoms is seen when comparing mechanisms of injury (e.g., blast vs. nonblast; Kennedy, Leal, Lewis, Cullen, & Amador, 2010). Overall, there appears to be a higher rate of symptom reporting when warriors are claiming the comorbid injuries of PTSD, mild TBI, and chronic pain (Walker, Clark, & Sanders, 2010).

In a number of studies (Jaffee & Meyer, 2009; Kennedy et al., 2010; Marx et al., 2009; Nelson, Yoash-Gantz, Pickett, & Campbell, 2009; Polusny et al., 2011), PTSD and mild TBI/concussive symptoms have been closely linked. In fact, there appears to be a stronger association between PTSD and mild TBI than any other type of injury (Jaffee & Meyer, 2009). On the other hand, mild TBI appears to be a risk factor for developing PTSD, especially reexperiencing symptoms (Kennedy et al., 2010), as well as a factor that complicates or aggravates recovery from PTSD (Hoffman & Harrison, 2009). In comparison to those wounded from injuries other then mild TBI, soldiers claiming symptoms resulting from mild TBI reported poorer general health, more missed days of work, and higher rates of concussive and somatic symptoms. However, when adjusting for PTSD and depression, all physical concerns (expect headache) were no longer significant (French et al., 2010). At 1 year postinjury, there does not appear to be any impact of mild TBI on psychosocial outcomes, concussive symptoms, depression, problematic drinking, social adjustment, or quality of life. Instead, postconcussive symptoms were actually found to be more strongly associated with PTSD than mild TBI; although more warriors with a history of mild TBI reported concussion symptoms than those with no TBI, this difference became nonsignificant when controlling for PTSD (Polusny et al., 2011). Even in the absence of frank PTSD, recent research suggested that the majority of the postconcussive complaints after combat-related mild TBI may simply be due to emotional distress (Belanger, Kretzmer, Vanderploeg, & French, 2010).

PTSD may also help explain the persistence of subjective cognitive dysfunction experienced after uncomplicated mild TBI. Chronic PTSD has been associated with attention impairments on neuropsychological measures. In fact, PTSD appears to have a greater effect on cognitive performance than depression, head injury, or combat exposure (Marx et al., 2009). In another study (Nelson et al., 2009), slowed speed of processing was found to be worse among warriors with comorbid PTSD and mild TBI, compared to mild TBI alone, even though the latter injuries appeared to be relatively more severe.

TREATMENT OF MILD TBI IN COUPLES THERAPY

Empirically validated psychological treatments aimed at the prevention of persistent postconcussive symptoms are primarily education based and therefore appropriate and adaptable for use in the context of couples counseling. Studies have shown that following civilian mild TBI, symptomatic patients who falsely believe that their symptoms will have severe and enduring negative consequences are at much higher risk of having persistent postconcussive symptoms (Whittaker et al., 2007). Therefore, psychological treatment, whether individual or marital, should, as a standard, begin as early as possible after injury and focus on education about mild TBI and expected recovery, as well as reassurance about and normalization of early symptoms (Belanger, Uomoto, et al., 2009; Iverson, Lange, Gaetz, & Zasler, 2007; Jaffee & Meyer, 2009). Education also entails direction on appropriate coping strategies (e.g., graded resumption of activities to assist with fatigue and cognitive inefficiency) and the avoidance of behaviors that can increase problems after mild TBI (e.g., alcohol abuse, behavioral inactivation or overactivation, and prevention of recurrent injury; Iverson, Lange, et al., 2007).

Special attention must also be given to the needs of children of warriors. Such children are generally resilient to the effect of deployment, but those with preexisting adjustment problems, and especially those with psychosocial adversities such as family violence or parental substance abuse, may have more significant difficulties coping with parental psychiatric symptoms (Lincoln, Swift, & Shorteno-Fraser, 2008). It has also been demonstrated that the mental health of the at-home parent during deployment is an important variable with regard to overall risk for child maltreatment as well as postdeployment child adjustment (Jensen, Martin, & Watanabe, 1996). Therefore, support services for families during deployment, as well as identification of deployed warriors who are at increased risk for postdeployment difficulties with family reintegration, due to factors ranging from psychological trauma to substance abuse, are strongly recommended (Lincoln et al., 2008).

Cognitive-behavioral techniques have been helpful in the treatment of civilian mild TBI and prevention of persistent concussive symptoms. These techniques can be easily adapted to a couples therapy framework. Couples should primarily learn cognitive restructuring techniques that assist with the reexamination of attribution of symptoms as solely related to mild TBI (Mittenberg et al., 2001; Mittenberg, Tremont, Zielinski, Fichera, & Rayls, 1996). For example, patients may be confronted about their oversensitivity or focus on concussive symptoms simply because of having sustained a "brain injury." In that regard, therapists help explain the concepts of expectation in illness or the "nocebo effect." Just because warriors or family members may have been informed that certain symptoms are common after a mild TBI, they may begin to falsely attribute fairly normal or non-TBI-related symptoms to "brain damage." This method of reattribution may be particularly relevant in the context of military mild TBI, in which, as mentioned, there are many associated comorbidities. Warriors and their spouses should be discouraged from blaming *all* of their symptoms on the brain injury.

Reattribution with returning soldiers, then, will often focus on helping them and their family member identify and seek treatment for the other relevant contributing factors; treatments will often consist of therapies or medications for pain, headache, sleep deprivation, depression and (most commonly) PTSD. Reattribution should also include education about the stressful factors that are common in military families, even in the absence of injury. One prevalent non-combat-related stressor facing many military couples is family separation. Even in those who are not injured, marital strain is frequently reported due to long deployments. Other widespread issues in military marriages, not specific to TBI, include domestic violence, child maltreatment (especially neglect during deployment), and alcohol abuse. The frequency and severity of domestic violence and child maltreatment have been shown to occur at higher rates in military marriages in comparison to civilian marriages, and longer deployment rates are associated with more severe levels of dysfunction (Clark & Messer, 2006; Gibbs, Martin, Kupper, & Johnson, 2007). Higher rates of alcohol abuse are also seen among military men versus their civilian counterparts, although drug use rates are significantly lower (Hall, 2008). Although no formal studies have been conducted on this form of education and reattribution techniques in military mild TBI, meta-analyses have shown satisfactory efficacy of this approach in civilians (Carroll et al., 2004; Mittenberg et al., 2001).

Symptomatic treatment of mild TBI and its comorbidities may also be helpful (Iverson, Zasler, et al., 2007). In civilians, this typically includes treatment of depression and anxiety, improving sleep, reducing stress, facilitating coping, and promoting resumption of normal activity. For warriors, especially those injured as a result of blast, concerted treatment for comorbid pain, concussive symptoms, and PTSD may be optimal. Walker, Clark, and Sanders (2010) have proposed a multifaceted and integrated model of treatment for those conditions; these treatments are proposed to include family education and support. For concussion treatment, symptom management and aforementioned education and reattribution techniques would be employed. For chronic pain, models similarly seen in interdisciplinary pain programs would be followed, in addition to close monitoring of opioid pain medication. For PTSD, treatments include medication, cognitive-behavioral restructuring, exposure therapy, stress inoculation training, and normalization of soldier reactions to trauma. In couples therapy, one of the most pertinent symptoms associated with concussion, PTSD, and chronic pain is irritability. Therefore, teaching cognitive-behavioral and conflict resolution strategies may be a necessary component of couples counseling for injured warriors. Since most warriors with mild TBI will not have pervasive cognitive deficits, the use of practical self-help books that have been written specifically for individuals with relatively recent injuries (e.g., Moore & Kennedy, 2011) may also be appropriate as an adjunct therapeutic approach.

Particular attention needs to be paid to two complicating factors that are frequently confounding the presentation of the warrior with mild TBI, and that may be particularly troublesome to his or her partner. The first is the warrior's struggle with morally injurious experiences that may result from having participated in, witnessed, or failed to prevent certain acts that transgress the warrior's own moral code. Litz and colleagues (2009) provided a working clinical care model that includes cognitive-behavioral strategies with real-time, emotion-focused event processing as well as experiential strategies to address such moral dilemmas. The second common complicating factor is encompassed by the feelings of anger and hostility with which the warrior may struggle. Elbogen and colleagues (2010) have demonstrated that these are frequently associated with hyperarousal symptoms of PTSD and suggest specific strategies for inquiring about specific behaviors and risk factors that may warrant direct clinical intervention.

COUPLES TREATMENT IN MODERATE-SEVERE TBI

Issues that are prominent for the spouses of people with moderate-severe TBI are quite divergent from those in the mild TBI population. In civilian marriages, spouses providing care for a person with this kind of TBI may report feeling burdened and emotionally distressed as early as 3 months post-injury and persisting up to many years. There appear to be fairly high rates of marital dissatisfaction, disrupted family role functioning, and poor communication (Davis et al., 2009). Spouses reported that the injured person's poor self-awareness, behavioral rigidity, emotional dysfunction, impaired self-control, apathy, and irritability contribute most to their own stress and emotionality (Kreutzer, Marwitz, Godwin, & Arango-Lasprilla, 2010); meanwhile, cognitive changes are only moderately related (Davis et al., 2009). Other contributors to caregiver distress include male patient gender, low levels of social support, and their own preinjury medical and psychological disorders (Davis et al., 2009). Spouses may also report problematic feelings of ambiguous loss, conflicted feelings about divorce, and unmet emotional needs. They may endorse feeling "trapped" in their marriage, being married to a stranger, and not having a husband (Kreutzer, et al., 2010). Many of the same issues will be seen in military couples with one spouse incurring a moderate-severe TBI.

When treating people with moderate-severe TBI and their spouses, the counselor should attempt to normalize and address these commonplace issues. In addition, it is imperative that the therapist explore unmet needs of the family and encourage peer support, self-care, and respite for the caregiver/spouse (Kreutzer et al., 2009). As in mild TBI, much of the counseling is educational in nature. However, in comparison to mild TBI, for which reassurance about total recovery is emphasized, education in moderate-severe TBI should focus on setting realistic expectations for recovery and rehabilitation, with descriptions of typical long-term TBI sequelae. In this context, it is important to be mindful of the cognitive deficits that the warrior may have; consequently, the interventions may need to use more concrete language, present information in only limited quantities at a time, break down longer-term goals into several shorter and intermediate ones, and include more frequent meaningful review. Marital therapists can also teach spouses behavioral strategies to assist them in coping with problematic behaviors, as well as stress management techniques to assist them in dealing with their own distress and emotionality. Other educational strategies that can be of benefit include teaching strategies for communicating with health care providers, and in finding appropriate TBI resources in the community. Finally, spouses of people with moderate-to-severe TBI may benefit from basic supportive techniques, which are often assistive in helping them process their ambiguous loss (Kreutzer et al., 2010).

Family-focused therapy is a systems-based approach that has been specifically modified for application with families of warriors with moderate-to-severe TBI. This approach combines psychoeducation, communication enhancement training, structured problem solving, and flexible goal setting (Dausch & Saliman, 2009). As has been emphasized by others, "recovery" to a precombat state is most often an inappropriate goal (Uomoto & Williams, 2009). Instead, a couples approach that responds to the personal experiences of suffering and that is responsive to the pragmatic needs of the warrior and his or her partner is more appropriate.

FUTURE DIRECTIONS

Research on prevalence, comorbid conditions, and outcome appears to dominate the current military TBI literature. A significant dearth exists in the area of treatment. At this point, in the absence of empirically validated techniques for the treatment of TBI sustained in the military, the most pragmatic practice appears to be the use of techniques validated in civilian populations. Research is sorely needed in the area of treatment of TBI sustained as a result of the OEF and OIF conflicts. First and foremost, studies are needed to ascertain whether the treatments used to prevent persistent concussive symptoms in civilians are similarly effective in military populations. One striking difference between these two groups is the fact that those incurring mild TBIs in combat often come to the attention of medical professionals many months, or even years, after injury (Belanger, Kretzmer, et al., 2009). As noted, the empirically validated prevention techniques are most effective when introduced soon after injury; it may be, then, that these techniques are not as effective for warriors who do not have the benefit of access to early intervention. Another issue that may be more common in military versus civilian TBI, leading to divergent treatment outcomes, is the prevalence of multiple physical injuries (including amputation), and the prominence of comorbid PTSD. Careful evaluation of the efficacy of current treatment models through randomized controlled clinical trials, with sufficiently long-term follow-up, remains a goal for future research. In the meantime, it behooves the mental health and rehabilitation communities to make use of the best available evidence-based methods from the civilian TBI literature to support the many men and women who have incurred TBI while serving their country during OEF and OIF.

REFERENCES

Belanger, H. G., Kretzmer, T., Vanderploeg, R. D., & French, L. M. (2010). Symptom complaints following combat-related traumatic brain injury: Relationship to traumatic brain injury severity and posttraumatic stress disorder. *Journal of the International Neuropsychological Society, 16*, 194–199.

Belanger, H. G., Kretzmer, T., Yoash-Gantz, R., Pickett, T., & Tupler, L. A. (2009). Cognitive sequelae of blast-related versus other mechanisms of brain trauma. *Journal of the International Neuropsychological Society, 15*, 1–8.

Belanger, H. G., Uomoto, J. M., & Vanderploeg, R. D. (2009). The Veterans Health Administration system of care for mild traumatic brain injury: Costs, benefits, and controversies. *The Journal of Head Trauma Rehabilitation, 24,* 4–13.

Bochicchio, G. V., Lumpkins, K., O'Connor, J., Simard, M., Schaub, S., Conway, A., … & Scalea, T. M. (2008). Blast injury in a civilian trauma setting is associated with a delay in diagnosis of traumatic brain injury. *The American Surgeon, 74,* 267–270.

Boone, K. B. (2009). Fixed belief in cognitive dysfunction despite normal neuropsychological scores: Neurocognitive hypochondriasis? *The Clinical Neuropsychologist, 23,* 1016–1036.

Carroll, L. J., Cassidy, J. D., Peloso, P. M., Borg, J., Von Holst, H., Holm, L., … WHO Collaborative Centre Task Force on Mild Traumatic Brain Injury. (2004). Prognosis for mild traumatic brain injury: Results of the WHO Collaborative Centre Task Force on Mild Traumatic Brain Injury. *Journal of Rehabilitation Medicine, 43,* 84–105.

Carty, H., & Pierce, A. (2002). Non-accidental injury: A retrospective analysis of a large cohort. *European Radiology, 12,* 2919–2925.

Clark, J. C., & Messer, S. C. (2006). Intimate partner violence in the U.S. military: Rates, risks, and responses. In C. A. Castro, A. B. Adler, & C. A. Britt (Eds.), *Military life: The psychology of serving in peace and combat* (Vol. 3, pp. 193–219). Bridgeport, CT: Praeger.

Clark, M. E., Walker, R. L., Gironda, R. J., & Scholten, J. D. (2009). Comparison of pain and emotional symptoms in soldiers with polytrauma: Unique aspects of blast exposure. *Pain Medicine, 10,* 447–455.

Corby-Edwards, A. K. (2009). *Traumatic brain injury: Care and treatment of Operation Enduring Freedom and Operation Iraqi Freedom veterans.* Washington, DC: Congressional Research Service.

Corrigan, J. D. (2005). Substance abuse. In W. M. High, A. M. Sander, M. A. Struchen, & K. A. Hart (Eds.), *Rehabilitation for traumatic brain injury* (pp. 133–155). New York: Oxford University Press.

Corrigan, J. D., Selassie, A. W., & Orman, J. A. (2010). The epidemiology of traumatic brain injury. *Journal of Head Trauma Rehabilitation, 25,* 72–80.

Dausch, B. M., & Saliman, S. (2009). Use of family focused therapy in rehabilitation for veterans with traumatic brain injury. *Rehabilitation Psychology, 54,* 279–287.

Davis, L. D., Sander, A. M., Struchen, M. A., Sherer, M., Nakase-Richardson, R., & Malec, J. F. (2009). Medical and psychosocial predictors of caregiver distress and perceived burden following traumatic brain injury. *Journal of Head Trauma Rehabilitation, 24,* 145–154.

Elbogen, E. B., Wagner, H. R., Fuller, S. R., Calhoun, P. S., Kinneer, P. M., & Beckham, J. C. (2010). Correlates of anger and hostility in Iraq and Afghanistan war veterans. *American Journal of Psychiatry, 167,* 1051–1058.

Faul, M., Xu L., Wald M. M., & Coronado V. G. (2010). *Traumatic brain injury in the United States: Emergency department visits, hospitalizations and deaths 2002–2006.* Atlanta, GA: Centers for Disease Control and Prevention.

Fear, N. T., Jones, E., Groom, M., Greenberg, N., Hull, L., Hodgetts, T. J., … & Wessley, S. (2009). Symptoms of post-concussional syndrome are non-specifically related to mild traumatic brain injury in U.K. Armed Forces personnel on return from deployment in Iraq: An analysis of self reported data. *Psychological Medicine, 39,* 1379–1387.

Flanagan, S. R., Hibbard, M. R., Riordan, B., & Gordon, W. A. (2006). Traumatic brain injury in the elderly: Diagnosis and treatment challenges. *Clinical Geriatric Medicine, 22,* 449–468.

Flashman, L. A., & MacAllister, T. W. (2002). Lack of awareness and its impact in traumatic brain injury. *NeuroRehabilitation, 17,* 285–296.

French, L. M., & Parkinson, G. W. (2008). Assessing and treating veterans with traumatic brain injury. *Journal of Clinical Psychology, 64,* 1004–1013.

French, L. M., Spector, J., Stiers, W., & Kane, R. (2010). Blast injury and traumatic brain injury. In C. H. Kennedy & J. L. Moore (Eds.), *Military neuropsychology* (pp. 101–125). New York: Springer.

Fritz, H. G., & Bauer, R. (2004). Secondary injuries in brain trauma: Effects of hypothermia. *Journal of Neurosurgery and Anesthesiology, 16,* 43–52.

Gibbs, D. A., Martin, S. L., Kupper, L. L., & Johnson, R. E. (2007). Child maltreatment in enlisted soldiers' families during combat-related deployments. *Journal of the American Medical Association, 298,* 528–533.

Goldstein, F. C., & Levin, H. S. (2010). Traumatic brain injury in older adults. In J. Donders & S. J. Hunter (Eds.), *Principles and practice of lifespan developmental neuropsychology* (pp. 345–355). New York: Cambridge University Press.

Hall, L. K. (2008). *Counseling military families.* New York: Routledge.

Hall, L. K. (2011). The military culture, language, and lifestyle. In R. B. Everson & C. R. Figley (Eds.), *Families under fire: Systemic therapy with military families* (pp. 31–52). New York: Routledge.

Hart, T., Seignourel, P. J., & Sherer, M. (2009). A longitudinal study of awareness of deficit after moderate to severe traumatic brain injury. *Neuropsychological Rehabilitation, 19,* 161–176.

Hoffman, S. W., & Harrison, C. (2009). The interaction between psychological health and traumatic brain injury. *The Clinical Neuropsychologist, 23,* 1400–1415.

Hoge, C. W., Goldberg, H. M., & Castro, C. A. (2009). Care of war veterans with mild traumatic brain injury—Flawed perspectives. *New England Journal of Medicine, 360,* 1588–1591.

Howe, L. L. S. (2009). Giving context of post-deployment post-concussive-like symptoms: Blast-related potential mild traumatic brain injury and comorbidities. *The Clinical Neuropsychologist, 23,* 1315–1337.

Iverson, G. L. (2005). Outcome from mild traumatic brain injury. *Current Opinion in Psychiatry, 18,* 301–317.

Iverson, G. L., Lange, R. T., Brooks, B. L., & Rennison, V. L. A. (2010). "Good old days" bias following mild traumatic brain injury. *The Clinical Neuropsychologist, 24,* 17–37.

Iverson, G. L., Lange, R. T., Gaetz, M., & Zasler, N. D. (2007). Mild TBI. In N. D. Zasler, D. I. Katz, & R. D. Zafonte (Eds.), *Brain injury medicine: Principles and practice* (pp. 333–372). New York: Demos.

Iverson, G. L., Langlois, J. A., McCrea, M. A., & Kelly, J. P. (2009). Challenges associated with post-deployment screening for mild traumatic brain injury in military personnel. *The Clinical Neuropsychologist, 23,* 1299–1314.

Iverson, G. L., Zasler, N. D., & Lange, R. T. (2007). Post-concussion disorder. In N. D. Zasler, D. I. Katz, & R. D. Zafonte (Eds.), *Brain injury medicine: Principles and practice* (pp. 373–396). New York: Demos.

Ivins, B. J., Kane, R., & Schwab, K. A. (2009). Performance on the Automated Neuropsychological Assessment Metrics in a nonclinical sample of soldiers screened for mild TBI after returning from Iraq and Afghanistan: a descriptive analysis. *Journal of Head Trauma Rehabilitation, 24,* 24–31.

Jaffee, M. S., & Meyer, K. S. (2009). A brief overview of traumatic brain injury (TBI) and post-traumatic stress disorder (PTSD) within the Department of Defense. *The Clinical Neuropsychologist, 23,* 1291–1298.

Jensen, P. S., Martin, D., & Watanabe, H. (1996). Children's responses to separation during Operation Desert Storm. *Journal of the American Academy of Child and Adolescent Psychiatry, 35,* 433–441.

Kennedy, J. E., Leal, F. O., Lewis, J. D., Cullen, M. A., & Amador, R. R. (2010). Posttraumatic stress symptoms in OIF/OEF service members with blast-related and non-blast-related mild TBI. *NeuroRehabilitation, 26,* 223–231.

Kothari, S. (2007). Prognosis after severe TBI: A practical, evidence-based approach. In N. D. Zasler, D. I. Katz, & R. D. Zafonte (Eds.), *Brain injury medicine: Principles and practice* (pp. 169–199). New York: Demos.

Kreutzer, J. S., Marwitz, J. H., Godwin, E. E., & Arango-Lasprilla, J. C. (2010). Practical approaches to effective family intervention after brain injury. *Journal of Head Trauma Rehabilitation, 25,* 113–120.

Kreutzer, J. S., Stejskal, T. M., Ketchum, J. M., Marwitz, J. H., Taylor, L. A., & Menzel, J. C. (2009). A preliminary investigation of the brain injury family intervention: Impact on family members. *Brain Injury, 23*, 535–547.

Kurth, S., & Bigler, E. D. (2008). Structural neuroimaging in clinical neuropsychology. In J. E. Morgan & J. H. Ricker (Eds.), *Textbook of clinical neuropsychology* (pp. 783–839). New York: Taylor & Francis.

Langlois, J. A., Rutland-Brown, W., & Thomas, K. E. (2004). *Traumatic brain injury in the United States: Emergency department visits, hospitalizations, and deaths.* Atlanta, GA: Centers for Disease Control and Prevention.

Lincoln, A., Swift, E., & Shorteno-Fraser, M. (2008). Psychological adjustment and treatment of children and families with parents deployed in military combat. *Journal of Clinical Psychology, 64*, 984–992.

Lippa, S. M., Pastorek, N. J., Benge, J. F., & Thornton, M. (2010). Postconcussive symptoms after blast and nonblast-related mild traumatic brain injuries in Afghanistan and Iraq war veterans. *Journal of the International Neuropsychological Society, 16*, 856–866.

Litz, B. T., Stein, N., Delaney, E., Lebowitz, L., Nash, W. P., Silva, C., … & Maguen, S. (2009). Moral injury and moral repair in war veterans: A preliminary model and intervention strategy. *Clinical Psychology Review, 29*, 695–706.

Maguen, S., Lucenko, B. A., Reger, M. A., Gahm, G. A., Litz, B. T., Seal, K. H., … & Marmar, C. R. (2010). The impact of direct and indirect killing on mental health symptoms in Iraq war veterans. *Journal of Traumatic Stress, 23,* 86–90.

Marx, B. P., Brailey, K., Proctor, S. P., MacDonald, H. Z., Graefe, A. C., Amoroso, P., … & Vasterling, J. J. (2009). Association of time since deployment, combat intensity, and posttraumatic stress symptoms with neuropsychological outcomes following Iraq war deployment. *Archives of General Psychiatry, 66,* 996–1004.

McCrea, M. A. (2008). *Mild traumatic brain injury and post concussion syndrome: The new evidence base for diagnosis and treatment.* New York: Oxford University Press.

McCrea, M., Iverson, G. L., McAllister, T. M., Hammeke, T. A., Powell, M. R., Barr, W. B., & Kelly, J. P. (2009). An integrated review of recovery after mild traumatic brain injury (MTBI): Implications for clinical management. *The Clinical Neuropsychologist, 23,* 1368–1390.

Meyer, K. S., Marion, D. W., Coronel, H., & Jaffee, M. S. (2010). Combat-related traumatic brain injury and its implications to military healthcare. *Psychiatric Clinics of North America, 33*, 783–796.

Mittenberg, W., Canyock, E. M., Condit, D., & Patton, C. (2001). Treatment of postconcussion syndrome following mild head injury. *Journal of Clinical and Experimental Neuropsychology, 23,* 829–836.

Mittenberg, W., Tremont, G., Zielinski, R. E., Fichera, S, & Rayls, K. R. (1996). Cognitive-behavioral prevention of postconcussion syndrome. *Archives of Clinical Neuropsychology, 11,* 139–145.

Moore, B. A., & Kennedy, C. H. (2011). *Wheels down: Adjusting to life after deployment.* Washington, DC: American Psychological Association.

Nelson, L. A., Yoash-Gantz, R. E., Pickett, T. C., & Campbell, T. A. (2009). Relationship between processing speed and executive functioning performance among OEF/OIF veterans: Implications for postdeployment rehabilitation. *Journal of Head Trauma Rehabilitation, 24,* 32–40.

Nelson, N. W., Hoelzle, J. B., McGuire, K. A., Ferrier-Auerbach, A. G., Charlesworth, M. J., & Sponheim, S. R. (2010). Evaluation context impacts neuropsychological performance of OEF/OIF veterans with reported combat-related concussion. *Archives of Clinical Neuropsychology, 25,* 713–723.

Nicholl, J., & LaFrance, W. C. (2009). Neuropsychiatric sequelae of traumatic brain injury. *Seminars in Neurology, 29,* 247–255.

Patterson, F. L., & Staton, A. R. (2009). Adult acquired traumatic brain injury: Existential implications and clinical considerations. *Journal of Mental Health Counseling, 31,* 149–163.

Pickett, T. C., Bender, M. C., & Gourley, E. (2010). *Head injury rehabilitation of military members*. In C. H. Kennedy & J. L. Moore (Eds.), *Military neuropsychology* (pp. 175–198). New York: Springer.

Polusny, M. A., Kehle, S. M., Nelson, N. W., Erbes, C. R., Arbisi, P. A., & Thuras, P. (2011). Longitudinal effects of mild traumatic brain injury and posttraumatic stress disorder comorbidity on postdeployment outcomes in National Guard soldiers deployed to Iraq. *Archives of General Psychiatry, 68,* 79–89.

Rao, V., Bertrand, M., Rosenberg, P., Makley, M., Schretlen, D. J., Brandt, J., & Mielke, M. M. (2010). Predictors of new-onset depression after mild traumatic brain injury. *Journal of Neuropsychiatry and Clinical Neurosciences, 22,* 100–104.

Roebuck-Spencer, T., Baños, J., Sherer, M., & Novack, T. (2010). Neurobehavioral aspects of traumatic brain injury sustained in adulthood. In J. Donders & S. J. Hunter (Eds.), *Principles and practice of lifespan developmental neuropsychology* (pp. 329–343). New York: Cambridge.

Ruff, R. L., Ruff, S. S., & Wang, X-F. (2008). Headaches among Operation Iraqi Freedom/ Operation Enduring Freedom veterans with mild traumatic brain injury associated with exposures to explosions. *Journal of Rehabilitation Research and Development, 45,* 941–952.

Ruff, R. L., Iverson, G. L., Barth, J. T., Bush, S. S., Broshek, D. K., & the NAN Policy and Planning Committee. (2009). Recommendations for diagnosing a mild traumatic brain injury: A National Academy of Neuropsychology education paper. *Archives of Clinical Neuropsychology, 24,* 3–10.

Selassie, A. W., Zaolshnja, E., Langlois, J. A., Miller, T., Jones, P., & Steiner, C. (2008). Incidence of long term disability following traumatic brain injury hospitalization in the United States. *Journal of Head Trauma Rehabilitation, 23,* 123–131.

Silver, J. M., Kramer, R., Greenwald, S., & Weissman, M. (2001). The association between head injuries and psychiatric disorders: findings from the New Haven NIHM Epidemiologic catchment area study. *Brain Injury, 15,* 935–945.

Smits, M., Hunink, M. G. M., Van Rijssel, D. A., Dekker, H. M., Vos, P. E., Kool, D. R., …., & Dippel, D. W. (2008). Outcome after complicated minor head injury. *American Journal of Neuroradiology, 29,* 506–513.

Teasdale, G., & Jennett, B. (1974). Assessment of coma and impaired consciousness: A practical scale. *Lancet, 2,* 81–84.

Terrio, H., Brenner, L. A., Ivins, B. J., Cho, J. M, Helmick, K., Schwab, K., … & Warden, D. (2009). Traumatic brain injury screening: Preliminary findings in a U.S. army brigade combat team. *Journal of Head Trauma Rehabilitation, 24,* 14–23.

Tsanadis, J., Montoya, E., Hanks, R. A., Millis, S. R., Fichtenberg, N. L., & Axelrod, B. N. (2008). Brain injury severity, litigation status, and self-report of postconcussive symptoms. *The Clinical Neuropsychologist, 22,* 1090–1092.

Tuerk, P. W., Grubaugh, A. L., Hammer, M. B., & Foa, E. B. (2009). Diagnosis and treatment of PTSD-related compulsive checking behaviors in veterans of the Iraq war: The influence of military context on the expression of PTSD symptoms. *American Journal of Psychiatry, 166,* 762–767.

Uomoto, J. M., & Williams, R. M. (2009). Post-acute polytrauma rehabilitation and integrated care of returning veterans: Toward a holistic approach. *Rehabilitation Psychology, 54*, 259–269.

Walker, R. L., Clark, M. E., Nampiaparampil, D. E., McIlvried, L., Gold, M. S., Okonkwo, R., & Kerns, R. D. (2010). The hazards of war: Blast injury headache. *Journal of Pain, 11*, 297–302.

Walker, R. L, Clark, M. E., & Sanders, S. H. (2010). The "postdeployment multi-symptom disorder": An emerging syndrome in need of a new treatment paradigm. *Psychological Services, 7*, 136–147.

Whittaker, R., Kemp, S., & House, A. (2007). Illness perception and outcome in mild head injury: A longitudinal study. *Journal of Neurology, Neurosurgery, and Psychiatry, 78*, 644–646.

16

Enhancing Resilience With Culturally Competent Treatment of Same-Sex Military Couples

MATTHEW PORTER and VERONICA GUTIERREZ

INTRODUCTION

This chapter presents information on how to work effectively with same-sex military couples.* Currently, federal law [Pub.L. 103–160 (10 U.S.C. § 654], better known as the Don't Ask Don't Tell (DADT) policy of the U.S. military, makes it impossible to know the number of LGB-identified service members currently serving throughout the U.S. military. However, estimates have ranged from 65,000 to 71,000 (Frank, 2010; Gates, 2004, 2010).

Mental health professionals, whether employed by the U.S. military or working in the civilian sector, are bound by the ethical codes established by the governing bodies of their professions (e.g., the American Psychological Association [APA], American Medical Association [AMA], American Psychiatric Association, the National Association of Social Workers [NASW]), which clearly establish the nonpathological nature of homosexuality and bisexuality (AMA, 1994; Fox, 1988; Spitzer, 1973) and the ethical responsibility of mental health professionals from

* The commonly used term homosexual has been identified as connoting a negative bias among some who use it (e.g., Atkinson & Hackett, 1998; Bhugra & Wright, 1995). To avoid this pitfall, we use the terms gay, lesbian and LGB (lesbian/gay/bisexual; a gender-neutral reference) to refer to individuals who self-identify as belonging to this sexual minority. For further clarity, we use the following terminology: (a) same-sex military couples (SSMCs) for gender-neutral reference; (b) lesbian military couples (LMCs); (c) gay male military couples (GMMCs). Any of these terms is understood to apply equally to couples with only one or both partners in the military. No distinction between active duty and former service is implied by these terms.

various disciplines to provide nondiscriminatory and culturally sensitive treatment to LGB clients (AMA, 1994; American Psychiatric Association, 2009; APA, 2010; NASW, 2008). The American Psychiatric Association removed homosexuality from the second edition of the *Diagnostic and Statistical Manual of Mental Disorders* (American Psychiatric Association, 1968). The APA followed by resolving that "homosexuality per se implies no impairment in judgment, stability, reliability, or general social or vocational capabilities" (Conger, 1975, p. 633). These changes are in direct contradiction to the initial versions of Department of Defense Instruction (DODI) 1332.38, implemented in 1996 and recertified by the Pentagon in 2003, which listed homosexuality as a mental disorder. Prompted by letters from the directors of both the American Psychiatric Association and the APA citing their respective organizations' declassification of homosexuality in 1973, DODI 1332.38 was updated in July 2006 (Hausman, 2006). This update removed homosexuality from the list of mental disorders but maintained its inclusion under the broader category Specific Conditions and Other Circumstances, along with such conditions as enuresis, learning disorders, mental disorders, and obesity (Department of Defense [DOD], 2006). There is no doubt that this contradiction between the expectations of the DOD and those of the professional organizations may place therapists employed by the military in a difficult situation. The professional, ethical, and legal implications of this dilemma are beyond the scope of the present chapter, which aims only to provide treatment recommendations to psychotherapists (miltary or civilian) who are working with SSMCs. The first author of this chapter has prepared a freely accessible, public domain continuing education training video that may be useful for therapists working with LGB military servicemembers, particularly at this time of U.S. military policy change (Porter, 2011).

The Need for Culturally Sensitive Treatment of Sexual Minorities

The need for culturally sensitive treatment for sexual minorities has been well established (e.g., MacDonald, 1998). Culturally sensitive treatment yields better outcomes for LGB individuals (e.g., Fassinger & Richie, 1997) as well as for same-sex couples (e.g., Boyle, 1993; MacDonald, 1998). Cultural sensitivity can guide therapy both specifically and nonspecifically. Specific interventions derived from cultural sensitivity may include psychoeducation on alternative models of sex and relationships (e.g., for serodiscordant male couples, Carballo-Diéguez & Remien, 2001; or for fused lesbian couples, Nichols, 1995). Nonspecific milieu interventions may consist of the therapist providing a gay-affirming treatment environment (e.g., personal comfort with the relationships of gay men and lesbians [Green, 2007] and knowledge of issues faced by LGB individuals [Eubanks-Carter, Burckell, & Goldfried, 2005]). In both cases, cultural sensitivity hinges on the therapist understanding the ways in which the same-sex couple's treatment needs can be the same as or different from those of heterosexual couples.

While LGB couples seeking psychotherapy have many of the same concerns as heterosexual couples, including problems with communication, infidelity, substance abuse, physical abuse, and making decisions about staying together or separating (Cabaj & Klinger, 1996), significant differences can also be identified.

Doing therapy with LGB clients often hinges on culturally specific issues as well as universal themes. Although these issues have mostly been researched in nonmilitary LGB populations (e.g., Bryant & Demian, 1994; Connolly, 2004; Green & Mitchell, 2008), they are likely to have an impact on the military LGB population as well. In reference to these issues, specific cultural competencies related to working with LGB clients have been well described (e.g., Bernstein, 2000; Green, 2007). Unfortunately, the majority of U.S. psychotherapists lack these competencies (Garnets, Hancock, Cochran, Goodchilds, & Peplau, 1991). Without specific training or clinical experience, the therapist working with LGB clients is ethically obligated to obtain the knowledge base, attitudes, awareness, and skill sets (Israel, Ketz, Detrie, Burke, & Shulman, 2003) necessary to work effectively with this population. While attitudes, awareness, and skills are best cultivated through practice, this chapter aims to cover the knowledge base pertaining to delivery of culturally competent therapy to same-sex couples.

The Need for Culturally Sensitive Treatment of SSMCs

For therapists working with SSMCs, becoming culturally sensitive toward same-sex couples is just the first step. There then follows a need to understand how the military service, particularly in the U.S. Armed Forces, may interact with LGB-specific cultural factors to create a unique pattern of treatment needs and strengths.

A further extension and refinement of the basic LGB competencies is needed to conduct therapy effectively with LGB service members, who often straddle two very different worlds (Barrett, 2003; Giordano, 2003; Kiritsy, 2004). Like any multicuturally competent therapy, this work requires great sensitivity, thoughtfulness, and flexibility. Therapy with SSMCs is impacted by all the treatment challenges presented by nonmilitary LGB couples (mentioned previously and further described in this chapter), all the challenges presented by heterosexual military couples (well described in the present volume), and by a unique set of treatment challenges that arise from the intersection of LGB and military cultures. This chapter aims to clarify the important points of intersection between these two very different societies and cultures to clarify how the intersection may have an impact on couples therapy. We rely on the little literature that exists in this area as well as on our own experience in private practice with this population. A video providing continuing education and training for psychotherapists working with this population can be freely accessed at http://www.ce-psychology.com/askingandtelling.html (Porter, 2011).

The heterosexual therapist who lacks experience treating SSMCs may initially feel as though the SSMC might fare better with an LGB-identified therapist. This need not be a concern unless the level of therapist expertise is very low or if the therapist is resistant to identifying and modulating his or her own biases that might have a negative impact on treatment. In these cases, the therapist could consider referring the SSMC to community service groups. Available data suggest that LGB clients benefit from treatment provided by heterosexual therapists, that therapist sexual identity is not an important part of the client's choice of therapist (Modrcin & Wyers,

1990), and the various supportive practices that a heterosexually identified therapist can implement (e.g., providing a gay-affirming treatment milieu) may be more important than therapist sexual identity to the outcome of therapy (Liddle, 1996).

SSMCs in Need of Therapy May Be Underserved and Difficult to Identify

Before a SSMC presents for couples therapy, extensive barriers to treatment must be overcome. LGB service members may not be able to gauge which of the existing resources and supportive networks within the military are LGB affirming or understand the psychological, social, economic, and legal implications of being LGB identified within the military. The widely publicized anti-LGB bias of the U.S. military that is made official in the DADT policy (1993) is certainly not universal (e.g., Bateman, 2004). However, at the time of the writing of this chapter, DADT is still in effect, and LGB service members cannot disclose their sexual orientation or the fact that they are in a same-sex relationship without risking discharge and all its concommitant losses (e.g., benefits, honor, friendships, career, meaning/purpose), including its psychological costs (e.g., Poulin, Gouliquer, & Moore, 2009; Rosenzweig, 1945).

Even if DADT is repealed and LGB service members are allowed to serve openly, it is unlikely that the culture of the military, heavily influenced by social conservatism and conventionalist Christian values (see Moore, Chapter 1, this volume) will be substantially affected. The official rules may change, but the unofficial attitudes and practices are likely to persist, albeit less overtly. This barrier can compound the stigma that has been identified among service members (irrespective of sexual orientation) surrounding seeking help for mental health issues (Hall, 2008). Hence, LGB service members in need of mental health services are likely underserved and may opt to seek treatment outside the mental health services provided by the military, particularly when seeking couples therapy, which would entail disclosing their sexual orientation.

On the other hand, LGB service members who manage to overcome the various barriers to treatment and who choose to seek help from a military psychotherapist are unlikely to present initially as an SSMC seeking couples therapy. Rather, in the interest of self-protection, LGB service members experiencing significant couples issues are likely to present initially for individual treatment. They may take several sessions before broaching the topic of their sexual orientation, given the seriousness of the risk constituted by disclosure of LGB identification.

In a climate of uncertain alliances, in which therapeutic goals may be at odds with military instructions (e.g., DOD, 2006, Keita, 2010), military client and military psychotherapist may engage in a subtle, complex, and tacit communication. In this way, the client is able to ascertain the psychotherapist's attitude toward LGB issues without full self-disclosure, and together the therapeutic dyad can develop a trusting working alliance before the client takes the risk of full self-disclosure (Sammons, 2010). It is, of course, only after the client discloses his or her LGB identification to the therapist that the topic of couples therapy may be broached. Military psychotherapists who encounter this type of material would do well to consider the advantages and disadvantages of referring the SSMC to an outside provider, given that the treatment needs are outside the purview of the military policy.

Overview of Chapter

Regardless of the path the SSMC takes to treatment and the barriers that have been overcome, this chapter is designed to enhance competencies of all psychotherapists (military or nonmilitary) who find a way to provide services to this population. Areas covered include challenges in society, unique strengths, history of LGB individuals in the military, the impact of military lifestyle and culture on LGB identity, coming out decisions, couples issues specific to lesbians in the military, couples issues specific to gay men in the military, specific difficulties posed by military service to same-sex couples, and therapeutic interventions and suggestions. Let us begin with some scenarios that may present in therapy:

- Amy is a communications officer in the Marines and had been seeing Liz, a civilian living in the LGB neighborhood 10 miles from base, for about 6 months. Although Amy knew that most of the other officers in the communications unit were well educated and relatively open-minded about sexuality, she still felt compelled to keep her relationship concealed for fear that rumors would reach the upper levels of command and bring professional difficulties. As Amy was preparing to deploy to Afghanistan, she and Liz decided mutually to end the relationship. Amy always wondered if their relationship could have had a chance had it not been for the stress of keeping their relationship quiet, a constraint that was challenging enough while she was stateside, but seemed insurmountable with her imminent deployment.
- Sam, a petty officer in the Navy working stateside, was spending a lot of time with his friend, Josh, after the end of each work shift. One day, a coworker asked him why he spent so much time with his friend and what they did together. Sam disclosed to his coworker that he was gay, and that he was interested in Josh, although he had never had the courage to approach Josh openly about his interest. Sam received a supportive reaction from the coworker, who also warned Sam to be careful because of rumors of hazing and other discriminatory acts. Several days later, Sam noticed that Josh stopped returning his calls and began treating him indifferently after work. Sam missed his relationship with Josh and wondered if the coworker had gossiped. He did not know whom to trust.
- After finishing high school, Ron, who was from a conservative, Christian background, joined the Army. Ron was deployed as an infantryman three times over the course of the next 4 years during Operation Iraqi Freedom. While overseas, Ron began to come to terms with his sexuality, a process that was especially challenging and confusing due to the blend of all-male camaraderie and explicit homophobia in his unit. Serving under very dangerous conditions, he managed to forge close friendships with the other young men in his unit, all the while concealing his growing awareness of

his sexual orientation. The unit lost several young soldiers during combat, and Ron and other survivors grieved together and made a pact to always support each other. When Ron returned from his third deployment and began serving at headquarters, he managed to start a long-term couples relationship with Mario, a civilian who had no military experience. Over time, Ron's secret created a widening gap between him and his friends from Iraqi Freedom. Ron began to feel increasingly isolated and his post-traumatic stress disorder (PTSD) symptoms worsened rapidly, affecting his relationship and his work.

- Luisa enlisted in the Air Force to pursue her dream of being a fighter pilot. She trained hard and did well, serving with distinction in South Korea. She was promoted to captain after years of disciplined service, in part due to the aggressive, no-nonsense stance she cultivated toward her subordinates and her hard-line respect of authority. When she returned to the states she rejoined her partner of 8 years, Sung. Over the course of the next few years, as Luisa settled into headquarters work, she became intolerant of Sung's more carefree ways. Sometimes, she became enraged at Sung's lackadaisical attitude and threatened her with physical force. On several occasions, she lost her temper and hit Sung.

Amy, Sam, Ron, and Luisa had experienced difficulties in their relationships resulting from the intersection of LGB and military cultures. Individuals who present to therapy with similar issues may try to salvage a romantic relationship or may instead seek satisfying closure to an untenable relationship. Whatever the treatment goal, it is the therapist's duty to help these couples resolve their problems with the understanding that SSMCs face unique challenges and draw on unique strengths.

SAME-SEX COUPLES

Despite the normative portrayal in both the popular media and among college undergraduates of same-sex couples as dysfunctional (e.g., Crawford & Solliday, 1996; Testa, Kinder, & Ironson, 1987), social scientific evidence suggests that same-sex couples have potential equal to heterosexual couples for closeness and affiliative emotions (e.g., Kurdek, 1998; Peplau & Cochran, 1990; Peplau, Cochran, & Mays, 1997) and sexual satisfaction (e.g., Blumstein & Schwartz, 1983; Kurdek, 1991; McWhirter & Mattison, 1984; Peplau & Cochran, 1981; Peplau et al., 1997). Same-sex couples also have the potential for relationship longevity (e.g., McWhirter & Mattison, 1984), although perhaps not quite to the extent of heterosexual couples (e.g., Kurdek, 2004; Gutierrez, 2002; see Peplau, 1991, for a review)—a difference that may reflect the fact that same-sex couples may face more institutional barriers to relationship longevity than heterosexual couples.

On the other end, same-sex couples are likely to deal with many of the same couples issues as heterosexual couples. They are equally likely to report arguments (Kurdek, 2005; Metz, Rosser, & Strapko, 1994), to problem solve (Kurdek, 1998), and to suffer from similar patterns of intimate partner abuse (e.g., Potoczniak, Murot, Crosbie-Burnett, & Potoczniak, 2003).

Coming Out

Coming out is a very important factor in LGB identity development and plays an important role in the health of same-sex couples. The term *coming out of the closet* or *coming out* refers to the process by which a person comes first to self-identify as LGB and then begins to disclose this identity to others. A person who comes out of the closet is understood to undergo a gay identity development process. In 1979, Cass proposed a stage-based model to help explain gay and lesbian identity development that is still in widespread use:

1. *Identity Confusion:* The individual feels different from other people and may alienate him- or herself.
2. *Identity Comparison:* The individual questions what is hard about being LGB and tries to see if this label fits.
3. *Identity Tolerance:* The individual wonders if he or she is LGB and has more contact with other LGB individuals and community.
4. *Identity Acceptance:* The individual begins to form a supportive network and decide to whom he or she wants to come out.
5. *Identity Pride:* The individual reacts to society's treatment of gay individuals and takes action to do something about it.
6. *Identity Synthesis:* Sexuality is integrated into the individual's overall identity.

Although some gay and lesbian individuals may come out in all contexts of their lives (e.g., family, home, work), others may choose to come out only in certain contexts (e.g., with friends only but not with family). It is important that the therapist inquire about the coming out process of each couple member as differences in this area can place strain on couples.

Same-Sex Couples: Unique Challenges

Heterosexism and *homophobia* are two widespread forms of cultural oppression (Brown, 1995) that affect same-sex couples (Klinger, 1996; see also Green & Mitchell, 2008). Heterosexism is the devaluation of any form of sexual expression or sexual identity outside the norm of heterosexuality. Homophobia is a fear-based hatred, dislike, or mistrust of LGB people (e.g., Brown, 1995). Heterosexism and homophobia have worked together in society to prevent same-sex couples from accessing the concrete social, religious, and legal supports that heterosexual couples have (Kitzinger & Coyle, 1995; Rutter & Schwartz, 1996). In addition, heterosexism and homophobia underlie the normative portrayal of same-sex couples as dysfunctional (e.g., Crawford & Solliday, 1996; Testa et al., 1987), which may covertly shape implicit attitudes toward same-sex couples, even among lesbians and gay men.

Therapists working with SSMCs need to be aware of concrete inequalities in the way same same-sex couples are treated legally in the United States, as all of these inequalities can take a toll on relationships. Same-sex couples cannot legally marry in most states and are often unable to obtain benefits for their partners through their jobs or hold some important religious positions (Brown, 1995; Rutter & Schwartz, 1996). LGB U.S. citizens cannot sponsor their non-U.S. citizen partners for permanent resident status (Basham & Miehls, 2004). Legal obstacles to having children vary from state to state, despite the fact that 49% of gay men and lesbians who are not parents report wanting to have or adopt children of their own (Kaiser Family Foundation, 2001). Heterosexism and homophobia can also skew legal processes and outcomes related to child custody, intimate partner violence, and workplace discrimination (Fassinger, 1991). These forms of discrimination are, of course, all the more apparent in the military, as described.

Importantly, gay men and lesbians tend to receive less social support from their families of origin (e.g., Elizur & Mintzer, 2003; Kurdek, 2004, 2006), which may lead to pervasive distress, low self-esteem, and maladaptive coping (Gillow & Davis, 1987). Lesser social support from one or both partners' family of origin may also be stressful for same-sex couples. This may take the form of homophobic reactions to the same-sex partner or concerns about societal misunderstanding (e.g., Kurdek, 1988, 1998; Lewis, Derlega, Berndt, Morris, & Rose, 2001). When heterosexism and homophobia in the family of origin is pronounced enough that the couple has chosen not to disclose their relationship, the toll on the relationship may be particularly heavy (e.g., Lewis et al., 2001; Ossana, 2000).

Finally, same-sex couples may perceive fewer barriers to leaving relationships than heterosexual couples (e.g., Kurdek, 1998; Kurdek & Schmitt, 1986). Lack of access to marriage, which can confer stability to relationships, may be particularly important in this regard (e.g., Lannutti, 2005). Furthermore, same-sex couples report fewer role models than heterosexual couples, hence have opportunities that are more limited to receive peer feedback and support during times of relationship stress (MacDonald, 1998) and hence may tend to disproportionately attribute relationship stress to sexual orientation, rather than seeing relationship stress as something that affects all couples (Spitalnick & McNair, 2005).

Same-Sex Couples: Unique Strengths

Same-sex relationships tend to be dual-earner relationships, and the majority of lesbians and gay men in relationships reported valuing equal distribution of power in the relationship (Kurdek, 1993, 2005, 2006; Peplau & Cochran, 1990), and they push toward an egalitarian relationship (Peplau & Spalding, 2000; Weeks, Heaphy, & Donovan, 2001). Equal sharing of power and household duties among gay and lesbian couples is more common than among heterosexual couples. Thus, these couples may tend to be flexible in their roles and domestic tasks at home as well as in other areas of the relationship (Peplau & Spalding, 2000). It is important to recognize that these data may be somewhat exaggerated due to self-report bias (Carrington, 1999), that the goal of exactly equal distribution of power may not be reached (Harry & DeVall, 1978; Peplau & Cochran, 1990; Reilly & Lynch, 1990), and that for some same-sex couples, ideas about conventional masculine and feminine gender roles may still structure the division of labor and power (e.g.,

Peplau, 2001). For example, income differences may have an impact on the power differential among gay male couples (Blumstein & Schwartz, 1983), although the evidence for this effect is mixed for lesbian couples (Blumstein & Schwartz, 1983; Caldwell & Peplau, 1984; Reilly & Lynch, 1990).

A further area of strength for same-sex couples is in the richly elaborated network of friends they tend to create, networks that tend to be better developed for same-sex couples than for heterosexual couples (Carrington, 1999; Oswald, 2002). In addition, gay men and lesbians are more likely than heterosexuals to remain friends with their former partners (Harkless & Fowers, 2005; Nardi, 1999; Solomon, Rothblum, & Balsam, 2004; Weinstock, 2004). SSMCs, however, who often need to be less public about their relationship due to pressure from the military, may have less access to this social support (see Clinical Issues Pertaining Uniquely to SSMCs, this chapter).

Issues Pertaining to Lesbian Couples

Development of Lesbian Romantic Relationships Clunis and Green (1993) proposed a six-stage theory for the development of lesbian relationships:

1. Prerelationship: getting to know each other
2. Romance: merging and fusion
3. Conflict: becoming disillusioned about the partner and relationship
4. Acceptance: accepting the partner as a separate person with own faults and areas for improvement
5. Commitment: making choices, and balancing togetherness and separateness
6. Collaboration: creating something together to share with the world

Clinical Issues Pertaining to Lesbian Couples Lesbian couples tend to bring strengths to their relationships and face relationship challenges that may differ somewhat from heterosexual couples. These are treated in more detail in the following section on treatment recommendations. Strengths reported in the literature include a higher value placed on emotional intimacy during sex (Downey & Friedman, 1995) and a greater frequency of nongenital sexual behavior, including cuddling (James & Murphy, 1998). Challenges include relationship fusion, a theoretical concept with mixed empirical support, wherein the two partners allow boundaries to become diffuse, thereby limiting the health of the attachment style between the two partners (e.g., Krestan & Bepko, 1980; Ossana, 2000; Roth, 1985). Another challenge is the tendency for lesbian couples to have sex less frequently than heterosexual or gay male couples (e.g., Blumstein & Schwartz, 1983; Hall, 1996; Lever, 1995; Nichols, 1995), a difficulty that may arise from women being socialized to be less sexual (e.g., Fassinger & Morrow, 1995; Peplau & Garnets, 2000), relationship fusion, or internalized homophobia (Brown, 1986; Downey & Friedman, 1995). Therapists working with LMCs need to be aware that these issues may arise during couples therapy and can be targeted with psychotherapeutic interventions.

Issues Pertaining to Gay Male Couples

Development of Gay Male Romantic Relationships McWhirter and Mattison (1984) proposed a six-stage theory of gay male relationship development:

1. Blending stage (first year): merging, falling in love or being romantically in love (limerence), equalizing of partnership, and having high sexual activity; sexual exclusivity common in this stage
2. Nesting stage (second and third years): homemaking, finding compatibility, decline of limerence, and being ambivalent
3. Maintaining stage (fourth and fifth years): moving toward the reappearance of each partner's self-identity, taking risks, dealing with conflict, and establishing traditions
4. Building stage (6th through 10th years): collaborating or working together, increasing productivity, establishing independence, and depending on each other
5. Releasing stage (11th through 20th years): trusting each other (i.e., a better quality of trust is present), merging of money and possessions, constricting, and taking each other for granted
6. Renewing stage (beyond the 20th year): moving toward achieving security, shifting perspectives, restoring the partnership, and remembering

Clinical Issues Pertaining to Gay Male Couples Therapists working with GMMCs need to be aware of a range of issues that pertain particularly to gay male couples to treat them effectively in psychotherapy. These are discussed in more detail in the following section on treatment recommendations. Strengths include a wider range of sexual behaviors than heterosexual couples, including less of a need for penetration (e.g., Cove & Boyle, 2002). Difficulties include the likelihood of conflict relating to monogamy (e.g., Cove & Boyle, 2002; Simon, 1996), although gay male couples often negotiate agreements about extradyadic sex (e.g., Hickson, Davies, Hunt, & Weatherburn, 1992).

Furthermore, HIV/AIDS has had a major effect on the gay male community. Gay male couples may experience psychological difficulties related to HIV/AIDS, including sexual dysfunction, decreased interest in sex, and (for couples wherein one or both partners have HIV) fear of infecting others (Bahr & Weeks, 1989; Catalan, Burgess, & Klimes, 1995; Meyer-Bahlburg et al., 1991; Tindall, Forde, Goldstein, Ross, & Cooper, 1994). HIV/AIDS may also lead to gay male couples keeping more secrets from friends and families, resulting in lower levels of social support. Some gay men engaging in extradyadic sex (within or outside agreements made with their partners) may become infected with HIV, another potential source of relational stress (Palmer & Bor, 2007).

Clinical Issues Pertaining Uniquely to SSMCs

To effectively treat SSMCs seeking couples counseling, the therapist must cultivate an understanding not only of all the issues outlined, but also the issues specifically relating to the intersection between LGB culture and military culture. The following sections focus on this knowledge base, including the impact of military lifestyle and culture on LGB identity, issues pertaining to lesbians in the military, gay men in the military, and SSMCs.

The Impact of Military Lifestyle and Culture on LGB Service Members While diverse political and social attitudes are certainly represented within the military, the majority of service members are politically right leaning and are likely to be intolerant of homosexuality (Moore, Chapter 1, this volume). This will continue to be true even if DADT is eventually repealed or implemented less restrictively. Therapists working with SSMCs need to be aware that the experience of antigay discrimination and hassles is a special stressor (Kaiser Family Foundation, 2001; Lewis et al., 2001), as are physical violence and threats to LGB individuals (Kaiser Family Foundation, 2001). Both of these are linked to psychopathology among LGB individuals (Mays & Cochran, 2001; Meyer, 2003) and are likely related to lower relationship satisfaction in same-sex couples (Mays, Cochran, & Rhue, 1993; Otis, Rostosky, Riggle, & Hamrin, 2006; Todosijevic, Rothblum, & Solomon, 2005).

On the other end, although not without exception, LGB communities tend to be politically left leaning and socially progressive, stances that tend to presumptively devalue the military. This sociopolitical devaluation tends to coexist with a certain reductive fetishizing of the military within the gay male (and to a lesser extent lesbian) sexual aesthetics. The widely popularized LGB military fetish may ultimately make LGB service members feel trivialized or marginalized within the nonmilitary LGB community. In other words, the LGB service member faces potential discrimination in both communities.

With all these differences and challenges, a very important question may arise: Why do LGB individuals join the military? The reasons are most likely the same as those for heterosexual individuals: family tradition; the benefits of traveling, education, equality, and money; the identity of a "warrior"; and separation or escape from their restrictive families or communities of origin (Hall, 2008; Smith, 2010). The military life may give gay men and lesbian women stability, independence, structure, and discipline (Greer & Morrow, 2006), just as it does for heterosexual individuals (Hall, 2008), or even a way out of a family environment that is seen as more homophobic than the military (Smith, 2010). These advantages must be considered by treating psychotherapists, who might otherwise recommend that LGB service members look for other employment to ease stress that may be adversely affecting their relationship.

Lesbians in the Military It is estimated that 14% of the military consists of women (Hall, 2008). Research has not documented what percentage of these women are lesbians. What we know about women in the military regardless of sexual orientation is that they may feel they have to prove they are tough and able to handle military work. They may be challenged by military men to the point of needing to balance their femininity with their military work (Hall, 2008). Although the stereotype of the masculine, "butch" lesbian seems ideally suited to military service, lesbians in the military report being hassled by coworkers and superiors who suspect their sexual identity (Sohn, 2010).

Women in the military may also be housed together due to the small numbers of women (Blaise & White, 2006). Thus, an advantage that lesbian women may have is the opportunity to have their partners nearby or right next to them if both couple members are in the military and in the same unit. Unfortunately, women in the military have reported incidents of sexual assault during their service (Hall, 2008). As discussed in this chapter, the probability of a couple experiencing relationship stress due to issues relating to past trauma is greater when the couple consists of two women rather than two men or a man and a woman (Gutierrez, 2004).

Gay Men in the Military Because of the masculine ideology that exists in the military, male service members may tend to be less verbally expressive and less willing to seek help for their problems (Hall, 2008; Moore, Chapter 1, this volume). This reality may be compounded by sexual identity issues for a gay man. A gay man has to balance his ideas and feelings about what it means to be a man and gay. Because these two aspects of his identity oppose each other, the gay man may find himself needing to split himself (i.e., time, places, and people) in both worlds (Cass, 1979). Thus, he may find he has to travel to another county to be with other gay men or to be open in public with his partner. Some gay men in the military may choose to date or form relationship ties with someone outside the military for fear of being caught, while others may find it easier to be with someone in the military as long as they are careful about their actions and behaviors and their relationship is not an obvious one.

COUPLES THERAPY WITH SSMCS

Highlighting Factors Contributing to Relationship Conflict

Following the review of major themes and issues with an impact on LGB individuals and same-sex couples, we now highlight key issues for clinical intervention with SSMCs. Like heterosexual couples, same-sex couples can be threatened by intimate partner violence (Farley, 1992; Kusian, 2007), substance misuse (Adam & Gutierrez, 2010), and conflict over negotiating sexual monogamy (Brown, 1995; Gutierrez, 2004). These issues, although common to all couples, may present differently in the same-sex couple than in the heterosexual couple. Gay male couples, furthermore, are at a higher risk of being impacted by HIV/AIDS (Gutierrez, 2004; Klinger, 1996). For any of these issues, one of the therapist's tasks is to elicit the extent to which the common contributing factors (sexual orientation, military service) have an impact on the couple's presenting problem.

Substance Use and Abuse Substance use is prevalent in the military regardless of sexual orientation, as evidenced by estimates indicating 12% of military personnel engage in illicit drug use, 20% in heavy alcohol use, and 31.7% in cigarette use. While military policies and efforts to decrease the use of substances have resulted in documented decreases in drug use, heavy alcohol use has remained relatively stable. Elevated use of substances has been similarly documented within the LGB population (Hall, 2008) and can complicate concomitant SSMC couples issues. For instance, substance abuse has been correlated with violence in lesbian relationships (Schilit, Lie, & Montagne, 1990).

Sexual Abuse and Relationship Violence Given the higher prevalence of histories of sexual abuse among women than men, female same-sex couples have a proportionately greater likelihood of having a member who is a survivor of childhood or adult sexual abuse (see Brown, 1995). Consequently, female same-sex couples may have difficulties in their relationships because of this past trauma (Gutierrez, 2004). Gay and bisexual men may also be survivors of incest or sexual abuse even though empirical evidence is lacking. Reasons for this lack of information have been attributed to males not reporting the incident to the authorities or denying the incident. In addition, they may have problems with memory retrieval (Gutierrez, 1992).

Furthermore, approximately 10–20% of the individuals in same-sex relationships experience violence that is similar to heterosexual battering (Renzetti, 1992). Some partners may not want to reveal their sexual orientation, discouraging them from seeking help (Hammond, 1988). Furthermore, there may be reluctance to discuss relationship violence for fear of the consequences of revealing their sexual orientation (Hammond, 1988) or contributing to negative attitudes toward homosexuality (Peplau, Veniegas, & Campbell, 1999) or because many professional and shelter services are not trained to work with same-sex couples (Hammond, 1988; Harris & Cook, 1994). Power imbalances seem to be connected to relationship violence among same-sex couples (e.g., Renzetti, 1992).

Sexual Monogamy Studies showed that gay male relationships are less sexually monogamous than are lesbian and heterosexual relationships (Blumstein & Schwartz, 1983; Klinger, 1996; Peplau, 1993). Sexual nonmonogamy becomes a problem when both partners in a relationship have different views about it, for example, when one partner wants to be sexually active outside the relationship while the other does not agree with this decision. Nonmonogamy can be negotiated among gay male couples just as can safer sex practices (McWhirter & Mattison, 1996).

HIV/AIDS The HIV/AIDS epidemic has had an impact on the gay male community, with the lesbian community being supportive in efforts to decrease this epidemic (Brown, 1995). Male same-sex couples have had to reevaluate their relationships with regard to commitment and monogamy because of the fear of infection with the human immunodeficiency virus (HIV) (Brown, 1995). This was particularly true during the first 15 years of the epidemic. Since the advent of highly active antiretroviral therapy (HAART) in 1996, HIV has become somewhat more manageable. With HAART, far fewer people with HIV are progressing to AIDS. However, HIV at best still requires daily medication management and negotiation of safer sex practices and at worst poses a fatal threat. Unfortunately, advances in HIV treatment have coincided, and perhaps precipitated, a resurgence of unsafe sexual behavior among gay men (Halkitis, Wilton, & Drescher, 2005). Most U.S. armed services branches require annual or biennial HIV tests, so there is a good chance that HIV-positive active service members will be relatively aware of their status.

It is not uncommon that one or both partners in a gay male relationship are HIV positive. When only one of the partners is HIV positive, the relationship is termed serodiscordant or magnetic. Such relationships are not rare and can be richly rewarding for men courageous enough to attempt them. With proper medication management, serodiscordant couples and healthy HIV-positive couples can certainly hope for a full lifetime together. Agreements about monogamy and safer sex practices need to be negotiated, sometimes with the help of a therapist, in a way that satisfies both the couple's need for sexual fulfillment and the HIV-negative partner's need for safety (see Hoff, Beougher, Chakravarty, Darbes, & Neilands, 2010). Furthermore, people who are HIV positive are more likely to fear losing a current relationship. In clinical practice, we have seen many go to great, and sometimes untenable, lengths to sustain their relationship, even when it is unhealthy. All of these issues, including the high levels of fear, social stigma, and secret-keeping that still surround AIDS can have an adverse impact on a relationship that might otherwise flourish and are appropriate targets for psychotherapy with SSMCs.

Challenges to SSMCs Resulting From Only One Member Being in the Military The same-sex partner who is not in the military may need help learning how to adjust and deal with the lifestyle of the member in the military, including demanding daily schedules when in town and lengthy and dangerous deployments. For nonmilitary partners of LGB service members, this may also include frustration about having to self-censor and not being able to attend their partner's work events or to fraternize openly with their partner's military friends and coworkers (Sohn, 2010). This is especially poignant in the case of the nonmilitary partner not being able to attend group farewells or welcome home parties surrounding dangerous deployments. A further challenge unique to SSMCs with one partner in the military is that the military partner may be reluctant to end a relationship due to fears about the nonmilitary member retaliating by disclosing the service member's sexual identity to the military.

When a military partner in a same-sex relationship returns from deployment, the nonmilitary partner may have difficulty understanding service-related symptoms. These are likely to include generalized anxiety disorder, depression, impulse control difficulties, survivor guilt, and PTSD (Hall, 2008). When symptoms related to deployment trauma present in the context of an SSMC, it is recommended that the couples therapy be enlarged to include addressing the specific symptoms in the individual (e.g., Sherman, Zanotti, & Jones, 2005).

Therapists working with SSMCs in this situation need to be aware that LGB service members often report a weakening of social support from military friends following return from deployment due to the inability to disclose their homosexuality (Smith, 2010). The problem of relational challenges arising due to symptoms related to deployment stress are especially complicated for SSMCs, as the returning LGB service member may end up isolated and without social support (Smith,

2010). Lack of social support has been identified as a powerful risk factor for mental health problems following war trauma (e.g., Porter, 2007; Porter & Haslam, 2005) and for LGB individuals and couples (MacDonald, 1998).

Interventions and Suggestions

Prior work on counseling military couples has articulated the benefits of relying on brief and direct problem-solving approaches, including cognitive-behavioral therapy (CBT), brief solution-focused therapy (BSFT), and family systems therapy (Hall, 2008; see also Part II, this volume). What we have found effective in our clinical practice has been a hybrid approach combining these three approaches in a way that is sensitive to both military and LGB cultures and directly involves both couple members.

When the barriers to treatment outlined are overcome, and the SSMC presents for therapy, the therapist must complete a thorough assessment of the challenges outlined (e.g., coming out issues, challenges in society and in the military as a result of sexual orientation, family of origin support for the relationship, discrimination) in addition to intake assessment questions that are asked of any couple (e.g., substance abuse issues, medical concerns). Having gathered the relevant cultural background information, the therapist can ask the couple directly about their perception of current obstacles to a healthy romantic relationship (i.e., define presenting problem), as well as what strategies the couple has already tried to fix the problem. The approach presented here basically involves the following for the therapist (note that these steps or suggestions are not in any order, and the therapist may choose to use only those that apply or are helpful):

- Ask and define the problem
- Ask the couple to envision the situation if the problem were resolved
- Ask the couple about the meaning behind the information disclosed
- Ask the couple what they have tried in resolving the problem
- Address any barriers in resolving the problem
- Ask the couple to meet halfway in resolving the problem and come up with some possible solutions

One important question to ask is whether they feel in control of the problem (e.g., the military has asked one member to deploy or the couple cannot move in together). If they do not, the therapist is to have the couple work out a plan that involves both members negotiating what each can do to make it easier or less painful (e.g., have one or both couple members make phone calls or e-mail at least twice a week if deployment is about to take place, work through past child abuse issues in individual therapy, or negotiate attending a gay bar in another city that a member feels more comfortable attending) or make the appropriate referrals (e.g., have one or both members seek psychiatric help for depression).

If the members feel they are in control of the problem, the therapist is to ask each member to envision how the situation would be if the problem were resolved, the meaning behind what is being disclosed, what they have tried in resolving the problem, and any barriers that get in the way of achieving the resolution of the problem. For instance, a member of the couple may disclose that he would like to have sex with his partner at least three times a week rather than once a month (problem defined and vision). The task of the therapist is to find out what the member means by "sex" (i.e., what would sex look like), ask the other member what he thinks, inquire about what the couple has tried, and rule out any barriers that get in the way (e.g., a partner's medical issues) of resolving the problem. The next step for the therapist is to help the couple meet halfway in resolving the problem (i.e., both members will do something to resolve the problem) and make the changes necessary to alleviate the problem. In doing so, the therapist is to make sure that each member of the couple feels that the proposed resolution to the problem is fair and reasonable. Thus, both members in the scenario may not be intimate in the way the partner desires three times a week, yet a satisfying compromise may be reached (e.g., one of the members is affectionate while the other masturbates, or both members decide that having sex once a week works for both of them).

Another example of a problem may involve a couple having a hard time finding time to be together due to their work shifts (presenting problem). In this situation, the therapist would ask for clarification (e.g., what do they mean by "finding time") and ask them to envision how the situation would look like if it were resolved and, again, what they have tried to fix the problem and discuss any barriers. Then, the therapist would help the couple think about what each can do to reach a compromise (e.g., they may be able to negotiate changing their work hours or taking short vacations throughout the year instead of taking long ones).

Case Vignette – Marcus

This vignette, which consists of a male client who is unsure about how to discuss his concerns about deployment involving his partner, is an amalgam of details from our own clinical practice. It illustrates the process of tentative client self-disclosure, followed by the more directive, culturally appropriate steps outlined in this chapter.

Marcus, a white male, age 25, in the Army Reserve, meets Dr. Tran, a non-military psychologist, for the first time to address his concerns about deployment. He is self-referred, and Dr. Tran gives him a demographic form to complete, asking him about his personal information, including sexual orientation, which he marks as "bisexual." Dr. Tran begins the intake assessment session by asking Marcus further questions about his work and role in the military as well as his sources of support. Marcus responds that the only person who "really cares about me is my buddy Anthony." "So you have no family that you are leaving behind?" asks Dr. Tran. "Oh, I do but they can take care of themselves."

Marcus does not know how to tell Dr. Tran that he is in a same-sex relationship with Anthony. Dr. Tran further questions him about his deployment, and when the session is about to end, Dr. Tran notices that Marcus is confused and quiet. "You'll be all right," states Dr. Tran. When Marcus leaves the office, Dr. Tran notices that Marcus marked the "bisexual" box on the form and keeps it in his mind for the next session.

In the next session, Dr. Tran asks Marcus how he is doing, and Marcus responds that "time is running out."

"And what is it that still needs to be resolved? Is it a special friend? We actually did not talk about your romantic life."

Marcus seems nervous and mumbles, "I-I don't ..."

"I have a question for you. In the demographic form, you marked your sexual orientation as 'bisexual.' What does being bisexual mean to you?"

"That I am attracted to men as well as women," responds Marcus.

"By any chance is there a close individual you are leaving behind who you worry about?"

"Yeah," responds Marcus.

"And is it a male or female?" asks Dr. Tran. "It's a male. ... It's Anthony," discloses Marcus.

"Well, tell me about Anthony," responds Dr. Tran. From this point, Dr. Tran was able to help Marcus about his concerns in relation to deployment and the specific problem involving "leaving Anthony behind." At the end of the session, Dr. Tran lets Marcus know that he is welcome to bring Anthony to the next session if he would like to bring him.

Marcus and Anthony show up for the third session, and Dr. Tran asks both of them how they are doing and what they would like to discuss during the session. Marcus begins by telling Dr. Tran that he is worried about Anthony staying behind because Anthony has no one to emotionally support him while he is gone. Anthony concurs, and they both seem unsure about what to do. Dr. Tran asks both of them what they can do while Marcus is gone, and they both agree to maintain contact through any possible avenue.

"But it is when there is no communication whatsoever that I worry about. ... Sometimes we cannot communicate with one another," states Marcus.

"Then, let's brainstorm," states Dr. Tran. "Why don't you and I look up resources on the Internet regarding deployment for family members and partners as well as counseling services for you, Anthony, while Marcus is gone," states Dr. Tran.

In the next session, Anthony announces that he found a hotline for individuals who feel depressed. Dr. Tran lets both of them know that individual counseling may be helpful for Anthony and gives him some referrals to LGB-affirming therapists he located through the local LGB community center. Dr. Tran utilizes the discussion of these concrete details to facilitate Marcus's expression of concern about Anthony's well-being during his deployment. At this point, the session becomes more emotional, and both partners become tearful. Knowing that agreements about monogamy or extradyadic sex can be important for many gay couples, Dr. Tran seizes the opportunity and becomes more directive, first recognizing the significance of the couple's emotional bond: "I see how closely emotionally linked the two of you are, and how much you care for each other's well-being, and the closeness of your relationship. Maybe now would be a good time to discuss what the two of you will do, sexually, during the 6 months that you will be separated."

The couple pauses, each sighs and looks at the other. Hesitatingly at first, and then more openly, they begin to disclose their feelings about "being tempted" to have sex with other men during the separation. Dr. Tran, as an LGB-affirming therapist, validates these concerns and normalizes them: "Concerns like these are very common among gay couples and can be very distressing, even when the couples are able to live together. I can only imagine how difficult this topic is given your upcoming separation."

Through the ensuing discussion, it emerges that this matter has been troubling the couple for some time. Dr. Tran senses that there is more to the story than the two are comfortable disclosing at present and offers to use the next session to discuss this matter further, including "how to stay safe" during Marcus's deployment. He notes that the feeling in the room has shifted from discomfort to appreciation, and when the couple leaves, Anthony mentions that he is relieved Dr. Tran brought up the issue of extra-dyadic sex.

Although the couple has committed to discussing this issue during the two remaining sessions, the matter remains unresolved before Marcus's deployment. However, both men affirm their willingness to continue discussing it by telephone. Dr. Tran again normalizes their concerns and further validates the idea that both men may be experiencing stress due to lack of psychological resources for sexual minority individuals. He brings up the possibility of computer-assisted couples therapy (e.g., using Skype) during Marcus's deployment. Because Marcus is unsure of the possibility of private computer access while away, he is unable to commit to this idea but agrees to explore the possibility when he arrives at his duty station. Dr. Tran and the couple agree to suspend sessions until further notice.

Four weeks later, Anthony calls Dr. Tran to inform him that Marcus does not have private computer time on base, but that the two of them do speak frequently by telephone. "At least it's out on the table," Anthony said, referring to the issue of nonmonogamy, "Now I feel like we can at least talk about what's going on." Dr. Tran and Anthony agree to schedule a session for the next time that Marcus is in town.

SUMMARY

Therapists working with SSMCs must find a way to negotiate the constraints and opportunities presented by the confluence of two distinct cultures. In writing this chapter, we have drawn on our clinical experience with the LGB military population as well as on the relevant social scientific literatures (see Porter, 2011, for a freely accessible training video). Therapists are encouraged to use this chapter as a starting point to develop basic cultural competence with SSMCs. This basic knowledge can be used to plan culturally sensitive assessments to determine which issues are most relevant to the presenting couple and to make certain that the important areas are covered in treatment. Once any initial barriers to client self-disclosure on the part of the LGB military client are overcome, more directive approaches are recommended, both in the assessment of the couple's current needs and in problem resolution.

The fact that the social science specifically targeting the psychological needs of LGB service members remains in its infancy represents both a challenge and an opportunity for clinicians and researchers. Working with SSMCs is an area of clinical expertise that will only grow in importance as the U.S. military rethinks its stance toward homosexuality. While the basic areas of concern have been noted in our review, clearly there is a need for innovation and empirical comparison of treatment approaches. More important, however, therapists willing to take the time to educate themselves cross culturally and to make themselves accessible to this population will be able to reach a historically underserved population in great need of psychological assistance.

REFERENCES

Adam, M., & Gutierrez, V. (2010). *Working with gay men and lesbian women with addiction concerns*.

American Medical Association. (1994). *Health care needs of the homosexual population (H-160.991)*. Retrieved from http://www.ama-assn.org/ama/pub/about-ama/our-people/member-groups-sections/glbt-advisory-committee/ama-policy-regarding-sexual-orientation.shtml

American Psychiatric Association. (1968). *Diagnostic and statistical manual of mental disorders* (2nd ed.). Washington, DC: Author.

American Psychiatric Association. (2009). *The principles of medical ethics with annotations especially applicable to psychiatry*. Retrieved from http://www.psych.org/mainmenu/psychiatricpractice/ethics/resourcesstandards/principlesofmedicalethics.aspx

American Psychological Association. (2010). *American Psychological Association ethical principles of psychologists and code of conduct.* Retrieved from http://www.apa.org/ethics/code/index.aspx

Atkinson, D. R., & Hackett, G. (1998). *Counseling diverse populations* (2nd ed.). New York: McGraw-Hill.

Bahr, J. M., & Weeks, G. R. (1989). Sexual functioning in a nonclinical sample of male couples. *American Journal of Family Therapy, 17*, 110–127.

Barrett, J. (2003, October 28). Reality sets in. *Advocate, 901*, 32–38.

Basham, K. K., & Miehls, D. (2004). *Transforming the legacy: Couple therapy with survivors of childhood trauma*. New York: Columbia University Press.

Bateman, G. W. (2004). *Military culture: United States. GLBTQ: An encyclopedia of gay, lesbian, bisexual, transgender, and queer culture*. Retrieved from http://www.glbtq.com/social-sciences/military_culture_us.html

Bernstein, A. C. (2000). Straight therapists working with lesbians and gays in family therapy. *Journal of Marital and Family Therapy, 26*, 443–454.

Bhugra, D., & Wright, B. (1995). Sexual dysfunction in gay men: Diagnosis and management. *International Review of Psychiatry, 7*, 247–252.

Blaise, K. & White, D. (2006). The heart of a soldier: A true story of love, war and sacrifice. New York: Gotham Books.

Blumstein, P., & Schwartz, P. (1983). *American couples: Money, work, sex*. New York: Morrow.

Boyle, M. (1993). Sexual dysfunction or heterosexual dysfunction? *Feminism and Psychology, 3*, 73–88.

Brown, L. S. (1986). Confronting internalized oppression in sex therapy with lesbians. *Journal of Homosexuality, 12*, 99–107.

Brown, L. S. (1995). Therapy with same-sex couples: An introduction. In N. S. Jacobsen & N. S. Gurman (Eds.), *Clinical handbook of couple therapy* (pp. 546–568). New York: Guilford Press.

Bryant, A. S., & Demian (1994). Relationship characteristics of American gay and lesbian couples: Findings from a national survey. In L. A. Kurdek (Ed.), *Social services for gay and lesbian couples* (pp. 101–117). New York: Haworth Press.

Cabaj, R. P., & Klinger, R. L. (1996). Psychotherapeutic interventions with lesbian and gay couples. In R. P. Cabaj & T. S. Stein (Eds.), *Textbook of homosexuality and mental health* (pp. 485–501). Washington, DC: American Psychiatric Press.

Caldwell, M. A., & Peplau, L. A. (1984). The balance of power in lesbian relationships. *Sex Roles, 10*, 587–599.

Carballo-Diéguez, A., & Remien, R. H. (2001). Sex therapy with male couples of mixed-(serodiscordant-) HIV status. In P. J. Kleinplatz (Ed.), *New directions in sex therapy: Innovations and alternatives* (pp. 302–321). Philadelphia: Brunner-Routledge.

Carrington, C. (1999). *No place like home: Relationships and family life among lesbians and gay men*. Chicago: University of Chicago Press.

Cass, V. C. (1979). Homosexual identity formation: A theoretical model. *Journal of Homosexuality, 4*, 219–235.

Catalan, J., Burgess, A., & Klimes, I. (1995). *Psychological medicine of HIV infection*. Oxford, UK: Oxford University Press.

Clunis, D. M., & Green, G. D. (1993). *Lesbian couples*. Seattle, WA: Seal Press.

Conger, J. J. (1975). Proceedings of the American Psychological Association, Incorporated, for the year 1974: Minutes of the annual meeting of the Council of Representatives. *American Psychologist, 30*, 620–651.

Connolly, C. M. (2004). Clinical issues with same-sex couples: A review of the literature. In J. J. Bigner & J. L. Wetchler (Eds.), *Relationship therapy with same-sex couples* (pp. 3–12). New York: Haworth Press.

Cove, J., & Boyle, M. (2002). Gay men's self-defined sexual problems, perceived causes and factors in remission. *Sexual and Relationship Therapy, 17*, 137–147.

Crawford, I., & Solliday, E. (1996). The attitudes of undergraduate college students toward gay parenting. *Journal of Homosexuality, 30*(4), 63–77.

Department of Defense. (2006). *Physical disability evaluation (DoD Instruction 1332.38)*. Retrieved from http://www.dtic.mil/whs/directives/corres/pdf/133238p.pdf

Don't Ask, Don't Tell Policy Act of 1993, 10 U.S.C. §654 (1997).

Downey, J. I., & Friedman, R. C. (1995). Internalized homophobia in lesbian relationships. *Journal of the American Academy of Psychoanalysis, 23*, 435–447.

Elizur, Y., & Mintzer, A. (2003). Gay males' intimate relationship quality: The roles of attachment, security, gay identity, social support, and income. *Personal Relationships, 10*, 411–435.

Eubanks-Carter, C., Burckell, L. A., & Goldfried, M. R. (2005). Enhancing therapeutic effectiveness with lesbian, gay, and bisexual clients. *Clinical Psychology: Science and Practice, 12*(1), 1–18.

Farley, N. (1992). Same-sex domestic violence. In S. H. Dworkin & F. J. Gutierrez (Eds.), *Counseling gay men and lesbians: Journal to the end of the rainbow* (pp. 231–242). Alexandria, VA: American Counseling Association.

Fassinger, R. E. (1991). The hidden minority: Issues and challenges in working with lesbian women and gay men. *The Counseling Psychologist, 19*, 157–176.

Fassinger, R. E., & Morrow, S. L. (1995). OverCome: Repositioning lesbian sexualities. In L. Diamant & R. McAnulty (Eds.), *The psychology of sexual orientation, behavior, and identity: A handbook* (pp. 197–219). Westport, CT: Greenwood Press.

Fassinger, R. E., & Richie, B. S. (1997). Sex matters: Gender and sexual orientation in training for multicultural counseling competency. In D. B. Pope-Davis & H. L. K. Coleman (Eds.), *Multicultural counseling competencies: Assessment, education and training, and supervision* (pp. 83–110). Thousand Oaks, CA: Sage.

Fox, R. E. (1988). Proceedings of the American Psychological Association, Incorporated, for the year 1987: Minutes of the annual meeting of the Council of Representatives. *American Psychologist, 43*, 508–531.

Frank, N. (2010). *Don't Ask, Don't Tell: Detailing the damage*. Palm Center, University of California, Santa Barbara. Retrieved from http://www.palmcenter.org/files/DetailingCostofDADT.pdf

Garnets, L., Hancock, K. A., Cochran, S. D., Goodchilds, J., & Peplau, L. A. (1991). Issues in psychotherapy with lesbians and gay men: A survey of psychologists. *American Psychologist, 46*, 964–972.

Gates, G. J. (2004). *Gay men and lesbians in the U.S. military: Estimates from Census 2000*. The Urban Institute. Retrieved from http://www.urban.org/uploadedPDF/411069_GayLesbianMilitary.pdf

Gates, G. J. (2010). *Lesbian, gay, and bisexual men and women in the U.S. military: Updated estimates*. The Williams Institute. Retrieved from http://www.law.ucla.edu/williams-institute/pdf/GLBmilitaryUpdate.pdf

Gillow, K. E., & Davis, L. L. (1987). Lesbian stress and coping methods. *Journal of Psychosocial Nursing and Mental Health Services, 25*(9), 28–32.

Giordano, S. A. (2003, April 10). Partners silenced under "Don't Ask, Don't Tell." *Bay Windows, 21*(17), 3–12.

Green, R.-J. (2007). Gay and lesbian couples in therapy: A social justice perspective. In E. Aldarondo (Ed.), *Advancing social justice through clinical practice* (pp. 119–149). Mahwah, NJ: Erlbaum.

Green, R.-J., & Mitchell, V. (2008). Gay and lesbian couples in therapy: Minority stress, relational ambiguity, and families of choice. In A.S. Gurman (Ed.), *Clinical handbook of couple therapy* (4th edition) (pp. 662–680). New York: Guilford Press.

Greer, P. L., & Morrow, D. F. (2006). The military life: The case of Saundra. In L. Messinger & D. F. Morrow, D. F. (Eds.), *Case studies on sexual orientation and gender expression in social work practice* (pp. 19–21). New York: Columbia University Press.

Gutierrez, F. J. (1992). Gay and bisexual male incest survivors. In S. H. Dworkin & F. J. Gutierrez (Eds.), *Counseling gay men and lesbians: Journey to the end of the rainbow* (pp. 191–201). Alexandria, VA: American Counseling Association.

Gutierrez, V. (2002). *Traditional theories and the formation, maintenance, and dissolution of same-sex couples*. Unpublished manuscript, Counseling/Clinical/School Psychology Program, University of California, Santa Barbara, Santa Barbara, CA.

Gutierrez, V. (2004). *Maintenance behaviors and conflict level, areas, and resolution strategies in same-sex couples.* (Doctoral dissertation, University of California, Santa Barbara, 2004). Dissertation Abstracts International, 65/09, 4896.

Hall, L. K. (2008). *Counseling military families: What mental health professionals need to know*. New York: Taylor & Frances Group.

Hall, M. (1996). Unsexing the couple. In M. Hill & E. D. Rothblum (Eds.), *Couples therapy: Feminist perspectives* (pp. 1–11). New York: Harrington Park Press.

Halkitis, P. N., Wilton, L., & Drescher, J. (2005). Why barebacking? *Journal of Gay and Lesbian Psychotherapy, 9*, 1–8.

Hammond, N. (1988). Lesbian victims of relationship violence. *Women and Therapy, 8*, 89–105.

Harkless, L. W., & Fowers, B. J. (2005). Similarities and differences in relational boundaries among heterosexuals, gay men, and lesbians. *Psychology of Women Quarterly, 29*, 167–176.

Harris, R. J., & Cook, C. A. (1994). Attributions about spouse abuse: It matters who the batterers and victims are. *Sex Roles, 30*, 553–565.

Harry, J., & DeVall, W. (1978). Age and sexual culture among homosexually oriented males. *Archives of Sexual Behavior, 7*, 199–209.

Hausman, K. (2006, July 21). Pentagon does about face on classifying homosexuality [electronic version]. *Psychiatric News, 41*(14), p. 9.

Hickson, F. C., Davies, P. M., Hunt, A. J., & Weatherburn, P. (1992). Maintenance of open gay relationships: Some strategies for protection against HIV. *AIDS Care, 4*, 409–419.

Hoff, C. C., Beougher, S. C., Chakravarty, D., Darbes, L. A., & Neilands, T. B. (2010). Relationship characteristics and motivations behind agreements among gay male couples: Differences by agreement type and couple serostatus. *AIDS Care, 22*, 827–835.

Israel, T., Ketz, K., Detrie, P. M. , Burke, M. C., & Shulman, J. L. (2003). Identifying counselor competencies for working with lesbian, gay, and bisexual clients. *Journal of Gay and Lesbian Psychotherapy, 7*(4), 3–22.

James, S. E., & Murphy, B. C. (1998). Gay and lesbian relationships in a changing social context. In C. J. Patterson & A. R. D'Augelli (Eds.), *Lesbian, gay, and bisexual identities in families: Psychological perspectives* (pp. 99–121). New York: Oxford University Press.

Kaiser Family Foundation (2001). Inside-OUT: A Report on the Experiences of Lesbians, Gays and Bisexuals in America and the Public's Views on Issues and Policies Related to Sexual Orientation (Kaiser Family Foundation Publication No. 3194). Retrieved from http://www.kff.org

Keita, G. P. (2010, October 28). *Letter to senators encouraging support for repeal of Don't Ask, Don't Tell.* Retrieved from http://www.apa.org/about/gr/issues/lgbt/dadt-support-letter.aspx

Kiritsy, L. (2004, October 14). From "Don't Ask, Don't Tell" to "I do." *Bay Windows, 22*(44), 1–17.

Kitzinger, C., & Coyle, A. (1995). Lesbian and gay couples: Speaking of difference. *The Psychologist, 8*(2), 64–69.

Klinger, R. L. (1996). Lesbian couples. In R. P. Cabaj & T. S. Stein (Eds.), *Textbook of homosexuality and mental health* (pp. 339–352). Washington, DC: American Psychiatric Press.

Krestan, J., & Bepko, C. (1980). The problem of fusion in the lesbian relationship. *Family Process, 19*, 277–289.

Kurdek, L. A. (1988). Relationship quality of gay and lesbian cohabiting couples. *Journal of Homosexuality, 15*, 93–118.

Kurdek, L. A. (1991). Sexuality in homosexual and heterosexual couples. In K. McKinney & S. Sprecher (Eds.), *Sexuality in close relationships* (pp. 177–191). Hillsdale, NJ: Erlbaum.

Kurdek, L. A. (1993). The allocation of household labor in gay, lesbian, and heterosexual married couples. *Journal of Social Issues, 49*, 127–139.

Kurdek, L. A. (1998). Relationship outcomes and their predictors: Longitudinal evidence from heterosexual married, gay cohabiting, and lesbian cohabiting couples. *Journal of Marriage and the Family, 60*, 553–568.

Kurdek, L. A. (2004). Are gay and lesbian cohabiting couples really different from heterosexual married couples? *Journal of Marriage and Family, 66*, 880–900.

Kurdek, L. A. (2005). What do we know about gay and lesbian couples? *Current Directions in Psychological Science, 14*, 251–254.

Kurdek, L. A. (2006). Differences between partners from heterosexual, gay, and lesbian cohabiting couples. *Journal of Marriage and the Family, 68*, 509–528.

Kurdek, L. A., & Schmitt, J. P. (1986). Relationship quality of partners in heterosexual married, heterosexual cohabiting, and gay and lesbian relationships. *Journal of Personality and Social Psychology, 51*, 711–720.

Kusian, J. (2007). An experimental look at gay male victims of intimate partner violence seeking formal services: A qualitative study. (Unpublished doctoral dissertation). Alliant International University, San Diego, CA.

Lannutti, P. J. (2005). For better or worse: Exploring the meanings of same-sex marriage within the lesbian, gay, bisexual and transgendered community. *Journal of Social and Personal Relationships, 22*, 5–18.

Lever, J. (1995, August 22). Lesbian sex survey. *The Advocate,* 22–30.
Lewis, R. J., Derlega, V. J., Berndt, A., Morris, L. M., & Rose, S. (2001). An empirical analysis of stressors for gay men and lesbians. *Journal of Homosexuality, 42*(1), 63–88.
Liddle, B. J. (1996). Therapist sexual orientation, gender, and counseling practices as they relate to ratings of helpfulness by gay and lesbian clients. *Journal of Counseling Psychology, 43,* 394–401.
MacDonald, B. J. (1998). Issues in therapy with gay and lesbian couples. *Journal of Sex and Marital Therapy, 24,* 165–190.
Mays, V. M., & Cochran, S. D. (2001). Mental health correlates of perceived discrimination among lesbian, gay, and bisexual adults in the United States. *American Journal of Public Health, 91,* 1869–1876.
Mays, V. M., Cochran, S. D., & Rhue, S. (1993). The impact of perceived discrimination on the intimate relationships of Black lesbians. *Journal of Homosexuality, 25*(4), 1–14.
McWhirter, D. P., & Mattison, A. M. (1984). *The male couple: How relationships develop.* Englewood Cliffs, NJ: Prentice-Hall.
McWhirter, D. P., & Mattison, A. M. (1996). Male couples. In R. P. Cabaj & T. S. Stein (Eds.), *Textbook of homosexuality and mental health* (pp. 339–352). Washington, DC: American Psychiatric Press.
Metz, M. E., Rosser, B. R. S., & Strapko, N. (1994). Differences in conflict-resolution styles among heterosexual, gay, and lesbian couples. *Journal of Sex Research, 31,* 293–308.
Meyer, I. H. (2003). Prejudice, social stress, and mental health in lesbian, gay, and bisexual populations: Conceptual issues and research evidence. *Psychological Bulletin, 129,* 674–697.
Meyer-Bahlburg, H. F. L., Exner, T. M., Lorenz, G., Gruen, R. S., Gorman, J. M., & Ehrhardt, A. A. (1991). Sexual risk behavior, sexual functioning, and HIV-disease progression in gay men. *The Journal of Sex Research, 28,* 3–27.
Modrcin, M. J., & Wyers, N. L. (1990). Lesbian and gay couples: Where they turn when help is needed. *Journal of Gay and Lesbian Psychotherapy, 1,* 89–104.
Nardi, P. M. (1999). *Gay men's friendships: Invincible communities.* Chicago: University of Chicago Press.
National Association of Social Workers. (2008). *Code of ethics of the National Association of Social Workers.* Retrieved from http://www.naswdc.org/pubs/code/code.asp
Nichols, M. (1995). Sexual desire disorder in a lesbian-feminist couple: The intersection of therapy and politics. In R. C. Rosen & S. R. Leiblum (Eds.), *Case studies in sex therapy* (pp. 161–175). New York: Guilford Press.
Ossana, S. M. (2000). Relationship and couples counseling. In R. M. Perez, K. A. DeBord, & K. J. Bieschke (Eds.), *Handbook of counseling and psychotherapy with lesbian, gay, and bisexual clients* (pp. 275–302). Washington, DC: American Psychological Association.
Oswald, R. F. (2002). Resilience within the family networks of lesbians and gay men: Intentionality and redefinition. *Journal of Marriage and Family, 64,* 374–383.
Otis, M. D., Rostosky, S. S., Riggle, E. D. B., & Hamrin, R. (2006). Stress and relationship quality in same-sex couples. *Journal of Social and Personal Relationships, 23,* 81–99.
Palmer, R., & Bor, R. (2007). The challenges to intimacy and sexual relationships for gay men in HIV serodiscordant relationships: A pilot study. *Journal of Marital and Family Therapy, 27,* 419–431.
Peplau, L. A. (1991). Lesbian and gay relationships. In J. C. Gonsiorek & J. D. Weinrich (Eds.), *Homosexuality: Research implications for public policy* (pp. 177–196). Thousand Oaks, CA: Sage.
Peplau, L. A. (1993). Lesbian and gay relationships. In L. D. Garnets & D. C. Kimmel (Eds.), *Psychological perspectives on lesbian and gay male experiences* (pp. 395–419). New York: Columbia University Press.
Peplau, L. A. (2001). Rethinking women's sexual orientation: An interdisciplinary, relationship-focused approach. *Personal Relationships, 8,* 1–19.

Peplau, L. A., & Cochran, S. D. (1981). Value orientations in the intimate relationships of gay men. *Journal of Homosexuality, 6*(3), 1–19.

Peplau, L. A., & Cochran, S. D. (1990). A relational perspective on homosexuality. In D. P. McWhirter, S. A. Sanders, & J. M. Reinisch (Eds.), *Homosexuality/heterosexuality: Concepts of sexual orientation* (pp. 321–349). New York: Oxford University Press.

Peplau, L. A., Cochran, S. D., & Mays, V. M. (1997). Psychological perspectives on lesbian and gay issues. In B. Greene (Ed.), *Ethnic and cultural diversity among lesbians and gay men* (pp. 11–38). Thousand Oaks, CA: Sage.

Peplau, L. A., & Garnets, L. D. (2000). A new paradigm for understanding women's sexuality and sexual orientation. *Journal of Social Issues, 56*, 329–350.

Peplau, L. A., & Spalding, L. R. (2000). The close relationships of lesbians, gay men, and bisexuals. In C. Hendrick & S. S. Hendrick (Eds.), *Close relationships: A sourcebook* (pp. 111–123). Thousand Oaks, CA: Sage.

Peplau, L. A., Veniegas, R. C., & Campbell, S. M. (1999). Gay and lesbian relationships. In J. P. Elia (Ed.), *Sex and relationships: An anthology* (pp. 145–168). Dubuque, IA: Kendall/Hunt.

Porter, M. (2007). Global evidence for a biopsychosocial understanding of refugee adaptation. *Transcultural Psychiatry, 44*, 418–439.

Porter, M. C. (2011). Psychosocial issues facing LGB military servicemembers: A continuing education training video. San Diego, CA: Alliant International University. Available from: http://www.ce-psychology.com/askingandtelling.html

Porter, M., & Haslam, N. (2005). Predisplacement and postdisplacement factors associated with mental health of refugees and internally displaced persons: A meta-analysis. *Journal of the American Medical Association, 294*, 602–612.

Potoczniak, M. J., Murot, J. E., Crosbie-Burnett, M., & Potoczniak, D. J. (2003). Legal and psychological perspectives on same-sex domestic violence: A multisystemic approach. *Journal of Family Psychology, 17*, 252–259.

Poulin, C., Gouliquer, L., & Moore, J. (2009). Discharged for homosexuality from the Canadian military: Health implications for lesbians. *Feminism and Psychology, 19*, 496–516.

Reilly, M. E., & Lynch, J. M. (1990). Power-sharing in lesbian partnerships. *Journal of Homosexuality, 19*(3), 1–30.

Renzetti, C. M. (1992). *Violent betrayal: Partner abuse in lesbian relationships.* Newbury Park, CA: Sage.

Rosenzweig, S. (1945). Emotional implications of military rejection and discharge. *Psychiatric Quarterly Supplement, 19*, 11–19.

Roth, S. (1985). Psychotherapy with lesbian couples: Individual issues, female socialization, and the social context. *Journal of Marital and Family Therapy, 11*, 273–286.

Rutter, V., & Schwartz, P. (1996). Same-sex couples: Courtship, commitment, context. In A. E. Auhagen & M. von Salisch (Eds.), *The diversity of human relationships* (pp. 197–226). Cambridge, UK: Cambridge University Press.

Sammons, M. (2010, April). The complexities of coming out decisions in the military. In M. C. Porter (Chair), *Asking and telling: Toward a critical psychology of Don't Ask Don't Tell.* Symposium conducted at the California School of Professional Psychology, Alliant International University, San Diego, CA.

Schilit, R., Lie, G., & Montagne, M. (1990). Substance abuse as a correlate of violence in intimate lesbian relationships. *Journal of Homosexuality, 19*, 51–65.

Sherman, M. D., Zanotti, D. K., & Jones, D. E. (2005). Key elements in couples therapy with veterans with combat-related posttraumatic stress disorder. *Professional Psychology: Research and Practice, 36*(6), 626–633.

Simon, G. (1996). Working with people in relationships. In D. Davies & C. Neal (Eds.), *Pink therapy: A guide for counsellors and therapists working with lesbian, gay and bisexual clients* (pp. 101–115). Buckingham, UK: Open University Press.

Smith, R. (2010, April). Personal history. In M. C. Porter (Chair), *Asking and telling: Toward a critical psychology of Don't Ask Don't Tell*. Symposium conducted at the California School of Professional Psychology, Alliant International University, San Diego, CA.
Sohn, J. (2010, April). Personal history. In M. C. Porter (Chair), *Asking and telling: Toward a critical psychology of Don't Ask Don't Tell*. Symposium conducted at the California School of Professional Psychology, Alliant International University, San Diego, CA.
Solomon, S. E., Rothblum, E. D., & Balsam, K. F. (2004). Pioneers in partnership: Lesbian and gay male couples in civil unions compared with those not in civil unions and married heterosexual siblings. *Journal of Family Psychology, 18*, 275–286.
Spitalnick, J. S., & McNair, L. D. (2005). Couples therapy with gay and lesbian clients: An analysis of important clinical issues. *Journal of Sex and Marital Therapy, 31*, 43–56.
Spitzer, R. L. (1973). *Homosexuality and civil rights* [Position statement]. Retrieved from http://www.psych.org/Departments/EDU/Library/APAOfficialDocumentsandRelated/PositionStatements/197310.aspx
Testa, R. J., Kinder, B. N., & Ironson, G. (1987). Heterosexual bias in the perception of loving relationships of gay males and lesbians. *Journal of Sex Research, 23*, 163–172.
Tindall, B., Forde, S., Goldstein, D., Ross, M. W., & Cooper, D. A. (1994). Sexual dysfunction in advanced HIV disease. *AIDS Care, 6*, 105–107.
Todosijevic, J., Rothblum, E. D., & Solomon, S. E. (2005). Relationship satisfaction, affectivity, and gay-specific stressors in same-sex couples joined in civil unions. *Psychology of Women Quarterly, 29*, 158–166.
Weeks, J., Heaphy, B., & Donovan, C. (2001). *Same-sex intimacies: Families of choice and other life experiments*. London: Routledge.
Weinstock, J. S. (2004). Lesbian FLEX-ibility: Friend and/or family connections among lesbian ex-lovers. In J. S. Weinstock & E. D. Rothblum (Eds.), *Lesbian ex-lovers: The really long-term relationships* (pp. 193–238). Binghamton, NY: The Haworth Press.

17

Cultural Differences

REBECCA TEWS-KOZLOWSKI and DESIREÉ KING

SCOPE OF THE MULTICULTURAL FAMILY PERSPECTIVE

Over 15 years of working in training clinicians on cultural awareness and intercultural psychology has reinforced the idea that speaking in culturally specific terms only ratifies stereotypes and propagates misinformation. Time and again students in these classes respond that they are different from the cultural statements being made about them. They express their own unique cultural perspectives and feel deeply offended when generalities are made about them based on one or two cultural factors. Time in the field has shown that the most functional approach is to view culture as multidimensional and to treat each client or couple as culturally unique. The training process then is broken into several key parts. First, basic training in the dimensions of culture and an overview of how the cultural differences play out with specific populations forms a framework for further study. Second, strategies for understanding the therapist's own cultural dynamics and how they contribute to the therapeutic process in a session and expand the quality of care. Finally, specific application to the military population takes this specific knowledge into practice.

EVERY FAMILY IS MULTICULTURAL

To begin, a discussion of culturally sensitive couples therapy with Ivey, Simek-Morgan, and Ivey's (1993) "multicultural or respectful cube" (Figure 17.1) is an essential reminder to step out of preconceived notions about who differs from whom and to embrace an understanding of each individual as unique and distinct from every other in a respectful and culturally insightful manner. It reminds each therapist to address their own personal cultural position and biases as well.

The cube itself reflects a multidimensional approach that is comprised of individual levels of development ranging from naïveté to multiperspective integration;

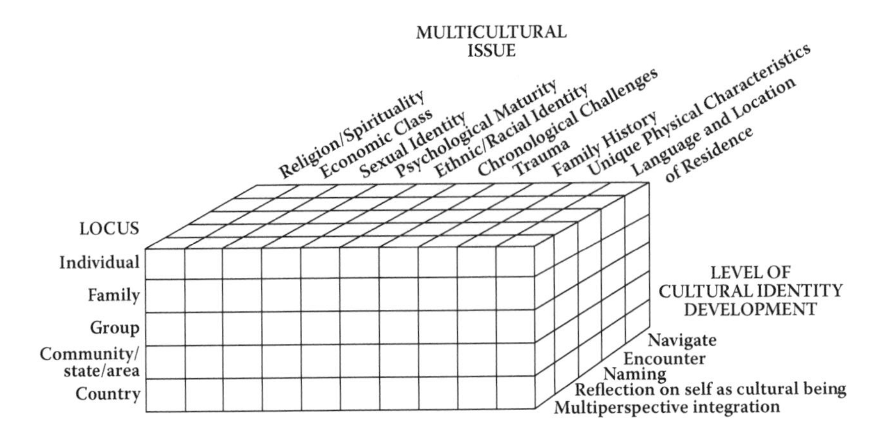

Figure 17.1 The respectful cube. (From Ivey, A., Simek-Morgen, L., & Ivey, M. B. *Counseling and psychotherapy: A multicultural perspective.* New York: Allyn & Bacon, 1993.)

locus-level development (individual, family, group, community/state/area, and country); and then dimensions of cultural difference. These dimensions include religion/spirituality, economic class, sexual identity, psychological maturity, ethnic/racial identity, chronological challenges, trauma, family history, unique physical characteristics, language, and location of residence (Ivey et al., 1993).

The importance of this model as a philosophical underpinning to working with couples is that it allows the treatment provider to view every couple as a multicultural couple. This respects the reality that no two individuals share exactly the same cultural experience. More important, it reflects awareness that individuals who choose to partner with our service members are already nontraditional when compared with their culture of origin and respects that these unique couples often break traditional molds even as they are still influenced by their cultures of origin. This stance begins the therapeutic relationship from a perspective of mutual respect and discovery and sets the tone for a knowledgeable collaboration of discovering what will work for these individuals rather than applying a one-dimensional, one-cultural-explanation-fits-all approach to the process. From the end-users' perspective, this is a highly desirable alternative to what is often perceived as a rigid, authoritarian interaction within the therapy setting.

MORE THAN JUST ETHNICITY OR PLACE OF BIRTH

The impact of remembering that culturally sensitive therapy is about much more than ethnicity and place of birth is that the sessions themselves model the type of communication, active listening, and dynamic acceptance of individual difference associated with both therapeutic change and client/patient satisfaction (Berg, 1994).

As experts on themselves, clients are often keenly aware of their sense of being accepted and understood or misinterpreted in the early sessions of therapy. This applies no less in couples work and indeed is often more pronounced if both members of the couple feel misunderstood or if there is a perception that the therapist is relating more strongly to one member of the couple rather than maintaining an equal stance with both members of the couple.

It also allows the couple to understand that the therapist is a person in his or her own cultural context and frees them from the perspective that they must have a cultural match to be understood. This awareness stems from open exploration of culture-based factors beginning from the initial intake session.

STEREOTYPE-FREE RELATIONSHIPS

The essential component of stereotype-free relationships is that global attributions of cultural experience or explanations of behavior based on perceived group norms is debunked in the worldview of the treatment provider and in the provision of supervision to those care providers. It involves a multitier commitment to cultural awareness, bias-free language, and adoption of an openness to the process of the unique cultural experience of each individual along with knowledge of culturally relevant information and how to apply it within clinical processes (Sue, Arrendondo, & McDavis, 1992; Sue, 1998).

DIFFERENCE IN PERSPECTIVE

Often, the difference in perspective comes to rest on taking the time to learn about cultural variants, to listen to the specific stories of the clients, and to ask the questions about how the cultural experience has had an impact on the current situation rather than making an assumption that it has or has not attributed a specific level of impact based on broad generalities. There is great disparity in viewpoints regarding emphasis on culturally specific interventions. Many of these approaches are too specific to the group in which they are developed and do not generalize to the broad array of individual differences within cultural groups. Sue (1998) suggested that it can be a helpful approach for those struggling with acculturation issues. In practical application, however, it is a broader, more open mind-set that seems most associated with favorable outcome across clinical populations (Sue, Zane, Hall, & Berger, 2009).

EFFECTS ON HOW BEHAVIOR IS INTERPRETED

This mind-set creates a mental filter through which the therapist interprets behavior of others. This is not merely aimed at the clients, but it is in fact infused into interpretation of all behavior. These assumptions often become buried and in that state create unspoken and often-unrecognized differences in the meaning attributed to specific behaviors. This can affect the nonverbal communication flowing between therapists and couples and alters the way in which the verbal information exchanged is interpreted (Hays, Prosek, & McLeod, 2010).

While it should go without saying that subconsciously obscured assumptions have an impact on the belief systems of clinicians with all levels of experience, it is often overlooked as a clinical issue for experienced care providers. It is essential, however, that the issues be revisited on a regular basis through individual and group consultation, self-journaling, workshops, and continuing education opportunities.

Therapists who allow the interpretation and meaning of behavior to be coconstructed by therapists and couples rather than assigned by the therapist are afforded the opportunity to gain deeper insight into the personal experience of the individuals involved. The payoff is that coconstruction leads to couples identifying therapists as having understood them, having a sense of being supported, and feeling that therapy was worth the effort. In contrast, assignment of meaning feels top down, dismissive, and negative. Rather than feeling understood, the clients often report feeling patronized, unsupported, judged, and hopeless about the resources available to them. This often ratifies the overall sense of despondency and hopelessness that the couple may be experiencing in relation to their experience of military culture and to their personal intimate culture-specific differences that may be affecting outcome (personal communications with veteran caregivers, 2010–2011).

CULTURAL BELIEFS AND EXPECTATIONS ABOUT MARRIAGE AND FAMILY LIFE

Generally, within the military community there is a wide range of attitudes toward gender and marital roles (Mittelstadt, 2010). These represent the range of attitudes in the broader population. To work effectively with military couples, an assessment of traditional versus nontraditional attitudes is essential. Often, the expectations of more traditional gender roles are challenged by frequent deployment or injury. This can be challenging enough for couples sharing the same socioethnic background. In multicultural couple pairs, these issues may be complicated by very traditional expectations arising from cultural values. These traditional values may involve themes of male leadership, female acquiescence, and gender-specific household responsibilities, including male as breadwinner/female as caregiver, among other expectations. In fact, these traditions may have originally been part of the couple's core value and the foundation of the attraction. If this is the case, the frequent deployment cycle and lengthy periods of relative isolation and disconnect from the partner can create even greater tension and disruption in the bonding process. Many women from cultures in which married females are expected to be dependent and subservient to their male family members may struggle heavily with developing the skills and mind-set needed for independent living while their partners are away. Further, once they attain more skills in independence it can be doubly hard for them to return to the position of deferring to their partners. For the partners, it can be hard to see a quality that was once a preferred value disappear.

Women especially may also struggle with negative feedback from immediate and extended family members with regard to their interpretation of the spouse's postdeployment and transitional behavior. This can also exacerbate struggles in coping with more serious challenges related to injury and disability, particularly personality changes due to posttraumatic stress disorder (PTSD) and mild-moderate traumatic brain injury (TBI) (Aranda & Knight, 1997; Landau & Hissett, 2008; Montgomery & Kosloski, 2009).

In rocking the couples' value system to the core, the military lifestyle may become the final destabilizing factor whereas once it was a mark of honor and excitement. In other words, the challenge to the value system, combined with the lengthy deployment commitments and concomitant residual effects, may have an extremely profound impact on the mental health of family members, interpretation of behavior, and relationships with extended family members, which may ultimately change the perceptions of the spouse.

ATTACHMENT AND LOSS

Time and again in clinical practice with military couples, there is observed a profound sense of loss that must be addressed at some level within the sessions. Often, a palpable sense of grief surrounds the couple as they tell their story and explore their current challenges and reactions. This grief may initially present as aggression or anger, and initial entry to therapy may be related to increasingly negative domestic interactions.

In fact, most anger-driven interaction has grief and perceived threat of loss at its core (Rosenberg, 2003). Zeroing in on the grief factors can often diffuse the situation sufficiently to allow the therapist to focus on the experiences that can be dealt with effectively in the here and now.

Addressing the disappointments, loss of cultural identity, loss of cherished roles, loss of innocence, loss of sense of coupleness, loss of intimacy, loss of trust, and lack of understanding about how to define themselves in the present can best be managed through acknowledgment of what has changed, normalizing, reframing loss into active statements, redefining the new cultural experience that is evolving, and restoring hope (Aranda & Knight, 1997; Ward & Wampler, 2010).

STRESSORS OF CULTURALLY DIVERSE COUPLES

Value/Belief Systems

Deployment/Postdeployment The attribution of meaning to deployment is remarkably affected by cultural factors related to gender roles and family connections. Amazingly, despite clear indicators in most marriages that one or more of the partners is a deployable troop, there still tends to be a cycle of reactive coping that affects the overall health of the couple/family and the specific health of the troop. In an ideal world, premarital counseling or orientation regarding what to expect would occur. Generally, while some bases have such options available, they are relatively rare and not compulsory. Few couples report ever having had such orientation, although there is a consistent predeployment briefing now available for those living on or contiguous to a base. Guard and Reserve troops are particularly vulnerable because they usually have no nearby base affiliation, and often they are isolated while going through the deployment cycle. Those who are partnered but not legally married also express significant challenges in being prepared for the rigors of deployment.

In the absence of a cultural interpretation presented by the base or unit, couples will automatically revert to their own patterns and interpretations. Commonly, when working with couples it is clear that issues of multigenerational loss and abandonment are triggered by the extended absence and limited contact of the couple. The spouse remaining at home may indeed struggle intensively with trying to manage the home front alone, and culturally based themes of the roles of male/female and the meaning of marriage will persist at the forefront. With peer support from other unit families, this can be mitigated; however, if this does not exist, individuals may reach out to extended families that neither understand nor normalize the deployment cycle experience. This results in intrusion of additional issues related to the roles of men/women and function of marriage that may include the unseen cultural input of people quite removed from the military experience.

Depending on cultural interpretation of this isolation in the relationship, many people become vulnerable to pathologizing "escapist" thinking. Common thoughts here are, "I deserve better than this"; "This relationship is not what a healthy relationship should be"; "My partner doesn't care enough about me to make this stop, so I should take care of myself and do what takes care of me"; "My partner is probably being unfaithful in the absence, so I should be, too"; "This sucks, and it's his [her] fault, so I can do ______________"; "If I do ______________, he [she] will see how upset I am"; or "If I do ________________, he [she] will see how much they needed me and what a big mistake they made."

This type of thinking can be viewed as a precursor to infidelity, negative guilt-based communications to the partner, and even parasuicidal and suicidal behavior. It appears to be culturally constructed in the larger sense of culture comprised of generational, ethnic, gender, religious, and community values and interpretations. It is helpful for the treating therapist to explore for these very common issues in a sensitive and supportive manner to preempt the latent anger and grief issues. When couples can address these cognitions openly and with therapeutic support that destigmatizes such thoughts and offers an interpretation of how these thoughts can be redirected to more useful, couple-supportive cognitions, it becomes a foundation for moving forward with a relationship-stabilizing program. Teaching the couple to understand that these ideas arise from their cultural traditions and how to forge a new, healthier culture that works for them is the critical intervention point.

Reality versus Unspoken Expectations An important note here is to address the meaning that the couple has attributed to the change in thinking. Some couples are observed to view this change in perception of themselves, their partner, and their relationship as an irretrievable breakdown in the quality of the relationship. In the words of one young soldier, "She looks at me differently now. The love, the trust, the unconditional happiness that was in her eyes when she used to look at me is gone. I feel like she is always judging, scared, wondering what is next and how bad I am gonna f*** up." He attributed that this meant his wife of 2 years would soon leave him. He had seen this look in his mother's eyes before she left his many stepfathers, he had seen this look in the eyes of former fiancées, and he was convinced that this relationship would be no different. From the spouse's perspective, that attitude was making things worse and was actually triggering the "escapist" thinking: "If he thinks like that, maybe I should go." In addition, her nonmilitary extended family support system was sending messages that his statements and behavior were controlling and abusive. He wanted her not to leave and to just be happy with him again. She wanted him to stop thinking the worst of her. Both of them were actively triggering each other's abandonment fears, which were generationally transmitted. The attributions of culturally and experientially based meaning, deeply internalized, were affecting the way this couple was interpreting and responding to the stressors around them. Each new challenge continued to be experienced as the "straw that broke the camel's back" rather than the next challenge to be solved together.

In working from a cultural perspective, it became possible for them to understand their hidden beliefs, the language of relationships that had been generationally transmitted, and to identify that even their previous experiences could not relate exactly to this unique situation; while that information was valuable, it did not serve to generalize into this situation. Although intermittently conflictual through serious new challenges, the relationship of the young soldier and his wife held up through deployments, hospitalizations, brain injury, and complete incapacitation on his part. Now, 10 years later, they report continuing to use this type of reframing strategy to understand their issues and to create safety within their marriage. At this point, they recently conveyed a sense that they have been creating their own culture and looking actively at what thoughts help them to do this and what relationships among family, friends, and community members best help them to do this. In other words, in becoming aware of how their cultural experience contributed to their shared meaning, they were able to develop a shared culture that freed them from roles that were not helping them meet their primary goal of remaining together. The therapist's understanding of how cultural dynamics had an impact on their growing together allowed them to reflect in a safe, supported space rather than feeling judged, blamed, or pathologized. The therapist's awareness of their own cultural space ensured that there was a suspension of cultural intrusion that ultimately fostered a sense that it was okay to develop their own unique sense of who they were and who they wanted to become.

ROLE OF EXTENDED FAMILY: APPLYING UNIQUE FAMILY CONTRIBUTIONS TO THE RELATIONSHIP

While there are many different cultural perspectives that can be analyzed, speaking in generalizations by cultural designator may be less useful than thinking about the extended family response as a cultural variant that occurs within many different ethnic groups. Arising from clinical observation, these fall into the following categories, and in some cases the attitudes can co-occur in various combinations (Tews review of clinical notes 2002–2011): stay and suffer the consequences alone, negative interpretation, overly solicitous of troop or injured/dismissive of caregiver, isolationism, collaborative collective, there if you need us, and extended family comes to the rescue.

Stay and Suffer the Consequences Alone

This family response is to withdraw support from the couple unless or until they remove themselves from the military; the couple will stay and suffer the consequences alone. Often, there is a tacit message that the marriage/partnership was a mistake for this couple, and that any difficulties they are experiencing are a result of that bad decision making. Frequently associated with stoic cultural traditions, the clear message is that if the couple chooses to stay together, any suffering they endure is their responsibility and their choice. The result is that the couple experiences increasing isolation, and one or both members feel pressured to leave the relationship to receive the reward of renewed family support and approval.

Negative Interpretation

In the family response of negative interpretation, the actions of one or both partners are viewed through a negative attribution filter. Parents, siblings, and extended family members may send the message that the partner is no good or act deliberately with intent to harm the relationship or the other individual. This may include real or imagined threats. These families may actively promote a revenge and retaliation model of interaction that has the effect of escalating the negative interaction between the partners.

Overly Solicitous of Troop or Injured/Dismissive of Caregiver

Families operating from the perspective of being overly solicitous if the troop or injured or dismissive of a caregiver tend to have been supportive of the military member at the beginning. The emphasis on the primary identification of the worth of the individual because of military service is then extended to an overwhelming and overly solicitous focus on the experience of the injured, with clear and definitive dismissiveness toward the spouse or partner, who is expected to derive his or her identity from being the partner of the troop or veteran. In many cases, this leads to a deep-seated feeling of isolation, loneliness, and internal conflict in the spouse or partner in the caregiver role. This caregiver role may exist prior to deployment, during deployment, or postdeployment and may not necessarily involve disability-related caregiving. For couples at risk for this model, the nonmilitary spouse or partner is encouraged to focus solely on his or her role as spouse or partner without developing personal or professional roles outside the relationship.

Isolationism

Often, isolationism is an intergenerational pattern in which the family sends the message that marrying or partnering means moving away from families of origin and into independent function with the couple responsible for their own experiences and not seeking support from the extended family or expecting the family to function as supports in time of crisis. There is no attempt made to coerce a change. Nevertheless, any expressed needs for support or attempts to engage the extended family in responding to crisis or distress are met with refusal to acknowledge, ridicule, judgments, or nonresponse. The focus here is that adults are independent, and family support is for children under 18. This model can lead to a strong sense of hopelessness and frustration and may be a risk factor for suicidal thinking and behavior.

Collaborative Collective

The collaborative collective is a more responsive model of family interaction. These families can often appear enmeshed to outsiders because there is a strong sense of not making a move without guidance from elders or more senior members of the extended family. With cultural awareness and insight, significant strengths can be observed in this type of family response. Individuals will experience strong support for crises, adapting to adverse circumstances and a sense that there is a safety net beneath them that will provide support during high-stress periods. The primary drawback in this model is that if a partner is perceived to be acting in a manner that threatens the collective good of the family group, the partner may have an intense out-of-group experience that shuns them into compliance or forces them to significantly alter behavior to experience restoration. It can at times be difficult to make decisions that violate the group norms; however, this family type does support couples in crisis more effectively than the previously discussed models.

There If You Need Us

Families that are "there if you need us" are perhaps aligned most closely with the ideal of resilient families with warmth, empathy, and healthy boundaries. This extended family group neither dictates course nor attempts to control members. The group aligns around needs, crises, and challenges in a supportive manner and extends the right level of support to meet the current need. Support is extended when requested and fades out as problems are solved. There is tacit belief in the couple's ability to resolve and move through experiences of life and an understanding that with appropriate support this process of resolution is made more efficient.

Extended Family Comes to the Rescue

Facilitating the couple's understanding of the culture of their extended family and how those voices influence their daily experience of their current relationship is a powerful tool in working with culturally diverse couples. When the extended family comes to the rescue, through the mirror of parents, siblings, and beliefs about family roles, functions, and support in time of crisis, couples can become more adept at focusing on what they are actually feeling, thinking, and believing about their relationship. Helping them to filter through the distortions and shadows they are experiencing allows them to refine the true nature and qualities of the relationship. This is a helpful adjunct in guiding a couple in identifying authentic goals and needs, which can then be addressed in the therapy process. While this is likely useful for every couple, it is an essential component when working with couples of differing ethnicity and national origin (McGoldrick, Gersen, & Shellenberger, 1999).

COMMUNICATION EXPERIENCE

Closely related to family of origin in the cultural context is the manner in which we communicate our experiences, feelings, needs, wants, and observations. Not only is this culturally unique within each family group, but also it varies by language spoken, ethnic group, and region.

Primary Language/Language Differences

Among couples with differences in native language it is useful to explore how the language differences have an impact on the way they think about a problem, infer meaning, and understand the nuances of their nonnative language. Misunderstandings can and do exist if choice of speech, fluency of response, and depth of emotional content are affected by the experience of being a nonnative speaker. In many military couples of differing nationalities, this can be a significant issue that affects not only conceptualization of the challenges being faced but also the interpreted meaning of the words chosen by the significant other.

Exploring complex feelings when language barriers exist may require extra time and attention. It is helpful to ascertain in what languages the individuals think and how the subtle differences in their translation skills have an impact on their understanding of each other. Taking time, for example, to listen to Latinos storytelling answers to questions may reveal better insight than attempting a traditional interview (Comas-Diaz, 2006). Linear, cognitive-behavioral-style questioning may need to be modified to a more emotion-focused style to facilitate progress among Hispanic and lower-income African American women (Miranda, 2003a, 2003b; Sue et al., 2009). The following case illustrates the point:

Case Vignette – Maria and Jose

Maria and Jose were both native Spanish-speaking individuals. Jose, an American citizen, had been in the Army for 10 years and spoke fluent English, thought in English, and was fully bilingual. His family originated in Mexico, and he had often visited there but was born and raised in Texas. He met Maria in Spain while visiting her family's hotel during an extended leave. United by the ability to speak two languages in common and obvious physical attraction, they married quickly, and Maria was soon relocated halfway around the world. Within a year, she found herself expecting a child, and shortly after his birth, she was single parenting as her husband was deployed repeatedly, often for a year with limited leave and with just 6 months between deployments. As the deployment cycles went on, the phone bill for calls to Spain got larger and larger, often creating financial distress. Maria's family, unable to afford travel to America, began to encourage her to return home to Spain and bring her child with her. Despite a shared language of Spanish, there were vast differences in the way that Jose and Maria expressed their feelings. Jose had very strong machismo notions about the role of women and expectations that Maria be keeping his home and child in his absence and doing so in America. He had great difficulty acknowledging Maria's differing viewpoints and felt threatened. Maria felt "like a fish in the wrong pond." She longed for home and family and was increasingly concerned about the way her son was developing in military base public schools. Her family was somewhat supportive of Jose's military commitments but also felt that he should have been more up front with Maria about his extended absences. Jose tried to explain that they were out of his control. The miscommunication and continued lack of understanding about military culture and the cumulative impact of absence created irreconcilable differences. Maria returned to Spain and refused to return to America. Jose exited the service at the first possible opportunity and spent some time in Spain attempting to restore the relationship but ultimately lost his marriage and custody of his son.

Culturally aware therapy during the initial period of distress and miscommunication or even at the intermediate stages might have educated the couple about how to manage their expectations versus the reality of their experience and to break through communication misfires that contributed to their distress.

UNEXPECTED OUTCOMES

PTSD/Mild-Moderate TBI: Caregiving in Multicultural Families

With over 1.64 million troops deploying to Afghanistan and Iraq since October 2001, Operation Enduring Freedom (OEF) and Operation Iraqi Freedom (OIF), respectively, have brought to light many significant issues that have been plaguing our veterans and military personnel for several years. The current war is most often described by a few novel features. There has been a change in military operations that has generally not existed in previous wars. Troops are experiencing more frequent and lengthier deployments with shorter rest periods between deployments. Service members who are wounded in combat have an increased likelihood of surviving these wounds than their counterparts in previous conflicts. The final novel aspect about this war is TBI, which is primarily caused by blasts sustained by deployed troops (Tanielian & Jaycox, 2008).

Invisible injuries such as TBI and PTSD have become signature wounds of service members who have served on either of these battlefield locations. During the first year of these conflicts, the Department of Defense (DOD) reported that there were 11,830 incidents of TBI (Defense and Veteran Brain Injury Center, 2010). These numbers more than doubled as of the third quarter of 2010, with reports being at nearly 24,000 for newly diagnosed TBIs (Defense and Veterans Brain Injury Center, 2010). TBI can be a result of some of the most common stressors associated with the current conflict, which include roadside bombs, improvised explosive devices (IEDs), and suicide bombers. In addition, a high percentage of service members have reported traumatic events such as being fired on, handling of dead personnel, or knowing someone who died or was seriously injured by an enemy combatant as part of service (Hoge et al., 2004). These experiences have the ability to increase a service member's likelihood of being diagnosed with PTSD. The National Center for PTSD (2010) estimated that PTSD occurs in 11–20% of OIF/OEF veterans, in 10% of Desert Storm veterans, and in 30% of Vietnam veterans.

One study indicated that more than a third of individuals with lifetime PTSD are unable to recover even after many years (Kessler, Sonnega, Bromet, Hughes, & Nelson, 1995). Many of these service members are going to require long-term care as a result of their injury, leading to an increase in the number of caregivers.

As a result of many service members receiving invisible war wounds, many spouses of young service members are thrust into the role of caregiver. Studies have shown that younger caregivers tend to experience a greater amount of burden when caring for another individual than does the older caregiver (Hughes, Giobbie-Hurder, Weaver, Kubal, & Henderson, 1999). Subsequently, when a partner is diagnosed at a young age, women may be caring for the individual in addition to having to care for any children the couple may have (MacKinnon, 2009). These issues may be considered significant in light of the fact that the majority of U.S. Armed forces are under the age of 40, and the majority are married or partnered (Obama, 2011). With younger individuals, predominantly young women, being placed in the role as primary caregiver, many of them may become isolated. These women are more often than not stationed far away from other family members and may not have the necessary support they need around them during the deployment cycle, and as they transition out of active duty this may be exacerbated.

Functioning as an individual caregiver may also be a time of great stress and difficulty for these women (MacKinnon, 2009). With the majority of primary caregivers being the spouses (Allen, Goldscheider, & Ciambrone, 1999) of wounded active duty service members and veterans, it is important to take into account cultural differences that may exist. Again with an understanding that specific cultural norms do not represent the gamut of individual experiences, a review of research on cultural pressures among caregivers of different nationalities does provide some helpful foundational information that adds dimension to the discussions of family impact, expectations, and communication styles.

Japanese individuals, especially females, may feel a tremendous amount of pressure to take care of their family members (Arai & Washio, 1999). Prior to World War II, the role of caring for the eldest son's parents was traditionally the responsibility of the daughter-in-law in Japan (Arai & Washio, 1999). Many Japanese do not report caregiving as a burden because they believe it would not be virtuous to do so; however, a study conducted by Arai and Washio (1999) in southern Japan using the Zarat Burden Interview indicates that some burden is felt by caregivers in Japan, particularly when it is correlated to behavioral disturbances. In addition to this finding, Japanese individuals who cared for someone with partially limited activities of daily living (ADL) appeared to experience a stronger caregiver burden than those who cared for someone who was completely dependent in ADL. This may be a result of the positive value that the Japanese place on interpersonal dependency, which may make caregiving more expected and less of a hardship for them (Arai & Washio, 1999).

Many similarities exist between the Japanese and Chinese in terms of obligation to care for elders in families. However, differences in the strength of this obligation seem to differ depending on which generation is being questioned. The younger generation seems to believe that having community support to care for older family members is acceptable (Cooney & Di, 1999). Those with less education and living in rural areas appear to be more traditional and are less burdened by their elder obligations, whereas those with higher education seem to express more burden, greater negative impact, and a need for more formal service supports (Cooney & Di, 1999).

Cultural differences in caregiving may also exist among minority spouses of service members within the United States. African Americans may rely on informal support more than the White population. This may be related to the fact that African Americans rely more heavily on extended family and fictive kin for support and assistance (Sue & Sue, 2008). Because there is extended family support, African Americans appear better able to cope with adverse life situations as a result of their value of interdependence. In addition, many African Americans hold strong beliefs that relatives, especially elderly ones, should be cared for by family members and therefore contribute considerable amounts of informal care to a family member in need (Bullock, Crawford, & Tennstedt, 2003). When addressing potential caregiver burden in this population, it is important to understand that African American adults tend to underuse medical care services and more often experience barriers to formal services because of an inability to afford or access such services (Bullock et al., 2003). In addition, when formal care services are used, some African Americans have reported dissatisfaction with them (Bullock et al., 2003). This may be due to the lack of trust that African Americans have in medical doctors (MacKinnon, 2009). The fact that African Americans feel cultural and social rewards from caregiving, such as a sense of belonging, self-worth, dignity, and companionship, may be a resiliency factor in coping with the burdens that are often associated with being a caretaker. African American caregivers were more likely to report discussing difficulties they were having with the care recipient with a clergy member. The use of prayer, faith, or religion was identified as an important way in which they care for their relative (Connell & Gibson, 1997). African American caregivers reported that their biggest difficulty in providing care was not having some sort of temporary relief from the demands of being a caregiver (Connell & Gibson, 1997). This may be particularly exacerbated in the military community, in which respite care resources are not yet fully developed.

Hispanic service members make up an estimated 9.5% of the DOD according to the Pew Hispanic Center (2003). Problems experienced by caregivers in this population may vary greatly from those of the Caucasian caregivers. Similar to that of the African American population, many individuals identifying as Hispanic reported strong filial bonds and felt it was their obligation to care for their family member without complaint. Gallagher-Thompson, Arean, Rivera, and Thompson (2001) have shown that Hispanic females who are also caregivers are at greater risk of experiencing depression. Depression levels may be higher in this population due to the greater amounts of stress that exist because of the lack of access to professional and community services, leading to delays in help seeking until a crisis arises and management is no longer possible at home (Gallagher-Thompson et al., 2001). Seeking assistance in time of acute need—as a last resort—may occur because there are underlying cultural perceptions that health care professionals have the tendency to shame and blame caregivers for not fully utilizing services (MacKinnon, 2009).

Gallagher-Thompson et al. (2001) have shown that active attendance and completion of psychoeducational classes relating to a family member's disease/disorder are better able to reduce depression, anger, and the level of caregiver burden reported by Hispanic caregivers.

Culturally sensitive interventions and support for caregivers of veterans and service members is imperative (Aranda & Knight, 1997). Education increases the caregiver's knowledge about what to expect as the disease or disorder progresses or recovery is made. Supportive therapists may want to ensure that they assist these caregivers in accessing training and informational materials in their native languages to ensure the highest level of support and understanding. Finally, this educational empowerment boosts the self-confidence of the caregiver and provides a foundation for resilience by supporting their self-defining cultural process and supporting the human experience of this unique journey.

Grieving Ambiguous Loss

Ambiguous loss as a concept has received relatively limited attention among military populations and has been more thoroughly addressed in health psychology research focusing on coping with long-term or chronic illness. Research in this area is informative about how couples cope with changing roles and life-altering and traumatic experiences and how social and familial support or lack of support alters the couple's developmental process (Landau & Hissett, 2008). The research suggested that clinicians should be looking more closely at these issues in working with couples struggling with life-changing experiences because they can have an impact on hope for the future, which plays a prominent role in therapy outcome with couples (Ward & Wampler, 2010).

While nearly half of couples dealing with TBI will separate or divorce, addressing the loss of self and loss of coupleness while reframing a "new normal" may be a way to tap into cultural differences positively to avoid relationship destabilization (Landau & Hissett, 2008)

Hidden trauma and distress may result from coping with the physical injuries and recuperation of a partner. Little research exists on how the physical injury and afteraffects are physically experienced by partners, but anecdotally in speaking with partners of injured military the same story is heard repeatedly about shared experiences of empathic pain and trauma. A frequent observation is the inclusion of trauma themes in dreams and a heightened sense of hypervigilance in couples managing posttraumatic stress. For most couples, finding a means of self-expression of these experiences helps to relieve the pressure and allows the couple to integrate the experiences into their new cultural reality. Without guidance in finding appropriate self-expression, the experiences can be highly pathologized, mysticized, or repressed. With guidance, they can be highly useful in building a stronger bond between the partners, and it is most likely a natural attempt to do so and a useful coping mechanism within the relationship. It is likely misunderstood because the couple has no frame of reference for the experience due to the unique situation in which they find themselves and the lack of exposure to others going through the same process (LeFebvre, Cloutier, & Levert, 2008). Group participation with some of the national wounded warrior support programs demonstrates the efficacy of a reinterpretation and empowerment model, although formal outcome data are still in process.

Deployment Experiences as a Factor in Cultural Awareness

The impact of facing challenging cultural experiences should not be overlooked in working with military couples. Obviously, spending extensive time in another culture changes one's worldview in general. Spending that time under great stress and constant threat alters those perceptions in ways that noncombat personnel and family find hard to truly understand. Allowing room for the expression of these experiences and opportunities to normalize and share the experience within safe boundaries is helpful to spouses and caregivers attempting to support the service member. It can also be helpful for the service member as well because it begins the process of destigmatizing the experience and integrating it into a sense of broad life experience. In effect, this may be useful for the service member to be able to start to rebalance his or her experiences and begin the process of evolving into a healthier new normal. Partners and family members will need help in understanding how the cultural experiences are now a part of their loved one's range of experiences, what will best support the unique experiences their troop encountered, and how best to safely and positively express these insights to other family members. Research in this area is still ongoing, and the observations about what works best are obviously still an ongoing understanding. In speaking with veterans, caregivers and family members of warriors, it is clear that the topic needs discussion early in the return from the deployment process, and that it will need to be addressed as both a behavioral and a cultural issue on an ongoing basis as memories and challenges arise.

HOW PEOPLE GROW TOGETHER

Bloom's Taxonomy of Change

Bloom's taxonomy of change (Granello, 2000) applied to the process of incorporating multicultural sensitivity into the therapeutic interaction provides a simple structure that incorporates well into a variety of treatment modalities and environments. The model itself contains six overlapping focal points that are often conceptualized as providing a feedback loop: knowledge, comprehension, application, analysis, synthesis and evaluation. This model partners extremely well with evidence-based intervention and quality assurance models.

Here, the knowledge construct corresponds to development of the awareness of differences among groups and a basic understanding of a multidimensional model. Characterized by awareness of and training in recognizing sociodemographic differences and how they present in relation to mental health concerns, this may involve learning about country of origin, nuances of language, traditional versus nontraditional roles, politics, religion, and formative social experiences of the various communities.

Comprehension addresses the active learning stage of moving knowledge into a position of meaning and incorporating strategies for culturally sensitive therapeutic exchange into a personal and professional worldview. Care providers will notice that they are more sensitive to inadvertent ethnocentrism, racism, gender bias, and other stereotypes.

In the application stage, the information acquired and internalized is brought into practical use with clients in session. Application is a dynamic process that transforms theoretical information into a working alliance. There is flow of real-world information mediating the basic foundational knowledge. It is in this process that the care provider learns about the individual contextual variations to the information that first informed their awareness of cultural distinctions.

As application and experience expand, a process of synthesis follows in which in the practitioner begins to develop a well-integrated sense of how to approach and adapt (global to specific) the knowledge and experience to meet the needs of each new client.

In the evaluation process, a feedback loop of identifying what works for whom under what circumstances (Newnham & Page, 2010) is created. This information becomes the foundation of expanding knowledge, increased comprehension, more effective application, more efficient synthesis, and the development of longitudinally meaningful evaluation.

Incorporation of this process in group and individual supervision is a critical part of the growth process and expands learning by including a variety of perspectives on the meaning and interpretation of the therapeutic exchanges. It is helpful as a framework for helping couples assimilate the effects of the deployment experiences and their impact on both individual and family culture.

TRAINING FOR THERAPISTS

Training in McGoldrick-style genograms (McGoldrick et al., 1999), which target areas of multicultural and experiential meaning that can influence the therapeutic process, is essential. Whether done as part of the session with clients present or conceptually outside the session, these help to clarify blind spots, core beliefs, coping strategies that have been generationally reinforced, strengths, and challenges. For couples struggling to understand their own cultural differences and locked in trying to change the "other," involving them in completing simple family genograms can be a useful homework assignment. Genograms can also be derived from recorded narrative reflection or short-paragraph descriptions of family members. The importance of this methodology in understanding cultural influences, unresolved losses, family strengths, and resources cannot be understated (Dunn & Dawes, 1999; Estrada & Hardy, 1998; McCullough-Chavis, 2004; McGoldrick et al., 1999; Thomas, 1998; White & Tyson-Rawson, 1995).

Ongoing cultural discussion groups raise awareness of emerging research trends and needs in specific sociodemographic groups. The opportunity for lively conversations via either face-to-face meetings or interactive webinars provides opportunities for clinicians to explore their own questions and reactions in a supportive environment. Further, the supervision process can become a multi-cultural interaction opportunity as well as a safe place to process and contemplate the role of basic assumptions and filters (Abe-Kim & Takeuchi, 1996; Constantine, 1997; Gavin et al., 2010; Sue, Zane, Hall, & Berger, 2009).

Finally, becoming educated about the culture of war, military family life, and the experience of injury, partner trauma, and living with the aftereffects of war as a cultural experience in and of itself should be a part of the ongoing training and development process. Pope (2011) maintains an excellent resource for those seeking additional information on these matters (http://kspope.com/torvic/war.php).

STRATEGIES FOR THERAPY: SIMPLE EXERCISES FOR COUPLES IN SESSION

Bronfenbrenner Circles

Utilizing Uri Bronfenbrenner's (1977) concentric circles, work with the couple to fill in the concepts, descriptors, and experiences that have shaped them at each level. Encourage them to create graphic representations of the items that are most important. Working at their pace encourages each member of the couple to describe in his or her own words the result of the work. Allow partners to respond to the content presented and then check for meaning and culturally sensitive interpretation.

Rosenberg's Nonviolent Communication

If communication issues seem to be the core of the problems facing a couple, utilize a culturally sensitive, nonaggressive communication model (like that of Rosenberg, 2003) and help couples create a shared communication style rather than arguing over which of the currently represented approaches is most right. Assigning easy-to-accomplish training exercises or listening to examples together in session helps couples to move toward a more universal mode of communication that improves understanding of latent (emotional) content (Connor & Kellian, 2005; Rosenberg, 2003; Sears, 2010).

Learning to Listen

Listening exercises involving turn taking, mirroring, responding to meaning rather than content, and clarifying what the speaker is seeking are important for all couples. Again, with couples of mixed cultural origins the early practices and experiences of listening and responding may be so disparate that creating a new culture of understanding must be formed for these to be successful in maintaining their relationship.

Keeping the environment light and fun but respectful is integral to getting these ideas to become part of internalized behavior change. This is often a good place to introduce ideas about problem solving (utilizing the five-step problem-solving model) or how to respond to feelings without necessarily agreeing with them perhaps through implementation of the nurtured heart approach (Glasser & Easley, 1999) or even applying Faber and Mazlish's (1990) approach. Both of these approaches focus more on communicating in families with children; however, in clinical practice consistent observation is that both approaches support insight and communication behavior change in the adults as well, and they are client-friendly adaptable strategies.

Celebrating Difference as Strength

In connecting across cultures, couples are seeking new experiences, challenges, excitement, and opportunity. These couples are not immune from family system challenges arising from family-of-origin experiences. They are, however, uniquely strong when they can learn to celebrate their differences as a strength and to value the unique experience set that each person brings to the couple. In the differences, they may have hidden assets in the form of skill sets they are able to draw on in times of challenge or crisis. They may be able to find purpose and meaning for their differences and learn to integrate them into their new, shared cultural definition (McCullough-Chavis, 2004).

Finding Shared Traditions Therapists can encourage the couple to embrace and share traditions rather than seeking to adopt one culture over another. Child rearing may include integrated aspects of both perspectives and can often provide rich and positive opportunities for fostering insight, appreciation, and celebration of the unique culture of both. Exploring the positives and negatives of each culture and creating a shared, integrated new culture is an important part of the therapeutic process. This process solidifies the couple's self-concept and relational skills in the context of a new family culture (Hong, Morris, Chiu, & Benet-Martinez, 2000).

Clarifying Expectations in Culturally Sensitive Ways Working collaboratively with therapists and clarifying expectations in culturally sensitive ways, clients may be able to see themselves in the context of their current life experiences. Through some of the other strategies outlined, the couple may understand that their ground rules and values belong to them and are able to be negotiated out of respect and commitment to each other. By identifying levels of importance and negotiability, they may find an increasing sense of tolerance and flexibility inside the relationship that translates into resilience and persistence in application (McGoldrick et al., 1999). This process may also improve a sense of marital support and satisfaction that counteracts the challenges of military life and the tendency toward being overwhelmed and isolated.

Strength-Based, Solution-Focused Problem Solving Arising from a better sense of themselves as cultural beings who are able to find and negotiate paths of agreement and new means of celebrating differences comes an opportunity to talk in terms of utilizing strengths in problem solving and developing a proactive, solution-focused model that keeps a couple moving toward shared goals and hopes for the relationship (Gordon, 2007).

Finding Ways to Extend Support Across Long Distances Couples may benefit from learning how to express their new ideas and understandings to extended family members. They may also need to strategize about how to keep in touch with each other across long distances to maintain ties, support, and corrective experiences. Technology can be useful for this purpose when it is coupled with ground rules about how that time will be used and how the couple will communicate within those precious minutes to ensure that the focus is on the relationship, commitment, and love rather than solely on discussion of what is wrong—even injuries, mistakes, or problems. Finding a means for dealing with those eventualities that is manageable, supportive, and reflexive is also a critical component of the marriage.

Long-Distance Relationships Between Couples Couples can and should be encouraged to discuss the means that they have at their disposal to continue to keep their relationship strong, even at long distances. While this may be strongly impacted by living situation, privacy factors, religious values, and personality, many couples find it possible to utilize cell phones, e-mails, Skype, traditional mail, intimate phoning, and brief leave opportunities to keep their relationships strong. When resources are scarce, service agencies may be tapped with the assistance of knowledgeable therapists and social workers to ensure that the connections remain healthy.

Long-Distance Relationships With Extended Family and Isolation A part of the psychoeducational process in couples work with military couples needs to be a discussion about how each person brings unique needs as part of a military couple to the attention of their families. Strategizing about how to best negotiate long-distance support from extended family and how to develop the relationships to be more supportive of their unique journey may require therapist support in the brainstorming, implementing, and maintenance phases. The couples who are able to do this step can often avoid further distress by educating and supporting their families in supporting them. This is particularly true for first-generation military families who have no frame of reference or experience with the military culture, what it means to be partnered with someone who is a deployable troop in wartime, and so on.

Mental Health at a Distance Developing a gauging system so that the partners can easily understand how they are doing in managing stress and take preventive measures to support each other and where to go for help before problems are too large to manage is another important function of the therapeutic process. This may involve prenegotiation of a coping plan to ensure that when the need arises a working process will be there.

Home/Culture Sickness Home and culture sickness is a normal part of the human experience. Longing for times and places of our happy experiences and our childhood is a normal function of memory. Interestingly, this can also occur for troops who have returned from their tours of duty. This can often be hard for partners to understand. After all, how can one miss what was so difficult or unpleasant? It is, however, a part of the growth and assimilation process. A helpful strategy is for couples to work with their care provider for one or both individuals to plan for how they will manage such feelings. This may take the form of planned intervals for keeping in touch with those important people from whom they are separated. It might also involve seeking out other expatriates or individuals with shared or similar cultural backgrounds and experiences. Maintaining ties via food, music, customs, holidays, and planned visits is integral to a feeling of positive cultural integration. Becoming a leader in connecting other individuals with similar experiences in communities where there is no formal group can also be therapeutic.

SUMMARY

Therapists and care providers need to take the time to develop cultural awareness and to pay attention to ongoing development and awareness of their internalized experience of cultural sensitivity. Their abilities in this area are a factor in the therapeutic process. As part of the complex dynamic processes occurring in therapy, clinicians need to be keenly aware of their own cultural contributions to the manner in which they interpret behavior of their clients and the attributions they make about the behaviors, including decisions about pathology. Above all, they must keep in mind how their cultural mind-set affects the language of the session and the cadence and pacing of the verbal interactions and the choice of intervention strategies utilized.

It is important to remember that there is no such thing as a one-size-fits-all formula, and this is also true when exploring the role of cultural differences. There are also no absolutes with regard to cultural experiences and the function of these experiences in the worldview of the individual. It is incumbent on the therapist or care provider to be open to therapy as a dynamic learning process of discovering who these people are and what they need to be best served in addressing their concerns. Being able to articulate an understanding of how culture affects the basic human process of intimate connection and security and to advocate for continued cross-cultural and multicultural training is an overarching responsibility of each clinician and supervisor providing couple and family support services.

REFERENCES

Abe-Kim, J. S., & Takeuchi, D. (1996). Cultural competence and quality of care: Issues for mental health service delivery in managed care. *Clinical Psychology: Science and Practice, 3*, 273–295.

Allen, S., Goldscheider, F., & Ciambrone, D. (1999). Gender roles, marital intimacy, and nomination of spouse as primary caregiver. *The Gerontologist, 39*, 150–158.

Arai, Y. Y., & Washio, M. M. (1999). Burden felt by family caring for the elderly members needing care in southern Japan. *Aging and Mental Health, 3*, 158–164.

Aranda, M. P., & Knight, B. G. (1997). The influence of ethnicity and culture on the caregiver stress and coping process: A sociocultural review and analysis. *The Gerontologist, 37*, 342–354.

Berg, I. K. (1994). *Family-based services: A solution-focused approach.* New York: W. W. Norton.

Bronfenbrenner, U. (1977). Toward an experimental ecology of human development. *American Psychologist, 32*, 513–530.

Bullock, K., Crawford, S., & Tennstedt, S. (2003). Employment and caregiving: Exploration of African American caregivers. *Social Work, 48*, 150–162.

Comas-Diaz, L. (2006). Latino healing: The integration of ethnic psychology into psychotherapy. *Psychotherapy Theory, Research, Practice and Training, 43* 453–463.

Connell, C., & Gibson. G. (1997). Racial, ethnic, and cultural differences in dementia caregiving: Review and analysis. *The Gerontologist, 37*, 355–364.

Connor, M., & Kellian, D. (2005). *Connecting across differences.* New York: Hungry Duck Press.

Constantine, M. G. (1997). Facilitating multicultural competency in counseling supervision. In D. B. Pope-Davis & H. L. K. Coleman (Eds.), *Multicultural counseling competencies: Assessment, education and training and supervision.* Thousand Oaks, CA: Sage.

Cooney, R., & Di, J. (1999). Primary family caregivers of impaired elderly in Shanghai, China: Kin relationship and caregiver burden. *Research on Aging, 21*, 739–761

Defense and Veterans Brain Injury Center. (2010). *TBI numbers.* Retrieved from http://www.dvbic.org/TBI-Numbers.aspx

Dunn, A., & Dawes, S. (1999). Spiritual focused genograms: A key to uncovering spiritual resources in African-American families. *Journal of Multicultural Counseling and Development, 27*, 240–255.

Estrada, A., & Hardy, P. (1998). Genograms in a multicultural perspective. *Journal of Family Psychotherapy, 9*, 55–62.

Faber, A., & Mazlish, E. (1990). *Liberated parents, liberated children.* New York: Harper Paperbacks.

Gallagher-Thompson, D., Arean, P., Rivera, P., & Thompson, L. W. (2001). Reducing distress in Hispanic family caregivers using a psychoeducational intervention. *Clinical Gerontologist, 23*, 17–32.

Gavin, A. R., Walton, E., Chae, D. H., Alegria, M., Jackson, J. S., & Takeuchi, D. (2010). The associations between socio-economic status and major depressive disorder among Blacks, Latinos, Asians and non-Hispanic Whites: Findings from the Collaborative Psychiatric Epidemiology Studies. *Psychological Medicine, 40*, 51–61. doi: 10.1017/S0033291709006023

Glasser, H., & Easley, J. (1999). *Transforming the difficult child: The nurtured heart approach.* Nashville, TN: Nurtured Heart Publications.

Gordon, A. B. (2007). *Families facing solutions: Mental health training module.* Retrieved from http://familiesfacingsolutions.org

Granello, D. H. (2000). Encouraging the cognitive development of supervisees using bloom's taxonomy in supervision. *Counselor Education and Supervision, 40*(1), 31–46.

Hays, D. G., Prosek, E. A., & McLeod, A. L. (2010). A mixed methodological analysis of the role of culture in the clinical decision-making process. *Journal of Counseling and Development, 88*, 112–119.

Hoge, C., Castro, C., Messer, S., McGurk, D., Cotting, D., & Koffman, R. (2004). Combat duty in Iraq and Afghanistan, mental health problems, and barriers to care. *New England Journal of Medicine, 351*, 13–22.

Hong, Y.-Y., Morris, M. W., Chiu, C.-Y., & Benet-Martinez, V. (2000). Multicultural minds: A dynamic constructivist approach to culture and cognition. *American Psychologist*, 55, 709–720.

Hughes, S., Giobbie-Hurder, A., Weaver, F., Kubal, J., & Henderson, W. (1999). Relationship between caregiver burden and health-related quality of life. *The Gerontologist, 39*, 534–545.

Ivey, A., Simek-Morgen, L., & Ivey, M. B. (1993). *Counseling and psychotherapy: A multicultural perspective*. New York: Allyn & Bacon.
Kessler, R., Sonnega, A., Bromet, E., Hughes, M., & Nelson, C. (1995). Posttraumatic stress disorder in the national comorbidity survey. *Archive of General Psychiatry, 52*, 1048–1060.
Landau, J., & Hissett, J. (2008). Mild traumatic brain injury: Impact on identity and ambiguous loss in the family. *Families Systems and Health, 26*, 69–85.
LeFebvre, H., Cloutier, G., & Levert, M. J. (2008). Perspectives of survivors of traumatic brain injury and their caregivers on long-term social integration. *Brain Injury, 22*, 535–543.
MacKinnon, C. (2009). Applying feminist, multicultural, and social justice theory to diverse women who function as caregivers in end-of-life home care. *Palliative and Supportive Care, 7*, 501–512.
McCullough-Chavis, A. (2004). Genograms and African-American families: Employing family strengths of spirituality, religion and extended family networks. *Family Practice: Innovations and Challenges, 9*, 30–36.
McGoldrick, M., Gersen, R., & Shellenberger, S. (1999). *Genograms: Assessment and interventions* (2nd ed.). New York: Norton.
Miranda, J., Azocar, F., Organista, K., Dwyer, E., Arean, P. (2003a). Treatment of depression among impoverished primary care patients from ethnic minority groups disadvantaged medical patients. *Psychiatric Services, 54*(2), 219–225.
Miranda, J., Duan, N. H., Sherbourne, C., Schoenbaum, M., Lagomasino, I. Jackson-Triche, M., & Wells, K. B. (2003b). Improving care for minorities: Can quality improvement interventions improve care and outcomes for depressed minorities? Results of a randomized, controlled trial. *Health Services Research, 38*(2), 613–630.
Mittelstadt, J. (2010, April 23). *Panelist: They also serve: Military families and the wars in Iraq and Afghanistan.* Keynote: Sutton, L., & Sherman, N. Retrieved from http://www.wilsoncenter.org/ondemand/index.cfm?fuseaction=Media.read&mediaid=693494CA-9B136C6FE0A3AB2158D7A55
Montgomery, R., & Kosloski, K. (2009). Caregiving as a process of changing identity: Implications for caregiver support. *Generations, 33*, 47–52.
National Center for PTSD. (2010). *How common is PTSD?* Retrieved from http://www.ptsd.va.gov/public/pages/how-common-is-ptsd.asp
Newnham, E. A., & Page, A. C. (2010). Bridging the gap between best evidence and best practice in mental health. *Clinical Psychology Review, 30*, 127–142.
Obama, B. (2011, January 14). *Strengthening our military families: meeting America's commitment*. Presidential statement. Retrieved from http://www.defense.gov/home/features/2011/0111_initiative/Strengthening_our_Military_January_2011.pdf
Pew Hispanic Center. (2003). *Hispanics in the military*. Retrieved from http://pewhispanic.org/files/factsheets/6.pdf
Pope, K. S. (2011). *Resources for troops and veterans, their families, and those who provide services to them*. Retrieved from http://kspope.com/torvic/war.php
Rosenberg, M. (2003). *Nonviolent communication: A language of life* (2nd ed.). Del Mar, CA: Puddle Dancer Press.
Sears, M. (2010). *Humanizing health care: Creating cultures of compassion with nonviolent communication.* Del Mar, CA: Puddle Dancer Press.
Sue, D. W., Arrendondo, P., & McDavis, R. (1992). Multicultural counseling competencies and standards: A call to the profession. *Journal of Counseling and Development, 70*, 477–489.
Sue, D. W., & Sue, D. (2008). *Counseling the culturally diverse: Theory and practice* (5th ed.). New York: Wiley.
Sue, S. (1998). In search of cultural competencies in psychotherapy and counseling. *American Psychologist, 53*, 440–448.

Sue, S., Zane, N., Hall, G. C. N., & Berger, L. K. (2009). The case for cultural competency in psychotherapeutic interventions. *Annual Review of Psychology, 60*, 525–548. doi: 10.1146/annurev.psych.60.110707.163651

Tanielian, T., & Jaycox, L. (2008). *Invisible wounds of war: Psychological and cognitive injuries, their consequences, and services to assist recovery.* Santa Monica, CA: RAND.

Thomas, A. J. (1998). Understanding cultural and world view in family systems: Use of the multicultural genogram. *Family Journal: Counseling and Therapy for Couples and Families, 6*, 24–32.

Ward, D. B., & Wampler, K. S. (2010). Moving up the continuum of hope: Developing a theory of hope and understanding its influence in couples therapy. *Journal of Marital and Family Therapy, 36*, 212–228.

White, M.B., & Tyson-Rawson, K. J. (1995). Assessing the dynamics of gender in couples and families: The genogram. *Family Relations, 44*, 253–260.

Section 4

Resources

18

Helping Military Couples Understand Their Legal Rights in Divorce

MATHEW B. TULLY

Many members of the armed forces, and especially their spouses, believe that it is possible to get a "military divorce" while in service.* In reality, there is no such thing as a military divorce, just as there is no such thing as a "military marriage." There are, however, "military married couples" who, for various reasons, may wish to end their marital relationship by divorcing. For purposes of this discussion, a military married couple is simply a married couple with one or both members of the couple in military service.

In addition to the religious aspects of most marriages, all marriages in the United States have a civil aspect. To get married, a couple must typically be eligible to marry under criteria established by the state in which they seek to marry. These criteria generally have to do with age and residency or time in the state. In any event, the couple must apply for and receive a marriage license. Only on the subsequent performance of a marriage ceremony, either civil or religious with civil approval, is the couple married under the laws of the state in which the marriage took place. This marriage is signified legally by a marriage certificate issued by an appropriate official. Once the marriage is in effect, the couple is legally bound to one another by a contract of marriage that can only be broken by a divorce. From the legal relationship established by marriage, each member of the couple has rights and expectations, often having to do with benefits, property ownership, inheritance, and legal–medical decision making. In addition, a marriage lawfully entered into in one state must, under the U.S. Constitution, be recognized as legally valid in each of the 50 states.

If a member of a married couple enters into the military or is in the military at the time of the marriage, certain additional marital benefits are conferred on one or both members of the couple. These benefits include typically higher housing

* This chapter is for informational purposes only. It should not be construed as legal advice.

allowance benefits or access to military family housing, health care benefits to all members of the family, and access to the commissary and exchange. The benefits might also include moving costs to and from new duty locations and access to family support programs.

When a military married couple chooses to divorce, they must look again to state law, and a state court legal process, to obtain that divorce. Just as the marriage was entered into under state law, it must be dissolved under state law. The military does not have jurisdiction over the marital contract and does not have any authority to dissolve that bond. Fortunately, a married person does not necessarily have to be in, or return to, the state where they were married to be divorced. They must, however, satisfy the eligibility requirements of the state in which they seek a divorce. These requirements may be different from state to state but generally have to do with residency, even under military orders, in that state for a requisite period. The key requirement is that the state is satisfied that it has jurisdiction over at least one member of the couple to dissolve that member's divorce.

When a person seeks a divorce, including a military member or spouse of a military member, that person must initiate a legal process that gives notice to the other party that his or her legal rights may be changed. This is called *filing for a divorce* and involves the filing of a petition in a court of appropriate jurisdiction. This divorce petition must set forth the basis for the court's jurisdiction, normally in a sworn statement that the petitioner has resided in the state for a requisite period or is in the state pursuant to military orders. The divorce petition must also set forth grounds for the divorce, often satisfied in a no-fault divorce state by simply claiming irreconcilable differences or whatever other appropriate declaration is called for under state law. The divorce petition must also set forth how the assets or property of the marriage should be divided and address other necessary issues, such as child custody and support, alimony or marital support, and distribution or maintenance of long-term benefits, such as life insurance or retired pay and survivor's benefits.

Many states will allow either one of the marital parties to file for divorce in the state where the military member is stationed regardless of whether the military member is a legal resident of that state. In addition, either party can file for divorce in the state where the military spouse resides or in the state where the military member claims legal residency if the parties, in fact, live or claim residency or are stationed in different states. This is important because the divorce will occur under the rules of the state where the filing took place, and because the rules for divorce vary widely from one state to the next, it may be more beneficial to file in one state and more detrimental to file in another state.

Ultimately, once the petition is prepared and filed, it must be served on the other member of the couple so that he or she can respond and protect his or her rights if there are contested issues. It is entirely possible to easily satisfy the service of petition requirement if both members of the couple want the divorce, have worked out all the details, and are accessible to one another. One party can simply consent in writing to the petition of the other party. Some states even allow for joint, uncontested petitions to be filed, with both parties joining in the same petition. Also, some states actually provide forms to help couples easily obtain a divorce without even involving a lawyer or lawyers.

When the marriage may be contested, however, proper service of the divorce petition is critical to initiating the process. This step is important because one party may not alter the rights of the other party without giving that other party notice of the divorce filing and an opportunity to respond to the petition. Service on the opposite party must be accomplished according to the requirements of the law in the state in which the divorce is sought. If the military member is overseas at the time, the military has the capabilities to serve the military member. Nevertheless, the military member can decline the service unless it comes from the court where the divorce is filed, and if the court is unwilling to send someone overseas to serve the military member, the spouse may have to wait until after the military member returns from active duty to begin the process. Once proper service has been accomplished, the opposite party must answer the petition or be deemed to have defaulted. In the case of a default, the party who filed for the divorce generally is granted a default judgment giving them what they requested.

When a party seeks to obtain a divorce from a military member, the Servicemembers Civil Relief Act (SCRA), found in Section 502 of the appendix to Title 50 of the *United States Code*, gives that military member substantial protections that may affect how the divorce proceeds. The stated purpose of the SCRA is to provide for, strengthen, and expedite the national defense through protection extended to service members of the United States to enable such persons to devote their entire energy to the defense needs of the nation and to provide for the temporary suspension of judicial and administrative proceedings and transactions that may adversely affect the civil rights of service members during their military service.

Two important features of the SCRA are that it allows a service member to stay certain civil legal proceedings against him or her for a period of time under certain conditions, and it allows a service member to reopen a default judgment taken against him or her, again under certain conditions. The SCRA applies to all military members on federal active duty. This includes the regular forces, the reserve forces, and the guard forces in Title 10 active duty. The SCRA also applies to the Coast Guard and officers in the Public Health Service and National Oceanic and Atmospheric Administration in support of the Armed Forces. In limited circumstances (i.e., evictions, joint leases), the SCRA may apply to dependents of the military member. The SCRA applies to all 50 states of the United States and to all territories (i.e., Puerto Rico, U.S. Virgin Islands, Guam, and the Marianas Islands) subject to U.S. jurisdiction.

The SCRA provides for an automatic stay of at least 90 days on a proper request from the military service member in civil administrative and civil matters. A member who is unable to appear in court on the date required, because of active military service, must request this protection in writing and include certain information with the request. After receiving the written request, the judge, magistrate, or hearing officer must grant a minimum 90-day delay. This delay is mandatory, and the military member's letter requesting postponement is not an appearance or waiver of any defense by the member. Any additional delay beyond the mandatory 90-day period is within the discretion of the judge, magistrate, or hearing officer. This protection does not apply to criminal court or criminal administrative proceedings.*

* Most of the information provided here on the SCRA was found at http://legalassistance.law.af.mil/content.

According to the SCRA Guide (United States Army and Civil Law Department, March 2006), prepared by the Administrative and Civil Law Department of the Judge Advocate General's School of the U.S. Army, a service member can reopen a default judgment by applying to the same court that rendered the original default judgment. The service member must apply, however, within 90 days of leaving service. A service member discovering a default judgment more than 90 days after termination of his or her military service is too late to invoke the SCRA. The default judgment must also have been rendered against the service member during his or her period of active duty service or within 60 days thereafter. This period excludes judgments rendered before the defendant entered military service or more than 60 days after separation from service. There are three main criteria that must be met if a service member is to reopen a default judgment. First, the service member must not have made an appearance in the case. Second, the service member's military service must be shown to have materially affected his or her ability to defend the suit. Third, the service member must have a meritorious or legal defense to the action or some part of it. Before seeking to invoke the protections of the SCRA, a service member should seek legal advice because many of the provisions are highly technical.

As mentioned, one important aspect of most divorces is the division of marital assets and property. In the divorce of a military married couple, the division of military retired pay can be a central issue. This division is important because military retired pay is considered to be marital property because of the sacrifices the nonmilitary spouse made in furtherance of the military spouse's career. Division of military retired pay assumes, of course, that at least one member of the couple is retired from military service or will be in the future.

The Uniformed Services Former Spouses' Protection Act (USFSPA)* recognizes the right of state courts to distribute military retired pay to a spouse, or former spouse, and provides a method of enforcing court orders for the distribution of that pay through the Department of Defense. The USFSPA does not, however, provide a former spouse with an automatic entitlement to a portion of a military member's retired pay. That former spouse must be awarded a portion of a military member's retired pay as part of the property settlement in their final decree of divorce or other court order. Put another way, the divorce decree or other court order must provide for the payment of military retired pay as property to a spouse or former spouse. In addition, the divorce decree or other court order must provide for the payment of an amount of money expressed in dollars or as a percentage of disposable military retired pay. Disposable military retired pay is gross retired pay minus allowable deductions. A qualified domestic relations order is not required to divide military retired pay as long as the former spouse's award is set forth in the pertinent court order.

In all cases when a military member is on active duty at the time of a divorce, the military member's rights under the SCRA must be observed during the state court proceeding. Also, to enforce orders dividing military retired pay as property, the state court must have had jurisdiction over the member by reason of

* See Title 10 of the United States Code, Section 1408.

(a) the member's residence in the territorial jurisdiction of the court (other than because of his or her military assignment), (b) the member's domicile in the territorial jurisdiction of the court, or (c) the member's consent to the jurisdiction of the court, as indicated by the member's taking some affirmative action in the legal proceeding.

An important consideration when dealing with the USFSPA is the overlap in years of marriage and years of military service. This overlap is used to determine the percentage of the military member's retired pay that may be awarded. For example, if 20 years of marriage overlap 20 years of military service creditable toward retirement, the former spouse is eligible for a maximum award of 50% of the military member's disposable retired pay. This outcome is because the total percentage may not exceed 50% of the military member's disposable retired pay. The formula is

(Years of Marriage)/(Years of Military Service) × 50% = Possible Maximum Award

A former spouse may not receive the maximum award, even if eligible, because the amount of any award is within the discretion of the court, based on equitable factors and all of the facts and circumstances of the couple's marriage and divorce.

If 10 years of marriage overlap 10 years of military service, the former spouse of the military member can apply to the Defense Finance and Accounting Service to have the awarded portion of the military retired pay awarded directly. This is called the 10/10 rule. This rule alleviates the need to rely on the former spouse to make recurring payments. Receipt of any portion of a military member's retired pay ends when that military member dies.

The overlap in years of marriage and years of service is important in determining other benefits after divorce as well. If a couple is married for at least 20 years and 20 years of that marriage overlap 20 years of military service, the unremarried former spouse is eligible for military medical benefits if the spouse does not have employer-sponsored medical insurance. The former spouse also qualifies for commissary, exchange, and theater privileges. This is called the 20/20/20 rule. If the former spouse does remarry, however, military medical benefits will be lost.

If a couple is married for 20 years and at least 15 years of that marriage overlap 20 years of military service, the former spouse may also be eligible for certain military medical benefits. This is called the 20/20/15 rule. In this case, unremarried former spouses are eligible for medical care for 1 year from date of divorce. The unremarried former spouse can then purchase a conversion health care policy, for up to 36 months, negotiated by the Department of Defense.

As previously stated, the maximum that can be paid to a former spouse under the USFSPA is 50% of a military member's disposable retired pay. If there are payments both under the USFSPA and pursuant to a garnishment for child support or alimony, the total amount payable cannot exceed 65% of the military member's disposable retired pay.*

---

* Most of the information provided here on the USFSPA was found at http://www.dfas.mil/militarypay/garnishment/fsfact.html.

Another possible issue in the divorce of a military married couple has to do with continuing benefits under a retired military member's Survivor Benefit Plan (SBP). The SBP pays an annuity to a military retiree's spouse, or other named beneficiary, after the military retiree's death. SBP benefits are not automatic, however. At retirement, a military member must choose whether to participate in the SBP. If a military member chooses to participate in the SBP, a plan premium will be deducted from his or her monthly retired pay amount. If a military member chooses not to participate in the SBP, he or she will receive a full monthly retired pay amount, but there will be no SBP annuity payments to the member's surviving spouse or other beneficiary. Without the plan, all military retired pay stops on the death of the retiree.

Generally, a spouse loses eligibility as an SBP beneficiary when he or she is divorced from the military member. A former spouse may, however, receive benefits under "former spouse coverage." A military retiree can voluntarily apply for former spouse coverage within 1 year of the date of a divorce. This voluntary application is not the only means for a former spouse to obtain SBP benefits. If a military retiree fails or refuses to apply for former spouse coverage, the formal spouse can still obtain the benefits if he or she has a court order, such as a divorce decree, and makes a written request to the Defense Finance and Accounting Service asking that the military retiree be deemed to have made an election for the coverage.

SBP benefits conferred on a former spouse will be suspended if that former spouse remarries before the age of 55. The benefits will be paid once again, however, if the new marriage ends. In addition, as long as the former spouse is alive, the military retiree may not name a current spouse as a beneficiary unless the former spouse waives the benefit in writing.[*]

Obtaining a divorce, especially between a military married couple, can be easy or very difficult and complex. It all depends on the facts and circumstances surrounding the particular couple's marriage, family, assets, and needs. It is important, therefore, to obtain the services of a qualified lawyer when needed. The first thing to note when considering the assistance of an attorney is that a military divorce is no different from a divorce in which neither party is a military member. Like any other dissolution of marriage, the action will take place in a civilian court in front of the same judges who preside over divorce cases involving civilians. Military divorce is simply an easy way to refer to a divorce involving at least one spouse who is a military member.

Also, there are no special certificates or qualifications for what constitutes a military divorce lawyer. Hiring an attorney will likely be an essential component of any military divorce and is a decision that should be handled with care. A family and matrimonial attorney who claims to understand the military, or even boasts of military service, does not necessarily have the experience or knowledge to do so. He or she may not understand the full scope of the issues affecting a divorce when one spouse is in the military, yet that attorney can still label him- or herself a "military divorce lawyer."

[*] Most of the information provided here on the SBP was found at http://www.divorcenet.com/states/nationwide/milart-03.

It may be helpful to talk to other military members or spouses who have gone through a divorce and to ask about the qualifications of their attorney. If their attorney was diligent and knowledgeable, chances are the attorney may make a high-quality effort on your behalf as well. Also, use search engines to your advantage. Law firms have highly established Web sites currently, and a scan of some of the top search returns should tell you how involved in military matters the firm in question is. No mention of the military on a site that contains matrimonial law may suggest the firm will handle a divorce involving a military member but may not necessarily be well versed in the practice.

Once your choices have been whittled down to a few, have consultations with each of the firms to judge their experience and determine what fit the firm might be for your particular situation. Doing a little bit of research in advance may help you make this determination. Asking military-related questions regarding your situation will quickly establish whether the attorney has suitable expertise or is merely masking a lack of knowledge about military divorce to procure a new client. In any event, care should always be taken to proceed cautiously and only after a great deal of forethought, separated from the emotional turmoil many divorces bring. A decision to divorce is a life-changing decision.

REFERENCE

United States Army and Civil Law Department of the Judge Advocate General's School, Charlottesville, Virginia (March 2006). *The Servicemember's Civil Relief Act's Guide* (JA260). Retrieved from http://www.miramar.usmc.mil/jlc/AAWebs.te/legal%20Assistance/Reference/SCRA%20guide%202006.pdf

19

Civilian and Military Programs in Psychosocial Rehabilitation for Couples With PTSD

WALTER PENK, DOLORES LITTLE, and NATHAN AINSPAN

INTRODUCTION

Psychosocial rehabilitation techniques are being empirically validated as beneficial for reducing symptoms and improving functioning among those surviving trauma in combat (e.g., Glynn, Drebing, & Penk, 2009). While couples and families may be impacted by trauma among partners and/or parents, simultaneously, couples and families are key in recovery and may need such services (e.g., Allen, Rhoades, Stanley, & Markman, 2010; Bates, Bowles, Kilgore, & Solursh, 2008; Figley, 1983, 1989; Gottman, Gottman, & Atkins, 2011; Park, 2011).

Several therapeutic approaches are available for couples when one partner—sometimes both—have survived trauma in combat (e.g., Riggs, Monson, Glynn, & Canterino, 2009). These include behavioral family therapy, behavioral marital therapy, cognitive–behavioral couples treatment, lifestyle management courses, emotionally-focused couples therapy, spousal education and support programs, family systems-based therapy, and critical interaction therapy. Most such therapies differ from techniques traditionally used in psychosocial rehabilitation.

To date, few psychosocial rehabilitation techniques, except for lifestyle management courses (Cahoon, 1984; Devilly, 2002) and family psychoeducation, have been demonstrated as beneficial for couples with posttraumatic stress disorder (PTSD) or for other disorders associated with trauma, such as depression, pain, traumatic brain injury (TBI), and addictions (e.g., Allen, Rhoades, Stanley, & Markman, 2010; Glynn et al., 2009). But, just as psychosocial rehabilitation techniques for individuals are being found to be effective based on findings from randomized clinical trials (see early review by Penk & Flannery, 2000), so we expect that results will be favorable once couples therapy interventions are integrated with psychosocial rehabilitation (Gottman, et al., 2011).

Combining treatment approaches for couples and families with psychosocial rehabilitation is essential since, in 2000, the American Psychiatric Association added Criterion F to the fourth edition of the *Diagnostic and Statistical Manual of Mental Disorders* (*DSM-IV-TR*) to classify PTSD. Criterion F—social, family, and work functioning—now is required for classifying PTSD and other mental disorders (e.g., Criterion B for schizophrenia). Previously, such dimensions of functioning were described in Axis IV of the third editions of the *Diagnostic and Statistical Manual of Mental Disorders* (*DSM-III*; American Psychiatric Association, 1980; *DSM-III-R*, American Psychiatric Association, 1987). But moving functioning from Axis IV to Axis I and Axis II criteria for classifying disorders—such as the aforementioned Criterion F on functioning for classifying PTSD—now transforms empirical validation to combine rehabilitation with treatments. Criterion F for PTSD now means testing efficacy may include combining therapies for individuals—and for couples—with psychosocial rehabilitation. Adding Criterion F to PTSD is transforming treatment and rehabilitation, bringing both forms of intervention together in an organized approach to recovery, as illustrated by Gottman et al. (2011), who combined couples therapy with social skills rehabilitation.

We discuss, in this chapter, then, basic approaches in civilian and military programs that now need to be pioneered by blending psychosocial rehabilitation in the treatment of PTSD with therapies for couples and their families. It should be noted that we are not speculating without any evidence that such combinations of therapies/rehabilitations can be helpful; rather, treating PTSD is grounded on empirical approaches based on clinical case studies, naturalistic observations, and randomized clinical trials demonstrating such treatments and rehabilitation as beneficial. Besides, the use of the term *psychosocial* paired with rehabilitation not only refers to symptoms within the individual but also requires interventions for the social context in which functioning takes place by each person in recovery, which, being psychosocial, includes each one's partner/spouse and family.

CHARACTERISTICS OF APPROACHES FOR COUPLES IN CIVILIAN AND MILITARY PROGRAMS

Combining couples therapy with psychosocial rehabilitation unites two theories of treatment models. Some forms of couples therapy may be characterized as akin to medical models based on "compensation" techniques, that is, therapies to remedy weaknesses (Snow, 1991). Psychosocial rehabilitation is based, more so, on public health models that use "capitalization" therapies, drawing on strengths within the individuals, couples, and families (e.g., Kudler, Straits-Troster, & Jones, 2006; Tedeschi & McNally, 2011). And, prevention is a significant feature for such capitalization/public health models in planning to treat and rehabilitate persons with PTSD (e.g., Reivich, Seligman, & McBride, 2011).

But, this contrast between compensation versus capitalization, while useful, oversimplifies rather than produces real differences, since everyday realities of treatment and rehabilitation are far more complex than even clinicians and researchers can imagine or practice. Besides, new treatment approaches introduce more capitalization into compensation than has been tried before. For example, Jenny Anderson and Paula Szuchman (2011) are adapting principles of behavioral economics (e.g., Diener & Seligman, 2004; Kahneman, Diener, & Schwarz, 1999) to form new approaches to couples therapies called "spousonomics," adding concepts of capitalization into overcoming weaknesses in relationships among those who are married or living with partners (see http://www.spousonomics.com).

Spousonomics translates principles of behavioral economics as a strategy to improve relationships. Thus, spousonomics transforms couples therapy more so into capitalization and, less so, compensation. Whereas most couples therapies seek to enhance relationships by improving communications that are weak and controlling emotions out of control for strains in relationships, spousonomics uses "positive psychology" for relationships among partners (Seligman, 2002). Spousonomics analyzes relationships between couples in terms of "allocation of scarce resources" and "division of labor" and improving "incentives," "trade-offs," "supply and demand" as couples cope with "moral hazards." Innovations in couples therapy like spousonomics provide new theoretical platforms into which psychosocial rehabilitation may be integrated. Such approaches move conflicts within couples beyond fears of losing ("loss aversion") to replacing losses with goals to resolve arguments, thereby linking couples to recovery and resilience that are essential in psychosocial rehabilitation.

TYPES OF PSYCHOSOCIAL REHABILITATION AMONG CIVILIAN AND MILITARY PROGRAMS

Types of psychosocial rehabilitation for PTSD include interventions with at least moderate empirical validation: social skills training; physical health/exercise training; supported education; supported employment; supported housing; self-care and independent skills techniques; family psycho-education; case management; and, Internet-based self-management training (see Penk & Flannery, 2000; Glynn et al., 2009; Penk & Ainspan, 2009). Such types of psychosocial rehabilitation will both increase and inspire new research designs and opportunities when integrated with approaches for couples and for families. Moreover, psychosocial rehabilitation has a long tradition in application (as we explain in historical notes), but the evidence validating such techniques is far too short and remains a major challenge and opportunity for our generation to accrue.

New forces are gathering—accountability, transparency, cost-benefit analyses—demanding that practitioners design and deliver services tailored specifically for individuals as individuals. But, likewise, as presented in this book, there are growing needs in the military and among veterans for treatment techniques that integrate therapies for couples and families with psychosocial rehabilitation (see, e.g., the series from American Psychological Association [APA] Books: Adler, Bliese, &

Castro, 2011; Moore & Kennedy, 2010; Kennedy & Williams, 2010; Ruzek, Schnurr, Vasterling, & Friedman, 2011). Health care systems, particularly the Veterans Health Administration (VHA), are now championing best practices as the standard for guiding decisions for treatment and rehabilitation. Best practices require evidence-based results, preferably results based on randomized clinical trials. And, best practices across many kinds of psychosocial rehabilitation still need to be carried out and assessed through meta-analyses (cf. Glynn et al., 2009; Penk & Flannery, 2000).

The DOD and VHA long ago began to coordinate their efforts to design military and civilian programs to foster resiliency and recovery among military and veterans. VHA summarizes these collaborative efforts with DOD for best practices in the Uniform Mental Health Services (VHA, 2008). Such techniques are indebted to psychosocial rehabilitation interventions that were first designed and published in the early 1990s, under the leadership of Thomas Horvath, MD, in the VHA, for serious mental disorders (see Penk & Flannery, 2000, and modules L–Z of the VA/DOD *Clinical Practice Guideline for the Management of Psychoses*). Decisions about the benefits of psychosocial rehabilitation techniques have been based primarily on clinical observation and naturalistic evaluations, using outcome data from many Veterans Affairs (VA) sites for assessing treatment outcomes (e.g., See Veterans Health Administration [VHA], 2008: North East Program Evaluation Center [NEPEC] at the VA Connecticut Health Care System in West Haven; the Program Evaluation Research Center, PERC, in Palo Alto, CA; HSR&D—Health Services Research and Development, CHQOER—Center for Health Quality, Outcomes, and Economic Research; MIRECC—Mental Illness Research, Education, and Clinical Centers, in other VA facilities).

These VHA outcome evaluation centers have amassed outcome results for several decades that can be attributed to treatment and rehabilitation. These findings likewise provide an empirical basis for operationalizing elements that constitute specific services defining types of psychosocial rehabilitation. And, such results are continuing to grow as the VHA continues to build its computer-based clinical records system, which includes standardized and objective classification of diagnostic categories for PTSD, along with process and outcome variables to determine results from best practices. Going beyond clinical case studies and naturalistic studies from large data set analyses, the mission of the VHA includes a Rehabilitation Research and Development section that funds randomized clinical trials (see VHA's *Journal of Rehabilitation Research and Development*).

Web sites have been created to link military and veterans to resources (see Penk & Ainspan, 2009, for more complete listings). Among the most frequently used Web site is MilitaryOneSource (http://www.MilitaryOneSource.com; 1-800-342-9647). An array of services is available, from such specifics as information on filing income tax forms to child care services, to more general outreach, such as availability of medical resources, and advocacy for resources for military and veterans in general. Another frequently used Web site is RecruitMilitary (http://www.RecruitMilitary.com). Consultation is available for job placement and job counseling, for such specifics as resume completion and job openings.

Key elements in military and civilian programs for individuals and for couples can be found in the *Key Elements of the Clinical Practice Guidelines* that the VHA Office of Mental Health Services has adopted, along with the DOD, as policy (for VHA see: https://www.lms.va.gov/plateau/user/login.jsp; for DOD, see: https://www.qmo.amedd.army.mil).

These key elements include the following:

> Each rehabilitation goal and treatment approach must be established with the veteran's active involvement.
> The safety of the veteran must be paramount.
> A proper discharge plan includes an arrangement for safe, stable housing—each and every veteran should have the option of work or productivity of some kind.
> Each and every veteran and family should be educated about his/her disorder(s), resources for both the veteran and the family, and support groups.
> Each veteran should be assigned a case manager, if needed.
> Each veteran should have access to job skills training, if so chosen.
> Each veteran should be assigned to a primary care team, either in a medical or mental health setting, to monitor medical conditions which may be masked by mental disorders.
> Each veteran should have access to psychiatrists, psychologists, social workers, and nurses, as indicated, for medical management and to provide other needed services. (See VHA Handbook 1160.01, p. 5. See, also: http://www.oqp. med.va.gov/cpg/cpg.htm.)

Embedded in these key elements of the VA/DOD clinical practice guidelines are services mandated by VHA's Mental Health Strategic Plan for the President's New Freedom Initiatives (New Freedom Commission on Mental Health, 2003). VHA and DOD mental health policies require psychosocial rehabilitation in military and civilian programs to provide therapies for couples and families. To repeat, VHA and DOD policies now include, for veterans and their families, such psychosocial rehabilitation services as patient education services, training in self-care and independent living skills, social skills training, supported housing, supported education, supported employment, family psychoeducation, peer counseling and vet-to-vet services, and intensive case management (VHA Handbook 1160.01, 2008). Each of these key elements constitutes its own unique form of clinical service, on a par with other elements in the system of health care that are more familiar, such as inpatient hospitalization or community-based outpatient clinics. And, these key elements in psychosocial rehabilitation must be offered to veterans and serve as resources for their families.

The policy of the VHA on key elements in psychosocial rehabilitation begins with the phrase, "with the veteran's active involvement," a mandate that providers must form active partnerships with those receiving services (VHA Handbook 1106.01, 2008). At the center of treatment and rehabilitation is always the person, the veteran, for whom services are tailored and provided.

But, as we know, the person, or each veteran, is different. The U.S. military has changed by eliminating conscription. The U.S. military no longer drafts citizens to serve, but rather has switched to a professional military, with the military, for many, a profession, a career. More than half the U.S. military now consists of professionals serving in a career. The other half consists of those in the Reserves and in the National Guard (Darwin, 2008), for whom the military is, at least, a part-time career, one that may take the National Guard and Reservists halfway around the world, away from family and from home, for several years at a time. Fifty percent in the military are married, 70% of whom have children (35% of the military are parents; Park, 2011). This change from conscription to professional military and National Guard/Reserves now means that treatment and rehabilitation of military recovering from exposure in combat involves the combatant as well as the family of the combatant. More so than in the past, planning for treatment and rehabilitation includes married couples and their family (see MilitaryOneSource at http://www.MilitaryOneSource.com and RecruitMilitary, at http://www.RecruitMilitary.com).

To cite one among many theorists who provided a theoretical framework to guide development and evaluation of rehabilitation services, Albert Bandura (2006), in his seminal article, "Toward a Psychology of Human Agency," provided the theoretical foundation for "the veteran's active involvement." Bandura specified principles that facilitate partnerships between providers and those receiving services, principles of alliances that address problems, principles of behaviors to learn how to overcome difficulties for recovering from illnesses, disease, and visible and invisible wounds in war. Bandura identified psychosocial rehabilitation techniques as experiences needed to unleash the agency of humans not just to be onlookers about events that shape their lives; rather, Bandura proposed those receiving treatment and rehabilitation services must be seen by providers as the center producing actions to influence and improve functioning. Psychosocial rehabilitation must be person-centered, recognizing that changes in behaviors to become pro-health and risk-averse are only carried out by human agents who have become and are "self-organizing, proactive, self-regulating, and self-reflecting" (Bandura, p. 164). Psychosocial rehabilitation techniques must focus on and engage the person as the agent to deliver changes to improve functioning. And the "self-agency" perspective applies to each individual and to each person who partners as a couple.

So, psychosocial rehabilitation in military and civilian programs cannot be carried out just for military and for veterans who have trained to fight in combat. Psychosocial rehabilitation must be designed so that it addresses the needs of the military and their families who are confronted with multiple stresses and traumas. As Park (2011) reminded us, "A common saying in the military is that when one person joins, the whole family serves" (p. 65). Stresses and traumas to warriors and their families arise from successive deployments, time and again, to war zones, as battles are enjoined in Iraq and Afghanistan. Such deployments create problems of isolation, tax the relative inexperience of the youngest in the military, and with multiple assignments to war zones, cumulatively build up stress for soldier and for the family of the soldier. Combat stress and trauma, then, require psychosocial rehabilitation for the military and veterans as well as for their families (e.g., Cacioppo, Reis, & Zautra, 2011; Gottman et al., 2011; Park, 2011).

Furthermore, psychosocial rehabilitation in the military and civilian programs, such as in the DOD and VHA, must be developed that not only address symptoms from wounds, illness, and disease but also, for most of the clientele, maladaptive behaviors learned from exposure to life-threatening experiences in military training and in combat situations. Many clients bring multiple co-occurring diagnoses: physical wounds, medical disorders, pain, serious mental illness, addictions, PTSD, and the signature wound of traumatic brain injury (TBI). As a consequence, psychosocial rehabilitation must promote recovery from diseases and illnesses as well as traumatic experiences. DOD and VHA psychosocial rehabilitation must focus on overcoming "learned helplessness" and regaining control in life by becoming agents of change in living.

A HISTORICAL PERSPECTIVE ON PSYCHOSOCIAL REHABILITATION

Literature over centuries contains collective wisdom that psychosocial rehabilitation, particularly education and work, is the royal road that leads to coping with illness and disease and assuaging symptoms of trauma experienced in war. To cite one early among thousands of examples, the first Benedict, coping with ravages of war, founded his monastic order on Monte Casino, in the sixth century, on the premise, "Ora et Labora" (Pray and Labor). The benefits of work, coupled with living a spiritual life as a mission, together, have long been acknowledged as essential for effectively coping with illness and trauma.

"Moral therapies" in 19th-century New England certainly prepared the infrastructure to develop psychosocial rehabilitation techniques later in the 20th and now the 21st centuries. We live in the tradition of " moral therapies" as both DOD and the VHA undertake to transform their mental health delivery systems, using these key elements to invest in such psychosocial rehabilitation techniques as intensive case management, supported education, supported employment, peer counseling, supported housing, social skills training, and Internet-based self-help rehabilitation.

While the history of research into psychosocial rehabilitation techniques is comparatively short, the history of design and application is long. Examples of techniques developed by past generations of practitioners can be found in many archives. For example, techniques promoting sublimation in response to illness and to trauma were designed and developed after the Great Fire of 1871 in the Boston area by disaster response programs to help large populations of citizens and new immigrants who had been devastated by a disaster of unprecedented proportions. Ideas from New England's Transcendentalism and the St. Louis Movement in 19th-century American education were put into practice for vulnerable populations in need. Concurrently, psychosocial interventions were also extended to other vulnerable populations—the seriously mentally ill, the incarcerated, the unemployed mill workers displaced by advances in 19th-century technology (see George Prochnik's 2006 book, *Putnam Camp: Sigmund Freud, James Jackson Putnam, and the Purpose of American Psychology*, for an extended discussion of the development of moral therapies for the seriously mentally ill in 19th-century Massachusetts).

That the VHA is directly indebted to the moral therapies in New England for its approach to treatment and rehabilitation is readily apparent when one sits in the VA committee room in the U.S. House of Representatives. On the front wall at the head of that august chamber where laws guiding and funding DVA were, are, and will be written, has been placed the portrait of Edith Nourse Rogers.

She wrote the Servicemen's Readjustment Act of 1944 and shepherded what came to be known as the "GI Bill" through the U.S. House and Senate to be signed by Franklin Delano Roosevelt on June 22, 1944 (Ainspan & Penk, p. 233). Edith Nourse Rogers was the daughter of mill-owning families in Saco, Maine. She married into mill-owning families in Lowell, Massachusetts. From 1927 until 1960, she was elected by citizens to serve the Fifth District of Massachusetts. In 1947, she became the first chair of the U.S. House's Veterans Affairs committee. She co-authored every major bill legislating the VA until she died in 1960. Her ancestors were victims of trauma: Her great-great-great-grandmother, Goody Nurse, was pressed to death in the Salem Witch Trials.

Edith Nourse Rogers' GI Bill legislation empowered one agency, the VA, to provide medical assistance, education, and employment training for World War II veterans and veterans of subsequent eras. The GI Bill integrated education and employment into medical treatment to heal medical and mental disorders and residuals of trauma, forming key principles in psychosocial rehabilitation (Bruun & Crosby, 1999). The first GI Bill developed templates building the VA., a template in which techniques in psychosocial rehabilitation are fused with medical treatment. Edith Nourse Rogers wrote the first GI Bill using the tradition of moral therapies for developing psychosocial rehabilitation techniques.

Histories of the VA—how psychosocial rehabilitation was integrated into medical treatments for veterans—have been described in several recent historical texts (e.g., Baker, 2007; Baker & Pickren, 2007). The events leading up to the introduction of psychosocial rehabilitation into the VA is recounted by the psychologist charged with developing the Counseling Service of the VA in the late 1940s (Waldrop, 2007). A history of initiating the first outcome evaluations of psychosocial programs in the 1960s was given by Lee Gurel (2007).

Currently, evidence-based practices, comparing effects of devices and chemicals, cognitive–behavioral techniques, and psychoeducational interventions, are demonstrating psychosocial rehabilitation techniques that are effective for symptoms of acute and chronic stress disorder, especially when treatments are integrated into supported education and supported employment (Glynn et al., 2009).

Efficacy may be stronger when couples and family therapies are integrated into psychosocial rehabilitation techniques designed to foster recovery and resiliency for those traumatized and for their partners and families. Psychosocial rehabilitation facilitates overcoming helplessness by increasing competence and mastery to cope with living shattered by trauma. Psychosocial rehabilitations address social isolation and avoidance that are hallmarks of stress and trauma. Psychosocial rehabilitations provide meaning and purpose changed by disease, illness, and trauma.

EVIDENCE-BASED PRACTICES COMBINING COUPLES THERAPY WITH PSYCHOSOCIAL REHABILITATION IN MILITARY AND CIVILIAN PROGRAMS

The January 2011 issue of the *American Psychologist* (Volume 66, number 1) presents a summary of US military training to prepare warriors and their families for war. In this special issue, "Comprehensive Soldier Fitness," authors describe different public health approaches that prepare military and their families how to recover from war-zone experiences when traumatized. As the lead author of this issue, General George W. Casey, Jr. (U.S. Army Chief of Staff) writes: "The army's Comprehensive Soldier Fitness program is an integrated, proactive approach to developing psychological resilience in our soldiers, in their family members, and in the army's civilian workforce" (Casey, 2011, p. 1). So, likewise, clinicians must integrate treatment with rehabilitation for posttraumatic growth.

Social Skills Training

One example of combining couples therapy with psychosocial rehabilitation is the Internet-based social skills training program devised at the Gottman Institute. This program was based on critical incidents collected from soldiers seen in combat stress clinics (Gottman, Gottman, & Atkins, 2011, p. 52). Social skills training is one form of psychosocial rehabilitation effective in reducing PTSD symptoms (e.g., Glynn et al., 2009, p. 408). Relationship difficulties in marriages increased when soldiers left home and went to battle. The Gottman Institute devised approaches to strengthen relationships, adapting *Seven Principles for Making Marriage Work* (Gottman & Silver, 1999) for dyadic interventions for military and their families. An Internet-based version was designed later for soldiers deployed to war zones, connecting to their families using laptops. The Internet form for building marital relationships evolved from earlier experiences in group meetings called "deployment relationship skills training," led by Captain Christopher Atkins before troops deployed to Iraq and Afghanistan. Internet-based interactions focus on family functioning problems:

> Creating and maintaining trust, safety, and secure attachment; creating and maintaining friendship and intimacy; increasing trust and honesty; having supportive phone conversations; managing conflict constructively and gently; avoiding conflict escalation leading to violence; cognitive self-soothing; containing managing physiological and cognitive flooding; soothing one's partner; managing stresses external to the relationship; dealing with and healing from betrayal; converting posttraumatic stress disorder to posttraumatic growth through the relationship; creating and maintaining shared meaning; building and maintaining a positive relationship with each child, including emotion coaching of each child; practicing effective positive child discipline; helping each child to learn at home; and supporting the child in forming healthy peer relationships. (Gottman, Gottman, & Atkins, 2011, page 55)

Such preventive interventions are more beneficial when carried out in "dyadic communications between partners" (Gottman, Gottman, & Atkins, p. 56), not delivered just for individuals or soldiers gathering in groups. Gottman's method (i.e., Sound Relationship House) focuses on what needs to be central for psychosocial rehabilitation to be effective (i.e., relationships). And, relationships are fostered by: "(a) building love maps, (b) sharing fondness and admiration, (c) turning toward instead of away or against, (d) creating a positive perspective, (e) managing conflict,

(f) making life dreams come true, and (g) creating shared meaning" (Gottman, Gottman, & Atkins, 2011, p. 53).

Devising techniques to foster relationships is what renders efficacious the social skills training form of psychosocial rehabilitation. Gottman et al. (2011) have devised a method of combining couples therapy with psychosocial rehabilitation. Outcomes evaluate emotions and cognitions within individuals and in relationships (See also Barak, Hen, Boniel-Nissim, & Shapira, 2008).

Supported Family Services

Supported family services (as distinguished from family therapies) more readily combine couples/family interactions in psychosocial rehabilitation. Again, such techniques are beneficial in reducing PTSD symptoms and increasing social functioning (see review in Glynn et al., 2009, pp. 406–408). Effect sizes are moderate to strong, exceeding 0.63 in meta-analyses of family psycho-education and other interventions. Shirley Glynn pioneered family therapy in VAs for combat veterans (Glynn et al., 1999). Sherman and Sherman (2005) have developed family psycho-educational approaches for combat veterans (see also Sherman et al., 2005). Techniques center mainly on educating family members how to understand and how to relate to a family member who has been traumatized. Figley (1983, 1989) long ago pioneered studies of PTSD to address family needs. Family psycho-education is essential and effective for military and civilians who have been traumatized, especially for those with partners and with children (e.g., Park, 2011). And new interventions and assessments are needed to improve relationships for partners and for families.

Supported Education

Education is one primary form of psychosocial rehabilitation. The revised GI Bill, along with financial support from states (e.g., Sabatier, 2008), funds tuition, books, and housing for veterans who return to school. GI Bill is administered through the Veterans Benefits Administration (VBA) of the Department of Veterans Affairs (DVA) while, simultaneously, the Veterans Health Administration (VHA) in DVA provides treatment and rehabilitation, including supported education, through VHA medical centers and clinics. VBA and VHA, both subdivisions within DVA, share responsibilities for delivering educational services, with most benefits provided by VBA through the revised GI Bill. VHA, with VBA, deliver treatment, rehabilitation, and support services to veterans and their families while in college and other forms of technical training. Supported education may include consultation about regulations to attend college or skills training and access to services for disabilities. One example is training for veterans with TBI to overcome difficulties in attention, memory, and concentration vital for performance in school. A comprehensive review of various forms of supported education services can be found in the work of Sabatier (2008; see his discussion of Montgomery Bill for Active Duty and Selected Reserves, Reserve Educational Assistance Program, Post-Vietnam

Veterans Educational Assistance Program, Survivors' and Dependence Assistance Program, DVA's Vocational Rehabilitation and Employment; service-connected disabilities training, 2009 revised GI Bill; and state programs).

The revised 2009 GI Bill is timely during an age of current economic difficulties and high unemployment in the United States. Many combat veterans are returning home from war during a "Great Recession," the most serious economic collapse since the Great Depression of the 1930s. Supported education interventions are being expanded through funding for Operation Iraqi Freedom/Operation Enduring Freedom (OIF/OEF) and Operation New Dawn (OND) combat veterans. And, such veterans returning home from war are experiencing more unemployment (14%) than among the U.S. population in general (9%).

Meta-analyses for combat veterans with PTSD showed effect sizes are indeed beneficial (Glynn, Drebing, Penk, 2009), such as peer support for student veterans, Internet-based self-management instructions for PTSD, supplemental education training for PTSD, TBI, and other disorders. Supported education treatment manuals are being empirically-validated in randomized clinical trials (e.g., Mueller, 2011; Smith-Osborne, 2011a, 2011b, in press).

However, supported education services have not been integrated into couples therapy for combat veterans with partners, even though education influences couples and couples contribute to educational attainments. Clinicians and educators, however, are answering calls for supported education from the National Institute of Education, Department of Labor, and VBA and VHA in the Department of Veterans Affairs (DVA). More needs to be learned about the role that relationships among couples and their families play in outcomes for supported education programs designed to enhance resiliency and recovery along with educational attainments.

Patient Health and Exercise Improvement Techniques

Patient education interventions have been demonstrated as effective for persons with combat-related PTSD, as well as with noncombat, civilian forms of trauma. But, treatment and psychosocial rehabilitation training manuals focus on individuals: Patient health improvement, along with exercise and nutrition, are not as yet developed for couples or for families (see Glynn et al., 2009, pp. 396–399). Internet-based training to assuage symptoms of PTSD have been shown to be effective, including for those who are seeking services shortly after civilian trauma has been experienced (e.g., Litz & Gray, 2004; see also www.T2health.org/mobile.apps, for Internet-based self-management for individuals and couples; PTSD Coach, Relax, Mild TBI, Mood Tracker, and Tactical Breather training). Such approaches are multiplying on Web sites (see review of Web-based resources in Penk & Ainspan, 2009, for many different forms of medical and mental health conditions). Work for the future needs to expand into dyadic approaches following the Gottman Institute model (see the discussion of social skills training) that designs Internet-based interventions (e.g., PTSD Coach, Mild TBI) to improve relationships, specifically, for example, to reduce social avoidance behaviors among veterans with PTSD and their spouses.

Further, families thrive when, as a unit, they increase their physical health through exercise and nutrition. Just as the military prepares for war through basic training, so, likewise, those who survived traumas must prepare for peace through physical conditioning. Raymond Flannery (1992) long ago grounded Project SMART (Stress Management and Relaxation Training) on aerobic exercises, relaxation training, and controlling dietary stimulants as a form of psychosocial rehabilitation to reduce life stress, gain mastery in everyday living, and caring relationships.

Supported Employment

Supported employment services are effective for psychosocial rehabilitation of PTSD (see review in Glynn et al., 2009, pp. 409–413; also Cole, Daly, & Mak, 2009). Work has a long history for encouraging recovery from trauma and building resiliency. Work is central in RecruitMilitary. "Work could cure almost anything, I believed then, and I believe now" (Ernest Hemingway from "Miss Stein instructs" in *The Moveable Feast*, 1996, p. 27, commenting on his recovery from the traumas he experienced in war zones during World War I). The Department of Labor, with VBA, VHA, and DOD, have developed formal programs in physical medicine and rehabilitation, and in mental health services, to foster recovery among those experiencing visible and invisible wounds from trauma in combat (e.g., Peffer, 1955; Baker & Pickren, 2007). VHA programs include compensated work therapy, job coaching, and vocational rehabilitation. Guidelines for supported employment are available (e.g., Becker & Drake, 2003; Penk, Drebing, & Schutt, 2002; Ainspan, 2008). Among the most creative approaches, ones that directly combine treatment for PTSD with interventions for work restoration, are those under way in several VA medical centers in Alabama, Massachusetts, and Texas (e.g., Davis, Drebing, Parker, & Lam, 2010). Treatment manuals are available to guide clinicians consulting with veterans to choose, get, and keep work as part of their recovery from trauma (www.va.gov/hoMeLeSS/docs/center/MiSSion_Veteran_Consumer_Workbook.pdf; http://www.va.gov/hoMeLeSS/docs/Center/MiSSion_treatment_manual_pdf).

Although work therapies impact families, less is known about how unemployment influences families or individuals (Cole et al., 2009). As mentioned, unemployment remains exceptionally high: To repeat, more veterans are unemployed (14%) than is average for the U.S. population in general (9%). More must be learned about how unemployment among those traumatized influences relationships among couples and families. So now, as demonstrated in the Internet-based social skills training developed by the Gottman Institute for OIF/OEF/OND combat veterans, we must all integrate couples therapy into vocational relationships. These are not the times when health services research in work restoration can concentrate only on work attainment attributable to vocational rehabilitation; rather, these are the times when we must add understandings about how work influences relationships among couples when veterans are recovering from trauma (see MilitaryOneSource and RecruitMilitary for guidelines and resources).

CONCLUSION

To summarize, we have concluded that psychosocial rehabilitation is essential for those who have survived wars only to return home with visible and invisible wounds to live again with spouse and family in the community. The Axis I Criterion F of *DSM-IV* requires clinicians to address social, family, and work functioning as well as other symptoms of PTSD. Delivering services to improve such functioning requires clinicians to expand the scopes of their practices: Clinicians must expand beyond VHA inpatient units, clinics, and Vet Centers and go to communities, working with couples as a way of serving military and veterans who are physically and psychologically traumatized. Services must be delivered in the community to couples, as mandated by the President's New Freedom Commission (2004) and the new Uniform Mental Health Services policies of the VHA (2008).

Reconceptualizing psychosocial rehabilitation for couples in communities, as a way to meet the requirements of *DSM-IV-TR*, must add functioning to criteria for classifying and evaluating interventions for PTSD. New perspectives on relationships among military and veteran couples are needed to determine whether services are efficacious and effective. Fortunately, such redesigns already are under way, using objective and standardized measures of functioning for assessing and evaluating PTSD (e.g., Marx, Schnurr, Rodriguez, Holowka, Lumney, Weathers, & Keane, 2010). New inventories specialized for the military's Comprehensive Soldier Fitness training are being field tested, such as the Global Assessment Tool (GAT), measuring emotional, social, family, and spiritual fitness. New scales to assess the long-standing impact of military deployment on soldiers, now veterans, are being researched—DRRI-2, second version of Deployment Risk and Resilience inventory (Vaughn, Vogt, King, King, Smith, Wang, & Di Leone, 2011; Vogt, Proctor, King, King, & Vasterling, 2008). The new DRRI-2 now adds measures of social support during deployment from friends and family; family stressors at home while deployed in war zones; and post-deployment family functioning.

All of these changes in assessment mark new attempts to prepare clinicians to integrate couples and family therapies with psychosocial rehabilitation that promote changes in relationships. Resources are available in military and civilian programs, as illustrated by the Comprehensive Soldiers Fitness program of the DOD (see Special Issue of *American Psychologist*, January 2011) and VHA and VBA in the Department of Veterans Affairs. All such efforts for military and for veterans embody the spirit of the old saying quoted by Nansook Park (2011), "When one person joins, the whole family serves" (p. 65).

REFERENCES

Adler, A. B., Bliese, P. D., & Castro, C. A. (2011). *Deployment psychology: Evidence-based strategies to promote mental health in the military*. Washington, DC: APA Books.

Ainspan, N. D. (2008). Finding employment as a veteran with disability. In N. D. Ainspan & W. E. Penk (Eds.), *Returning wars' wounded, injured, and ill: A reference handbook* (pp. 102–138). Westport, CT: Greenwood/Praeger.

Ainspan, N. D., & Penk, W. E. (Eds.). (2008). *Returning wars' wounded, injured, and ill: A reference handbook*. Westport, CT: Greenwood/Praeger.

Allen, E. S., Rhoades, G. K., Stanley, S. M., & Markman, H. J. (2010). Hitting home: Relationships between recent deployment, posttraumatic stress symptoms, and marital functioning. *Journal of Family Psychology, 24*, 280–288. doi: 10.1037/a0019405.

American Psychiatric Association. (1980). *Diagnostic and statistical manual of mental disorders* (3rd ed.). Washington, DC: Author.

American Psychiatric Association. (1987). *Diagnostic and statistical manual of mental disorders* (3rd ed., rev.). Washington, DC: Author.

American Psychiatric Association. (2000). *Diagnostic and statistical manual of mental disorders* (4th ed., text revision). Washington, DC: Author.

Anderson, J., & Szuchman, P. (2011). *Spousonomics: Using economics to make love, marriage, and the dirty dishes*. New York: Random House.

Baker, R. R. (Ed.). (2007). *Stories from VA Psychology*. Bloomington, IN: Author House. Available from http://www.authorhouse.com

Baker, R. R., & Pickren, W. E. (2007). *Psychology and the Department of Veterans Affairs*. Washington, DC: APA Books.

Bandura, A. (2006). Toward a psychology of human agency. *Perspectives on Psychological Science*, 1, 164–180.

Barak, A., Hen, L., Boniel-Nissim, M., & Shapira, N. (2008). A comprehensive review and a meta-analysis of the effectiveness of Internet-based psychotherapeutic interventions. *Journal of Technology in Human Services, 26*, 109–160. doi: 10.1080/15228830802094429.

Bates, M. J., Bowles, S. V.,Kilgore, J. A., & Solursh, L. P. (2008). Fitness for duty, recovery, and return to service. In N. D. Ainspan & W. E. Penk (Eds.), *Returning wars' wounded, injured, and ill: A reference handbook* (pp 67–101). Westport, CT: Greenwood/Praeger.

Becker, D. R., & Drake, R. E. (2003). *A working life for people with serious mental illness*. New York: Oxford University Press.

Bruun, E., & Crosby, J. (1999). *Our nation's archives: The history of the United States in documents*. New York: Black Dog and Leventhal.

Cacioppo, J. T., Reis, H. T., & Zautra, A. J. (2011). Social resilience: The value of social fitness with an application to the military. *American Psychologist*, *66*, 43–51.

Cahoon, E. P. (1984). *An examination of relationships between PTSD, marital distress, and response to therapy by Vietnam veterans.* Unpublished doctoral dissertation, University of Connecticut, Storrs.

Casey G. W. (2011). Comprehensive soldier fitness. *American Psychologist*, *66*, 1–3.

Cole, K., Daly, A., & Mak, A. (2009). Good for the soul: The relationship between work, well-being, and psychological capital. *Journal of Socio-economics, 38*, 464–474. doi: 10.1016/j.socec.2008.10.004.

Darwin, J. (2008). Disabilities and injuries among the members of the National Guard and Reserve units. In N. D. Ainspan & W. E. Penk (Eds.), *Returning wars' wounded, injured, and ill: A reference handbook* (pp. 160–172). Westport, CT: Greenwood/Praeger.

Davis, L. L., Drebing, C., Parker, P. E., & Lam, A. C. (2010). *Occupations for persons with PTSD: Results from clinical investigations.* Paper presented at the International Society for Traumatic Stress Studies, 26th meeting, Montreal, Canada.

Diener, E., & Seligman, M. E. P. (2004). Beyond money: Toward economy of well-being. *Psychological Science in the Public Interest*, 5, 1–31.

Devilly, G. J. (2002). The psychological effects of a lifestyle management course on war veterans and their spouses. *Journal of Clinical Psychology*, 58, 1119–1134.

Figley, C. R. (1983). Catastrophes: A overview of family reactions. In C. R. Figley & H. I. McCubbin (Eds.), *Stress and the family, volume 2, Coping with catastrophe* (pp. 3–20). New York: Brunner/Mazel.

Figley, C. R. (1989). *Helping traumatized families*. San Francisco: Jossey-Bass.
Flannery, R. F. (1992). *Post-traumatic stress disorder: The victim's guide to healing and recovery*. New York: Crossroad.
Glynn, S. (2008). Impact on family and friends. In N. Ainspan & W. Penk (Eds.), *Returning wars' wounded, injured, and ill: A reference handbook* (pp.173–190). Westport, CT: Greenwood.
Glynn, S., Drebing, C., & Penk, W. E. (2009). Psychosocial rehabilitation. In E. B. Foa, T. M. Keane, M. J. Friedman, & J. Cohen (Eds.), *Effective treatments for PTSD: Practice guidelines from the International Society for Traumatic Stress Studies* (pp. 383–426). New York: Guilford Press.
Glynn, S. M., Eth, S., Randolph, E. T., Foy, D. W., Urbaitis, M., Boxer, L., ... Crothers, J. (1999). A test of behavioral family therapy to augment exposure for combat-related posttraumatic stress disorder. *Journal of Consulting and Clinical Psychology, 67*, 243–251.
Gottman, J. M., Gottman, J. S., & Atkins, C. L. (2011). The comprehensive soldier fitness program: Family skills component. *American Psychologist, 66*, 52–57.
Gottman, J. M., & Silver, N. (1999). *The seven principles for making marriage work*. New York: Three Rivers Press.
Gregory, W. (2008). Peer support services. In N. D. Ainspan & W. E. Penk (Eds.), *Returning wars' wounded, injured, and ill: A reference handbook* (pp. 191–204). Westport, CT: Greenwood/ Praeger.
Gurel, L. (2007). Reflections on the VA years. In R. R. Baker (Ed.). *Stories in VA Psychology* (pp. 73–82). Bloomington, IN: www.authorhouse.com
Hemingway, E. *The moveable feast*. New York: Scribner Classics.
Kahneman, D., Diener, E., & Schwarz, N. (Eds.). (1999). *Well-being: The foundations of hedonic psychology*. New York: Russell Sage Foundation.
Kennedy, C. H., & Williams, T. J. (2010). *Ethical practice in operational psychology: Military and intelligence applications*. Washington, DC: APA Books.
Kudler, H., Straits-Troster, K., & Jones, E. (2006). *Strategies in the service of new combat veterans*. Paper presented at the ViSN 17 PTSD Conference, San Antonio, TX, April, 2006, Available from howard.kudler@va.gov
Litz, B. T., & Gray, M. (2004). Early intervention for trauma in adults. In B. T. Litz (Ed.), *Early intervention for trauma and traumatic loss* (pp. 87–111). New York: Guilford.
Marx, B. P., Schnurr, P. P., Rodriguez, P., Holowka, D., Lunney, C., Weathers, F., & Keane, T. M. (2010) *Development and validation of a PTSD-related Functional Impairment Scale*. Paper delivered at the International Society for Traumatic Stress Studies, Montreal, Canada, November, 2010.
Moore, B. A., & Kennedy, C. H. (2010). *Wheels down: Adjusting to life after deployment*. Washington, DC: APA Books.
Mueller, L. (2011). *Supported education: Motivational interviewing for entry and outcomes*. Bedford, MA: Study in process, funded by VA Rehabilitation Research and Development. Available from lisa.mueller@va.gov
New Freedom Commission on Mental Health (2003). Achieving the promise: Transforming mental health care in America: Executive summary. DHHS Pub. No. SMA-03-3831:Rockville, MD. Available from www.mentalhealth.samhsa.gov
Park, N. (2011). Military children and families: Strength and challenges during peace and war. *American Psychologist, 66*, 65–72. doi: 10.1037/a0021249.
Peffer, P. A. (1955). *The member-employee program*. DS&M Program Guide for Psychiatry and Neurology Services, Department of Veterans Affairs, G-1, M-2, Part X, March 15, 1955, pp. 3–10.
Penk, W. E., & Ainspan, N. D. (2009). Community response to returning military. in S. M. Freeman, B. A. Moore, & A. Freeman (Eds.), *Living and surviving in harm's way: A psychological treatment handbook for pre- and post-deployment of military personnel* (pp. 417–436). New York: Routledge/Taylor & Francis Group.

Penk, W. E., Drebing, C. E., & Schutt, R. (2002). Post-traumatic stress disorder. In J. Thomas & M. Hersen (Eds.), *Handbook of mental health in the workplace* (pp. 215–248). Thousand Oaks, CA: Sage.

Penk, W. E., & Flannery, R. B. (2000). Psychosocial rehabilitation. In E. B. Foa, T. M. Keane, & M. J. Friedman (Eds.), *Effective treatments for PTSD: Practice guidelines from the International Society for Traumatic Stress Studies* (pp. 224–246). New York: Guilford Press.

Peterson, C., Park, N., & Castro, C. A. (2011). Assessment for the U.S. Army Comprehensive Soldier Fitness program: The Global Assessment Tool. *American Psychologist, 66*, 10–18.

Prochnik, G. (2006). *Putnam Camp: Sigmund Freud, James Jackson Putnam, and the purpose of American psychology*. New York: Other Press.

Reivich, K. J., Seligman, M. E. P., & McBride, S. (2011). Master resilience training in the U.S. Army. *American Psychologist, 66*, 25–34.

Riggs, D. S., Monson, C. M., Glynn, S. M., & Canterino, J. (2009). Couple and family therapy for adults. In E. Foa, T. Keane, M. Friedman, & J. Cohen (Eds.), *Effective treatments for PTSD: Practice guidelines from the International Society of Traumatic Stress* (2nd ed., pp. 456–478). New York: Guilford.

Ruzek, J.I., Schnurr, P. P., Vasterling, J. J., & Friedman, M. J. (2011). *Caring for veterans with deployment related disorders: Iraq, Afghanistan, and beyond.* Washington, DC: APA Books.

Sabatier, C. (2008). Educational options. In N. D. Ainspan & W. E. Penk (Eds.), *Returning wars' wounded, injured, and ill: A reference handbook* (pp. 139–159). Westport, CT: Greenwood/ Praeger.

Seligman, M. E. P. (2002). *Authentic happiness*. New York: Free Press.

Sherman, M. D., Sautter, F., Lyons, J. A., Manguno-Mire, G. M., Han, X., Perry, D., & Sullivan, G. (2005). Mental health needs of co-habiting partners of Vietnam veterans with combat-related PTSD. *Psychiatric Services, 42*, 213–219.

Sherman, M. D., & Sherman, D. M. (2005). *Finding my way: A teen's guide to living with a parent who has experienced trauma*. Edina, MN: Beaver Pond Press.

Smith-Osborne, A. (2010). Does the GI Bill support educational attainment for veterans with disabilities? *Journal of Sociology and Social Welfare, 36*, 111–124.

Smith-Osborne, A. (2011, in press-a). Mental health risk and social ecological variables associated with educational attainment for Gulf War veterans: Implications for current veterans returning to civilian life in communities. *Journal of Sociology and Social Welfare*.

Smith-Osborne, A. (2011, in press-b). A randomized clinical intervention trial of supported education for veterans. *Psychiatric Rehabilitation Journal*.

Snow, R. (1991). Aptitude-treatment interaction as a framework for research on individual differences in psychotherapy. *Journal of Consulting and Clinical Psychology, 59*, 205–216.

Tedeschi, R. G., & McNally, R. J. (2011). Can we facilitate posttraumatic growth in combat veterans? *American Psychologist, 66*, 1924.

Vaughn, R. A., Vogt, D., King, D. W., King, L. A., Smith, B. N., Wang, J. M., & Di Leone, B. A. L. (2011). Measuring deployment and resilience among military personnel and veterans. *Texas Psychologist, 61*, 6–8.

Veterans Health Administration. (2008). VHA Handbook 1160.01 *Uniform mental health services policies*. Washington, DC: U.S. Government.

Vogt, D., Proctor, J., King, D., King, L., & Vasterling, J. (2008). Validation of scales for the Deployment Risk and Resiliency inventory (DRRi) in a sample of Occupation Iraqi Freedom (OIF) veterans. *Assessment, 15*, 391–403. doi: 10.1177/1073191108316030.

Waldrop, R. S. (2007). The beginning of counseling psychology in VA hospitals. In R. R. Baker (Ed.), *Stories in VA Psychology* (pp. 127–134). Bloomington, IN: www.authorhouse.com.

Index

E

F

G

J

K

T

U

V